TWENTIETH CENTURY HISTORY

The World Since 1900

Tony Howarth

Second Edition
by Josh Brooman

D1419720

ADDISON WESLEY LONGMAN LIMITED
Edinburgh Gate, Harlow,
Essex CM20 2JE, England
and Associated Companies throughout the world.

Published in the United States of America
by Longman Inc., New York

© Longman Group Limited 1979
© Longman Group UK Limited 1987

First published 1979
Second edition 1987
Third impression with additions 1989
Twelfth impression 1997

Set in 10/12 point Ehrhardt (Lasercomp)
Produced by Longman Singapore Publishers Pte Ltd
Printed in Singapore

British Library Cataloguing in Publication Data
Howarth, Tony
    Twentieth century history: the world
    since 1900.—2nd ed.
    I. History, Modern – 20th century
    I. Title   II. Brooman, Josh
    909.82   D421

ISBN 0-582-33209-5

Library of Congress Cataloging in Publication Data

Howarth, Tony
    Twentieth century history.
    "By arrangement with the British Broadcasting
Company" — T.p. Verso.
    Includes index.
    Summary: Describes the political and social
changes throughout the world from 1900 to the
present day.
    I. History, Modern — 20th century — Juvenile
literature. [I. History, Modern — 20th century]
    I. Brooman, Josh.   II. Title.
    D421.H59 1987 909.82   86-33788

ISBN 0-582-33209-5

By arrangement with the British Broadcasting Corporation

The publisher's policy is to use paper manufactured from sustainable forests.

Acknowledgements

We are grateful to the following for permission to reproduce copyright material:

André Deutsch and Holt, Rinehart and Winston for a table from *The Second World War* by Henri Michel © 1968 by Press Universitaires de France, Translation © André Deutsch 1975, reprinted by permission of Holt, Rinehart and Winston and AndréDeutsch and Press Universitaires de France; Cambridge University Press for figures from *China's Economic Revolution* by A. Eckstein (1977) and *Cambridge Economic History of Europe*, Vol. VI, Part 1, by D.V. Glass and E. Grebenik; Frank Cass & Co. Ltd for figures from *A Short History of Economic Progress* by Y.S. Brenner (1969); Cassell plc for the map 'The Allies Meet' from *History of the Second World War* by B.H. Liddell-Hart; Wm. Dawson & Sons Ltd for figures from *A Political Geography of Post-War Europe* by Dr M. Blacksell; Delacorte Press Inc. for extracts from *Europe 1919–45* by R.A.C. Parker; The Hamlyn Group for figures from *War Memories of D. Lloyd George* by D. Lloyd-George, Odhams, Vol. 1 (1938); Harper and Row Publishers Inc. for extracts and Figure 2 (p. 18) from *America's Greatest Depression 1929–1941* by Lester V. Chandler © 1970 by Lester V. Chandler, reprinted by permission of Harper and Row Publishers Inc; Her Majesty's Stationery Office for figures from *Race Relations in Britain*, 2nd edition 1977, by Central Office of Information, Reference Pamphlet 108; Dr Walter Kumpman for figures from *History of the World Economy in the 20th Century*, Vol. IV–*The World in Depression 1929–1939* by C.P. Kindleberger, published by Penguin Books Ltd; Alfred A. Knopf for map redrawn from *The Emergence of the Middle East: 1914–1924* by Howard M. Sachar, 1969; figures from *Impact of Western Man*, Copyright © 1982, 1966 by William Woodruff, University Press of America Inc.; *China and the World since 1949* by Wang Gung Wa, by permission of Macmillan, London and Basingstoke; Macmillan, St. Martin's Press Inc, for figures from *Weimar and the Rise of Hitler* by A.J. Nicholls (1928); Campbell, Thompson, McLaughlin Ltd, for material from *Independent Eastern Europe* by © C.A. Macartney and A.W. Palmer 1962; Monthly Review Press for figures from *China's Economy and the Maoist Strategy* by J.G. Gurley © 1976 by John G. Gurley, reprinted by permission of monthly Review Press; Penguin Books Ltd for figures from *An Economic History of the USSR* by Alec Nove (Allen Lane, The Penguin Press, 1969; Pelican Books 1972), pp. 146, 180, 186, 191, 225, © Alec Nove 1969, and an extract from a table in *The Economic History of World Population* by C.M. Cipolla (Pelican original, 1974), p. 96, 1978, p. 98, © C.M. Cipolla, 1962, 1964, 1965, 1967, 1970, 1974, reprinted by permission of Penguin Books Ltd; Rand McNally & Co. for an adapted version of the map 'The Years Between World Wars' from *These States United*, Rand McNally Atlas of American History © 1974; The Twentieth Century Fund for figures from *World Population and Production: Trends and Outlook* by W.S. Woytinsky and E.S. Woytinsky © 1953 by the Twentieth Century Fund Inc., New York; United Nations for figures from The United Nations Demographic yearbook from p. 405 © United Nations 1948; pp. 558–73 © United Nations 1957; pp. 138–41 © United Nations 1962; pp. 280–95 © United Nations 1966; pp. 139–46, 392–413 © United Nations 1975; and *The United Nations Statistical Yearbook* form pp. 19–20, 273–74, 306 © United Nations 1948; pp. 67–78, 98–101, 102–03, 486–92, 568–71, 689–91, 893–97 © United Nations 1976; Topham for map redrawn from Purnell *History of the Twentieth Century* Vol. 5; Weidenfeld and Nicolson for a table from *The War Against the Jews* by Dawidowicz, figures from the *First World War Atlas* by Martin Gilbert, and map redrawn from *Recent History Atlas*, 1966.

We are grateful to the following for permission to reproduce additional copyright material.

The author's agents for the poem 'Bombardment' by Richard Aldington from *The Collected Poems of Richard Aldington* © Catherine Guillaume; Harper and Row Publishers Inc for an extract from the article 'The Decision To Use The Atomic Bomb' by Henry L. Stimson from pp. 38–39 *The Atomic Age: Scientists in National and World Affairs* ed. M. Grodzins and E. Rabinowitch; Oxford University Press Inc. for an extract from pp. 112–118 *The German Inflation of 1923* by Fritz K. Ringer (1969); Southern Music Publishing Co Ltd and Cromwell Music Inc for an extract from 'The Coffee Song' words and music by Bob Hilliard and Dick Miles TRO – © Copyright 1946 & renewed 1974 Cromwell Music Inc., New York.

We are grateful to the following for permission to reproduce photographs:

Associated Press, page 176; BBC Hulton Picture Library, pages 29, 97, 155, 205 (UPI/Bettmann Newsphotos); Bettmann Archive, page 101; British Library, page 9; Camera Press, page 199; Alex Henderson for Dupont/Colorific, page 232; The John Hilleslon Agency Limited, pages 151 (photo: Robert Capa), page 249 (photo: Marc Ribound/Magnum), page 285 (photo: Ernest Cole), page 302 (photo: Sebastio Salgado/Magnum); Imperial War Museum, London, pages 24, 154, 178, 183; The Keystone Collection, page 181; David King Collection, page 34; Landesbildstelle, Berlin, page 193; Library of Congress, Washington, page viii; London Express News Service, page 267; Mail Newspapers p.l.c., page 274; National Archives, Washington, page 84; Novosti Press Agency, page 136; Popperfoto, pages 163, 171, 229; Press Association, page 72; Süddeutscher Verlag Bilderdienst, pages 49, 117, 156, 194; Topham, pages 61, 210; Ullstein Bilderdienst, page 111; USIS, page 222; Roger-Viollet, page 57 (photo: Harlingque-Viollet).

Cover: Refugee family from Frankfurt-on-Oder rest in street in Berlin. Possible date, 1945. BBC Hulton Picture Library.

Contents

BBC Television Series 'Twentieth Century History'

This television series is associated with this book. The series is designed primarily for pupils aged 14 to 17, many of whom will be following examination courses; but it is hoped that some programmes will be useful to pupils in current affairs or contemporary studies courses.

Fifteen programmes are broadcast during the school year. Most are in colour and each lasts for twenty minutes. The programme titles and the chapters which relate to them are given below.

Programme	chapter	page
1 Make Germany Pay! (events in Germany 1918–29)	11	47
2 Boom and Bust (USA 1920–30)	21	81
3 Hitler's Germany, 1933–36	23 and 25	90, 110
4 Roosevelt and the New Deal	26	119
5 Stalin and the Modernisation of Russia (1924–37)	27	128
6 Why Appeasement? (Europe 1937–39)	29 and 30	152, 159
7 Britain Alone (1939–42)	30	162
8 Pearl Harbour to Hiroshima (1931–45)	31 and 34	169, 198
9 The Road to Berlin (1942–45)	31 and 33	173, 177, 191
10 The Third World	16, 17, 19, 34, 43, 46 and 47	68, 71, 75, 202, 277, 295, 299
11 Cold War – Confrontation (Berlin Airlift and the Korean War)	35	209, 210
12 Mr Kennedy and Mr Khrushchev	36	221
13 One Man's Revolution (Mao Tse-tung)	18, 34 and 39	73, 204, 246
14 China since Mao	39	250
15 The Arabs and Israel since 1947	45	288

Most of the programmes cover short time spans and concentrate on those aspects of the subjects which television can best illustrate. They are therefore selective and do not attempt to deal with whole periods or topics. Archive film forms the bulk of the broadcast material, although other visual techniques are used, and in some programmes eye-witnesses relate their personal experiences of events. The BBC has produced a booklet for teachers to accompany the series. Dates and times of transmissions are listed in the BBC's leaflet, *Radio and Television for Schools and Colleges.*

Author's Note

Author's Note

I would like to express my thanks to all the people who helped in the making of this book. In particular I am grateful for the advice and assistance of John Robottom, Janet Howarth, Marguerite Dupree, and Peter Campbell who designed the book. I wrote it, and therefore accept all responsibility for what follows.

Tony Howarth

Tony Howarth died in 1980. In revising and updating his book, I too have incurred debts, and owe thanks especially to John Robottom.

Josh Brooman

The framework of a childhood: a ten-year-old spinner in a cotton mill in North Carolina, USA, in 1909. The photographer, Lewis Hine, worked for the National Child Labor Committee, collecting evidence of children's working conditions. Because factory owners feared such photographs could lead to charges of exploitation, Lewis Hine had to pretend to be interested only in photographing the machinery, asking for a child to stand in 'for a sense of scale'. While arranging the scene, he measured the child's height against his coat buttons, making notes of her age, working conditions and years of experience.

1 People and Societies I

When the twentieth century began, not everyone got the date right. In the so-called 'Western world' time was measured in the Christian fashion (AD – in the Year of Our Lord) and its people knew for a fact that 1st January was New Year's Day.

But 1st January 1901 must have been supremely unimportant to Hindus, Buddhists, Jews, Muslims and Chinese. They had their own festivals on which to celebrate new beginnings. Exactly when the New Year began was a matter on which even Christians did not agree; the Russian calendar was thirteen days behind ours in Britain. While people in Moscow were preparing for the last Christmas of the nineteenth century, in Glasgow they were drinking in the twentieth century. Whether they got the time right is yet another matter – few people had watches.

That's just one example – though not in itself a very important one – of differences between peoples of the world at the beginning of the period this book will cover. You can, however, develop ideas of other, more important, differences from that one example. Obviously, industry did not yet have the technology to turn out mass-produced wristwatches. And religion mattered. Unlike today, there were very few Christians who were prepared to accept that one man's faith was as good as the next's; Hindus, Muslims and Buddhists could easily be dismissed as heathens.

But there were also greater differences which you can begin to imagine. The Russians hadn't yet changed from the old, Julian calendar to the new Gregorian calendar, used in Western Europe, and neither had the Greeks, Serbs and Romanians. This suggests isolation, the separateness of peoples and countries. It suggests old ways of thinking and behaving. It suggests people who dressed according to custom, not according to fashion. It brings to mind small communities where change was not welcome, where it would have been meaningless to set out to measure time accurately in minutes and seconds.

Such a picture, of an old-fashioned, slow-moving world, was partly true, but that picture was having to make room for increasing numbers of people to whom time, accuracy and the development of technology did matter. The rest of this chapter will provide information from which you should get a clearer view of that picture – a view which should help you to see

patterns of change, and of continuity, in the story of the world which was preparing to welcome your great-grandparents as babies.

The People

With a total of 1,608 million people (distributed as you can see below) the world seemed crowded after a century of rapid population growth.

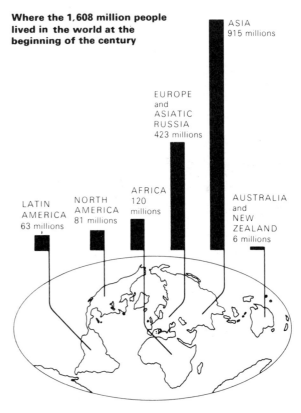

Where the 1,608 million people lived in the world at the beginning of the century

ASIA 915 millions

EUROPE and ASIATIC RUSSIA 423 millions

AFRICA 120 millions

LATIN AMERICA 63 millions

NORTH AMERICA 81 millions

AUSTRALIA and NEW ZEALAND 6 millions

Let's put it another way: out of every 1,000 people in the world, 570 lived in Asia, 260 in Europe and the Russian Empire, 75 in Africa, 50 in North America, 40 in Latin America and 5 in Australia and New Zealand.

1

The most densely populated part of the world, then as now, was Europe. Germany had 56 million people, the Austrian Empire 46, the United Kingdom (including Ireland) 42 million, France 39, Italy 33, Spain 19. There were more people in tiny Belgium than in Australia and New Zealand combined. In the vastness of Russia lived 133 million people.

Coming into the world was a hazardous business. It was much safer to be born in Sweden than in Russia, in Japan rather than in Chile.

Death in infancy: the number of children who died before the age of one (out of every 1,000 born alive)

SWEDEN 96
GREAT BRITAIN 145
FRANCE 149
JAPAN 151
USA 162
SPAIN 195
INDIA 232
RUSSIA 260
CHILE 264

The prospect facing a newly born child could be grim. In Western Europe or the USA he or she could expect to live, on average, until nearly 50; but a Russian baby could expect to reach only just over 30; an Indian about 23. Artificial techniques of contraception were already being used in the more industrialised countries of the West. Elsewhere – as you have seen – the most reliable family planner was Death.

Town and Country

Most of the world's workers (7 out of every 10) still made their living from farming. In some countries almost the entire population still worked on the land: in South East Asia and Russia 8 out of every 10; in the poorer parts of Eastern Europe, 9 out of 10. In Western Europe (5 out of 10) the pattern was very different. Only *one* out of every 10 British workers was employed in agriculture.

By the beginning of the twentieth century, Western Europe had become industrialised. Farmers still farmed – in East Anglia and East Prussia, in the Loire Valley and in Lombardy, in Sicily and in Sussex – and they still do. But the wealth and strength of Western European countries now lay in their ability and capacity to manufacture goods – to mass-produce a bewildering variety of things, from cotton sheets, woollen trousers and bicycles to shoes, saucepans, rifles and railway lines.

In a century of booming population growth, peasants and farm labourers had been drawn from the land to work in the factories, mines and shipyards. New cities were still growing and old towns rapidly expanding to house them. By 1914, Western Europe had more than 140 cities of over 140,000 inhabitants. They sprawled across the maps, linked by railways and fed by farmers who had begun to mechanise the cultivation of the land. In 1900, the world had only eleven cities with populations of over one million: four of them (London, Berlin, Vienna and Paris) were in Western Europe, two were in western Russia, and two in Asia. The other three (New York, Chicago and Philadelphia) were all in the USA – and that fact alone gives us a hint of the power of America's industrial muscle. The USA had become the world's top industrial heavyweight and the UK had already been pushed down to third position in the world in terms of industrial output.

In 1913, Americans produced 36 per cent of all the world's manufactured goods. Germany produced 16 per cent and the UK 14 per cent.

Trading Nations

Unlike Western Europe, North America had a variety of natural resources available for easy exploitation. The most obvious of those was the land itself, and in the second half of the nineteenth century large areas were opened up for the cultivation of crops, especially grain, and the rearing of animals. It was the golden age of the cowboys, the gun-toting guardians of the vast cattle ranges. Chicago became a slum city, reeking with the stink of blood and fat from factories where underpaid workers – many of them slowly dying from tuberculosis – canned meat for consumption by other workers in other cities of the Western world.

The three industrial heavyweights in 1913

Coal
(millions of tonnes)

Steel
(millions of tonnes)

Railway
(thousands of km of track)

478	292	190	31.3	18.7	9.0	309	52	29
U S A	U K	GERMANY	U S A	GERMANY	U K	U S A	GERMANY	U K

From the wide open spaces of Argentina and Australia came wheat, beef, mutton and lamb in abundance. The technology of refrigeration made possible the export of millions of carcasses a year. The journey of the lamb, from the pastures of New Zealand to the dinner tables of Britain, began. It was carried cheaply in the holds of iron, and then steel, steamships.

As the people of industrialised Western Europe provided much of the demand for grain and meat from the USA, Argentina, New Zealand and Australia, so they affected patterns of agriculture throughout most of the world. To meet their demands, tea plantations were laid out in India, Ceylon (now Sri Lanka) and China; farm land in the West Indies was taken up with cane fields; coffee was cultivated in Brazil, and cocoa in West Africa. Tea, sugar, coffee and cocoa were (like rice, rubber and tropical fruits) labour-intensive crops – but there was plenty of cheap labour available to plant and harvest them.

The steam locomotive had created national, and even continental, markets by transporting goods and raw materials more quickly and more cheaply than ever before. Now the steamship enlarged world markets in food, raw materials and manufactures. And by 1903 those markets were connected by a world-wide network of submarine telegraph cables. Before cables, it took three weeks for a German or Italian to get a reply to a question he'd sent to New York; a reply from India took two months, and from Australia four months. Now questions about quantities, qualities and prices were answered on the same day.

Countries' economies (and the lives of their peoples) became more dependent on each other as they specialised in the production of the things they could grow, or could make better, or more cheaply or in greater quantities, than anyone else. The primary producers of raw materials, minerals and food, depended on the industrial nations for supplies of manufactured goods:

3

the countries of town-dwellers depended on the primary producers for cheap food and for some of the raw materials they used in the manufacture of finished goods. The USA, already highly industrialised, and blessed with most of the valuable things to be found on this earth and beneath it, had it both ways.

The food, the raw materials and the manufactured goods which the nations of the world sold to and bought from each other were paid for in gold, or in currencies whose values were linked to gold, which was given a fixed price. This 'gold standard' meant that a manufacturer or trader knew, with reasonable certainty, what one pound, one dollar, one mark or one peseta was worth – in anybody's money. It made for stability and ease of trade, but it benefited mostly those countries already well-off.

At the centre of the world's financial system was London, the capital of the world's greatest trading nation – a nation which earned a great deal more abroad than it spent on importing goods and services. This huge balance of payments surplus was earned not only from the export of goods but also from 'invisible' exports such as shipping, insurance and dividends on overseas investments. Not surprisingly, this rich trading nation had become a great creditor nation, earning yet more money by lending her surplus abroad. It was in Britain's interests to stimulate world trade by lending money to those in need, provided they were

thought to be credit-worthy enough to be able to pay it back. But the world's poorer countries were not good credit-risks and so loans were not always easy for them to obtain – and in any case they had to be repaid, with interest.

Migrants: New Faces, New Places

Not only goods were moved from country to country, continent to continent, in greater quantities than ever before. People moved too – by railroad and steamship – and in particular they moved out of Europe. Unemployed town-dwellers (in an age when governments didn't provide social security to fall back on), and farmers who couldn't produce food as cheaply as the beef and grain barons overseas, looked for a better life elsewhere.

Many of them were attracted by the wealth and promise of the USA, though large numbers of Italians and Spaniards preferred Latin to North America, and considerable numbers of Britons went to stock the great emptinesses of Canada and Australia. But the USA gained most from the great European exodus. At the start of the twentieth century American society was a unique mixture of peoples of all nationalities, races and religions. Out of a population of 92 million Americans in 1910, well over 13 million were foreign-born.

There were population movements within and out

1901–10 Eleven million leave Europe

NETHERLANDS	28 thousand
BELGIUM	30 thousand
SWITZERLAND	37 thousand
FRANCE	53 thousand
DENMARK	73 thousand
FINLAND	159 thousand
NORWAY	191 thousand
SWEDEN	224 thousand
GERMANY	274 thousand
PORTUGAL	324 thousand
RUSSIA	911 thousand
SPAIN	1,091 thousand
AUSTRIAN EMPIRE	1,111 thousand
UK (including IRELAND)	3,150 thousand
ITALY	3,615 thousand

of Asia too. Millions of Chinese were moving, some into South East Asia, especially to Malaya and Singapore; while substantial numbers of Chinese and Japanese emigrated across the Pacific, to Hawaii or the USA – yet more good Americans in the making. Other Japanese made their way to Latin America. White Australians took fright at the prospect of a yellow invasion and the twentieth century's first immigration laws put the shutters up against the Asians. Meanwhile, on a smaller scale, Britain was receiving immigrants. As well as the continued influx of Irishmen and women, there were Jews from Eastern Europe, and ice-cream sellers from Italy – in a way, blazing the trail for the Indian restaurants and shops and Chinese take-aways of the future.

The Other Half

For most women in the world at the start of this century the purpose of life was marriage, and the purpose of marriage was to bear and rear children. Some societies kept women out of the business of public life altogether. Religion and custom affected them in ways which seemed odd, and sometimes perverted, to Western eyes. In Muslim lands women were kept in 'purdah', hiding their faces as well as their bodies from strangers. In China little girls' feet were mutilated to satisfy a male sense of what was attractive: small was beautiful. In India the murder of baby girls and the practice of 'suttee' – widows burning themselves alive on their husbands' funeral pyres – secretly continued despite the attempts of the British to stamp out these practices.

In the West male attitudes to women were hypocritical rather than cruel: men who believed that respectable ladies didn't like sex could enjoy themselves with child prostitutes. With few exceptions, women's influence was restricted to the home. Only in Australia, New Zealand and Finland did women have the vote before 1910.

However, such long-established anti-feminist traditions were gradually being weakened in the West. Industrialised economies called women into paid employment – in factories, offices, shops and schools. Marriage and domestic service were no longer the only careers open to the majority of women. For those who did marry, artificial techniques of contraception offered some the prospect of being able to limit the years they would spend in the bearing and rearing of children. The first modern domestic appliances, such as gas cookers, held out the hope of a little relief from the daily drudgery of housework.

The more politically minded women began to organise their sex to fight for the right to vote and the right to control their own property. In the West at least the battle against male domination had begun.

The Shape of Things to Come

As the world entered the twentieth century it was clear that Western man was re-inventing transport – only the shape of the wheel remained from the original idea. Although the horse still had a lot of life left in him, his days were numbered. In 1900 there were 36,000 horses pulling tramcars in the towns of Great Britain: by 1914 only 900 were left. Motor-cars were already in mass-production; by 1914 there were a million of them on the roads of the USA. The age of the internal combustion engine had arrived. In 1903 the Wright brothers made the first powered flight in what was just recognisable as an aeroplane. In 1909 Blériot flew across the English Channel.

Along with the new forms of transport marched the new technology of communications. The telephone was invented in 1876 and was commonplace by the end of the century. In 1901 Guglielmo Marconi transmitted the first radio signal across the Atlantic, and so began the age of distant 'wireless' communications.

Much of the apparatus of modern Western society had already appeared – the typewriter, the sewing machine, the phonograph (ancestor of the record-player), the box camera, and, more ominously, the revolver and machine-gun. Perhaps most important of all, Western man knew how to generate and distribute electricity to his home and to his place of work.

The world doesn't change overnight. Only a small proportion of the world's population were directly affected by the new marvels of technology such as those mentioned above. Habits, customs and ways of thinking die hard. To a majority of the people of the world, the future looked very much the same as the past. Their lives were regulated by the seasons and the sun, not by the railway timetable or the factory whistle. But the twentieth century would not leave them for long in their sometimes grim, and sometimes peaceful, ignorance of its novelties.

2   Lines on the Map

When you look at the map of the world you sometimes get a feeling that things have always been like that. The shapes are familiar: Italy is putting the boot into Sicily; Africa looks like a pear upside down; the two Americas float between two oceans; and Wales resembles a pig.

Geologists will tell you it hasn't always been like that: some of the free-floating bits were once joined together. But for historians that's neither here nor there. For them the shapes have always been the same. It has been the lines on those shapes – the frontiers or borders – which have altered, time after time. And the twentieth century has seen them change more often than in any previous century.

We in Britain have seen very little change. The only big change in the British Isles this century occurred when a line was drawn in the north of Ireland and the British kept the little bit at the top while the rest became the Irish Free State (and later the Republic of Ireland). In contrast, practically everything has changed in Africa – the names of countries as well as their frontiers. And there have been great changes in Asia too. For example, at the beginning of the century what we now know as Bangladesh was part of British India: in 1947 it became part of Pakistan; and only in 1971 did it become its independent self.

In Europe there has been an almost continuous game of musical borders. Take Czechoslovakia as an example. In 1901 it didn't exist; in 1919 it was created; in 1939 it was split into three; and in 1945 the pieces were put back together again. To the west of the River Rhine, in Alsace, there are towns and villages which began the century as German; they then became French, then German again, and now they're French. People were born, lived, worked and died in those places while the frontiers moved about them, first one way, then the other, and then back again. They may have thought of themselves as Bohemians, Slovaks, Germans or Frenchmen, but they were rarely asked for their opinions about where the lines should be drawn on the maps. It was the rulers who used armies, either to invade and conquer or to back up their demands in negotiations, who decided where the lines would run.

We have to accept that maps, like people's faces, change. We know that maps show us, roughly, where the Russians, the Poles, the Indians, the Chinese and the British live. But they also show us *power* – the power of nations, of their armies, navies and traders. Power decides where the lines are drawn – and changes of power mean that those lines change too.

Nations and Nationalism

In distant times it hadn't mattered much to most people who ruled them – a king, an emperor, a native or a 'foreigner' – unless the ruler was unjust, cruel, or asked for too much in the way of taxes. The main business of life had been making a living; the main issues had been local.

At the end of the nineteenth century, such attitudes were still common. You have already seen that many of the world's people had their work cut out to scrape a bare living for themselves and their children in isolated communities. Yet by that time most people were at least dimly conscious (and many were keenly aware) of what they shared with some people and what made them different from others – for example, religion, language, customs, dress.

That feeling (or 'consciousness') of sharing a common past and the closeness of speaking the same language makes people into nations. We call the feeling itself *nationalism*. By the start of the twentieth century the lines on the map of the world had been drawn into patterns of power which didn't take all that much notice of many nations' feelings. But the time was coming when nationalism would be a very potent force in world affairs.

The World's Empires

In 1901 the world seemed well stocked with emperors. Russia had one, Germany had one, Austria had one; China was ruled by an Empress; and Queen Victoria of England was also, by grace of God, Empress of India. And there were states whose rulers were not called emperors but which still had empires – for example, France, Holland, Spain, Portugal and Belgium.

The map at the top of the next page shows four of the world's great empires. You can see at a glance how they dominated most of the great land-mass of Asia and much of Eastern Europe, as well as the hundreds of different peoples living there.

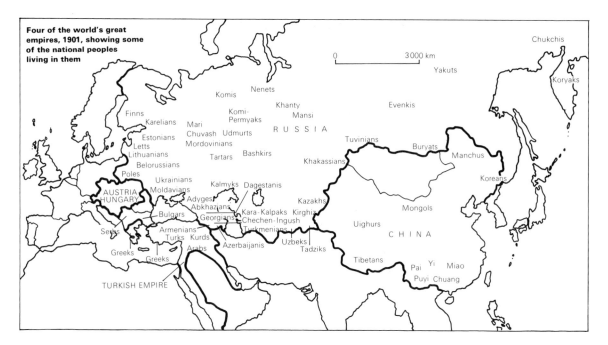

Four of the world's great empires, 1901, showing some of the national peoples living in them

0   3000 km

Chukchis
Yakuts
Koryaks
Komis
Nenets
Khanty
Mansi
Evenkis
Finns
Karelians
Komi-Permyaks
Mari
Chuvash
Udmurts
Estonians
Mordovinians
R U S S I A
Tuvinians
Buryats
Manchus
Letts
Lithuanians
Tartars
Bashkirs
Khakassians
Koreans
Belorussians
Poles
Ukrainians
Moldavians
Kalmyks
Dagestanis
Kazakhs
Mongols
AUSTRIA-HUNGARY
Adyges
Abkhazians
Kara-Kalpaks
Kirghiz
Uighurs
Bulgars
Georgians
Chechen-Ingush
Turkmenians
C H I N A
Serbs
Armenians
Turks
Kurds
Azerbaijanis
Uzbeks
Tadziks
Greeks
Arabs
Tibetans
Pai
Yi
Miao
Greeks
Puyi
Chuang
TURKISH EMPIRE

The map below shows one of those empires in more detail. It reveals how it was made up of various peoples of different nationalities. It makes the idea of empire clear: a dominant nation or people (in this case, German-speaking Austrians) conquer and then rule over subject nations or people.

Unlike the Russians or the Austrians, the nations of Western Europe had nowhere to expand – except overseas. At first they had traded with foreign lands; then they had come to dominate the lands they traded with; and finally they had transformed many of those lands into 'colonies'. In the second half of the nineteenth

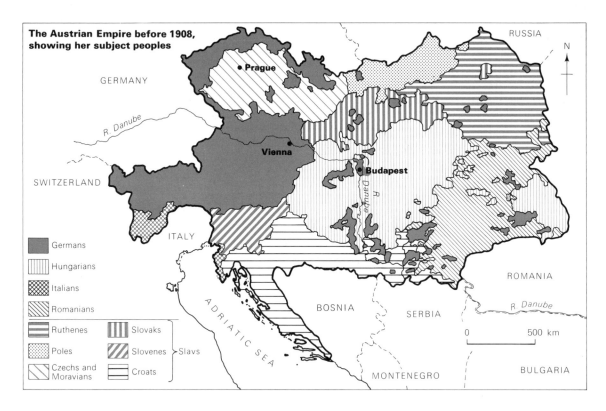

The Austrian Empire before 1908, showing her subject peoples

RUSSIA
GERMANY
Prague
R. Danube
Vienna
SWITZERLAND
Budapest
ITALY
ROMANIA
R. Danube
BOSNIA
SERBIA
ADRIATIC SEA
MONTENEGRO
BULGARIA

0   500 km

Germans
Hungarians
Italians
Romanians
Ruthenes
Slovaks
Poles
Slovenes   Slavs
Czechs and Moravians
Croats

century that gradual enlargement of the European empires had become a scramble to take over those parts of the world which had not yet been colonised – especially in Africa and Asia.

You can see from the map on page 9 that by the start of this century half a dozen nations in Western Europe ruled much of the rest of the world. Their white Christian rulers, soldiers and civil servants lorded it over blacks in Africa, Arabs in the Middle East, and vast numbers of Hindus, Muslims and Buddhists further east still. Lands had been claimed for this or that Western European nation with a total indifference to the wishes of their native populations (except that the local rulers often found that it paid them to do as the powerful foreigners wished.)

Why did the nations of Western Europe go on adding bits, and then yet more bits, to their empires? Sometimes they did it because it was easy to do. Naval and military commanders of expeditions from Europe often found that the locals made no great objection when they ran up their flags over Pacific atolls or African jungles. And once you had run up one flag it seemed only sensible to put up more flags over any other unclaimed land nearby.

Then there were the matters of power and prestige: the bigger you were, the better you felt and looked; and the more people you ruled, the more powerful you appeared. A Britain which could call on the resources (say in wartime) of not only Canada and Australia but on India too was much more imposing than a Britain which depended entirely on the English, Scots, Welsh and a minority of Irishmen.

Then came the matter of strategic security – which meant that you felt safer if your trade routes to distant parts of your empire were protected by colonies along those routes. Again, take the example of British India. After 1869 the main trade route to India was through the Suez Canal. What was more probable than the British then taking over not only Egypt but also other nearby lands to protect their Indian trade?

Underlying the steady growth of empires was also the fact that Western Europe had come to depend on them for its continued industrial development. To Europeans the expansion of plantations and mines had become essential to provide much of the food for the tables of their growing populations and raw materials to fuel their industries. Such considerations meant that no place in the world then seemed too small on which to stick a European flag. Their effect on Africa in par-

ticular was extraordinary. It was owned, practically lock, stock and barrel, by white Europeans.

If the behaviour of the Western Europeans now looks outrageous, we have to remember that they acted as they did not only for hardheaded commercial and strategic reasons, but also because they felt they were bringing advantages to their subject peoples. They believed they were better administrators, more just rulers than the native leaders they either displaced or worked with – and judged by Western standards, in many cases they were. When Joseph Chamberlain, Britain's Colonial Secretary, declared that "the British race is the greatest governing race the world has ever known", many Britons warmly agreed with him.

Finally, there were the missionaries – the men and women who set out to bring the word of Christ to the heathen. Deeply devout people (why else would they have gone?), they also believed their duty lay in taking the light of their civilisations to the 'dark' corners of the world. But the empire-builders followed in their footsteps. After all, the missionaries had to be protected – like the trade routes.

Profits and Losses

The Europeans who wanted to expand their empires thought that they could not only control sources of vital raw materials in the colonies but also use the colonies as markets for their own manufactured goods. But it is not at all clear whether that idea paid off as fully as the Europeans hoped. Certainly, as you saw in the previous chapter, the industrial nations, like those of Western Europe, imported cheap food and raw materials from abroad; but the countries which exported the rice, tea, sugar, tin, jute and rubber did not turn out to be an expanding market for manufactures. Quite simply, they couldn't afford all that many of them.

In general, what happened was that standards of living in the industrial nations rose more quickly than standards in the primary-producing countries. These were lands where almost the only work, apart from subsistence farming, lay in producing raw materials and/ or food for export. Most of these primary-producing countries were colonies. If the colonies had had enough money to invest in the improvement of their own mines, farms and plantations, and *if* they had had more technical know-how, they would obviously have done better. But they didn't have the cash or the skills to

A snapshot of British imperialism: Lord Curzon, Viceroy of India, seated in a gold-embossed howdah on an elephant (left), watches the arrival of his guests at the Delhi Durbar in 1903.

The colonial empires of Western Europe by 1910

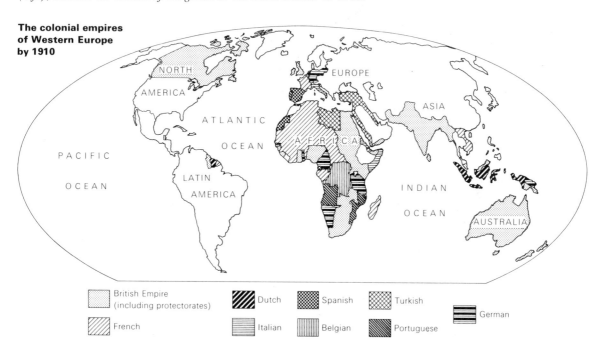

go it alone. It was only recently, when they became independent, that some of them were able to band together and make the industrial nations pay higher prices for their products.

Meantime, the glories of empires were not cheap for the nations which ran them. It cost a great deal to employ civil servants to administer colonies, soldiers to defend them against internal disorder and threats from outside, and sailors to keep the trade routes open. Frequently, however, the colony, not the 'mother country', paid some of those salaries and wages. The British ruled and defended India: in return for those services they taxed the Indians.

Who, then, benefited from the colonial empires? You've met some of them already – the civil servants, the judges, the soldiers and the sailors, who benefited by being employed. And no admiral has ever grumbled about being given a bigger fleet to play with.

Among the others were European business men and investors who struck it rich – either in diamond mines, rubber trees or tea plantations. But investment in the cheap-labour colonies was not a sure way to riches: failures were more common than fortunes. Merchants prospered, in general, as they were bound to when world trade was expanding. And the missionaries benefited too. In the security of a colony they could begin to educate as well as to convert, to give medicine to the bodies as well as to comfort the souls.

Independence and Dominions

More than four thousand kilometres across the Atlantic from Western Europe, the USA had, in the nineteenth century, spread from the east to the west coast of North America. The Americans had behaved rather like the European 'imperialists'. The Mexicans, as well as the Apache, Shoshone, Cheyenne, Sioux and other 'Indian' peoples, had been pushed aside, resettled or simply exterminated in the Union's advance to the Pacific. As Red Cloud, a chief of the Sioux people, said, "The white man made us many promises, more than I can remember, but they never kept but one; they promised to take our land, and they took it." But the conquered peoples and their lands were included in the enlarged Union, and that alone made the United States of America (think carefully about that name for a moment) very different from Russia or Turkey. It was *not* an empire. Indeed, ever since the original thirteen states had fought their way out of the British Empire the Americans had been against imperialism, and especially against Western European imperialism. The 'Monroe Doctrine' (declared early in the nineteenth century) told Europeans to keep their noses out of the affairs of the whole American continent, and in that century the old Spanish and Portuguese empires in Latin America collapsed. Brazil, Argentina, Chile, Bolivia, Peru, Columbia, Venezuela – all became independent countries.

If you look back at the map on page 9 you will see that the Europeans were left with a shaky hold on a few colonies in and around the Caribbean. Compare that with the grip they had on Asia and Africa, which lacked protection from a big brother like the USA.

During the early nineteenth century the former colonies of Latin America had freed themselves by war from Spain and Portugal. In the later nineteenth and early twentieth centuries certain territories in the British Empire achieved a different kind of independence. They were the 'white colonies'. Canada, Australia and New Zealand were settled almost entirely by Englishmen and Scotsmen. There was no difficulty in allowing them to become virtually self-governing Dominions within the Empire.

South Africa, also a 'white colony', was different. Most of her white farmer settlers, the Boers, were Dutch, yet the commerce, the gold and diamond mines and the government of the colony were in the hands of the British. After the Boers had settled in new areas in the interior, they refused to submit to British government. In the Boer War (1899–1902) Britain imposed her will by force. In 1910 the British government persuaded the two Boer provinces of the Transvaal and the Orange Free State to join together with the two provinces of the Cape and Natal in the Union of South Africa, to which Britain granted self-government. The Boers, or Afrikaners as they were also known, only agreed to join the Union, however, if the British agreed to their demand that only Europeans should be able to sit in their parliament, and that the qualifications for voting should be so strict that hardly any Africans would be able to vote. Britain agreed because she was anxious to keep the four provinces within the Empire, but she hoped that eventually the English settlers would outnumber the Boers and that they would be able to change the laws.

Japan and the USA: New Imperialists

The traffic was not all one-way – out of empires. While the British were granting self-government to the white settlement colonies, they and other European powers were taking over more of Africa and Asia. Even China with her 400 million people was forced to allow European traders to settle in her cities, sail freely along the rivers, and build railway lines from which the traders took the profits.

But while Western European powers were still taking over foreign territories, two newcomers appeared in the empire-building business – Japan and the USA. Japan was the more extraordinary of the two. Midway through the nineteenth century, that country looked as if she would suffer the same fate as China and see her trading wealth trickle ever faster into the pockets of foreigners. The Japanese saw, however, that the best way to beat the Westerner was at his own game. By the start of the twentieth century they had developed the industrial power and the military and naval strength to make war on – and defeat – the might of the Russian Empire in the Russo–Japanese War of 1904–1905.

Like the British the Japanese could expand nowhere but overseas. By 1910 they had created an empire at the expense of the Russians and Chinese – and that had whetted their appetite for more.

If Japan's new empire was a startling development, America's policy of grabbing foreign land for herself looked like barefaced hypocrisy. While using the Monroe Doctrine to keep Europe at arm's length from the New World, the USA took over Hawaii, the Philippines and other Pacific islands and gained control of Cuba. Most of this was done in the name of 'liberating' these lands from Spanish rule. The US government backed up American business men and trading companies by openly interfering in the affairs of other Caribbean and Latin American countries.

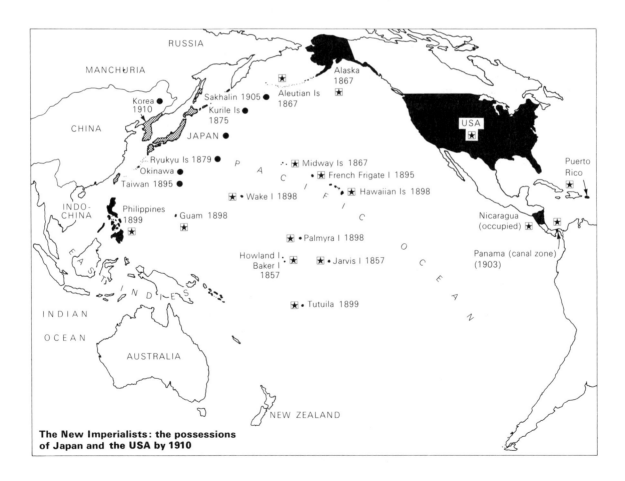

The New Imperialists: the possessions of Japan and the USA by 1910

The reason for American imperialism was much the same as that for European imperialism – the protection of commercial interests and of trade routes. At the very beginning of the twentieth century the USA negotiated with Colombia for the rights to build and fortify a canal through the Isthmus of Panama, which Colombia controlled. Colombia asked too high a price. In 1903 a convenient revolution in the Panama region against Colombia led to the setting up of a new independent state of Panama – which agreed to accept the USA's terms of ten million dollars for permanent rights over a sixteen-kilometre-wide canal zone. The waterway was opened in 1914 – under US control.

Hints of Things to Come

Earlier in this chapter we touched on feelings of 'nationalism' – people's sense of belonging to a distinct 'nation', of sharing the same history, traditions, religion and, above all, the same language. Administrators and soldiers of the great empires often trod heavily all over such feelings. Many of them believed they understood the culture of those they ruled, but such understanding as they had was usually very limited. The only nationalists who gloried in empire were the aggressive nationalists of the imperial countries themselves. Just as they imposed their taxes and laws upon foreign peoples, so they imposed their own languages too. Africans and Asians who wanted to do well found they had to leave their villages, take on European dress and customs and speak English, French or German.

But while the imperial countries were still redrawing the lines on the map in their own interests, nationalists were already undoing some of their old work. In Eastern Europe nationalists fought for and won their independence from the Turkish Empire. As that empire shrank back towards the east, the new nations of Serbia, Greece, Romania and Bulgaria were established. It would be Austria's turn next to deal with aggressive Balkan nationalists.

Nearer home, nationalists had almost succeeded in persuading Britain to give Ireland to the Irish – although the whole question of Ireland's future was about to be darkened by Protestant nationalists in Ulster, who threatened revolution if the British dared to leave them to sink or swim in an independent, mainly Catholic, Ireland.

Far away, in British India, extreme nationalists were already turning to terrorism – to assassination and bombings – in their attacks on the ruling foreigners. At the same time two moderate nationalist organisations, the Indian National Congress and the Muslim League, were pressing for a share in governing their country. But, as long as most Englishmen denied that Indians were their equals, there was little hope of much progress in allowing Indians to take a more responsible part in the government of their own country.

At the beginning of the twentieth century nationalism was stronger in Asia than in Africa. The Japanese defeat of Russia in the war of 1904–1905 provided Asian nationalists with a model of how to deal with Western imperialists.

The Japanese slogan of 'Asia for the Asians' was taken up by the Chinese nationalists. Their leader, Sun Yat-sen, was pledged to drive Westerners out of China, and after a revolution in 1911 he became the first President of a new Chinese Republic. In the following year a nationalist party was set up in Indonesia with the aim of driving out the Dutch colonialists. In Indo-China the French were trying to groom upper-class Indo-Chinese into Catholic, French-speaking rulers; but the majority of their subject people remained *Asian* Asians in culture, religion and language.

With few exceptions, nationalists did not yet pose a severe threat to the stronger empires, those of the British and the French. But their time would come, especially after a great war in which nationalists in Europe would help that continent to tear itself apart. But before we come to that we have to look at another aspect of the world as it marched into the twentieth century – its politics.

3 Politics Old and New

Critics of Capitalism

The growth of industry in the advanced countries of the West had affected not only the ways in which people earned their daily bread, their expectations of life, the survival rate of their children, their entertainments and habits of religious observance – it had also greatly altered their political attitudes, and it was beginning to change the forms of government under which they lived. The 'industrial revolution', which had made farm labourers into factory hands, was also developing, under its own steam, a political revolution.

The power of the old political masters – kings and queens, great landowners, bishops and priests – was fast fading. The capitalists, the men who owned the factories, mines and railways, demanded political power to match their economic power. And the workers they employed also had ambitions. For many of them, industrial employment, with its relatively high wages, was a distinct improvement on rural poverty. But city life could be grim, with its often squalid living conditions and long hours of disciplined work. They had been recruited into industry to create new wealth for their masters. Now they were beginning to claim their own share of that wealth; and some of them were seeking the political power they thought was their due.

The new political questions about how people should live and be governed in industrial societies were answered in different ways. There were reformers who wanted to improve working conditions in factories, to abolish child labour where it still existed, to develop 'social welfare' schemes and better housing to make city life tolerable and decent. Others, however, wanted much more radical changes. They saw capitalism as nothing but the exploitation of the many by the few. The capitalist was in business for profit, not to do good. The aim of the workers, or proletarians, should be, therefore, to destroy the capitalists, and then take over for themselves the means of production and distribution. That would be the next, and the last, political struggle. After the 'workers' revolution', all property and all power would be in the hands of all the people.

Marx and the Workers

The man who had made the most eloquent and forceful appeal for a workers' revolution was Karl Marx, a German Jew. Chased out of his own country, he had finally settled down in London to write his book, *Capital*. But by the time of his death in 1883 the revolution he worked for had not happened in either Britain or Germany, the two most advanced industrial countries in Europe, where he had expected that the worst injustices of capitalism would goad the workers into action. Marx was dead, but he had left behind in his *Communist Manifesto* one of the great battle-cries of history:

"Let the ruling classes tremble at a Communistic revolution. The proletarians have nothing to lose but their chains. They have a world to win.
WORKING MEN OF ALL COUNTRIES UNITE!"

That call to action was taken up by Marx's followers – Marxists – who believed that revolutions in the industrialised countries would lead, in the end, to the triumph of workers throughout the world. Such people would, in the twentieth century, be known as communists. However, in the late nineteenth century, Marx's ideas also gave many industrial workers a sense that the working class was on the way up, and that they didn't have to accept oppression and exploitation as part of an unchangeable pattern of life. They came to believe that if they were well organised and ably led, they could claim their right to a share in political power.

Such men were not out-and-out revolutionaries. They had little desire to turn the world upside down; but they were determined to improve the position of workers in their own countries. In Britain, in Germany and in France, they encouraged working men to band together in trade unions to press for higher pay and better working conditions; and in those countries there grew up non-revolutionary socialist parties, seeking to attract the votes of working-class men. These parties were independent of the small, revolutionary communist groups, and they proposed their own candidates for election to national parliaments.

Broadly speaking, the contestants in the struggles for power that we know as politics were changing. The new parties which claimed to stand for the interests of the workers began to compete with the old parties which represented the traditional ruling classes. Put in terms which are easy to remember, the new parties of the Left began to challenge the established parties of the Right.

Patterns of Power

We can now look at politics in particular countries to see how, if at all, industrialisation had affected them; and see what other factors had given them their character by the beginning of the twentieth century.

In Britain, industrialisation had already had profound effects, for the great landowners no longer controlled Parliament. Some of them still sat in the House of Lords – by hereditary right, not by election – but that body was about to have its powers severely trimmed in 1911. The government was formed by the party which won most seats in a general election to the other House of Parliament, the Commons. At the start of the century that chamber was dominated by two parties, the Liberals and the Conservatives, both of which had learnt how to appeal to a population in which most adult males had the vote. A third party was formed, which claimed to represent the demands of the working class for a share in law-making. Yet for a time that new organisation, known as the Labour Party from 1906, had little effect. Its representation in Parliament was small compared with over eighty Irish Nationalist MPs, most of whom had only one concern – to win Home Rule (self-government) for Ireland.

The politics of other industrialised countries in Western Europe looked similar to those of Britain. For example, both France and Germany had parliaments elected by the adult males in their populations. But there were important differences too, as we should expect, since each country had developed in its own way, politically as well as economically.

In France, organised religion still played an important part in political life. The Catholic Church's involvement in politics raised questions such as whether the state or the Church should control education; and France's political parties were either 'clerical' or 'anti-clerical', for or against the influence of the Church. There was nothing quite like that on the main island of Britain. Then again, there were more people who made their living from the land in France than in Britain. The interests of large numbers of conservative peasants were not the same as those of industrial workers; and French politics reflected that deep conflict of interests.

The British monarch had been stripped of power well before the beginning of the twentieth century and no longer played an active part in politics. In contrast, the German Kaiser (Emperor) wielded great power and appointed the ministers of his government without consulting the *Reichstag* (Parliament). Those ministers came from the old ruling class of Germany and most of them were from landowning families in Prussia, the powerful state which had forced the smaller German states to unite with her into one empire. The weak and divided opposition to the government came from the members elected to the Reichstag from the smaller states and from liberals who believed that Germany should be more democratic. There was also a fast-growing Social Democratic Party. The government had tried to prevent the spread of socialism in the industrial cities by introducing the first unemployment benefits and old-age pensions of any country in Europe, but it could not stop the industrial workers voting for the Social Democrats.

In contrast to both Britain and Germany, Russia had been slow to industrialise and most wealth was still in the hands of the imperial family, the landed nobility and the Church. The main business of the government of the Tsar (Emperor) was to keep law and order, to control the subject peoples of the Russian Empire, and to protect landowners against the frequent outbreaks of peasant violence. The Fundamental Law of the Russian Empire said: "The Emperor of all the Russias is an autocratic [all powerful] and unlimited monarch. God himself commands that his supreme power be obeyed. ..." God might command obedience to the Tsar, but in that immense empire obedience had to be enforced by a large civil service, the Russian Orthodox Church, the secret police and the Cossacks – peasant warriors from south Russia who were allowed to rule themselves in return for helping out the Tsar in time of trouble.

The most spectacular opponents of the Tsar's government were the terrorists who wanted to smash the system, not tinker with it. In 1881 they blew up Tsar Alexander II, an act which merely made the next Tsar set his face against reform of any kind. The non-violent opposition to the power of the Tsar came from the Liberals, who believed that Russia should be modernised on the lines of France and Britain. That would have meant industrialising, improving public services such as schools and roads, and setting up a more modern form of government, responsive to the needs of the people. Eventually, in 1906, after the Tsar's government had been weakened by disastrous defeat in the war with Japan (see Chapter 2, page 11), Russia did get a parliament, or 'Duma'. It was a sham, it had no real power and the Tsar sent its members away every time they tried to discuss political questions seriously. But the Duma was never finally disbanded.

Meanwhile, as industrialisation got under way in western Russia, workers in the cities formed trade unions; and a Social Democratic Party, influenced by the ideas of Karl Marx, was started – but it met in secret and had next to no effect on Russian politics. In 1903 a small group, calling themselves the Bolsheviks, and led by Vladimir Ilich Lenin, set off on their own to plan a Marxist revolution in Tsarist Russia. However, even Lenin thought they hadn't a hope of succeeding during his lifetime.

Across the Atlantic, or across the Bering Sea, was the USA, whose form of government was as unlike that of Russia as people could imagine. Many Russians did imagine it and promptly left Russia on a one-way ticket to 'the land of the free'. America was democratic: the people (provided they were neither female nor black) elected their President as well as Congress (Parliament). Indeed, Americans seemed addicted to voting, as they also elected their state governors and parliaments, their town mayors, sheriffs, police chiefs, judges and school boards.

There was, however, a darker side to American politics. The southern states, which had lost the Civil War against the more industrialised North only forty years before, were still plagued with a vicious racialism: negroes were systematically denied their civil rights. In the northern cities immigrant workers and children were ruthlessly exploited in factories and sweatshops. But there was little chance of Marx's ideas making much headway there. Trade unions found it difficult to recruit new members among a highly mobile working population, many of whom were recently arrived immigrants. And although hours of work in America were long, rates of pay were generally much higher than in Europe. Both main political parties, the Democrats and the Republicans, supported a more or less unrestrained capitalist system. They believed that it offered unique incentives to hard work and opportunities for all – even though there was plenty of evidence that it left many people very poor and a few grotesquely rich.

As you saw in Chapter 2, much of the rest of the world had been gathered into the colonial empires of Western European states, such as France, Britain and Germany. Colonies were ruled directly by the mother countries, or indirectly through local princes and chiefs. Within the British Empire the exceptions were India and the white Dominions.

India was provided with a complete system of government and an army. Her people were controlled by British civil servants and British officers; and at the head of that system of rule was the 'Viceroy', appointed by the British government in London. The former white colonies of Australia, New Zealand and Canada had become self-governing countries (South Africa achieved the same status in 1910) and, reasonably enough, they adopted the British way of governing themselves, through elected parliaments. As in any other country whose government was not controlled from outside, the political struggles inside the Dominions were about their own peculiar circumstances and people. For example, in Australia the battle was about the powers of the federal government and the rights of the individual states which made up the 'Commonwealth of Australia'. In South Africa the struggle for power was restricted to a contest between the Boers and the English settlers, with the black population looking on to see who would be their eventual masters.

You have now seen something of the variety of the world's politics as it entered the twentieth century. You have seen how communism and non-revolutionary socialism were beginning to emerge as alternatives to capitalism; and how some Western European countries enforced their rule over much of the rest of the world. We ended the last chapter with a look at nationalist opposition to the European imperialists. Among the leaders of that opposition were men who admired much of what they saw or read of Western Europe. Some of the Asians who wanted the French out of Indo-China admired the French ideals of 'Liberty, Equality, Fraternity'. And many of the Indians who wanted to expel the British were deeply impressed by British parliamentary government. In a sense they wished to destroy the power of the West in order to spread what many of them believed to be good Western values – such as liberalism and democracy – in their own lands. We must now turn to see how the West tried to help them, unintentionally, by an attempt to destroy itself.

4 Towards Disaster: Causes of the Great War

Europe Under Stress

At the beginning of this century Europe was at peace and parts of it, especially in the West, were prosperous. No-one was fighting anyone else of importance. Indeed, ever since the defeat of the French Emperor, Napoleon, at Waterloo in 1815, there had been no war in which all the major powers of Europe – France, Austria, Russia, Britain and Germany (Prussia before 1871) – had been involved.

But if there had been no general continental conflict, there had been many smaller wars; and behind most of the troubles that had flared into fighting had been something we have come across before – nationalism. It had expressed itself in two forms: the nationalism of great powers, who wanted to extend their boundaries and their influence to make themselves even more powerful; and the nationalism of groups of subject peoples who wanted to set up their own independent national homelands and states. In the nineteenth century nationalism had provoked only local wars: in the early twentieth century it would drag Europe down the path to disaster.

In the West

Germany was a new country, a collection of German-speaking peoples forged into one state by Prussia. The rise of a united Germany, with its powerful Prussian army, had been feared and resented by the French; and hostility had erupted into war in 1870. The French lost the war; and in 1871, when the lines on the map were re-drawn, France lost the provinces of Alsace and Lorraine. Although only a minority of the people of those provinces was German, the Prussians decided that the new German Reich needed the territories to make its western frontier more secure. In the very act of creating their new empire, German nationalists had made for themselves a long-term enemy – France.

Over the next thirty years, German nationalists pressed for expansion overseas, for Germany to build the same kind of colonial empire that France and Britain already had. Their reasons were familiar: Germany needed colonies to provide raw materials for her new industries; and German prestige was at stake. When the young Wilhelm II became Kaiser in 1888, he actively encouraged the ambitions of German nationalists. While Germany claimed colonies overseas, in Africa and in the Pacific, Kaiser Wilhelm tried to persuade Britain and France that Germany was not out to compete with them.

For a time it seemed that the two established Western European empires and the newcomer could co-exist peacefully. But friction and rivalry were almost inevitable. Both Britain and France regarded the Mediterranean as an area of great strategic and commercial importance. Britain controlled the entrance to it at Gibraltar; France, whose empire included Algeria and Tunisia, controlled much of the coast of North Africa, and it had been generally agreed that she should also be the predominant European power in Morocco. In 1905 Kaiser Wilhelm stirred up the waters of the Mediterranean by claiming that Germany would guarantee Morocco's independence. At a conference in Algeciras one year later it was agreed that Morocco should remain independent but that France should still retain her special position there. Five years later, in 1911, Germany plunged into Mediterranean affairs once again by protesting against a likely French takeover of Morocco. The French did complete their takeover – and Germany got nothing out of the two crises she had provoked, except the hostility of both France and Britain, now drawing ever closer together to protect their common interests.

In the meantime, another, more ominous, contest had developed: a 'naval race' between Britain and Germany. Early in the century Germany had expanded her navy, much to the delight and pride of German nationalists – and to the alarm of the British. As you have already seen in Chapter 2, Britain's economy depended on her trade routes, and the safety of those routes depended on the unchallenged supremacy of the Royal Navy. The British had a song, 'Rule Britannia', which they felt made their position perfectly clear to anyone who cared to listen:

"When Britain first, at Heaven's command,
Arose from out the azure main,
This was the charter of the land,
And guardian angels sang this strain:
'Rule Britannia, Britannia rule the waves;
Britons never, never, never shall be slaves.'"

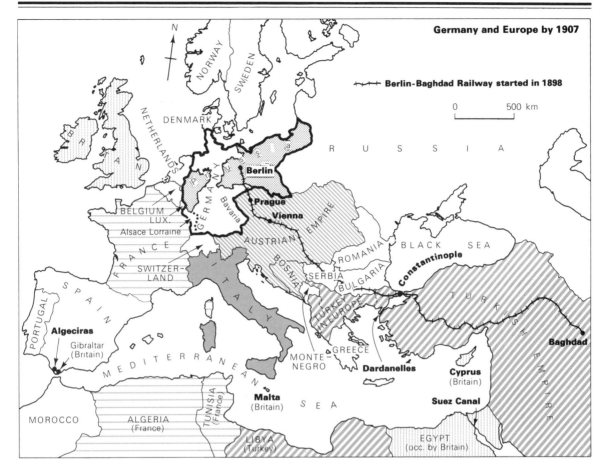

Germany and Europe by 1907

+++ Berlin-Baghdad Railway started in 1898

0   500 km

But German nationalists turned a deaf ear to that kind of music. Their protests that they were not competing with the empires in the West had already begun to sound hollow before 1906, when Britain launched HMS *Dreadnought*, the first of a new class of powerful battleships. In 1909 the Germans launched the *West-falen*, which looked remarkably similar. The 'naval race' was becoming more and more expensive for both powers – and more dangerous.

In the East

You will see from a glance at the map above that there was no state of Poland at the start of this century. That doesn't mean to say, of course, that there were no Poles. The people of that nationality, without a state of their own, were subjects of the three great empires which met in Central Europe – those of Germany, Austria and Russia. Because the Poles were members of the Slav race they had more in common with their rulers to the east (the Russians were Slavs) than with

their Germanic overlords to the west and south. This did not mean, however, that the Poles preferred Russian rule to German or Austrian rule. On the contrary, Polish revolts against Russia in 1830 and 1867 had shown how powerfully they detested their eastern rulers. What it did mean was that German rule of Polish Slavs was already a sore point with Russia and that the issue of Polish independence was therefore a possible source of international discord.

The rulers of the new Reich had also begun to push German influence further into South Eastern Europe, into the area we call the Balkans, where Russia had long-standing interests. First, Russia's trade route from the Black Sea to the Mediterranean was through the Dardanelles: it was vitally important that control of those straits didn't pass from a weakening Turkish Empire into the grip of a power hostile to Russia. Second, two of the nationalities in the Balkans, the Serbs and Bulgars, were not only Slavs but shared the same religion as the Russians – Orthodox Christianity.

17

To the Russians this seemed a natural justification for expanding their influence into the Balkans.

It was into that hotbed of Slav nationalism that Germany drove the Berlin–Baghdad Railway. Many Bulgarians were pleased by this new stimulus to trade in their poverty-stricken corner of Europe; it was also some guarantee against being swallowed up by Russia. The Russians saw the railway as a threat to their hope of influence in the Balkans.

By both ruling over Polish Slavs and penetrating into the Balkans, Germany made herself the natural ally of the Austrian Empire – that great Central European jumble of races and nationalities which was also ruled by Germans, included many Slavs and took a keen interest in Balkan affairs. The rulers of Austria were particularly disturbed by the second kind of nationalism we mentioned at the beginning of this chapter – the nationalism of subject peoples. And if you refer back to the map of the Austrian Empire before 1908 on page 9, you don't have to look very hard to see why.

The most aggressive nationalists in the Balkans were the Serbs. The kingdom of Serbia had been set up late in the nineteenth century when its people had won their independence from the decaying Turkish Empire. But that was not enough for Serbian nationalists: they planned to create a Yugoslavia (South Slavia) by joining to Serbia all the Slav peoples who lived in the south of the Austrian Empire, and the northern tongue of the Ottoman Empire. To the German-speaking rulers in Vienna, the creation of a Yugoslavia would mean the end of their empire: if the Southern Slavs were allowed to break out it would be only a matter of time before the Czechs, Poles, Hungarians and Slovaks went their separate ways.

Two Power Blocs and a Plan for War

When countries share common interests, and especially when they feel they share common enemies, they become allies – they sign 'alliances' with each other. Shortly after Prussia had hammered together the German states, the new German Empire formed an alliance with Austria. That 'power bloc', stretching across Central Europe and later joined by Italy, scared the French and Russians into each other's arms. They signed an alliance in 1892: in the unlikely event of war, Russia promised to support France if she were attacked by Germany. But, as you have seen, aggressive nationalism in the early twentieth century began to make war more, rather than less, likely.

The generals of the German army took the prospect of war in their stride. They believed they must plan to win it on two fronts – first, quickly in the west against France, and then in the east against Russia. Any plan which involves the movement of hundreds of thousands of men and their equipment, by rail, on horse and on foot, through the home country, then through enemy territory, and then back again, takes a long time to settle. When the German war-plan, named after General von Schlieffen, was finally settled, it set like concrete. Germany was stuck with it. Even if war broke out over a dispute in the east or the south of Europe, the German war machine could respond only by striking *west* first. And that would make a general European war far more likely.

Britain had tried to remain aloof from the two hardening power blocs. Separated by the sea from continental Europe, she had believed that her future lay in the development and protection of her overseas empire. But the growing menace of the German navy had forced the British to change their attitude. In 1904 and 1907 they had signed 'ententes' with France and Russia respectively. The 'ententes' were general agreements rather than firm alliances. For example, the entente with the French did not mean that Britain agreed to support France, unconditionally, against any enemy. But it did bring Britain and France closer together by clearing up disagreements between the two countries over colonial matters, and by encouraging the heads of their armed forces to discuss what joint action they might take if war did break out.

So, the five great powers of Europe had aligned themselves in two opposing blocs; and the great power in the centre of it all – Germany – had already developed a war-plan capable of turning a local conflict into general disaster. That local conflict would eventually break out between Austria and Serbia; and the incident to spark it off would happen in a place called Bosnia. The people who struck the spark would be what you would expect – extreme nationalists.

The Bosnian Connection

In the year 1908 Austria extended her boundary to the south by taking over the province of Bosnia from the Turks. The people of Bosnia were Slavs; and since most of them were Serbian Slavs, the takeover was a slap in the eye for Serbian nationalists and for their

Russian sympathisers. Russia reacted by increasing her support for Balkan nationalism and encouraging Serbia, Romania, Bulgaria and Greece to form the 'Balkan League', an instrument which Russia hoped to turn against Austria. The members of the League, however, turned instead on Turkey in the First Balkan War of 1912; and then on each other in the Second Balkan War of 1913. The most important result of those struggles was that Serbia, the most intensely nationalist of the Balkan states, had roughly doubled in size by the end of 1913. It appeared that the Serbian dream (and the Austrian nightmare) of an independent Yugoslavia might be coming true.

On 28 June 1914, in Sarajevo, the capital of Bosnia, Serbian nationalists shot dead the heir to the Austrian throne, Archduke Francis Ferdinand, and his wife. The man who pulled the trigger, Gavrilo Princip, was a Bosnian Serb, but the Austrian government blamed the killings on the kingdom of Serbia. It was convenient to do so: encouraged by Germany, the

The changed face of the Balkans by 1914

The Balkans before 1912

Austrians decided to use the murders as the excuse to smash the homeland of Serbian nationalism. After making unacceptable demands on the Serbian government, Austria declared war on 28 July.

Suddenly, the two power blocs found themselves eyeball to eyeball, unable to prevent a war down in the south-east spreading like a plague across the continent. As Austria opened fire on Serbia, Russia prepared all her armies for war – the one in the north which would attack Germany as well as the central and southern armies which could help the Serbs. Austria's ally, Germany, promptly declared war on Russia and then (remember General Schlieffen's plan?) attacked France. The easiest line of attack in the west was through the lowlands of Belgium, well equipped with roads leading to France. By invading neutral Belgium on 4 August, the Germans not only shocked public opinion in Britain; they threatened to occupy the ports on the other side of what was, after all, the *English* Channel. On the same day Britain declared war on Germany.

Whatever their political opinions, whatever the form of government they shared in or endured, most of the people of the five great powers of Europe greeted the

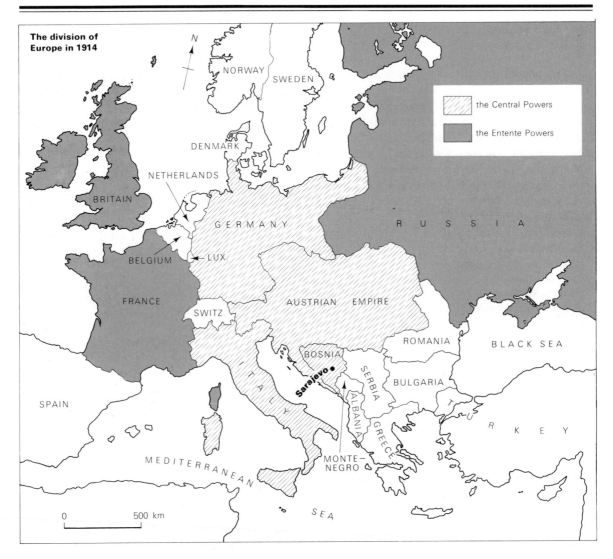

The division of
Europe in 1914

N

the Central Powers

the Entente Powers

NORWAY

SWEDEN

DENMARK

NETHERLANDS

BRITAIN

GERMANY

RUSSIA

BELGIUM

LUX.

FRANCE

SWITZ.

AUSTRIAN EMPIRE

ROMANIA

BLACK SEA

SPAIN

ITALY

BOSNIA

Sarajevo

SERBIA

BULGARIA

ALBANIA

GREECE

TURKEY

MONTE-
NEGRO

MEDITERRANEAN

SEA

0   500 km

outbreak of war with loud enthusiasm. Each country had its reasons for thinking the war was just and necessary. The soldiers went forth joyfully to do battle, and their mums and dads and children proudly waved them goodbye. They expected them to be back in time for the Christmas pudding.

5 The Great War of 1914–18

The Making of the Fronts

The Great European War began with three great blunders. First, after a successful start to the Schlieffen Plan when the Germans marched confidently through Belgium and into northern France, their armies were slowed down and a change was made in the great warplan. Instead of sending their First Army to the west of Paris and then rolling up the French armies from the rear, the Germans attacked with all their forces to the east of Paris and were stopped dead in their tracks at the Battle of the Marne.

Despite their success at the Marne, the French generals didn't have the strength to follow it up. This was because they had made the second mistake of the war in the very first week. Believing that attack was the best form of defence, they had thrown their best troops against the Germans in the centre and the south. They had suffered appalling casualties and had been beaten back.

The Russians made the third mistake. Their two northern armies lumbered into eastern Germany, with little idea of what to do once they got there, except to occupy German territories along the Baltic coast. But

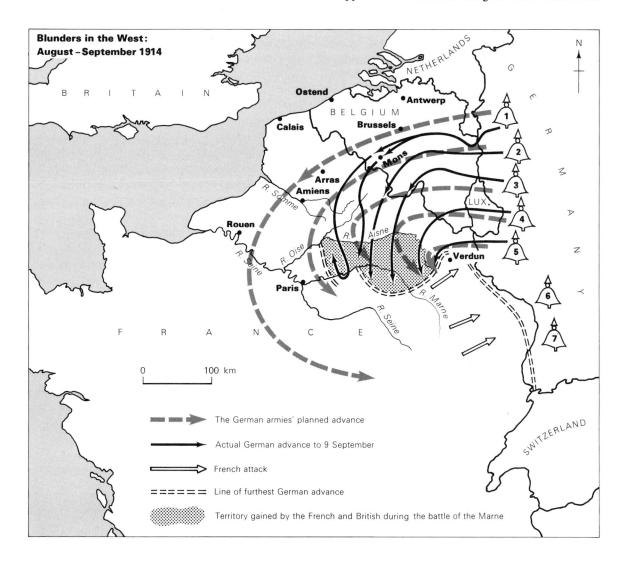

Blunders in the West:
August – September 1914

0   100 km

━ ━ ▶ The German armies' planned advance

───▶ Actual German advance to 9 September

═▷ French attack

= = = = = Line of furthest German advance

▒▒▒ Territory gained by the French and British during the battle of the Marne they had no plans for defending the land they had occupied and were promptly clobbered by the Germans in the battles of Tannenberg and the Masurian Lakes.

In the west, the two sides searched for each other's weak points to break through. They found none. By November 1914 they faced each other along a line which stretched from the Channel to the Swiss frontier. The Western Front had been drawn on the map. In the east, the Germans advanced into Russia, the Russians advanced into Austria, and then the armies of the three powers paused for the winter. The Eastern Front, much longer and in places much more vague than the front in the west, had been only roughly sketched out.

A New Kind of War

Over the next three years the great powers of Europe fed their men, money and munitions into those two fronts. There were plenty of men available – and mostly willing – to fight. At first the densely populated countries of Western and Central Europe recruited millions of soldiers without much difficulty. Russia was a human reservoir. Governments of the great powers spent all the money they dared to raise in taxes and then borrowed more – from their own citizens and from any other countries prepared to lend it. They geared their industries to the new markets of human destruction and turned out weapons and ammunition in unbelievable quantities. In those three long years the Germans pushed part of the Eastern Front further east and the Russians pushed another part further west – neither overwhelmed the other. And the shorter Western Front stood still.

A modern historian has described the reason for the stalemate of the Great War like this: "There was ... a twentieth-century delivery-system, but a nineteenth-century warhead." The delivery system of the armies was the railway network of Europe. Trains could deliver masses of men speedily to the fronts and supply them with food, armaments and equipment. But beyond the railheads the armies could move only at the speed of a marching man or of a horse pulling a wagon or gun. And if an army did threaten to break through at some point on the front, the opposition could rush its reserves by rail to reinforce that point. Just one example should help you to appreciate the scale of railway operations. When the German Fourth Army came

under attack in Flanders between June and November 1917, it used a total of 6,591 trains, pulling 242,185 wagons to feed, supply and reinforce itself. The railways, which, in the nineteenth century, had brought the people of Europe closer together in peaceful trade, now held them fast in war – and the generals could think of no way out, except to demand more men, more guns, more shells to hammer the enemy.

To protect themselves from rifle and machine-gun fire and the explosions of artillery shells, the soldiers of the front-line armies sheltered in trenches, which were soon extended into elaborate systems of defence and communication. The Western Front became probably the most extraordinary spectacle in the history of warfare. The two sides, each made up of millions of men, confronted each other, below ground level, in trench systems so complicated that only the birds and daring young men in their flying machines could fully appreciate them.

Generals planned the most deliberate battles the world had ever witnessed, monotonously following the same pattern of intense artillery bombardment of enemy barbed wire and trenches before the PBI (Poor Bloody Infantry) were sent 'over the top' into the attack. And the enemy reinforced the sector of their line under stress and eventually the attack would stop, after gaining maybe a few kilometres of worthless territory. With few exceptions, the great battles of the war ended in neither victory nor defeat, but in exhaustion. Verdun, the Somme, Passchendaele – they were all massacres whose futile horrors sickened the imagination. "We shall bleed the French to death", said the Germans before the battle of Verdun; and the world watched, astounded, as the 'civilised' countries of Europe opened each other's veins.

The Sideshows

The Great European War was not restricted to the five great powers and little Serbia and Belgium. Anyone could join in. In time a number of the lesser powers either seized the opportunity of war to pay off old scores against their neighbours, or were bribed to enter the fighting, or jumped on the bandwagon of the side they thought would win. The most important of the new entrants were the Turkish Empire and Italy.

Turkey entered the war on the side of Germany and Austria, mainly with the intention of halting Russian expansion around the Black Sea. The British attacked

The Great War of 1914–18

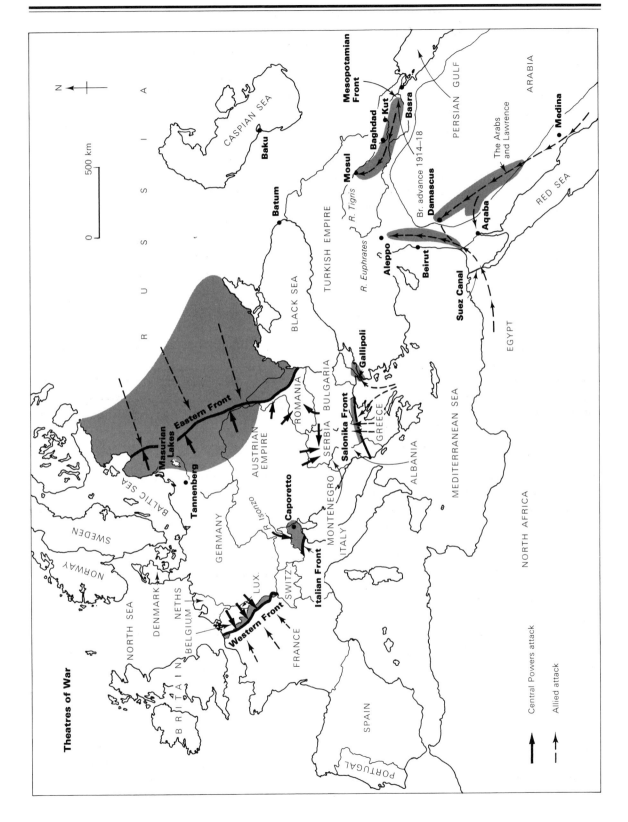

Theatres of War

500 km

N

RUSSIA
CASPIAN SEA
• Baku
• Batum
BLACK SEA
TURKISH EMPIRE
R. Tigris
R. Euphrates
Mosul
Baghdad
• Kut
Basra
Mesopotamian Front
PERSIAN GULF
Br. advance 1914–18
The Arabs and Lawrence
ARABIA
• Medina
RED SEA
Damascus
Aleppo •
Beirut
Aqaba
Suez Canal
EGYPT
MEDITERRANEAN SEA
Gallipoli
GREECE
Salonika Front
BULGARIA
SERBIA
ROMANIA
MONTENEGRO
ALBANIA
AUSTRIAN EMPIRE
Eastern Front
Masurian Lakes
Tannenberg •
Caporetto
R. Isonzo
Italian Front
ITALY
SWITZ.
LUX.
Western Front
BELGIUM
NETHS
FRANCE
GERMANY
DENMARK
BALTIC SEA
SWEDEN
NORWAY
NORTH SEA
BRITAIN
SPAIN
PORTUGAL
NORTH AFRICA

Central Powers attack
Allied attack

23

British soldiers resting in a captured front line trench at Ovillers on the Somme in July 1916.

the Turkish Empire in three separate campaigns. The first, the Gallipoli Campaign, was intended to force a way through the Straits of the Dardanelles into the Black Sea. This would have enabled Britain to attack Germany and her allies from the east and to send supplies to Russia. Just as important, the Gallipoli Campaign seemed to offer the possibility of a quick and unexpected success, in contrast to the deadly stalemate which had already set in on the Western Front. It was an attractive alternative to what Winston Churchill (then the Minister in charge of Britain's navy) described as "sending our armies to chew barbed wire in Flanders".

The first stage, a naval bombardment of the Turkish forts protecting the narrow Straits, was a failure. So to provide the navy with a safe passage through the Straits the British now planned to invade the Gallipoli Peninsula and clear the Turks out altogether. But the build-up was slow; some commanders were too timid and back at home the government was no longer confident that the scheme would succeed. Not enough troops were sent (many of those who were came from the Australian and New Zealand Army Corps – the ANZACS) and the Gallipoli Campaign ended in total failure and withdrawal.

The second campaign was perhaps the first in history which was fought to win control of oil supplies. The expedition to Mesopotamia was to bring the oil of the countries we now know as Iran and Iraq under British control. The Turks resisted fiercely at first, but by the end of the war British forces were in control of the three cities of Basra, Baghdad and Mosul. The third campaign was more glamorous, though its outcome was not at all honourable. The British planned to support the Arabs in a revolt against their Turkish rulers and promised that after the war they would help to create independent Arab states in Iraq, Syria, Palestine and Arabia (today's Saudi Arabia). T. E. Lawrence, a British Intelligence officer, became a military adviser to the Arabs, and helped the Arab rulers to build and lead a guerrilla force in attacks on Turkish railways and supply lines. The daring exploits of this young officer, who became known as 'Lawrence of Arabia', were a strange, romantic episode in the war. In the end, the Arab units linked up with the British force which set out from Egypt, and drove through Palestine and Syria to the frontiers with Turkey. However, that joint Arab and British success was spoilt by news of the Sykes-Picot agreement (signed in 1916) in which the British and the French governments planned to divide much of the Middle East between them with little thought for the interests of the Arabs.

Britain and France enticed Italy into the war by promising her a share in the spoils which would come from the defeat of Austria. The Italians had a miserable war fighting the Austrians along the Isonzo river. After a crushing defeat at the battle of Caporetto in late 1917, the Italian war effort had to be propped up by the British and French.

We left little Serbia back in July 1914, threatened by the might of the Austrian Empire. The Serbs held out until the autumn of 1915 when they were crushed from the north by Austria and Germany and from the east by Bulgaria, whose dislike of the Serbs made her a natural ally of the Germans.

The defeat of Serbia by overwhelming force was the tragedy of the war in the Balkans. Light relief was provided by the British–French force which was sent to Salonika to help the Greeks to help the Serbs: however, the Allies could not persuade Greece to enter the war until 1917. But the full comic turn was put on by the Romanians. Encouraged by Russian successes against Austria, Romania entered the war in August 1916, hoping to get out of it Transylvania (from Austria) and the Dobruja (from Bulgaria). Here was an example of a small nation seeing war as an opportunity for expansion. But Romania was poorly served by a large, almost completely illiterate army – a very odd army in which "officers above the rank of major had the right to use

make-up". It took the Germans, Austrians, Turks and Bulgarians just a little over three months to defeat them at the end of 1916.

Empires at War

The conflict in Europe was bound to affect countries outside. Just as the Russians and Austrians conscripted soldiers from the mixtures of nationalities which made up their great land empires, so the British, French and Germans involved their colonial territories in the war.

The British Dominions entered the war of their own free will. British India, too, fought for the mother country – though the Indian people were not asked whether they loved mother well enough to go to war for her. Taken together they made a vast contribution of nearly three million troops to the British war effort – made up as follows:

India	1,400,000
Canada	640,000
Australia	417,000
New Zealand	220,000
South Africa	136,000

Many of them fought and died on the Western Front. The Indian army manned the expedition to Mesopotamia; and the ANZACS suffered great losses in the futile Gallipoli Campaign. In a grisly kind of way, the graveyards of Gallipoli were the most remarkable of all memorials to the Western European empires. Men from 'down under' died in a remote corner of south-east Europe, fighting for a king and country many of them had never clapped eyes on.

If the Dominions entered the war freely, the colonies were dragged in. France, Britain and Germany all had colonies on the continent of Africa; and in the German colonies the world was treated to the spectacle of great European powers fighting each other with armies made up largely of Africans, with some Indians added by the British. German South-West Africa was attacked, for the British, by the South Africans. It turned into an even more interesting struggle when large numbers of Boer soldiers decided they preferred to fight for the Germans rather than against them. In the Far East, Japan joined the war on the side of the British, French and Russians, and took the opportunity to occupy German colonial possessions in the Pacific and to seize the

Chinese port of Kiaochow, previously controlled by Germany.

The campaigns in colonial Africa, like those in the Middle East, were side-shows to the main events on the two fronts in Europe. But before we turn back to those vast killing grounds we must look at one more aspect of the European conflict which spilled over the borders of that continent.

War at Sea

You will remember that the original reason for Britain drawing closer to France and Russia had been the growing naval threat from Germany. On the outbreak of war in 1914 many people expected that a battle between the two naval giants, Britain and Germany, might decide the outcome of the war. By any standards, the two navies were colossal: between them they had over a hundred battleships, not counting cruisers, battle-cruisers, destroyers and torpedo-boats.

The great fleets clashed once – at the Battle of Jutland in the North Sea in 1916. And that was enough to convince them they were better off threatening each other than actually fighting. Defeat for one side would have meant much more than the loss of a fleet: it would have given to the other side complete control of the trade routes to and from Europe.

So, instead of a naval war waged by the bull elephants of the seas – the battleships – there developed a war of blockade. Both sides tried to disrupt each other's trade routes and prevent vital foods and raw materials reaching the enemy by laying minefields at sea and by using a new kind of warship – the submarine. The raids of German submarines on British merchant shipping caused havoc until by mid-1917 the British had organised their ships into 'convoys', escorted safely across the seas by warships. The British blockade of Germany tightened as the war went on. While the German navy forced the British government to ration their people's food, the British navy ensured that Germany's people suffered even worse shortages. In the last bitter year of the war that was to be one of the factors that tipped the scales in favour of Britain and her Allies.

6 Peoples at War I

The importance of the steam locomotive on land and the steamship on the world's sea-routes was part of a larger pattern. For this was the first great war fought between industrialised countries; and as soon as the hopes of a quick finish disappeared, it became a struggle in which the stamina of the armies depended largely on the industrial strength of the economies behind them.

The soldiers often complained that they were merely things to hang other things on – helmets, rifles, ammunition pouches and bandoliers, grenades, water-bottles, packs, groundsheets, gas-masks and entrenching tools: the list seemed almost endless. Dressed to kill, the soldier of the Great War looked more like a pack-mule than a warrior.

There were millions of such pack-mules spread out along the Eastern and Western Fronts; and industry made it all possible. The European soldier of 1914–1917 was dressed, booted, armed, blinded, gassed and blown to bits by mass-produced articles from the factory lines. Industry protected him with barbed wire, stuck him with best-quality bayonets and carried him from the field on the very latest line in stretchers. In other words, industry adapted itself to the demands of a new kind of warfare as quickly as the conscript soldier did. The figures for British munitions production on the right tell their own tale.

Throughout Europe industry advanced to meet the requirements of armed forces. Russia, previously regarded as industrially backward, greatly expanded her chemical, engineering and munitions industries. The numbers of workers employed in the cities grew rapidly. Russia's imports of machine-tools and other sophisticated products of Western European countries declined. The war was beginning to make it possible for the industrialists of Petrograd and Moscow to look forward to the day when Russia would be a modern, self-sufficient, industrialised country.

Old and New Technologies of War

Inevitably, the Great War stimulated the application of human intelligence to the development of more efficient methods of killing people. The most spectacular development was that of the aeroplane.

The Wright Brothers had first flown in a powered

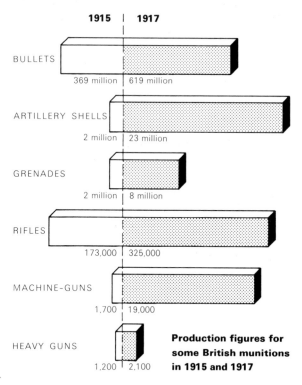

Production figures for some British munitions in 1915 and 1917

1915 | 1917

BULLETS — 369 million | 619 million
ARTILLERY SHELLS — 2 million | 23 million
GRENADES — 2 million | 8 million
RIFLES — 173,000 | 325,000
MACHINE-GUNS — 1,700 | 19,000
HEAVY GUNS — 1,200 | 2,100

machine in 1903. Now the war transformed the primitive 'kites' of wood, wire and canvas into a range of fighting machines with distinct purposes: the scout-reconnaissance 'plane, the fighter and the bomber. It didn't take men long to realise that if you could fly above people, you could also drop things on them. Although casualties and damage caused by bombs in the Great War were not extensive, for the first time in history civilian populations far away from the front lines of battle became vulnerable to enemy attack.

In 1914 the British air services could muster a total of 272 primitive aircraft. By October 1918 the newly formed RAF would possess over 22,000 'planes. Fighters could reach a height of over 4,000 metres, fire deadly accurate machine-guns through their propellers, harass ground troops, and photograph enemy positions. The Great War gave birth to new branches – or, if you prefer, wings – of the world's armed forces.

For the war at sea modern industry added to the *Dreadnought* class of battleships the super-dreadnoughts and hyper-super-dreadnoughts. The last of these were steel monsters of over 27,000 tonnes, armed with eight guns, each of which could hurl a high explosive shell more than fifteen kilometres. For submarine warfare the factories of the great sea-powers produced the moving sea-mines (torpedoes) to sink enemy vessels, while the shipyards built more ships to replace those destroyed – and more submarines to do more damage.

The generals of the European armies believed that the only way to open up the enemy front was by a massive artillery bombardment followed by an overwhelming infantry attack. As you have seen, they demanded, and got, vast quantities of 'conventional' artillery and infantry weapons and ammunition. It was quantity they were after – not novelty.

They were prepared to use poison gas – after all it could be fired in shells from guns. They were even prepared to use it when the wind was blowing the wrong way. But most of them could not appreciate the new weapon which lurched on to the battlefields of the Somme in 1916 – the tank. Perhaps they were right to distrust it at first: it moved very slowly, often broke down, and almost suffocated its crews with petrol fumes. The tank was a revolutionary weapon which required generals to think out new battle tactics – and generals preferred to stick to what was familiar rather than experiment in the middle of the strain of war. The tank, like the bombing plane, was a weapon for future wars.

Paying the Price

War is the most expensive of all human activities. It costs money to train and equip men to take other men's lives; it costs money to support the living casualties when war comes to an end; and it involves the cost of lost production – that is, what countries could have produced if they had not had to concentrate most of their efforts on supplying their armed forces. In this chapter we are concerned only with the 'immediate' costs of the war – the money spent to wage it at the time. Any government which is suddenly faced with the need to take on millions more paid employees (soldiers), to feed them, arm them, transport them here and there, suddenly needs a lot more money.

There are three ways in which a government can raise the enormous amounts needed; by taking money from its people, in taxation; by borrowing it from them; and by borrowing it from other sources.

The governments of all the countries engaged in the Great War used all those three ways of getting money.

The proportion of the total sum spent on war that was raised in taxes varied greatly from country to country. People throughout Europe had long been used to paying 'indirect' taxes on the things they bought. Some of them were now made to pay a 'direct' tax on their earnings.

The British had long been used to this 'income tax'. The Russians had their first experience of it in 1916 and the French in 1917. To be fair, a government should have taken more money from citizens with large incomes to pay for the war; and that was the case in Britain, where the government got a quarter of all its money from direct taxation. In Russia, where the gap between the well-off and the poor was very wide, the new tax on high incomes was hardly noticed. In one year it brought in a pitifully small sum, "less than enough to pay for a weekend of war". The Russian war effort was financed by borrowing and by 'indirect' taxes which bore heavily on the poor. The burden of the Great War was not being fairly shared.

All governments borrowed immense sums to finance their war efforts. For example, the Russians, French and Italians borrowed heavily from the British; they and the British borrowed heavily from the USA. The governments of all combatant countries borrowed from their own people through 'war loans', which would be repaid with interest after the war.

In some cases government borrowing to meet vast increases in government spending led to rapid inflation as the amount of money in circulation increased. In Russia, by 1917, people's need for more money with which to buy goods at inflated prices was so great that the State Bank did not have time to cut and number its notes: the money was paid out by banks in printed sheets for the customers to cut up. In the end the heaviest burden of all fell on the German people, although few realised this until the war was over. The Kaiser's undemocratic government never told the people the true cost of the war they were waging. Instead of asking the Reichstag to agree to extra taxes, Kaiser Wilhelm ordered his finance ministers to raise the money for the war almost entirely from loans and government savings bonds which would be repaid when victory came. The government never seriously considered the possibility of defeat. But when that defeat came and Germany was bankrupt, there was no hope of repayment. Hundreds of thousands of Germans lost all their savings.

The 'new woman' in London in 1917: short hair, knee-length skirt, gaiters, and a job on the No. 19 bus.

Changes on the Home Fronts

You have seen some of the effects of war on Russia by 1917 – the rapid growth of industries making use of a previously neglected labour-force; and mounting inflation. The already industrialised countries of Western Europe experienced changes too.

As the men went to fight, women took over their civilian jobs. Although some men objected to the employment of females in engineering and munitions works, on railways and buses, there was really no alternative if the war effort was to be maintained. In Britain, women's organisations which had been de-

manding the right to vote now demanded the 'Right to Serve'. The war was undermining many old notions about women as the inferior, weaker, gentler sex. In contrast, in rural villages throughout Europe there was no need to claim the right to work. Who else could have farmed the land but the women, assisted by the children and old men who were left behind?

You will remember from Chapter 3 that the people of Russia and Germany were used to living under powerful 'authoritarian' governments. Now the governments of Britain and France gave themselves new powers to mobilise their peoples in the war effort. In particular they established controls over industries, and especially over vital industries such as munitions, coal and railways. News from the fronts was officially censored. In Britain the Defence of the Realm Act (known unaffectionately as DORA) gave the government wide powers over the individual citizen, including not only the power to take over private land and property for military purposes, but also to control, and change, the hard-drinking habits of the people (the opening hours of pubs were severely restricted). The French government took similar powers into its own hands, directing the economic life of the country and closely regulating the behaviour of its citizens. The people of Britain and France, two liberal democracies, were getting their first real taste of 'state control'.

Changes in Attitudes

The longer the war went on the more it separated whole peoples from each other in hatred. Governments used propaganda to whip up people's cruder emotions and direct them not only against the vile, inhuman enemy but also against the 'shirkers' and 'conshies' (conscientious objectors) at home. Civilians were, by and large, the fiercest haters – it was their substitute for actually fighting. At the fronts the war sharpened men's wits, infested them with vermin and maimed them. It killed them every day and night, without warning; and in that awful uncertainty they lived as close as men could be to each other, as 'mates', and wondered why they were there at all. They knew whom they were fighting against, but whom and what were they fighting for? Some of them came to believe they were fighting not to defeat 'the enemy' but to ensure a better future for themselves and their children in a world without war.

By 1917 the bright and spirited patriotism of the distant summer of 1914 had taken a bloody beating. The loss of millions of men had brought merely the prospect of further agony – repeat performances of failed offensives by unimaginative or incompetent generals. In the west, the British army was disillusioned. The French army fell apart under the strain. Some soldiers simply packed up and went home; others mutinied. The habit of obedience had been stretched beyond endurance; and traditions of respect for superiors, duty, loyalty, all lay in tatters. The army was pulled together by General Pétain: the ringleaders of the mutinies were shot; the complaints of the rest of the troops were treated with some sympathy. The French army held its positions on the Western Front – but it was never the same again as a fighting force.

The German army was still held together by remarkably tight discipline, despite shortages of food and other supplies. But the Austrian army had not recovered from the shattering blow of losing over a third of its men as prisoners of the Russians in the summer of 1916. Many of the men had surrendered willingly for they were not German-speaking Austrians but Slavs from the subject peoples of the Austrian Empire. They hoped that the Empire would suffer a defeat which would bring freedom to its nationalities. Czech and Ruthene soldiers came to despise their incompetent Austrian commanders. Only those Austrian battalions and divisions stiffened with German troops could now be considered effective units. If Germany lost the war, there would be nothing left to hold the Austrians' army or empire together.

In the east the war was about to shatter the government of an empire even bigger than Austria's. We must now turn to look at how the war brought about the end of the rule of the Tsars in Russia and at the beginning of something quite new.

7 1917: Russia in War and Revolution

Russia in Crisis

By the winter of 1916 there was a serious military crisis in the Russian armies. From the beginning of the war there had been repeated complaints (most of them genuine, some of them invented by generals playing at politics) about shortages of ammunition and equipment for the soldiers at the front. By July 1915 about nine million men had been called into the Tsar's forces. It was not enough to stop a terrible series of defeats and retreats. Morale sank to rock bottom. Ill-trained, under-fed troops surrendered to the enemy in their thousands. Generals took revenge on their own men by cancelling leave, by floggings and by murder. For example,

"at Opatow [in Poland] in June 1915 a batallion, ordered to attack, fell into uncut wire and enemy machine-gun fire. The survivors fell into shell-holes and were bombarded by enemy artillery. A few white flags then appeared above the shell-holes; and Russian officers, in the rear, ordered Russian guns to fire on the troops, as well as the German ones."

In the autumn of 1915 the Tsar had taken over as Commander-in-Chief of the Russian armies; and since then he had been in charge of the war effort from his headquarters at Mogilev, far to the south of Petrograd. His presence made not the slightest difference to the performance of the Russian army. In the military campaigns of 1916 more than two million Russian soldiers were killed or wounded, and a third of a million were taken prisoner. Furthermore, Nicholas's absence from Petrograd quickly led to a serious government crisis. His German-born wife, Tsarina Alexandra, had taken control of the imperial government; and she, in turn, had been taken over by Gregory Rasputin, a drunken, lecherous 'holy man', who claimed that he had the power to cure the Tsarina's only son of haemophilia, an incurable disorder of the blood.

In Rasputin's heyday the imperial government had been turned into a farce. In under two years, twenty-one ministers were sacked and replaced by Rasputin's favourites—most of them incompetent old men. Eventually, in December 1916, Rasputin was murdered by a group of noblemen; but by then a great deal of damage had been done. The Tsarina's foolish antics had brought accusations that the imperial government was, of all things, pro-German!

The crisis in government was accompanied by a growing economic crisis. By the start of 1917 prices were, on average, four times higher than they had been in August 1914. One of the main reasons for this rapid inflation was that the government had put heavy taxes on goods to pay for the war. In all the towns and cities food became scarce and more expensive; and there were now more mouths to feed since great numbers of peasants had left their villages to work in the munitions industries. In the countryside the poorer peasants demanded land, while the better-off ate or hoarded much of their surplus food rather than sell it to the towns for paper money which quickly lost its value.

The war-time economic crisis was the final disastrous peak in changes that had been eating away at traditional society for twenty years before 1914. There had been a massive migration from the countryside to the towns. Some peasants had uprooted themselves because a rising population left too little land to feed everyone in the villages of their district. Others had abandoned cottage industries, such as making rope and sacks or weaving cloth, which had been ruined by competition from town factories. Yet others had been attracted by the higher wages paid in the booming centres of industry. Whatever the cause, an urban working class (or, as Marxists called it, a 'proletariat') was growing steadily and irresistibly. The extra war-time demand for labour in arms factories and on the railways swelled the numbers while inflation and food shortages deepened the discontent. Nearly all of this new working class, by 1917 seething with discontent, was concentrated in the cities and towns of European Russia, west of the Urals, and especially in Moscow and Petrograd.

The March Revolution

Petrograd (whose pre-war name of 'St Petersburg' had been changed because it sounded German) was an extraordinary place. Its industrial areas were all that a revolutionary communist could hope for—filthy, disease-ridden, bulging at the seams with the families of poor workers. Yet the city was also the centre of Russian high society, the hive of the civil service, and the city of the Tsar's court. From Petrograd the Tsar ruled Russia through an unholy combination of church, bureaucracy and brute force. His power to rule was unlimited, and he shared it with no group or class of the Russian people; although since 1906 he had had to accept the existence of a Duma, a sort of parliament with no real law-making powers. The Duma's chief importance was as a training-ground for politicians who sought liberal reforms in the way Russia was governed. They wanted a genuine parliament, a cabinet and ministers able to take their own decisions, and the modernisation of the country's educational and economic systems.

Before the war it had been easy for the Tsar to ignore the opinions of liberals. But, as the military failures became evident, there were widespread demands for a more democratic and efficient system of government to cope with the problems made more acute by the war. By the end of 1916 the Duma had ceased to be a mere 'talking-shop' and liberal politicians openly criticised the Tsar and Tsarina. In March 1917 (according to the Russians it was February, but they were still using that old calendar – see Chapter 1, page 1), serious disorders began in Petrograd. The managers of the gigantic Putilov steel works in the south of the city locked out 20,000 workers after pay talks between them broke down. This put 20,000 tough, angry steelmen out on the streets with nothing to do and in a mood for trouble. Workers in nearby factories quickly came out on strike in sympathy until some 90,000 were out on the streets.

The next day, 8 March, bakeries in some parts of Petrograd ran out of bread. Bread rationing had already been introduced, bringing discontent and long queues with it. Now the queues of hungry shoppers began smashing up the empty bakeries.

By the weekend, 250,000 workers were out on strike, surging around the streets in giant demonstrations. Although police managed to disperse one crowd by firing on it, Cossacks in another part of the city refused to attack a procession of strikers when ordered to do so. The President of the Duma, Michael Rodzianko, sent off an urgent telegram to the Tsar:

"The situation is serious. The capital is in a state of anarchy. The government is paralysed; the transport system is broken down; the food and fuel supplies are completely disorganised. Discontent is general and on the increase. There is wild shooting on the streets; troops are firing at each other. It is urgent that someone enjoying the confidence of the country be entrusted with the formation of a new government."

Rodzianko believed that such a government would come from the Duma. But the Tsar behaved – as he often did – as if he lived on a different planet from his people: he ordered the Duma to stop meeting. Early next morning, however, on Monday 12 March, soldiers in Petrograd joined the workers' protests. They were sick of a war in which the army had suffered enormous casualties; they were also hungry. Riots were turning into revolution.

For the first time in its short history the Duma had a real political choice to make. It could either take the leadership of the revolution or be swept away by it. Twelve of its members disobeyed the Tsar and formed a Provisional government which demanded that Nicholas should abdicate. Nicholas, still in army headquarters at Mogilev, 500 kilometres from Petrograd, at last decided to return to take control of the situation. However, the leading generals of the army informed him that he no longer had their support. Nicholas had no real alternative but to abdicate. On 16 March he gave up his throne and power. There was suddenly a great political hole in Russia.

Between Revolutions

There appeared to be no shortage of answers to the question of who would fill the hole. The Provisional government planned to rule the country until the people elected a Constituent Assembly which would work out a new system of government. But there were rivals to its claims to power. In Petrograd a Council of Workers, Peasants and Soldiers (the Petrograd Soviet) was determined to share power with the Provisional government. The Soviet was dominated by Marxists, mostly trade unionists from the *Menshevik* groups who believed that the workers should band together to defend their rights but that they were not yet powerful enough as a class to run the state. At this time the Soviet included only a few of the *Bolsheviks* – revolutionary communists whose leader, Lenin, believed in overthrowing the liberals at once and setting up a new government which would rule in the name of the working class.

The Soviet declared in Order No. 1 that soldiers

in the Russian army should not take their orders from officers but from committees elected by each regiment. The government's control of the army was thus weakened. But beyond that the parties in the Soviet didn't know how far to go. Although popular opinion was in favour of an end to the war, the government planned to continue the fighting on the Eastern Front; and the Soviet accepted that Russia must be defended from German aggression. Neither the government nor the Soviet had a clear idea of what to do about the peasants' demands for land.

The Bolsheviks' leader, Lenin, had been in exile in Switzerland, planning a revolution on paper. When the real revolution broke out he made a deal with the Germans who allowed him to pass through their land from Switzerland in a sealed train, not inspected by police or customs officers who would otherwise have arrested him as a citizen of an enemy country. Lenin, the hard, professional revolutionary, was now appalled by the unwillingness of the Soviet to declare open war on the Provisional government. Most Russian Marxists were still saying that their revolution, when the working class would seize complete control, could come only after a long period of capitalist development. Lenin couldn't wait that long. His arrival at the Finland Station in Petrograd in April 1917 was one of the decisive moments in the history of the twentieth century. He brushed aside the committee that had turned up to welcome him and the next day, 17 April, made it clear what he intended the Bolsheviks to do. In a speech to a meeting of Bolshevik leaders he outlined a set of new policies for them to follow – the 'April Theses'. There must be an immediate end to the war, he said; Bolshevik agitators must go to the trenches and persuade soldiers to desert. There must be no cooperation with the Provisional Government: the Soviets must have all power. Industry must be put under the workers' control. Land must be nationalised, along with all banks. And a new Communist International must be set up to spread revolution outside Russia.

The April Theses alarmed other Bolshevik leaders. Most thought that Lenin was being hopelessly unrealistic and that they could achieve more by working with the Provisional Government. Lenin replied in a famous slogan that 'Peace, Bread and Land' were what the peasants, workers and soldiers wanted, and that the Provisional Government could not, or would not, meet those wants. If the Bolsheviks

told the people that they could give them what they wanted, then the people would support the Bolsheviks in elections to the Soviets. After that, Lenin said in another famous slogan, the Bolsheviks should demand 'All Power to the Soviets!' and confront the Provisional Government from their new position of strength.

Events ran out of Lenin's control. In June the Russian army launched a major offensive against their enemies. Within days it was halted and turned into a miserable retreat. In mid-July, mutinous soldiers and sailors joined hungry workers in demonstrations in Petrograd. Their slogan was 'All Power to the Soviets!' – Lenin's new battle-cry: but they were shouting it before the Bolsheviks were strong enough to do battle with the Provisional Government. On 16 and 17 June government troops restored some kind of order to the streets at the cost of 400 deaths. The government and the majority of the Soviet seized the chance to label the Bolsheviks as traitors. Many were arrested, and Lenin escaped only by putting on a wig and slipping out of Russia to Finland.

Lenin's Revolution

Conditions in Russia grew worse. Neither the government nor the Soviet could control inflation. The government failed to announce schemes for the transfer of lands to the peasants, and by harvest time many peasants were seizing landlords' fields and crops for themselves. The government sent troops to stop them while, in contrast, Lenin deliberately supported the peasants. As the war went on, the Bolsheviks spread their propaganda view that the struggle against Germany and Austria benefited only the ruling class in Russia. Peasant soldiers were already deserting from the army in their thousands.

General Kornilov, the new army Commander, decided to put a stop to all this revolutionary nonsense and march to Petrograd. He intended to replace the Provisional government by a military one which would act firmly against the Soviet, and especially against the Bolsheviks. The government, however, had no desire to be kicked out: it turned for help to bands of Bolsheviks in the large factories (the Red Guards), and distributed weapons among them. Kornilov was defeated. Shortly afterwards, in the elections to the Soviet, the newly popular Bolsheviks won control. Leon Trotsky, Lenin's right-hand man, was already chairman of the Soviet.

Bolsheviks guarding the Smolny Institute in Petrograd, their military headquarters in the November Revolution of 1917.

Lenin slipped back into Petrograd. He now had over 20,000 armed men to command. The government couldn't even rely on its own troops in the capital (remember Soviet Order No. 1?). The Bolshevik Revolution began on 6 November. Under Trotsky's leadership, bands of Red Guards took over key points in the city – the telephone exchange, the arsenal, government buildings. There was hardly any resistance. By the evening of the next day the Red Guards controlled the city. Within a week, Bolsheviks had seized power in Moscow and other major

centres, and so had control of most of European Russia.

Straightaway Lenin announced two decrees. The decree on land gave the land to the peasants: they would divide it up among themselves. Although the decree gave the peasants the right to do what they were doing already, it brought Lenin the support of many people in the countryside. The decree on peace declared that the war would be ended at once. To the amazement and anger of her allies Russia was abandoning the Eastern Front.

8 The End of the Great War

The USA Enters the War

In March 1917 no-one could have foreseen the outcome of the bread riots in Petrograd – that within eight months Russia would have a communist government which would take Russia out of the war and take the pressure off Germany's Eastern Front. Perhaps if it could have been foreseen, the German admirals and soldiers who persuaded their government in March 1917 to unleash unrestricted submarine warfare on the high seas would not have had their way. Their argument was simple. Britain and France could not be beaten into submission by the German artillery and infantry on the Western Front: but it was just possible that they could be starved into defeat.

For a time, in the winter of 1916, the war's most important new naval weapon, the submarine, had looked as if it might turn the war in Germany's favour. British merchant ships were being sunk at an alarming rate:

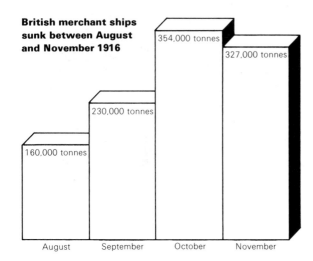

British merchant ships sunk between August and November 1916

160,000 tonnes — August
230,000 tonnes — September
354,000 tonnes — October
327,000 tonnes — November

In November there was a time when London had only two days' supply of wheat left.

Soon the British government under Lloyd George would take steps to counteract the U-boat menace: merchant ships would be organised into convoys protected by the Royal Navy; British shipbuilding would be speeded up, and farmers would be encouraged to plant more wheat. But, in the meantime, Britain survived only because of a steady flow of shipping from outside the UK – from the Dominions and, above all,

from the USA. Woodrow Wilson, the President of this great neutral power, favoured Britain but was reluctant to enter the war unless the action of the USA could lead to an early compromise peace – which was unthinkable to Britain and France.

Long before, in May 1915, a German submarine had sunk the British liner *Lusitania*: 128 American civilians (and 1,073 other passengers and crew) had gone down with her. Few people knew that the *Lusitania* was also carrying arms to Britain. That sinking had provoked outrage but not war. Since then, however, the Germans had sunk a number of American ships – and every attack brought Woodrow Wilson closer to military action against Germany.

Now, in 1917, the German High Command could hardly doubt that if they set out to destroy *all* American shipping making its way to Britain, they would drive the USA into war. But to desperate men who believed that the war could not be won on land, it seemed a risk just worth taking. In the early months of unrestricted submarine warfare enough American ships might be sunk to destroy the British war effort.

The USA declared war on Germany on 6 April 1917. She had no army worth speaking of, but a quick glance at Chapter 1 will tell you what Germany had taken on – the world's greatest industrial power, with a population fast approaching one hundred millions. In 1917, while she trained her recruits, America was only a distant threat to Germany. By 1918, when the Eastern Front had collapsed and it was obvious that the war would be decided in the west, America was ready to feed her fresh young men into the line of battle.

More than any other event, the entry of the USA into the Great European War appeared to turn it into a *world* war: indeed, we often refer to it as the 'First World War'. In fact, what happened was not that the fighting spread further afield, but that Americans crossed the Atlantic to help settle Europe's problems for her. The soldiers would come first, and later their President would follow. The Americans were coming – fit, confident and, of course, with the very best intentions.

Fourteen Points for a Just Peace

Woodrow Wilson's declaration of war would

send hundreds of thousands of American boys to face death and mutilation in Europe. The causes for which he was asking them to put aside the view that the USA was a refuge from the misery and hardship of Europe had to be good ones. In January 1918 he announced them – his Fourteen Points. The first five, taken together, suggested a complete change in the ways governments should deal with each other in the future.

1 There should be no more secret treaties: governments should make their deals openly with each other.

2 They should allow freedom of navigation on the high seas.

3 They should encourage free trade between countries.

4 They should reduce their armaments.

5 When future claims for colonies were made, the interests of the people must be taken into account.

The other nine showed clearly that in Wilson's opinion the war had been caused by disregard for the right of every man to live in his own national home. The first step was to make it clear that Germany would not be allowed to hang on to any of the lands she had conquered.

6 German troops should move out of Russian territory.

7 German troops should move out of Belgium.

8 Alsace and Lorraine should be handed back to France.

The rest of the Fourteen Points showed that Wilson sympathised with the principle of national self-determination and that he had listened to the committees of Poles, Czechs, Serbs and other minority peoples who had been campaigning in the USA for the right to set up their own independent national states.

9 Italy's frontiers should be restored along clear lines of 'nationality'.

10 The peoples of the Austrian Empire should be given the opportunity of self-government.

11 Serbia, Montenegro and Romania should be restored, and Serbia given access to the sea.

12 People in the Turkish Empire who were not Turks should be given the opportunity of self-government.

13 An independent Poland should be created and given access to the sea.

14 An international organisation should be set up to protect the independence of all states.

Before America came in, the war aims of the Allied powers had been vague, to say the least. They boiled down to something like defeating Germany and her supporters, rubbing their noses in it, and then sharing out the spoils of victory. The governments of Britain and France had not considered the possibility of breaking up the Austrian Empire (Point 10) or re-creating a free Poland which had disappeared from the map of Europe nearly 150 years before (Point 13). The effect of the Fourteen Points on the people of Europe was even more shattering. Until then only a handful of men, mostly Marxists, had said that the war had been caused by the greed of governments for more territory and power. Now Wilson was saying just that and offering the chance of a peace which would make future wars impossible. But in the spring of 1918 the chances of that just peace coming about seemed as slim as ever, as German successes thrust the war into a new phase of danger for the Allies. In March Germany forced Russia into signing the Treaty of Brest-Litovsk: it was more like an act of rape than an agreement. A vast portion of western Russia, containing a third of the Russian people, a third of the railway system, most of the coal mines, and the rich grain-lands of the Ukraine, were torn away from the new Bolshevik republic. In the same month the Germans attacked on the Western Front and drove the Allied armies back towards Paris.

Break-up of the Austrian Empire

Germany and Austria had refused Wilson's peace proposals. Germany now hoped that the Treaty of Brest-Litovsk would take the pressure off Austria. She would no longer have to face Russia in battle: and the grain from the Ukraine could be used to feed the millions of non-Germans in the Empire who had been brought to the edge of revolt by their sufferings in a war started by their masters. But bread was no longer enough. Throughout 1918 Austria's chances of survival as an empire were being undermined by a series of promises which Wilson made to the Slav nationalities.

In June 1918 he declared that "all branches of the Slav race should be completely freed from German and Austrian rule" (compare that clear statement with his rather cloudy Point 10 earlier in the year). In September he went further and recognised a group of men who called themselves the Czechoslovak National Council as a separate government. In October America recognised "in the fullest manner the justice of the nationalistic aspirations of the Yugoslavs for freedom" – in other words, the Serbs and Croats should be free to form their own independent state. The President of the USA was writing out the death warrant of the old Empire. Late in October, the Czechs and Slovaks and the southern Slavs signed it – they declared their independence.

Revolt in Germany and a Cease-fire

Meanwhile, the Allies had launched a counter-offensive on the Western Front in August and had driven the German armies back. The Allied blockade had already weakened the will of the German people to continue their war effort. Weary and hungry, they saw their allies surrender in quick succession. Bulgaria caved in on 29 September, Turkey on 30 October. By then the Austrian Empire had broken up with the declaration of independence by the Slav peoples. There was nothing for the German Austrians to do but sign an armistice (cease-fire) on 3 November.

A month earlier Germany's military leaders had told the Kaiser, but not the people, that there was no hope that the armies could fight on. The Kaiser's chief minister, the Chancellor, saw one faint chance of avoiding total disaster, by making peace speedily before the advancing Allies pursued retreating armies on to German soil. He asked Wilson for an armistice to be followed by a peace made on the basis of the Fourteen Points. Wilson consulted other Allied leaders, but they could see no reason why Germany should be treated to an equal share in the better world promised by Wilson. The British would not accept the second Point: the nation which sang 'Rule Britannia' would not accept that the seas should be free to all nations. Italy's claim on some Austrian territory was at odds with Wilson's principle of self-determination. France was determined to get compensation for the damage the German armies had done.

So the terms of the armistice which were offered on 5 November were harsh. Germany should compensate all the Allies for the damage done to their civilian populations and property. Further, the Germans should agree to get out of all occupied territory, to withdraw from their overseas colonies, hand over vast supplies of armaments and railway rolling stock and surrender their navy and merchant fleet to the Allies. Those terms would mean that Germany would no longer be able to

fight on and her people would depend absolutely on the goodwill of the Allies – even for supplies of food.

Wilson had made it clear that he would not sign a peace with the Kaiser, but only with a government which he thought more truly represented the German people. By November such a government was available. A wave of strikes, revolts and mutinies had swept the country. They had begun when the sailors at the Kiel naval base refused to put to sea and control of the town was taken over by a Council of Sailors, Soldiers and Workers, modelled on the Soviets in Russia. Other cities followed that lead, and in a series of revolts the kings and princes who had ruled the provinces of Germany were replaced by republican governments controlled by socialists. In the capital, Berlin, socialist politicians forced the Kaiser to abdicate, declared they had set up a new Republic with a provisional government headed by Friedrich Ebert – and were ready to sign the armistice. At 11 o'clock on the morning of 11 November 1918 the guns on the Western Front fell silent.

The people of the victorious powers let themselves go in a frenzy of relief and delight. They celebrated their own survival and their victory, and they looked forward to their first taste of vengeance. The German people were depressed and confused. Their old form of government had collapsed under the weight of their own suffering and anger; and their new one had signed away the means of protecting Germany against hurt. The generals had advised the government to ask for an armistice before their armies had been pushed back on to German soil. In that way the generals had avoided taking responsibility for defeat and could blame the politicians for asking for peace. It was all very puzzling for the German people to see their armies marching back from France in good order and yet to learn that their supplies of daily bread depended on the Allies who now controlled their shipping and their railways.

Casualties and Creditors

Before the war, the slaughter of *millions* of people would have been unthinkable. The war did slaughter them, but *millions* were, and still are, unthinkable. No-one can imagine a million, or five million, or ten million dead human beings.

If you do want to know how many died, you will have to put up with guesses. We know that Britain and her Empire suffered nearly 950,000 deaths, France

1,400,000, Germany, 1,800,000. We estimate that Turkey lost 300,000 people – though it may have been twice as many as that, or three times. Maybe two million Russians died, or maybe it was four or even six millions. In Petrograd they didn't count deaths as carefully as in London or Paris – and for the Russians the Great War was followed by a Civil War between Reds and Whites – the Bolsheviks and their opponents. Who's to say for certain whether Ivan was killed by the Germans, the Austrians, the Bulgars, the Turks, the

Allied debts to Britain and the USA in 1918

Reds or the Whites? Obviously it mattered to Ivan; to his wife, his parents, his children – or maybe they were destroyed too. But the exact figures, even if we had them, could not tell us any more than this – that in the Great War, Europe was sick, and that recovery would take a long, long time.

You will remember from Chapter 6 that the Great War was paid for on the never-never. Compared with their rough estimates of the numbers of people killed or wounded, governments had kept accurate records of how much money they had borrowed and lent. By the end of 1918 most of them owed vast sums to their own people. The Allied states on the mainland of Europe were deeply in debt to Britain and the USA. Britain was in a special midway position: she had borrowed heavily from the USA, partly so that she could lend money to her continental allies.

Russia was no longer an ally and the Bolshevik government had no intention of repaying the debts of the old Tsarist government. The rest were expected to pay back what they had borrowed.

There were all kinds of accounts to settle, claims to be made, old scores to be paid off. Central Europe had fallen apart; Eastern Europe and the Middle East were in turmoil; Bolshevism could no longer be dismissed as the raving of a few exiled cranks. So far there was only a cease-fire. Europe was no longer at war, but neither was it at what you and I would call 'peace'. The making of the peace would take nearly as long as the waging of the war.

9 The Peace Settlement of 1919–20

In January 1919 the representatives of twenty-seven countries came together in Paris to begin drawing up the terms they would impose on the defeated powers in the form of 'treaties of peace'. As usual, at the end of a war, the first prize for the winners was the right to use their pencils on the map. The winners were France, Britain and the USA – the Big Three who would make the major decisions in Paris. For the present, their armies were the masters of Europe.

The lesser allies and the nationalities of Central and Eastern Europe were in Paris to press the Big Three to confirm that they were independent and to draw the most favourable boundaries for their states. But the first question that had to be answered was the same one that Britain and France had faced before the Great War began – what to do about Germany?

The Road to Versailles

Although the leaders of the three great Allied powers believed Germany was to blame for the war, they disagreed about what to do with her in defeat. The French Prime Minister, Georges Clemenceau, and the French people knew what they wanted to write into the treaty of peace – revenge, compensation for all they had suffered, and guarantees that a similar war would never happen again. For four years they had believed that the only good German was a dead German. Now they felt that the only safe Germany would be a crippled Germany, stripped of her wealth and most of her armed forces, and separated from France either by the creation of a new state between them or by making sure that what remained of the German army stayed well away from the French border. In the east, a line of new states able to defend themselves would take care of any future German ambitions in that direction.

Woodrow Wilson had already revealed, in the Fourteen Points, what he wanted to see emerge out of the war – a Europe whose nationalities would rule themselves as open, democratic societies. Before the end of the war he had declared that the peace should show "no discrimination between those to whom we wish to be just and those to whom we do not wish to be just. It must be justice that plays no favourites ..." But any Germans who thought that Wilson's 'justice' meant that they would be treated generously were in for a shock. In the President's eyes Germany had

been wicked, and 'justice' demanded that Germany be punished.

The British had probably never before felt so close to the mainland of Europe: most of them knew someone lately buried there. Now they too wanted revenge on Germany; and the Prime Minister, David Lloyd George, appeared to agree with them. But at the Paris Conference he had no time for those who wanted to put the boot into Germany. It didn't matter *now* that the Germans had been wicked. What did matter was that Germany should not be humiliated or made bankrupt, for then she would not be able to help get European industry and trade moving again. Britain had fought the war to destroy the German threat to her navy and overseas Empire. It was now in her interests to help rebuild a healthy *continental* Germany.

Above all, Lloyd George feared the spread of communism in Europe. In January 1919 there had been a communist uprising in Berlin. In March there was a short-lived communist government in Hungary. In April communists took control of the state of Bavaria in southern Germany. Obviously, it couldn't make sense for a British government to send help to the White armies fighting the Reds in Russia, and at the same time to make Germany so poor that more of her people would be driven into the arms of her home-grown Bolsheviks.

After several months of haggling the Big Three proposed their terms to Germany on 7 May 1919. The German Chancellor resigned in protest. German sailors made a more spectacular protest: they sank their warships in their watery prison camp at Scapa Flow in the Orkney Islands, rather than see them turned over to the Allies. It was all very patriotic to protest; but that was all the Germans could do while Europe was in the grip of the Allied armies. They were hardly in a position to re-start the war. Instead, two representatives of the German government took the road to the Palace of Versailles, not far to the west of Paris. There, on 28 June 1919, they signed a treaty of peace with Germany's former enemies.

For many Germans, especially those who had lost fathers, sons and brothers among the 1,800,000 soldiers killed, additional distress was caused by Article 231 of the treaty which laid all the blame for starting the war on Germany and her allies:

The Peace Settlement of 1919–20

The Treaty of Versailles

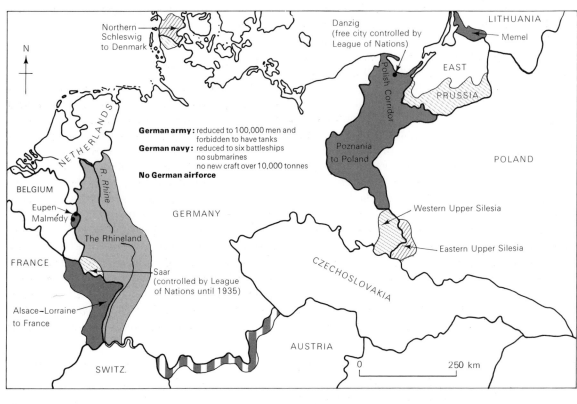

German **army:** reduced to 100,000 men and forbidden to have tanks
German **navy:** reduced to six battleships
no submarines
no new craft over 10,000 tonnes
No German airforce

Northern Schleswig to Denmark

Danzig (free city controlled by League of Nations)

LITHUANIA — Memel

Polish Corridor

EAST PRUSSIA

Poznania to Poland

POLAND

Western Upper Silesia

Eastern Upper Silesia

NETHERLANDS

R. Rhine

BELGIUM

Eupen Malmédy

The Rhineland

GERMANY

FRANCE

Saar (controlled by League of Nations until 1935)

Alsace–Lorraine to France

CZECHOSLOVAKIA

SWITZ.

AUSTRIA

0   250 km

Land taken from Germany

Germany forbidden to unite with German-speaking Austria

areas whose future was decided by the votes of their people, one way to remain part of Germany the other way to leave Germany

Demilitarised zone: no German troops or fortifications permitted

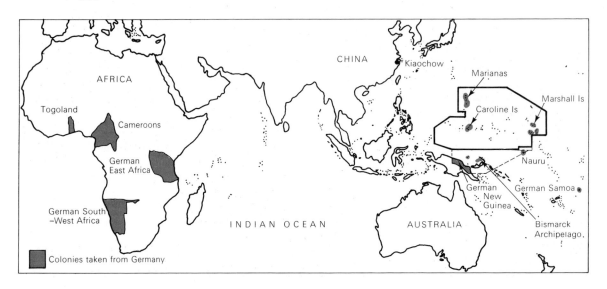

CHINA — Kiaochow

AFRICA

Togoland

Cameroons

German East Africa

German South –West Africa

Marianas

Marshall Is

Caroline Is

Nauru

German New Guinea

German Samoa

Bismarck Archipelago

INDIAN OCEAN

AUSTRALIA

Colonies taken from Germany

"The Allied and Associated Governments affirm and Germany accepts the responsibility of Germany and her allies for causing all the loss and damage which the Allied and Associated Governments and their nationals have been subjected to as a consequence of the war imposed upon them by the aggression of Germany and her allies."

Further, Germany would have to pay for her sins. The full amount to be paid would be decided later by a Reparations Commission.

The treaty satisfied no-one. It didn't cripple Germany – as the French had hoped. It was at odds with Wilson's principle of nationalities ruling themselves – otherwise, why were so many Germans being forced to live in the new Poland? And most Germans bitterly resented the treaty – as Lloyd George had feared. It seemed to them that all the talk of justice had been a sham. Hadn't the famous Fourteen Points now come to mean (in the real world, not in Wilson's Wonderland) that the defeated countries should be permanently stripped of their power to defend

themselves? The Germans felt humiliated. The 'peace' they had been offered was not generous: worse than that, it was not even sensible.

In Place of Empires

When their arms were not being twisted by Italians, Poles, Czechs and Greeks, the Big Three tried to deal sensibly with the rest of Europe. The trouble was that the continent's problems were too knotty to be unravelled quickly and to everyone's satisfaction.

The principle of national self-determination meant that new frontiers should be drawn according to the wishes of the peoples concerned. But the peoples of Central and Eastern Europe did not all live in tight compartments labelled 'Polish' or 'Czech' or 'Hungarian' or 'Italian'. There were places in which a few people of one nationality (for example, Hungarians) dominated a majority of, say, Romanians. One man's idea of a part of Poland could very well be another man's idea of a part of Czechoslovakia.

There was also the question of whether the frontiers

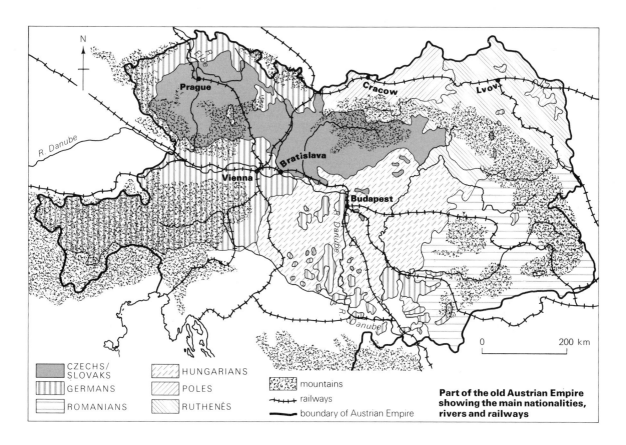

CZECHS/SLOVAKS
GERMANS
ROMANIANS
HUNGARIANS
POLES
RUTHENÈS
mountains
railways
boundary of Austrian Empire

0   200 km

Part of the old Austrian Empire showing the main nationalities, rivers and railways

proposed for a new state made military and economic sense. Surely, wherever possible, a country should have access to the sea or to a major navigable river? Surely it made military sense to draw lines on the map along 'natural' boundaries such as rivers and mountain ranges? But what if, for example, by granting Czechs and Slovaks access to the River Danube, you included in their new state lands where most of the people were Hungarians? What kind of self-determination would that be?

Try the exercise for yourself. On page 41 is a map of the northern half of the old Austrian Empire, showing its nationalities and physical features. Imagine that you (like the Big Three) have agreed that there shall be an independent Czechoslovakia. Copy the map and then draw on it what you think should be the frontiers of the new state. Whose interests do you put first when drawing your lines? Does your state have 'natural' or 'artificial' boundaries? Does it have outlets for its trade? Later you can compare it with the Czechoslovakia drawn at the Paris Conference.

There was little that was wrong with the principle of national self-determination – on paper. Europe was going to be re-shaped, in the interests of her nationalities – or in the interests of as many groups of them as possible. Under great pressure, the statesmen in Paris did their best. To their credit they didn't try to solve awkward problems by ordering minorities out of their homes and shunting them to lands where most people spoke their language. Indeed, the Allies insisted that the governments of Czechoslovakia, Poland, Yugoslavia and Romania should all sign treaties in which they promised to treat their 'minorities' on the same terms as the rest of their citizens.

Eventually, between the summers of 1919 and 1920, the Allies imposed their new frontiers on old Europe in the peace treaties which they signed with the other defeated powers: the Treaty of Saint-Germain with Austria; the Treaty of Trianon with Hungary; and the Treaty of Neuilly with Bulgaria. The settlement they had worked out was not brutal: it was just shortsighted.

Central and Eastern Europe were cut up and parcelled out to the nationalities. In place of the two old, multi-national empires of Austria and Russia, there were now no fewer than ten 'successor' states. The corpse of the Austrian Empire was dismembered to form three whole new states (Austria, Hungary and Czechoslovakia) and parts of three others (Poland, Yugoslavia and Romania). From Russia were carved

the Baltic states and part of Poland: Bessarabia was cut off and given to Romania. Russia was not only separated from the Balkans: she was isolated from the West by a barrier of newly independent countries.

Looking at the map of Europe after the Paris Peace Settlement on page 43 you could convince yourself that at last the Poles, Czechs, Slovaks, Hungarians, Latvians, Lithuanians and all now ruled themselves. It appears that they should have been satisfied. But already an alarming number of the new states were eager to bite chunks out of each other. As you will discover later in this chapter, some of the conflicts which flared up among the new nations were almost inevitable. Much of the dissatisfaction arose simply because the Big Three were unable to form new countries which did not include minorities. The problems were particularly acute when minorities found themselves forced to live in a country alongside people who had perhaps been their enemies before the war; for example, many people from eastern Hungary were placed in the new enlarged Romania.

Let us take just one example of the Big Three at work. As you know, they had encouraged the breakup of the Austrian Empire during the war, and they had confirmed it afterwards. But the Empire had not been just a collection of oppressed nationalities dominated by a government in Vienna: it had also been a complete economic system, held together by a railway network and free trade between all the regions. The Paris Conference carved up the Empire but could find no way to preserve the economic system which would have pleased everyone. Under pressure from those against the idea, the Conference would have nothing to do with a proposal that all the states which had been formed from, or had gained land from, the old Empire should form a free trade area. (You might care to look back at the third of Wilson's Fourteen Points on page 36, and wonder, as the government of the Austrian republic wondered in 1919, what it was supposed to mean.) If the small powers concerned had agreed to the proposal, and if the Big Three had also been prepared to push it through, the scheme might have changed the whole history of Central and Eastern Europe. It would have made economic and political sense by giving the new states a cause for cooperation in place of reasons for conflict. The opportunity was thrown away. Europe would have to wait nearly forty years and pass through another great war before its first 'common market' was set up.

Europe after the Paris
Peace Settlement:
the new frontiers

ference's hopes for the future would be realised – that the new states would stand together in the event of a threat from Germany.

In contrast, the Poles were not stopped by the Allies when they tried to extend their frontier to the east at the expense of a Russia still licking the wounds of civil war. In April 1920 the Polish army attacked and by early May had penetrated deep into western Russia. The Red Army counter-attacked, collapsed near Warsaw and was driven back a second time before the two sides agreed to a cease-fire in October. The war satisfied Poland: she had pushed her frontier further east than the line laid down in Paris. It rammed home a hard lesson to Bolshevik Russia – that she would have to grow much stronger if she was to survive in a hostile world.

The statesmen in Paris created separate, vulnerable states, whose peoples had long histories of mutual dislike and whose very creation gave them new grievances to quarrel over. To their west lay Germany, deeply offended but by no means crippled. To the east was massive, unpredictable Bolshevik Russia, whose interests had been ignored by the Big Three. There would be no certainty that Eastern Europe would not once again provide the flash-point for the outbreak of another general European war once the Allies no longer controlled Germany or Russia renewed her strength.

Cracks in the Peace

The Big Three in Paris proposed no new forms of economic cooperation or other ways in which the newly independent states might work together to take the heat out of European politics. Individual countries claimed, and in some instances tried to grab, what they could. If the name of the game was not cooperation to build a new peace, then everything was to be played for and won. Even while the Paris Conference was still going on, serious conflicts broke out between Germans and Poles, Czechoslovaks and Hungarians, Romanians and Hungarians.

For example, both Poland and Czechoslovakia felt they had strong historic claims to the area around Teschen, its railways and coalfields. The Czechs needed Teschen's coal for their industries, but most of the people in the place were Polish. Early in 1919 the Czechs moved into the area, and the Poles were bullied by the Big Three into accepting the situation. But the dispute poisoned future relations between the two states, and made it unlikely that one of the Con-

The Polish land-grab: new frontiers in Eastern Europe

area of dispute between Poland and Czechoslovakia

seized by Poland from Lithuania in 1920

transferred by Russia to Poland in the Treaty of Riga, in 1921 after the Russian-Polish war

10 The Fourteenth Point: a League of Nations

Wilson's League

President Woodrow Wilson arrived at the Paris Peace Conference with a draft of an agreement by which the powers would bind themselves by solemn promises into a new body to be called the League of Nations. Wilson called this agreement the Covenant of the League; it was, in effect, his grand scheme for the international organisation he had proposed in the last of his Fourteen Points.

Lloyd George and Clemenceau were not enthusiastic about the League, but Wilson pressed home his view that there had to be some organisation to make the peace permanent and to deal with future disputes between nations. In the end Wilson had his way and the Covenant was included in each of the peace treaties. This meant that the powers which signed the treaties were therefore bound to support the League.

The League was to be a guarantee against war. The terms of the treaties might leave a lot to be desired by some countries: but the League would see to it that all the powers, great and small, would no longer set about achieving desired changes, or any others, by war. And the League was to be a *world* organisation. Wars could and did flare up between countries outside Europe; so there was every reason for making the new body truly international.

The Covenant set out the League's aims. Among them were the reduction of armaments "to the lowest point consistent with national safety"; and mutual respect for all countries' frontiers and independence. Aggressors would be dealt with, first by the peaceful weapon of economic sanctions, such as refusing to sell them fuel or other vital supplies. But if all else failed, the League would be justified in using armed force.

Rather like our present-day United Nations Organisation, the League was to have an Assembly, in which all its members would be represented; and a smaller Council, whose permanent members would be the representatives of the great powers. The Permanent Court of International Justice would settle arguments between countries; and the League would have its own permanent staff of employees which was called the Secretariat. Unlike UNO, the League of Nations emerged out of a belief that *all* wars could be avoided if world opinion was mobilised against an aggressive nation. Wilson was not the only believer: there were many other people who shared his optimism. In the present-day UNO there are few signs of such idealism, but it works with some success and we don't expect it to prevent all international disagreements ending up in war: first, because we realise that there are some quarrels between countries which are too bitter to be settled by talk and compromise; second, because no one any longer seriously believes that there is a 'world opinion' which can be brought into effective, threatening action – even against the evils of war.

The United Nations has become useful because, unlike the League, it has not been asked to do an impossible job. Wilson's organisation, however, was a 'League Against War'. It grew out of a terrible conflict and it carried the hopes and good wishes of many people in many countries. In the end it failed to match up to their hopes.

A League of Some Nations

A body which was set up to defend international order and guarantee world peace obviously needed the support of the great powers. Yet only two of the Big Three became members: the USA, of all countries, refused to join. While Wilson was making the peace and the League, American public opinion hardened against any further entanglement in the affairs of Europe. America had brought the Great War to an end and she had helped the European nationalities towards independence. But many Americans believed that membership of the League would turn that temporary involvement into a permanent responsibility for the affairs of a continent from which many new Americans had only recently fled. The American Senate refused the USA's signature to the Treaty of Versailles; and by that refusal, of course, they rejected the American President's League of Nations. Without America the League was unlikely to be strong enough to stand up to a powerful aggressor. Yet Wilson had persuaded the other powers at the Paris Peace Conference to make the League the only body responsible for seeing that the terms of the treaties they had drawn up were observed. The USA's absence from the League might therefore be very serious if any power chose to challenge, for example, the terms of the Treaty of Versailles.

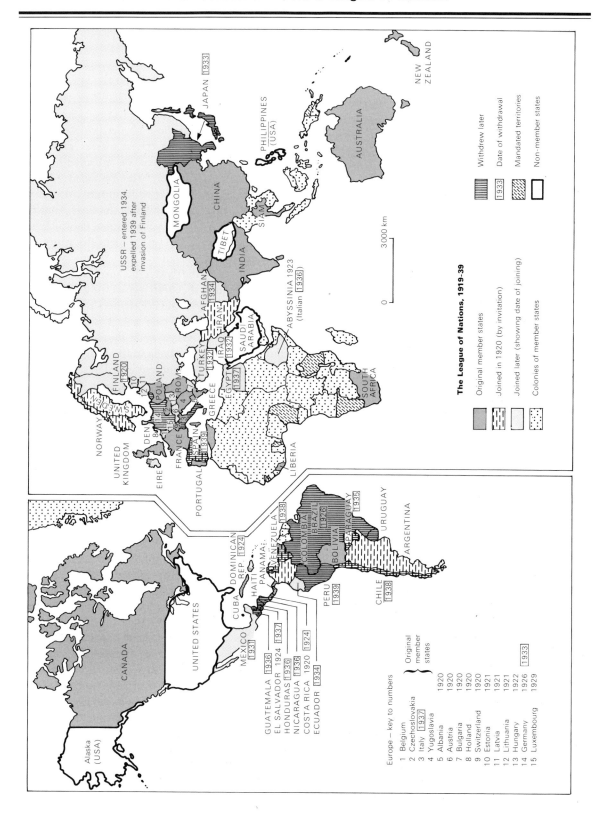

JAPAN 1933

NEW ZEALAND

PHILIPPINES (USA)

AUSTRALIA

MONGOLIA

CHINA

SIAM

USSR – entered 1934, expelled 1939 after invasion of Finland

TIBET

INDIA

ABYSSINIA 1923 (Italian 1936)

AFGHAN 1934

IRAN 1932

IRAQ 1932

TURKEY

SAUDI ARABIA

GREECE

EGYPT 1937

SOUTH AFRICA

FINLAND 1920

SWEDEN

NORWAY

POLAND

ROM

SPAIN 1939

FRANCE

PORTUGAL

LIBERIA

UNITED KINGDOM

EIRE

DEN

3000 km

0

The League of Nations, 1919-39

Original member states

Joined in 1920 (by invitation)

Joined later (showing date of joining)

Colonies of member states

Withdrew later

1933 Date of withdrawal

Mandated territories

Non-member states

Alaska (USA)

CANADA

UNITED STATES

MEXICO 1931

GUATEMALA 1936

EL SALVADOR 1924

HONDURAS 1936

NICARAGUA 1936

COSTA RICA 1920

ECUADOR 1934

CUBA

DOMINICAN REP. 1924

HAITI

PANAMA

VENEZUELA 1938

COLOMBIA

BRAZIL 1926

PERU 1939

BOLIVIA

PARAGUAY 1935

URUGUAY

CHILE 1938

ARGENTINA

Italy 1937

Original member states

Europe – key to numbers

1 Belgium
2 Czechoslovakia
3 Italy 1937
4 Yugoslavia
5 Albania 1920
6 Austria 1920
7 Bulgaria 1920
8 Holland 1920
9 Switzerland 1920
10 Estonia 1921
11 Latvia 1921
12 Lithuania 1922
13 Hungary 1922
14 Germany 1926 1933
15 Luxembourg 1929

45

Russia, too, was out. In 1919 no state in the world recognised Lenin's Communists as the lawful government of Russia; so Russia was not invited to sign the treaties drawn up at the Paris Peace Conference. The world's first, and at the beginning of the 1920s the world's only, Communist state could hardly be invited to join a body which promised to preserve the peace while the official policy of the Russian government was world revolution. Unlike Russia and the USA, Germany had signed the Treaty of Versailles, but she too was excluded from the League. Who could believe that Germany was interested in keeping the peace until she accepted her responsibility for starting the Great War and learned to live with the conditions of her defeat?

The League began its life with forty-two members: by 1924, that number had increased to fifty-five. But the admission of new members like Finland, Luxembourg, Latvia, Hungary and Ethiopia could not make up for the absence of three world powers. Their absence meant, in practice, that the duties of preserving peace and of guaranteeing the frontiers and independence of small nations depended on the only two great powers actually in the League – Britain and France. From what you already know of those two countries before, during and after the Great War, you can well imagine that neither of them was able, or even willing, to take on the job of 'world policeman'. The 'League Against War' had to include all the great powers, or it was nothing.

However, the very fact that it had been set up, even in a limited fashion, encouraged many people to believe that it *had* to work. Another Great War was unthinkable: even if the League could not solve every problem, it could persuade nations to disarm and to settle their quarrels openly. The people who believed that – and set up League of Nations Associations in their own countries – were neither stupid nor blind, but they might be criticised for thinking that there were no ways of working for peace other than through the League.

The League at Work

The new organisation settled into temporary accommodation in Geneva, Switzerland. There it set up agencies for forms of international social work, such as dealing with the plight of refugees and prisoners-of-war. Later it would try to get nations to cooperate in the control of dangerous drugs and in the abolition of slavery and forced labour. The International Labour Organisation aimed to improve conditions of work, to raise the minimum age at which children could be employed, and to encourage the development of social welfare schemes. In those ways the League concerned itself with matters which had previously been the business of individual countries and their governments.

You will remember that as a result of the peace settlement Germany and Turkey had been stripped of their colonies and that those former possessions had been shared out between the victorious powers as 'mandates'. That arrangement was intended to mean that the new ruling powers were responsible to the League for the development of the former colonies. In other words, they held the lands 'in trust', and the League set up a special Commission to which the powers reported each year on the mandates which had been entrusted to them. That was all very proper in theory. In practice, the powers did not regard their new territories in quite the same way as the League. And how could the League enforce changes in the ways in which, for example, Britain and France ran their Middle Eastern mandates when those two European countries were the backbone of the League itself?

In the 1920s the League succeeded in settling some territorial disputes between countries; for example between Finland and Sweden in 1921, between Turkey and Iraq in 1924, and between Greece and Bulgaria in 1925.

In 1923, an incident took place which seemed just the sort of event which the League was designed to stop escalating into war. Five Italian officers were shot by Greeks while investigating the frontier between Greece and Albania. The Italian dictator, Mussolini, used this as an excuse to attack and then occupy the Greek island of Corfu. The Greek government appealed to the League. The British and French governments helped Mussolini to save face by arranging a compromise settlement in the name of the League. Italy agreed to leave Corfu, while the Greeks paid heavy compensation for the incident which had sparked off the quarrel.

By the late twenties the League had achieved some modest successes and nothing had yet happened to shake the confidence of people who saw the international organisation as the best hope of mankind. In 1929 work began on the building of the League's new permanent headquarters in Geneva – the Palace of the Nations. By 1936, when that great symbol of international cooperation and harmony was complete, the League had already failed to prevent two wars and was powerless to stop the great powers re-arming for the next great war in Europe.

46

11 Make Germany Pay!

Threats to the New Republic

Long after the armistice of November 1918 the German people found it difficult to adjust themselves to the fact of their defeat in war and to the changes which quickly followed. The peace treaty had declared them solely responsible for a war in which very many had lost relatives; it had reduced their nation's wealth and strength; and it had left them with Allied armies of occupation on German soil.

In place of the old authoritarian government of ministers chosen by the Kaiser, they were now ruled by an elected President and ministers who needed the support of the democratically elected Reichstag. But the system did not work smoothly, for a bewildering range of new parties appeared on the scene. Among them were extremist groups who wanted to overthrow the new democratic constitution agreed at Weimar in mid-1919. The attacks came from two anti-democratic extremes: on the left were those who wished to set up a communist system modelled on that of Bolshevik Russia; and on the right were those who yearned for a return to the old authoritarian régime controlled by a handful of ministers and generals. Several times a naked struggle for power took place.

In 1920 bands of extreme nationalists, people who supported the idea of an enlarged and militarily strong Germany, were led by Wolfgang Kapp in the Berlin *putsch* – an attempt to seize power from Ebert's government. Kapp's men were reinforced by ex-soldiers who had formed themselves into groups of Freikorps (free corps), led by officers of the old Imperial Army. They were men who hated the new Weimar Republic, who felt its politicians had betrayed the German Empire when they had called for an armistice in 1918. The Freikorps despised these parliamentary democrats as men unfit to rule the German nation.

Kapp's putsch was only checked by the trade unions, who called a general strike and paralysed the city. The workers and the civil servants – the people who made the city tick – refused to cooperate. Kapp was left with a dead Berlin on his hands, not an active centre of power. Four days after they had marched into Berlin, Kapp and his supporters fled.

In the years after the Kapp putsch, the citizens of German cities would be regularly treated to the spectacle of parades of uniformed party supporters barely troubling to hide the fact that they were the private armies of the Nationalists, the Communists, the Socialists. Political murders became commonplace.

All that was bewildering and frightening enough for comfortable and respectable Germans – the shopkeepers, the clerks, the middle-aged craftsmen – but what was left of their confidence in their country and its rulers was being shaken by rapid inflation. Prices of goods were rising faster than wages or salaries and cutting into the value of savings and pensions. And over the heads of the German people hung the threat of the reparations they would, as a nation, be forced to pay to their former enemies. Eventually, in 1921 they were told the sum they would have to pay – 132,000,000,000 gold marks (the equivalent of £6,600,000,000) – in cash and in deliveries of goods. Not surprisingly, they were not enthusiastic about keeping up their monthly payments.

In the Allied countries attitudes to reparations varied. John Maynard Keynes, an English economist, thought they were a brutal nonsense:

"The policy of reducing Germany to servitude for a generation, of degrading the lives of millions of human beings, and of depriving a whole nation of happiness should be abhorrent and detestable ... Some preach it in the name of justice. In the great events of man's history ... justice is not so simple."

To some people, however, there *was* a simple justice in Germany being made to pay for a war she had started. And, in any case, if Allied governments had to repay the money they had borrowed to fight a war started by Germany, surely they had the right to make the German people share the cost? As you have seen (on page 38), the French owed money to Britain and both countries had borrowed from the USA. An obvious solution to that was to appeal to the Americans to wipe out all war debts. The British government suggested exactly that, and the Americans turned them down. The money would have to be repaid; and if the British and French couldn't screw money out of Germany, they would have to find it some other way.

To the French government the issue was very clear.

They had not been permitted to trample all over Germany at Versailles, and now there were many people agreeing with Keynes that the Germans should be let off reparations altogether. Germany may have lost the war, but France was in danger of losing the peace. Early in 1922 Raymond Poincaré became Prime Minister of France. He had no intention of letting Germany off the hook. Later that year the Germans informed the Allies they could not keep up their payments. The scene was set for the extraordinary events of 1923.

1923–The Year of Reckoning

On 20 February 1923 the President of the Reich Department of Health made his report to the Reichstag, the German parliament:

"... health levels are deteriorating ever more seriously.... oedema is re-appearing, the so-called war dropsy, which is a consequence of a bad and overly watery diet. There are increases in stomach disorders and food poisoning, which are the result of eating spoiled foods. There are complaints of the appearance of scurvy, which is a consequence of an unbalanced and improper diet....

In medical circles, there have been complaints about specially sharp increases in infant mortality particularly for the time since August 1922 – that is, since the especially steep rise in the price curve. There are also frequent reports of an increase in sicknesses among infants, of rickets and digestive disorders.... In some places up to twenty per cent of the children who register to begin school must be turned back, because they can be regarded as not yet ready for enrolment in view of their bodily weakness....

In the selection of children for supplementary meals at school last year, it was found that on the average no less than fifty per cent of the children were undernourished.... A municipal school inspector from Leipzig reports that during an unannounced visit to a school class of twenty-seven girls, only three had proper shirts, only two had stockings without holes in them and only four were nourished in a moderately satisfactory way.

... Tuberculosis is on the increase ... tuberculosis, like hunger, is known to be a slow murderer, which does not kill its victims immediately.... A municipal welfare officer from western Germany reports that the spread of tuberculosis and scrofula is especially great among the children....

... From week to week, the table of medicine rates lists higher prices for medicines. 100 grams of surgical cotton in 1914 cost 45 pfennigs,* today 2,552 marks; a bandage in 1914, 20 pfennigs, today 1,270 marks. This clearly indicates that many thousands of sick people must at present do entirely without medicines or be only very marginally supplied with them....

Now all this misery is doubly and cruelly sharpened in those parts of the fatherland which have already been subjected to foreign occupation for four years, but more particularly for the inhabitants of *the Ruhr region, which has recently been invaded by French and Belgian troops in violation of the peace treaty of Versailles.*"

French 'patience' had run out. On 11 January 1923 French and Belgian troops had marched into the Ruhr, the major coal and steel producing region of Germany, to extract reparations for themselves. Suddenly, the German people and politicians were united in a common cause – hatred of the French. The people of the Ruhr refused to cooperate with the enemy; the government supported their passive resistance, and refused to pay any reparations to the Allies.

Fritz Thyssen, a leading German industrialist, described what followed:

"The government had forbidden the coal deliveries. The officials had been instructed to refuse to obey the order of the occupation authorities. The railway employees went on strike. Navigation on the Rhine was stopped. The French themselves had to provide the means of transporting passengers and goods by rail, road and water. The French army occupied the mouths of the mine pits belonging to the Prussian state. When this happened, the miners quitted work. In the other collieries the work continued, but the coal accumulated in great heaps on the surface. No train, no boat transported any of it to Belgium or France ... In order to break the resistance, the occupation authorities established a customs cordon between the occupied territories and the rest of Germany. No merchandise was allowed to leave."

Another kind of traffic penetrated that 'cordon' in the opposite direction. Konrad Heiden, then a German student, told how

* 100 pfennigs = 1 mark.

"in the Ruhr, little troops of men crept at night through the industrial territory. They laid dynamite on railroad trestles, bridges and junctions. French military trains were blown up. In the canals ships sank, and for days the westward stream of coal was interrupted."

There were outbreaks of violence between French troops and German workers. The French expelled or imprisoned the leaders of the resistance. The British tried to persuade the French that this was no way to make the peace work, but Poincaré said:

"Since the signature of the peace, England has always tried to seek a basis of conciliation on which Germany could negotiate as an equal with the Allies. . . . We are persuaded, on the other hand, that if Germany, so far from making the slightest effort to execute the treaty of peace, has only sought to evade her obligations, it

Germany, 1923, when money was worthless. Two young German women use the family silver to buy flour.

is because she has not yet been convinced of her defeat. . . . In fact, the Allies have never got anything from Germany, except when, together, they have threatened to use force."

This time, the use of force had a grotesque side-effect. To pay for the upkeep of their people in the Ruhr, the German government printed more and more paper money. You already know that the German people were troubled by inflation, but nothing had prepared them for the disaster which now hit them. Konrad Heiden described how:

"On Friday afternoons in 1923, long lines of manual and white-collar workers waited outside the pay-windows of the big German factories, department stores, banks, offices . . . staring impatiently at the electric wall clock, slowly advancing until at last they reached the window and received a bag full of paper notes. According to the figures inscribed on them, the paper notes amounted to seven hundred thousand, or five hundred million, or three hundred and eighty billion, or eighteen trillion marks – the figures rose from month to month, then from week to week, finally from day to day. With their bags the people moved quickly to the door, all in haste, the younger ones running. They dashed to the nearest food store, where a line had already formed. Again they moved slowly, oh, how slowly, forward. When you reached the store, a pound of sugar might have been obtainable for two millions; but, by the time you came to the counter, all you could get for two millions was half a pound, and the sales-woman said the dollar had just gone up again. With the millions or billions you bought sardines, sausages, sugar, perhaps even a little butter, but as a rule the cheaper margarine – always things that would keep for a week, until next pay-day, until the next stage in the fall of the mark. . . .

The printing presses of the government could no longer keep pace. . . . You could see mail-carriers on the streets with sacks on their backs or pushing baby carriages before them, loaded with paper money that would be devalued the next day. Life was madness, nightmare, desperation, chaos. . . . Communities printed their own money, based on goods, on a certain amount of potatoes, of rye, for instance. Shoe factories paid their workers in bonds for shoes which they could exchange at the bakery for bread or the meat market for meat."

Germany was sliding rapidly towards economic disaster as she defied the French. It looked brave and patriotic, but it couldn't go on. A new Chancellor, Gustav Stresemann, came to power, and at the end of September he called off passive resistance in the Ruhr and announced that Germany would resume the payment of reparations.

It was the only sensible thing to do, but to the extreme nationalists in Germany it looked like another pathetic surrender to the enemy. First the armistice, then Versailles – and now this! Early in November there was an attempt at revolution by various small nationalist parties gathered in Munich, the capital of the state of Bavaria. The extremists failed: their leader, Adolf Hitler, was sent to prison.

Stresemann's government could now concentrate on solving Germany's most urgent problems. At the end of 1923 a new currency was introduced – the *rentenmark* – and the old paper money was destroyed.

Stresemann also had success in the international field. Having proved his intention to make Germany financially respectable again he could count on the support of the British – and of the Americans, who had an interest in the payment of reparations to France and Britain, since much of the cash was passed on by them to repay American war loans. The real power of the USA in international trade and finance was shown by the appointment of an American banker, Charles Dawes, to head a committee to put reparations on a sensible footing.

The Dawes Plan and the Locarno Pact

In August 1924, Germany and the other powers agreed to the Dawes Plan – a new scheme for the payment of reparations by which Germany paid over a proportion of her industrial output each year. At the same time the French agreed to withdraw their troops from the Ruhr within twelve months.

In October 1925 the Western European powers signed new agreements, together called the Locarno Pact. Germany, France and Belgium promised to respect the frontier between them, the line on the map which had been drawn in 1919 at the Paris Conference. Britain agreed to come to the aid of any one of those countries attacked by its neighbours. On the face of it, Locarno looked like a good deal from everyone's point of view. But in fact it meant different things to different people – depending on whether they lived in Western or Eastern Europe. It meant safety to some and it provoked anxiety in others. In the West, in contrast to the years before 1914, the French now had a guarantee of British support if the Germans should attack. The Locarno Pact removed the sense of fear felt by Germany's western neighbours and it was possible for the French and British foreign ministers to treat Stresemann as a friendly equal. Of even greater importance to Germany was the fact that Locarno protected her border in the west: there would be no repeat of the French invasion of 1923. But if Stresemann had soothed the powers in the West with promises of Germany's good behaviour, he had promised nothing of the kind to the countries in Eastern Europe, especially Poland and Czechoslovakia. The result of the Pact was to divide Europe into a guaranteed West and a newly insecure East. If you look at the map on page 43 of Europe after the Paris Peace Conference, you will see how this division could become of vast importance to the future peace of the continent, particularly if Germany became powerful and ambitious enough to demand the return of those lands in the east which the Treaty of Versailles had taken from her.

12　The Establishment of Fascism in Italy

The story of Italian politics in the twenties is a very sorry one. We shall look at it in some detail, not because Italy was a particularly important continental or colonial power, but because it was the birthplace of a new 'ism' of the twentieth century – fascism.

Italian Fascism was an ugly, violent political movement. Unfortunately, the term 'fascism' itself has since been used to describe a variety of political movements and forms of government in other countries, in recent times as well as in the 1920s and 1930s. The result has been that the word has become overloaded – it has been made to describe too much – and has ended up as a vague term of abuse. When we hear the slogan 'fascist!' these days, it usually tells us more about the ignorance of those who shout it than about the nature of the people, the party or the government they are against. This part of the book is about Italian Fascists. When we come to deal with other movements which have been labelled 'fascist' – for example, the German National Socialists in Chapter 23 – we shall describe them for what they were – in some ways similar to the Italian Fascists, but by no means just late developers north of the Alps: there were important differences.

Problems of Italian Democracy

The Italian state, like the pre-war German Reich, was a fairly new creation, pieced together in the 1860s and early 1870s. Like the Germans, the Italians were touchy nationalists, quick to feel offended; and at the beginning of the twenties many Italians felt that their country had done badly out of winning a war which had cost them an immense military and economic effort. As you can see from the map below, some of the lands which had been promised to Italy by Britain and France as rewards for entering the war in 1915 were not handed over in the Paris peace settlement. Italian nationalists felt that they had been slapped in the face by the Allies, and that they needed a strong government with the muscle and the nerve to slap back.

Italy's war gains

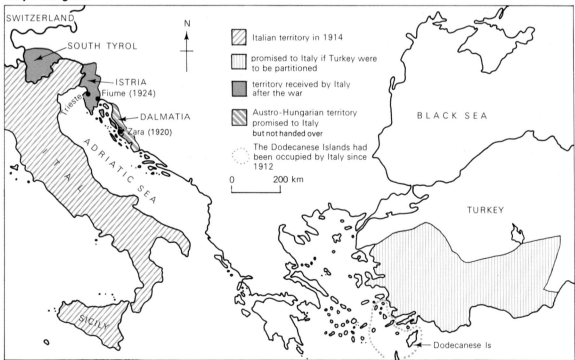

If the Italian state was a recent creation, a democratically elected Italian parliament was an even newer development: only in 1912 had the vote been given to almost all adult males. The traditional ruling classes had had little time in which to learn how to live with and use a mass electorate to their own advantage. Now they were being asked to come to terms with parliamentary democracy in times of widespread social unrest in a semi-industrial country which had Fiat car factories in the north and a mediaeval system of agriculture in the south. In the countryside peasants were being driven by hunger and over-population to reform the pattern of land ownership by simply taking land for themselves; rural labourers banded together to force employers to pay them more and improve their conditions of work. In the towns workers went on strike and occupied factories in attempts to push up wages which had been eaten away by the inflation of the war years. Both inside and outside parliament Italian socialists spoke of the revolution that was bound to come – though without any real idea of how they would bring it about. By 1920 those people who feared that there was a chance that they might lose their property and power – landowners, industrialists, the owners of small businesses – were strongly anti-socialist. They would be prepared to abandon democracy (much good that had done them!) if only someone would come and set all their fears at rest.

The Rise of the Fascists

They found him, or, to be more accurate, he found them in 1920. Benito Mussolini, former revolutionary socialist and journalist, ex-soldier, ambitious rogue, liar and bully, had set up a national organisation of *Fasci di Combattimento* (combat groups) in the troubled Italy of 1919. At first its programme for action was vaguely socialist, and opposed to big business, its behaviour strikingly violent. It gained no support among the workers and Mussolini was still far from the power he craved. He drew the obvious conclusion: if the workers wouldn't have him, the enemies of the workers would. Suddenly the anti-socialists were offered a leader and an organisation which would strike back at their enemies. The leader (*Il Duce*) made that clear:

"One hears it said that the masses must be won over. We do indeed wish to serve them, to educate them, but we also intend to flog them when they make mistakes."

Mussolini had made the startling discovery that there was considerable support for a movement *against* the masses of the people.

That was the start of Fascism. It was against socialism, against liberalism, against democracy, against people thinking for themselves. It had perhaps only two positive principles – and both of them were mean, and in the end despicable: aggressive nationalism, and a belief in the superiority of action over thought. And last, but by no means least among the attractions the Fascists offered their supporters, was the uniform – the black shirt of the *Fasci*. For many of its active supporters Fascism was dressing up in black to look and feel more important than they were either at work or at home. Psychopaths and sadists joined the movement too, of course: they came for the blood.

Mussolini's rise towards power in the state was fast and violent. At the end of 1920 there were 88 Fascist groups, with 20,615 members: exactly one year later numbers had grown to 834 *Fasci* and over a quarter of a million members. In four and and a half months at the beginning of 1921, Fascist attacks on their opponents resulted in 207 deaths and over 800 woundings. As a general rule the police and army didn't interfere: they tended to believe that they and the Fascists shared the same enemies. The Liberals in the government didn't crack down on the *Fasci*, partly because they were frightened more by the threats of a Red revolution than by the murderous activities of the blackshirts; and partly because they thought they could control Mussolini, if and when he agreed to join in a coalition government.

In the elections of May 1921 the Fascists gained only thirty-five seats out of a total of 535 seats in the Italian Parliament. But at the end of October 1922 Mussolini threatened to march on the Italian capital with 26,000 armed Fascists to insist that the country was given strong government: "either the government is handed over or we take it by attack on Rome". The government hesitated, then prepared to resist and asked the King to sign a decree declaring a state of emergency. Victor Emmanuel III refused to sign. Perhaps he feared that resistance to the Fascists would lead to civil war; and in addition there was the threat that Mussolini might turn him off the throne and put in his place the king's pro-Fascist cousin, the Duke of Aosta. On 29 October the King asked Mussolini to form a government. The leader and his Fascist bands then made their 'march on Rome' in true twentieth-century fashion: Mussolini arrived by overnight sleeper and 25,000 of the Black-shirts by local trains.

Mussolini's Dictatorship

Although the Fascist revolution had begun, Mussolini remained head of a coalition government made up of Fascists and representatives of the old parties, until in 1923 a new electoral law, the Acerbo Law, was forced through Parliament, which ensured that the party which got the most votes in a general election would receive two-thirds of the seats in the Chamber of Deputies (the Italian version of our House of Commons). After the general election of April 1924 the Fascists became by far the largest party in parliament. On 30 May, one of the Socialist leaders, Giacomo Matteotti, openly denounced Fascist corruption and violence: eleven days later he was murdered. Socialists, Christian Democrats and Communists called on the King to restore the rule of law and dismiss Mussolini. Victor Emmanuel, the supposed guard-dog of the Italian constitution, behaved like the *Duce's* lap-dog; he refused to bite.

Mussolini was now sufficiently confident to establish his dictatorship. In 1925 the freedom of the press was destroyed. In 1926 all anti-Fascist political parties were suppressed, and the free trade unions followed them into oblivion. In 1927 a secret police force, the OVRA, was set up; and in 1928 what was already a mockery of a parliament was turned into a farce – its members were no longer elected but chosen by the Fascist Grand Council, presided over by the *Duce*. In 1929 the Roman Catholic Church set the seal on Mussolini's success by signing the Lateran Pacts with the Fascist government. The Church got what it wanted: virtual control over religious education in schools and recognition of Roman Catholicism as "the only State religion" in Italy. The Italian government also acknowledged the Pope's right to rule over his own state – Vatican City in Rome. Mussolini got much more: in many people's eyes he had the approval of the head of the Catholic Church. If the Pope found Mussolini acceptable, why should ordinary Italian Catholics turn up their noses?

It is often worth asking the question 'what might have happened if ...?' It is certainly worth asking what might have happened in Italy in the late 1920s and 1930s if the Church of Rome had openly opposed the moral corruption, the brutality and the sickening emptiness of the Fascist régime. Since the Fascists could not have crushed the Church, we are entitled to wonder why the Church lent its authority to a government of thugs led by a self-confessed anti-clerical.

Italy entered the 1930s under the control of a man whose only fixed principles were his belief in his own importance and in the effectiveness of violence as a form of persuasion. Obviously, not all Italians took at their face value the Fascist slogans they heard on the radio, read in the newspapers, saw on the cinema screens and street posters:

'Believe! Obey! Fight!'

'War is to the male what childbearing is to the female!'

'A minute on the battlefield is worth a lifetime of peace!'

They saw, they could hardly fail to see, that these were remarkably silly messages. The urban workers and the rural labourers, whose standards of living improved very little, were being terrorised into obedience. The anti-socialists who had welcomed the *Duce* in 1920 had not the slightest desire to spend even half a minute on the battlefield: they had believed the *Fasci* would do all their fighting for them, against those whom they thought were enemies of a stable, orderly and respectable society. They had prayed for a strong man to take away nasty politics, rather as small children ask Daddy to take away the pain. Once the struggle to control the masses of the people was over, they found themselves in the grip of a political loudmouth who asked them to accept the absurdity that 'Mussolini is always right'. By that time of course, as we have seen, they had thrown away their right to disagree.

Yet there was an appearance of order about what the Fascists called the 'Corporate State', in which industries, agriculture and even film-making were each run by a Corporation which supposedly was made up of both owners and workers. In fact those organisations were largely shams, aimed at taking away the rights of workers to join trade unions. But despite the sham, Mussolini's Corporate Fascist State appealed to some Europeans outside Italy. He seemed to them to have succeeded in abolishing fruitless political argument and the violence which entered politics in times of stress. He had replaced it with another kind of violence and repression. *Il Duce* had his admirers in industrialised countries such as Britain, but in the end the style of Fascism would appeal most in poor countries where political violence was common.

13 The Establishment of Communism in Russia, 1917–24

The government which Lenin and the Bolsheviks set up after the revolution of November 1917 was called 'Sovnarkom', short for Council of People's Commissars. During the next few weeks, Soviets all over Russia joined in the revolution and took control of most towns and cities. By the end of 1917 nearly all Russia was in Soviet hands.

This did not mean, however, that the Bolsheviks controlled Russia. Far from it: only fourteen of the twenty-five members of Sovnarkom were Bolsheviks; not all Soviets were run by Bolsheviks; and in the countryside most peasants supported the Socialist Revolutionary Party. Even more awkward from the Bolshevik point of view, the long-awaited elections for a Constituent Assembly (arranged by the Provisional Government earlier in the year – see page 32) gave a large majority to the Socialist Revolutionaries.

Lenin had no intention of sharing power with others in an elected parliament. When the Constituent Assembly met for the first time in January 1918, armed Bolsheviks closed it down – for good. In Lenin's view, his first tasks were to establish the authority of Sovnarkom and to crush any other parties or organisations that either demanded a share in government or threatened to undermine the Bolshevik Party.

Sovnarkom had already put an end to the private ownership of land (see page 34). It had gone on to issue a decree on work, establishing an eight-hour day and a forty-eight hour week; a decree on unemployment insurance, outlining plans for workers' insurance against injury, illness and unemployment; a decree on workers' control, putting all factories under the control of elected committees of workers; and a decree on banking, putting all banks in Russia under state control. Now Sovnarkom issued more decrees which pointed the way to the kind of Russia that Lenin intended to create. All titles and ranks were abolished: from now on, people were to call each other 'Comrade' or 'Citizen'. Women were declared to be the social equals of men. The Orthodox Church, which had already been stripped of its lands, was to stop teaching religion.

Some of this was merely tinkering with the old Russia. The new Russia could not be built until the Bolsheviks had swept away the enemies within, who were already recruiting armies for the struggle. Even more urgent was the problem of the German armies still on Russian soil. For any Russian government that continued the war would risk losing whatever support it had among the people. The Provisional Government had made that mistake and Lenin was determined not to repeat it.

The Treaty of Brest-Litovsk

Late in 1917, Trotsky, now Commissar for Foreign Affairs, led a team of negotiators to the headquarters of the German army in the Polish town of Brest-Litovsk. The German demands were so savage that Trotsky returned and advised Lenin to carry on with the war. But the Bolshevik leader was convinced that the future of Bolshevik Russia depended more than anything else on peace. He said to Trotsky:

"You yourself say that our trenches are deserted . . . At the moment there is nothing more important in the world than our revolution; the revolution has to be safeguarded no matter what the price."

In February 1918 the German armies rolled forward again: the Russians were unable to stop them. On 3 March the Russian negotiators were back in Brest-Litovsk to sign a peace treaty whose terms were even more humiliating than the Germans' original demands. Russia had to give up all her western territories – Finland, Estonia, Latvia, Lithuania, Poland, the Ukraine and Georgia. As these were the richest areas of the country, Russia lost 62 million people – 26 per cent of the entire population – along with 27 per cent of her farm land, 26 per cent of the railway system and 74 per cent of her iron ore and coal. Russia also had to pay an indemnity of 300 million gold roubles to Germany.

Reds and Whites: the Russian Civil War

No sooner had the Russian people shaken off the horrors of the Great War than they were plunged into the most vicious of civil wars. The new government was attacked from all sides by the 'Whites', the enemies of the Bolsheviks, who included supporters of the former Tsar, landowners and Tsarist generals, as well as groups such as the Socialist Revolutionaries and the Mensheviks with whom the Bolsheviks refused to share power. In the Ukraine, nationalists formed their own army and government to resist the Bolsheviks as well as the Germans who occupied their land. In the north, the Socialist Revolutionaries set up a government in Archangel, and troops led by General Mannerheim cleared the Bolsheviks out of Finland; while by the end of 1918 much of Siberia was controlled by a former Tsarist admiral, Kolchak, and his forces.

Sovnarkom was merely one government among many by the middle of 1918. Even the Treaty of Brest-Litovsk seemed to have backfired on Lenin. It had bought off the Germans but it had also aroused the wrath of Russia's wartime allies. They feared that the Germans would now be able to transfer their eastern armies to the Western Front. So, hoping to bring down Lenin and to establish a new, friendly government which would start fighting the Germans again, the British, French, Americans and Japanese sent troops to Russia to help the White armies fight the Bolsheviks.

The story of the fighting in the Civil War can be quickly told. The White armies were never a united force. They fought separate campaigns against a Red Army, created and commanded by Trotsky, which had the great strategic advantage of controlling the heartland of western Russia. The allied armies of intervention, made up of the odds and ends left over from the Western Front, fell into disorder when mutinies broke out among the French forces in Odessa, and were withdrawn early in 1919. The war lasted nearly two years. Both sides committed terrible atrocities, on each other and on the suffering people.

The Bolsheviks were prepared to use any means to survive and win the Civil War. One of those means was a new security police force which had been established in December 1917, the 'All-Russian Commission against Counter-Revolution, Sabotage and Speculation', known and feared by its short name – the Cheka. Led by Felix Dzerzhinsky, the Cheka organised a 'Red Terror' during the summer of 1918. Cheka units in the countryside hanged, beat, shot and tortured anyone who helped the Whites or fought for them. They spied on the Red Army and drove its soldiers into battle with machine-guns trained on their backs. Probably 50,000 people, Reds as well as Whites, died at the hands of the Cheka.

War Communism

The Bolshevik government was equally harsh in its direction of the Russian economy. Sovnarkom took strict measures to organise industry and agriculture in the areas under its control. Its aims were to keep the Red Army supplied with food and with weapons, and to introduce a system of communism – the equal sharing of wealth. Under this 'War Communism' of 1918–21, Sovnarkom banned private trade, took (not bought) surplus food produced by the peasants to feed the hungry towns and the Red Army, and nationalised all factories and workshops which employed more than ten workers. The Supreme Council of National Economy (VSNKH) took over the management of industry, the Commissariat of Transportation managed the flow of goods and foodstuffs on the railways and waterways, while the Food Commissariat (Narkomprod) organised the rationing of food in the towns.

War Communism kept the Red Army going but it had grim, sometimes appalling, effects on the people in the towns. The Russian newspaper *Pravda* summed up the situation in an article on 26 February 1920:

"The workers of the towns and of some of the villages choke in the throes of hunger. The railroads barely crawl. The houses are crumbling. The towns are full of refuse. Epidemics spread and death strikes to the right and to the left."

The figures below will show you how near the Russian economy was to complete collapse in 1921.

Pig-iron production was only 2·4 per cent of the 1913 figure.

Iron ore production was only 1·7 per cent of the 1913 figure.

Coal production was only 27 per cent of the 1913 figure.

The harvest of food crops was 40 per cent below pre-war levels.

For every 100 horses in 1916, there were now only 75.

For every 100 cattle in 1916, there were now only 79.

For every 100 pigs in 1916, there were now only 72.

For every 100 sheep and goats in 1916, there were now only 55.

Then, in March 1921, the sailors in the port of Kronstadt, near Petrograd, rebelled against the government. The sailors demanded free elections for new soviets, freedom of speech, freedom of association and the right for peasants to farm their land freely. Trotsky, still Commissar for War, sent loyal Red Army troops against the sailors and after a battle that raged for ten days in blinding snowstorms, the mutineers were defeated and their leaders were shot.

The New Economic Policy

The Kronstadt mutiny had failed; but it was, in Lenin's words, "the flash which lit up reality better than anything else". Lenin could see that government controls must be relaxed, and War Communism brought to an end. So in March 1921 the New Economic Policy (NEP) was launched. Private trade was permitted once again, peasants were allowed to sell their surplus produce, and many small factories returned to private ownership.

If we measure the effects of the NEP on agriculture by looking at how much more food was produced, then the following statistics show definite improvements:

	1922	1925
Grain harvest (million tonnes)	50·3	72·5
Horses (million head)	21·7	27·1
Cattle (million head)	45·8	62·1
Pigs (million head)	12·0	21·8

However, these figures don't tell the full story of what was happening to the Russian peasants. For a start, NEP came too late to affect the sowing of crops in 1921, and a dry summer ruined what was already a disastrous harvest. The result was a massive famine. Over five million peasants died of starvation. According to Pravda, more than 27 million people were living at below subsistence level. Cannibalism became common in the worst affected areas.

Even after the famine of 1921–22, NEP did not solve the problem of food shortages in the towns – and that was its primary aim. Although there was an increase in the amount of grain produced, the amount of grain sold by the peasants remained low – about 20 per cent of the total output. One very obvious reason for this was that as the peasants produced more, they also ate more – a very natural thing to do. They were using the NEP to fill their own bellies.

Just as the NEP benefited the peasants, it also encouraged those industries which produced goods for the peasants to buy. So, in the early 1920s, the leather and textile industries made good recoveries; while the heavy industries, on which the country's strength was built, progressed little, if at all. Russia's development as an industrial power was therefore severely retarded in the early 1920s. For this reason Sovnarkom felt it necessary to sign trade agreements with some of the industrial countries, including Britain and Germany. Imports of German steel were vitally important to the Russian economy, so Germany and Russia signed the Treaty of Rapallo in 1922: Russia was to get German steel and help with the reconstruction of her armaments industry; and a secret part of the Treaty arranged for Germany to manufacture in Russia the weapons the Treaty of Versailles forbade her to make openly in her own factories. For the first time, but not the last, necessity had brought together those strange bedfellows.

Party Control

We should now look briefly at the way in which Russia was governed if we are to understand later developments in that country in the 1920s. In 1922 Bolshevik Russia was re-named the Union of Soviet Socialist Republics (the USSR or the Soviet Union)– a federal state in which each of seven republics had, although mostly only in theory, some degree of control over its own internal affairs. (Today there are fifteen republics in the USSR.) In theory, government was the business of elected Soviets, or Councils, at every level – from the village to the government of the republics. At the centre of the system of government of the whole Soviet Union was the Supreme Soviet and a Council of Ministers.

The Soviet Union had only one political party, so you won't be surprised to learn that Russian voters had only the choice of electing either Communists or Communist sympathisers in Soviet elections. Of course, not everyone in Russia was a Communist, and the members of the Communist Party were a political élite who had numbered a quarter of a million by the end of 1917. By 1922 there were over a million members but, more important, the number of full-time Party officials had risen to twenty-five thousand – enough to fill every important post in the USSR, from the Council of Ministers down to the position of

War, civil war, and now starvation. Just four victims among the millions, during the famine of 1921.

Chairman of each of the Soviets of remote villages in the back of beyond.

The Party could say that it operated a Soviet democracy: people stood for election; people turned out to vote. It was just that the result of any election was bound to be a Communist victory. Real power lay in the hands of the Party officials – the 'apparatchiks'. The man who hired and fired those officials, who could promote a man's career in the Party 'organs' or ruin him, was the real ruler of the new Russia.

Lenin established a dictatorship which he and the Communist Party claimed to exercise on behalf of the Russian workers and peasants, but in doing so he established a system which could be corrupted into a dictatorship of one man.

Lenin died in January 1924, Petrograd was renamed Leningrad in his honour, and his mortal remains were embalmed and placed in a mausoleum in Red Square, Moscow – where they have remained on public display ever since.

14 Europe in the Twenties

The Search for Security

The new Europe of the early 1920s was an explosive mixture of dissatisfied, angry and anxious states. In the three years after the signing of the Treaty of Versailles, violent disturbances continued to shake Central and Eastern Europe. A chain of new states, from Finland in the north to Yugoslavia in the south, had been created to satisfy nationalists' demands for the right to govern themselves – yet there were still well over 20 million people living as minorities in states ruled by other nationalities. Out of Czechoslovakia's total population of some 14 millions, well over 4 millions were Germans, Poles, Hungarians and Ruthenes. Among 12 million 'Yugoslavs' were nearly 2 million Germans, Romanians, Albanians and Hungarians. As a direct result of the peace settlement Romania had taken over more than a million and a half Hungarians.

It was obvious that neither Germany nor Russia would be prepared to let things stand as they were. Both powers had lost lands which had been extremely valuable to the economies of their pre-war empires. For example, Russian oil fields had been given to Romania, and German coalmines in the east now belonged to the Poles. No European statesman could fail to see that one day Germany and Russia would try to re-draw the lines on the map which had taken land, people and power from them. To a casual observer, the Europe of, say, 1923 would have looked a much more dangerous place to live in than the Europe of June 1914. But the continent did not explode into war in the twenties – mainly because neither Germany nor Russia was strong enough to use force to alter the map. Instead those years were a period in which European countries tried to make themselves more secure by seeking alliances to protect themselves against likely enemies.

It was inevitable that the majority nationalities dominated the new states of Central and Eastern Europe: the Czechs in Czechoslovakia, the Serbs in Yugoslavia, the Poles in Poland. In some places minorities were treated fairly, as equal citizens: in others they got a raw deal. In good times – when most workers in the towns and cities had jobs, and when peasant farmers received a decent price for their surplus produce – minority peoples shared in the general well-being. When times became hard, as they did at the end of the twenties, it would be a different story – of job discrimination in the interests of majorities; of new grievances on both sides to sharpen old dislikes.

Meanwhile, although complaints about the ill-treatment of minorities were often to be heard (especially from Germany, where a propaganda campaign was started against the treatment of brother Germans living in Poland), the new states survived and searched for friends who would guarantee their survival. In 1921 Poland formed a defensive alliance with France: a glance at the map of Europe on page 43 will tell you the enemy they would defend each other against. In 1922, Czechoslovakia, Romania and Yugoslavia came together in a 'Little Entente' to discourage Hungary from trying to take back the lands and peoples they had all seized from her at the end of the war. Two years later Czechoslovakia also formed an alliance with France. It looked as if a determined effort was being made by France in the West and four states in the East to make the new lines on the map permanent.

France wanted Britain to support the effort. But while Britain was willing to go to almost any lengths to defend her empire in Asia, she was not prepared to guarantee frontiers in 'faraway' Eastern Europe. Britain still thought of herself first as a great imperial, sea-going power: the idea that her future could be closely bound up with the goings on of Poles and Czechs came a very bad second.

58

Any disagreement between Britain and France was good news for Germany: it weakened the alliance against her in the West. Germany's aim in the mid-twenties was to separate France from her new friends in the East, the Poles and the countries of the Little Entente. That separation began with the Locarno Pact of 1925, which at first sight seemed to put an end to more than ten years of hostility in Europe, but which alarmed the leaders of the Eastern European states.

At the end of Chapter 11 (page 50) we noted that the agreements signed at Locarno included a promise by Germany, France and Belgium to respect the frontier between them which had been set down in the Treaty of Versailles. The results were that France at last began to feel safe from the awful possibility of a German attack; and Germany at last looked sufficiently respectable to be invited to join the League of Nations (an invitation she accepted in 1926). But you also saw on page 50 that the Locarno agreements did not carry a German guarantee to respect the frontiers of Poland or Czechoslovakia. And now that France's frontier with Germany was guaranteed by the Locarno Pact, some French politicians began to think that France would be safer if she avoided alarming Germany by becoming too friendly with Poland and Czechoslovakia. In 1929 the French began to build massive fortifications – the Maginot Line – along their border with Germany, just in case the Germans didn't take the Locarno Pact as seriously as they had promised. And as they felt themselves more secure from attack, they attached less importance to their treaties with Poland and Czechoslovakia. The French were turning their backs, instead of their bayonets, to the East.

Communist Russia and the Comintern

Far to the East lay the great new unknown factor in European politics – a Russia which had lost much of her territory but which now lay under communist rule. Perhaps only two things were certain about that country – its desperate need for breathing space in which to rebuild a shattered economy, and its leaders' fears of attacks from the West. The Western intervention in the Civil War of 1918–20 strengthened the communist belief that the state could not survive for long if the industrial countries of the West decided to patch up post-war quarrels and turn on Russia in an attempt to destroy communism before it could seriously threaten their capitalist societies.

Following the example set by the Bolsheviks, communist parties quickly developed in several Western European countries – especially in Germany and Italy – and you will remember from Chapter 9 (page 39) that there were very real fears among the Allies of a wave of communist revolutions sweeping over Europe while the Big Three were still trying to agree on a peace settlement. Early in 1919 the Comintern (Communist International) was set up to oversee the actions of Marxist parties throughout the world. Socialist groups from most European countries joined the Comintern, calling themselves 'communist' parties, and committed to international revolution. After all, Marx had called for workers of *all* countries to unite and overthrow their masters. The Russian Soviet leaders may not have believed that international revolution would happen immediately, but they certainly hoped that the countries of the West would be weakened by strikes and disturbances in which the new communist parties would play a leading part.

The leadership of the Comintern was clearly in the hands of the Russians, who saw it as an instrument for weakening their European enemies. At the second congress of the Comintern, held in Moscow (the new capital of Russia) in 1920, a number of conditions were laid down for the parties who wished to join. Each party must be tightly disciplined and obey its leaders; all the parties must agree to the decisions of the Comintern; and every party was "obliged to give unconditional support to any Soviet republic in its struggle against counter-revolutionary forces". 'Soviet' here meant communist, and at that time the only communist republic in the world was Russia.

There was nothing very surprising about the Russians taking over the leadership of the international communist movement. But it meant that what the Comintern did in future would be decided by the policies and personalities of the Russian Communist Party. However, as early as 1921 communist rebellions had been defeated in Hungary and Germany and it was becoming clear that the non-revolutionary socialist parties (which were not members of the Comintern) had far more support than the communist parties among workers and peasants outside Russia. Despite the strenuous efforts of its Chairman, Grigori Zinoviev, the Comintern never stood any real chance of lighting the spark of revolution in Europe.

The New States of Eastern Europe

Between 1914 and 1918 European governments had called on their peoples to join in the immense military, economic and financial efforts which the new kind of warfare demanded. Whole peoples had taken part in war – as soldiers, as workers, as lenders of money. Subject peoples had used the war as an opportunity to claim their independence and freedom. And, as you saw in Chapter 6 (page 29), the war had weakened old traditions of respect for superior authorities. When the slaughter ceased and statesmen began to make the peace, it was not possible to put the clock back to 1914 and deny most people the opportunity of taking part in their own government.

Democracy became the new fashion in Europe. Even in an old parliamentary democracy such as Britain there were changes: in 1918 the Representation of the People Act gave the vote to nearly all men over the age of twenty-one and women over thirty. The changes in Central and Eastern Europe appeared much more remarkable. The new states began their lives with new systems of parliamentary government and their creators and well-wishers (such as President Wilson) expected that they would, before too long, develop into true working democracies – governments of the people, by the people, for the people. But things were not to turn out as simply and neatly as that. If the masses of the people were now going to have a much greater effect on government, the critical question to be answered was this: who was going to get control of the masses?

There were plenty of people with answers ready. In the mainly peasant lands of Eastern Europe the traditional rulers – such as the landowners, the churches, the army leaders – were not going to give up their power without a struggle. In the West, non-revolutionary socialist parties (such as the Labour Party in Britain and the Social Democrats in Germany) saw their opportunity to reform and improve industrialised societies. In both the East and West of Europe, as you have already seen, there were also the new communist parties, planning to imitate the Bolshevik Revolution of 1917.

In most of the new states of Central and Eastern Europe the democratic forms of government with elected parliaments, which had been imposed by the Paris peacemakers, soon proved to be unworkable. There the people and their leaders had no tradition of government through freely elected parliaments, no sense of the duty of majorities to protect the rights and property of minorities. Their politics were struggles for power between different national and social groups – between Poles and Germans, Serbs and Croats, Romanians and Hungarians; between peasants and landowners, and between peasants and the middle classes of the towns.

The struggles were often violent and strongly tinged with anti-Semitism – for Jews were a minority to be found in every country in Europe and had no state of their own. Because they rarely owned land Jews valued education as a way of entering city occupations, as doctors, lawyers, civil servants and journalists. In the main cities of Austria, Hungary and Poland there were often more Jews in those professions than other groups of people. That had led to resentment from educated non-Jewish people, and sometimes to restrictions on the numbers of Jews allowed into universities. In the countryside many Jews lived in desperate poverty, but the activities of some of them as moneylenders earned the hatred of the peasant farmers. All that was nothing new: the Jews were long used to persecution. But the point was that in most of the new states the Jews had little more protection than they had had under the old empires. It was just one more indication that traditions of intolerance and illiberalism could not be wiped out, or even weakened, by a pretence of parliamentary government.

In some of the states even the pretence at democracy was soon given up. In the late 1920s Poland (1926) and Yugoslavia (1929) were taken over by dictators who ruled with the aid of the upper classes and the army, and who used their control of the state to reward their supporters with jobs – in the civil service, in the professions, and on the state-owned railways. Often these supporters came from one national group. In Yugoslavia there were six nationalities, but almost every important post in the government service and the armed forces was held by a Serb. With few exceptions, such as Czechoslovakia (a more industrialised country in which the leaders of the various national groups agreed to cooperate in making parliamentary government work), control of the peoples of Central and Eastern Europe passed into the hands of small, unrepresentative cliques. Elections continued to be held, but the use of bribery and terror meant that no government in Eastern Europe lost an election in the twenty years after the Great War.

This German poster of the early 1920s warns of the menace of Bolshevism. The Archangel Michael cries; "People of Europe! Protect your most sacred possessions!" – property and religion.

Competitors for Power in Western Europe

In contrast, the societies of the industrialised West seemed capable of accepting big political changes. Mass electorates were not new; old established parties might not welcome the participation of more of the people in government, but they didn't fear them. As a result, the struggle for political power in the West became a three-cornered competition between the communist parties, the non-revolutionary socialists, and the old parties who had accepted democracy as something they had to come to terms with. In France, in Britain and in Germany, most of the people who still regarded themselves as the 'ruling classes' had long since realised that the surest way to commit political suicide was to try to ignore the voting power of the working classes. A fourth competitor for political power – the revolutionary nationalist parties, such as the National Socialists in Germany and the Fascists in Italy – waited in the wings. Their time would come if and when democracy no longer seemed capable of coping with social and economic distress.

The nearest the communists came to success was in their short-lived revolutions in some of the German states in 1919 and the early 1920s. Thereafter, although the German Communist Party (the KPD) was supported by a large minority of the electorate (it had over three million votes in each of the elections of May 1924 and May 1928), it was never within reach of coming to power by democratic methods. The Social Democrats, the communists' chief rivals for the support of the working class, did much better. Friedrich Ebert, President of the German Republic from 1919 until his death in 1925, was a Social Democrat. His party, the SPD, always won more votes than any other party in the elections of the twenties; and the leaders of this non-revolutionary socialist movement became ministers in coalition governments with other parties from 1919 to 1923 and again in 1928.

You may have gathered by now that there was no love lost between communists and non-revolutionary socialists. They were rivals for the workers' affections; and the Comintern, which wanted to weaken other states, forbade its member parties to enter into alliances with any other parties which claimed to represent the interests of the working class. Thus, in France, as in Germany, the communists and the socialists were enemies, not allies. Both groups were smaller

than in Germany because France was less industrialised and had a smaller working class; but political disagreements between communists and socialists were no less bitter. The communists refused to consider sharing power with any other group, while the more popular socialists were willing and able to form alliances with other parties. In the elections of 1924 they made an alliance with the Radicals (a non-socialist, anti-clerical party of the centre) to defeat the coalition of conservative parties led by Poincaré, and then supported the new Radical government led by Edouard Herriot. (It was this government which agreed to end the French occupation of the Ruhr and to accept the Dawes Plan which revised Germany's payments of reparations – see Chapter 11, page 50.)

The conservative parties regained power in France in 1926, but the socialists were given little to criticise in the new government's policies, which included 'socialist' measures such as higher public expenditure on social services. The old parties had not only come to terms with democracy; they had learned that to appeal to the masses it was sometimes necessary to pinch their opponents' political clothing.

In Britain the Communist Party was too small to make serious threats of revolution. After the war the Labour Party in the House of Commons steadily overtook the Liberals as the main opposition party to the Conservatives. Conservative newspapers and politicians frequently raised alarms about communists penetrating the trade unions and the Labour Party – 'the Reds under the bed'. But neither the unions nor Labour wanted revolution: both were committed to the reform of British society through a democratically elected Parliament which could make changes in the law.

In January 1924 Labour leaders had their first taste of power when Ramsay MacDonald became Prime Minister of a government which did not have an absolute majority in the House of Commons. This meant that the number of all MPs in the opposition parties was larger than the total number of Labour MPs. The minority government lasted only until November, when a general election not only gave the Conservative Party a landslide victory but pushed the Liberal Party into a very poor third place behind Labour. It appeared that the British, unlike the French and the Germans, preferred a two-party system, with clear winners (who became the government) and equally obvious losers (who formed the Opposition). The next general election, in May 1929, appeared to confirm that preference: Labour won 288 seats, the Conservatives 260, and the Liberals only 59. On the other hand, Liberals could complain that the British electoral system of 'first past the post' didn't give them a fair representation in Parliament. Then, as today, in each constituency the winner was the candidate who won most votes, even if a majority of electors in the constituency voted for the other candidates. In May 1929 both Labour and Conservative parties received over eight million votes, and their MPs dominated the new House of Commons. The Liberals looked done for with fewer than sixty MPs – yet they had polled over five million votes throughout the country in the election.

But whatever could be said for or against the elec-toral system, one thing was clear – a new force in British politics had matured: a non-revolutionary socialist party. The main support of the Labour Party and most of its funds came from the trade unions, who accepted the British system of parliamentary democracy. Ramsay MacDonald became Prime Minister again, and the Conservatives duly became His Majesty's Opposition. The system of government had been proved strong and flexible enough to contain the struggle of new and old parties to gain the support of the people. Except for some isolated incidents, British politics remained a contest of votes, in polling booths and in Parliament – not a conflict of broken heads in the streets.

15 The Middle East between the Wars

In the last chapter we looked at Europe in the 1920s; at a continent deeply scarred by the Great War, where one great empire had been dismembered and another severely cut about. The new states made for the nationalities had not become the sturdy democracies their creators had hoped for: nationalism was still the most powerful disruptive force in European politics; and the post-war political struggles for control of the people had already produced authoritarian régimes in much of Eastern Europe and the vicious, anti-democratic backlash of Fascism in Italy. In the new countries of the Middle East many of the same forces were at work in the 1920s. We can begin our survey of this region by looking at a country where nationalists were determined on the one hand to reject European imperialists, and on the other to welcome European ideas.

The Break-up of the Turkish Empire

You have seen (Chapter 4, page 17) that the Turkish Empire was in retreat well before the Great War began. In the First Balkan War of 1912 Turkey was expelled from most of her European territories, retaining only Thrace, on the tip of the Balkans, and the Turkish Straits. Although in the Great War the Turks scored some major victories over the British at Gallipoli and in Mesopotamia (see Chapter 5, page 24), they were driven out of their Arab territories in the south by the Arab Revolt of 1917, and by the joint Arab-British offensive in 1918. When Turkey signed an armistice on 30 October 1918, there was no prospect whatever of the Empire remaining intact: Emir Feisal, the military commander of the Arabs, was in control of Syria, Lebanon and Jordan, while the British controlled Iraq and Palestine.

Although the defeated Turkish Empire was not European (except for Thrace) the British and French felt free to divide it between them. Despite Feisal's pleas at the Paris Peace Conference for Arab independence, the British and French had already made arrangements for the Arabs in the Sykes-Picot Agreement of 1916 (see page 25). As you can see from the map opposite, the British took the lion's share of the land. However, they didn't want to spend money on troops and officials to rule directly over their new territories (except in Palestine), and so they set up Arab governments under their protection in Iraq and Transjordan. The French took a firmer grip on Syria and the Lebanon, deposing Feisal, who had proclaimed himself King of Syria earlier in 1920.

Oil was not the motive that prompted Britain and France to assert themselves in the Middle East: in 1920 the Middle East produced only about one per cent of the world's oil. But you will remember from Chapter 2 how seriously the great colonial empires regarded the protection of their trade routes. The British, in particular, were determined to secure control of an area which included the Suez Canal, the Red Sea and the Persian Gulf, and which was vital for the protection of their traffic to and from India.

Turkish Nationalism

Allied plans to take over the Turks' homeland of Anatolia completely misfired. In 1919 the Big Three encouraged the Greek government to send troops to Anatolia to control not only the Turks but also the Italians, who were already at work in Anatolia trying to snatch a large chunk of Turkey for themselves. The Greek government had grand ideas of re-creating the ancient Greek Empire in a land in which there were large numbers of Greek-speaking people. Turkish nationalists, led by General Mustafa Kemal, had the simpler intention of kicking out all Europeans.

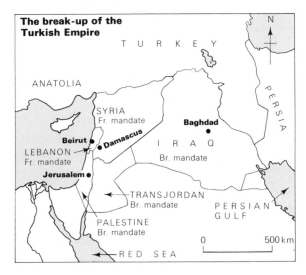

The break-up of the Turkish Empire

Then, in August 1920, the Allies presented the Turkish government with the Treaty of Sèvres, the fifth and last of the Paris peace treaties. You can see from the map below that it dealt harshly with Turkey. Anatolia, the Turkish heartland, was divided into French, Italian and American spheres of influence, with Smyrna becoming a Greek protectorate. The Turkish Straits were made into an international zone under the League of Nations, while Thrace was given to Greece: this meant that Turkey's western border now extended only a little further than the suburbs of Constantinople, bringing the capital within range of Greek artillery in the event of war.

Rather than accept the dismemberment of Turkey by the Allies, Mustafa Kemal and the nationalists had already set up a breakaway government in Ankara, in the heart of Anatolia, in March 1920. Their survival looked doubtful when a large Greek army suddenly advanced from Smyrna in June 1920, defeating Kemalist forces in a series of battles, and occupying the province of Brousa.

The war which followed between the Greeks and the Turkish nationalists ended in total victory for Kemal in 1922. Kemal smashed the Greek army in a major battle at Afion Karahissar on the River Sakarya (26–30 August 1922), and drove the remnants of it back to Smyrna. There, Turkish civilians promptly set upon the Greek population of the city in a series of massacres. Pursuing the Greek army northwards, Kemal then came up against a British garrison at Chanak, guarding the Turkish Straits. Rather than risk battle with Kemal, the British commander at Chanak signed an agreement with him, the Convention of Mudania, promising a revision of the Treaty of Sèvres in Turkey's favour. Out of this came a new treaty, the Treaty of Lausanne, in 1923: Turkey regained Eastern Thrace from Greece, and the frontier between them was demilitarised. Turkey was left free of all foreign troops. The Straits were returned to Turkish control although they were to remain demilitarised. And no restrictions were placed on Turkey's armed forces.

The Treaty of Lausanne didn't quite finish the

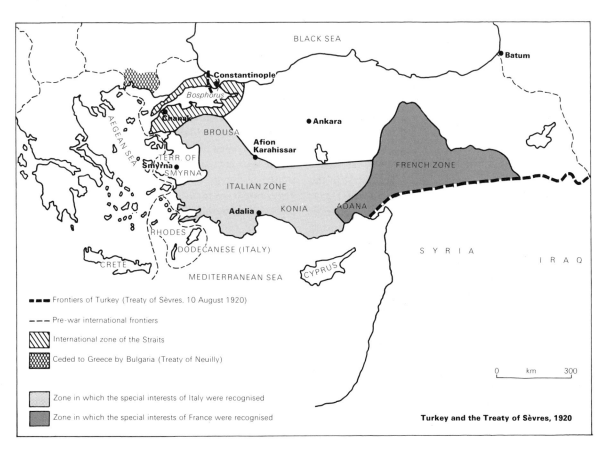

■■■ Frontiers of Turkey (Treaty of Sèvres, 10 August 1920)

――― Pre-war international frontiers

International zone of the Straits

Ceded to Greece by Bulgaria (Treaty of Neuilly)

Zone in which the special interests of Italy were recognised

Zone in which the special interests of France were recognised

Turkey and the Treaty of Sèvres, 1920

tragedy of the conflict between Greeks and Turks. All Greeks still living in Turkey and all Turks living in Greece were sent 'home'. Nearly a million and a half people were uprooted from places in which their families had lived for generations. The Turks had set a brutal example for the more crude nationalists of the twentieth century.

Mustapha Kemal, who later altered his name to Atatürk ('Father of the Turks') declared a Turkish Republic in October 1923, and ruled it as President until his death in 1938. Atatürk's major achievement was the rapid modernisation of Turkey along Western European lines. He declared that Islam was no longer the state religion; he introduced the Western alphabet and forbade writing in Arabic; polygamy (the practice of a man having more than one wife) was abolished. If male Turks wished to wear headgear they had to wear Western-style hats or caps, not the traditional 'fez'. In 1934 a law was passed which gave women the vote. A new word entered the language: from 1 p.m. on Saturday to midnight on Sunday became the Turkish 'vikend'.

Persian Nationalism

Persia was also taken over by aggressive, reforming nationalists. In 1921 Reza Khan, with the support of the army, led a rebellion to overthrow the Persian government, which had accepted the presence of Russian and British troops, officials and business men. The Russians withdrew from north Persia, and the British left the Persian Gulf area – though they did so rather more reluctantly and kept a controlling interest in the Anglo-Persian Oil Company which had already begun the serious exploitation of the wealth that lay beneath Persian sand and soil. In 1925 Reza Khan made himself Shah of Persia and started a programme of reform similar to that of Kemal in Turkey. Industrial growth was encouraged, communications were improved, and education was re-organised along Western European lines. In 1935 the Shah changed the name of his country to its ancient name of Iran. In the following year European dress was made compulsory for both sexes. As in Turkey, it was declared that women need no longer obey the Islamic rule about completely covering their faces and bodies in public. In both countries, of course, many women continued to do so, and it was mostly the daughters of the educated and better-off families who accepted Western fashions. In

both Turkey and Iran the Westernising, modernising movement was much stronger in the main towns than in the rural communities, where very little changed.

Arab Nationalism

Britain made no really determined effort to stay in Turkey or Iran in the face of nationalist opposition. She and France faced even fiercer resistance from nationalists in the Arab lands of the Middle East, but there the two European powers were not prepared to give up their interests.

We saw on page 64 how the Arab lands of the former Turkish Empire were divided between the British and French and Arabs friendly to the Allied powers. Five new states emerged from that arrangement – Syria and the Lebanon were French mandates; Transjordan, Iraq and Palestine were British. Only in the Arabian Peninsula were any of the Arab peoples truly independent. Egypt had been occupied by British troops since 1914, and for all practical purposes the British government regarded that country as part of the British Empire. France imposed direct rule on her Arab territories, Syria and the Lebanon, while the British arranged that friendly princes ruled Transjordan and Iraq.

Britain's control of Egypt was vehemently opposed by Saad Zaghlul, the leader of the local nationalist party, the Wafd. When Zaghlul proved to be too effective in whipping up nationalist feeling, the British spirited him off to Malta – whereupon the Wafd led an uprising against the British in Egypt. Although the revolt was not successful, violence and unrest continued in Egypt until early 1922, when the British government decided that the only way to put a stop to it (short of getting out altogether) was to grant Egypt a kind of semi-independence. The Egyptians were given a form of parliamentary democracy, Sultan Fuad became King Fuad I, and the number of British officials in the country was steadily reduced. But the British army remained in occupation, and the Wafd remained a dissatisfied nationalist party, committed to the overthrow of Europeans who wouldn't go away.

It was obvious that neither Britain nor France was prepared to give up control of Arab lands. In 1925 France had to deal with a revolt in Syria when nationalists rebelled against the French policy of supporting Christian Syrians at the expense of the Muslim Arabs who formed the majority of the population. After the revolt was put down France granted Syria a new constitution, making her (like the Lebanon) a parliamentary republic: but France kept control of Syrian foreign policy and the armed forces. Similarly, although Iraq achieved a kind of independence by the end of the 1920s, Britain insisted on her 'right' to maintain forces in that country. The security of Suez and the potential oil-wealth of that part of the world were too important to be left to the chances of friendship.

The exception to the European domination of Arab lands was the Arabian Peninsula. In the early 1920s, it was rapidly taken over by Ibn Saud, a ruler who had sided with the British during the war. In 1924 his forces invaded the Hejaz (see map below) and captured the holy Muslim city of Mecca. In 1926 he was proclaimed King of the Hejaz, a title he changed to King of Saudi Arabia in 1932.

Independent Saudi-Arabia in a European-dominated Middle East

The problem of Palestine

To the north of Ibn Saud's enlarged kingdom, between British Egypt and French Lebanon and Syria, lay the land which was to become the focus of Arab nationalism. Back in 1917 the British Foreign Secretary, Arthur Balfour, had stated that:

"His Majesty's Government view with favour the establishment in Palestine of a National Home for the Jewish people, and will use their best endeavours to facilitate the achievement of this object, it being clearly understood that nothing shall be done which may prejudice the civil and religious rights of existing non-Jewish communities in Palestine, or the rights and political status enjoyed by Jews in any other country."

The British had been attracted by the prospect of having a stable, friendly Jewish community in Palestine as well as by the more romantic idea of helping the Jews to return to their promised land after nearly two thousand years in exile. The trouble was that the Arabs were not consulted about the plan.

At the end of the Great War there were only 60,000 Jews in Palestine, out of a total population of 750,000; or roughly about seven Jews to every ninety-three Arabs. Yet the Palestine mandate made Britain responsible for establishing a Jewish National Home there while at the same time protecting the rights and position of the rest of the population. It was, of course, an impossible undertaking, and it would poison relations between the Arabs and the British for many years to come. As Britain was responsible for Palestine, she was also held responsible by the Arabs for both the legal and illegal immigration of Jews. By 1931 there were 175,000 Jews in Palestine – or nearly eighteen per cent of the population. It's possible that the Arabs might have been willing to accept even that sizeable minority, but sinister developments in Europe in the 1930s would soon bring a massive influx of Jews to the Middle East. By 1939 there would be nearly 430,000 Jews in Palestine, making up twenty-eight per cent of the population. Arab nationalists had rightly complained about their treatment at the hands of the Western powers after the war: the Palestinian problem inflamed their sense of injustice.

16 Africa between the Wars

Until the nineteenth century Africa had remained a continent which Europeans touched and knew only at the edges. The land, peoples and civilisations of the African interior had remained largely unknown to them. Only when new paths into the interior were cleared by explorers and missionaries, and when the Western imperialists stepped up their search for new colonies in the later nineteenth century, did the Europeans begin to penetrate beyond the African coast.

Before the Great War most of the European colonies in Africa were largely unaffected by the trade and industry of the rest of the world. Few had much in the way of communications systems except the bare 'spinal columns' of the railway networks of the future. Only in South Africa was there anything like a complete rail system linking industrial centres (mostly mines) with farming areas as well as ports. Quite simply, much of

Africa had not been in the hands of Europeans long enough for them to organise the colonies in ways which would bring maximum benefits to the mother countries. For example, British East Africa had only been taken over in 1895, the Belgian Congo in 1908, and French West Africa in 1909. The Great War had interrupted the exploitation of the continent almost before it was really under way. Once the war was over, the imperial powers (except Germany, of course) returned to the business of getting Africa to earn its keep.

The Economics of Colonialism

Throughout the 1920s and 30s the story of colonial Africa was one of Western investment in a wide range of agricultural produce, in mining, in the extension of the railway networks and the development

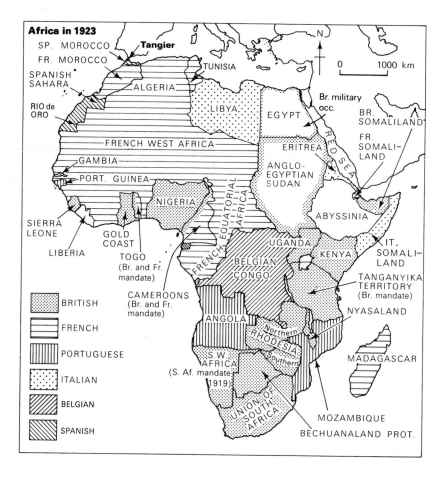

of harbours. Except in South Africa there was little, if any, attempt to develop industries whose products could compete with European manufactures.

By the end of the twenties the merchants and traders of the Western empires had developed two kinds of economy in Africa. The colonies of West Africa and most of East Africa exported crops grown on the small-holdings of peasant farmers: the colonies of Southern and West-Central Africa (and of Liberia in the West and Kenya in the East) exported mineral ores and crops grown on plantations by wage-earning labourers.

Most colonies specialised in one or more primary products – for example, cocoa in Western Nigeria and the Gold Coast; ground-nuts in Northern Nigeria and Senegal; cotton in the Sudan and Uganda; rubber in Liberia; coffee in Kenya and Tanganyika; copper in Northern Rhodesia; copper, diamonds and palm-oil in the Congo. The money invested in the new planta-tions and mines, and in the necessary railway and harbour facilities, came from the USA as well as from Western Europe; and many parts of Africa soon ex-perienced their first taste of Western 'big business' when small trading firms either joined together or were taken over by bigger ones. An outstanding example was the United Africa Company, formed in 1929, which handled most of Nigeria's foreign trade and and a large part of the Gold Coast's. UAC was itself part of a Euro-pean 'multi-national' company, the Anglo-Dutch Uni-lever organisation, which also had a stake in the palm-oil and palm-kernels export trade of the Belgian Congo.

Social and Political Effects of Colonialism

All this exploitation of the colonies had profound effects on their African populations. The small-holders of West and East Africa brought new land under cultivation, purchased new tools, invested in transport to get their produce to market, and began to employ extra men at harvest times. To be a wage-earner, moving from job to job, became a common way of life for many Africans. In the mining and plantation colonies there were, of course, more wage-earning labourers; and if there were not enough men *willing* to work for low wages, colonial governments applied pressure to the labourers to volunteer. Taxation was one form of pressure: if a man wouldn't work for a wage, however low, he wouldn't have the cash to pay the taxes demanded from him. Such techniques of

persuasion were gentler than in the past. Not so many years before, in the Belgian Congo, workers who didn't produce sufficient rubber had their hands cut off. By and large that kind of forced labour was, in the 1920s, a sour memory of the bad old days before 1914. Only in the Portuguese colonies of Angola and Mozambique was it still practised on a large scale. There, an African could be harshly punished or imprisoned if he broke his contract with an employer.

At the end of the twenties, most African peoples were still coming to terms with their new economic roles, as suppliers of foods and raw materials to the din-ner-tables and factories of Europe and the USA. They were not encouraged to develop political ambitions. With few exceptions, they were more conscious of belonging to tribes than to the artificial colonies drawn on the African map by European imperialists. Even in the more prosperous colonies the European powers didn't encourage the Africans to take any part in government, and they took little notice of black Afri-cans' first attempts to create nationalist movements. For example, in 1920 black Nigerians set up the National Congress of British West Africa, and demanded a degree of self-government: all they got was the vote for a limited number of Africans in elec-tions for an advisory council which had little real power. That was in vivid contrast to the British govern-ment's treatment of white settlers. In 1923 the territory then known as Rhodesia was divided in two. The northern half, where there were few settlers, remained under direct British rule as the protectorate of North-ern Rhodesia (today it is the independent state of Zambia). The other half, in which white settler-farmers were already well established, became the colony of Southern Rhodesia (today it is the inde-pendent state of Zimbabwe). Both lands were to become very prosperous by African standards – the North exploited its copper mines while the South exported flue-cured tobacco to British cigarette manu-facturers. The difference was that the whites of South-ern Rhodesia were given virtual self-government over their own internal affairs.

The Union of South Africa

At the very tip of the dark continent, South Africa soon began to develop a distinct kind of white-domi-nated society. In 1912 the National Party was formed by Afrikaners (whites of Dutch origin) who didn't want to retain close links with Britain or share power with the blacks. In the same year, the African National Congress was set up to defend the rights of black men in a country where they had no vote and where the land would soon be divided up in the proportion of one-eighth for the blacks and seven-eighths for the whites.

The early prosperity of South Africa had been based on the mining of gold and diamonds. During the Great War the South African government had encouraged new industries and now their owners looked to the political leaders for protection from European competition in the post-war period. White workers, and those Afrikaners who moved into the towns for employment, also wanted protection from the black workers in the competition for jobs. In 1924 the Afrikaner National Party joined with the Labour Party, which represented the mainly English-speaking white urban workers. One of the first measures passed by the new coalition government was the Mines and Works Act of 1925, which meant that the government could reserve skilled jobs for whites and coloureds (people of mixed race) only. The pattern was set for black South Africans to remain in low-paid, unskilled work. Tariff barriers were also raised to protect the new industries from European competition, and in 1928 the South African government set up a state-run Iron and Steel Corporation. The foundations had been laid for the development of the first industrialised society in Africa, in which the unskilled labour was provided by poorly paid black Africans who were allowed no share in the running of what had been their country.

The Impact of the Depression

The countries of the African continent became involved in international trade just in time to be hit by the international slump – and although the economies of the African countries were not as badly affected as those of Latin America, they undoubtedly suffered. Between 1929 and 1932, their earnings from exports fell, on average, by over forty per cent; and by 1938 most of them had still not recovered their relative prosperity of the late twenties. Throughout Africa thousands of labourers lost their work and income; those who kept their jobs had their wages cut.

Among the few African countries which recovered quickly from the Depression were Southern and Northern Rhodesia and Kenya. All three of them benefited from protected access to the British market after 1932. Southern Rhodesia was also helped by the fact that she had large quantities of a mineral whose price actually *rose* in the 1930s – gold. When many of the world's trading nations abandoned the gold standard in the early thirties, the price of gold was no longer artificially fixed: it was free to move, and it moved rapidly upwards – from 85 shillings (£4.25) an ounce in 1931 to 140 shillings (£7) an ounce in 1939. Southern Rhodesia experienced a 'gold rush' as European companies sank mines to excavate the metal, for the profit of their shareholders back home and to the benefit of Southern Rhodesia's export trade.

The most spectacular recovery, however, was that of the Union of South Africa. It would not be too fanciful to say that she was pulled out of depression by gold-miners' picks. The number of men employed in the mines rose from 232,000 in 1931 to 364,000 in 1939. Between 1931 and 1938, the value of South Africa's gold exports rose from £48 million to £71 million – and those export earnings were pumped into the new industries which had been started in the Great War, developed in the twenties, and then threatened by the world Depression. The iron and steel, food, tobacco, chemicals, textiles and construction industries all expanded; and between 1932 and 1939 South Africa more than doubled her industrial production.

In the gold-boom of the 1930s the Union was ruled by a coalition government made up of the South Africa Party (supported by people of both British and Dutch descent) and the National Party (supported mainly by Afrikaners – descendants of the Dutch Boers), which together formed the United Party. But as the economy recovered, so the more extreme Afrikaners kept the National Party alive as an anti-black and anti-British political movement. Blacks were already second-class citizens in the Union; they were made to live apart from whites, they had to have 'passes' to travel in their own country, and they were forbidden to join trade unions. If yellow metal was one of the two chief props of South Africa's industry, the other was cheap black labour – and the Afrikaner Nationalists were determined to keep it that way.

Across the border, in Southern Rhodesia, the ruling whites were already aping South African ways of treating blacks. By the late 1930s, the richer parts of southern Africa were well on the way to creating societies in which the wealth of white minorities depended on keeping black majorities poor and powerless.

17   India between the Wars

The British in India

If most of Africa was only now, in the early twentieth century, being thoroughly penetrated by European business men, India had already a long history of white man's rule. For there, for well over a hundred years the British had dominated the peoples of civilisations more ancient than their own.

In that vast land of huge population and many religions, the majority of the people were Hindus, segregated by their 'caste' system into hereditary social classes which defined their occupations and whom they might marry. The largest religious and cultural minority was made up of Muslims, descendants of earlier conquering peoples who long ago had controlled much of the sub-continent.

Within the British Empire India had a unique system of government, and as you saw in Chapter 5 (page 25) hundreds of thousands of Indian troops fought on Britain's side in the Great War. By that time demands for Indian independence had become so loud and insistent that in 1917 the British government accepted, in principle, that one day India would become a dominion (i.e. a self-governing country within the Empire).

In 1919, the Montagu–Chelmsford reforms introduced a system of government called 'dyarchy' into the eleven provinces into which India was divided. In each province there were now to be two levels of power and responsibility: Indian ministers were responsible for programmes of health, education and agriculture; while the British kept control of finance and of the forces of law and order (the army, the police and the courts). It was not enough. Angry Indians resorted to anti-British campaigns which sometimes ended in disorder, and the British over-reacted in enforcing their law. The most sickening example of 'law-enforcement' occurred at Amritsar in the Punjab, where troops opened fire on a mob, killing 379 and wounding over a thousand other people. It was unforgivable. It was also out of character: British officials in India had generally set out to be humane, not barbarous, although this had not prevented them from frequently misunderstanding Indian customs and traditions. Now that the process of allowing Indians to take part in government had begun, the pace was always too slow

for the Indians, always too fast for the reluctant British. Human behaviour alters, becomes cruder and less rational, under stress. In the twenty years after 1919 the sub-continent was to suffer much crude and violent behaviour.

Gandhi and the Congress Party

It was fortunate for the people of India, and for their British rulers, that in those crucial years the independence movement was led by a Hindu who was both a wily politician and as near to a saint as a good British Christian could admit. Mohandas Gandhi was the leader of the Congress Party, the Hindu-dominated nationalist organisation. Instead of violent reprisals against the British, he preached (and practised) non-violent resistance; for example, disobeying British laws, and refusing to pay taxes to the occupying power. Both he and his right-hand man, Jawaharlal Nehru, were imprisoned by the authorities and the strikes and demonstrations of his followers sometimes collapsed into ugly, brutal spectacles. Yet Gandhi's moral leadership gave the Indian struggle for independence a massive dignity. His ideal was one of an independent India in which Hindus and Muslims could live and work peacefully together and in which the lowest of the Hindu social groups, the 'Untouchables', would be raised above the grim, indecent misery in which the caste system forced them to live.

But Gandhi's ideal was not wholeheartedly shared by all members of Congress nor by the more extreme Hindu nationalists outside the party. The traditionalists in Congress were offended by Gandhi's love for the Untouchables, whom he called *Harijans*, 'Children of God'.

Jinnah and the Muslim League

The other problem was that Hindu extremists would not consider sharing power with Muslims in a future independent India. The Muslims too were wary of Gandhi's grand and humane plan. By the early 1930s some of them had become so worried by the threat of Hindu domination that they campaigned for the independence not of one but of two Indias. Their organisation, the Muslim League, had been set up

Gandhi sets out on yet another challenge to British power—this time an attempt to break the government's monopoly on the manufacture and sale of salt. In 1930 he led a march to the sea to collect free salt. "The honour of India", he declared, "has been symbolized by a fistful of salt in the hand of a man of non-violence. The fist which held the salt may be broken, but it will not yield up its salt."

in 1906 to counter the Hindus' growing political influence. Now it began to be attracted by the idea of a separate state for Muslims. In January 1933 a Muslim Indian called for the creation of a separate state based on the Muslim homelands of the Punjab, Kashmir, Sind, the North West Frontier and Baluchistan (which you can see on the map in 'India—"that most truly bright and precious jewel"' on page 203. Elements of those names blended easily into one word—*pakistan*—'land of the pure'. The first man to demand its creation was called Rahmat Ali: at the time he was living at No.3 Humberstone Road, Cambridge.

Eventually, in 1935, the British Parliament passed the Government of India Act. Indians were to have full control of the provincial governments: the British and the Indians would share control of the central government. In the elections of 1937, the Congress Party gained control of six of the eleven provinces; the Muslim League came out on top in two; and there was no clear majority for either in a further three. Arrogantly, Congress declared that the Muslims elected should take their orders from Congress, not from the Muslim League. And from that point on, the League's leader, Mohammed Ali Jinnah, was convinced that the Muslim people would never be well treated in an India run by the Congress Party.

By the end of the 1930s the question of who would rule the sub-continent had still not been finally settled, even though it was more or less certain that the British would leave, sooner or later. Gandhi and Nehru found themselves in the strange position of nationalists who wanted to get rid of the only people who appeared able and willing to hold the country together—the alien British.

18 China between the Wars

The Warlord Years 1911–27

At the end of Chapter 2 we noted that a man called Sun Yat-sen led a successful nationalist revolution in China in 1911. The revolution ended the rule of emperors, but that was about the limit of its success. There was nothing left to hold together what had once been an empire, no single central authority which all the people would accept. The new Chinese republic entered a long period of lawlessness in which local warlords fought for power. The great majority of the population – the peasants – got nothing out of the 1911 revolution except war and more misery. Their numbers increased, their pressure on the land available for cultivation increased; they became poorer, not better off.

Such industry as China had was mostly in the hands of foreign business men – especially the British, Americans and Japanese. Indeed, the degree to which foreigners controlled China's commercial life led Sun Yat-sen to describe his country as a 'hypo-colony' – a land exploited like a colony without being brought under the formal rule of a foreign power. Among the workers in China's cities and towns there was a deep sense of humiliation which a well-organised nationalist party would be able to use to its own advantage.

Sun's Chinese National People's Party (the *Kuomintang*) had a bad time in the early years of the warlord period. In 1917 Sun re-established himself as President of China; but he and his party actually controlled only the city of Canton and part of Kwantung province in the south. To be able to drive north in an offensive against the warlords who controlled the rest of China, the party needed to be larger, better organised and to have a trained fighting force. In 1922 Sun accepted the Soviet Union's offer to help improve party organisation and military training. He was determined that China should become a truly democratic socialist state, not a communist dictatorship – but he and the Kuomintang could find no-one else to support them. A small Chinese Communist Party had been formed in 1921. In 1924 Sun persuaded the Kuomintang to accept Communists as members.

Chiang Kai-shek and the Kuomintang

Sun died in 1925. Shortly afterwards, a young, ambitious officer called Chiang Kai-shek was appointed commander of the Kuomintang army; and a thirty-two-year-old Communist organiser called Mao Tse-tung was put in charge of the Kuomintang's propaganda and political agents. It was a successful and short-lived partnership. The Kuomintang set out on its Northern Expedition late in 1926. The urban workers rose to greet their deliverers from humiliation at the hands of foreigners; the peasants would have welcomed almost anyone who encouraged them to turn on the hated landlords. By the end of March 1927 Chiang's army was in control of Shanghai and all China south of the Yangtse River.

It was then that Chiang decided to deal with the Communists and their supporters in the trade unions, whom he saw as a future threat to the Kuomintang. In Shanghai and other occupied cities the Communists and their supporters were simply hunted down by Chiang's soldiers and massacred. After that savage extermination of most of their former allies the Kuomintang continued their march to the north and entered the capital city, Peking, in 1928. Chiang made Nanking, a city further south, his new capital and by 1930 could regard himself, not without good reason, as the new ruler of China.

Chinese communism seemed a lost cause. In Moscow, Joseph Stalin was not at all disappointed by the way things had turned out. He wanted a strong government in China, able to stand up to the world's great powers, and to Japan, which was now the biggest threat to the security of the USSR's eastern lands. The Kuomintang appeared likely to provide such a government: Stalin was not interested in supporting international communist revolution, in China or anywhere else, unless it directly benefited the USSR.

Mao Tse-tung and the Communists

Mao Tse-tung had escaped Chiang's bloodbath. He led a few other survivors to a remote, mountainous area in southern China. There Mao was to rebuild the Party, create an army and plan his revolution. He was a Marxist without an urban working class, a 'proletariat', to lead: his only possible allies were the peasants. But hadn't the great Lenin taught that

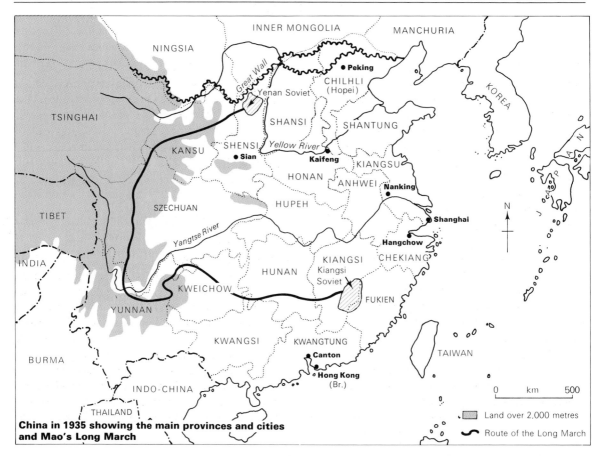

China in 1935 showing the main provinces and cities and Mao's Long March

imperialism makes *all* subject peoples 'proletarian'? If that were so, then all Chinese were proletarian and ready for revolution: Mao would make his revolution among the peasants.

In his southern stronghold Mao set up China's first Communist state – the Kiangsi Soviet. By late 1931 Mao's army had beaten off three attempts by Chiang's forces to destroy the small Communist state, using the tactics of guerrilla warfare.

But in September 1931, Japanese forces committed a major act of international aggression: they invaded Manchuria, China's most industrialised province. The League of Nations condemned the invasion but took no action; and despite evidence that the Japanese intended to dominate China, Chiang Kai-shek took no action either. Instead he preferred to continue his efforts to destroy the Communists' stronghold.

This time he was determined not to be drawn into another round of guerrilla warfare, but first to blockade and then to crush Mao's smaller forces. The Communists responded by setting out, in October 1934, on the

longest and most extraordinary military retreat in history. As you can see from the map above, their 'Long March' took them over some of the highest mountains in the world, on their journey from the south to a new base in the caves and hills of Shensi province in the north of the country. Their ordeal lasted over a year, and three-quarters of the Red Army died along the 9,000-kilometre route, many of them from starvation, disease and exposure.

But Mao survived and so did Chinese communism. The Yenan Soviet was set up, which attracted to it many Chinese who believed that Mao, not Chiang, was capable of both building a better China and giving the lead in resistance to the Japanese invaders. By the middle of the 1930s there were three competitors for power in China – Chiang's Kuomintang; the Japanese, firmly based in the north-east; and the Communists in the new Yenan Soviet. "Political power", said Mao, "grows out of the barrel of a gun." The three rivals armed themselves to the teeth for the struggles to come.

74

19 Latin America and the Caribbean between the Wars

To the south of the USA lay the under-developed half of a vast continent. The countries of Latin America (that is, those countries in which the people spoke Spanish or Portuguese – both of which were derived from the Latin language) already had long histories of independence from the Spanish and Portuguese empires, but they depended heavily on Western Europe and the USA for trade and for money. Mountain ranges (the Andes were the largest), swift rivers and impenetrable jungle were formidable obstacles to trade within Latin America at a time when air travel was still hardly used, and in a sub-continent where there were as yet few international railways. It meant that the 'natural' markets for Latin America's primary products were overseas. The poverty of the people meant that there was not enough spare money (capital) available to invest in the development of industry and communications. For that kind of development the Latin Americans had to attract capital from abroad.

In the nineteenth century, Britain had been the chief foreign investor, especially in Argentina where British money had tamed the *pampa* (grasslands), built the railways and frozen the beef ready for export. An American visitor to Argentina in 1908 declared that

"In Buenos Aires one looks in vain for an American bank … American financial institutions are like the American merchant steamers, conspicuous by their absence. The Anglo-Saxons that you see briskly walking along the sidewalks are not Americans, but clean-shaven, red-cheeked, vigorous Britishers."

But after the Great War, which left Britain and other Western European countries much poorer and therefore with less money to invest, the USA quickly took their place and became the dominant business and financial power south of the Rio Grande.

The investment of American money – in agriculture, in mining, in oil-wells, in construction industries – was not always popular. Latin Americans had, and still have, a strong respect for American industrial power, and an equally powerful suspicion of American money. There was always the feeling that *Yanqui* dollars might bring with them *Yanqui* interference in politics; that 'dollar imperialism' would make the independent republics of Latin America little more than satellites of

their powerful neighbour to the north.

In the first thirty years of this century most of the Latin American republics remained relatively poor and under-developed. Only four countries – Argentina, Mexico, Brazil and Chile – showed any marked industrial development. And only in the southern lands – Argentina, Chile, Uruguay and southern Brazil – was there any rapid growth of urban populations.

Argentina and Chile

Argentina stood out as much the most 'modern' of the Latin American states, with a large urban working class based on her capital city and biggest port, Buenos Aires. From the late nineteenth century the people of Argentina had some of the apparatus of democratic government – political parties, votes for adult males and a secret ballot – but real political power still remained in the hands of the country's great landowners. Similarly, the Chilean landowners kept their control over a country in which an urban working class developed as more miners were needed to extract first the nitrates and then the copper ore which Chile sold abroad.

Brazil

Brazil too had a form of democracy, but the real power in the land was the army, supported by the landowners. For a short time, before the Great War, Brazil had been the world's biggest exporter of rubber. But competition from new plantations in the Far East, especially in Malaya, had led to the collapse of the Brazilian rubber industry; and in the 1920s the country's economy, and therefore the day-to-day lives of most of the people, depended almost entirely on the cultivation and export of coffee and cotton.

Uruguay

To the south of Brazil lay Uruguay, a much smaller country whose people were mostly of European origin, and whose democratic system of government was to become much more than a form of words. In the 1920s, President Batlle y Ordóñez's government introduced an impressive programme of reforms – old-age pensions, reductions in working hours, abolition both of capital punishment and of censorship of the press. It was an extraordinary attempt to create a 'welfare state' in a sub-continent whose ruling classes, in general put their own welfare first and last.

Venezuela

Perhaps most people would regard the early twentieth-century history of two countries to the north of Brazil, Venezuela and Mexico, as more typical of Latin America. Between 1908 and 1935 Venezuela was in the hands of a dictator, Juan Gómez, whose achievements included setting up a savage secret police force, fathering over a hundred children, and presiding over one of the first great 'oil-booms' of the century. By the end of the 1920s, Venezuela had become the second largest producer, and the biggest exporter, of oil in the world. As the oil flowed out, the money flowed back in – to Gómez and his government. The mass of the people had little share in the new national wealth: there were no noticeable improvements in health services, in education or in general living standards.

Mexico

Oil-wealth had already played its part in Porfirio Diaz's corrupt dictatorship in Mexico before Gómez began exploiting the Venezuelan wells. Diaz had brought a kind of political stability to lawless Mexico by imprisoning or murdering opponents of his government. He had encouraged foreigners (especially the British and North Americans) to invest in oilfields, in mines, in railroads; and in doing so he had started his country on the path of industrialisation. But the mass of the people benefited not at all: the wealth of the country was in the hands of the great landowners and foreign business men. Just two statistics should help you to grasp the situation: more than three-quarters of Mexico's people had to scratch their living from the land: yet ninety-five per cent of them owned no land of their own.

A revolution which began in 1910 soon brought an end to Diaz's dictatorship, which had lasted for over thirty years; but it didn't stop there. It turned into a ten-year civil war in which Emiliano Zapata led the landless peasants against the central government and its army, and in which a quarter of a million people died. The bloodbath didn't end with the victory of the

Latin America and the Caribbean after 1920

'good guys' who wanted land returned to the peasants from whom it had been taken and with the vast estates broken up to provide more land for the poor. The great landowners and the army remained in power, but they realised that Mexico's rulers couldn't behave as they had done in the days of Diaz. In a sense they 'adopted' the Revolution they had fought against, and wrote into the new Mexican constitution the principle of *national* ownership of the land and of the minerals and oil beneath it.

The first two Presidents of the new Mexico, Alvaro Obregón (1920–24) and Plutarco Calles (1924–34), made haste very slowly to practise that new principle. The transfer of land to the peasants on a large scale had to wait until the presidency of Lázaro Cárdenas, who was in power from 1934 to 1940. Meanwhile, Mexico became a one-party state after the formation of the *Partido de la Revolucion Institucional* (PRI) in 1929. The Party ruled; the Party would accept as members people of very different political opinions, provided they didn't want to start a revolution against the 'adopted Revolution'.

The Caribbean

As you can see from the map on page 76, most of the islands of the Caribbean had not tasted the independence enjoyed by the Latin American republics. With the exceptions of Haiti, Cuba and the Dominican Republic, the Caribbean islands were firmly under the rule of foreigners.

The British West Indies, with their slave-manned sugar plantations, had once produced by far the greatest profits of any part of the Empire – but those days were long past. At the end of the 'sugar boom', over a hundred years before, the islands' economies had gone into a long, dismal decline, and it was only just before the Great War that they began to show signs of recovery. Instead of relying almost entirely, for employment as well as for an export trade, on the cultivation of sugar cane, a variety of tropical fruits was grown and shipped overseas. It was a shaky new prosperity, in which not all the people shared. Just as

Britain dominated the political life of the islands, so their economic well-being and living standards depended on the capacity of the British and American markets to absorb their produce. If they didn't, it meant unemployment and hunger for many.

As far as the USA was concerned, 'empire' was chiefly a matter of protecting trade. You saw in Chapter 2 (page 11) how the Americans took control of lands in the Pacific, Central America and the Caribbean early in the century. In the 1920s and early 1930s, when they saw that there was no likelihood of foreign threats to their security in the Caribbean or to their control of the Panama Canal, the Americans withdrew from all the lands they had occupied in that area – except for Puerto Rico and the Canal zone itself.

By now you will have read enough to make you wary of generalisations about the governments, societies and economies of Latin America and the Caribbean. By the end of the 1920s the independent republics had reached very different levels of economic development, and their peoples were living with (and sometimes suffering under) a variety of forms of government. It's true that democratic government through elected parliaments was not widely practised in the sub-continent, but then neither had it become well established in independent Eastern Europe.

Even so, one generalisation about Latin America has to be made: it was becoming more closely tied to the USA, as a market for manufactured goods, as a source of foods and raw materials for industry, and as an area of investment for North American money. The sugar plantations of Cuba, the oil-fields of Mexico and Venezuela, the tin mines of Bolivia, the copper mines of Chile, the coffee plantations of Brazil and Colombia – all came to depend more and more heavily on the USA as their chief consumer and money supplier. And North American money was invested in Latin America for the same purpose as it was invested in Europe and Africa and Asia – to make a profit. If the USA's demand for food and raw materials went down, if the supply of *Yanqui* dollars dried up, Latin America would be in trouble.

20 Imperial Attitudes: Colonies and Dominions between the Wars

You have seen in previous chapters something of the determination with which the European imperial powers held on to their overseas possessions after the Great War, even in the teeth of organised opposition. That determination was not just stiff-necked obstinacy, nor did it mean that the imperial powers thought only of their own narrow commercial and strategic interests. Gradually they were coming to think of their colonies as lands they were holding in trust for 'backward' peoples who were, as yet, not within sight of being able to fend for themselves.

Nowadays, in the last years of the twentieth century, such an attitude is often dismissed as hypocrisy, as a thin excuse for Western whites to continue lording it over Africans and Asians. But you have to consider whether the Western European powers in the 1920s were behaving in ways which were reasonable for those times. If Britain or France *had* given up their African colonies, would the new states have been strong enough, in military and economic terms, to remain independent for long? Wouldn't they have been simply left open to political and financial penetration by other powers – not excluding the USA and the USSR, those two great anti-imperialists who didn't always practise what they preached? In the 1920s, as you have seen, real trouble erupted only when a colonial power took the same paternalistic attitude towards peoples who considered themselves, rightly, far from 'backward' or 'uncivilised' and among whom nationalism had become a powerful force – for example, the peoples of Egypt and Syria, and of India.

Before we begin our survey of the colonies and dominions between the World Wars, we should note an important development in the British idea of empire. You know that the Dominions were already virtually self-governing; indeed, they signed the peace treaties of 1919 and 1920 as individual states and were founder-members of the League of Nations. In 1926 an Imperial Conference in London led to a declaration by Balfour in which he defined the status of the Dominions. They were

"equal in status, in no way subordinate to one another – though united by a common allegiance to the Crown, and freely associated as members of the British Commonwealth of Nations".

In 1931 the Statute of Westminster declared the Dominions to be completely independent of the British Parliament: no future British laws should apply to them. Until 1947 that Commonwealth was to remain a select club, only part of the vast British Empire. But it was a club into which other peoples of the empire would be able to move easily once they had become self-governing. Independence would not have to mean a complete break with the mother country – and that, in the end, would allow Britain to deal more generously, more flexibly than, for example, France, with nationalist movements among her colonial peoples.

Britain in Ireland

Ireland was a peculiar British problem. There had been rebellions against the British before, but this time the struggle was not just between Irish nationalists and the British. The Irish themselves didn't agree about the kind of independence they wanted. The Catholics wanted to break away completely from Britain, but the Protestants, who were in the majority in six of the northern counties of Ulster, wanted to remain within the United Kingdom.

In the 1918 British general election, out of a total of 105 Irish seats seventy-three were won by members of a movement called Sinn Féin ('Ourselves Alone'), who wanted to set up an independent Irish Republic. They refused to take their seats in the British House of Commons and in 1919 they met in Dublin and set up an independent Assembly of Ireland (the Dáil Éireann). No matter what the British said, Sinn Féin were determined that Ireland should be an independent Republic and declared Eamon de Valera its first President. The British refused to accept this act of rebellion: they were prepared only to grant 'Home Rule', which would have given the Irish control over all internal matters but not over foreign policy and defence. A clash was inevitable. The British Parliament passed the Government of Ireland Act of 1920, which set up separate parliaments in Belfast and Dublin. The Unionists reluctantly accepted the proposal for a six-county unit in the north (although they would have preferred the full nine counties of Ulster). The twenty-six counties in the south, however, turned the plan down flat. The British government declared the Sinn

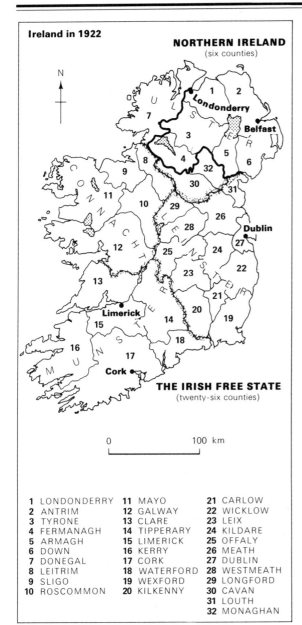

Ireland in 1922

NORTHERN IRELAND
(six counties)

N

Londonderry

Belfast

Dublin

Limerick

Cork

THE IRISH FREE STATE
(twenty-six counties)

0   100 km

1 LONDONDERRY	11 MAYO	21 CARLOW
2 ANTRIM	12 GALWAY	22 WICKLOW
3 TYRONE	13 CLARE	23 LEIX
4 FERMANAGH	14 TIPPERARY	24 KILDARE
5 ARMAGH	15 LIMERICK	25 OFFALY
6 DOWN	16 KERRY	26 MEATH
7 DONEGAL	17 CORK	27 DUBLIN
8 LEITRIM	18 WATERFORD	28 WESTMEATH
9 SLIGO	19 WEXFORD	29 LONGFORD
10 ROSCOMMON	20 KILKENNY	30 CAVAN
		31 LOUTH
		32 MONAGHAN

counties in the south would become a self-governing Dominion (to be known as the Irish Free State) but remain within the British Empire. Straight away the members of Sinn Féin who had negotiated the Treaty were labelled traitors by those members of the Dáil, led by de Valera, who would accept nothing less than complete independence from Britain. A civil war between the pro-Treaty and anti-Treaty factions flared up, and lasted until 1923 when the Irish Free State army defeated de Valera's republican, anti-Treatyite, wing of Sinn Féin.

In 1925 a Boundary Commission confirmed the border that had been laid down by the Government of Ireland Act in 1920 between the twenty-six southern counties and the six northern counties. Irish nationalists and Unionists, Catholics and Protestants, had a new line on the map to make their divisions clearer. By 1926 de Valera was convinced that the way to fight for full independence was through the Dáil, and when Sinn Féin still refused to take their seats, he set up a new party, Fianna Fáil ('Soldiers of Destiny'). Many members of Sinn Féin then followed de Valera into the new party, and it gradually gained support, winning a majority in the Dail in the 1932 elections. De Valera became Prime Minister and set about dismantling Ireland's remaining links with Britain. In 1937 he took advantage of the Statute of Westminster and pushed a new constitution through the Irish parliament. In effect this made the Irish Free State virtually an independent republic, but the new Republic of Ireland was not finally recognised by Britain until 1949.

South-East Asia

We noted in Chapter 18 that China in the 1920s and 1930s was emerging slowly but surely out of its condition as a 'hypo-colony' exploited by European and American traders. Whoever won the three-cornered struggle for power, China would, in future, be ruled by Asians. But to the south of China nearly all the signs pointed to the determination of the Western European powers to hold on to their possessions. Like the territories in Africa, the colonies in South-East Asia were becoming more valuable as suppliers of food and raw materials to Europe.

In 1921 the British government announced its plans to build a great naval base at Singapore, on the tip of the Malay peninsula, from where the Royal Navy would be able to defend British possessions and trade

Féin government illegal and guerrilla warfare broke out. The British strengthened the Royal Irish Constabulary with ex-soldiers, who were known as the 'Black and Tans' from the colour of their uniform and were feared and hated for their brutality. Eventually the small, dirty War of Independence came to an end with a truce in July 1921, followed by a treaty in December, which was approved, after bitter debate in the Dáil, in January 1922.

In the Treaty it was agreed that the twenty-six

in the Indies and the Pacific. Malaya itself was prospering from the development of the rubber and tin industries: as early as 1920 this British possession was exporting half the world's supply of rubber. There was little open opposition to the presence of Europeans; and the native Malays appeared to be more concerned about the steady influx of Chinese and Indian immigrants, especially into Singapore, than about the desirability of getting rid of the British.

Before the war the French had treated the subject people of Indo-China roughly, damaging native culture and local forms of government as they imposed French ways on the territories. After the war, in an attempt to repair some of the harm done, they began to involve local rulers (mandarins) in government and to recognise native laws as well as to enforce French ones. But opposition to their rule mounted swiftly in the twenties. Among the dissidents was a young Marxist, Ho Chi Minh, who had visited Russia and China before organising the Revolutionary Youth Movement from Canton. In 1927, when the Kuomintang turned on the Chinese Communist Party, Ho moved first to Moscow and then back to South East Asia, a shadowy, subversive figure rousing opposition to the French from outside the borders of his native land.

Meanwhile, a nationalist People's Party had been founded in Indo-China, and in 1930 (the same year in which Ho Chi Minh set up the Indo-Chinese Communist Party) tensions erupted into a large-scale revolt of the native population against their European masters. The rebels were crushed and their few remaining leaders fled to China.

The disruptive force of nationalism affected the Dutch East Indies too. In 1917 the Dutch had allowed the native population a limited share in government through a parliament which had only the power to advise, not to decide policy. It was not enough. The Indonesian Communist Party, set up in 1919, attracted the support of the more determined nationalists, and in 1926 organised a revolt in Java and Sumatra. The revolt failed, the Party was declared illegal, and its role as the standard-bearer of opposition to Dutch rule was taken over by the Nationalist Party, set up in 1927 by Ahmed Sukarno. But the Dutch were determined to stamp out resistance: Sukarno and other leading nationalists were imprisoned, and opposition to colonial rule was forced underground.

The Comintern and World Revolution

Besides the various nationalist movements within the colonial empires, the most vocal critics of imperialism were, of course, the Marxists. They were out not only to destroy the capitalist exploitation of workers in industrialised Western Europe but also to deny the capitalist his cheap colonial labour and raw materials.

You will remember the organisation whose task it was to spread communist revolution – the Comintern. At its second congress in 1920, that body called for "the closest possible union of the West European communist proletariat with the revolutionary movement of the peasants in the East"; and in the September of that year the 'First Congress of Peoples of the East' was held at Baku, on the shore of the Caspian Sea. There, Gregory Zinoviev, President of the Comintern, declared that

"a new page in the history of humanity has opened; the sun of communism will shine not only on the proletarians of Europe but on the working peasantry of the whole world".

He ended with a call to battle:

"The real revolution will blaze up only when the 800,000,000 people who live in Asia unite with us, when the African continent unites, when we see that hundreds of millions of people are in movement."

Yet ten years later there was no sign of a world revolution 'blazing up'. The African continent was still, by and large, docile; communism in China was hanging on by Mao Tse-tung's finger-nails; and as you have seen – in India, in Egypt, in Indo-China – the 'ism' which fired the imagination of subject peoples was nationalism, not Marxism. Zinoviev's call for an international communist crusade was merely words: he might just as well have whistled for a red moon. The Comintern was, in reality, a department of the Russian Foreign Ministry: revolutionary comrades in other lands would be helped only if and when it suited Stalin's Russia.

21 'Boom and Bust' – the USA in the Twenties

Closing the Door

To begin the story of the USA in the twenties we should remind ourselves that it was home for a bewildering variety of people – a mixture of all the world's races, nationalities and religions; a jumble of long-established American families and newly arrived immigrants (see Chapter 1, page 4). But now many Americans wanted to restrict immigration, to close their 'Open Door'. Already the Immigration Act of 1917 had established a literacy test for immigrants and had barred the door to newcomers from Asia. In the elections of 1920 the Republican Party called for an even stricter exclusion of 'undesirables':

"The immigration policy of the U.S. should be such as to insure that the number of foreigners in the country at any one time shall not exceed that which can be assimilated with reasonable rapidity, and to favour immigrants whose standards are similar to ours.

The selective tests that are at present applied should be improved by requiring a higher physical standard, a more complete exclusion of mental defectives and criminals, and a more effective inspection applied as near the source of immigration as possible, as well as at the port of entry....

The existing policy of the United States for the practical exclusion of Asiatic immigrants is sound, and should be maintained."

The Republicans' candidate, Warren Harding, won the election and became President. In 1921, Senator Heflin of Alabama made it very clear why he wanted no more immigration:

"The steamship companies haul them over to America, and as soon as they step off the decks of their ships the problem of the steamship companies is settled, but our problem has but begun – bolshevism, red anarchy, black-handers, and kidnappers, challenging the authority and the integrity of our flag.... Thousands come here who never take the oath to support our Constitution and to become citizens of the United States. They pay allegiance to some other country while they live upon the substance of our own. They fill places that belong to the loyal wage-earning citizens of

America.... They are of no service whatever to our people. They constitute a menace and a danger to us every day...."

In that year an Act was passed which limited immigration to 357,000 persons in one year. In 1924 another Act reduced even that number: by 1929 only 150,000 newcomers would be allowed to enter the USA each year. Both Acts discriminated against Catholic and Jewish immigrants from Southern and Eastern Europe, making it particularly difficult for them to enter.

You have already seen in Chapter 10 (pages 44–7) that the USA did not join the League of Nations. American policy in the 1920s was one of 'isolationism' – keeping out of foreign entanglements which did not directly affect the security and prosperity of the USA. The new President, Warren Harding (1921–23), had proclaimed that "America's present need is ... not submergence in internationality, but sustainment in triumphant nationality". But at home the sense of 'nationality' sometimes had an ugly, intolerant look.

Between 1920 and 1925 nearly five million Americans joined the Ku Klux Klan, a movement which had its own limited and prejudiced view of who belonged to the 'triumphant' American nation. In the eyes of the Klansmen, blacks, Jews, Catholics, socialists, and non-English-speaking immigrants did not belong. Their leader, Wesley Evans, used some grand mumbo-jumbo to explain why not:

"There are three great racial instincts, vital elements in both the historic and the present attempts to build an America which shall fulfil the aspirations and justify the heroism of the men who made the nation.... They are condensed into the Klan slogan: 'Native, white, Protestant supremacy!' The Klan is intolerant of the people who are trying to destroy our traditional Americanism ... aliens who are constantly trying to change our civilisation into something that will suit themselves better."

On the face of it the Klan was absurd: its members dressed up in white sheets; its officers called themselves Klaliffs, Klokards, Kludds, Kligrapps and Klabees; Evans, a Texas dentist, called himself the 'Imperial Wizard'. But its activities were far from funny: beatings-up, tar-and-feathering, and lynching.

Closing the Bars

As well as the aggressive bullies of the KKK, America had many 'progressive' organisations which campaigned for a wide variety of causes. Before the war, many of those 'progressives', such as the Women's Christian Temperance Union, had joined in a crusade against what appeared to be one of the great evils of the times – alcoholism. They believed that the only way to end drunkenness was to ban drink; and in 1917 a nation-wide campaign, led by the Anti-Saloon League, brought sufficient pressure to bear on Congress for it to pass a law which forbade the use of grain for either distilling or brewing.

That victory encouraged the supporters of the League to push towards their final goal – an amendment to the Constitution of the USA itself, which needed not only the approval of two-thirds of both Houses of Congress but also of three-fourths of all the States of the Union. In December 1917 the amendment was approved by Congress, and in January 1919 it was ratified by the States.

Amendment XVIII to the Constitution of the United States (1919)
"After one year from the ratification of this article the manufacture, sale, or transportation of intoxicating liquors within, the importation thereof into, or the exportation thereof from the United States and all territory subject to the jurisdiction thereof for beverage purposes is hereby prohibited."

That amendment to the Constitution was backed by the Volstead Act, which defined 'liquor' as one half of one per cent alcohol by volume. The amendment came into force in January 1920 and America went 'dry'. The age of Prohibition had arrived.

The first Prohibition Commissioner, John F. Kramer, had no doubts that he and the amendment together would stamp out the curse of drink:

"This law will be obeyed in cities, large and small, and in villages, and where it is not obeyed it will be enforced.... The law says that liquor to be used as a beverage must not be manufactured. We shall see that it is not manufactured. Nor sold, nor given away, nor hauled in anything on the surface of the earth or under the earth or in the air."

To help Kramer in his work the government appointed 1,500 prohibition agents: by 1930 that number had almost doubled. An American writer, Frederick Lewis Allen, was anything but impressed by this body of law enforcers:

"Anybody who believed that men employable at thirty-five or forty or fifty dollars a week would surely have the expert technical knowledge and the diligence to supervise successfully the complicated chemical operations of industrial-alcohol plants or to outwit the craftiest devices of smugglers and bootleggers, and that they would surely have the force of character to resist corruption by men whose pockets were bulging with money, would be ready to believe also in Santa Claus, perpetual motion and pixies."

In 1928 the Republican candidate in the Presidential election, Herbert Hoover, declared that Prohibition was "a great social and economic experiment, noble in motive and far-reaching in purpose". By that time there were more than 30,000 'speakeasies' (illegal saloons) in the city of New York – more than twice the number of bars open in the 'bad old days' before 1920. In the great American cities, gangsters like Dutch Schultz, Frank Costello and Al Capone had turned the evasion of Prohibition into big, violent business. It's difficult to know how much they 'earned' – they didn't tell the tax-man – but it's estimated that in his heyday Capone made between 60 million and 100 million dollars a year from sales of beer alone; and he could afford to run a private army of between 700 and 1,000 mobsters to control the Chicago booze trade and profitable 'rackets' in prostitution and 'protection'.

"Prohibition is a business," said Capone. "All I do is supply a public demand. I do it in the best and least harmful way I can." The 'least harmful' bit was funny: Capone was a murderous thug. But then the age of Prohibition was like that: humour could be deadly. 'Jackass Brandy' caused internal bleeding, while 'Soda Pop Moon' contained poisonous alcohol. Machine-guns were called 'typewriters', and Capone's men chose St Valentine's Day 1929 to type all over the rival O'Banion gang.

Thirteen years after going 'dry', America went 'wet' again. In the new hard times of the thirties many people came to think it more sensible for the government to tax legal liquor than to stand by, more or less helpless, while bootleggers made fortunes out of illegal booze. The 'great experiment' had failed. Perhaps its worst, and most long-lasting, effect had been to turn many otherwise respectable people into law-breakers. Once you break one law, what price the rest?

The Business of America

But the face of America which startled the world in the twenties was not that of the racist bully hiding behind the white sheet of the Klan, nor that of the booze-rich mobster making fools of President and Congress. It was, instead, the extraordinary face of an industrialised society which threatened to make all its citizens rich.

In 1927 a Frenchman, André Siegfried, suggested that America was becoming, once again, a 'new world'.

"European luxuries are often necessities in America.... One could feed a whole country in the Old World on what America wastes. American ideas of extravagance, comfort and frugality are entirely different from European.... In America the daily life of the majority is conceived on a scale that is reserved for the privileged classes anywhere else...."

James T. Patterson, an American historian, said

"the years between 1917 and 1929 witnessed major industrial breakthroughs, such as the manufacture of continuous strip-sheets in steel and tin, and of machines to make glass tubing.... New machines revolutionising the construction industry included power shovels, belt and bucket conveyors, pneumatic tools, concrete mixers and dump trucks. The communications industries developed automatic switchboards, dial phones, and teletype machines. Innovations in chemicals and synthetics included rayon, bakelite, and cellophane. George Washington Carver, a pioneer in developing farm products for industrial use, found ways of turning peanuts into axle grease and shaving lotion, and sweet potatoes into shoe blacking, library paste, and synthetic tapioca ... consumer goods industries boomed as never before. Moderately priced products included radios, wristwatches, cigarette lighters, hand cameras, linoleum, vacuum cleaners, and washing machines."

The following statistics should help you to grasp the dimensions of that industrial 'boom':

	1920	1929
Kilometres of surfaced roads	620,000	1,000,000
Motor cars on roads	9,000,000	26,000,000
Telephones in homes and offices	13,000,000	20,000,000
Radios in homes	60,000	10,000,000

The most spectacular development was that of the mass-produced motor-car. By 1925 Henry Ford's factories were producing one new car every ten seconds. By the end of the twenties there was one American car to every 4·5 American people; or, to put it another way, more than two cars for every three American families. The car industry devoured 20 per cent of America's steel, 80 per cent of her rubber and 75 per cent of her glass. It employed millions of workers – either directly in the factories of Detroit, or indirectly in other major industries, in road-building, in the rash of new roadside restaurants, motels and service stations.

The rise of the motor-car and the lorry marked the beginning of the long-drawn-out decline of the railways. It hurried along the growth of American cities with their sprawling suburbs. Many people saw the car as a machine which freed them to discover the vastness of their country for themselves. Others saw it as a menace to American moral standards: for them the 'automobile' was a 'house of prostitution on wheels'. But whatever else it did, for good or ill, one thing was certain: the automobile "built oil into a major industry and ultimately created the fateful dependence of the economy on petroleum".

The Never-Never Land

"The business of America is business," declared Calvin Coolidge, President from 1923 to 1929. Business was not just a matter of mass-producing motor-cars, refrigerators, vacuum cleaners and other 'consumer durables': it meant the industrialisation of entertainment too. As early as 1915, the film *Birth of a Nation* had made 18 million dollars – big money in anybody's language. In 1929, the first year of the new 'talkies', cinema receipts totalled 720 million dollars; and in 1930 the average weekly attendance at American cinemas was a staggering 90 million! Radio too was big business – unlike in Britain, where broadcasting was a non-profit-making public service. From the beginning American radio was 'commercial', a mass medium for advertising the products of American industry.

"The man who builds a factory," said Coolidge, "builds a temple. The man who works there, worships there." A worshipper is not supposed to tell priests how to run a temple – and neither were American workers supposed to interfere in the running of American industry. Membership of trade unions shrank from five millions in 1920 to less than three millions in 1932. The banding together of working men to press for higher wages and shorter working hours was somehow

Switchboard operators of the Chesapeake-Potomac Telephone Company in 1927. The photograph shows three features of life in America in the 1920s: the expansion of work opportunities for women, the new technology of the telephone, and the silk dresses and bobbed hair that were fashionable among 'flappers' in 1927.

thought to be 'communistic' or 'un-American'.

Other observers, like Richard Müller-Freienfels, believed that American industrialism was making men less than human. "They [the workers] too are machines, which indefatigably exercise the same function – without any personal relation to the thing which they are making. Strictly speaking, the factory worker is not even a complete machine, but only a portion of a machine, with no more independence than a cogwheel or driving-belt." But however their employers or foreign observers regarded them, the factory workers' jobs depended on advertisers persuading consumers to buy more goods by spending money they hadn't got. The age of instalment credit (hire purchase) dawned in the USA in the twenties. America became the first of the never-never lands.

In 1928 Herbert Hoover declared, "We in America are nearer to the financial triumph over poverty than ever before in the history of our land. The poorhouse is vanishing from among us." Hoover was to be the next President of the USA (1929–33), and he was convinced, as were many others, that American economic progress was unstoppable. Already many Americans had bought themselves a stake in the continued prosperity of American business by investing their savings in company stocks and shares. As American industry boomed, so the value of stocks and shares rose, and more people were tempted to invest in the hope of getting rich quick. The stock markets – the places where shares in companies were bought and sold – suddenly looked like short-cuts to happiness.

Just as automobiles, fridges and vacuum cleaners could be bought on the never-never, so company shares could be bought on the 'margin' – which meant that the buyer paid only a small percentage of the purchase price in cash, and the remainder was covered by loans. The loans were usually provided by 'brokers', men who bought and sold shares in the markets on behalf of their customers. In turn, the brokers borrowed the money from banks, from industrial companies and from abroad. The buyer 'speculated' – that is, he hoped the value of his shares would rise so that he could sell them at a profit before he had to repay his debts. He would then re-invest his money and profit in more shares, bought 'on the margin'.

Throughout the twenties trading in the stock markets grew heavier. Anyone with spare capital could join in. There was no shortage of money to borrow: between 1926 and 1929 brokers' loans jumped from 3·5

billion dollars to 8·5 billion dollars. Share prices continued to rise.

The End of the Dream

By 1927 there were already signs that the American economy was slowing down. Fewer new houses were being built, and sales of motor-cars declined. Industrial workers' wages were not rising fast enough for them to buy (even on the never-never) all the consumer durables the factories could produce. American farmers had over-expanded their production of food: food prices went down, farmers' earnings decreased – and so, inevitably, did their purchases of goods.

The stock markets took no notice. Speculators continued to indulge in what the humorist Will Rogers later called a 'financial drunk'. Though the car industry recovered for a while in 1928, by the summer of 1929 it and the construction industry were again feeling the pinch. Early in October doubts finally began to affect the stock markets. More and more investors tried to sell their shares while prices were still high. The wave of selling gathered pace until on 'Black Tuesday', 29 October 1929, more than sixteen million shares were sold on the New York Stock Exchange in Wall Street. The stock markets crashed and share prices continued to fall as panic set in. Investors sold shares at a loss; banks and foreign lenders demanded their money back from the brokers; brokers called for the money they had loaned to their clients, and their clients sold more shares – which sent prices down even further.

The 'financial drunk' was over. Many speculators were ruined, but most Americans were not at first directly affected by the 'Wall Street Crash': only about one American in a hundred had been actively 'playing the market'. But the collapse of the stock markets had serious effects on an already sagging economy. Many banks went bust – they couldn't recover all the money they had lent; others sharply reduced their lending to industry and the money they provided for instalment credit.

After the 'boom' years of the twenties, in which Americans had thought they were in sight of the final triumph of capitalism over poverty and want, they staggered into the blackness of economic depression. It was almost unbelievable. As Will Rogers put it, "We are the first nation in the history of the world to go to the poorhouse in an automobile."

22 The Great Depression: Causes and Consequences

Into the Dark

The history of the world economy in this century is a tale of ups and downs, of good times and bad. Looking back, we can see a rough pattern of periods of growth, when trade increased, more goods were produced and people were better off, and between those 'booms' we can see periods of decline which we call 'recessions'. But that pattern was interrupted in the 1930s by a particularly severe period of decline, when the world economy sagged into a condition much worse than a recession; when trade, production of goods, levels of employment and standards of living sank to alarmingly low levels.

In 1929 the American economy started to go bust. By 1932 the economies of most other countries were to go bust too: the world was to plunge into what has since been called the 'Great Depression' or the 'World Slump'. It was a dark period in which many ordinary people throughout the world realised for the first time just how much their own lives and jobs had come to depend on economic relationships between countries and on the economic policies of governments. They became newly aware of 'economics' as something which affected *them*; and economic terms began to come into everyday language.

Those people were bewildered and many of them were hurt. Some of them thought they knew what or who lay behind it, and they lashed out – with appalling consequences, for themselves as well as for their victims. Others suffered the Depression more or less quietly, seeing it as yet another disaster which ordinary human beings could do nothing to avert. They hoped and waited for better times to come. Yet they, like most other people, felt that the effects of the Great Depression would be of the same magnitude as the effects of the Great War: that when it was over the world would never be quite the same again.

The World Economy after 1918

You will remember from Chapter 1 (page 4) that before the Great War the world's trade had been paid for in gold, or in currencies whose value was fixed in gold. The 'gold standard' made for stability and for confidence among traders and governments alike, whether they were buying or selling goods, asking for loans or making them. The Great War smashed that stability. Governments of countries fighting for their lives borrowed and taxed money from their own people, borrowed from each other, and printed vast quantities of paper money to cover their debts. For the first time in the twentieth century, though certainly not for the last, people became aware of a new, impersonal and frightening enemy – inflation. You have already seen it at work in Russia and in Germany (Chapters 7 and 11). It hit other countries too, less spectacularly but enough to make nonsense of fixed relationships between dollars, pounds, francs, marks and yen; and more than enough to make the gold standard unworkable.

After the war, governments and peoples yearned for a return to stability, to the security of knowing what money was worth. A return to fixed relationships between currencies, based on the gold standard, seemed to most people who had any influence on governments' policies the only way to achieve that stability. Eventually, in 1925, Britain went back on the gold standard (at the rate of £1 = $4.86); and in 1926 France fixed the value of her currency at the rate of 120 francs = £1. Other European nations followed quickly, and the 'return to gold' was soon complete among the world's most powerful trading nations – except for Japan, which didn't return to gold until January 1930.

The world economy now looked more stable. In reality, it was anything but secure, for too much had changed since 1914 to be put right by a 'return to gold'. One of the most important changes was that Britain was no longer the supreme trading and money-lending power she had once been: the USA had emerged from the war as the world's greatest money-power.

If you glance back at Chapter 8 (page 38), you will remember the pattern of international debts which the Great War had created. To pay their debts to each other and to the USA (and, in the case of Germany, to pay reparations), the nations of Europe needed to make more money from trade; they also needed to borrow large sums – some as straight loans to their governments and some as capital for investment in the industries they were trying to revive. Britain continued to lend money to all parts of the world, and especially to

Latin America, Australia and Europe; but in the five years from 1924 to the end of 1928 the USA lent nearly twice as much as Britain – a massive $5,758,000,000. Europe took the largest proportion of American loans – which was to Europe's benefit unless, for some reason, Americans should ever want their money back quickly.

In the mid and late 1920s there was a boom in production in most of the industrialised countries of the West – in France, Italy, Germany, Canada and, of course, in the USA. The only major industrial nation which didn't enjoy the boom was Britain, a country whose older industries no longer had the 'sales-pull' they once had. World markets could take only so many British railway engines and ships, so much coal and cheap cloth. That was a severe handicap because Britain depended more than any other country on the export of manufactured goods. But despite the general boom in other nations, international trade in the late 1920s did not reach pre-war levels; and among the obstacles to growth were new 'tariff barriers' (taxes or duties on imports) which countries erected to protect their own industries against foreign competition.

As you might have expected, the new states of Central and Eastern Europe followed a policy of 'economic nationalism'. Their aim was 'autarky' – self-sufficiency in the production of food, basic manufactures and goods necessary for their defence should war break out again. To depend on each other for the import of vital raw materials and manufactures would, they felt, be rather like inviting a strangler to put both hands round your neck. You saw in Chapter 9 (page 42) how the Paris Peace Conference failed to investigate the possibility of setting up a free trade area among those new states. The price of failure was high. As early as 1919 the most highly industrialised of the new states, Czechoslovakia, slapped customs duties on imported goods. Hungary did the same in 1924. Romania had the highest duties on textile imports in all Europe by 1926, and Bulgaria the highest duties on manufactured goods.

Developing the industries of those new states, behind high tariff barriers, was a slow and expensive process – after all, the machinery had to be imported. Industrialisation didn't keep pace with the growth of population, and therefore it didn't draw enough people away to the towns from an already over-populated countryside. And meanwhile, the American Immigration Acts of 1921 and 1924 (see Chapter 21, page 81) suddenly closed a traditional outlet for surplus population – that of emigration to the New World. By the end of the twenties, only Czechoslovakia and Austria among the new states did not depend primarily on agriculture to earn their living. Nearly all of them were heavily in debt (to the USA and to Western European countries) at high rates of interest, and they could continue to pay off their loans and make some kind of economic progress only as long as they could earn money from their exports.

But it was not only the small states of Central and Eastern Europe which sheltered their economies behind tariff barriers. Every great trading nation in the world, except Britain, built a similar kind of protection for itself. The most formidable obstacle of all to the free flow of international trade was the Fordney-McCumber Act of 1922 which raised American customs duties on imported goods so that imports would normally be more expensive than goods produced in the USA itself. As an expression of American 'isolationism' that Act was the economic equivalent of refusing to join the League of Nations, or of drastically cutting the annual quota of immigrants. As an act of economic nationalism it was short-sighted and selfish. The USA was not Bulgaria: its industries had a huge, increasingly wealthy domestic market in which to grow; and if the USA wouldn't admit imports from foreigners, how could foreigners earn dollars to repay their American loans?

First Signs of Danger

From 1925 another very disturbing trend appeared in international trade: between the end of that year and the autumn of 1929 the prices of agricultural produce fell by about thirty per cent. The reason was simple: the world's farms and plantations were producing too much. During the Great War, European agriculture had suffered a setback, and other countries had expanded their production to supply a new demand. Now, by the mid-twenties, European agriculture had returned to pre-war levels, and as foodstuffs and raw materials flooded on to world markets in ever-increasing quantities, so producers were forced to sell at lower and lower prices, if they wanted to sell at all. The farm and plantation workers of the world (including those in industrialised countries) began to suffer a long-term decline in their standards of living.

Although, at first, industrialised communities and nations benefited from cheaper food and raw materials, the fall in farm prices soon began to have unpleasant effects on them too. As the earning power of the producers of food and raw materials went down, so did their buying power, and so did their purchases of manufactured goods.

Crises and Collapse

From June 1928 the USA began to lend a lot less money abroad. The main reason was that extraordinary 'financial drunk' you read about in Chapter 21 (page 85). Investment in the American stock markets became more profitable, and it was thought to be safer than lending money to foreign borrowers – especially to those borrowers who were now being hit by falling prices on world markets.

Europe was badly affected by the American stock market boom. As less money found its way across the Atlantic, so European business started to decline. By the summer of 1929 over one million German workers were without jobs and the number of unemployed people in Britain was nearing a million. And then, in the autumn of 1929, the Wall Street Crash shook to its foundations an American economy already unsettled by a decline in demand for manufactured goods and by falling farm prices.

As American industry slowed down its jazzy pace, as more American producers (of manufactured goods as well as of food and raw materials) went further into debt to their banks, so Europeans, Canadians and Latin Americans were faced by the awful spectacle of the world's most advanced industrial country suddenly unable to cure its own economic ills. If the USA could not buy its own industry and agriculture out of trouble, it would no longer make enough money available in loans for other countries to tackle their problems.

In 1929 US lending to other countries more than halved as the Wall Street Crash of that year helped to dry up the flow of money on which other countries had come to depend.

In June 1930 President Hoover signed the Smoot–Hawley Tariff Bill, which raised American customs duties still further. It was a desperate policy: Congress and President persuaded themselves that if even more foreign goods were kept out of the States, maybe the business of America would pick up again. But its only effect was to goad other countries into raising their tariffs – Australia, Cuba, France, India, Italy, Mexico, New Zealand, Spain and Switzerland; a roll-call of countries frightened and angered into taking measures which could only harm international trade even more. The USA, the world's leading industrial and financial power, was refusing to lead. The message was already becoming clear: every nation should be prepared to look after itself.

As the prices of goods (especially those of food and raw materials) continued to fall in 1930 and the early months of 1931, business profits and share prices sank with them. In the USA one effect of a fall in prices and production was the failure of many banks: much of the money they had lent was no longer there to be paid back by ruined farmers and business men. Pressure now mounted against banks everywhere, and especially against those that had lent too much money or had lent it unwisely to bad business risks – and there were a large number of such banks in Europe. If one large bank was seen to be unable to pay back what it owed to its creditors, and went bust, a panic would start: everyone would want their money back, knowing that not everyone would get it. When banks started to close, the supply of money available for lending to business men and traders would simply dry up.

The crisis of European banking started in Austria. As a result of the break-up of the Empire in the Peace Settlement, Austrian banks no longer made profits from investment in industry in places such as the Sudetenland and Trieste. To lend money to what remained of Austrian industry they had to borrow heavily from Britain and the USA. In May 1931 the Credit-Anstalt, the largest of the Austrian banks, announced that it had suffered grave losses and was in danger of being unable to repay money to its creditors. Immediately British and American creditors moved in to claim what they could from the Austrian wreck – and they also began to pull their money out of Hungary, Czechoslovakia, Romania, Poland and Germany. Two months later, the large German bank, the Darmstädter und National-bank, went bust.

The panic spread as people feared for the value of their money. Was it, for example, safe for foreigners to hold their money in pounds? What was a pound? – was it really worth $4.86? The general decline in world trade had gravely damaged British exports, and in 1931 Britain was heavily in debt – the country paid more for its imports than it earned from its exports. The pound suddenly looked unstable: its gold-standard price was too high and would have to come down. Foreigners exchanged pounds for other currencies which looked as if they would hold their value. As the reserves of gold and foreign currencies drained out of the country, the British government decided to take the pound off the gold standard in September 1931. With international trade shrinking, Britain hoped to get an advantage over her competitors by letting the value of the pound sink, which would make her goods cheaper and more attractive in world markets. By December the pound, no longer fixed in relation to gold, was worth less than $3.50.

Twenty-five other countries hoped to increase their trade by following Britain off the gold standard and devaluing their currencies. They included countries in the British Empire, in Scandinavia, in Eastern Europe, and Britain's long-standing trading partners, Argentina and Portugal. The USA left the gold standard later, in 1933. Germany, South Africa and the countries in the so-called 'gold bloc' (France, Belgium, the Netherlands, Switzerland and Italy) did not. In Germany devaluation was simply not on: it would have reduced the value of the mark, and that was a prospect which provoked nightmares of a repeat of the inflation of 1923 (see Chapter 11, page 49). To protect the value of the mark, and to avoid inflation at any cost, the German government, under Chancellor Brüning, took desperate measures, including cutting wages and restricting imports. One result was almost predictable: as Germany raised her tariff barriers, Denmark, Sweden, the Netherlands, France, Belgium and Switzerland all raised theirs in late 1931 and 1932. And in 1932 the long tradition of British free trade came to an end at the Imperial Economic Conference in Ottawa. In its place was a new British trade policy – that of Imperial Preference: tariffs were imposed on foreign goods entering Britain, while goods from the Empire continued to come in free of customs duties.

The Failure to Find an International Solution

In the 1920s people had hoped that international trade would once again be stimulated by stable currencies with fixed values and that the richer nations would lend to others the money they needed to manufacture or to grow products more efficiently and in increasing quantities. Before the Great War such a system had been supported by Britain – a nation whose wealth depended on a high level of international trade. But after the war, Britain was no longer wealthy enough to bail out other countries when their economies began to go wrong; and the USA (the new financial giant) was unwilling to come to the rescue of other nations once her own economy had started to sag. Instead of working to improve the worsening international situation, both Britain and the USA retreated – Britain into her Empire, and America behind her tariff wall.

In the second half of the twentieth century we have become used to international organisations, like the World Bank and the IMF (International Monetary Fund), helping countries out of their financial and economic difficulties. It is generally agreed that it is in nobody's interests for any country to go bust, for its workers to line up in dole queues and for its money to lose value. When the Great Depression got under way there was only one international financial organisation in existence – the Bank for International Settlements, set up in 1930 to provide machinery for the payment of German reparations which had been renegotiated for a second time in the Young Plan of 1929. Britain proposed that the Bank's powers should be extended to make it a kind of central 'World Bank' which would lend money to countries in temporary difficulties. But the plan failed, chiefly because the USA and France saw no good reason why their gold should be used to help anyone else out of a mess. At the World Economic Conference in the summer of 1933 the British suggested the creation of an international fund with enough money to lend to countries in difficulties. Again the Americans and the French blocked the idea.

Largely because of that American attitude, the World Economic Conference ended in failure. There would be no truly international attempt to drag the world economy out of the slump. The nations would have to go it alone.

23 Industrial Nations in the Slump

The Great Depression was like a long, slow and immensely powerful earthquake which shook the foundations and the fabrics of whole societies, and whose most critical effects were on the world's industrialised nations.

Before the Depression, many of the people in the primary-producing countries had low standards of living; and that was particularly true in those countries which had only recently begun to produce food and raw materials for world markets. Their expectations of life had not been raised so high that they would feel shattering disappointment when either their incomes fell or they lost their jobs. In contrast, the people of the industrialised nations had come to expect relatively high standards of life, some security of employment or profession, sufficient food and clothing, and the prospect of improvement. In the USA, in the heady optimism of the 1920s, many people had even come to believe that capitalism was about to put an end to want itself.

In short, the industrialised societies were the richer societies, and their people believed they had 'riches' to lose – whether it was a factory or a chain of shops and a mansion in the country, or a job in the civil service and a mortgaged 'semi' in the suburbs, or a weekly wage packet and two rented rooms in a decaying tenement near the city centre. If the Dépression undermined and then ruined their businesses, if it threw them out of work, their ways of life would lie in tatters.

In this chapter we shall look at the effects of the Depression on five of the world's industrialised countries – Germany, Britain, France, the USA and Japan – and we shall see how people reacted to their new insecurity in very different and sometimes violent ways. Three of those countries – Britain, France and the USA – would, in the end, emerge with their traditional forms of government intact: the slump would put to the test, but not break, people's attachment to democratic institutions. But both Japan and Germany would go through political upheavals brought about by despair and a sense of outraged nationalism.

Germany – Down the Road to the Third Reich

After the bewildering inflation and the French occupation of 1923, the German economy had re-

covered in the second half of the twenties; and the boom had attracted investment from the USA which, in turn, stimulated further industrial development. Workers' average earnings rose by nearly one-third between 1925 and 1929, and industrial production overtook pre-war levels. The wild political extremism of the immediate post-war years appeared to have died down; and when the first President of the Republic, the Social Democrat Friedrich Ebert, died in 1925, the people elected as his successor none other than Field-Marshal Paul von Hindenburg, the most revered relic of the old Imperial Army. Parliamentary democracy appeared to be working. Although the extremist parties of both the Right and the Left continued to oppose the system, the more moderate parties were willing to join together in coalition governments. And Gustav Stresemann (see page 50) worked to restore some of Germany's influence and prestige in European affairs.

But by the time Stresemann died in October 1929, the Depression was already rocking the economy: the number of registered unemployed workers was well over the million mark. As American bankers and investors called for their money back (see Chapter 22, page 88), as world demand for manufactures and foodstuffs declined, as prices slumped, as banks went bust, so the lines of the unemployed in Germany grew longer, until by September 1932 over five million people were out of work.

They were not all factory employees: the Depression took down with it the middle class – bank clerks, civil servants, office personnel – as well as the working class. And it overwhelmed many of the self-employed – shopkeepers, small farmers, independent professional men. It directly affected one out of every two German families; it brought back the fearful memories of 1923; and it dredged back to the surface of German politics those extremists who had been submerged in the brief years of prosperity. Among them was the man who would become the most terrifying political figure of our century – Adolf Hitler. You will remember him from the end of Chapter 11 (page 50) – a nationalist revolutionary who had been jailed for his messy failure in Munich in 1923. So far we have needed to know nothing of him as a man. It is now time to learn something about his life and character.

Born in 1889 and brought up in the German-speaking part of what was then the Austrian Empire, he later drifted dreamily from place to place – a failed artist, a layabout, a nobody – until in 1914 war broke out while he was in Germany and he volunteered for service in a German infantry regiment. During the next four years it appears that, for the first time in his life, the young Hitler found a purpose – in the discipline of war. But when the Great War ended his world threatened to collapse around him. He was convinced that the army had been betrayed, that Germany's will to fight on had been sapped by the enemies and aliens within – by Bolshevik revolutionaries and, above all, by the Jews. The dreamer who became a soldier now became a fanatic who would carry on the struggle against his own and his Fatherland's enemies.

The failed artist turned to politics. He joined and soon became leader of a new, small political party based in Munich – the *Nationalsozialistische Deutsche Arbeiterpartei* (NSDAP), the National Socialist German Workers' Party – the Nazis. 'National Socialism' itself was a hotch-potch of political ideas. It was against large-scale capitalism but utterly opposed to international communism; it was aggressively nationalist and violently anti-Semitic (hostile towards Jews).

In that post-war period of rising tension and violence, which you read about at the beginning of Chapter 10, the Nazis formed their own private army – the brownshirted *Sturmabteilung* (SA) – for the political struggle that was being waged in the streets; and they carried their new flag – blood red with a black swastika (a hooked cross) on a white circle. On 9 November 1923 they carried it into the centre of Munich to begin their ill-fated revolt against the government of the Republic.

While serving a short prison sentence for his part in the Munich *putsch* (armed uprising), Hitler wrote the first volume of *Mein Kampf* (My Struggle), the story of his life and the history of his ideas. In it he described what he was by saying what he was against: he was against the new Republic, against democracy, against Marxism, against liberals and pacifists, against Christian moral values and the rule of law, and against the Jews. Much of it was half-baked; and even its racialist claptrap about the 'Aryan master-race' and an 'international Jewish-Marxist conspiracy', was second-hand, lifted from other, earlier writers. But among the jumble of hysterical ideas Hitler showed an alarming confidence in his ability to organise a disciplined political movement, and a sure sense of how to appeal to the lowest instincts of frightened masses.

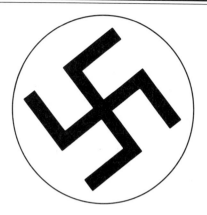

The Swastika: a sign whose history can be traced back to the religious art of a number of ancient civilisations but which Hitler used as a symbol of the supremacy of the Aryan 'master-race' over all other peoples.

Hitler was released from Landsberg Castle in December 1924, just when Germany was beginning her economic recovery and everyday life was returning to normal. In a land which offered much less scope to political extremists, Hitler's aim could no longer be immediate, violent revolution carried out by a few fanatics. Instead he set to work to rebuild his shattered Nazi Party into a tightly knit movement with branches throughout the country. The SA was reorganised and expanded; in 1926 the black-shirted *Schutzstaffel* (SS) appeared, as did the Hitler Youth, the Nazi German Student League, the Nazi Teachers' League, the Nazi Women's League, and the Nazi Physicians' League.

By 1928 Hitler was in control of a party with 100,000 members. But it was not a political party as we understand that term; its aims and policies were not decided democratically by its members. It was a political 'movement', whose members were united by fanatical loyalty and unconditional obedience to their *Führer* (leader). The only challenge to Hitler's absolute control of the movement had come from the Strasser brothers, Gregor and Otto, who had their own power base in the industrialised regions of northern Germany and who took the term 'national socialism' seriously and favoured the public ownership of heavy industry and big estates. Hitler himself had no interest in such 'red' policies: his aims were to seize power and then to destroy. Perhaps Hitler himself didn't know precisely what or whom he would destroy, if ever he got the chance. Obviously, Jews and communists would be dealt with, but in 1928 they looked safely out of his reach.

Results of the May 1928 Reichstag election
(main parties only)

Party	Votes	Seats in the Reichstag
Social Democrats	9,153,000	153
Centre and BVP*	4,658,000	78
Nationalists (DNVP)	4,382,000	73
Communists	3,265,000	54
DVP†	2,680,000	45
Nazis	810,000	12

* BVP – Bavarian People's Party
† DVP – German People's Party

Hitler had already tried his hand at violent revolution, and failed. In 1928, as you can see above, his party held a mere twelve seats in the German parliament (Reichstag). Despite all the fancy-dress ceremonials and demonstrations of his followers, he was still nowhere in sight of coming to power by legal means.

You have already seen something of the effects of the Depression on Germany. In March 1930 the 'Grand Coalition' split apart under the mounting strain of rising unemployment: the Social Democrats would not accept the cuts in unemployment benefits which their partners in government proposed. But that disagreement didn't only bring about the end of an effective coalition government: it brought into the open all the festering dislike which many influential Germans felt for parliamentary democracy itself. You will remember from the beginning of Chapter 11 that to Germans this form of government was not only new, it was associated in many people's minds with defeat in war and humiliation in peace. In the minds of President Hindenburg and his advisers, and in the opinion of Kurt von Schleicher and other army generals, it was now obvious that parliamentary democracy was incapable of dealing with a national emergency.

The German President had the authority to appoint and dismiss the Chancellor and government ministers without the approval of the Reichstag; he also had the power to dissolve the Reichstag and call for new elections. In addition, Article 48 of the Weimar Constitution gave him the right in a national emergency to sign decrees submitted by the Cabinet and give them the force of law, without having to ask for the Reichstag's agreement. Armed with those formidable powers, and with Schleicher's approval, Hindenburg chose as the next Chancellor Heinrich Brüning (one of the leaders of the Centre Party) and made it clear that if a majority of the Reichstag opposed Brüning's policies, not only would he push them through by presidential decree, but he would also dissolve the parliament and call new elections. The Social Democrats refused to give in to the President's threat, and blocked the new government's policies in the Reichstag. Hindenburg dissolved the Reichstag, and Germany prepared for a general election.

The results of the September 1930 election were alarming. They showed how badly the slump had affected people's morale, how in their anger and frustration many people had come to think that only desperate measures, and men, could pull them out of a desperate situation. Large numbers of working-class men without jobs gave their support to the Communist Party (KPD), which polled over four-and-a-half million votes (compared with three-and-a-quarter million in 1928) and increased its number of seats in the Reichstag from fifty-four to seventy-seven. In contrast, Stresemann's old party, the German People's Party (DVP), lost over a million votes and fifteen seats in parliament; while the Social Democrats (SPD) lost over half a million supporters and ten of their Reichstag seats. But the really staggering feature of the election was the sudden rush of support to the Nazis.

The Twenty-Five Points of the Nazi Party Programme had first been announced in 1920. Now, in 1930, they appeared to offer something for nearly everyone – for the unemployed workers, the worried farmers, the anxious middle classes, the bored and dispirited young.

"Point 11. We demand the abolition of all income unearned by work.

Point 14. We demand profit-sharing in large industrial enterprises.

Point 15 We demand the generous development of old age insurance.

Point 16. We demand the creation and support of a healthy middle class . . .

Point 17. . . . We demand the abolition of ground rent, and the prohibition of all speculation in land."

The Nazis even had a ready-made scapegoat for Germany's ills – the Jews. And Hitler put it all across with incomparable flair; for he was the supreme public speaker, the orator who went straight to the gut feelings of an audience. The result in September 1930 was over 6⅓ million votes – more than seven times the number the Party had received in 1928. With 107 Reichstag seats, the Nazis had become the second biggest party in a parliament they intended to destroy.

For the first time Hitler had the mass support he needed, and it seems that it came chiefly from three sources. First, some of his backing came from the panic-stricken middle classes – people who not only feared the loss of their businesses or jobs but also believed that the Communists and Social Democrats intended to ruin them by bringing them down to the level of the proletarian masses. Second, the Nazis attracted the votes of small landowners, whose property and way of life were threatened by the sudden fall in prices for agricultural produce, and who were attracted by Nazi election promises of higher tariffs on imports of foreign foods and lower interest rates on loans. And third, there were many new young voters – university students as well as unemployed working-class youths – who saw no future for themselves in a weak democracy, despised by its army, its business men, and even by the President himself.

Chancellor Brüning stayed in power as head of a government supported in the Reichstag by the Social Democrats, who were now thoroughly alarmed at the wave of anti-democratic feeling that was sweeping the country. Brüning was determined to use the slump to put an end to reparations, by proving that a depressed Germany could no longer afford to pay them. His policy was, therefore, one of *deflation* – of making life in Germany even harsher than before. His government would not spend money on public works to create jobs for the unemployed, who would then have spent more on the products of German industry. Instead, by 'emergency decrees', Brüning reduced wages, cut unemployment benefits and increased taxes.

Eventually the Allies did agree, at a conference in July 1932, to bring an end to reparations; but that relief came too late. By that time many German banks had already gone bust in the financial crisis of 1931 (see Chapter 22, page 88); industrial production had sunk to little more than half its level of 1928–29; five million workers were out of a job – and so was Heinrich Brüning.

Meanwhile, Hitler had taken another opportunity to test his popularity in Germany: in April 1932 he had challenged Hindenburg in the seven-yearly presidential elections. Hindenburg had won, but Hitler (who

had become a German citizen in order to stand for election) had emphasised the growing support for the Nazi movement by polling thirteen-and-a-half million votes to the old Field-Marshal's nineteen-and-a-half million.

One month after his re-election Hindenburg had felt secure enough to get rid of a government which relied on the cooperation of the Social Democrats he despised. In May 1932 he sacked Brüning and appointed in his place Franz von Papen – another Centre Party man and another friend of Schleicher. Papen was much more interested in doing a deal for the support of the Nazis than in asking for the support of the SPD. The deal was arranged: after new elections, Hitler would be invited to join the government.

Results of the July 1932 Reichstag election
(main parties only)

Party	Votes	Seats in the Reichstag
Nazis	13,769,000	230
Social Democrats	7,960,000	133
Centre and BVP	5,782,000	97
Communists	5,283,000	89
Nationalists (DNVP)	2,177,000	37
DVP	436,000	7

Now Hitler, the leader of the largest Reichstag party, laid down *his* condition on which he would join the government: he demanded the position of Chancellor for himself. Papen refused and went ahead with his policies to inject new life into the German economy. Instead of the misery of Brüning's deflation, Papen's government prepared to spend its way out of the Depression with new programmes of public works. The Nazis refused to cooperate unless they were given power, so Papen asked Hindenburg to dissolve the Reichstag and call yet another general election in November. The election did not, as Papen hoped, destroy the Nazis; although they did lose votes (over two million) and won only 196 seats. But the Communists ended up with 100 Reichstag seats. Papen was still faced by two large extremist parties who were determined not to let the Reichstag work.

Papen, the Chancellor with opposition in the Reichstag and no mass support in the country, believed that he could continue to rule with the backing of Hindenburg and Schleicher – and behind them, the army. He was mistaken. In December Schleicher himself took over as the new Chancellor. But the wily general had also made enemies – among them influential industrialists who were suspicious of Schleicher's attempts to win trade union support for his government. Behind Schleicher's back Papen now approached Hindenburg with yet another scheme for a new government – to bring in Hitler while the Nazis still had a mass following in the country, while the Social Democrats were still doing badly in elections, and before the Communists gained any more ground. Hitler should be used. Why not make him Chancellor of a coalition government which contained only a few other Nazis, and give the other ministries to good, conservative politicians who would do as Vice-Chancellor Franz von Papen told them to do?

At last Hindenburg was persuaded that Papen could control the Nazi leader. On 30 January 1933 he appointed Adolf Hitler Chancellor of the German Republic. "I have Hindenburg's confidence," Papen boasted. "Within two months we will have pushed Hitler so far into a corner that he'll squeak."

At this crucial moment in German history – perhaps the most fateful moment in the history of the world in our century – there was no determined opposition to the foolish plottings of Hindenburg and Papen. Hitler was not elected Chancellor, he was not chosen by a majority of the people: he was put in power by a senile President, a retired Commander-in-Chief who had never even had the courage to admit he lost a war. Yet no-one lifted a finger to stop him. The army stood to one side. More important, there was no attempt by the parties which represented the working class (the Social Democrats and the Communists) to form a common front against the Nazis. Yet in the election of November 1932 they had together polled more votes and won more Reichstag seats that Hitler's party.

You will remember from Chapter 14 (page 62) that throughout the 1920s in the industrialised countries of the West the communists and the non-revolutionary socialists had fought bitterly for the political leadership of the workers; and that the Comintern had forbidden its member parties to join forces with any other parties which claimed to represent the interests of the working class. But now the rivalry of the parties of the Left was becoming self-destructive: they fought each other instead of fighting the dark enemy that threatened to destroy them both. In February 1933 Max Brauer, the Social Democrat who was mayor of Altona, asked Ernst Torgler, chairman of the Communists in the Reichstag, if the KPD would join the SPD in a common front. Torgler replied, "It doesn't enter our heads. The Nazis must take power. Then in four weeks the whole working class will be united under the leadership of the Communist Party."

The German Communists' attitude was simpleminded to the point of idiocy. Their first aim was to control the working class – and they thought Hitler would help them to achieve it: after a few weeks of Hitler as Chancellor, the workers would, as a man, flock to the bright red banner of communism. The Communists had failed to learn anything from the experience of Fascist Italy, where Mussolini had used the power of the state to crush the Left – and yet here, in Germany, they were dealing with a man whom they labelled 'fascist' and who was a thousand times more dangerous than the pompous *Duce*. For very different reasons Franz von Papen and the KPD intended to make use of Adolf Hitler. Within two months Hitler would have made fools of them all.

Early in February 1933, Hitler called for new Reichstag elections. The German people had become used to violence in the streets at election time; but even they were unprepared for the terror which the Nazis unleashed. Hermann Goering, Hitler's right-hand man, had been appointed Prussian Minister of the Interior, a position from which he controlled the police in almost two-thirds of Germany. Goering now appointed 50,000 'auxiliary policemen', mostly from the SA and the SS: they were nothing less than Nazi gun-slingers in the pay of the government.

Worse was to come. On the night of 27 February the Reichstag building went up in flames. A young Dutch Communist, Marinus van der Lubbe, was arrested and later charged with arson. Chancellor Hitler claimed that a communist revolution was at hand and persuaded Hindenburg to sign an emergency law, "for the Protection of the People and the State", which swept away the freedom of speech and the freedom of the Press. As Nazi propaganda was stepped up, Goering's bully-boys terrorised German towns and cities. On 5 March German voters went to the polls, and Hitler's Nazis won their greatest electoral victory – over seventeen million votes and 288 seats in the Reichstag. But a majority of the electorate – twenty million of them – declared themselves against National Socialism and all its works by voting for other parties. Given the circumstances, it was an amazing last fling for German democracy.

On 23 March, the new parliament met in the Kroll Opera House to act out a tragic farce. All of the Communist deputies and some of the Social Democrats were either already in prison or in hiding. Hitler demanded an Enabling Act which would give him the power to make his own laws, and only the ninety-four Social Democrats who remained had the courage to oppose him. The Act was passed, and what little life there was left in German democracy was killed stone dead.

That was how the 'Third Reich' (Empire) came into being. The first Reich had been the Holy Roman Empire of the Middle Ages; the second had been that short-lived German Empire which plunged to defeat in 1918. This new 'Third Reich', the Nazis boasted, would last for a thousand years. We have described its beginnings in some detail for three reasons. First, the Nazi movement in Germany would become a model for radical groups in other countries gripped by the Depression of the thirties. Second, the German revolution of 1933 let loose a destroyer who would eventually set off another great war. And third, the Nazi seizure of power is, even for us today, history's most terrible lesson in the speed and ease with which democracy and the rule of law can be overthrown.

Britain – MacDonald, Means Tests and Mosley

Between 1921 and 1938, at least one out of every ten British citizens of working age was without a job. In the worst of those years one out of every five was out of work. Unemployment ranged from just over one million in September 1929 to just under three million in 1932. At its height it claimed 34 out of every 100 coalminers, 47 out of every 100 steelworkers, and 62 out of every 100 shipbuilders and ship-repairers.

The blight of unemployment was not evenly spread throughout the land, but concentrated in areas which became grim, derelict: South Wales, central Scotland, the north-east, parts of Lancashire, Cumberland and Northern Ireland. When Palmers' shipyard in the north-east town of Jarrow closed down in 1933, eight out of every ten workers there were without jobs.

The twenties had been a bad time for Britain as world trade had struggled to recover to pre-war levels and as old-established industries had been faced with shrinking world markets. In the early thirties the Depression aggravated those ills, and in particular the running sore of long-term unemployment. They were bleak years of poverty and misery for many people. Yet they did not end in revolution, did not spark off a violent reaction against 'the system', against the established form of government. As the historian Alastair Parker has pointed out: "Between 1919 and 1939 no single life was lost in Britain in political or industrial conflict." (You can compare that with the turbulence in Germany, where, for a start, 356 political murders were committed between 1918 and 1922.)

In Britain parliamentary democracy was long-established; as a form of government it had proved capable of ruling and expanding an empire, of winning the war, of improving the general quality of life and of setting up a primitive 'welfare state' to care for its most needy citizens. In 1924 the Labour Party, which claimed to represent the interests of the working class, had formed a government for the first time. Parliament had already granted unusual legal privileges to the workers' trade unions – for example, protection against being sued by employers for damages if they went on strike. And the leaders of the unions in the 1920s and 1930s were, on the whole, men who were not attracted to revolutionary politics – as was made clear in their non-violent leadership of the 'General Strike' of 1926.

If the British middle classes had little reason to fear the unions, they had even less cause to worry about the communists. The membership of the Communist Party never rose above 20,000, even in the darkest days of the Depression. And the record of the Communist Party in parliamentary elections was one of continual failure: in 1924, one Communist MP was elected; in 1929, none; in 1931, none; in 1935, one. Hitler could frighten shopkeepers, lawyers, doctors and civil servants with tales of the 'Bolshevik menace': by the 1930s, no British politician could seriously scare the electorate with threats of a 'red peril'. In general, the failure of the communists to make much progress among the working class, and the way the British political system actually worked, made for stability and not for revolution.

The world crisis had hit the second Labour government, under the Prime Minister, Ramsay MacDonald, as soon as it came to power after the general election of 1929. Government spending was rising sharply as the cost of paying out benefits to the unemployed went up; and meanwhile, as people earned less, the government's income from taxation was falling. In 1931 a committee appointed by the government recommended what then seemed to be massive cuts. Public spending was to be cut by £96 million, mainly by reducing unemployment benefits and the wages of public employees (such as teachers). Rather than carry out all those measures, a majority of Labour ministers resigned, and the Labour government was replaced by a coalition called the National government, made up mostly of Conservatives. MacDonald remained Prime Minister – and his name has remained mud in the Labour Party ever since.

In that same year, when MacDonald left the Labour Party, and Britain left the gold standard (see Chapter 22, page 89), the economist John Maynard Keynes gave a talk on BBC radio on 'The Problem of Unemployment'. We have met Keynes before, in Chapter 11, when he was criticising the bill for reparations imposed on Germany. Now he told his startled listeners, who had been brought up to believe in the virtue of saving money, that the best way out of depression was not to save money but to *spend* it. This increased demand for goods would, in turn, increase employment. "The best guess I can make," said Keynes, "is that whenever you save five shillings, you put a man out of work for a day." Later, in his *General Theory of Employment, Interest and Money* (published in 1936, and one of this century's most influential books), Keynes went on to say that a government should *manage* demand to make sure that a nation's resources (including its labour force) were fully employed.

According to Keynes and his followers a government faced with a depression should be prepared to spend more than its income in order to create jobs, which in turn would raise demand for goods. The National governments of the thirties, however, took what seemed to be the common-sense view that to spend more than they received (creating a 'budget deficit') would eventually lead to bankruptcy. Neville Chamberlain, Chancellor of the Exchequer from 1931 to 1937, believed in 'sound finance', in balancing the books – and so did the Labour Party in opposition. However, even though British governments did not do as Keynes proposed, they did develop new policies in attempts to stimulate employment, industry and trade.

Interest rates on loans were reduced from 1932 onwards, which made industrial investment cheaper. The electrical, chemical and motor-car industries all

benefited, but the most spectacular development was in the construction industry in general, and in house building in particular. The figure of 275,000 houses built in 1933 was, until then, an all-time record; by the year 1937 it reached 362,000. Unfortunately, although the new houses were cheap, they were not cheap enough for poor people with large families: as part of its cuts in spending, the government had stopped paying subsidies for council housing.

MacDonald's National government attempted to protect British industry by tariffs, and by the scheme of Imperial Preference (see Chapter 22, page 89), which gave Britain cheap imports from the Empire. But 'protection' was not, could not, be any kind of solution to the problems of a nation whose industrialised economy really needed a high level of world trade. Its effect was to reduce world trade even further. And since Britain could not absorb all the primary products of her Empire and imposed quotas on imports of food, the policy was resented in the Empire as well as by countries outside.

At home, the National governments of the thirties intervened directly in industry for the first time since the Great War. Firms in old, depressed industries (such as iron and steel, coal mining, cotton and shipbuilding) were encouraged to join together to regulate output and fix prices. Even nationalisation (taking firms into public ownership) was undertaken if there was a good case for it: BOAC (later to be known as British Airways) took off in the Depression years. And the Special Area Acts of 1934 and 1937 aimed to revive the depressed areas of the country by offering firms subsidies to settle in the areas and provide new jobs. Although only £4 million was actually spent on those subsidies in the thirties, the two Acts marked the beginning of modern 'regional' policy, on which large sums would be spent in later years.

Despite those new policies, unemployment did not go away; and that, in itself, raised a new issue in British politics. The system of providing poor relief through separate, local Public Assistance Authorities had led to wide variations in the rates of relief made to those out of work. It was not coping fairly or efficiently with the hundreds of thousands of long-term unemployed. In 1934 this system was scrapped and the Unemployment Assistance Board (UAB) was set up to pay national rates of 'assistance' to those in need. Eventually the UAB gave the unemployed a fairer deal than they had got under the old system, and by the end of the thirties

Jarrow approaches London. In 1936 a deputation of unemployed workers marched from that depressed town in the north-east to ask the government and Parliament for help. Here they halt near Bedford for a meal of corned beef and potatoes.

Britain was spending a higher proportion of her national income on social security than any other country in the world.

The unemployed in Britain could not complain that they were callously treated by their government, but they could, and did, protest against the 'means test' snoopers – the people whose job it was to enquire into the 'means' of men and women who claimed assistance from the Board. The 'means test' penalised people who had saved money in the days when they had jobs, or whose sons and daughters were still in work. It was hated by all people who disliked the invasion of their privacy, and by many who were now coming to believe that in a rich, industrialised society they should be able to claim relief from poverty as a *right*.

Parliamentary democracy in Britain was not undermined by the Depression. Yet there were people who believed that Britain's best way out of the slump was not by the cautious measures of coalition governments but by strong, authoritarian rule on the model of the German National Socialists or the Italian Fascists. In the 1920s there had been a number of small, ineffective fascist groups in Britain. In the early thirties they found their leader in Sir Oswald Mosley, a former Labour minister who had left the party in 1930. Mosley founded the British Union of Fascists in October 1932 – just three months after Hitler's Nazis had hit the jackpot in the German elections.

The British fascists aped their European models – dressing up in black shirts, riding-breeches and jack-boots, parading through the streets, distributing propaganda against democracy and socialism, and making their most vicious attacks on the Jews. It is possible that the money to finance Mosley's activities came from Mussolini's Italy as well as from some British industrialists. It is a fact that for a short time in 1934 the *Daily Mail* openly gave its support to the fascists. It is also a fact that as part of a European fascist crusade, Mosley's movement was a dismal failure. After riots in the East End of London in October 1936, the Public Order Act was passed, which forbade (and still forbids) the wearing of military-style uniforms, and limited the right to march in the streets. Until the end of the decade, the Union of Fascists remained in the background of British politics, little more than an ugly reminder of the creatures across the sea, dancing on the corpse of German democracy.

France – *Le Front Populaire*

Like the British, the French did not abandon their democratic form of government during the Depression; but there were times in the 1930s when France seemed to be teetering on the brink of civil war. In the 1920s the French economy had done well, mainly because the French franc had been 'undervalued' (its real value had been greater than the rate at which it had been fixed by the French government for exchange with, say, pounds or marks) and French products were therefore cheap enough to sell well in world markets. But when, in the early thirties, other countries left the gold standard and devalued their currencies (which brought down the prices of *their* goods in world markets), France and the other countries which stayed in the 'gold bloc' were left high and dry: their goods became relatively expensive in a world in which trade was shrinking fast. Between 1929 and 1933 French exports of manufactured goods fell by forty-two per cent.

Stubbornly, French governments refused to leave the gold standard or devalue the franc: it all seemed to be a matter of protecting French prestige; an unwillingness to admit that France was not as strong as she pretended to be. And to pay for that prestige, French governments (rather like the British in 1931 and the Germans under Brüning) tried to balance their budgets by raising taxes and by cutting public spending on, for example, civil servants' wages and the pensions of war

veterans – the kind of policy we have come to know as deflation.

The Depression had affected French agriculture, as it had affected agriculture throughout the world. Deflation on top of Depression hit French industry, although in comparison with Britain and Germany the figures for unemployment in France seemed low – only half a million people out of work in early 1935. However, such figures in themselves are rather misleading when we consider that France solved part of her unemployment problem by rounding up about a million Polish, Italian and Algerian workers and packing them off home. In addition, many city dwellers who couldn't find work simply migrated back to the countryside where families and relatives could at least offer them beds and food.

Meanwhile, a succession of weak coalition governments was finding great difficulty in coping with the crisis. Between 1932 and 1934, five successive governments tried, and failed, to balance the budget – and, as in Germany, there was much criticism of parliament as a mere talking shop, where political parties protected the interests of the groups they represented and seemed to care little about the fate of the nation as a whole. Fascist-type groups had been formed in the 1920s. The largest of them was the *Croix de Feu*, set up in 1927 by François Coty, a man with a unique place in history as the purveyor of two very different sorts of smell – women's perfumes and the stink of political extremism. Other groups were *Action Française*, the *Camelots du Roi*, and a body called the *Cagoule* which was set up to resist an imagined communist take-over and was helped by senior officers such as Marshal Pétain to form secret groups inside the French army.

On 6 February 1934 extremist groups demonstrated in Paris against the failure of the National Assembly to cope with the nation's problems. They clashed with the police, and seventeen people were killed and well over two thousand injured. In the months which followed there was an alarming increase in the membership of the *Croix de Feu*, and in the activities of the movement's shock troops, which seemed to threaten a revolution of the kind by which Mussolini had come to power in Italy in 1922. But the most important, and in some ways extraordinary, development in the period which followed the Paris riots was the coming together of the Radicals, Socialists and Communists to form a common front – the Popular Front – against the fascist threat. To explain why those three parties embraced each other we shall have to make some comparisons between French and German politics in the early thirties.

The Radical Party in France was "the party of the small independent proprietors, farmers, shopkeepers, artisans, civil servants, men of the liberal professions" – the kind of people who in Germany between 1930 and 1932 had been drawn in large numbers, in fear and despair, to support Hitler's Nazis. But in France they were among the chief supporters of a parliamentary democracy which, until recently, had brought them stability and prosperity. They were in no hurry to hand over the Republic to gangs who might end up treating Frenchmen in the same ways the Nazis were now treating Germans.

The French Communists were a different matter altogether: they owed no loyalty to the Republic or to parliamentary democracy; and as you saw in Chapter 14 (page 62) they were the bitter enemies of the French Socialists. In 1932, Maurice Thorez, the French Communist leader, was still standing firm on the old Comintern line: "We do not wish agreement with the socialist chiefs, we do not wish understanding with the socialist organisations. We wish to lead the socialist workers to battle." It all sounded remarkably similar to the speechifying of the German Communist leaders in the same year. Yet little more than two years later Thorez's Communists were arm in arm with the Socialists in the Popular Front. What happened to change their minds?

That question has a one-word answer – Hitler. The Nazi leader lasted a lot longer than von Papen and the KPD had foolishly expected (see page 94). The Enabling Act of March 1933 had led to a reign of terror in which German Communists had been destroyed – and it soon became clear to Stalin that the new, fanatically anti-communist German government was a threat to the Russian state itself. If France went the same way as Germany (and France still had considerable influence in Eastern Europe), Russia might soon find herself faced by a powerful new alliance on her western borders. A new message went out from the Comintern to the French Communists: stop the fascists by joining a common front with other anti-fascist parties – and the Communists obediently hopped into bed with their old enemies to form the Popular Front.

The Popular Front won the elections of April and May 1936; and Léon Blum became Prime Minister of France, the first Socialist to hold that office. And the industrial workers came out on strike to show that they expected good socialist reforms from the new government – not just more of the old deflation. They got their reforms: by the Matignon Agreement employers were made to raise wages and to give their workers three weeks' annual holiday with pay; and a rigid forty-hour working week was introduced. But the forty-hour week was a failure – in some instances it deprived industries of skilled labour and discouraged investment – and Blum's government persisted in refusing either to devalue the franc or to create a budget deficit: it continued trying to balance the books. French industry did not prosper under the Popular Front: in 1937 France was producing fewer motor cars than she had turned out in 1929 – while Britain was producing nearly twice and Germany more than twice their 1929 outputs.

The problems became too great, Blum's government fell in June 1937, and in July the franc was devalued. New governments staggered on with Popular Front support, but the French economy remained depressed until the Popular Front itself broke up towards the end of 1938 and a new government was formed by a Radical, Edouard Daladier. Paul Reynaud, the new Minister of Finance, set about reversing previous governments' policies: in particular the forty-hour week was gradually abandoned, and interest rates on loans were brought down to encourage investment. Industrial production and prices began to rise again.

Despite outbreaks of political violence and the dark menace of fascist-style movements, France survived the years of the Depression without falling victim to revolution from the Right or the Left. In 1936 Blum's government had outlawed the *Croix de Feu* and other extremist organisations: the *Croix* reappeared almost at once in the form of the *Parti Social Français*, but from then on it behaved more like an ordinary party in a parliamentary democracy. That in itself tells us a lot about France in the thirties, a world apart from its Nazified next-door neighbour. One historian has summed it up like this: "France remained until 1940 a country in which an intelligent and free man might reasonably choose to live."

'Hooverville', USA

By 1932 many Americans had been forced to leave the homes on which they could no longer afford to pay the rent. If they were fortunate, they moved their few belongings into the homes of sympathetic relatives; if they had no-one to turn to, they slept out of doors or in shacks and tents on the outskirts of the cities. They called those shanty-towns 'Hoovervilles' – which was, perhaps, a shade unfair on Herbert Hoover; but back in 1928 Hoover had asked to be President, he had become President, and now, four years later, he was presiding over the worst depression in American history – and, to most Americans, he seemed prepared just to watch things get worse.

In Chapter 21 you read about the American boom of the 1920s, about an advanced industrial society which had appeared capable of bringing prosperity within reach of all its citizens. But the American economy had depended on the demand for manufactured goods and agricultural produce growing as swiftly as supply. At the end of the twenties, however, demand had slackened, the Wall Street Crash had seriously injured the banking system and the supply of credit, and the decline in international trade had reduced America's ability to sell abroad what she couldn't sell at home. The results were appalling. Depression was more severe, and lasted longer, in the USA than in any other industrialised nation, as you can see on page 101.

The unemployment figures for some of America's great cities were even worse than the national average: for example, in the autumn of 1931 there were 624,000 people out of work in Chicago – roughly forty per cent of the work-force. And, throughout the country, as the table on page 102 shows, unemployment hit blacks harder than it hit whites.

The USA had no national system of relief against poverty. Many unemployed workers and their families depended on private charity (such as 'soup kitchens' financed by rich citizens); and on the public charity of town and city governments, whose relief programmes were cut back as their incomes from local taxes fell. The face of charity could be hard; a Chicago welfare officer said: "We insist that the people who come to our private and public agencies shall use up, absolutely and completely use up and come to us empty-handed, all their available resources." That was a 'means test' with a vengeance.

Somehow, millions of Americans avoided both the humiliation of public charity and the degradation of the 'Hoovervilles' by living off the 'invisible relief' of friends, relatives and neighbourhood stores. Those at the bottom of the pile stayed alive by living like ani-

mals. According to the American historian, William Manchester:

"In the Pennsylvania countryside they were eating wild weed-roots and dandelions; in Kentucky they chewed violet tops, wild onions, forget-me-nots, wild lettuce, and weeds. . . . City mothers hung around docks, waiting for spoiled produce to be discarded and then fighting homeless dogs for possession of it."

While American industry had been booming in the 1920s, American farmers had been complaining of lower prices for their produce. They had increased their production during the Great War and had continued to do so in the years that followed. Their incomes were, therefore, already depressed before the Great Depression; and many small tenant-farmers in the southern and mid-western states had already been forced off their land by a combination of high rents and low prices for their crops.

But in the early 1930s American farmers would look back to the twenties as the 'good old days'. Between 1929 and 1933 their net incomes (what they had left as 'profit' after paying all expenses) fell by nearly seventy per cent. Inevitably they went into debt – or further into debt – and to meet their debts, taxes and costs of living they had to try to sell more produce at lower and lower prices. Neither the home market, nor a world market already glutted with agricultural produce, could take all they had to offer. Many of them went under: unable to repay loans and the mortgages on their land, they joined the new army of migrants who roamed their own country in search of work. And as farmers went under so did the banks which had lent them money. Between 1930 and 1932, over five thousand banks went bust in the USA; and well over half of them were country banks in places with populations of under 2,500. Small-town America, like big-time Chicago and New York, took a frightful beating.

It was not that President Hoover did nothing, but that what he did was too little, and it came too late. In 1930 he persuaded Congress to cut taxes by $160 million; in 1931 he increased public expenditure on the building of river dams which would eventually generate electricity, and in the short term provided jobs in the construction industry. In the same year the Reconstruction Finance Corporation (RFC) was set up, with funds to provide relief for ailing banks and insurance

As the Depression deepened, men of all ages, all social classes, found themselves out of work. Here some of them shop for jobs in a New York street. Among the unemployed were many who felt it was their own fault that they couldn't find work. "Sometimes I feel like a murderer", one of them told a New York Daily News *reporter in February 1932. "What's wrong with me, that I can't protect my own children?"*

Unemployment in the USA, 1929–32

Year	Numbers of unemployed	Unemployed as % of the labour force
1929	1,550,000	3·2
1930	4,340,000	8·7
1931	8,020,000	15·9
1932	12,060,000	23·6

Unemployment of blacks in early 1931

City	Blacks as % of population	Blacks as % of total numbers of unemployed
Chicago	4	16
Philadelphia	7	25
Pittsburgh	8	38
Baltimore	17	32
Memphis	38	75
Charleston	49	70

companies. But, in general, the government's policies were deflationary. For example, interest rates were raised, and the higher cost of borrowing further discouraged business men from investing in the re-equipment of their industries. The dollar was not devalued, and American goods remained expensive in world markets. And Hoover was determined to keep public spending as low as possible in his attempts to balance the budget at a time when the government was bound to receive less from taxation. In 1930 the American government agreed to the Hawley–Smoot Tariff, which raised customs duties on imports to record levels. This simply provoked other countries to do the same, and American exports suffered as much as those of other countries.

Hoover had not created the slump which forced Americans into 'Hoovervilles', but he showed precious little sympathy for the misery of millions of his fellow-countrymen. Only in July 1932 did he sign the Emergency Relief and Reconstruction Act, which gave the RFC power to lend $300 million to the states for the relief of the unemployed. Yet by the end of 1932, when over twelve million Americans were out of work, only $30 million had been paid out by the RFC!

In that same year a ragged army of unemployed ex-servicemen came to the American capital, Washington DC, to ask Congress and the President to pay them their bonuses for war service now instead of when they were due, in 1945. Congress rejected their appeal and many of them returned home. The rest of the BEF (Bonus Expeditionary Force) set up camp on the outskirts of the city, hoping their President would do something for them. He did – he sent them General Douglas MacArthur, who hounded them away from the capital with tanks, cavalry, infantry and tear gas.

America had a new hit song in 1932: 'Brother, Can You Spare a Dime?'

"Once I built a railroad, made it run,
Made it race against time.
Once I built a railroad,
Now it's done–
Brother, can you spare a dime?

Once I built a tower, to the sun.
Brick and rivet and lime,
Once I built a tower,
Now it's done –

Brother, can you spare a dime?

Once in khaki suits,
Gee, we looked swell,
Full of that Yankee Doodle-de-dum.
Half a million boots went sloggin' through Hell,
I was the kid with the drum.
Say, don't you remember, they called me Al–
It was Al all the time.
Say, don't you remember, I'm your pal–
Buddy, can you spare a dime?"

The BEF asked Hoover for a dime: he gave them tear gas. Unemployed and ruined Americans asked Hoover for hope: he gave them only empty words. In the summer of 1932 the Democrats nominated Franklin Delano Roosevelt, Governor of New York, as their candidate for the Presidential election in November. In his acceptance speech he said, "I pledge you – I pledge myself to a new deal for the American people. . . . This is more than a political campaign; it is a call to arms. Give me your help, not to win votes alone, but to win in this crusade to restore America to its own people."

In the November election twenty-two million Americans accepted Roosevelt's pledge, against fifteen million who voted for Hoover. Many Americans knew next to nothing about the man who was to be their next President, yet like the nation itself, he was a cripple. When he was thirty-nine, Roosevelt's legs had been paralysed by polio. Now, at the age of fifty, his legs locked in steel braces when he stood to speak, he was offering new hope to a stricken land. In Chapter 26 you will see how his 'New Deal' affected the USA and how it made Roosevelt perhaps the best-loved, and most bitterly hated, President in American history.

Japan – The Aggressive Way Out

Japan was the only independent Asian power with her own colonial empire – an empire that had been extended in 1920 when Japan took over the Mariana and Caroline Islands as 'mandates'. Japan was also Asia's greatest industrial and trading power, producing and exporting a wide range of manufactured goods as well as factory-spun silk yarn. In 1923 the capital city, Tokyo, was destroyed by an earthquake in which over a hundred thousand people died. Six years later the man-made disaster of the Great Depression began to flatten the Japanese economy. The decline of international trade and the raising of tariff barriers soon had savage effects. Japan's exports of manufactured goods dropped by two-thirds; and by 1931 half her factories were idle. In the countryside millions of peasants were ruined as demand for and prices of food and raw materials fell.

Japan attempted to solve her problems in two ways. The first involved using the desperate measure of war against a foreign power – and we have already looked at the beginning of that policy in Chapter 18 (page 74).

Japan had important economic interests, such as the mining of coal and iron ore and the cultivation of soya beans, in the northern Chinese province of Manchuria. To protect those interests she had insisted on keeping an army in the Port Arthur region of the province. Nationalist officers in that army and on the Japanese General Staff now planned the take-over of the whole province, and faked an incident between Japanese and Chinese soldiers near Mukden in September 1931 as an excuse to launch an invasion of the interior. The civilian government in Tokyo was appalled, outwitted and unable to stop the troop movements. By December Manchuria was in Japanese hands. Soon it was to be renamed Manchukuo and provided with an emperor: Japan had at last found a use for Pu Yi, the Chinese Emperor who had been overthrown in Sun Yat-sen's revolution of 1911. But Pu Yi was merely a figurehead: the real rulers of Manchukuo were the jubilant officers of the Japanese army.

The invasion of Manchuria had two important effects – putting aside for the moment its dreadful revelation that the League of Nations was powerless in the face of a determined aggressor. First, it raised the prestige and power of the Japanese army, in which nationalist extremists were now dominant. Second, it made it possible for the army to begin putting massive pressure on the civilian government to undertake a policy of imperial expansion, backed up by enlarged and well-equipped armed forces.

Japan's second way out of economic depression was the work of a remarkable Minister of Finance, Korekiyo Takahashi, a kind of Asian Keynes. Not for him the policies of deflation and penny-pinching followed by the Brünings, MacDonalds and Hoovers of the Western world! Takahashi was, quite simply, a big spender. In each of the years 1932, 1933 and 1934 he increased government spending by no less than twenty per cent, and so provided workers with jobs, and with wages to

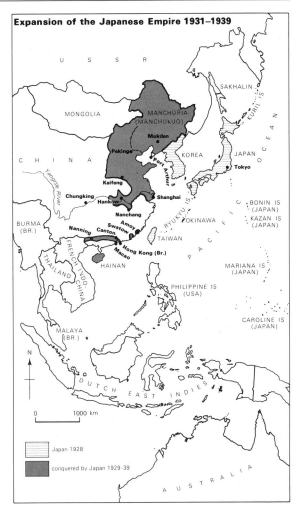

Expansion of the Japanese Empire 1931–1939

Japan 1928

conquered by Japan 1929-39

create new demands for manufactures and food. In 1936, as the Japanese economy was booming and the end of unemployment was in sight, Takahashi prepared to restrict government spending. Army officers, who were now demanding almost unlimited expenditure on armaments, made their opposition clear by murdering him.

The civilians in the government were no longer able to check the more dangerous ambitions of army leaders. In July 1937 the second stage of Japan's new drive for a greater empire opened as troops swept south from Manchukuo. The targets this time were China's ports and great cities, and control of traffic on the Yangtse River. In a little over a year they forced Chiang Kai-shek's forces far into the interior, to the new Kuomintang capital of Chungking.

The Japanese declared that they had established in the east of China a 'New Order', which promised efficient government in the interests of the local people. In fact, it was a simple occupation of foreign land, which depended on the presence of large numbers of Japanese troops and on the willingness of many Chinese landlords and civil servants to collaborate with the invaders.

By the end of 1938 Japan dominated the richest parts of the Chinese mainland. At home, Takahashi's policies and rapid rearmament had brought about full employment and an end to depression. Most of Japan's trade was now with the 'yen bloc' of Korea, Taiwan and Manchukuo – to which she now sold over half her exports, and from which she bought over forty per cent of her imports.

But Japan's new prosperity and her expensive armed forces would be difficult to maintain if her empire was kept within even its 1938 limits. She needed larger markets in which to sell her goods; and she looked enviously at the Dutch, French and British colonies which could provide not only markets but rich resources of raw materials for industry – especially the rubber of Malaya and the oil of the Dutch East Indies. The very forces which had pulled Japan out of depression – aggressive nationalism and the rapid development of her military power – would soon pull her into a war of conquest throughout East Asia and the Pacific. But that part of our story comes later, in Chapter 31.

In this chapter we have looked at the effects of the Great Depression on five industrialised countries. Of those five, Britain and France still had vast colonial empires which straddled the world. Germany, defeated in the Great War and feeling humiliated in the peace, was Europe's most disturbed and restless nation. Japan, as you have just seen, set out to cure her economic ills by rearmament and aggression. And the USA, despite her severe mauling in the Depression, remained the world's greatest economic and financial power. Taken together, those five countries could exert enormous influence on the rest of the world – for good or ill.

In Chapters 25 and 26 we shall return to two of them – Germany and the USA – to follow their history through to the end of the 1930s. And in Chapter 27 we shall look at the government and people of the Soviet Union, who have so far touched only the edges of our story of the world in the period of the Great Depression. That period emphasised the Soviet Union's unique position as the world's only communist state, for she was now faced by capitalist countries weakened by the slump. By cutting off all imports of non-essential goods, the government of the USSR isolated and protected the Soviet economy from the collapse of world trade in the 1930s. The international depression was, for the Soviet Union, a national opportunity to develop her industrial power while the capitalist countries struggled to recover the ground they had lost.

Meanwhile, to complete our picture of the worldwide effects of the slump we shall turn to look at those countries whose economies depended first and foremost (though not in every case entirely) on the production and sale of food and raw materials.

24 Depression Round the World

Between 1925 and 1929 world prices for agricultural produce had fallen steadily. Now you can see from the examples below how prices plunged still further in the period 1929 to 1932.

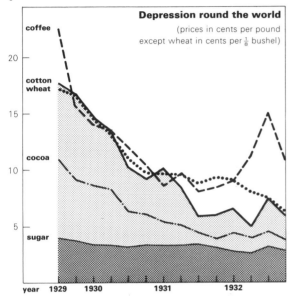

Depression round the world
(prices in cents per pound
except wheat in cents per $\frac{1}{8}$ bushel)

coffee
cotton
wheat
cocoa
sugar

year 1929 1930 1931 1932

As the depressed industrial countries reduced their imports of food and raw materials, as their governments raised tariff barriers to protect their own producers, so the primary producers found they couldn't sell what they had produced – even at giveaway prices.

Primary-producing countries classified by percentage decline in exports, 1928–29 to 1932–33:

Exports down by over 70 per cent
Chile, China, Bolivia, Cuba, Malaya, Peru, Salvador

by over 65 per cent
Argentina, Canada, Ceylon, Dutch East Indies, Estonia, Guatemala, India, Irish Free State, Latvia, Mexico, Thailand, Spain

by over 60 per cent
Brazil, Dominican Republic, Egypt, Greece, Haiti, Hungary, the Netherlands, Nicaragua, Nigeria, Poland, Yugoslavia

by over 50 per cent
Australia, Bulgaria, Colombia, Costa Rica, Denmark, Ecuador, Finland, Honduras, New Zealand, Panama, Paraguay

Not all the people in those countries affected by the slump in prices and exports suddenly found themselves in poverty and want. Many were already in that position before the Depression came to drag others down to their level. In some of the European colonies (for example, in parts of the Dutch East Indies), business men and planters fared relatively worse than their labourers – who were paid most of their 'wages' in goods, not money. And not everyone who lived in a primary-producing country depended for his or her living on exports. But in general the living standards of people did suffer – dreadfully in some places – and the Depression left its mark on politics and forms of government, as well as on economies, around the world.

Latin America

"Way down among Brazilians
Coffee beans grow by the billions,
So they've got to find those extra cups to fill.
They've got an awful lot of coffee in Brazil!

You can't get cherry-soda
'Cause they've got to sell their quota,
And the way things are I guess they never will,
They've got a zillion tons of coffee in Brazil!

No tea, or tomato-juice,
You'll see no potato-juice,
'Cause the planters down in Santos
All say 'No, no, no!'

A politician's daughter
Was accused of drinking water,
And was fined a great big fifty-dollar bill.
They've got an awful lot of coffee in Brazil!

And when their ham and eggs need savour,
Coffee ketchup gives them flavour;
Coffee pickles way outsell the dill!
Why, they put coffee in the java in Brazil!"

Pop-songs are historical documents. This American song tells us, with a certain grim satisfaction, about the plight of just one country in Latin America. It could have been written about Colombian coffee, or Argentinian wheat, or Cuban sugar, or Bolivian tin, or

105

Chilean copper and nitrates – for a glance at the table on page 105 will show that from the Rio Grande to Cape Horn the staple exports of the countries of Latin America were the victims of Depression.

Prices fell, loans from the USA dried up, and there was little money available to pay for the storage which would have kept some of the produce out of glutted markets until better times came. Producers were forced to sell on shrinking markets at lower and lower prices; they cut wages and sacked workers. Workers rioted, and revolutions were commonplace. New governments appeared, which mostly depended on the support of the armed forces; but there was little they could do, except by raising tariffs, to protect their nations from the effects of the world slump.

However, some Latin American countries tried to develop their own industries to provide substitutes for the manufactured goods they could no longer afford to import, and to protect themselves against any future depressions in world trade. In general, it was a slow process, but for the first time in Latin American history several national governments got themselves into the business of forcing the pace of economic change. In 1939 the Chilean government established a Corporation for the Development of Production, which organised steel, oil and other industries. In 1940 the Brazilian government set up a National Steel Company.

New Problems for Colonial Empires

As we have seen in Chapter 16 (page 70), the international slump quickly found its way into the African colonies of the western European imperial powers. Although their economies were not, on the whole, as badly affected as those of Latin America, they undoubtedly suffered: their earnings from exports were almost halved, throwing many thousands of labourers out of work. Some African countries recovered remarkably quickly, however. The British colonies of Northern Rhodesia, Southern Rhodesia and Kenya benefited from the Ottawa Agreement (see page 89) which imposed customs duties on produce imported into Britain from outside the Empire. This gave, for example, the copper mining companies in Northern Rhodesia a trading advantage over Chile, the world's leading copper producer. And, as we have noted, Southern Rhodesia and the Union of South Africa were able to make spectacular recoveries from

the slump through the rapid growth of their gold exports.

Meanwhile, way across the Atlantic, the descendants of the black slaves who had once been West Africa's chief exports were beginning to demand power. In Chapter 19 (page 77) we saw how the living standards of the people of the West Indies depended almost entirely on the export of foods to the British and American markets. Now the Depression of the late twenties and thirties reduced those markets for the islands' produce. Wages were cut, many plantations were closed down and unemployment rose sharply. To make things worse, the annual migration of tens of thousands of West Indians to find work in the USA and in Cuba was no longer possible. The misery and frustration of the people erupted in riots, strikes and a wave of opposition to white, British rule. Depression in the West Indies brought into being new trade union movements which formed the bases for the political parties that began to campaign for the end of colonial rule.

Australia and New Zealand, the two Dominions furthest from the European heart of the British Empire, were bound to be hard hit by the Depression. The world prices of New Zealand's chief exports – wool, meat and dairy produce – all went down sharply. The country's problems were best illustrated between 1932 and 1933 when both she and Denmark reduced the prices of their butter in a commercial fight over the British butter market. There was only one winner – the British housewife, who got cheaper butter from both countries.

The Australians had similar problems – low prices and glutted world markets. They were not helped by the policies of their Labour government, which came to power in the autumn of 1929. A campaign to 'Grow More Wheat' raised the amount of wheat produced by more than twenty per cent in 1930; and since Australian wheat-farmers could not afford expensive storage facilities, almost the entire crop had to be unloaded on an already over-supplied world market! Other Labour policies were more familiar: deflation, wage cuts, and devaluation of the currency to encourage exports. The results were familiar too: over thirty per cent of the work-force unemployed in 1933, and the rejection of the Labour government at the next general election. Free trade within the British Empire could not compensate Australians for the fact that they were producing too much for the world of those depressed times to buy: too much wool and too much wheat.

The world slump obviously put the colonial empires under a new kind of stress. In the past, colonies had earned their way by supplying foods and the raw materials of industry to the mother countries; and surplus money from those countries had been invested in their colonies. Now investment was no longer profitable (except in isolated cases such as Southern Rhodesia); and the imperial powers were seen to have no other ways of protecting their overseas subjects from the effects of the slump.

Already we have seen (in Chapter 22, page 89) how the British tried to protect themselves and their colonies by making their empire into a free trade area by Imperial Preference. But the very size of that empire was now seen to be a weakness as well as a source of pride. It was too widespread to make into a manageable, exclusive trading system; and at its centre Britain was not big enough to buy in all its surplus produce, and she was no longer rich enough to lend sufficient money for investment or to tide countries over a bad patch.

Eastern and Central Europe

If the collapse of the prices of primary products – like Australian wheat, West Indian sugar and Malayan rubber – put new stresses on the British Empire, they had even more unsettling effects nearer home, on the continent of Europe. In Chapter 22, page 87, we looked at some of the economic problems of the Eastern European countries – over-population, slow rates of industrial growth, and an unhealthy dependence on the export of primary products (chiefly wheat) to earn the money they needed to pay off debts to Western European nations and the USA. We also saw how tariff barriers were erected to protect new industries and to encourage national self-sufficiency. Now we shall see how the Depression magnified those problems and brought with it new miseries.

As a result of the European financial crisis of 1931 (Chapter 22, pages 88–9), governments, business men and farmers in Eastern and Central Europe had to pay back their loans to Western European and American bankers; and they were no longer able to borrow new money to pay off old debts as they had done in the twenties. The only way to get money was to earn it, by increasing exports and reducing imports. The trouble was that they all tried to earn more and buy less at the same time – and at a time when the world

slump was driving down the prices of wheat, tobacco and timber. The result was economic disaster. Exports, especially of wheat, went down. Farmers couldn't sell their produce at a profit, even at home. The bigger farmers were ruined; and peasant-farmers either went back to their old ways of payments 'in kind' or did without the goods which they could no longer afford. Industries could no longer sell manufactured goods to the people of poverty-stricken villages, and tariff barriers prevented sales abroad. As production went down, people were thrown out of work. The middle classes suffered too: many civil servants were dismissed or forced to retire early on half-pensions; while even fewer people than before could afford the services of lawyers or doctors.

The peoples of Eastern Europe endured terrible hardship in the 1930s, but it was a misery which forced them further apart rather than closer together. It exaggerated the economic nationalism of the separate states. Austria actually increased her production of wheat while Yugoslavia was bursting at the seams with the stuff. And Poland, Hungary and Romania all hastily built new factories to manufacture the kinds of goods they had in the past imported.

The only Western European country which showed any interest in helping the depressed economies of Eastern Europe was Germany, who turned the situation to her own advantage. From 1934 onwards the German government negotiated trading agreements, one by one, with the Eastern European states. Germany agreed to import large quantities of agricultural produce and raw materials, and paid for them in special currencies that could only be used to buy German manufactured goods. Obviously, Germany gained a lot from the agreements – not only valuable outlets for the products of her own industries but also political influence in Eastern Europe. As Germany bound the Eastern states to her with economic ties those states could not afford to break, so the influence of Germany increased at the expense of the influence of France. The figures on the next page should give you a clear idea of how the agreements helped Germany to dominate Eastern European trade in the later 1930s.

People in other Western European countries could, and did, complain about this German policy – claiming, for example, that the Reich sucked Eastern Europe dry of valuable resources and in return dumped useless manufactured goods – such as mouth organs and typewriters – onto peasant economies. There was much

Germany's percentage share in the trade of Eastern European countries

Country	1934	1935	1936	1937	1938
Hungary:					
Imports	18·3	22·7	26·0	25·9	40·9
Exports	22·2	23·9	22·8	24·0	40·0
Romania:					
Imports	15·5	23·8	36·1	28·9	40·0
Exports	16·6	16·7	17·8	22·3	26·5
Yugoslavia:					
Imports	13·9	16·2	26·7	32·4	39·4
Exports	15·4	18·6	23·7	21·7	42·0
Bulgaria:					
Imports	40·2	53·5	61·0	54·8	52·0
Exports	42·8	38·0	47·6	43·1	59·0

truth in such complaints but the fact remained that Germany provided what Eastern Europe needed above all – markets for primary produce – and so helped to relieve some of the pressures of the slump.

We saw in Chapter 14 some of the problems of the minority peoples in the states of Central and Eastern Europe in the 1920s. Not surprisingly, the majority nationalities had quickly dominated the economic and political life of the new states; and the old, powerful prejudice against the Jews (anti-Semitism) had stayed firmly rooted throughout the area. As long as the states were fairly prosperous, dislike and distrust of Jews and other minority groups could be kept under control. But once the Depression set in to ruin many people's livelihoods and threaten others, old prejudices took shape as new and dangerous political forces.

You have already seen (page 105) that the Depression affected all levels of society in the new states. The urge to find a scapegoat – some thing or some people on whom to fix the blame – was overwhelming, especially among those middle classes of people who lost jobs or army commissions or who became hopelessly in debt to banks or to local moneylenders. Jews were the most obvious candidates as scapegoats – despite the fact that many of them were as badly affected as anyone else by the slump. Eastern European anti-Semitism was, therefore, a home-grown prejudice which thrived in the Depression years: it was not imported direct from Germany. But some of the new political movements which developed in this period of economic crisis resembled German Nazism.

In Hungary a National Socialist Workers' Party was set up by Zoltan Böszörmény, who chose crossed scythes as the movement's emblem. Böszörmény preached a familiar fascist message: he was against communists, against liberals, and against democracy; but his Scythe Cross movement appealed less to people in the cities than to the poverty-stricken peasants of eastern Hungary who were attracted by the leader's vague promises of land reform and 'justice for the poor'. Böszörmény described his followers as "Gardeners of the Hungarian race, fateful Death Reapers of the Jewish swine and their hirelings", and in 1936 he planned a march on Budapest. The 'revolution' fizzled out in the arrest of 700 half-starved peasants and the imprisonment of the party's incompetent leaders.

More serious was the Arrow Cross movement, led by Ferenc Szálasi. At first its members came mainly from unskilled industrial workers in the depressed towns, but later the movement attracted support from the professional classes and army officers. Szálasi's ideas, when they were clear enough to be understood, appeared to combine bits of Nazism with bits of Italian Fascism in a perverted vision of a new Hungary which would be based on what he called a "Christian moral order" – which, of course, excluded Jews. The Arrow Cross, although increasingly popular in the late 1930s, was resisted by the government and failed to gain power.

Romania produced what was perhaps the most extraordinary of all the fascist movements in the Europe of the 1930s. The Legion of the Archangel Michael had been founded in 1927 by Corneliu Codreanu, a young man whose deep religious faith was matched only by his desire to rid Romania of the Jews, communists and foreign capitalists who, he believed, were responsible for widespread poverty and injustice. Codreanu's instrument for the work of destroying the 'oppressors and betrayers' of Romania was the Iron Guard, an organisation whose methods of operation included torture and murder. It was hardly surprising that Codreanu admired nationalist leaders outside Romania who were not squeamish about using the same methods to ensure obedience to their wills – Hitler and Mussolini.

As the Legion grew more popular and widely feared it became a kind of 'rival dictatorship' to that already set up by King Carol; and in 1938 and 1939 the struggle between the Legion and the royal government ended in a bloodbath. Codreanu was murdered; and as teams of terrorist Legionaries planned to avenge his death, the police tracked them down and either strangled or shot them. Eventually, in September 1939, Legionaries

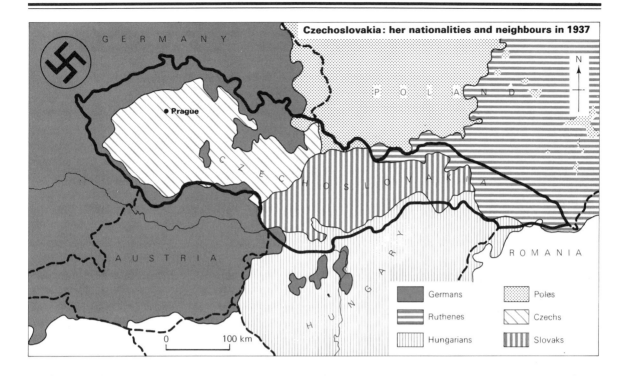

Czechoslovakia: her nationalities and neighbours in 1937

Germans
Ruthenes
Hungarians
Poles
Czechs
Slovaks

0   100 km

assassinated the Prime Minister – and in return the government forces hanged Legionaries in the market-places of towns the length and breadth of the land.

Throughout Eastern Europe, in the misery of the Depression years, the nationalities who had been forced to live cheek by jowl with other nationalities in the new states grew more suspicious and intolerant of each other. Majority nationalities were openly hostile to the 'foreign' minorities in their midst; and the minorities responded with a new determination to join up with the national states dominated by their own people. And of all the countries in Europe, Czechoslovakia was the one which had most cause to be alarmed by these ambitions among its minority peoples.

In the 1920s most of the bad feeling about the share-out of power and jobs had been between the Czechs, who got most of both, and the Slovaks and Ruthenes in the east. The Germans of the western border area, the Sudetenland, had been loyal to the central government while their industries, shops and tourist businesses had prospered. But the slump in world trade hit them hard and they blamed unemployment and a fall in their standard of living on the government in Prague. But this was a long way from calling for the separation of the Sudetenland from Czechoslovakia – until 1933. Then Hitler came to power in Germany with the promise of a single 'Reich' for all Germans. The Sudeten Germans turned from voting for the Czechoslovak parties of their choice – whether conservative, liberal or socialist – towards the Sudeten German Party led by Konrad Henlein, an admirer of Hitler who was in the Führer's pay. In the elections of 1935, Henlein's party won forty-four of the sixty-six parliamentary seats in the German-speaking parts of Czechoslovakia.

By 1936 it had become clear that Henlein and his party had their eyes fixed on something much more ambitious than the better protection of Czech-German citizens by the Czech state. In almost everything but name the leaders of the Sudeten German Party were Nazis. Their eventual aim was nothing less than to make the Sudetenland part of Germany.

109

25 Hitler's Germany

Führer, Party and People

Before Hitler came to power, a German citizen – like the citizens of other democratic Western countries – had a variety of loyalties, interests and responsibilities. In his daily life he was probably most concerned about his family, his neighbours, his church and the people he did business with or worked for.

His freedom to live his own life within the law was protected by a variety of powerful forces within the German Republic. Firstly, the Republic was a federation of states, or *länder*, each with its own democratically elected government. Those second-level governments worked as a check on the power of the federal government in Berlin: for example, the largest of the states, Prussia, was ruled for many years by Social Democrats while the federal government was in the hands of right-wing coalitions. Secondly, as in all modern democratic states, a citizen could join an organisation which protected his interests: a worker could become a member of a trade union; a farmer could join a co-operative, which tried to sell his produce for him at the best price. Thirdly, a citizen had the right to speak, listen to and read criticism of those who ruled him: political argument was carried on in public, in a vast number of local and national newspapers and magazines. And finally, there was the crucial principle that no person or government was above the law.

There was nothing extraordinary about all that. What was extraordinary was Hitler's determination to sweep away that rich variety of life in which free citizens could express themselves as individuals and the *länder* could preserve their traditions and differences. Hitler's vision of the people belonged to the distant past, before written history; to dark forests inhabited by warriors who survived in their struggles against rival people by blind obedience to their leader. He himself was to be the new German leader, or *führer*, and his will was to be above the law. Sixty million Germans were to be moulded into a *volk*, a racially pure people, whose only loyalty was to him.

Once he was in power, Hitler moved to destroy whatever stood in the way of his domination of the minds and bodies of the people. By the middle of March 1933 all the governments of the *länder* had been taken over by local Nazi leaders. The new State Presi-

dent of Württemberg, Wilhelm Murr, staged a massive victory demonstration on 15 March, at which he made clear the facts of life in Nazi Germany:

"The government will brutally beat down all who oppose it. We do not say an eye for an eye, a tooth for a tooth. No, he who knocks out one of our eyes will get his head chopped off, and he who knocks out one of our teeth will get his jaw bashed in."

On 23 March, what was left of the Reichstag passed the Enabling Act (see also Chapter 23, page 95), which gave Hitler the authority to make his own laws. On 2 May, the trade unions, which had consistently opposed the Nazis, got their 'heads chopped off' when union offices throughout the country were raided by the SA and SS. In their place the German Labour Front (*Deutsche Arbeitsfront* – DAF) was set up, led by Robert Ley, which both workers and employers were forced to join. The DAF was basically a means of stopping German workers organising themselves in their *own* interests.

And on 14 July a new law destroyed the German people's democratic right to disagree openly with those who ruled them.

"Law Against the New Formation of Parties
July 14, 1933

Article 1
The sole political party existing in Germany is the National Socialist German Workers' Party.

Article 2
Whoever shall undertake to maintain the organisation of another party, or to found a new party, shall be punished with a sentence of hard labour of up to three years, or of prison between six months and three years, unless other regulations provide for heavier punishment."

The NSDAP itself became a mass party. It had grown from just over 100,000 members in 1928 to nearly one-and-a-half million in 1932: within the next two years it would grow again by almost 200 per cent. For many people it was convenient, and prudent, to join the Nazis: there were all kinds of benefits for Party members, such as being first in line for jobs. For some people it became essential: by 1939 Party membership was a condition of entry into the civil service.

Everyday life in Germany was dominated by the Party organisations, and the affairs of its citizens were open to the interference of Party officials. By 1937 there were 700,000 political leaders in Germany. They ranged from the *gauleiter* (the regional Party chiefs), through the *kreisleiter* (the area bosses), the *ortsgruppenleiter* (the local leaders) and the *zellenleiter* (the cell leaders), down to the *blockleiter* (block leaders), the local eyes and ears of the Party, the subscription collectors, the snoopers.

Through these 'mini-führers' of his mass party Hitler could regulate and spy on the nation. If the Nazis could smash the unions and other political parties, they could also alter people's public behaviour – even how they greeted each other in the streets.

"If people belong to the same social group, it is customary to raise the right arm at an angle so that the palm of the hand becomes visible. The appropriate phrase that goes with it is 'Heil Hitler' or at least 'Heil'. If one espies an acquaintance in the distance, it suffices merely to raise the right hand in the manner described. If one encounters a person socially ... inferior to oneself, then the right arm is to be fully stretched out, raised to eye-level; at the same time, one is to say 'Heil Hitler'."

That stiff-armed salute was officially known as the 'German greeting'.

For a time the Nazification of Germany and the smashing of the known opponents of the new régime obscured a struggle for power within the NSDAP itself. Control of the Party and, through the Party, control of the people had appeared to be in Hitler's hands from the very beginning. In fact, after he had come to power in January 1933, his authority was soon challenged by Ernst Röhm and other leaders of the SA,

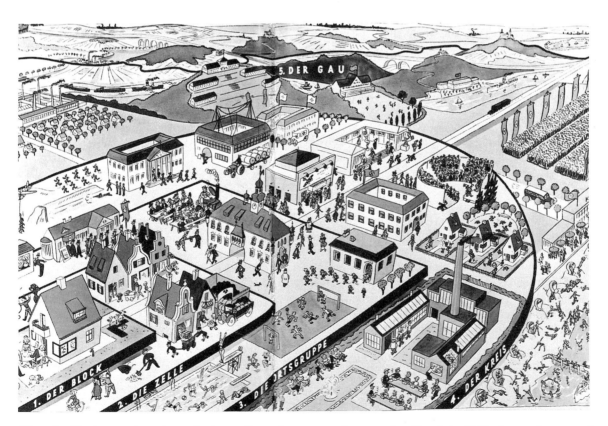

How the Nazis saw themselves. A picture from the propaganda magazine Signal *in 1941 shows a happy and harmonious people living in 1. the block, 2. the cell, 3. the locality, 4. the area, and 5. the region.*

the Nazis' uniformed force of stormtroopers, which had swollen to over two million men. Röhm's ambition to take over the *Reichswehr*, the regular German army, not only alarmed the generals: it was a direct threat to the unique authority of the Party leader. If Röhm were allowed to control the armed forces as well as the stormtroopers, he would be the greatest power in the land. And while Röhm was plotting to bring the army under his authority, other SA men were demanding that the 'socialist' part of the National Socialist revolution should begin.

On the 'Night of the Long Knives', 30 June 1934, Hitler dealt with his challengers. Röhm and over 150 others were murdered. The victims included General von Schleicher, who paid the price for his intrigues of 1932 (see page 94), and Gregor Strasser, the 'socialist' Nazi who had opposed Hitler once too often (see page 91). The intruments of death were the black-shirted SS, commanded by Heinrich Himmler.

Hitler made no bones about who was responsible for the massacre. He told his mockery of a parliament:

"I ordered the leaders of the guilty shot. If someone asks me why we did not use the regular courts I would reply: at that moment I was responsible for the German nation;... it was I alone who, during those twenty-four hours, was the Supreme Court of Justice of the German People!"

He could have added that the army had stood aside and let him do it, and that President Hindenburg had sent him a telegram of congratulations.

On 2 August, Hindenburg died. Straight away Hitler announced that the offices of Chancellor and President were combined, and on the same day the soldiers of the German army swore their loyalty to a new chief:

"I swear by God this holy oath, that I will render unconditional obedience to Adolf Hitler, Führer of the German Reich and People, Supreme Commander of the Armed Forces, and will be ready as a brave soldier to risk my life at any time for this oath."

Within the space of a few weeks Hitler had finally answered all the questions about who ruled the Party and Germany. And the events of the night of 30 June had made clear *how* he ruled – by the methods of a gangster boss, served by men who were prepared to cut each other's throats to gain favour in his eyes.

"Your Child Belongs to Us"

It takes time to teach old dogs new tricks – even to say "Heil Hitler" – and the Führer was aware of resistance among older generations. In the short term they could be squashed: in the long term Hitler was sure they wouldn't even matter.

"When an opponent declares, 'I will not come over to your side,' I calmly say, 'Your child belongs to us already.... What are you? You will pass on. Your descendants, however, now stand in the new camp. In a short time they will know nothing else but this new community.'"

In 1932 only 35,000 German children had 'belonged' to the Leader as members of the Hitler Youth movement. By the end of 1934 membership of the Hitler Youth had soared to over three-and-a-half million; and at the end of 1936 Hitler finally gathered in all Germany's youngsters by making membership compulsory.

This was to be the real education of German youth: all else was mere book learning. Twelve years before, in *Mein Kampf*, Hitler had written, "The bodies of the young will be systematically trained from infancy onwards, so as to be tempered and hardened for the demands to be made on them in later years." By "young" Hitler had really meant 'boys', although he had a few words to say about the girls: "In the education of the girl the final goal always to be kept in mind is that she is one day to be a mother." Now the *Bund deutscher Mädel* would teach her all she needed to know: how to be a good Nazi, a fit Nazi; and, as far as possible, an attractive mate for a good, fit Hitler Youth.

The Hitler Youth movement emphasised above all else physical fitness, endurance and participation in team-games. Its members attended regular camp meetings and took part in mass demonstrations of loyalty to the Führer.

Some children were selected to complete their secondary education in special Adolf Hitler Schools, where the emphasis on physical fitness was carried to extraordinary lengths. And from those special schools a small number of students were selected to go on to the four *Ordensburgen* (Order Castles) whose job it was to complete the education of the young people who had been picked out as the future Party leaders.

Early in 1933 the Nazis had celebrated their seizure of power with bonfires of literature. Into the flames had gone everything they disliked or despised – books by Jews, books by socialists, books about the merits of democracy, about the old morality of protecting the weak from the strong. And along with them had gone many of the textbooks used in the schools of the Republic – especially the history textbooks. History would be re-written by the Nazis, and for the time being pupils would have to make do with cheap pamphlets. In any case a Hitler Youth was not expected to spend too much time in the company of books. Even the books that had not been burnt might give him ideas, might encourage him to think for himself.

The Organisation of Terror

Let's begin with an example of what happened to one man – a former member of the SPD – soon after Hitler came to power.

"An unknown man knocked at Leidler's door and asked for him by name. Leidler took him in. It was raining and the man was wet. The man showed Leidler a *Reichsbanner** membership book and told him that he was a fugitive from the Gestapo. He told Leidler that the *Reichsbanner* had risen in the Ruhr and was fighting the Nazis. Would Leidler have any weapons? Could he supply the names of any loyal *Reichsbanner* men in the area? Leidler answered 'no' to each question and added, 'I'm through. I've had the shit kicked out of me. All I can do is put you up overnight and feed you, which I'd do for any human being on a night like this.'

In the morning, after breakfast, the man went to the door and, just before he left, turned his lapel back and showed Leidler an SS button. Then he left wordlessly."

Thousands of Germans had similar experiences. Some of them were lucky: they kept their mouths shut, their opinions to themselves, and they survived. Others were not so fortunate: they were caught up in the system of terror and spat out at the other end, dead.

In the summer of 1934 Heinrich Himmler, chief of the SS, had helped Hitler in the bloody business of the Röhm massacre. Less than a month later, Himmler re-

* *Reichsbanner* = a para-military organisation which had supported the democratic Weimar Republic.

ceived his first reward: the SS was made independent of the SA. Two years later, in June 1936, the grateful Führer gave Himmler the greatest prize he had to offer – control of all Germany's police. Hitler had placed himself above the law: now he put his chief murderer in charge of the forces of 'law and order'.

Like all the other Party organisations, the SS was responsible to no-one but its own leader, and he was answerable only to Hitler. As long as Himmler remained faithful to the Führer he was free to do as he wished, to subject the German people to organised terror.

Perhaps the most widely feared branch of Himmler's organisation was the *Gestapo*, controlled by Reinhard Heydrich (who was also head of the SD – the Party police). His deputy, Dr Werner Best, described how this new body was different from any previous police force in German history:

"The National Socialist Führer State has created for the first time in Germany a political police which we regard as modern, i.e. as meeting our present-day needs; an institution which carefully supervises the political health of the German body politic, which is quick to recognise all symptoms of disease and germs of destruction … and to remove them by every suitable means."

The most suitable means of removing the "germs of destruction" was to place them in 'protective custody' – Nazi shorthand for arresting suspicious characters and handing them over, without trial, to the concentration camps run by the *Totenkopfverbände* of the SS. Many camps had been hastily set up in 1933 to cope with the flood of victims of the SA and SS terror, but gradually their numbers were reduced until there were just four large camps left – at Dachau, Sachsenhausen, Buchenwald and Lichtenburg.

From the end of 1937 the political prisoners in 'protective custody' were joined by more and more people roped in by the police under their new powers of 'preventive detention'. The argument behind this new development was brutally simple: certain types of people were always causing trouble, refusing to behave like everyone else – so why not lock them up? The 'anti-social' elements included beggars, gypsies, prostitutes, 'grumblers', alcoholics, hooligans, and what the Nazis called 'mental cases'. Homosexuals were definitely 'anti-social', and so were people who refused to work.

By the summer of 1939 there were about 25,000 prisoners in the camps. They were 'marked' men and women in more than one sense of the word, for each prisoner had a coloured triangle of cloth sewn on to his or her uniform for easy identification. Political prisoners wore red triangles; Jehovah's Witnesses, blue; anti-socials, black; criminals, green; and homosexuals, pink. We know all that now, long after most of the prisoners are dead. We don't know how many Germans, outside the SS, knew of those things at the time; but we can guess that most people, given a choice between ignorance and finding out, preferred not to know. The "fear and horror" (Heydrich's own words) which surrounded the very name *Gestapo* was enough to discourage most people from asking questions.

Werner Best put the situation in a nutshell: "Provided the police are carrying out the will of the Leadership, they are acting legally." Germany was in the grip of a kind of political rabies: the disease of Nazism had penetrated the central nervous system of the state – its law-making and law-enforcing agencies. The Law was now the will of the Führer, and the whims of his obedient underlings.

The Empire of the 'Poison Dwarf'

"The broad masses of the people are not made up of diplomats or professors of public law nor simply of persons who are able to form reasoned judgment in given cases, but a vacillating crowd of human children who are constantly wavering between one idea and another."

"The chief function [of propaganda] is to convince the masses, whose slowness of understanding needs to be given time in order that they may absorb information; and only constant repetition will finally succeed in imprinting an idea on the memory of the crowd."

Those two quotations are taken from Adolf Hitler's *Mein Kampf* (see also Chapter 23, page 91), the book which sold hundreds of thousands of copies after January 1933 and made a fortune for the Führer. They reveal a contempt for "the masses", and at the same time a realisation that the fickle "crowd of human children" must be numbed into Nazi ways of thinking by the constant repetition of Nazi propaganda.

You have already seen how little respect Hitler had for the people he ruled and how he encouraged Himmler and Heydrich to create an empire of terror

within the Reich. On 13 March 1933 (ten days before the Enabling Act was forced through the Reichstag) Hitler appointed Dr Joseph Goebbels as his Minister of Popular Enlightenment and Propaganda, responsible for "all tasks of spiritual direction of the nation". Goebbels was physically small, but what he lacked in inches he made up for in ambition. Before long he had created his own empire – of newspapers and magazines, of film studios and radio transmitters. He was perhaps the cleverest and most unscrupulous manipulator of mass media in history. He was a bigger liar than the master he served. Behind his back he was called "poison dwarf" and "Wotan's Mickey Mouse"; and he was likened to a tadpole – all mouth and tail (*Schwanz*, the German word for tail, is also slang for 'penis').

The two most important media were the press and radio. German broadcasting was already centralised and Goebbels took it over in 1933 as a ready-made instrument of propaganda – or, as the Minister himself put it, "a spiritual weapon of the totalitarian state". All that was required was to 'Nazify' its programme output and to ensure that people listened in. The first task was quickly completed; success in the second was guaranteed by the very novelty of wireless broadcasting and by the efforts of manufacturers to produce cheap sets. In 1933 fewer than one out of every four German households had a wireless. By 1942, seven out of every ten German families owned radios.

But broadcasting was not aimed just at the home: offices, factories, restaurants and cafés were equipped with wirelesses through which the Minister or his Führer could reach out to the German people. Nor did Goebbels neglect the world outside the Reich: by early 1935 he had under his control a network of short-wave transmitters which could broadcast to any part of the world. Australians, Brazilians, Portuguese and Japanese – all could listen in to the voices of the new Germany. More important, Goebbels' propaganda penetrated the homes of Germans who lived outside the Reich – in Poland, in Czechoslovakia, in Austria.

The press presented the Nazis with very different problems. When they came to power they controlled only 121 newspapers and periodicals out of a total of 4,700. There were, of course, crude ways of selling papers: the *Fränkische Tageszeitung*, controlled by Julius Streicher, sent this circular to readers unwilling to renew their subscriptions:

"Your intention expresses a very peculiar attitude towards our paper, which is an official organ of the National Socialist German Workers' Party ... We shall continue to forward copies of it to you, and hope that you will not want to expose yourself to unfortunate consequences in the case of cancellation."

By the end of 1934 Goebbels had extended direct Nazi control of the press from 121 papers to 436; but he had also taken indirect control of all the others. No longer were German news agencies independent: Goebbels made them put out Nazi versions of the news. And a law of October 1933 forbade any newspaper editor to criticise the government. As the historian Z. A. B. Zeman has pointed out, "There was no need for censorship because the editor's most important function was that of a censor."

If the *Gestapo* was the Nazis' secret service, the job of Goebbels' Propaganda Ministry was to reinforce the terror by convincing the people that the Party was everywhere. It was difficult, if not impossible, to avoid the Party: even if you avoided its opinions in newspapers and on radio, it was still there in the streets – its uniforms, its parades, its flags hung out in 'spontaneous demonstrations' of loyalty to the Führer. Only for a brief period, in the summer of 1936, was the output of propaganda restrained. The Olympic Games were being held in Berlin – and while Germany was on show to the world, some of the more strident Nazi posters disappeared.

Nevertheless, the Games were a massive propaganda success. Their organisation was faultless, the Führer turned up in person to award medals, and the radio facilities provided for foreign commentators were lavish. Only one man spoiled the effect – Jesse Owens, the American sprinter and long jumper, who won four gold medals. For the Games were not staged by the Nazis to "promote international understanding" or "to bring the youth of the world together in friendly competition": their purpose was to reveal to the world the new Germans, Hitler's 'master-race', in action. Owens, the supreme Olympic athlete, was American: worse still, he was black.

"My daddy says Jews are not damnably vile"

Way back in 1920 Adolf Hitler, the unknown politician of Munich's back streets, had announced the Nazi Party Programme (see also Chapter 23, page 92). The fourth of its Twenty-Five Points read as follows:

"None but members of the nation may be citizens of the state. None but those of German blood, whatever their creed, may be members of the nation. No Jew, therefore, may be a member of the nation." And so it followed that a Jew could not be a citizen of the German state, with the same civil rights as anyone else.

Even when Hitler became a national political figure, not everyone took his anti-Semitism at face value. And if anything shows how badly Hindenburg, Papen and the other intriguers of January 1933 had miscalculated when they lifted Hitler to power, the following letter does:

Berlin, April 4, 1933

Dear Mr Chancellor,

In recent days, a whole number of cases were reported to me in which judges, lawyers and justice officials who are wounded war veterans, and whose conduct of office has been flawless, were forcibly retired and are to be dismissed because of their Jewish descent.

For me personally ... this sort of treatment of Jewish officials, wounded in the war, is quite intolerable. I am convinced, Mr Chancellor, that you will share this human feeling with me, and I ask you, most cordially and with the utmost urgency, to look into this matter yourself. ...

If they were worthy of fighting and bleeding for Germany, they must be considered worthy of continuing to serve the fatherland in their professions. ...

Your devoted
Von Hindenburg

There was no "human feeling" to appeal to. Those legal officials were merely some of the first victims of the Nazis' systematic persecution of the Jews.

Some Dates in the Calendar of the German Jews

1933   *1 April* – First official boycott of Jewish shops, doctors and lawyers.

   7 April – Law for the Re-Establishment of the Career Civil Service excluded Jews from government jobs.

1934   *22 July* – Jews forbidden to take legal examinations.

   8 December – Jews forbidden to take pharmaceutical examinations.

1935 *15 September* – Reich Citizenship Act: "No Jew can be a Reich citizen. The right to vote on political questions is not extended to him and he may not be appointed to any office of State."

15 September – Law for the Protection of German Blood and German Honour: "Marriages between Jews and citizens of German or kindred blood are hereby forbidden. . . . Extramarital intercourse between Jews and citizens of German or kindred blood is forbidden."

1936 and 1937 Professional activities of Jews severely restricted or prohibited – including vets, chartered accountants, teachers, dentists, surveyors, auctioneers and nurses.

1937 *12 June* – Secret order from Heydrich: Jewish women who had had sexual intercourse with Germans to be sent to concentration camps.

1938 *17 August* – All male Jews to add the name 'Israel' and all female Jews the name 'Sara' to their non-Jewish first names.

30 September – Cancellation of qualifications of Jewish doctors.

7 November – Ernst von Rath, a German diplomat, murdered in Paris by Herschel Grünspan, a Jew.

9 November – 'Kristallnacht' (Crystal Night). Destruction of Jewish shops, homes and synagogues throughout Germany. Over 30,000 Jews sent to the concentration camps: they were later released, after they had promised to leave the country.

15 November – Jewish children excluded from German schools and universities.

3 December – Closing and compulsory sale of Jewish businesses and shops.

1939 *21 February* – Jews to hand over all gold and silver objects and jewels in their possession.

1 September – Curfew on the Jews after 8 pm in winter and 9 pm in summer.

23 September – Confiscation of all radios owned by Jews.

As you can see, the sickness of rabid anti-Semitism became a feature of everyday life in Germany. Towns and villages put up notices on their approach roads - "Jews not wanted here". Holiday resorts advertised themselves as "free of Jewish taint". By 1935 local authorities were banning Jews from public parks and playing fields: it was not unusual to see outside a local swimming pool the notice "Bathing Prohibited to Dogs and Jews".

Hatred of the Jews was taught in schools. Jewish children were repeatedly humiliated in front of their classmates until they were excluded from the German education system altogether in 1938. And not only the Jews were harmed by the campaign against them. In 1934 a Berlin schoolboy interrupted his teacher's anti-Semitic lecture with the remark, "My daddy says Jews are not damnably vile." His daddy was put in prison. In a land where a father could be punished for the innocent words of his child, it was safer to keep your opinions to yourself – even at home.

In Chapter 15 (page 67) you read that there was a massive migration of Jews to Palestine in the 1930s. Now you know where many of them came from, and why. Between 1933 and 1939 roughly half the Jewish population of Germany emigrated, mostly to Palestine, the USA and Britain. The other quarter of a million German Jews stayed behind – to wait.

The Intentions of Nazi Germany

Where was Nazi Germany going? What would Hitler do with a state over which he now had total control?

Let's look first at *Mein Kampf*, at some of the ideas Hitler put forward in his chapter called 'German Policy In Eastern Europe'.

"Our Movement must seek to abolish the present disastrous proportion between our population and the area of our national territory. . . . In striving for this it must bear in mind the fact that we are members of the highest species of humanity on earth. . . . For the future of the German nation the 1914 frontiers are of no significance. They did not serve to protect us in the past, nor do they offer any guarantee for our defence in the future. With these frontiers the German people cannot maintain themselves as a compact unit, nor can they be assured of their maintenance. . . . The soil on which we now live was not a gift bestowed by Heaven on our forefathers. But they had to conquer it by risking their lives. So also in the future our people will not

116

"He who would live must fight. He who does not wish to fight in this world, where permanent struggle is the law of life, has not the right to exist." – Adolf Hitler in Mein Kampf. *Here, young men of the* Reichsarbeitsdienst *(RAD – the National Labour Service), gripping their spades like tools of war, parade in front of their Führer at Nuremberg.*

obtain territory, and therewith the means of existence, as a favour from any other people, but will have to win it by the power of a triumphant sword.... We National Socialists put an end to the perpetual Germanic march towards the South and West of Europe and turn our eyes towards the lands of the East.... when we speak of new territory in Europe today we must principally think of Russia and the border States subject to her."

It is clear that Hitler believed the German people had to have more territory (*lebensraum* – living space) in Europe and that they would have to take it by "a triumphant sword", or, more accurately, by the weapons of modern warfare. But *Mein Kampf* was written nearly ten years before Hitler became Führer; and ten years are a long time in a man's life – time enough in which to change opinions, cool down, limit his ambitions. We have to look at what he did in the 1930s as well as at what he believed in the mid-1920s.

As soon as he came to power, Hitler acted quickly to deal with Germany's unemployment problem. A National Labour Service was set up to employ people on a wide range of public works – in agriculture, land reclamation, the building of schools and hospitals, and the construction of the *autobahnen*, Germany's new motorways. The results of Hitler's approach to unemployment – using government money to create jobs – looked spectacular.

Unemployment in Germany, 1933–37

Date	Numbers of unemployed
October 1933	6,000,000
October 1934	4,100,000
February 1935	2,800,000
February 1936	2,500,000
February 1937	1,200,000

However, the rapid decrease in unemployment was only one side of the coin. From the very beginning the Nazis had been spending money on rearmament. Admittedly, it was not a lavish outlay at first – only 4,000 million Reichsmarks in the first two years of Nazi rule. But in March 1935 Hitler announced the start of universal military service and the creation of a new German air force, the *Luftwaffe*. The money made available for equipping the armed forces was suddenly doubled; and in the years 1936–39 a total of 42,000 million Reichsmarks was spent on rearmament.

The conscription of young men into the armed forces and the expansion of the armaments industry both helped to reduce Germany's unemployment figures. And more jobs were created by Hitler's policy of autarky – his attempt to reduce Germany's dependence on world markets for essential raw materials. Particularly from 1936 onwards, more and more people were employed in the metal-processing industries and in plants producing synthetic oil, rubber and textiles.

Policies like these – conscription, the development of an air force, massive expenditure on rearmament, autarky – were obviously preparations for a war, though they didn't necessarily mean that Hitler was determined to start one. We have to leave it to Hitler to tell us that.

On 10 November 1938 Adolf Hitler made a secret speech to representatives of the German press.

"The prevailing circumstances have obliged me to speak, for a decade or more, of almost nothing but peace. Only, in fact, by continuously declaring the German desire for peace and Germany's peaceful intentions was I able, step by step, to secure freedom for the German people and to provide Germany with the armaments which have, time and time again, always been the essential precondition for any further move. ... It was sheer necessity that made me speak for years of peace alone. It has now, however, become necessary to submit the German people to a gradual change in its psychological state of mind, and to make it plain to the Germans that there are things which, if they cannot be achieved by peaceful means, *must* be achieved by means of force. ..."

26 Roosevelt and the New Deal

The '100 Days'

On 4 March 1933, just a little over a month after Hitler had become Chancellor of Germany, Franklin Delano Roosevelt took the oath of office as President of the United States. In his Inaugural Address he told the American people that "the only thing we have to fear is fear itself – nameless, unreasoning, unjustified terror which paralyses needed efforts to convert retreat into advance".

Around fifteen million Americans were without jobs, ruin was staring farmers in the face, banks were going bust, and an army of migrants was already on the highways – refugees from poverty in a land of plenty. Yet the cripple who now replaced Herbert Hoover in the White House seemed to welcome the awesome responsibility for putting things right. To walk, Roosevelt had to have his legs harnessed in steel braces, and most of his day was spent in a wheelchair. It appears that many Americans never knew the full extent of his handicap – that to get upstairs their new President had to be carried in men's arms, like a helpless child. To those who did know it was not important: what mattered was that he seemed to have the guts and the will to lead the nation, not that he couldn't dance the waltz at a White House ball.

Roosevelt's first actions as President were not imaginative, nor did they solve America's most pressing problems. But they did stop the feeling that feeble government was allowing the country to slide further into depression. To begin with, the banking system had to be made to work again, and Roosevelt did it by 'old-fashioned' means. On his second day in office he ordered the banks to close – all of them. On 9 March, Congress did as it was asked and passed the Emergency Banking Act, which extended government aid to the stronger banks and arranged for the re-organisation of the rest. On 10 March, the President asked Congress to slash government expenditure by $500 million, and Congress obliged with the Economy Act. On 13 March, he asked for the legalisation of beer and a quick end to Prohibition: again Congress did as it was asked and voted in the Beer Act.

Meanwhile, on 12 March, Roosevelt had spoken to the nation on radio in the first of his 'fireside chats',

saying there were no longer good reasons for withdrawing money from the banks and hoarding it: "I can assure you that it is safer to keep your money in a re-opened bank than under the mattress." And they believed him. When the banks opened in the following week, people deposited more money than they took out. They were prepared to believe almost anything he said, to accept anything he did, even those actions which could do nothing to lift them out of the slump – like cutting government spending.

But he was no dictator: there were limits to his power. Under the American Constitution, Congress was the law-maker and it was the President's job to carry out those laws. And alongside President and Congress were the nine justices of the Supreme Court with the power to crush any law of the Congress, any action taken by the President, if they judged it to be 'unconstitutional' – if they believed, for example, that such a law or action violated the rights of individual people or states as laid down in the Constitution.

Roosevelt had no 'Enabling Act', as Hitler did, to allow him to make his own will the law of the land. He began his work in 1933 with no special Presidential powers to meet the emergency; but he did start off with the good will of Congress, which was eager to work with him to translate his ideas for a 'New Deal' into law.

In his first '100 Days' as President, Roosevelt asked for and got from Congress an extraordinary burst of activity – making laws, voting money for new government programmes, setting up new agencies to carry them out. The first of the 'alphabetical agencies' appeared – the organisations through which Roosevelt would tackle the Depression – the CCC, the NRA, the AAA, the PWA, the TVA. In 1934 more agencies were set up, and yet more still in 1935. The list seemed endless – FERA, CWA, RA, FCA, WPA, NYA, REC, NLRB.

But for millions of Americans, who remembered all too vividly the dispiriting years when Hoover was President, these new agencies represented action instead of empty words. For many people they represented relief from starvation, the chance of a job and holding on to the family home: for some they meant the difference between life and death.

Acts and Agencies of the First New Deal

CCC
(Civilian Conservation Corps: 31 March 1933)

Organised activity for unemployed young men

Camps set up and organised by the army. In all 2,500,000 young men took part in the 1930s. As America's greatest re-foresters, they planted trees on eroded lands and on lands previously stripped of timber. They stocked rivers and lakes with one billion fish, built 30,000 wildlife shelters, dug canals, built networks of fire-lookout towers and roads through forests.

AAA
(Agricultural Adjustment Administration: 12 May 1933)

To control the growth of crops and livestock and guarantee farm prices

Farmers in each area decided what the total production of each crop should be and then set an average quota for each farmer. Farmers who agreed to participate in the scheme and who reduced their acreage under cultivation would benefit by (a) higher prices for what they produced, and (b) government subsidies.

FERA
(Federal Emergency Relief Administration: 12 May 1933)

Organisation to provide relief, quickly, to those in need — and, where possible, to provide some kind of public employment. Headed by Harry Hopkins, who would become Roosevelt's most influential adviser

It gave money to the states (on the basis of one dollar of federal money to every three dollars of state money spent on relief of poverty). It also had power to spend money on relief when states were reluctant to finance it.

Its lasting achievements included the construction or improvement of 5,000 public buildings and 7,000 bridges. It financed the clearing of streams and dredging of rivers. It organised nursery schools for children of poor families and helped one-and-a-half million adults to learn to read and write.

TVA
(Tennessee Valley Authority: 18 May 1933)

Government development of a poverty-stricken region which included lands in seven separate states (see map on page 133)

The Authority was given power to build dams to control floods and generate cheap hydro-electric power throughout the valley.

HOLC
(Home Owners' Loan Corporation: 13 June 1933)

To assist home-owners unable to keep up mortgage payments on their houses

Mortgages were re-financed by buying them from banks and offering home-owners long-range terms for repayment. This Agency would eventually help to re-finance one fifth of all mortgaged urban houses.

NRA
(National Recovery Administration: 16 June 1933)

To stabilise prices of manufactures and to improve the standing of organised labour

Management and workers in each industry were to agree on 'codes' of production and prices. Section 7A of the Act which set up the NRA said that codes should guarantee minimum wages, maximum hours of work and union rights of collective bargaining. Eventually, codes were drawn up by two-and-a-half million firms and covered twenty-two million workers. Firms which took part had the right to display the 'blue eagle' insignia: "In war, in the gloom of night attack, soldiers wear a bright badge on their shoulders to be sure that comrades do not fire on comrades. On that principle, those who cooperate in this program must know each other at a glance. That is why we have provided a badge of honor for this purpose, a simple design with a legend, 'We do our part', and I ask that all those who join with me shall display that badge prominently." – F. D. Roosevelt.

One of the NRA's great achievements was to wipe out child labour in the USA. But because many firms soon began to violate the codes, and because it was not a *compulsory* organisation, it failed in its two main purposes.

PWA
(Public Works Administration: 16 June 1933)

To provide employment on large-scale public works

Between 1933 and 1939 it built seventy per cent of the country's new schools; sixty-five per cent of new court-houses, city halls and sewage plants; and thirty-five per cent of new hospitals, as well as bridges, tunnels and harbour facilities. PWA funds were also used to build the aircraft carriers *Yorktown* and *Enterprise* as well as other warships for the navy. The Army Air Corps got grants for building over a hundred planes and fifty military airports.

FCA
(Farm Credit Administration: 16 June 1933)

To aid farmers unable to keep up mortgage payments on their land

In under two years one-fifth of all farm mortgages were re-financed with the help of government loans.

CWA
(Civil Works Administration: 8 November 1933)

Temporary work relief programme which paid wages, not relief doles

In the winter of 1933–34 it had over four million people on its payroll. It closed down in 1934. In its short life it built or improved 800,000 kilometres of roads, 40,000 schools, 3,500 playgrounds and athletics fields, and 1,000 airfields. It employed 50,000 teachers to keep rural schools open and to teach adults in cities.

Acts and Agencies of the Second New Deal

In 1933 Roosevelt had provided relief for the unemployed, particularly through FERA and CWA. It had been absolutely necessary. But in January 1935 the President declared:

"I am not willing that the vitality of our people be further sapped by the giving of cash, of market baskets, of a few hours of weekly work cutting grass, raking leaves or picking up papers in the public parks. ... The Federal Government must and shall quit this business of relief."

He asked for, and Congress passed, the Emergency Relief Appropriation Act of 1935. The Act provided a first instalment of $5,000,000,000 which the President was authorised to spend as he saw fit. Much of the money (and further sums voted later by Congress) was divided between existing agencies; but a vast new agency – the WPA – was formed to put as many unemployed people to *work* as quickly as possible.

WPA
(Works Progress Administration: 8 April 1935)

Harry Hopkins in charge

Its main achievement was to provide some kind of work for about three million of America's ten million unemployed. They were paid, on average, about $52 a month – barely enough to keep a family. Because of the haste to get the unemployed off relief and back to work, many WPA projects were "make-work assignments of scant value". But by 1941 the WPA had pumped $11,000,000,000 into the economy; had built or improved over 2,500 hospitals, 5,900 school buildings, 1,000 airport landing fields, and nearly 13,000 playgrounds. The WPA also ran three cultural organisations. The Federal Theatre Project employed actors, artistes, directors and craftsmen to produce plays, circuses and other entertainments throughout the land. In four years its audiences totalled thirty million people. The Federal Writers' Project produced about a thousand publications, including guides to cities and to the countryside. And the Federal Art Project gave work to unemployed artists to produce paintings and statues for public buildings, and to teach classes in painting, weaving, modelling, carving, etc.

Finally, the WPA ran an organisation aimed at solving the problems of youth unemployment: the NYA (National Youth Administration) gave part-time work to 600,000 college students and 1,500,000 high-school pupils in the seven years of its existence. It also aided 2,600,000 youths who had left school but had not gone on to college.

RA (replaced by FSA)
(Resettlement Administration: 1 May 1935)

Attempted to deal with the problem of rural poverty

It aimed to give poverty-stricken farmers and share-croppers new starts on good land. It planned to resettle 500,000 families, but, mainly because of shortage of funds, resettled fewer than 5,000.

The agency would be replaced in 1937 by the FSA (Farm Security Administration) which granted long-term, low-interest loans to enable poor farmers to buy family-sized holdings, and which also set up clean, well-run camps for migrant workers and their families.

REA

(Rural Electrification Administration: 11 May 1935)

Attempted to bring electricity to the countryside

In 1932, nine out of every ten American farms were without electricity. The federal government now gave loans to private power companies to encourage them to run their lines out to the farms. If the companies refused, the government was willing to lend money to farmers' cooperatives instead. By 1941, four out of every ten American farms had electricity.

NLRB

(National Labour Relations Board)

Set up by the Wagner Act of 5 July 1935

The Act protected workers who wanted to bargain collectively with employers for better wages and conditions of work. The NLRB was set up to prevent management practices such as sacking workers because they were members of trade unions, or setting up employer-dominated company unions.

Social Security Act: 14 August 1935

The start of the American 'welfare state'

The Act was passed in August 1935. It set up a national system of old-age pensions for most employees. At sixty-five workers would get pensions financed by taxes on their wages and on their employers. The rate of benefit would vary according to what they earned during their working lives. The government would start to pay pensions in 1940.

The federal government also offered to share equally with the states the cost of the care of people over sixty-five who couldn't take part in the pensions scheme; to cooperate with states in a system of unemployment insurance; and to help states with the care of dependent

mothers and children, the crippled and the blind.

Achievements and Failures

What did it all add up to? Well, first it was the most extraordinary burst of law-making in American history; and those laws gave the federal government powers to affect every aspect of American life. President and Congress had once seemed remote from the people. Now it was difficult, if not impossible, to avoid the doings of a national government whose agencies directly affected how millions of people earned or were given their daily bread, whether they held on to their homes or farms, whether their young children got an education and a hot lunch, whether their boys and girls fresh from school or college were provided with a job to do.

For many people the 'alphabetical agencies' were far from a joke: they seemed like a godsend. Former President Hoover could make wisecracks about FERA, CWA and the rest, but then he hadn't been hungry in the winter of 1933–34. Nor had he been in danger of losing his home by failing to keep up the payments on a mortgage. Hundreds of thousands of American citizens had felt that chilling fear and they took a very different attitude to Roosevelt's 'New Deal'.

Dear Mr. President,
This is just to tell you that everything is all right now. The man you sent found our house all right, and we went down to the bank with him and the mortgage can go on for a while longer. You remember I wrote you about losing the furniture too. Well, your man got it back for us. I never heard of a President like you.

Nor had anybody else. Roosevelt received between 5,000 and 8,000 letters a day. He and his staff were available, accessible to the people. One of his first orders as President had been that people in distress who telephoned the White House should never be cut off: someone must be found to talk to them about their problems. Roosevelt himself explained the programme of the New Deal to the people on radio, in his 'fireside chats', when he talked "like a father discussing public affairs with his family in the living room". He had a growing 'family': between 1930 and 1940 the number of American households with wireless sets rose from twelve million to twenty-eight million.

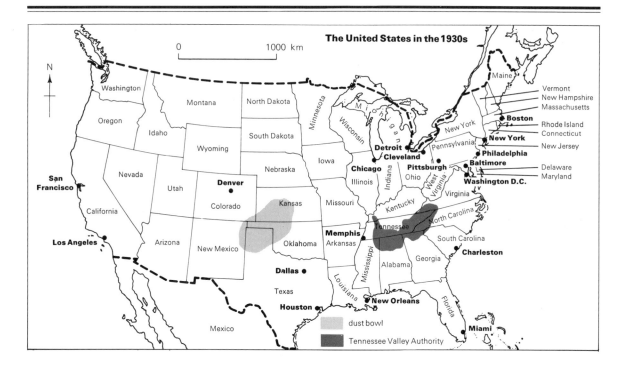

The United States in the 1930s

0   1000 km

dust bowl

Tennessee Valley Authority

Some people admired Roosevelt to the point of adoration: "when he locked his [leg] braces and appeared in public, people literally reached out to touch the hem of his cape". One Congressman compared him to Jesus Christ, and "in a poll among New York schoolchildren God ran a poor second to FDR". One working man, probably with the Wagner Act in mind, expressed his admiration for the President less reverently: "Mr. Roosevelt is the only man we ever had in the White House who would understand that my boss is a sonofabitch."

Unemployment in the USA, 1933–36

Year	Numbers of unemployed	Unemployed as % of the labour force
1933	12,830,000	24·9
1934	11,340,000	21·7
1935	10,610,000	20·1
1936	9,030,000	16·9

These figures begin to tell another part of the story. Four years after Roosevelt was elected President, nine million Americans were still out of a job. The agencies had worked no miracles for them: they remained on relief, many of them living in states that were unwilling to spend much on unemployment assistance. The

Social Security Act of 1935 had laid down no national rates of benefit for people in need – for the unemployed or for the 'unemployables' – nor had it set up an insurance scheme for workers who lost their jobs because of illness. Roosevelt's social security programme was little more than a promise of 'jam tomorrow'. Nor did his Works Progress Administration substitute jobs in place of relief for most of the nation's unemployed: it affected only a large minority of them – roughly about a third.

In the countryside, the AAA had got off to an unpopular start with its policy of destroying crops and livestock in an attempt to keep up agricultural prices. In 1933 vast amounts of cotton were ploughed back into the earth, and six million piglets and 200,000 sows were slaughtered – and that in a land where the poor were desperately short of both clothing and food. Even more serious was one side-effect of the AAA's policy of persuading farmers to reduce the acreage under cultivation: many tenants and share-croppers were simply driven off the land.

Between 1933 and 1935 many of the poorer people of the American countryside must have wondered whether the New Deal wasn't, in fact, a 'raw deal'. And to cap their misfortune, drought and wind turned a vast area of land into a 'Dust Bowl'.

Many of the small tenant-farmers, like the Joad

family in John Steinbeck's novel *The Grapes of Wrath* (published in 1939), fled with their belongings west to California. They went from Texas, Kansas, Colorado, Oklahoma, lured by offers of work at decent rates of pay. They were the 'Okies', and Steinbeck described how they were welcomed into a land of plenty:

"In the West there was panic when the migrants multiplied on the highways. Men of property were terrified for their property. Men who had never been hungry saw the eyes of the hungry.... And the men of the towns and of the soft suburban country gathered to defend themselves.... They said: These goddamned Okies are dirty and ignorant. They're degenerate, sexual maniacs. These goddamned Okies are thieves. They'll steal anything....

... they formed units, squads and armed them – armed them with clubs, with gas, with guns. We own the country ... And the men who were armed did not own the land, but they thought they did. And the clerks who drilled at night owned nothing, and the little storekeepers possessed only a drawerful of debts. But even a debt is something, even a job is something. The clerk thought: I get fifteen dollars a week. S'pose a goddamn Okie would work for twelve? ...

And the migrants streamed in on the highways and their hunger was in their eyes, and their need was in their eyes.... When there was work for a man, ten men fought for it – fought with a low wage. If that fella'll work for thirty cents, I'll work for twenty-five.

If he'll take twenty-five, I'll do it for twenty.

No, me, I'm hungry. I'll work for fifteen. I'll work for food. The kids. You ought to see them. Little boils, like, comin' out, an' they can't run aroun'. Give 'em some windfall fruit, an' they bloated up. Me, I'll work for a little piece of meat.

And this was good, for wages went down and prices stayed up."

As you saw on page 121, the RA, and later tha FSA, tried to help some of these people. But New Deal aid to the 'Okies' was a mere drop of government goodwill into an ocean of misery.

Opponents of the New Deal

There were those who believed the New Deal went too far and spent too much in the interests of people who wouldn't try to stand on their own two feet.

There were others who believed it didn't go half far enough to provide solutions to America's economic problems and glaring social inequalities. And there were millions of Americans, from the desperate 'Okies' in the West to the haggard victims of long-term unemployment in the eastern cities, who *knew* that the New Deal was not enough: they proved it by the wretchedness of their lives. Many of them kept their early faith in Roosevelt, convinced that he would do more for them. Others were tempted away by 'messiahs' who preached the need for radical changes throughout American society. Of the three 'messiahs' who threatened to wrench the support of ordinary Americans away from Roosevelt, one was a Catholic priest (Father Charles Coughlin), and one was a country doctor (Francis Townsend). The third was a spectacularly ambitious Senator from Louisiana – Huey 'Kingfish' Long, who declared:

"All the people of America have been invited to a barbecue. God invited us all to come and eat and drink all we wanted. He smiled on our land and we grew crops of plenty to eat and wear.

He showed us the earth, the iron and other things to make anything we wanted. He unfolded to us the secrets of science so that our work might be easy. God called: 'Come to my feast'. Then what happened? Rockefeller, Morgan and their crowd stepped up and took enough for 120,000,000 people and left only enough for 5,000,000, for all the 125,000,000 to eat. And so many millions must go hungry and without these good things God gave us unless we call on them to put some of it back.

I call on you to organise Share Our Wealth societies."

Long had started his national political career as a supporter of Roosevelt. In January 1934, disappointed by the New Deal, he set up his own 'Share Our Wealth' movement. By early 1935 he claimed it had over 27,000 branches and a mailing-list of 7,500,000 people. Maybe it had, maybe it hadn't (Long was never a modest man), but the Senator's political programme certainly appealed to very large numbers of poor people. He proposed to redistribute wealth: to take away the fortunes of the very rich (like the Rockefellers and the Morgans) and to give to every family enough money to buy a house, a car and a radio. All the old people would get pensions, there would be a national minimum wage and a shorter working week. And for those people who said that it all sounded marvellous but they didn't understand how such a share-out of the nation's wealth could be achieved, Long had a simple answer: "You don't have to. Just shut your damned eyes and believe it. That's all."

There were enough Americans willing to shut their eyes (after all, it felt better than keeping them open on familiar scenes of poverty) to make the 'Kingfish' a powerful figure in the land. But in September 1935 their dream came to an abrupt end when Long was assassinated. 'Share Our Wealth', the movement he had created to sweep him into the White House, died with him.

Like Huey Long, Father Charles Coughlin started off as a Roosevelt supporter. Like the President himself, Coughlin had a talent for broadcasting – only he was even more successful than Roosevelt. By 1934 he had the largest regular radio audience in the world, and he received more letters than any other person in the USA. Gradually he moved away from support of the New Deal into outright opposition, and in November 1934 formed his own 'National Union for Social Justice', which offered Americans a political programme strikingly similar to Italian Fascism – it was violently anti-communist, anti-trade union and anti-freedom of speech.

The historian William Manchester has described Coughlin as "exploiting aspects of the national character which were then but little understood: American innocence, the nation's yearning for simple solutions, ... and the carnival instinct for collecting shiny junk". In return for sending him money, Coughlin's supporters received a tiny chrome-plated crucifix which, the Radio Priest assured them, had "touched a relic of [Christ's] True Cross".

In the 1936 Presidential election, Coughlin and others put forward William Lemke as the candidate of the 'Union Party'. He polled fewer than a million votes. Coughlin dropped Lemke and moved further to the Right as a pedlar of political hate. He became openly anti-Semitic, referring to the New Deal as the "Jew Deal"; and his 'platoons' beat up Jews in the streets of American cities. He was a self-styled 'messiah' whose vision was, in the end, empty of anything but vicious intolerance. "When we get through with the Jews in America", he proclaimed in 1937, "they'll think the treatment they received in Germany was nothing!"

If Coughlin stood out as the fascist who attracted most support in the USA in the 1930s, Dr. Francis Townsend was, quite simply, unique. He appealed to people whom most politicians ignored – the old – and he organised them into a political crusade. In 1934 he set up an organisation which sounded like a weak joke, 'Old Age Revolving Pensions, Limited', through which he proposed to pay $200 a month to every citizen over the age of sixty, provided that he or she retired from work and promised to spend every last cent of his or her 'pension' within the month – whereupon he or she would get another $200. The money for the scheme was to come from a two per cent tax on business transactions, which would be paid into a "revolving fund".

The scheme looked impractical, unworkable, daft; but it was supported by many otherwise sensible people. It appealed to a belief that America still had immense wealth which, somehow, all her citizens could tap. It put forward the far from ridiculous notion that if all the old folk retired from work, there would be more jobs for the young.

In 1935 America's old people finally got their cut of the New Deal – the Social Security Act introduced old-age pensions, but not for all. Because the new federal scheme left vast numbers of elderly Americans *without* pensions, they joined Townsend's movement in their millions. But in 1936 'Old Age Revolving Pensions, Limited' fell apart as a political organisation after Townsend's partner, Robert Clements, was found to have been revolving some of the funds into his own pocket. In the Presidential election Townsend, like Coughlin, supported Lemke; but to his credit he denounced the fascists who were trying to use the 'Union Party' for their own ends. Gradually, the man who had been called "the outstanding political sensation" of 1935 faded away as a national political figure.

The Other Opposition

Long, Coughlin and Townsend all challenged Roosevelt's influence over the broad mass of the American people. But more important, the popularity of their movements clearly revealed that many citizens were not satisfied with the President's package of New Deal reforms.

It was easy to understand why the New Deal was opposed by many employers, bankers and Republican politicians. They dismissed 'relief' as a waste of taxpayers' money and saw government regulation of industry as a sure sign that communists were running the White House. Good old President Coolidge (see Chapter 21, page 83) had declared that "the business of America is business", and these men believed that no damn fool of a Democratic President had any business sticking his interfering nose in it. When he did interfere – especially when he appeared to support organised labour against employers – some of them were almost incoherent with rage.

Among those who kept their tempers were some whose attacks on "that man" in the White House were revealing as well as funny. This one was printed on the back of business cards:

"Four thousand years ago Moses said to his people: 'pick up your shovels, mount your asses, load your camels, and ride to the Promised Land.'

Four thousand years later Mr. Roosevelt said to HIS people: 'Throw down your shovels, sit on your asses, light up a Camel:* THIS IS the Promised Land.'"

The following jibe against FDR and all his works began with definitions of some of the other 'isms' of the 1930s:

"SOCIALISM – If you own two cows you give one to your neighbour. COMMUNISM – You give both cows to the government and the government gives you back some of the milk. FASCISM – You keep the cows but give the milk to the government, which sells some of it back to you. NEW DEALISM – You shoot both cows and milk the government."

However, most of the opposition from business men and bankers was anything but funny. Few of them would have recommended, as Father Coughlin did, that the President should be removed by "the use of bullets"; but just as few would have shed any tears over his grave. Roosevelt recognised their feelings and in his 1936 campaign for re-election he lashed back at his enemies:

"... business and financial monopoly, speculation, reckless banking ... organised money.... Never before in all our history have these forces been so united against one candidate as they stand today. They are unanimous in their hate for me – and I welcome their

* Camel – a brand of American cigarette.

hatred. ... I should like to have it said of my first administration that in it the forces of selfishness and of lust for power met their match. I should like to have it said of my second administration that in it these forces met their master!"

But well before that time President Roosevelt had met *his* master – the Supreme Court of the United States of America. In May 1935, in what became known as the "sick chicken" case, the nine justices of the Supreme Court struck down the NRA (National Recovery Administration) and threatened the rest of the New Deal. A firm which bought and sold poultry, Schechter Brothers, had been convicted of breaking an NRA 'code' by selling diseased chickens and not abiding by regulations on workers' wages and hours of work. The justices said that the power to prescribe 'codes' of employment belonged to Congress, not to the President and his agencies. They also ruled that the federal government had no authority to regulate working conditions in the Schechter Brothers' firm, since that was the business of the state in which the firm sold putrid poultry to its unfortunate customers. The "sick chickens" would stink in Roosevelt's nostrils for a long time to come.

President Again

In November 1936 Roosevelt won the Presidential election by a landslide: 27,700,000 votes to Republican Alf Landon's 16,600,000. William Lemke was simply buried in the avalanche. Despite Coughlin and Townsend, despite the opposition of "organised money", Roosevelt had triumphed. America prepared for another '100 Days', for a burst of reforms even more radical than those of 1933 to 1935. Instead, in 1937, the New Deal stopped dead in its tracks. Roosevelt asked Congress not for laws to aid the unemployed and the poor, but for reform of the Supreme Court.

According to the President, the Court was getting behind with its work and its justices were too old. He therefore recommended that if a justice didn't resign six months after his seventieth birthday, the President should be allowed to appoint an extra justice to the Court – up to a total of six extra justices in all.

His plan was a sham. What Roosevelt wanted was to 'pack' the Court with justices who would not oppose him. The Court knew it, Congress knew it, and most of the people knew it. The Court was the defender of the Constitution, the protector of the people against

Presidents who wished to be tyrants. Even if Roosevelt didn't want to be a dictator, what guarantee could he give that he wouldn't become one if the Supreme Court was packed by 'all the President's men'?

Roosevelt's case for reforming the Court lost any force it might once have had when in March and April 1937 the Court reversed the decision of the Schechter case; and in May it declared that old-age pensions and unemployment insurance, as set up by the Social Security Act of 1935, were *constitutional*. The New Deal was safe from destruction by a conservative Court, and Roosevelt was persuaded to abandon his plan. But the damage had been done. The Democratic Party had torn itself apart over the issue; and an angry Congress would now resist making more New Deal reforms into law.

Sit-downs and Recession

Back in 1935 militant trade unionists had formed the Committee for Industrial Organisation (CIO), whose aim was the formation of single unions for each major industry in America to bring pressure to bear on employers for higher wages and better working conditions. The CIO and its members backed Roosevelt in the 1936 election – and they gave him $770,000 to help pay for his campaign, as well as their votes. When Roosevelt was re-elected, the trade unionists decided the time was ripe for taking on their most powerful enemies, America's biggest industrial corporations – US Steel, the Ford Motor Company, General Motors, Firestone Tire and Rubber, General Electric, American Woolen, and the rest of the giants. Walk-out strikes were no longer effective enough so trade unionists organised 'sit-downs', occupations of factories by strikers. Company bosses up and down the country responded by taking new employees on their payrolls – strike-breakers. A striker in a General Motors factory in Flint described one of the inevitable clashes:

"A hundred of us started walking through the plant calling a sit-down. The company police and thugs sprung up from nowhere. They kept them shut in the employment office and sprung them loose on us. In a moment there was fighting everywhere. Fighters were rolling on the floor. They had clubs and we were un-armed. They starting shooting off tear gas. I saw one fellow hit on the head and when he swung backwards he cut his head on the machinery. He started to stagger out. Two of the thugs knocked him down again. I let go on a couple of thugs. You kind of go crazy when you see thugs beating up men you know."

Some employers, notably Henry Ford, were prepared to fight to their last hired hoodlum, but most gave in rather than risk pitched battles in factories stuffed with expensive machinery. By 1938 it was clear that the trade unionists had come out on top, but it was far from a complete victory of the workers against the bosses: by 1940 only twenty-eight per cent of America's non-agricultural workers were members of trade unions. Even so, it was a vital battle to have won and one in which Roosevelt indirectly helped the workers by refusing to use force to eject sit-down strikers.

But if 1937 was a good year for the organisers of industrial unions, it meant disaster for millions of others. In June Roosevelt, worried about inflation, cut government spending on two of his major relief agencies, the WPA and the PWA. At the same time the federal government was taking large sums of money from people in new social security taxes. This meant that demand for goods went down, which put more and more people out of work. America lurched back into the darkness of the worst Depression years.

In April 1938 Roosevelt altered course. Instead of cutting spending further, he asked Congress for huge funds with which to face the new emergency. Congress obliged, with nearly $1,000,000,000 for the PWA and $1,400,000,000 for the WPA; and slowly the economy began to recover.

Over in Germany, the Nazis crowed gleefully that the New Deal had failed and that its failure was one more proof that democratic governments could not cope with economic depression. In Washington DC Roosevelt believed the New Deal had not failed, that it had bought Americans time to think out ways of coming to grips with profound economic and social problems. He knew that the events of 1937 and 1938 had severely harmed his own reputation; that the New Deal was beginning to look old and tarnished. No American had ever been elected President three times. It was unlikely that he would break that record.

27 Stalin and the Modernisation of Russia

Hammer and Sickle

In an extraordinary period of ten years, between 1928 and 1938, Joseph Stalin forced the people of the Soviet Union through the most rapid and far-reaching changes in their ways of life that any people in history had ever been made to accept and take part in. But before we can understand what Stalin did to the Soviet Union and why, we have to grasp some of the features of that country as it was before he came to power.

Back in 1925 (a date well within the lifetimes of some of your grandparents) the country had been ruled by Communists for only eight years. In the first three of those eight years, Russia had been grievously mutilated by a vicious civil war and her people had spent the next five years picking up the pieces of their shattered lives. Lenin's New Economic Policy (see Chapter 13, page 56), which in 1921 allowed private trade and small-scale private industry to start up again, was an admission that together the Great War and the civil war had reduced the Russian economy to a shambles. There was little to suggest that in the rubble there were the makings of a thrusting, industrialised super-power.

In the vastness of the new USSR there were few great cities: the land east of the Ural Mountains was, for the most part, an under-populated wilderness. Russia's rivers flowed unused or under-used to the seas; and enormous mineral deposits lay untouched underground. There were railways – even from Leningrad to Vladivostock – but other modern forms of transport were rarely to be seen. In 1925, in the whole of the Soviet Union, there were 7,448 cars, 5,500 lorries, and just 263 buses!

Just pause for a moment to think about that emblem of the new Communist state. The hammer was the symbol of the industrial workers, the proletariat; and the sickle represented those who worked on the land: together they would forge a new society of equals, a new prosperity in which all would share. But if we used those symbols to represent the real Russia of 1925, and not the dream, the sickle would be a great deal larger than the hammer: fewer than twenty out of every hundred people lived in towns or cities. Apart from a few nomads, the rest were peasants – 120 million of them – and to a fervent Communist they felt like the dead weight of Russian history: conservative, narrow-minded and superstitious; working from sunrise to sunset in the summer, and spending the long Russian winter on top of the stoves in their wretched hovels, counting fleas.

In contrast, we can make a less one-sided generalisation. Most peasants were desperately poor, and many farmed the land as if the twentieth century had not yet begun. As late as 1928, five-and-a-half million families still broke the earth with a *wooden* plough; half the grain harvest was reaped by scythes and sickles; and forty per cent of the crop was threshed with flails.

There were, of course, the richer peasants, the *kulaks*, who owned farm machinery, employed other peasants or labourers, and produced surplus food to sell to the towns. Some of them acted as the local moneylenders – and the very word *kulak*, which meant 'fist', was originally a term of abuse for peasants who made loans at high rates of interest. The *kulaks* were hated by some peasants and envied by more. They were the local boys who had made good – though it was a very poor 'good' by Western standards: most of them owned no more than two cows and two horses and employed no more than one labourer, and even then for only a few months in the year.

Left and Right

Somehow the Communist Party had to make the hammer and the sickle work together. But as agriculture recovered from the civil war more quickly than industry, so food prices went down and the prices of manufactured goods continued to go up. Peasants had no incentive to sell their surplus food to the towns, so they either ate it themselves, fed it to their animals or kept it in store. It seemed that if the peasants could not get the manufactured goods they wanted from the towns at reasonable prices, then the towns could starve. Yet many Communists believed that to develop the production of such things as clothing, footwear and kitchen utensils, at the expense of heavy industries (such as coal, oil, iron and steel), would be a suicidal policy. Their new state *had* to be made stronger to resist armed attacks which might soon come from the capitalist nations of Western Europe.

Within the Party two groups emerged, each with its own approach to the problem. The moderates (later to be damned as "right-wing deviationists") were led by Bukharin and Rykov, and they believed it essential to continue with Lenin's NEP, perhaps for as long as twenty years. They thought that any attempt to force the peasants to part with their surplus crops would lead to rebellion in the countryside and starvation in the towns. Communism could not be built in the Soviet Union in a fortnight or six months, but only at a pace which 120 million peasants would accept.

The 'Left Opposition' was impatient. Its leading figures included Trotsky, Preobrazhensky and (from 1925) Zinoviev and Kamenev; and they believed that Russia must be industrialised more rapidly than the NEP would allow. They were convinced that the capitalist nations would try to destroy the new Communist state; so the safety and development of the Soviet Union depended first and foremost on the international revolutionary movement bringing communists to power in the advanced countries of the West. They insisted that, in the meantime, Russia could not afford to wait for the NEP to create enough wealth to pay for massive investments in heavy industry. The Party must take the lead by mobilising shock troops, groups of dedicated Communists, to build new factories, railways and canals, and sink new mines. But they offered no real solution to the basic problem of how to persuade the peasants to provide the grain needed for export and to feed the towns.

Where did Stalin stand in all this? Between 1923 and 1927 he supported the moderates because he needed their support to defeat his chief rivals for supreme power – most of whom, like Trotsky, were members of the Left Opposition. Stalin was considered by most people in the Party a rather dull committee man – from 1921 he was General Secretary of the Party Central Committee, member of the Politburo, the Party's policy making body, and member of the Orgburo, which ran the Party organisation. What they didn't realise was that dull bureaucrats are capable of quietly acquiring a great deal of power for themselves. As General Secretary of the Party Central Committee, Stalin was able to appoint his supporters as full-time Party officials throughout the country. This meant that he could easily call on his supporters to vote against Trotsky's schemes. At public meetings, for example in factories, he instructed his yes-men to boo and shout down Trotsky and his followers. In the Politburo and in meetings of the Party Central Committee, Stalin's creatures made sure that Trotsky's proposals were always rejected.

Trotsky had once been second only to Lenin in the Party leadership. He was a hero of the Revolution, the founder of the Red Army, Commissar for War. But as Stalin's control of the Party increased, so Trotsky's power and prestige declined. In 1925 he was forced to give up his post as Commissar. In 1927, along with Kamenev and Zinoviev, he was removed from the Politburo and then expelled from the Party. A year later he was forced into exile abroad. Now Stalin was able to push the Soviet Union further to the left than the Left Opposition had ever dared to propose, but under a different slogan. Trotsky had spoken of Russia as the headquarters of "International Socialism": Stalin was going to industrialise the USSR under the banner of "Socialism in One Country".

The Plan

From the earliest days the Russian Communists had believed in planning. As soon as they came to power, the Bolsheviks had set up VSNKH (the Supreme Council of National Economy) (see page 55). In 1921 *Gosplan* (the State Planning Commission) had been created as a kind of board of management for all the major industries and public services. The work of VSNKH and *Gosplan* was to estimate the production and profits likely to be made by different sections of agriculture and industry and to decide the best ways of increasing them.

In 1927 they were asked to do something different. There was to be an "all-union plan, which ... would facilitate the maximum development of economic regions on the basis of their specialisations, ... and the maximum utilisation of their resources for the purpose of industrialisation of the country" – a plan not to guide but to force through economic change. When the Plan was published in 1929 it was clear that the government of the Soviet Union had abandoned planning in the old sense. The first Five-Year Plan was a blue-print for a *command economy*: it was a list of targets for industries, power supplies and transport; targets which were not just expected but demanded.

Under Joseph Stalin plans would now have the force of government orders. A look at the chart which follows will tell you that considerable force would be needed. The first column records what was actually produced in the year 1927–28; the second column shows what the government wanted to achieve by 1933; and the third column reveals what was called the "optimal variant" – or, in everyday language, the Communist Party's wildest dreams.

Some industrial targets in the first Five-Year Plan

Industry	1927–28	Target for 1933	'Optimal variant'
Electricity *(milliard kWh)*	5·05	17·0	22·0
Coal *(million tonnes)*	35·4	68·0	75·0
Oil *(million tonnes)*	11·7	19·0	22·0
Pig-iron *(million tonnes)*	3·3	8·0	10·0
Steel *(million tonnes)*	4·0	8·3	10·4

To come within reach of even the lower targets of the Plan would require immense efforts from the Russian people. It would also require answers to be given to the questions which had been raised earlier in the twenties by Bukharin and Trotsky about the relationships between the industrial hammer and the peasant sickle. For example, how could the government guarantee supplies of food to the towns if they developed heavy industries at the expense of those producing goods for the peasants to buy? How could the government buy vital foreign-made machinery if the peasants would not release enough grain to sell abroad? And how could the targets of the Plan be met unless there was an enormous increase in the numbers of industrial workers? The stock answer to those questions was that the peasants should be persuaded gradually to join their small plots of land together to make farms large enough to use modern machinery and advanced agricultural techniques. Production would increase; and since fewer farm-workers would be needed, the surplus labour could be released for work

in industry. In 1927 Stalin had publicly given his support to the idea:

"The way out is to unite the small and dwarf peasant farms gradually but surely, not by pressure but by example and persuasion, into large farms based on common, cooperative, collective cultivation of the land ... there is no other way out."

But that was before the first Five-Year Plan had made it clear that methods of gradual persuasion had been abandoned in the Soviet Union. In late 1929 Stalin announced his unexpected and brutal answer to all the questions about the peasants: they were to be 'collectivised' at once.

Collectives and Kulaks

But what was 'collectivisation'? What was a *kolkhoz* (collective farm)? That was the curious thing about this farming revolution that happened slap-bang in the middle of the Plan: no-one had prepared for it; no army of experts had worked out what to do with 120 million bewildered peasants.

As the orders were sent to local party leaders to carry out collectivisation, only one thing was clear: the peasants of a village must pool their land and their equipment and work in future under the orders of a collective farm committee over which the Party would keep a tight control. But no other details were given: it was left unclear whether a collective should pay its workers 'by eaters' (according to the number of mouths in a worker's family), according to the work they did, or according to the tools they contributed. In some areas peasants were allowed to keep their livestock: in others, the cows, pigs, sheep, goats, horses and chickens were all collectivised. And the same was true of the peasants' small vegetable plots.

In February 1930 it was announced that half the peasant population of the Soviet Union had joined collective farms. Just think what that meant: sixty million people uprooted and re-settled in less than two months! And then suddenly Stalin put a stop to it. He declared that on the collectives "small vegetable gardens, small orchards, the dwelling houses, some of the dairy cattle, small livestock, poultry, etc. are *not socialised*". Well, well, well! – if the cows were allowed to leave the collectives, maybe the peasants were too. Some villagers decided to break up the collectives, and to their astonishment no-one stopped them (except in key grain-producing areas such as the Ukraine). By June half the collectivised peasants had withdrawn. And Stalin had got what he wanted – with the Party officials off their backs, the peasants got on with the vital spring sowing of Russia's crops.

It was only a temporary halt. When the harvest was in, collectivisation started up again. By July 1931, fifty-three per cent of all peasant families were on collective farms; by July 1932, sixty-two per cent. Some peasants resisted as best they could, determined to hand nothing over to the local Party tyrants. In his novel *The Soil Upturned*, Mikhail Sholokov described what happened in just one village:

"Stock was slaughtered every night in Gremyachy Log. Hardly had dusk fallen when the muffled, short bleats of sheep, the death-squeals of pigs, or the lowing of calves could be heard. Both those who had joined the *kolkhoz* and individual farmers killed their stock. Bulls, sheep, pigs, even cows were slaughtered, as well as calves for breeding. The horned stock of Gremyachy was halved in two nights. The dogs began to drag entrails about the village; cellars and barns were filled with meat ... 'Kill, it's not ours any more ...' 'Kill, they'll take it for meat anyway ...' 'Kill, you won't get meat in the *kolkhoz* ...' crept the insidious rumours. And they killed ..."

And the government took away from the peasants more grain than ever to feed the towns and to sell in exchange for foreign currencies. You can see below the effects of collectivisation on grain production, and imagine the effects of the government biting into harvest yields with its "state grain procurements".

Grain harvests and procurements
(in millions of tonnes)

	1928	1929	1930	1931	1932	1933
Grain harvest	73·3	71·7	83·5	69·5	69·6	68·4
State grain procurements	10·8	16·1	22·1	22·8	18·5	22·6

In places the chaos caused by collectivisation, the smaller harvests (except for that of 1930) and savage state procurements led to famine. Many peasants could not feed themselves, let alone save the seed for next year's sowing or feed their animals. You have already read something of a massive butchery of animals in Russia's villages. You can now see the effects of that

great blood-letting and of the shortage of fodder on Russia's livestock population.

Livestock
(million head)

	1928	1929	1930	1931	1932	1933
Cattle	70·5	67·1	52·5	47·9	40·7	38·4
Pigs	26·0	20·4	13·6	14·4	11·6	12·1
Sheep and goats	146·7	147·0	108·8	77·7	52·1	50·2

If the ways of life of most of Russia's peasants were brutally and permanently changed by collectivisation, the *kulaks* suffered worse: they were obliterated. In a speech in December 1929 Stalin had described the fate he had in store for those better-off peasants whose 'wealth' we described on page 128:

"We have passed from the policy of restricting the exploiting tendencies of the *kulaks* to the policy of eliminating the *kulaks* as a class. . . . To launch an offensive against the *kulaks* means that we must prepare for it and then strike at the *kulaks*, strike so hard as to prevent them from rising to their feet again. . . ."

Stalin's language was unmistakable. It was a declaration of war against a million Russian families. To those who argued that the *kulaks* should be allowed to enter the collectives, Stalin's answer was firm: "Of course not, for they are sworn enemies of the collective farm movement."

The "enemies" were divided into three categories. Those described as "actively hostile" to the government were handed over to the OGPU (the political police) and put in concentration camps, while their families were deported to the north, the Far East and Siberia. The wealthiest were also rounded up and deported. The third category, the poorer *kulaks*, were allowed to stay in their own regions but given the poorest land to farm and required to hand over to the state large quantities of grain and to pay very high taxes. If they failed to deliver their produce or their taxes, they were deported. In reality, it didn't seem to make much difference which category you were in. According to the historian Alec Nove, "it is quite probable that in the end all the persons described as *kulaks* were in fact deported".

You will notice that Professor Nove is not *certain* about the fate of all the *kulaks*. No-one can be: we do not have all the facts. Deportation must have been, in most cases, a sentence of death, by cold or by hunger, in forced-labour camps where the *kulaks* helped to build, among other things, new industrial cities. Professor Nove has calculated that in 1929 there were about four-and-a-half million people in *kulak* families. A French historian, Professor Sorlin, has estimated that three million of them died as a result of deportation. We can only guess at what happened to the other one-and-a-half million – and our guesses can hardly be anything but gloomy.

The *kulaks* performed a last service for their country: the treatment dealt out to them frightened other, poorer peasants 'voluntarily' into Stalin's collectives. The sickles had been forced into a new relationship with the hammers of the proletariat. Watched over in the collectives by Party officials and police, their task was now to pay for the industrialisation of the Soviet Union. They would pay in taxes and in the proportions of the crops the state took from them. The *kulaks*, who would not have bent easily, had simply been broken and discarded.

The Plan and the People

On page 130 we described some of the targets set for various industries in the first Five-Year Plan. Let us now look at what was actually achieved by 1932. (You could, at this stage, make your own chart or block graph to record the differences between the planners' targets and actual outputs.)

Some industrial production figures in 1932, at the end of the first Five-Year Plan

Electricity *(milliard kWh)*	13·4
Coal *(million tonnes)*	64·3
Oil *(million tonnes)*	21·4
Pig-iron *(million tonnes)*	6·2
Steel *(million tonnes)*	5·9

It will not have taken you long to work out that only one of those industries, oil, reached its target. But before you are tempted to write off the Plan as a failure, consider these facts. Late in 1929 it had been decided to 'complete' the Five-Year Plan in a little over four

years. In that short time the output of electricity had been more than doubled, while the output of oil, coal and pig-iron had all been nearly doubled. And in 1932 there were factories and power stations still being built, and oil-wells and mine-shafts being sunk, which would all pay off handsomely in the future. Consider also that much of the work had been done by uneducated, and often illiterate, peasants who had been recruited or had fled in terror from the collectivised countryside – men and women who had never seen an electric light before, let alone a lathe, a conveyor belt or a furnace.

The planners had expected to add an extra 800,000 workers to an industrial labour force of just over three million. Instead, by 1932, there were nearly six-and-a-half million people employed in large-scale industries. It was a sharp contrast to what was happening in the depressed capitalist countries of the West, but it brought its own fearsome problems of how to feed, how to clothe and how to house vast numbers of new industrial workers and their families. You have already seen that the peasants were made to 'solve' the food supply problem: by the end of 1929 the allocation of that food to the people in the towns was being made through a system of rationing. And gradually rationing was applied to manufactured consumer goods as well as to food, which meant, in many cases, that if you needed a new coat or a pair of boots, you didn't get them. The footwear and clothing industries came a long way down Stalin's list of priorities.

Altogether, something like thirteen million men, women and children were added to the populations of the USSR's towns and cities in the period of the first Five-Year Plan. Many were brought to established cities in the western and central regions, cities such as Moscow, Leningrad, Kazan and Gorki (the new name of Nizhni Novgorod). Others volunteered or were forced to move to the Urals, to Siberia, to the Far East, where the first task was to build the new industrial towns they were to work in – towns like Magnitogorsk, Karaganda and Stalinsk.

In the old cities there was appalling overcrowding, with several families sharing one room and kitchen-space in apartment-buildings that came to look more like warrens than living quarters. And Professor Sorlin has described what a typical new town (in this case Stalino, in the west) looked like:

". . . endless streets laid out on the grid pattern ran right up to the mine shafts; the persistent smell of coal and smoke fouled the air; outside the city centre, there were no pavements and hardly any roads, only huge avenues – which were too wide and usually untarred – where carts and trucks raised clouds of dust. The new quarters were almost always ugly. ... housing was still extremely scarce; a family of five with two rooms considered itself fortunate. ... The government erected two or three prominent public buildings in each city – a university, a 'palace of culture' and a department store – and, having made this bow to the concept of public, proletarian luxury, it finished off with the cheapest possible housing."

Everywhere the impression was one of haste, of building tomorrow today and never mind the petty comforts of everyday life. In a speech to industrial managers in February 1931, Stalin explained why speed was essential, why a slow-down was unthinkable:

"Do you want our Socialist fatherland to be beaten and to lose its independence? If you do not want this you must put an end to this backwardness as speedily as possible and develop genuine Bolshevik speed in building up the Socialist system of economy. There are no other ways. ... We are fifty to a hundred years behind the advanced countries. We must make good this lag in ten years. Either we do it or they crush us."

Anything could be, and would be, sacrificed in the cause, and that included the Marxist principle of 'egalitarianism', of treating men as equals. Marx had taught that in a communist society people would work for the common good, not for selfish, private gain: "to each according to his need; from each according to his ability". Stalin now taught that until the Soviet Union could produce enough to satisfy *everyone's* needs, egalitarianism was mere pie in the sky. Workers who acquired new skills and stayed in their jobs were paid the highest wages. But in times when even high wages could not buy (openly or on the black market) scarce foods and consumer goods, the government also rewarded the more valuable workers and, of course, the ever-increasing numbers of officials with 'perks'. Such benefits included permission to buy scarce goods in shops which were closed to ordinary citizens, the allocation of a decent place to live in, and permits to buy clothes which would not fall apart after a couple of months. Nadezhda Mandelstam, the wife of the poet, Osip Mandelstam, recalled in later years how

deeply privileges and 'perks' bit into the new Soviet Communism:

"... even the medicine you get depends on your status. I once complained about this in the presence of a Soviet official who held high rank before his retirement. I said medicine was something everybody needed. 'What do you mean, everybody?' he asked. 'Do you expect me to get the same treatment as a cleaning woman?' He was a kind and perfectly decent person, but nobody was unaffected by the 'fight against egalitarianism'."

Saboteurs and Slaves

If workers in factories and mines, on building sites and collectives reached or surpassed their targets, they were rewarded. But how could the government deal with those who failed? And an even more difficult question: how could it explain the apparent failure of whole sectors of Soviet industry?

It could not be admitted, in public, that the planners, or the Great Planner himself, had made mistakes. If Stalin was seen to have made or approved impossible targets, then how could he justify the terrible sacrifices he had demanded of the people? The answer was that the finger was never pointed openly at him. Nor was it pointed at the other real reasons for failure to achieve targets – at peasants who broke machines, not out of malice but because they hadn't a clue how to work them; at Russia's inability to pay for all the foreign machinery she desperately needed; at a transport system which could not meet the new demands made upon it.

Instead, the blame was placed on "them" – on murky enemies who worked silently and in the dark to sabotage the great work of Comrade Stalin and the Soviet people. Let us take just one example – the official explanation of why the railway system could not do what was asked of it by 1933. The real reasons were fairly clear: there was not enough railway track (only 5,500 kilometres of new track had been laid down, while the first Five-Year Plan had demanded an extra 16,000 kilometres); there were not enough spare parts for the old and overworked engines and wagons; and there were not enough skilled technicians to repair and run the system. But the official explanation put the blame squarely on "them":

"Until now many party cells show class blindness and

do not unmask class enemies who creep into the railways and attempt to wreck and disrupt. As a result, class enemies, white guardists [anti-Reds], *kulaks*, still have the opportunity here and there on the railways to creep into 'modest' and 'insignificant' jobs, like those of greasers, and ... they carry on their wrecking, becoming organisers of crashes and accidents, destroying essential parts of the railway and disorganising its work. ... To raise the level of watchfulness over the class enemy which has crawled into transport, to show up and unmask every kind of open and hidden saboteur so that ... their criminal activities can be ended, that is the duty of every communist ..."

It would have been laughable if it had not been so threatening: for "watchfulness" was not just the "duty of every communist"; it was at the very heart of the job of the secret police, once called the Cheka and now vastly enlarged as the OGPU, headed by Genrikh Yagoda. Like the *Gestapo*, which was soon to be set up in Hitler's Germany (see Chapter 25, page 113), the OGPU's task was not only to root out and destroy opposition but to terrorise ordinary people into silence and passive obedience.

The OGPU's job did not end with the close supervision of the Soviet people going about their daily business. When the People's Courts dealt out sentences of death, Yagoda's men did the shooting; and when prisoners were sentenced to exile or to periods of forced labour they were handed back to the police who had arrested them. The shadow of the *gulag* (the system of forced labour camps) spread over the land. No-one knows exactly how many prisoners (or *zeks*) they held, though the historian Martin Gilbert has estimated a minimum of three-quarters of a million as early as 1930.

The *zeks* may have been sentenced to five years or ten, or to longer periods, in the camps. In effect they were slaves at the disposal of the OGPU, and their lives were lavishly spent by their masters on construction sites and in mines. Machinery was expensive; *zek* labour was free and easily replaced. Between September 1931 and April 1933 a canal was built between the White Sea and the Baltic Sea. Altogether about 300,000 prisoners worked on its construction of whom it is 'estimated' (again that hazy word when we try to count Stalin's victims) that at least 100,000 died.

Victors and Victims

As night followed day, so a second Five-Year Plan was to follow the first. Drawn up in 1932, the plan was to cover the period 1933–37, and the Party planners showed all their old enthusiasm for making other people work harder. By 1937 the Soviet Union would be producing, so they said 22 million tonnes of pig-iron, 250 million tonnes of coal and 90 million tonnes of oil, not to mention 100 milliard kWh of electricity.

It was just not on. The Soviet people could not maintain the frantic pace of the first plan, could not shrug off the widespread famine which killed peasants like flies in 1933. The targets for the second five-year period had to be scaled down, and new figures were finally agreed at the 17th Congress of the Communist Party which met early in 1934.

Some of the revised targets for industries in 1934

Electricity (*milliard kWh*)	38·0
Coal (*million tonnes*)	152·5
Oil (*million tonnes*)	46·8
Pig-iron (*million tonnes*)	16·0
Steel (*million tonnes*)	17·0

That congress was called the 'Congress of Victors', a meeting of a Party which had put an end to the NEP, liquidated the *kulaks*, collectivised seven out of every ten peasants, and taken the first giant strides along the road to industrialisation. But there were people present, powerful people, who believed that enough was enough – that now was the time to end the bloodshed, relax the terror and cut Comrade Stalin down to size. Again, no-one knows *for certain* what happened, but we are now reasonably sure that at a secret session of Party leaders it was decided to reduce Stalin's influence and increase the power of Sergei Kirov, the popular secretary of the Leningrad Party organisation.

On 1 December 1934, Kirov was shot, almost certainly on Stalin's orders. The assassin and thirteen others were tried in secret and executed. Two old Bolsheviks, Kamenev and Zinoviev (do you remember them from page 129 as leaders of the Left Opposition in the twenties?), were tried and imprisoned. And that was merely the beginning of Stalin's purge of the

Party: where once he had paddled in blood, now he would swim in it.

The OGPU (renamed the NKVD in 1934) began its work of rounding up those suspected of opposition. Two of Stalin's chief supporters, Zhdanov and Khrushchev, took over as the party chiefs in Leningrad and Moscow; and in 1936 police-chief Yagoda was replaced by another of Stalin's creatures, the unspeakable Yezhov. In that year and in 1937 'show trials' were held in Moscow. To the astonishment of the Soviet people, old heroes of the Bolshevik Revolution stood up in open court and 'confessed' their parts in plots to overthrow the government and kill Stalin. The NKVD had worked on them for months: they knew what they had to say.

One by one they followed Kirov to the grave. Kamenev and Zinoviev were shot in 1936, Bukharin and Rykov in 1938. Of the seven men who had controlled the Party after Lenin's death in 1924, only three escaped being gunned down: Tomsky took his own life in 1936; and Trotsky was finally hunted down and his head smashed with an ice-axe in Mexico in 1940. Which left Stalin.

One of those who survived the purge of the Party leadership, Nikita Khrushchev, would later tot up the 'victors' who became 'victims':

"Of the 139 members and candidates of the Party's Central Committee who were elected at the Seventeenth Congress, 98 persons, i.e. seventy per cent, were arrested and shot. . . . Of 1,966 delegates . . . 1,108 persons were arrested on charges of counter-revolutionary crimes, i.e. decidedly more than half."

The old leaders did not just confess and disappear: they were rubbed out of history. Nadezhda Mandelstam described how a little girl showed her one way in which that was done.

"She showed us her school textbooks where the portraits of Party leaders had thick pieces of paper pasted over them as one by one they fell into disgrace – this the children had to do on instructions from their teacher. . . . At this time the editors of encyclopaedias and reference books were sending subscribers . . . lists of articles that had to be pasted over or cut out. . . . With every new arrest, people went through their books and burned the works of disgraced leaders in their stoves."

It could not, and did not, stop there. The Red Army

was purged (at least one-fifth of all its officers were shot); the NKVD was encouraged to purge itself; and local Party officials disappeared by the thousands. And what happened to the ordinary people of the Soviet Union? They were at the mercy of a state which used imprisonment and murder as political weapons to discipline citizens into obedience and to punish slackers and critics. Millions disappeared into the *gulag*; and the rest trembled, especially at night, for that was when the police called. Osip Mandelstam was taken at night. "Why do you complain?" he had once asked his wife. "Poetry is respected only in this country – people are killed for it. There's no place where more people are killed for it."

They were killed for all kinds of reasons – for having known the wrong people, for saying the wrong thing, or not saying the right thing. Nadezhda heard how:

". . . mothers prepared their children for life by teaching them the sacred language of their seniors. 'My children love Stalin most of all, me only second,' Pasternak's* wife, Zinaida Nikolayevna, used to say. Others did not go so far, but nobody confided their doubts to their children: why condemn them to death?"

Everyone 'loved' Stalin: in the public worship of the Leader lay the hope of safety from his terror. Solzhenitsyn has described how people loved him at a district Party conference in Moscow Province in 1938.

"At the conclusion of the conference, a tribute to Comrade Stalin was called for. Of course, everyone stood up (just as everyone had leapt to his feet during the conference at every mention of his name). The small hall echoed with 'stormy applause, rising to an ovation'. For three minutes, four minutes, five minutes, the 'stormy applause, rising to an ovation' continued. But palms were getting sore, and raised arms were already aching. . . . However, who would dare be the *first* to stop? After all, NKVD men were standing in the hall applauding and waiting to see *who* quit first! And in that obscure, small hall, unknown to the Leader, the applause went on – six, seven, eight minutes! . . . They couldn't stop now till they collapsed with heart attacks! At the rear of the hall, which was crowded, they could of course cheat a bit, clap less fre-

*Boris Pasternak, author of the novel *Dr. Zhivago*.

The cult of the Leader: Stalin in 1937.

quently, less vigorously, not so eagerly – but up there with the presidium where everyone could see them? The director of the local paper factory, an independent and strong-minded man, stood with the presidium. Aware of all the falsity and all the impossibility of the situation, he still kept on applauding! Nine minutes! Ten! In anguish he watched the secretary of the District Party Committee but the latter dared not stop. Insanity! ... Then, after eleven minutes, the director of the paper factory assumed a businesslike expression and sat down in his seat. And, oh, a miracle took place! ... To a man, everyone else stopped dead and sat down. They had been saved! ...

– That, however, was how they discovered who the independent people were. And that was how they went about eliminating them. That same night the factory director was arrested. They easily pasted ten years [in a labour camp] on him on the pretext of something quite different."

Soviet Progress and its Price

Let us now look at what the people actually achieved during the Great Terror, and at how near they came to reaching the targets of the second Five-Year Plan. (If you made a chart or block graph of the targets and achievements of the first plan, you might do a similar exercise for the second plan, using the figures on page 134 and the ones below.)

Some industrial production figures in 1937, at the end of the second Five-Year Plan

Electricity
(*milliard kWh*)   36·2
Coal
(*million tonnes*)   128·0
Oil
(*million tonnes*)   28·5
Pig-iron
(*million tonnes*)   14·5
Steel
(*million tonnes*)   17·7

Again the targets had not been reached, except for steel. But look back to Russian production figures for 1927–28, the year before the first plan, and consider just how much had been done in less than ten years. By any standards, it was a staggering achievement.

Russian society had been wrenched out of its old patterns. By 1937, nine out of every ten peasants had been collectivised: and the countryside was cultivated by the workers of 243,000 *kolkhozes* and nearly 4,000 state farms. Production of food had begun to recover from the chaos of the early thirties: the grain harvest of 1937 yielded 97·4 million tonnes; and by 1938 there were in the Soviet Union nearly fifty-one million head of cattle, well over twenty-five million pigs and more than sixty-six million sheep and goats – most of them the private property of collectivised peasants.

The urban population had continued to expand very rapidly: during the period of the second Five-Year Plan. another sixteen million people were added to Russia's already overcrowded towns and cities. By 1939, when the total population of the USSR had risen to over 170

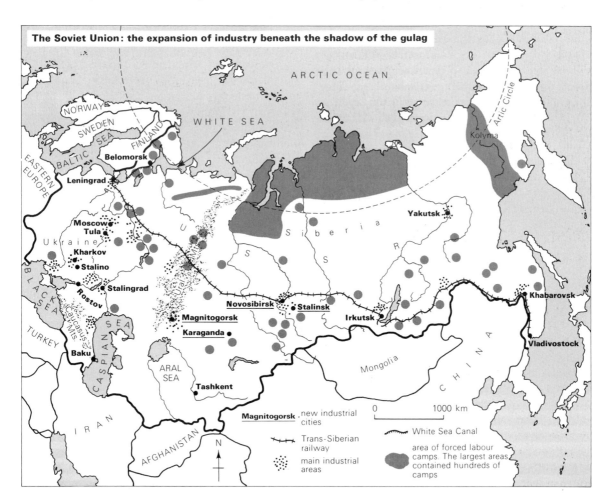

The Soviet Union: the expansion of industry beneath the shadow of the gulag

Magnitogorsk — new industrial cities

⊢⊣⊢⊣ Trans-Siberian railway

main industrial areas

White Sea Canal

area of forced labour camps. The largest areas contained hundreds of camps

0   1000 km

million, 33 out of every 100 people were town-dwellers. And gradually, after the rationing of food was ended in 1935, workers' standards of living began to improve, although they nowhere near approached those of the country's seven million civil servants and officials. A factory director or a government planning specialist could earn up to 4,000 roubles a month in 1937 – twenty-five times as much as an ordinary workman.

But even so, many workers were given opportunities to train for skilled, higher-paid jobs; all workers' children now got a free primary education; and increasing numbers of people had access to better medical facilities. Much of that was good – it was what we can all recognise as 'progress'. The Soviet Union was still a poor country, but by 1938 it was no longer poor as old Russia had been. Although many of its people were hungry, ill-clothed and crowded into inadequate housing, they no longer lived under the old threats of periodic famine and epidemic disease.

But that progress had been bought at an appalling price. We have counted some of the cost in earlier sections of this chapter. The map on the previous page will tell you more about what was achieved and how people paid for it with their freedom and their lives.

Let us remind ourselves of the price in human terms. There is no point in trying to estimate the total number of *zeks* in the *gulag* in 1938, or 1939, or 1940. No-one knows – or if someone does, he hasn't yet dared to print it. Still, would it be worse if the number turned out to be ten million instead of five million?

According to the map, the Kolyma is a place in the USSR – distant, bleak and cold, but still just a place. According to a man, Ivan Karpunich-Braven, the Kolyma meant the destruction of all civilised values, the descent of man below the level of the beasts.

"The prisoners were so famished that at Zarosshy Spring they ate the corpse of a horse which had been lying dead for more than a week and which not only stank but was covered with flies and maggots. At Utiny Goldfields the *zeks* ate half a barrel of lubricating grease, brought there to grease the wheelbarrows. At Mylga they ate Iceland moss, like the deer. Multitudes of 'goners', unable to walk by themselves, were dragged to work on sledges by other 'goners' who had not yet become quite so weak. Those who lagged behind were beaten with clubs and torn by dogs."

In these pages we have met Nadezhda, wife of the poet Osip Mandelstam. In June 1940 she learnt that she was a widow when Osip's death certificate was passed on to her.

"The issue of the death certificate was not the rule but the exception. To all intents and purposes, as far as his civil status was concerned, a person could be considered dead from the moment he was sent to a camp, or, indeed, from the moment of his arrest, which was automatically followed by his conviction and sentence to imprisonment in a camp.... Nobody bothered to tell a man's relatives when he died in a camp or prison: you regarded yourself as a widow or orphan from the moment of his arrest. When a woman was told in the Prosecutor's office that her husband had been given ten years, the official sometimes added: 'You can remarry.' – ... In the circumstances, death was the only possible deliverance. When I heard that M. had died, I stopped having my nightmares about him."

It was as if he, and all the other victims, had disappeared in war.

28 People and Societies II

In the first chapter of this book we surveyed the world at the start of this century, the world into which your great-grandparents were about to be born. In this chapter we shall look over the world in which your grandparents were born and in which they grew up.

The People

The number of people in the world was increasing at a faster and faster rate. An extra 200 million people were added to the total population in the first twenty years of the century; but the addition of a further 200 million took only ten more years. For every four people alive in 1900, there were five in 1930. And the next ten years, to 1940, saw the arrival of another 230 million mouths to feed.

In 1930, the world population was distributed as follows:

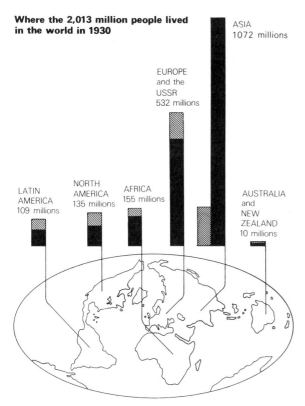

Where the 2,013 million people lived in the world in 1930

ASIA
1072 millions

EUROPE
and the
USSR
532 millions

LATIN
AMERICA
109 millions

NORTH
AMERICA
135 millions

AFRICA
155 millions

AUSTRALIA
and
NEW
ZEALAND
10 millions

Out of every 1,000 people in the world, 533 lived in Asia, 264 in Europe and the Soviet Union, 77 in

Africa, 67 in North America, 54 in Latin America, and 5 in Australia and New Zealand. If you compare these figures with those in Chapter 1 (page 1) you will soon see that the population was growing faster in the Americas than anywhere else. In fact, by 1940 the countries of Latin America together would have more than twice the number of people they had at the start of the century.

In Europe the rate of population growth varied enormously. The French hardly increased their numbers at all; while the Russians recorded a massive increase. By 1930 there were 170 million people in the USSR, 65 million in Germany, 46 million in the UK, 41 million in France and 40 million in Italy. Of the new European states, Poland had 32 million people, and Czechoslovakia and Yugoslavia had about 14 million each.

More people didn't mean that more babies were being born: indeed, in some Western countries the birth rate was going down. What was happening was that fewer babies were dying, while adults were living longer. In general, people were eating more and better food and keeping themselves and their dwellings cleaner; while effective medical care was being brought to larger numbers of the sick.

Such improvements to the human condition were not equally spread among all the world's people. Doctors, hospitals, high-protein diets, social security benefits, adequate housing – these were the privileges of people in the richer, mostly industrialised countries. And as we shall learn, not all the citizens of those lands were equally privileged.

Let's look now at infant mortality rates. The figures at the top of the next page are averages for the period 1930 to 1934, and they tell us how many children out of every 1,000 born alive died before the age of one. It was obviously much safer to be born in England than in India, in Scotland than in Spain. Or was it? Those national averages hid some disturbing truths. For example, the infant mortality rate for the Spanish province of Catalonia was 74, compared with a rate of 84 for County Durham in England. While in the slums of the Mile End district of Glasgow in the 1920s, the rate had been 163 – worse than the national averages of Bulgaria and Portugal!

No-one in his right mind would say that every child

Death in infancy: the number of children who died before the age of one (out of every 1,000 born alive)

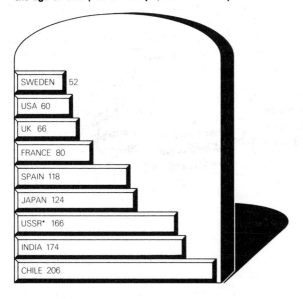

SWEDEN 52
USA 60
UK 66
FRANCE 80
SPAIN 118
JAPAN 124
USSR* 166
INDIA 174
CHILE 206

born in the UK this week has an equal chance of survival, no matter where he or she is born. The same was true of the 1930s – only more so. While the infant mortality rate was going down *on average*, large pockets of overcrowded humanity were not getting much benefit. If your grandmothers had had the choice of where to give birth to and bring up your mothers and fathers, they couldn't have done better than take the ferry to the Isle of Wight, where the infant mortality rate was 30 per 1,000.

As the grim figures for baby deaths were going down, on average, throughout the world, so the expectation of life was going up – though in some countries it was still more a matter of how early to expect death than of how long you could hope to live.

We noticed earlier that national averages can conceal as well as reveal information. The figures given opposite for the USA are the averages for all Americans in the years 1929–31: yet even by 1935 the life expectancy of a *non-white* American male was only 49 years, and of a *non-white* female 52 years. We have already seen that regional and class differences could give you a better start in life and the expectation of a long innings:

* The figure given for the USSR is an average for the period 1935–39, since an estimate for the years 1930–34 would not be reliable. If you would like to remind yourself of the reason why, look at Chapter 27, pages 131–34.

in some societies, the colour of your skin could have an important effect too.

It is worth remembering at this point that by the early 1930s some of the less well-off and more needy citizens of Western European countries were being helped by welfare provisions such as insurance against unemployment and sickness, old-age pensions and family allowances. No country had, as yet, a complete system of provision; but by 1930 the UK and Germany were the clear leaders in this developing field of 'social security'.

Town and Country

The movement of people off the land and into industry continued. In those countries which already had large industrial work-forces and had begun to mechanise agriculture by the start of the century, the pace of the movement hotted up. At the same time, the growth of industry called for the employment of more people in 'service' jobs, ranging from typists to accountants, from sales representatives to telephonists. In the Soviet Union (as we saw in Chapter 27) a much slower rate of movement out of agriculture into industry was being speeded up in the 1930s – by order of the government. Elsewhere in the world, and especially in Africa and Asia, the movement of labour into industry was still very slow, and the majority of people worked on the land – most of them to produce their own food, and some to raise crops for world markets.

By the mid-1930s, 64 out of every 100 workers in the world made their living from the land. And if we tried to show those areas of the world which had higher than average agricultural populations and those which

Life expectancy at birth in the early 1930s		
Country	Males	Females
India	32	31
Chile	40	42
British Guiana	40	43
Japan	46	48
Poland	48	51
France	56	62
USA	58	61
England and Wales	59	63
Germany	60	63
Australia	63	67

had lower, it would look something like the map at the top of page 142.

It is a crude but interesting way of looking at the people of the 1930s. Yet once again we must be cautious of averages – and in this case particularly cautious of an average for *all* the countries of Europe. As you know, parts of Western and Central Europe were already highly industrialised, while in much of Eastern Europe most people still made their living from the land. In Great Britain, in the early 1930s, only 6 people out of every 100 worked in agriculture, compared with 36 out of every 100 in France, and 79 out of every 100 in Romania.

Industrialisation stimulated the growth of towns and cities. By 1930, 16 out of every 100 people in the world lived in localities with 20,000 or more inhabitants – and that figure jumped to 19 out of every 100 by 1940. Inevitably, the average figure was higher in the industrialised parts of the world than elsewhere. For example, by 1930, 46 out of every 100 North Americans were town-dwellers, compared with only 6 out of every 100 Africans. Most of the world's big cities were in the industrialised countries, and so were most of the 'multimillion' cities, those with populations of more than 2,500,000.

The development of industry, and in some countries the practice of efficient, large-scale farming, created wealth. A huge gap had opened up between the people of affluent, developed countries and those who lived in under-developed lands. The map below should give you a picture of contrasts between the rich, the not-so-well-off, and the poor parts of the world, measured in terms of *per capita* income (that is, the sum we end up with when we divide the total income of a country by the total number of its people).

Again, it must be emphasised that we are dealing with *averages*. If you keep that in mind, you will not read into the map the notion that the yearly income of a South Wales miner was the same as that of a London solicitor.

Among the world's industrial powers, the USA was still way out in front. The chart on page 142 below, which shows some of the industrial outputs of the four leading powers, gives yearly averages for the period between 1936 and 1938 – which, as you saw on page 128, was not a good time for the United States.

Even in those difficult years the United States produced thirty-two per cent of the world's manufactured goods, compared with Germany's eleven per cent and the UK's nine per cent. A further example of her

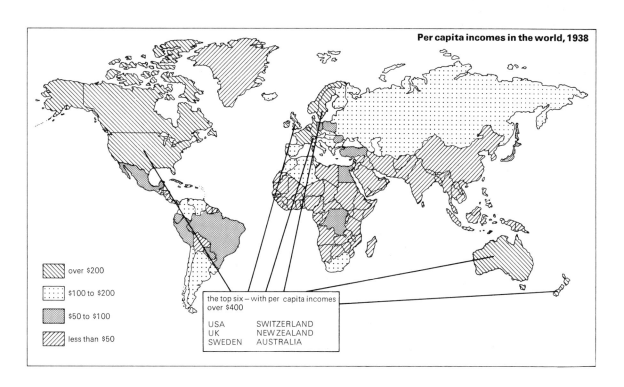

Per capita incomes in the world, 1938

over $200

$100 to $200

$50 to $100

less than $50

the top six – with per capita incomes over $400

USA   SWITZERLAND
UK   NEW ZEALAND
SWEDEN   AUSTRALIA

Agricultural populations as percentages of total populations in the mid-1930s

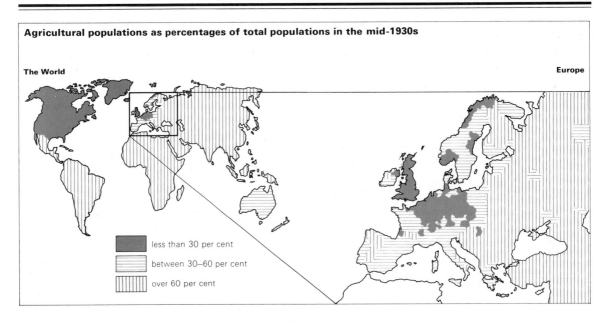

The World

Europe

- less than 30 per cent
- between 30–60 per cent
- over 60 per cent

The four industrial heavyweights 1936–38

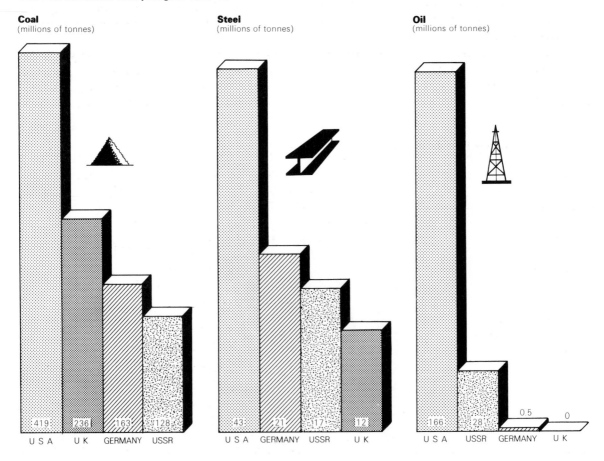

Coal
(millions of tonnes)

U S A	U K	GERMANY	USSR
419	236	163	128

Steel
(millions of tonnes)

U S A	GERMANY	USSR	U K
43	21	17	12

Oil
(millions of tonnes)

U S A	USSR	GERMANY	U K
166	28	0.5	0

industrial power was the production in the late thirties
of a yearly average of well over three million motor cars—
nearly ten times the number produced in the UK and
twelve times the output of German car factories. Despite the Depression, surfaced roads in America were
extended from about one million kilometres in 1930 to
over two million kilometres in 1940.

While the German and the British shares of total
world manufacturing output were declining by the late
1930s, Japan's share rose to 3·8 per cent. But the real
success story was that of the Soviet Union. By 1938
she was producing over eighteen per cent of the world's
manufactured goods, an output second only to that of
the United States. The price the Soviet people paid
for that success has already been described in Chapter 27.

New Faces, New Places

Emigration from Europe, especially to the USA
and Latin America, had reached its peak in the first
ten years of the twentieth century, and over the next
twenty years it steadily declined. Even so, in the 1920s,
no intercontinental movements of population anywhere else in the world compared with the continuing
flow of Europeans overseas. Yet in the 1930s, as you
can see, the numbers of European emigrants shrank
dramatically.

Among the most important reasons for the decline
in the 1930s was the new immigration policy of the
USA (see Chapter 21, pages 81–2). The figures below
show how tightly the Americans closed their doors to
foreigners.

Total numbers of immigrants (from all parts of the world) entering the USA

1901–10	8,813,000
1921–30	4,107,000
1931–40	528,000

By 1940 only nine per cent of the population of the
USA was foreign-born. But we should note that
although the American government could severely
limit the numbers of European immigrants who sailed
across the Atlantic, they found it much more difficult
to stop Latin Americans swimming the Rio Grande
(the river between Mexico and the USA). From the
mid-1920s hundreds of thousands of Mexican 'wet-
backs' entered the USA each year – illegal immigrants
who hired themselves out as cheap labour on American
farms.

Apart from the USA, the countries to which the
majority of emigrants went in the first forty years of
the twentieth century were Brazil and Argentina and
the British Dominions of Canada, Australia and New

Emigrants from selected European countries 1921-30 and 1931-40

	1921–30	1931–40
FRANCE	4,000	5,000
BELGIUM	17,000	16,000
NETHERLANDS	32,000	4,000
SWITZERLAND	50,000	47,000
DENMARK	64,000	100,000
FINLAND	73,000	3,000
NORWAY	87,000	6,000
SWEDEN	107,000	8,000
IRELAND	167,000	10,000
AUSTRIA, HUNGARY AND CZECHOSLOVAKIA	357,000	57,000
SPAIN	560,000	132,000
GERMANY	721,000	124,000
PORTUGAL	995,000	108,000
ITALY	1,370,000	235,000
UK	1,984,000	252,000
TOTAL	6,588,000	1,107,000

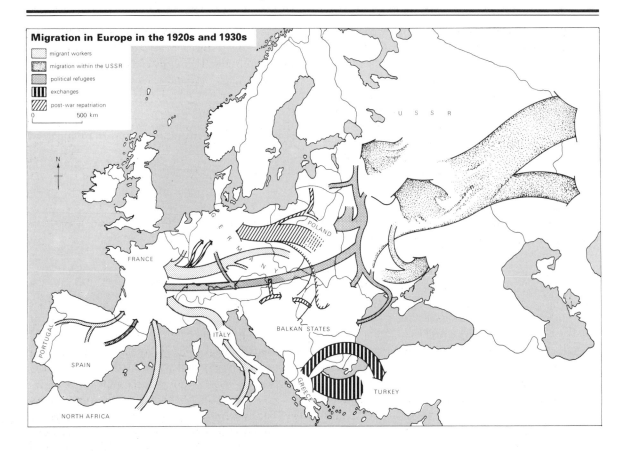

Migration in Europe in the 1920s and 1930s

migrant workers
migration within the USSR
political refugees
exchanges
post-war repatriation

0   500 km

N

USSR

GERMANY

POLAND

FRANCE

PORTUGAL

SPAIN

ITALY

BALKAN STATES

GREECE

TURKEY

NORTH AFRICA

Zealand. There was also the special case of emigration to Palestine, a movement which gathered pace in the 1930s when the Nazis began their systematic persecution of German Jews (see also Chapter 15, page 67, and Chapter 25, pages 115–18).

We shall now look at migration within the continent of Europe itself, where people moved or were uprooted for a variety of reasons.

You can see from the map above how people were taken up and whirled about by political events and economic circumstances. After the Great War, one-and-a-quarter million Germans came 'home' from lands outside the Reich – from Poland, the Baltic states, the Balkan countries and Alsace-Lorraine. During and after the Peace Settlement there was a great re-shuffling of Central and Eastern European peoples, as many of them chose to leave their old homes and move to the new countries dominated by their own nationalities.

You can see too how many Italians left the poverty-stricken lands of the south and moved north to the industrial cities of Milan and Turin – and how some of them moved further north still, to France. Poles,

Spaniards and rather smaller numbers of Portuguese also migrated to France in search of work, as did over 100,000 people from French North Africa. The UK increased her immigrant population, but it remained small compared with that of her next-door neighbour. By 1938, over three million foreigners were living in France.

Finally, you can see on the map two examples of forced migration – the 'exchange' of foreign nationalities between Turkey and Greece in the early 1920s (for details see Chapter 15, page 66), and the massive re-settlement of people in the USSR of the 1930s. The practice of moving human beings over the map – like pawns in a chess game – was already established.

The Other Half

How do we measure the influence of women and their progress towards the goal of being treated as the equals of men? If we use the right to vote as a measurement, then by the late 1930s women had more influence in the world than they had had before the Great

144

War. They now had the vote in the USA and Canada, in the UK, Belgium and the Netherlands, in Germany and Austria, in Poland, Czechoslovakia and the USSR, and in all the Scandinavian countries.

But the right to take part in elections did not, in itself, change women's economic position or their expectations of the future. It didn't qualify them for skilled jobs or for careers in the professions, and it certainly didn't mean that employers had to fork out equal pay for what was (judged by any other standard than male hypocrisy) equal work.

The women of industrialised countries such as the UK had benefited from the Great War, in which they proved their ability to do men's work. They also gained from the growing number of jobs in service industries, which we noted on page 140. Just as important, artificial means of contraception were being more widely publicised and – so far as we can guess – used. Obviously, the thin rubber sheath – or condom – could be used to prevent conception only with the agreement of the male; but men as well as women were now thinking of the advantages of 'family planning'. Large families were no longer an economic asset in countries where young children had to go to school; and a wife might be more 'valuable' as a wage-earner than as a child producer and rearer.

If industry called many women out to work, it was also making the job of home-management easier for some by producing domestic appliances such as electric cookers, refrigerators, vacuum cleaners and washing machines. Few women, as yet, possessed those modern marvels – but think for a moment of the work saved in millions of households in the USA, in Britain, Germany and France by the humble electric light, the electric iron and the piped water supply to a kitchen sink.

Slowly but surely the women of the industrialised countries, and those of the wealthy Dominions of the British Empire, were making a kind of progress which could be observed in terms of their becoming freer to decide how to spend their own lives and control their own property. And in the 1930s, Stalin mobilised women as well as men to launch the Soviet Union's gigantic industrial 'leap forward'. The majority of Russian doctors, nurses and teachers were women – but there were female factory workers and engineers too, as well as millions employed in the construction of new roads, canals and towns.

Despite those changes, some of the old notions of male superiority – of men as 'breadwinners' and 'natural leaders' – were taking a long time to undermine, even in the industrialised countries. Girls, like boys, received an elementary education, but fewer girls went on to secondary schools, and there were far fewer female students than males in the universities.

But outside those countries there was little, if anything, that we would call progress. Women laboured, brought children into the world and grew old before their time – unless, of course, they died young in childbirth. In lands where religion and custom put women out of public view there was little prospect of change until old societies and cultures were more thoroughly penetrated by Western ideas and Western technology.

The Shape of Things to Come

To a woman, or a man, in a village in central India, to a farmer high up in the mountains of Peru, or even to a peasant in southern Yugoslavia, the world would have looked much the same in 1938 as it had to her or his grandparents. The novelties of the twentieth century still had made little impression on the style and pace of their lives. The nearest many people came to being caught up in a technological wonderland was watching the sleek new flying machines overhead: it probably never occurred to some of them that there were human beings inside the planes.

For every 1,000 Americans there were nearly 200 cars on the roads: in Peru there was one car to every 5,000 people. Americans treated the telephone as part of the furniture, both at home and at work: there were three of them to every twenty people. In Yugoslavia the telephone barely interrupted life: there the ratio was one telephone to every 2,500 people. News, advertising, entertainment and politics were broadcast 'wireless' to Americans – and there were three sets to every ten listeners to make sure they could hear whatever it was wherever they were. Indians hadn't yet been hooked: there was only one set to every 5,000 people.

Motor cars and lorries, telephones and radios, aspirins, anaesthetics, comics, disposable razor blades, fountain pens, pasteurised milk, tinned goods, plastics and X-rays – all these things and many more had been absorbed into the Western way of life. And Western industry needed to export them to stay in business. In some respects at least the shape of tomorrow was clear enough – in many parts of the world it would be rather like yesterday in the USA. The American idea of the good life was already being exported – on film. There, on the movie screen, was something to look up and forward to. And a new form of mass communication and persuasion had made its appearance: in 1936 the BBC opened the world's first regular television service.

That was about as much of the future as men could foresee. Most people were not in the business of prophecy: they hoped their future would somehow be better, but in the meantime they carried on with the work of living. The human race was bigger than at any time in history. Even if they weren't all personally aware of it, people now shared a common interest in the development of the world economy. They were beginning, in a limited way, to share the benefits of invention and technology; they were living longer and burying fewer babies. In Europe, where industrialised countries were climbing back out of Depression, there was even cause for optimism about the future – provided you didn't enquire too closely into the ambitions of those political leaders who were going to decide it.

29 Down the Road to War: International Relations, 1933–39

First Responses to the German Führer

When the Austrian-born nationalist fanatic, Adolf Hitler, became Chancellor of Germany in January 1933, it was clear that European politics were about to be jolted into a new and perhaps dangerous phase. Even those people who believed that Hitler had mellowed since he wrote *Mein Kampf* (see Chapter 23, page 91) expected that the new German leader would demand at least the return of what the Treaty of Versailles had taken away in 1919; and there were some who thought that it was time to treat such German claims reasonably. Others feared something much worse: that Germany had fallen into the hands of new barbarians, the Nazis, who would make a bid for the domination of the continent.

If *Mein Kampf* were taken at all seriously, Austria, Czechoslovakia and Poland had good reason to be alarmed. Austria was the homeland of German people, and in Hitler's eyes she 'belonged' to the Reich; Czechoslovakia had three million Germans living in the Sudetenland along her western border; and despised Poland not only had a large German-speaking minority but her 'corridor' to the sea cut the Reich in two. Beyond them lay the Soviet Union, who feared that if Germany did enter those lands she would be poised to carry out the National Socialist threat to destroy Bolshevism by invading Russia.

In the south the Italian dictator, Mussolini, had mixed feelings. A powerful Germany, prepared to break up the Paris Peace Settlement, was to his advantage. If Hitler kept to northern and Central Europe, Mussolini would be left free to develop Italian power in the Mediterranean region. On the other hand, he too feared an expansion of Germany into Austria, a country which Italy regarded as within her sphere of influence and wanted to keep out of the hands of any other strong power. While in the west, France was acutely conscious that between her and the new hard men of Germany lay only the demilitarised Rhineland and the still incomplete Maginot Line (see Chapter 14, page 59). For military support on a serious scale the French could only look to Britain.

Their terrible losses in the Great War had convinced most Britons that they should avoid getting tangled up again in the affairs of Europe. Moreover, in the Depression of the early thirties Britain had turned away from Europe and sought to safeguard her future in a closer economic relationship with her Empire. Even so, many British people believed that their government should take an active lead in any international action which might prevent another European war breaking out.

The British were not the only people who shrank from the prospect of another Great War, a war in which the new bombing planes would terrorise civilian populations as surely as the new tanks would cut down the infantry at the battlefronts. But how were the nations of Europe to stop all that happening? How could they control Germany?

There was no shortage of alternative strategies. They could, for example, hit Germany in a 'preventive war' before Germany hit them. Poland could attack from the east while the French invaded the Reich from the west. But that kind of pre-emptive strike to rid Europe of Nazism was simply not on: after all, Hitler had come to power by legal means, and the German government was being careful to make only reasonable demands against the Versailles settlement. In any case, if such a war was fought, the victorious powers would still have to hold down an outraged Germany.

The second alternative was massive rearmament. Threatened nations could call up enormous armies, build huge air forces and navies, but use them only as deterrents to frighten a would-be aggressor. But even if people believed that such rearmament could prevent war, there would still be political objections to the cost. Large armed forces with modern equipment had become ruinously expensive.

At the other extreme was the third alternative of disarmament, of making a war less likely by reducing the numbers of men and machines available to take part in it. The nations were already trying to work out something along those lines in Geneva, where the World Disarmament Conference had been meeting since February 1932. But in 1933 Germany demanded 'equality' with the most heavily armed powers, and in the October of that year Hitler made clear his intention to rearm the Reich, when he withdrew Germany's representatives from the Conference. The Conference itself was wound up in June 1934, having achieved nothing.

A fourth alternative was to settle problems and

maintain collective security through the League of Nations. As we have already seen (Chapter 10) the League was not an independent force in world politics: it depended entirely on the goodwill and support of its members, of whom Britain and France were the most powerful. Nor did the League include all the great powers: the USA had never joined, and the USSR would not become a member until September 1934. Worse still, the League had only recently been shown to be powerless in the face of aggression. It had criticised the Japanese invasion of Manchuria in 1931 (see Chapter 13, page 103) but not stopped it. Japan left the League in February 1933, and Germany followed in October. Many ordinary people continued to hope that the League could prevent another war; but to Europe's troubled statesmen the Palace of the Nations in Geneva was obviously not the place in which the great questions of war and peace were going to be settled.

Meeting the Threat

If a preventive war was out of the question, if world disarmament was merely a pious hope, if massive rearmament was too expensive, the nations would have to find other means of containing German ambitions.

Back in the 1920s you saw how France had negotiated insurances against German aggression. In the Locarno Pact (see Chapter 11, page 50) she and Germany had agreed to respect their common frontier. But even if the Nazis now attacked in the West, France's treaties with Poland and Czechoslovakia (see Chapter 14, page 59) should ensure that Germany would again have to fight a war on two fronts. Britain too had signed the Locarno Pact as a guarantor, which meant that she was obliged to go to France's aid if German troops crossed the French frontier. But that did not necessarily mean that Britain would have to fight if France triggered off a war by supporting one of her Eastern European allies against Germany.

In 1934 Hitler made his first move to break out of France's encirclement of Germany. In January the German government signed a non-aggression pact with Poland: it was a cheap way of undermining France's influence in Eastern Europe, for the Poles were now afraid that too close a relationship with the French would give Hitler an excuse for saying they had broken the spirit of their pact with Germany. In the rest of Eastern Europe Hitler was also about to increase

German influence by means of bilateral trading agreements with countries hard-hit by the Depression (Chapter 24, page 107–8).

After the pact with Poland, Hitler's next move was to try to weaken Austria. Since 1919 both conservatives and socialists in Austria had been in favour of remaining independent of their brother Germans in Germany: only a small Nazi Party believed in *Anschluss*, or union, with the Reich. In July 1934 those Austrian Nazis tried to overthrow the conservative government of Chancellor Engelbert Dollfuss and replace it with one loyal to Berlin. Dollfuss was killed, but the revolt was put down by the Austrian army, after Mussolini said he would move Italian troops to the frontier to help them resist a Nazi takeover.

The Führer now turned to the rearmament of Germany. In March 1935 Goering announced the existence of the *Luftwaffe* (the air force), to be followed only a week later by Hitler's announcement of compulsory military service – both flagrant breaches of the Treaty of Versailles. It would be a matter of only a few years before Hitler had his armed forces ready to back up his meddling in the affairs of Germany's neighbours.

The governments of democratic France and Britain had a common interest with Fascist Italy in wanting to keep Nazi Germany out of Austria. In April 1935 their representatives met at Stresa and declared they would uphold Austrian independence. One month after that 'Stresa Front' was formed, France and Russia signed an alliance of mutual assistance against aggression; while a Czech–Russian alliance was also agreed, to come into effect once the French–Czech alliance was activated. It might be helpful at this stage if you copied the map on page 149 and, using a key, showed on it the alliances and agreements made between European states by early 1935. You should be able to see clearly from your map the network of insurances that had been formed against a developing threat of German aggression.

However, the Stresa Front soon crumbled as Britain and Italy looked to their own self-interest. In June 1935, without consulting either France or Italy, Britain negotiated the Anglo-German Naval Agreement with Hitler's government by which the size of the German navy would be allowed to reach thirty-five per cent of the navies of the whole British Empire. Britain wanted to ensure that Germany's navy remained smaller than hers, but her way of ensuring it involved breaking the Treaty of Versailles, which had forbidden Germany to

Europe in 1935

build a war fleet. The Germans were delighted.

The Stresa Front was soon to be far more seriously damaged by Italy. Mussolini had long dreamt of re-creating a 'Roman Empire'. Of course, it would have to be done quickly, on the cheap and at the expense of weak opposition, since Italy could not afford a long, costly war. In October 1935 his troops invaded Abyssinia (Ethiopia), one of only two countries in Africa not under European control (the other was Liberia). The *Duce*'s tanks and planes took on Emperor Haile

Selassie's cavalry – it was that kind of war – but the Italians found it surprisingly difficult to win.

The Emperor's appeal for help from the League of Nations put Britain and France in a pretty fix. They were bound to support the League in its condemnation of aggression; yet they were desperately anxious not to offend Italy for fear of driving the *Duce* into the open arms of the German Führer. They did as you might expect: in public they supported the League's imposition of economic sanctions against Italy; in private they blocked the imposition of the sanctions that really mattered – on iron, steel, coal and, above all, oil; and in secret they put forward a deal to give Mussolini much of what he wanted. A plan was drawn up by Sir Samuel Hoare and Pierre Laval (the British and French Foreign Ministers) to give Italy some Abyssinian territory as well as a "zone of economic expansion and settlement". In December 1935 the plan was discovered by the press, its publication roused deep public anger, and Hoare was forced to resign. But both Western governments continued their double game of public support for the League and private compromise with Mussolini until the *Duce* won his war in May 1936.

But by that time Europe had already passed through another crisis: in March 1936 German troops had been sent into the demilitarised Rhineland. It was not so much that Nazi Germany again flouted the Treaty of Versailles (after all, that had become something of a habit): this time Hitler tore up the promise Germany had made in the Locarno Pact not to station troops west of a line running fifty kilometres to the east of the River Rhine.

The French had the choice of fighting to drive the German forces out of the Rhineland or of accepting Hitler's unilateral act. Even if they had wanted to fight they would have got no material support from the British; and it was pointless asking the Italians to help, for Mussolini was still fighting his own ugly little war in Africa. So the French took no action but hoped they would remain safe behind their new fortifications, the Maginot Line. In early 1935 France had appeared as the great champion of European security against the threat of German aggression: the Rhineland crisis showed that the spirit of the champion was weak.

A Spanish Connection

It may seem odd to move at this point from an international crisis to the domestic affairs of Spain, a militarily weak and economically backward country. But there is a reason. Until the 1920s Spain had been dominated for centuries by landowning grandees, the Catholic Church and the army. Now she began to face the challenge of new forces. Land-hungry and oppressed peasants were joined by workers, some of them organised in socialist trade unions, others belonging to anarchist groups which wanted to overthrow the authority of the 'state' and the privileges of those who supported it. Add to that one other particularly Span-

ish problem, the call for self-government by people of Catalonia and the Basque country, and you begin to see why revolution was just around the corner.

In 1931 the King abdicated in the face of widespread opposition to his monarchy and the semi-dictatorial government. Spain became a Republic and her people elected a new government, in which the leading part was played by well-meaning socialists and liberals. Their programme of reform was bold. The Catholic Church was to have much less control of education; the provinces were given some powers of self-government; and poorer peasants were promised that land would be transferred to them from the owners of great estates. Such promises angered the Church, army leaders and landowners but did not go far enough to satisfy the anarchists, who were the strongest political force among the poor. They, together with the more extreme trade unionists and Spain's few communists, carried out a series of violent strikes, riots and church burnings. Public opinion then swung against these left-wing groups and brought a right-wing government to power in 1933.

The Left tried to bring this government down with four general strikes and then a strike of coal-miners. This was put down savagely by army units from Spanish Morocco led by General Francisco Franco. The savagery aroused a new sympathy for the Left and in February 1936 an election brought the socialists back to power – this time in a Popular Front alliance with anarchists and communists. The Popular Front's determination to carry out a programme of reforms encouraged right-wing opposition forces to draw closer together. Under the general heading of 'Nationalists' were now the leaders of the Church and the army and members of the *Falange*, Spain's fascist party.

In July the army took the lead against the government by rising in revolt, first in Morocco and then in towns on the Spanish mainland. The Spanish Civil War had begun, a struggle between the 'Nationalist' army and the forces of the 'Republican' government.

Franco, the Nationalist leader, was a narrow-minded conservative, not a fascist: he fought to defend the privileges of the army, the landowners and the Church, and he absorbed the Falangists into his movement and made use of them. Outside Spain the war was seen differently. Hitler and Mussolini saw the right-wing revolt against an elected government as a crusade against the communists. Both sent troops to support the Nationalists, and bombers of the new *Luftwaffe* de-

The bombers are coming. Mother and child in Madrid.

stroyed the small Basque town of Guernica.

Britain and France adopted a policy of non-intervention: although they condemned Guernica as barbarous, military help was not to be offered to either side. The leading advocate of this policy was the socialist prime minister of the French Popular Front government, Léon Blum (see Chapter 23, page 99). Although he himself supported the Republicans he was afraid that if his government intervened in the war in Spain, the French fascist parties might start a civil war in France – a very real risk. The British government were anxious not to get involved in a European war. They believed that any British naval activity off the Spanish coast in the western Mediterranean might lead to clashes with Italian forces; and they still

clung to the idea of keeping good relations with Mussolini.

Of the non-fascist powers only the USSR sent aid to the Republican government; although communists and socialists from all European countries (and some Americans) volunteered to serve in international brigades in the Republican army. For Britons and Frenchmen service in such brigades was illegal, because of their countries' policies: but the volunteers took the 'underground' routes across the Pyrenees to fight – and many of them to die – in Spain. The war ended in a Nationalist victory in March 1939 after three years of bloody and vicious fighting. It had cost over half a million lives. The war's losers were the Spanish people – who suffered cruelly from atrocities by both

151

sides, and who were forced to live under Franco's dictatorship from 1939 to 1975.

So there was a Spanish connection with the rest of the story told in this chapter. For every major European country there was a lesson to be learned from Spain. Hitler learned that the Western democracies were not yet ready to oppose the aggressive activities of Germany and Italy. The USSR drew pretty much the same unpleasant conclusion: if Germany started a war, Britain and France might again follow a policy of non-intervention. Britons tended to say either that non-intervention had avoided war or that it had made it more likely by encouraging further acts of aggression by Nazis and Fascists. The second of those opinions was the more important because it was new; from 1937 onwards many people in Britain, especially liberals and socialists, ceased to believe in the idea they had held since 1919 – that no future war could be justifiable. In the autumn of that year the Labour Party, for the first time, supported British rearmament.

The man who was most misled by the Civil War was Mussolini. He sent 60,000 troops to Spain, convinced that here was another Mediterranean country where he was a major influence. It was, he managed to persuade himself, a further achievement for Italian Fascism to add to his victory over Abyssinia and his success in Albania, where he had installed a puppet king. Britain and France, however, were also powers with major interests in the Mediterranean. France had a Mediterranean coastline, colonies in North Africa and mandates in the Middle East; Britain controlled Gibraltar, Malta and Egypt and had long been friendly with Greece. Given those circumstances Mussolini decided to draw closer to Hitler and encourage him in his defiance of Britain and France. The *Duce* fooled himself into believing that German expansion could be restricted to northern Europe, leaving the Italians free to act in the south. In November 1936 Mussolini spelt out his view of the relationship between Italy and Germany: the two powers did not have a firm alliance, but they did have an 'axis'. Austria was no longer something that need come between them.

Why Appeasement?

In the same month that Mussolini and Hitler came to that understanding, Germany and Japan signed the Anti-Comintern Pact, a treaty in which each of them promised, secretly, not to help the Soviet Union attack the other. The Pact was obviously directed against Russia, but it alarmed the British too, for it linked together the aggressive Asian nation that might soon threaten their Empire in the Far East with the power that had started to undermine the peace in Europe.

The National government in Britain, under the Prime Minister, Stanley Baldwin, had already begun to increase spending on the armed forces, especially on the navy and the RAF, but British rearmament was a slow and cautious affair. It had been opposed by those who still believed that the best way to preserve the peace was through firm support of the League of Nations. Many of them were members of the Labour Party which was opposed to rearmament until 1937. The rearming and expansion of Britain's forces could not be rushed through in six months. For example, some of the new planes intended for the RAF were still in the prototype stage: they would not be ready until 1939.

In May 1937 Baldwin resigned and was succeeded as Prime Minister and leader of the Conservative Party by Neville Chamberlain. As Chancellor of the Exchequer since 1931, Chamberlain was known to be an active, clear-sighted, forceful politician: and it was soon evident that, unlike Baldwin, he was determined to direct British foreign policy himself.

Chamberlain saw, as did most other people who could read a map, that Britain would face insoluble strategic problems if war broke out simultaneously in the Far East and in Europe. It was not just that she had only a small 'peacetime' army: the Royal Navy could not be in two places (for example, Scapa Flow and Singapore) at the same time. When Japanese forces launched their second invasion of China in July 1937 (see Chapter 23, page 103) and the threat to British colonies in the Far East became acute, there was little the British government could do. The situation looked even more grave when in November Italy joined the Anti-Comintern Pact. Any attempt to halt the expansion of the Japanese Empire, however, called for American cooperation – and the USA refused to emerge from her self-imposed isolation.

On the other hand, Chamberlain felt sure that a British statesman could make all the difference between peace and war in Europe. He disliked the Nazis but believed you did not have to like people to live alongside them. It was now essential to find out what the Nazis wanted, what they would accept as the price of peace, and (if necessary) give it to them before they dragged the continent into war. This was Chamberlain's new strategy for dealing with Hitler. It did not mean that he was prepared to surrender Europe to Nazi domination: it meant that he believed all the German government's claims could be met without them going to war. The strategy was summed up in one word – 'appeasement'. For the most part, Chamberlain's desire to avoid war matched the anxiety of the British people about being brought into a conflict like that of 1914–18 which had led to the death and mutilation of so many. To this was added the new awareness that bombers could bring the war to their cities. It was not, after all, surprising that fear for the future should lead to a public mood which favoured peace at almost any price. Only a small number argued that failing to face up to the dictators could lead to a general war within a short time.

In February 1938, under pressure from Hitler, Kurt Schuschnigg, Chancellor of Austria, allowed the Nazis much more influence in his country. Schuschnigg soon began to have doubts about an agreement which weakened his own authority and threatened Austria's independence – an independence which Mussolini would no longer help to preserve. On 9 March he announced that a plebiscite (a nation-wide vote) would be held on 13 March, when voters would be asked whether or not they wanted Austria to remain independent of Germany. Hitler, afraid that Schuschnigg might win a large majority in favour of remaining independent, threatened to invade the country if plans for the plebiscite went ahead. The vote was called off, but the German invasion began on 12 March. There was no resistance. On the 13th a jubilant Hitler announced the *Anschluss* of Germany with Austria, the land of his birth. Chamberlain had no opportunity to put his strategy to the test. The *Anschluss* was a lightning move, and most Austrians appeared to welcome being swallowed up in a Greater Germany – that is, unless you counted nearly half of the people who voted Socialist, and the tens of thousands of Austrian Jews.

In Chapter 24 we saw how in the Depression a majority of the Germans living in the Czech Sudetenland were weaned away from loyalty to the Czech state by Konrad Henlein and the Sudeten German Party. Now that Greater Germany surrounded the western half of Czechoslovakia, it was clear that Hitler would demand a 'solution' to the Sudeten problem. And Chamberlain was quick to make it just as clear that Bri-

tain would not organise collective resistance to Germany's claims. In the House of Commons on 24 March 1938 he declared that Britain would not promise to support France if France attacked Germany after a German attack on Czechoslovakia. That same afternoon another politician (a trouble-maker this one, always sniping at his leader) openly criticised Chamberlain's policy.

"The Nazification of the whole of the Danube States is a danger of the first capital magnitude to the British Empire. Is it all to go for nothing? ... If so, we shall repent in blood and tears our imprudence and our lack of foresight and energy."

The speaker was Winston Churchill, former Cabinet Minister and now just a backbench Conservative MP.

At about the same time, when Churchill was making savage attacks on appeasement, the head of the Civil Service, Sir Warren Fisher, was making some frightening comparisons between current British and German air strength. "For the first time in centuries," he told the Prime Minister, "our country is (and must continue to be) at the mercy of a foreign power." Despite the facts that in December 1937 the government had stepped up the production of fighter planes to protect British towns from bomber attacks and had ordered the first RDF (Radar) stations to be erected along the east coast to give advance warning of enemy air attacks, Chamberlain believed he had to take account of Fisher's gloomy conclusion. The threat of German bomber attacks on the British Isles was by now almost too awful to contemplate. The government had calculated that a sixty-day offensive would cause 1,800,000 casualties – a third of them dead. Using the same grim arithmetic, the Home Office had worked out that twenty million square feet of seasoned timber would be needed each month for coffins, then decided the country could not afford it and recommended instead burial in mass graves and burning with lime.

When the French Prime Minister, Edouard Daladier, came to London in April he was told that British support for military action against Germany was out of the question. Even together Britain and France would not be able to save Czechoslovakia if Germany attacked; and the British Dominions would not enter a war to defend a remote country in Central Europe. President Beneš of Czechoslovakia "must

German rearmament: U-boats at Kiel, 1938.

seize this opportunity ... to make a supreme effort to reach a settlement".

There was a false alarm in May, when reports of German troop movements scared the Czech government into a partial mobilisation of their army, but a major Czech crisis broke out on 12 September when Hitler demanded self-determination (by which he meant the right to unite with Germany) for the Sudeten Germans. Chamberlain responded with what he called Plan Z: he, the British Prime Minister, would fly to Germany and talk to the Führer, man to man.

On 15 September Chamberlain met Hitler at Berchtesgaden, where the Führer described the Sudetenland as the "last major problem to be solved" and declared that he would risk war to bring the Sudeten Germans into the Reich. Chamberlain returned to London, having decided that the Czechs must give in to Hitler's demand that areas in which more than half the population was German should be handed over. Between 18 and 21 September he and the French persuaded the Czechs to agree to a handover, with compensation and an international guarantee of Czechoslovakia's defences.

On 22 September Chamberlain flew to Bad Godesberg for his second meeting with Hitler and was welcomed with the diplomatic equivalent of a punch in the mouth. The new frontier was to be drawn at once! There would be no time for an agreement between Czechoslovakia and Germany. Hitler's troops were to occupy the new territories by 1 October! The Czechs must also give in to Polish and Hungarian claims on their land!

Chamberlain returned home bitterly disappointed. The Czechs could not be told to agree to the virtual destruction of their state by force of arms. It seemed that the great prize of peace was slipping away, even though Hitler had told the Prime Minister that once this issue was settled he had "no more territorial ambitions in Europe". And then, dramatically, on 28 September Chamberlain announced to the House of Commons that Hitler had agreed to Mussolini's suggestion of a Four Power Conference. On the next day, in Munich, Chamberlain, Hitler, Daladier and Mussolini agreed to transfer the mainly German areas of Czechoslovakia to the Reich by 10 October, while Polish and Hungarian claims were to be settled later. Nothing of any value had been gained for the Czechs by this conference which they were not allowed to attend. They were left to choose between signing the Munich Agreement or fighting the Germans alone. Beneš signed: what else could he have done?

Now that the Sudeten problem had been solved in such a shabby way, Chamberlain felt he had to show proof that he had removed the threat of European war, that in Munich he had brought about peace "with honour". Hitler, of course, had no objection to putting his name to a document, drawn up by the British Prime Minister, which cost the Germans no more than a few vague promises. On 30 September, Chamberlain returned triumphantly to London, bearing his piece of paper.

He received a hero's welcome. That evening he declared from Downing Street, "I believe it is peace for our time."

The price of peace was paid by the Czechs. They lost not only the Sudetenland, their western fortifications and vital industrial resources: Poland soon paid off an old score and seized the area around Teschen (see Chapter 9, page 43); and Hungary was granted a long, thin slice of land in the south. Beneš resigned in October. In November Czechoslovakia was divided into the three autonomous areas of Bohemia-Moravia (the home of the Czech people), Slovakia and Ruthenia.

For a few months it was possible to believe that appeasement had succeeded. Munich had removed the threat of war. Then, in March 1939, Hitler destroyed the feeble remnants of Czechoslovakia. After he had urged the Hungarians to invade Ruthenia and persuaded Slovakia to declare herself independent, leaving only the Czech homelands of Bohemia and Moravia, Hitler bullied the new Czech President, Emil Hacha, into signing a document in which he "confidently placed the fate of the Czech people and country in the hands of the Führer of the German Reich". German troops marched into Prague, and on 16 March Hitler announced the creation of the German

We, the German Führer and Chancellor and the British Prime Minister, have had a further meeting today and are agreed in recognising that the question of Anglo-German relations is of the first importance for the two countries and for Europe.

We regard the agreement signed last night and the Anglo-German Naval Agreement as symbolic of the desire of our two peoples never to go to war with one another again.

We are resolved that the method of consultation shall be the method adopted to deal with any other questions that may concern our two countries, and we are determined to continue our efforts to remove possible sources of difference and thus to contribute to assure the peace of Europe.

September 30. 1938.

Protectorate of Bohemia and Moravia. A week later Slovakia placed itself under the protection of the Reich.

Even Chamberlain no longer believed that Hitler could keep a promise. The Czechs had been taken into the Reich against their will: it was no longer possible to argue that Hitler was merely bringing Germans under his government. He had clearly started a programme of conquest; and an outraged Chamberlain was now determined to draw a line beyond which Britain would not allow Germany to go unopposed. Because of the gains she had made at Germany's expense in the Treaty of Versailles, Poland was obviously going to be Hitler's next victim; and the Polish frontier with Germany was where the British government drew their line. On 31 March 1939 Chamberlain told the House of Commons,

"in the event of any action which clearly threatened Polish independence and which the Polish Government accordingly considered it vital to resist with their national forces, His Majesty's Government would feel themselves bound at once to lend the Polish Government all support in their power. They have given the Polish Government an assurance to this effect. The

155

The price of appeasement. Prague, March 1939.

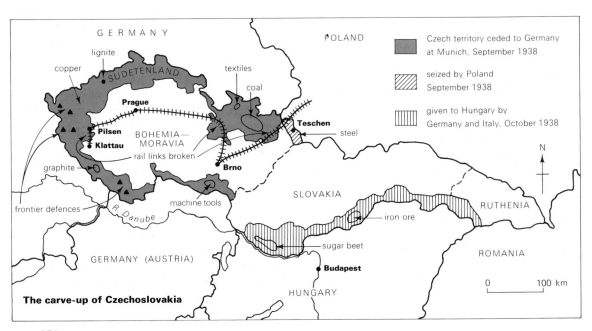

The carve-up of Czechoslovakia

French Government have authorised me to make plain that they stand in the same position."

It was an extraordinary change in policy. Whereas the British government in the early thirties had firmly resisted any idea of forming an alliance with an Eastern European state, here was a Prime Minister committing his country (and, by implication, the British Empire) to the defence of Poland. More was to come. On 13 April after Italian troops had overrun Albania in the previous week, Britain and France gave Romania and Greece similar guarantees to the one they had given Poland.

Guarantees to Poland and the two Balkan States would not be enough, however, to stop Hitler. In Eastern Europe there was only one power big enough to make him think twice about forcing along his policy of conquest. That power now put Britain and France to the test of deciding how far they were prepared to go to stop Hitler. On 18 April the government of the Soviet Union asked Britain and France to join them in making a treaty of mutual military assistance.

A glance at the map on page 149 would suggest that the British government should have jumped at Stalin's proposal. They did not. They were suspicious of the Communist leader's motives; they believed the efficiency of the Red Army had been gravely damaged by Stalin's purges; above all, they could not persuade the Poles to allow Soviet troops to enter Poland if and when war broke out. In contrast to the haste with which they had offered guarantees to Poland, Romania and Greece, the British government sent only a minor official to negotiate with Viacheslav Molotov, the Soviet Foreign Minister. For the all-important talks about cooperation in the event of war, the British government despatched a military mission on a slow boat to Russia.

On 23 August Molotov signed a non-aggression pact – but the other signature on the paper was that of Joachim von Ribbentrop, the German Foreign Minister. While the Russians had been negotiating with the British and French, they had also been sounding out what the Germans could offer them. Now, in radio and newspaper accounts of the most astounding international agreement of modern times, the world's public was told that Nazi Germany and Communist Russia had agreed not to fight each other. It was obvious to many people that Hitler was now free to

enter Poland without fear of Russian resistance, and had time to attack before winter when the weather might slow down his tanks. What the public did not know was that the two powers had also agreed, in a secret protocol (addition to the Pact) to carve up Poland between them.

In what was left of August, Hitler, Goering and Ribbentrop tried to persuade Britain and France that German claims on Poland were reasonable, perhaps hoping that Chamberlain and Daladier would be prepared to sell Poles as they had once sold Czechs to pay for an extension of peace in Europe. It did not work, and by now Hitler was in a hurry to begin his war. At 4.45 a.m. on 1 September the German army invaded Poland.

To the astonishment of MPs of all parties, Chamberlain seemed in no hurry to go to war, and Daladier insisted that his government could not send an ultimatum (final warning) to Germany without the consent of the French parliament. On 2 September he proposed an ultimatum with a 48-hour time limit. Chamberlain was prepared to wait that long but the rest of his Cabinet and many MPs in the House of Commons were not. Their anger at what they considered a shameful delay forced the Prime Minister to act. At 11.15 a.m. on 3 September 1939 Chamberlain broadcast to the nation:

"This morning the British Ambassador in Berlin handed the German Government a final note stating that unless we heard from them by eleven o'clock that they were prepared at once to withdraw their troops from Poland, a state of war would exist between us. I have to tell you now that no such understanding has been received and that consequently this country is at war with Germany."

The French declared war at 5.00 p.m. on the same day. It was all over: appeasement had failed. Chamberlain told the House of Commons:

"Everything that I have worked for, everything that I had hoped for, everything that I have believed in during my public life, has crashed in ruins."

Later that day the Prime Minister met his new War Cabinet at No. 10 Downing Street. Reluctantly he had given his most persistent critic the job of directing the Royal Navy in war. Winston Churchill was back in the British government, as First Lord of the Admiralty.

30 The Last European War

Allied and Axis Strategies

The political and military leaders of the countries which went to war in September 1939 believed they had learnt the lessons of the Great War of 1914–18. They were determined not to fight a war of attrition, of wearing down the enemy until he had no more human sacrifices left to make; they would not re-live the nightmares of Verdun, the Somme and Passchendaele. As you will see, some had learnt their lessons better than others.

The French and British could see no further than fighting a defensive war, in which they would protect themselves against air attack and weaken Germany by naval blockade. They hoped that the USA would one day enter the conflict; but meanwhile they believed that their greatest strengths were their defences: the French had the Maginot Line; the British had the Royal Navy and the English Channel – the widest anti-tank barrier in Europe. In contrast, the Germans were to become aggressors; and to suit their strategy of conquest they had developed the new technique of *blitzkrieg* – lightning war.

The essence of *blitzkrieg* was surprise, speed and weight of attack; its novelty was in the way it made use of two modern weapons – the tank and the warplane. First the air force would attack, bombing enemy positions and airfields and dropping paratroops behind their lines; then heavy tanks would smash through the front. Medium tanks would open up the gap, followed by motorised infantry whose job was to consolidate the new positions and mop up any enemy resistance. Throughout the attack the air force would continue to support the armour advancing on the ground, its dive-bombers acting as a kind of swift-moving airborne artillery.

From Lightning to 'Phoney' War

The workings of the two strategies meant that, as Hitler's armies attacked Poland in the East, British and French forces remained on the defensive in the West – despite their guarantees of support to the Poles. The German Führer in this war already had one enormous advantage over the German Kaiser in the last: he had to fight on only one front.

Hitler launched his *blitzkrieg* with a vast superiority in men and machines: 63 divisions, six of them armoured, against the Poles' 20 divisions and 12 cavalry brigades (only one of which had given up its horses and been mechanised); 2,000 aircraft against 600. Most of the Polish air force was destroyed on the ground, and the army was unable to cope with the speed of the German attack. By 17 September the Poles were defending just three separated areas around Warsaw, Lublin and Lvov. Now was the time for Soviet forces to march in and take over eastern Poland as had been agreed in the Nazi–Soviet Pact. On 1 October, just one month after the outbreak of war, German troops entered the Polish capital, Warsaw. On the next day resistance came to an end, and before the month was out the state of Poland disappeared from the map – parcelled out between the German Reich and the Soviet Union.

The gain for the Russians was a front line further to the west, 160 extra kilometres for German troops to travel should Hitler one day turn against Stalin. The Russians now tried to bully another neighbour, Finland, into parting with territories which would improve the defensive position of Leningrad. The Finns refused and the Russians invaded, only to get themselves involved in a surprisingly long little war – the 'Winter War'. Eventually, the Red Army brought the unequal struggle to an end, and the Finnish territories were added to the Soviet Union in March 1940. By that time the working relationship between Russia and Germany had been strengthened by the signing of a commercial treaty in February 1940. Russia agreed to supply Germany with grain and vital raw materials such as copper, nickel, tin, tungsten and iron ore; while in return Germany provided the Soviet Union with technical know-how and machine tools for her armaments industry.

Meanwhile, in the West, the governments of France and Britain had called up conscripts and stepped up the pace of munitions production. They had issued civilians with gas masks and steel sheets for back-garden shelters in preparation for the onslaught. They had watched, embarrassed, as Poland went under, and then stiffened themselves to meet the Nazi assault – and nothing had happened.

The British called it the 'Phoney War', the French 'La Drôle de Guerre'; and it was indeed a very odd kind of war to be fighting – or, rather, not fighting. At sea the Allied blockade looked anything but a serious threat to the German economy: enough neutral countries were now willing to supply Hitler with all he wanted – from Romanian oil to Swedish iron ore. On land the French disposed their armies along the frontier, and the British sent nearly all the soldiers they had to help them (although by January 1940 the British Expeditionary Force – BEF – in France consisted of only five divisions). Together the French and the British tried to persuade the Belgians and the Dutch to join them in a common plan for the defence of the West, but the Dutch were unwilling to give up their neutrality. Even though most people believed that a German attack in the West was bound to follow a similar path to that of the offensive of August 1914 the Belgians refused to throw in their lot with the Allies.

The countries which did join the alliance against Germany were those of the British Empire. The British declaration of war on 3 September 1939 automatically brought in the colonies and India; and the Dominions all joined in during the same month – except for Ireland, which stayed neutral. It would, however, take a long time before those additions to the alliance could have much practical effect: none of the Dominions had a large standing army.

And what of Germany's allies? You may have been puzzled by the absence of any mention of Italy (the other end of the Berlin–Rome Axis) in the story of the first few months of the war. Mussolini had warned Hitler in May 1939 that Italy could not undertake a major war before 1943. She was not only much weaker han Germany in military terms; she was also far more vulnerable to attack by the combined navies of France and Britain. So, until the Western Allies were weakened by Germany, Mussolini was happy to keep out of the war.

Eventually, in March 1940, after more than six months of 'Phoney War', the British and French decided to tighten the blockade of Germany. Their plan was to land an expeditionary force in Norway to seize the port of Narvik, through which Swedish iron ore was shipped to Germany. But by the time the plan was put into action in mid-April, Hitler had got in first. On 9 April German troops had landed in the chief Norwegian ports, and the Allied forces now faced an enemy for whom they had not prepared. Their attempts to change an expedition to Narvik into a series of attacks on German positions failed miserably. Norway sur-

rendered and Hitler set up a puppet government there headed by the leader of the Norwegian Nazi Party, Vidkun Quisling. There were to be other 'quislings' in the months to come.

After so many months of inaction, the British failure in Norway was humiliating. By early May the British Prime Minister, Neville Chamberlain, had lost the confidence of the House of Commons and was considering resignation. Then, as the war suddenly lurched much nearer home, members of both the Conservative and Labour Parties made it clear that they would no longer support him in office. On 10 May he was persuaded to hand over at once to the man who had been the most outspoken critic of appeasement. Winston Churchill became Prime Minister on the day that Hitler's armies invaded the Netherlands and Belgium.

Disaster in the West

Churchill quickly formed a new National government, a coalition which included members of the Labour Party as well as Conservatives and Liberals.

But by the evening of 15 May, less than a week later, the survival of all Western Europe was already in doubt. The German *blitzkrieg* had swept through the Netherlands and Belgium and had cracked the French defences.

Once again Hitler was able to fight his war on only one front: he left behind only ten divisions to guard Germany's frontier with Russia. And once again the German *blitzkrieg* overwhelmed the opposition by its speed and weight after Hitler and his generals had chosen to launch their attack on France along a section of the frontier where the Western Allies least expected it.

The Maginot Line and the armies behind it provided a strong defence only as far north as the border with Luxembourg: the defence of the north-east of France was left in the hands of armies which contained almost all the most powerful and highly mobile French divisions, together with the BEF. Between the armies in the north-east and the Maginot Line was an area which the French had not troubled to protect either with concrete fortresses or large numbers of troops: they believed that this sector had more than adequate natural fortifications – the River Meuse and beyond it the Ardennes Mountains. It was exactly there that Hitler made his thrust spearheaded by no fewer than

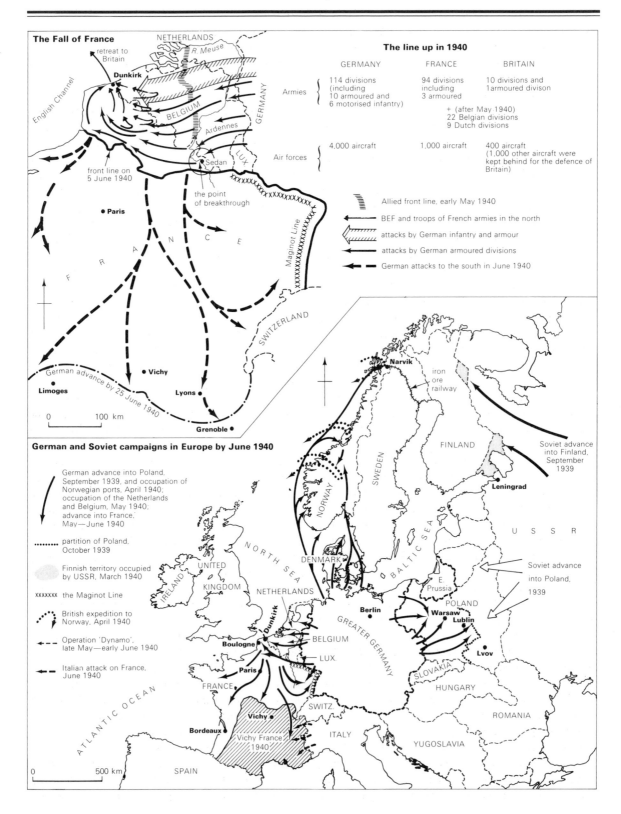

seven armoured divisions. The *Luftwaffe* destroyed much of the French air force early on 10 May; the massive German tank force rumbled undisturbed along the narrow, twisting roads of the Ardennes, paused for the capture of bridges across the Meuse, and then punched a hole in the French front line.

Suddenly the roads to the west were open and in true *blitzkrieg* style the German armoured divisions swept along them. Their devastating assault turned the Maginot Line into an expensive stretch of useless concrete and steel, and it trapped 13 French divisions, 9 divisions of the BEF and the whole of the Belgian army against the sea.

In an attempt to strengthen national unity in France, Prime Minister Reynaud, who had replaced Daladier in March, invited into his government right-wingers, left-wingers and military experts. Among the newcomers were the aged and revered hero of Verdun, Marshal Pétain, and the young commander of a tank division, General Charles de Gaulle. But political changes could not stop tanks.

The British had sent the whole of their, admittedly small, fighting army to France. Despite Reynaud's pleas Churchill now refused to commit the whole of the air force to the battle for France: he believed that most of the RAF's fighter planes must be held back to resist any future invasion of the home islands. By 22 May the Germans had reached Boulogne. On the 25th the commander of the BEF, Lord Gort, gave up hope of breaking out to the south and ordered his troops to withdraw to Dunkirk. On the 27th, as British troops retreated and lost contact with their Belgian allies, King Leopold asked for an armistice. On the next morning the Belgian army surrendered, unconditionally, to the Germans.

By that time the British Admiralty had put into action 'Operation Dynamo' – a plan to lift what they could of a trapped British army and their French allies from the beaches of Dunkirk. Deeply pessimistic, they expected to save only about 45,000 men before the German armour and air force closed in for the kill. For a change, success exceeded all expectations. By 4 June, over 330,000 men had been ferried to safety across the Channel by the Royal Navy, merchant ships and an armada of pleasure boats from the riversides and resorts of southern England. Some 200,000 British and 130,000 French soldiers escaped to fight another day, though for some time to come they would have nothing to fight with: their transport, tanks and guns had been

left behind, wrecked or deliberately destroyed on the shores of wounded France.

On the day that 'Dynamo' ended, Churchill addressed the House of Commons.

"Even though large tracts of Europe and many old and famous states have fallen or may fall into the grip of the Gestapo and all the odious apparatus of Nazi rule, we shall not flag or fail. We shall go on to the end. We shall fight in France, we shall fight in the seas and oceans, we shall fight with growing confidence and growing strength in the air; we shall defend our Island whatever the cost may be. We shall fight on the beaches, we shall fight on the landing-grounds, we shall fight on the fields and in the streets, we shall fight in the hills; we shall never surrender . . ."

The "old and famous states" that had fallen to the Nazis were Norway, Denmark (overrun on 9 April), Belgium, and the Netherlands (surrendered on 15 May). As for fighting in France – well, her days were numbered.

On 10 June Mussolini attacked in the south-east. The *Duce* feared that if he waited until 1943 he would be too late to share in the spoils of Hitler's victory: "I need a thousand dead in order to take my seat at the table with the victors." He was to get his thousand corpses in the most humiliating way: a French force, outnumbered by more than two to one, stopped the Italian invasion in its tracks. Meanwhile the Germans had swung south through France driving before them millions of refugees and the remnants of French armies who were given no time to re-group and counter-attack. Among the refugees were Paul Reynaud and his government, who fled from Paris on 10 June and reached Bordeaux five days later.

By now the government was deeply divided. A minority supported Reynaud, who was determined not to surrender and had vague plans for carrying on the war from France's overseas empire in North Africa. The majority formed a 'peace party' led by Pétain. On 16 June Reynaud resigned, and Pétain took over as Prime Minister. On the 22nd France's new government signed an armistice with Germany.

The battle for France was over. The Germans occupied the whole of the north and the Atlantic coast: Pétain was left with a rump state which Hitler allowed him to govern from the spa town of Vichy. To the French people, dazed after a six-week defeat, Pétain explained that the disaster had been brought about not only by the French having fewer troops and fewer aircraft than the Germans, but also by the moral weakness of democracy – a form of government for which the Marshal had no respect.

It was true that France had not built an air force capable of clawing Hitler's *Luftwaffe* out of the skies. It was also true that her defeat owed much to the defensive strategy of her army generals. They had been made to look foolish by an enemy that fought its crucial battles with concentrated masses of fast-moving tanks. Whether France fell because democracy had made her morally weak is more arguable. True, France had had many changes of government in the inter-war years, but much of her political instability had been due to the threats of violence from the right-wing and fascist groups now supporting Pétain, the French 'quisling'. The story of the French resistance would show whether it was Pétain and his friends or thousands of brave, more humble Frenchmen who had a spirit of sacrifice.

As Pétain set up shop in Vichy, Charles de Gaulle escaped to Britain. But the British refused to accept him as they accepted other leaders in exile – King Haakon of Norway, Queen Wilhelmina of the Netherlands, General Sikorski of Poland – as representatives of the rightful governments of their countries. Churchill's government did not want to see the whole of France under Nazi occupation; but by accepting the partition of the country they had to recognise the Vichy régime as the government of unoccupied France. Consequently, they could not recognise de Gaulle as the leader of the whole nation, only as the head of a fighting group, the Free French. Such treatment would rankle in the General's mind for a very long time to come.

Meanwhile, there was one last act to be played out in the tragedy of France. Her fleet had been sent to French ports in North Africa, but the British feared that the Germans might decide to call on it for use against them. On 3 July the Royal Navy attacked the ships of their former allies and friends at Mers el-Kebir: 1,300 French sailors were killed and only one of their battleships escaped serious damage or destruction. It was a savage act of war by a country which now stood alone against the Nazis.

Britain Alone

On 16 July Hitler issued orders for the preparation of 'Operation Sea-Lion', an assault on Britain to be carried out by his land, sea and air forces. If the invasion were to succeed, German air superiority had to be established over the Channel and the south of England, and the greater part of Goering's *Luftwaffe* was therefore moved to bases in northern France and the Low Countries. Across the narrow seas the RAF's Fighter Command prepared to meet an attack in which its own airfields would be prime targets, an attack whose outcome could well decide whether the British survived as a free people or were brought under Nazi rule – or maybe that of a British 'quisling'. The leader of the British fascist movement, Sir Oswald Mosley, had been put in prison, but there would have been a place for him in a pro-German government.

The Battle of Britain and the Blitz

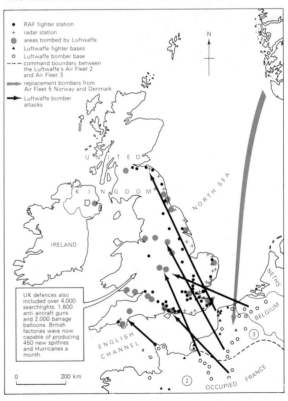

- • RAF fighter station
- + radar station
- ● areas bombed by Luftwaffe
- ▲ Luftwaffe fighter bases
- ○ Luftwaffe bomber base
- --- command boundary between the Luftwaffe's Air Fleet 2 and Air Fleet 3
- ➡ replacement bombers from Air Fleet 5 Norway and Denmark
- ➡ Luftwaffe bomber attacks

UK defences also included over 4,000 searchlights, 1,800 anti-aircraft guns and 2,000 barrage balloons. British factories were now capable of producing 450 new spitfires and Hurricanes a month.

0   200 km

By August 1940 German Air Fleets 2 and 3, based in France and the Low Countries, had 875 bombers, 316 dive-bombers and 930 fighters (mostly Messerschmitt 109s) Air Fleet 5 in Norway and Denmark had over 100 bombers – to be used mainly to replace the

Iris Cox goes to war, with her suitcase and her gasmask. As a precaution against air attacks many children were evacuated from the cities to the countryside on the outbreak of war. By the time of the 'blitz', many of the evacuees had returned to their homes.

losses of Fleets 2 and 3. The RAF had 650 fighters (mostly Hurricanes and Spitfires).

The preliminary stage of the Battle of Britain started on 10 July 1940 when the *Luftwaffe* attacked convoys in the Channel. On 13 August, 'Eagle Day', German pilots set course for new targets and prepared to repeat the tactics which had helped bring Germany victory in Poland and France: they were to attack the fighter bases of their enemy. The next three weeks were critical. Although radar gave the RAF advance warning of raiding bombers, many of them found their way through British defences and inflicted severe damage on the airfields, while German fighter escorts took a heavy toll of British aircraft and pilots. The *Luftwaffe* lost more planes and more men; but given the advantage of numbers with which they started, they could

'afford' the casualties. By the beginning of September Fighter Command was down to 840 pilots (compared with over 1,400 a month earlier); and young aviators, fresh from the RAF's schools, were being shot out of the sky faster than their replacements could be trained.

During those weeks when the fate of Britain appeared to depend on a few very young men, not long out of school, a German error changed the course of the battle and probably decided its result. On 23 August a flight of bombers lost its way and dropped its cargo on the East End of London. Churchill immediately ordered a revenge raid, and on the 28th the first Berliners were killed by British bombs. Hitler now ordered the *Luftwaffe* to turn away from its strategic attack on airfields to the bombing of London. As the 'blitz' on the British capital began, so Fighter Command was spared from destruction. London had attracted the wrath of the Führer; and first Londoners and then citizens in other parts of the kingdom began to pay with their lives for the survival of their country.

As Fighter Command was released from the daily strain of defending its own widely dispersed bases, it began to inflict heavier casualties on the German bombing squadrons. German hopes for air superiority began to fade, and on 17 September Hitler postponed his invasion "until further notice". On 12 October he postponed it until January 1941, and in that January 'Sea-Lion' was finally called off. In the Battle of Britain, from July until the end of October, the Germans lost a total of 1,733 aircraft and the British lost 915 fighters.* It was a famous, and a decisive, victory. Britain had survived as a base from which attacks might later be made on the mainland of Europe.

If the battle was over, the war still went on and with it the 'blitz'. From early September to mid-November London was subjected to intensive bombing. Over 13,000 tonnes of high explosive were dropped on the capital, and over 13,000 people were killed. Waging war on civilians was expensive: one tonne of steel-wrapped high explosive, delivered by air, for each corpse. Damage to property, from blast and fire, was both extensive and spectacular.

On the night of 14 November the *Luftwaffe* temporarily turned its attention away from the suffering capital: 449 bombers attacked Coventry in the single biggest air-raid on a British city; 554 people were killed, 865 were injured – it was a devastating opening to the 'blitz' of the provincial cities and ports. Plymouth, Southampton, Hull, Bristol, Liverpool, Manchester, Birmingham, Glasgow – the targets were all obvious; and they were either well or ill prepared for their fate according to whether their local councillors and officials were well or ill prepared. In all, 43,685 citizens would die in raids before the end of 1941, just over 20,000 of them in London.

It is not possible to describe here in any detail what it was like to experience the 'blitz': for that you will have to read elsewhere. Instead we will look at the hole it made in the life of an old man from Hull. As you read the following passage, try not to think of it as 'typical'. All the tragedies of the 'blitz' were personal, and therefore different.

*Some historians give different figures. These are taken from B. H. Liddell Hart's *History of the Second World War* (published in 1970 by Cassell).

"I just went down to the Post an' when I come back it was as flat as this 'ere wharfside – there was just my 'ouse like – well, part of my 'ouse. My missus was just making me a cup of tea for when I come 'ome. She were in the passage between the kitchen and the wash-'ouse, where it blowed 'er. She were burnt right up to 'er waist. 'er legs were just two cinders. And 'er face ... the only thing I could recognise 'er by was one of 'er boots ... I'd 'ave lost fifteen homes if I could 'ave kept my missus. We used to read together. I can't read messen. She used to read to me like. We'd 'ave our arm-chairs one either side of the fire, and she read me bits out o' the paper. We 'ad a paper every evening. *Every* evening."

Even after Hitler had removed his invasion fleet from the Channel ports, Britain had no means of carrying the fight against the Axis Powers into occupied Western Europe. Only in the Mediterranean and in Africa were the British able to strike against the enemy alliance, and then only against its weaker half, Italy.

In November 1940 aircraft from the carrier *Illustrious* attacked the Italian fleet at Taranto, severely damaged three out of six battleships, and silenced Mussolini's boast that his navy was a formidable fighting force. In January 1941 Haile Selassie returned to Abyssinia (see Chapter 29, page 149) to lead an uprising against the Italian occupying forces. The Abyssinians were helped by an invasion from the Sudan and Kenya of British, South African and Free French Forces. By November, the five-year-old Italian Empire in Abyssinia was at an end (see the map on page 173).

To the north of Abyssinia a large force of British and Dominion troops had the vital task of protecting Egypt, the Suez Canal and the oil-fields of the Middle East which provided the fuel and the lubricants for all the armed services. In September 1940 a much larger Italian force had advanced from Libya against the British positions, had been halted and then forced into headlong retreat. By early February 1941 the British had captured 130,000 Italians and appeared to be undisputed masters of North Africa. But later that month Hitler sent to the aid of his Axis partner a light-armoured division commanded by General Rommel. The arrival of this expert in tank warfare swung the balance back in favour of the Axis: his rapid offensive in April pushed the British towards Egypt and surrounded the vital port of Tobruk.

By the end of May 1941 Britain's position as the last surviving enemy of the German Reich was by no means secure. From Manchester to Malta she was under attack from the *Luftwaffe*. From Southampton to Suez her trade routes were in danger. German submarines now operated from bases perilously close to the British Isles and were gaining the upper hand in the long and crucial Battle of the Atlantic, the struggle to keep open the sea routes to the Americas and the British Empire along which most of the UK's food and arms had to come. The German raids on Britain's shipping and on her cities were made doubly effective by the use of bombers from airfields along the coastlines of Nazi-dominated Western Europe. Nor could the British take any comfort from developments in Eastern Europe, where the war had freed both Germany and Russia from the old restraints on their ambitions.

A New Map of Eastern Europe

When Czechoslovakia and Poland were dismembered in 1939, the writing was on the wall for the rest of Eastern Europe. There was nothing to stop the two great powers of Germany and Russia re-drawing the map to suit their own purposes.

In August 1940, while Hitler was still giving most of his attention to the West, the Russians absorbed Lithuania, Latvia and Estonia into the Soviet Union, having first seized the territories of Bessarabia and the northern Bukovina from Romania. Hitler made himself effective master of the countries to the south of his enlarged Reich. The friendship of Bulgaria and Hungary was bought by allowing each to take a part of what the Russians had left of Romania. Romania then asked Germany to guarantee the rump of her territory – so

Hitler's mastery of Europe, by early June 1941

Hitler's guarantee replaced the one given by Britain in April 1939 (see Chapter 29, page 157).

In September 1940 Germany signed a Tripartite Pact with Japan and Italy, in which each country promised to support the others if they were attacked by any new enemy. The possible enemy of the future whom the Germans and Japanese had chiefly in mind was the USA. But to the small states of Eastern Europe the creeping extension of Russian territory was a much more alarming threat, and a number of them decided to secure German 'protection' by asking to join the Tripartite Pact. Hungary, Slovakia and Romania would all become members by November.

Hitler could hardly have asked for more: Eastern Europe was falling into his lap without any need for him to pull his armed forces away from the West. But Mussolini disturbed this quiet takeover by invading Greece in October. The Italian troops were soon forced back into Albania, but not before the Greeks had invited Britain to intervene. The British sent aircraft to the mainland and occupied the island of Crete, where Hitler saw them as a potential threat to the oilfields of Romania. The Führer decided that he must smash Greece and evict the British.

To do this he needed to control the roads through Bulgaria and Yugoslavia. Bulgaria was already firmly in the German camp and willingly joined the Tripartite Pact in March 1941. So did Yugoslavia, but there the government's decision to back Germany led to its overthrow in a revolt led by air force and some army leaders. Hitler immediately decided to attack Yugoslavia as well

as Greece, and on 6 April launched his armed forces against both countries.

The German victory took less time than even Hitler had anticipated. The Yugoslavian troops surrendered on 16 April, although the resistance groups were not crushed; Athens, the capital of Greece, fell on the 27th. The British forces that had been sent to help the Greeks were evacuated to Crete – and the Germans captured Crete on 2 June. Germany, Italy, Hungary and Bulgaria all took a cut in the share-out of the Balkan spoils. Greece was occupied by Axis (mainly Italian) forces; and Yugoslavia disappeared from the map to be replaced by areas occupied by Italy and Germany and a puppet state in Croatia run by local pro-fascist politicians and churchmen.

Hitler now had an economic empire. From France and the Netherlands in the West to Romania and Greece in the East, he could control, directly or indirectly, the economies of a continent in the interests of the Reich. Towards the peoples of the conquered and 'client' states the Nazis did not act in a uniformly barbaric way. In general, their behaviour was harsher in the East than in the West. In France and the Netherlands they kept to some of the codes of civilised conduct: in the 'incorporated territories' and 'General Government' of what had once been Poland, the Gestapo and the SS set up a reign of terror and racial persecution. Many of the people of Britain, thankful for their sruvival in the summer of 1940, still did not realise the full horror of the fate from which they had been saved.

31 The Second World War

Between September 1939 and May 1941, countries in both Eastern and Western Europe had taken on Nazi Germany in war, and they had lost. Others had caved in without a fight, and yet others had only avoided full military occupation by joining the Tripartite Pact. Nearly all the action had been confined to the continent of Europe itself. Germany had no overseas colonies for her enemies to attack; and after a year and nine months of Hitler's war the rest of the world was hardly ruffled. Tanks had churned up the sands of North Africa, and U-Boats had stained the waters of the Atlantic and the Mediterranean – but that was about all. Of the two great powers that stayed out of the war, one in the East and one in the West, the Soviet Union had an understanding with Germany, and the USA was protected by 5,000 kilometres of ocean.

The USSR's leaders worried about how long their understanding with Germany would last, but for the time being they could claim that the war was no real concern of theirs. Their propaganda called it a war between capitalist and imperialist powers, ignoring the fact that they had helped themselves to the Baltic States, and parts of Finland and Romania. Everywhere in Europe, communists took their line (as they had done since 1919) from Moscow: this war, they parroted, was of no concern to 'the people'. That they took that line said more for their discipline than for their common sense.

In the USA the argument which most appealed was the one that said America should steer well clear of the war and let the Europeans fight it out for themselves. When we last looked at the USA, Franklin D. Roosevelt was still grappling with the problems of the Depression that he had only partially solved in two terms as President (see Chapter 26, pages 119–27). In July 1940 he was nominated by the Democratic Party to stand for election for an unprecedented third term; but his re-election this time was very far from the 'certainty' of 1936. Above all, he had to tread very carefully round the issue of possible American involvement in the war.

In the grim days of May and June 1940, when Hitler's assault on Western Europe looked unstoppable, both France and Britain appealed to the USA for help. The fall of France shocked American public opinion, and in September the US government did send help to Britain, in the shape of fifty old destroyers in exchange for rent-free naval bases in British colonies from Bermuda to British Guiana. It was an act that to some people looked more like hard bargaining than aid to a hard-pressed friend.

Roosevelt had his electorate to consider. In a speech in Boston at the end of October he declared, "And while I am talking to you mothers and fathers, I give you one more assurance. I have said this before, but I shall say it again and again and again: your boys are not going to be sent into any foreign wars." In November he was re-elected President by a majority of five million votes.

With four more years of power ahead of him Roosevelt could set out to strengthen Britain's resistance to Hitler. By the middle of March 1941 the Lend-Lease Bill was passed through Congress, giving the President power to lend or lease arms to any nation whose own defence was considered vital to American security. The USA would be, in the President's words, "the great arsenal of democracy" – but it was doubtful how long the American people could limit their involvement in the war to just earning a decent wage in an arsenal.

However, the most alarming threat to American influence and security was now coming from the East rather than from the West. In Chapter 23 (page 103) you saw how the generals of the Japanese army brought about war against China, took the province of Manchuria and then occupied vast territories to the south. In July 1941 they occupied French Indo-China with the agreement of Pétain's government in Vichy. From their new bases in South-East Asia the Japanese now threatened the colonies of the Western imperialist Powers; the Dutch in the oil-rich East Indies, the British in Malaya and Burma – and the Americans in the Philippines.

Roosevelt responded by freezing all Japanese cash and property in the USA and tightening economic sanctions. The American government had already imposed an embargo on scrap iron and scrap steel: now they joined with the Dutch and the British to place an embargo on oil. The 'war party' in Tokyo prepared to take action, and in October the civilian Prime Minister, Fumimoro Konoye, was replaced by the former War Minister, General Hideki Tojo. The Japanese were well prepared for war in Asia and in the Pacific: they were allied to the Axis Powers in Europe; they had signed a non-aggression pact with Russia in April 1941; and they possessed a large army and a powerful modern navy. If they felt they had to go to war to clear the Westerners from their path, they must strike quickly before the "arsenal of democracy" built up her own armed forces to wartime levels. The value of a massive surprise attack had already been demonstrated in this war; in Poland, in the Netherlands and France, in Yugoslavia. But while the Japanese were considering where and when they should make their move, Hitler had already struck once more – against Russia.

Barbarossa

On 22 June 1941 the armies of Nazi Germany poured across the frontiers of Soviet Russia. They were the greatest invasion force Hitler had ever set in motion: their objective was the conquest of the largest country on the face of the earth; the code-name for their assault was 'Operation Barbarossa'. Obviously, an attack on this scale (nearly 200 divisions of infantry and armour, 3,500 tanks, 3,000 aircraft) was not an adventure the Nazi leader dreamt up overnight: in fact, Hitler had ordered the plans to be prepared eleven months back, when the *Luftwaffe* was fighting the preliminary skirmishes of the Battle of Britain. The great question is why Hitler went ahead with 'Barbarossa', when by June 1941 he was already master of Europe.

Some historians have suggested that 'Barbarossa' was merely part of a monstrous plan for the Nazi domination of the world. Others have said that it was a predictable grab for *lebensraum*, for more 'living-space' for the German people. Another argument is that Hitler knew that the Russians were playing for time when Molotov signed the non-aggression pact of August 1939 with Ribbentrop (see page 157). July 1941 was Hitler's view of the best time for him to strike before the Russians consolidated their strength. If that was so, three months before the attack, he left his generals with no doubts about the aims of the war which would start with 'Barbarossa':

"The Communists never have been and never will be our friends. The fight which is about to begin is a war of extermination. If Germany does not embark upon it in this spirit she may well defeat the enemy but in thirty years from now they will once again rise up and confront her."

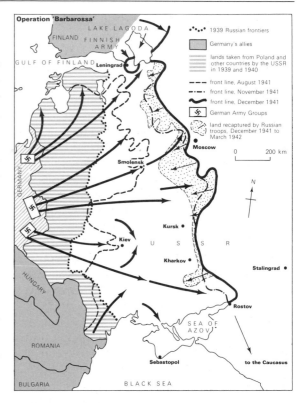

Germany	USSR
116 infantry divisions (14 of them motorised)	88 infantry divisions
19 armoured divisions (with 3,500 tanks)	7 cavalry divisions
15 divisions from Finland	54 tank and motorised divisions (with a claimed total of over 20,000 tanks, more than half of which were in western Russia – and many of which were obsolete)
20 divisions from Romania	
10 divisions from Hungary	
10 divisions from Italy	
3,000 modern aircraft	
	6,000 aircraft – most of them obsolete

Look at Russia on any map (for example page 137). The sheer size of it had defeated the greatest of all modern European warlords: in 1812 Napoleon had been forced to retreat in humiliation from Moscow. One hundred years later, in the Great War, even the Kaiser's armies had barely made a dent in it. But Hitler was not impressed. Napoleon didn't have Stukas and Messerschmitts; the Kaiser didn't have tanks. *Blitzkrieg* had done for Poland in five weeks, France in six weeks, Yugoslavia in under a fortnight. Russia – whose armies had been weakened by Stalin's purges, and whose minority peoples in the west would not all struggle to defend a Communist dictatorship – would take longer, perhaps as much as six months. Hitler was confident to the point of cockiness; and military experts in both Britain and the USA thought he had every reason to be so. No one, except perhaps the Russian Communists, gave the Red Army much of a chance.

The three German army groups punched massive holes in the Russian defences. On all fronts the Red Army reeled back, its generals outwitted by the battle-hardened veterans of the *Wehrmacht*. Early in July Stalin made his first radio broadcast to the Russian people and ordered them to stand firm against the invaders of the fatherland: the "imperialists' war" had become, in the twinkling of a dictator's eye, the Great Patriotic War against the Fascist hordes.

Standing firm was impossible: those Russian armies that tried it were surrounded and then hauled off into captivity. Collaboration turned into a nightmare: soldiers and citizens who welcomed the Germans as liberators were tortured, forced to work for their new masters, or shot. The only realistic tactic was to hold on until defeat was imminent and then to retreat, destroying anything that might be of use to the enemy and carting off industrial plant to distant, safe regions of the country. The Germans advanced over a. 'scorched earth'; by the end of November they had captured lands that contained over sixty per cent of Russian coal and pig-iron production, and over half the output of steel. And the Russians evacuated over 1,500 industrial enterprises to the east.

By the beginning of December 1941 Hitler's armies had advanced beyond the Sea of Azov in the south; they had surrounded the city of Leningrad in the north; and they had penetrated the suburbs of Moscow itself. On 6 December General Zhukov launched a Russian counter-attack which drove the Germans away from the capital. As 'Barbarossa' came to a temporary halt in the depths of a Russian winter, far away to the east the Japanese launched their attack on the United States of America.

Pearl Harbour and Japan's Onslaught in Asia and the Pacific

On the morning of 7 December 1941, between 6 o'clock and 7.15, 360 aircraft took off from six Japanese carriers sailing about 440 kilometres due north of the US naval base at Pearl Harbour. They were picked up by American radar, but intelligence officers mistook them for planes coming in from the States. The radar station was closed down at 7 a.m., and the operators went off to church parade. It was Sunday in Hawaii.

At 7.55 a.m. the first wave of dive-bombers and torpedo-bombers attacked the undefended American fleet: the second wave went in at 8.40. By 10 o'clock it was all over. Of eight American battleships, four had been sunk and four severely damaged. Ten other warships had been sunk or put out of action; 188 planes had been destroyed and another 159 damaged; 2,403 Americans had been killed and 1,178 injured. Only the American carriers had escaped: they were at sea during the raid. In the space of two hours Japan had become the greatest naval power in the Pacific: it had cost her a mere twenty-nine aircraft.

On the following day, 8 December, both America and Britain declared war on Japan. They were followed in the next few days by the Latin American states of Costa Rica, the Dominican Republic, Haiti, Honduras, Nicaragua, El Salvador, Cuba, Guatemala and Panama. On 11 December the circle was completed when Germany and Italy honoured (if that's the right word) the promise they had made in the Tripartite Pact, and declared war on the USA. Hitler's war had at last spilt right across the globe.*

In crippling the American fleet at Pearl Harbour, Japan carried out the first crucial stage in her plan to force Western imperialists out of Asia. The maintenance and defence of European and American colonies in Asia and the Pacific were not possible without control of the seas. The Americans knew it and the British knew it: the Japanese now demonstrated it at a speed that left their enemies flat-footed.

On 8 December, in three separate offensives, they bombed American positions in the Philippines, attacked the British in Hong Kong on land and from the air, and began to land troops in Thailand to prepare for an assault on British Malaya and the great naval base at Singapore. On the 10th, Japanese aircraft struck at British warships sailing to intercept the troop transports: the battleships *Prince of Wales* and *Repulse* were sunk – and so were any remaining hopes of the Royal Navy being able to defend Singapore. In mid-December Japanese troops invaded Burma.

* The conflict which began in 1939 would now become known as the 'Second World War'; which meant that the Great War of 1914–18 would be referred to as the 'First World War'.

Battleships burning after the raid on Pearl Harbour: the West Virginia, *and behind her the* Tennessee.

On Christmas Day and Boxing Day, Hong Kong and 12,000 prisoners fell into Japanese hands. Less than a fortnight later, on 6 January 1942, Japanese troops entered the Dutch East Indies. Before the end of the month British, Australian and Indian forces had retreated from the tip of the Malay peninsula to Singapore; on 8 February the great base itself was attacked. One week later it was surrendered, along with 80,000 men, to an enemy force of no more than 35,000. Singapore, "the outstanding symbol of Western power in the Far East", collapsed with more of a whimper than a bang.

So it went on. By the end of the first week of March nearly 100,000 Dutch East Indian troops had surrendered. On 6 May the USA gave up the struggle to keep the Philippines after losing 110,000 Filipino and 30,000 American troops. In the same month the British abandoned Burma. The Japanese now held the country through which Chiang Kai-shek had his only access to the outside world. The Chinese had been at war with Japan since 1937 (see page 103) and they now lost any chance of joining forces with Japan's new enemies.

Together with their other conquests of Pacific islands, the Japanese now held a vast empire on the

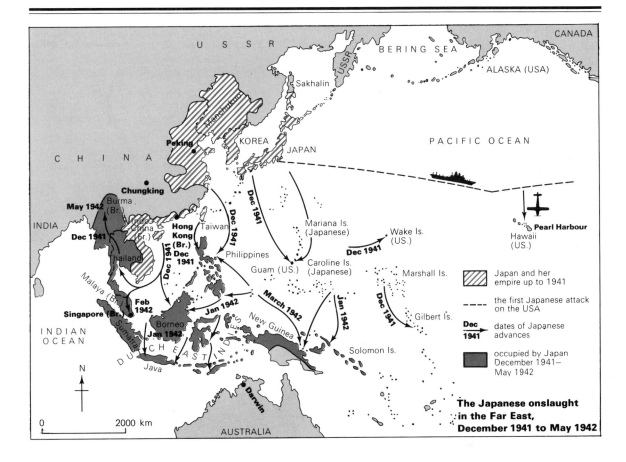

The Japanese onslaught
in the Far East,
December 1941 to May 1942

mainland of Asia, in the East Indies and dispersed over the sea. They called it the Greater Asia Co-Prosperity Sphere, a propaganda title that suggested a working partnership between the Asian Japanese and their new Asian subjects. It was a sham: Japan milked her empire for all it was worth. Subject peoples soon discovered that Asian imperialism was no better than Western imperialism: indeed, in some places the behaviour of the Japanese made it markedly worse.

The Allies: a Second Front or 'Torch'?

The three great powers – Britain, the Soviet Union and the USA – that faced the Axis at the start of 1942 soon began to refer to themselves as the "United Nations". In fact, they were closely united on only one major issue – the need to defeat Nazi Germany, quickly. Even though it had been Japanese aggression that brought the USA into the conflict, Roosevelt had agreed with Churchill and Stalin that the war against Germany should be given first priority.

But in answer to the question as to how they should set about defeating the Reich, the three powers had prepared different replies.

The Russians foresaw a bloody struggle between themselves and the Germans. They had no other choice but to defend, to counter-attack and then, if successful, to pursue. Stalin wanted his new allies to hit Germany where she too would bleed: in his opinion that could be done only by Britain and the USA opening up a second front in Western Europe.

The American Chief of Staff, General George Marshall, also believed it was the only way to win quickly: but the earliest that the Americans would be ready to make the attack would be the spring of 1943. Roosevelt, however, wanted action before that.

The British were not ready to open a second front either. The only direct action planned for 1942 was a bombing campaign master-minded by Air Marshal A. T. Harris. The result was large-scale bombing of factories and civilian populations in German towns; and that was the only kind of direct attack the British

171

made on Hitler's Europe during 1942.

Apart from that, Churchill was determined to carry on fighting Britain's war in North Africa, where the Eighth Army was facing German and Italian forces in Libya. In May and June 1942, however, Rommel's Afrika Korps thrust the British Eighth Army back to El Alamein, less than a hundred kilometres from Alexandria; and Malta was still taking a severe battering from the *Luftwaffe*. To make matters even more gloomy for the British, the Battle of the Atlantic (see page 165) was going very badly. Germany was sinking ships faster than the Allies could build them.

Churchill badly needed a win somewhere: for the first time since he had become Prime Minister people were beginning to doubt his ability to lead them in war. Eventually, in the high summer of 1942, he persuaded Roosevelt to agree to a joint American–British invasion of French North Africa. The President was attracted by the prospect of an offensive, to begin in early November: the Prime Minister was eager to draw German pressure away from Malta and the Eighth Army. The operation was to be called 'Torch'. To the American generals it looked like anything but a light in the dark: if it failed, Germany would not have been harmed; if it succeeded, and the offensive was carried on across the Mediterranean, 'Torch' might begin to suck in more men and resources and further delay the opening of a second front in Western Europe.

The Russians would have been hard pushed to think of anything less helpful than 'Torch'. In March 1942 their counter-attacks on the German lines had been halted; their front-line soldiers were exhausted. On 28 June Hitler launched a new attack, this time to the south, towards Stalingrad. When the Germans were within reach of the city, Hitler divided his forces; half to take the 'City of Stalin', half to advance further south to the oilfields in the region of the Caucasus Mountains. The southerly movement of the German armies was halted in October, just short of their objective. All eyes turned to Stalingrad where the German Sixth Army, commanded by General von Paulus, was engaged in the bloodiest fighting of the war so far.

As Germans and Russians came to grips in the streets of Stalingrad, the Americans and the British were putting together their gear for the trip to French North Africa; and General Bernard Montgomery, the new commander of the British Eighth Army, was collecting a formidable mass of men and armour with which to beat Rommel away from the Egyptian border.

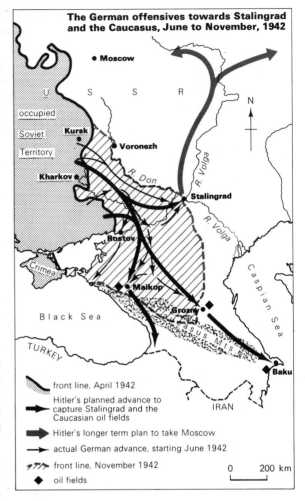

By 23 October, when the Battle of El Alamein began, Montgomery had 230,000 men and 1,440 tanks to Rommel's 80,000 troops (of whom only 27,000 were German) and 540 tanks (of which 280 were out-of-date Italian models). On 4 November the British tanks broke through the remnants of Rommel's defences and started to chase his Axis troops back through Libya.

It was four days later that 'Torch', the operation originally designed to take the pressure off the Eighth Army, was started. The Americans landed in Morocco, the British in Algeria. Both places were held by Vichy French armies which stubbornly resisted for a day until Admiral Darlan, their commander-in-chief, ordered them to stop and began to negotiate with the Allies. The next day Pétain's Vichy government dismissed Darlan. Their effort to save themselves from German anger failed: on the same day German and Italian

The Second World War

The war in Africa and the defeat of the Axis Powers

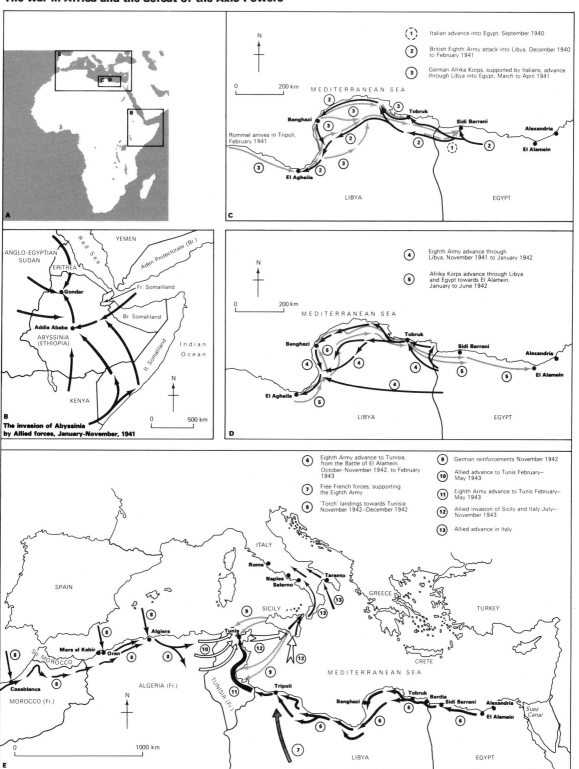

C

N

0 200 km

MEDITERRANEAN SEA

- ① Italian advance into Egypt, September 1940
- ② British Eighth Army attack into Libya, December 1940 to February 1941
- ③ German Afrika Korps, supported by Italians, advance through Libya into Egypt, March to April 1941

Rommel arrives in Tripoli, February 1941

Benghazi Tobruk Sidi Barrani Alexandria El Alamein
El Agheila LIBYA EGYPT

A

E C D B

B

ANGLO-EGYPTIAN SUDAN YEMEN Red Sea Aden Protectorate (Br.)
ERITREA Fr. Somaliland
Gondar Br. Somaliland
Addis Ababa It. Somaliland Indian Ocean
ABYSSINIA (ETHIOPIA)
KENYA
N
0 500 km

The invasion of Abyssinia by Allied forces, January–November, 1941

D

N

0 200 km

MEDITERRANEAN SEA

- ④ Eighth Army advance through Libya, November 1941 to January 1942
- ⑤ Afrika Korps advance through Libya and Egypt towards El Alamein, January to June 1942

Benghazi Tobruk Sidi Barrani Alexandria El Alamein
El Agheila LIBYA EGYPT

E

- ⑥ Eighth Army advance to Tunisia, from the Battle of El Alamein, October–November 1942, to February 1943
- ⑦ Free French forces, supporting the Eighth Army
- ⑧ 'Torch' landings towards Tunisia November 1942–December 1942
- ⑨ German reinforcements November 1942
- ⑩ Allied advance to Tunis February–May 1943
- ⑪ Eighth Army advance to Tunis February–May 1943
- ⑫ Allied invasion of Sicily and Italy July–November 1943
- ⑬ Allied advance in Italy

SPAIN ITALY GREECE TURKEY
Rome
Naples Taranto
Salerno SICILY
Tunis CRETE
Mers el Kebir Oran
Algiers MEDITERRANEAN SEA
Sp. MOROCCO ALGERIA (Fr.) TUNISIA (Fr.)
Casablanca Tripoli Benghazi Tobruk Bardia Sidi Barrani Alexandria
MOROCCO (Fr.) El Alamein Suez Canal
N
0 1000 km
LIBYA EGYPT

troops entered Vichy France, and the whole rotten structure of Pétain's 'independent' government came tumbling down.

The Western Allies, however, had Algeria and Morocco and were ready to attack Tunisia. German and Italian troops were moved in quickly, but there was not much need for haste. The advance of American and British forces towards Tunisia was a shambles. Many of the troops were inexperienced, and some of their commanders were too timid to make effective use of superior numbers against the small Axis armies. The Commander-in-Chief of the combined operation, Major-General Dwight D. Eisenhower, was appalled. On 7 December 1942 he confided to a friend, "I think the best way to describe our operations to date is that they have violated every recognised principle of war." On Christmas Eve, with the Axis still defending stoutly, and the rains pouring down, Eisenhower called a halt to the affair for the time being.

There was, however, much better news coming in from the USSR. In November, while the Americans and British had been tying themselves in knots in French North Africa, Russian armies had broken through the German lines north and south of Stalingrad and joined up in the rear to encircle the German Sixth Army. Hitler refused to allow any attempt at withdrawal from the trap and promoted General von Paulus to field-marshal as an incentive to carry on fighting. But the German position was impossible to hold, and the new field-marshal surrendered himself, twenty-four generals and 91,000 soldiers on 31st January 1943. For the first time in Hitler's war a German army in Europe had been beaten.

The Allies on the Move

Roosevelt and Churchill met at Casablanca in January 1943. Roosevelt insisted on making the 'Casablanca Declaration', which stated that the Western Allies would accept only unconditional surrender from Germany. This was intended as a plain message to Stalin that the USA and Britain would not make a separate peace with Germany and leave Stalin to face Hitler alone. At the same time, the two leaders were still not ready for the only war measure which would help Stalin in the short term: a second front in Western Europe. Instead they agreed to carry the 'Torch' campaign to its obvious conclusion and drive the Germans and Italians out of North Africa. By February, Eisenhower's

forces in the West had been reinforced and the British Eighth Army was already at the north-eastern border of Tunisia. The Axis forces had to fight a defensive action with their backs to the sea against much larger numbers of Allied troops. By 13 May the battle for Tunisia was over, and Allied control of the air over the North African coast ensured that the beaten Axis troops could not be evacuated across the Mediterranean. Altogether, about 130,000 German and Italian soldiers were taken prisoner. In his determination not to give up Tunisia, Hitler had sent to North Africa thousands of experienced troops whom he couldn't pull out once the battle was lost. They would be sorely missed.

The Allies now controlled the Mediterranean and the whole of Italian and French North Africa. Barely two weeks after the fall of Tunis, Charles de Gaulle arrived in North Africa and, together with General Giraud, whom the Americans regarded as the leader of the French Resistance, set up the French National Liberation Committee. To the Americans' dismay, de Gaulle soon out-manœuvred Giraud as leader and began to act as if the Committee were the French government: Roosevelt had already taken a violent dislike to the self-appointed 'saviour of France'.

In that early summer of 1943 Roosevelt and Churchill had more important matters to consider than the bickerings of Frenchmen. They had to decide what to do with their armies in North Africa, and they didn't have much choice. It was too late in the year to move the troops to Britain and prepare to open a second front in Western Europe: the obvious target to aim them at was Sicily. Marshall and Eisenhower had been right back in 1942: 'Torch' had led the Western Allies away from the battleground the American generals would have preferred to fight on.

In July 1943 the Americans and British launched a massive invasion of Sicily: the Axis armies badly missed their troops imprisoned in North Africa. Progress was slow and the island was only captured on 17 August. By that time Italy was in turmoil. Most Italians were sick of the war; and there were strikes in the northern industrial cities. Even the Fascist Grand Council deserted Mussolini. On 25 July General Badoglio took over as head of the government and the former dictator was removed from Rome.

The Allies' hopes that they would be able to occupy Italy without a fight were short-lived. They began to cross the Straits of Messina on 3 September, and Italy's new government signed an armistice on the 8th. But German soldiers promptly disarmed the Italian troops in Rome; and by the time the main Allied landings took place at Salerno on the 9th, Hitler was sending troops to the north of Italy and reinforcing his armies in the south.

On 12 September, Mussolini was spirited out of Italy by German paratroops, taken to see Hitler, and then returned to Salo on Lake Garda, where he proclaimed a new Fascist Social Republic. Once more he strutted about as *Il Duce*, but in reality he was the Führer's puppet, looking on while the SS terrorised the northern regions. The overthrow of the Fascist régime in July had simply led to more suffering for the Italian people: they now had war in the south and German occupation in the north. And in the south the advance of the Allies was painfully slow. By the end of 1943 they were still 120 kilometres from Rome.

Meanwhile, across the Adriatic Sea, Italian troops in what had once been Yugoslavia were disarmed by Communist partisans led by Josip Broz (known as Tito). The Communists set up a Revolutionary Army of National Liberation, and Churchill decided to encourage and supply their movement to harass German troops. It was worth it: Tito's 200,000 partisans would keep eight German divisions fully occupied.

During 1943, as the Allies were entering Hitler's Europe by the back door in the south, Air Marshal 'Bomber' Harris intensified his 'area' (or indiscriminate) attacks on German cities. In 1942, 48,000 tonnes of bombs had been dropped on Germany: in 1943, helped by Americans in their new Flying Fortresses, Harris managed to unload 207,000 tonnes. By this time it was well understood that it was impossible to pinpoint an industrial target such as a factory, let alone a military target, such as a line of tanks on a particular road; and the main effect of the bombing was the killing of German civilians.

A more sophisticated use of aircraft was in long-range flights to cooperate with naval support groups (equipped with new radar systems) in hunting and destroying U-boats in the Battle of the Atlantic. In March 1943 the British were near to losing that battle: 107 Allied ships were sunk in the first twenty days of that month. But in the last third of the month only 15 ships went down; and between June and August the German navy destroyed only 58 merchant ships, at an alarming cost to them of 79 submarines (58 of them sunk by aircraft). Compared with that kind of perform-

ance, 'area' bombing was a useless extravagance. By the end of May 1944 there were only three U-boats in the North Atlantic – to report the weather!

While the British and Americans had been preparing their invasion of Sicily, Hitler had been deciding his next move in Russia. On 5 July 1943 at Kursk he sent his armour into what was to become the greatest tank battle of the war – roughly 1,500 on each side. Within a week, German losses forced Hitler to call off his offensive, and the Russians counter-attacked.

Hitler was no longer fighting the kind of war he liked. The Red Army was calling the shots. It was an extraordinary fighting force, headed by élite units, well trained in tank and artillery warfare, whose breakthroughs were consolidated by what has been described as "an inexhaustible mass of infantry ... like a barbarian horde on the march", living off the country and wrecking the towns and villages in the path of the remorseless advance of the Russian front.

In November 1943, Stalin, Churchill and Roosevelt met as a group for the first time at Teheran. The 'Big Three' appeared to get on well together: the Communist tyrant, the British imperialist, and the President of 'the land of the free'. A major war objective for Churchill was that Britain should end up powerful in Greece and the eastern Mediterranean. He may also have hoped that the Western powers, rather than the USSR, would be the ones to liberate the Balkans. So he tried to divert his partners to the 'Mediterranean Strategy' of advancing on Germany through Italy and the Balkans. But Roosevelt came down in favour of the plan that Stalin wanted: a second front in France, which it was agreed should be opened in the early summer of 1944. Looking further forward, the three leaders agreed that when the war in Europe was over Russia should be allowed to move her frontier west at the expense of Poland, while the Poles would receive in compensation part of eastern Germany. That was a foretaste of the treatment Germany could expect after defeat – and the Poles after victory. The Allies did not, however, draw up at Teheran a list of the exact terms they would impose on Germany or tell the unfortunate Poles just what they would receive after the war. Finally, Stalin declared that Russia would enter the war against Japan once Germany was defeated. Roosevelt was pleased by that. Although the Americans had held to their promise to give the European war priority, much had happened in the Far East since the spring of 1942 – as we shall now see.

American soldiers dead on Buna Beach, New Guinea, 1943. This was one of the first photographs to show American servicemen killed in action.

The War against Japan

After their successes in late 1941 and early 1942 (see pages 169–71), the Japanese now suffered two serious setbacks at the hands of the Americans when they failed either to capture Port Moresby on the south coast of New Guinea (which would have brought the north coast of Australia within reach of their bombers) or to take Midway Island (where they had hoped to destroy the US Pacific Fleet).

The USA had divided the Pacific into two areas of command – the Pacific Ocean area under the command of Admiral Chester Nimitz and the South-West Pacific area under General Douglas MacArthur, to whose forces had been added Australian troops recalled from the British Eighth Army. First the Japanese were cleared out of the Papuan Peninsula of New Guinea and then out of Guadalcanal in the Solomon Islands by early 1943. From then on the Japanese were gradually swept out of the Pacific by a two-pronged assault on the Japanese Empire, with Nimitz advancing through the Central Pacific while MacArthur continued along a south-western route from New Guinea. Using combined air and sea power Nimitz's forces took the Gilbert Islands in late 1943, the Marshall Islands in February 1944 and began landing in the Marianas in June 1944, after the Battle of the Philippine Sea. The way to the Philippines, the islands which controlled Japan's sea route to oil supplies in the East Indies, was now open. In October 1944, in the largest naval battle of all time, 282 warships and hundreds of aircraft clashed in the Battle of Leyte Gulf. Under the protection of the victorious US navy, MacArthur's forces now began the bloody business of clearing the Japanese out of the Philippines. It was a grim struggle against an enemy for whom surrender was dishonourable, and the Americans were to face the same fanatical resistance when they fought for the islands of Iwo Jima and Okinawa in 1945. (See map on page 198.)

Meanwhile, as Americans and Australians were destroying the Japanese Empire in the Pacific, the Allies had set up a new South-East Asia Command under Admiral Lord Louis Mountbatten, whose objective was to clear the Japanese out of Burma and open the 'Burma Road' to China. In 1943 the British forces in the Far East had little success, but in early 1944 they stopped a Japanese offensive into Assam, counterattacked and began to push back the Japanese in Burma. From the middle of October 1944 until May 1945 General Sir William Slim's 14th Army (made up of British, Indian, and African soldiers), supplied by American cargo aircraft, drove the enemy south and finally out of Burma.

Now that the 'Burma Road' was open, it might have been expected that Chiang Kai-shek's Nationalist armies would take the offensive against Japanese occupying forces and drive them towards the sea. Roosevelt had faith in Chiang; he'd sent him vast quantities of military supplies. Rarely has faith in an ally been so utterly misplaced. Chiang had no intention of frittering away his troops in attacks on the Japanese.

He was waiting for the Americans to drive out the foreign enemy and leave him free to turn against Mao Tse-Tung's Communists.

It was obvious in the early summer of 1945 that island-hopping through the Co-Prosperity Sphere had destroyed Japan's Empire and gravely weakened her armed forces; the only question was how much it would cost in lives – American as well as Japanese – to force a surrender.

Closing in on the Reich

At the start of 1944 the British and Americans continued their war against Hitler in Italy, the place to which 'Torch' had led them. Churchill hoped for a great, primarily British, success here. The American generals, again, believed that this urge to hit Germany from below was little more than an evasion of the much harder job of invading France. After the Teheran conference (see page 175) they were determined not to allow more troops and resources to be sucked away from preparations for a second front.

On 22 January the Allied armies landed a large force on the coast at Anzio behind the 'Gustav Line', the main front of the German armies in southern Italy, and began their slow, piecemeal liberation of a sorely tried people. Perhaps the most that could be said of the Italian campaign was that it tied up German troops who might otherwise have been used to oppose 'Overlord', the long-awaited invasion of Western Europe, which began on D-Day, 6 June 1944.

General Eisenhower, the man appointed to command 'Overlord', had to put on the beaches of northern France a large force of Allied soldiers sufficiently well equipped and supported to break through the 'Atlantic Wall' – the Germans' coastal defences. The organisation of the Allied armada was meticulous – it had to be. Once under way, it was an operation that went according to plan – although not according to timetable. By the evening of 6 June, 156,000 men had landed in France together with their equipment, transport, fighting vehicles and fuel. With the aid of naval bombardment and control of the skies above the coast, they held and secured their beaches. But the caution of their commanders and fierce resistance from the Germans slowed down their advance inland.

Hitler would not admit the possibility of defeat in France nor give his soldiers the opportunity to withdraw to positions they were capable of defending. There

Death in a fine summer sky. A 'flying bomb' or 'doodle-bug' over Central London.

would be no retreat, no surrender! His new terror weapons would destroy the British people's will to fight on! On 13 June the first V 1, a pilotless plane carrying a charge of high explosive, crashed on Gravesend. Soon more than a hundred 'flying bombs' a day were being sent over, and in July and August a million school-children and mothers migrated or were evacuated from their homes in the target areas of London and the south-east.

On 20 July, as the V 1 offensive was reaching a peak, and while the Allies were still consolidating their positions in the north of Normandy, a German officer, Colonel Claus von Stauffenberg, tried to assassinate Hitler at his headquarters in East Prussia. He placed a bomb in a briefcase beneath the Führer's map-desk, waited outside to watch the explosion, then flew to Berlin to take part in the overthrow of the Nazi régime. Orders were sent out to arrest the chief Nazis, and in Paris SS and SD chiefs and their men were arrested. Field-Marshal von Kluge, the Commander-in-Chief of the German armies fighting in Normandy, was involved in the plot, but he refused to order his troops to cease fire until he was sure that Hitler was dead.

The Führer was alive, with burns and a shattered eardrum, and spitting for revenge. Stauffenberg was shot: about 5,000 other people were executed. Von Kluge came under suspicion and he was sacked; shortly afterwards he committed suicide. The most famous name to fall was Rommel, who was made to take poison, then given a lavish official funeral so that

no-one would think a war hero had turned against his Führer.

Hitler's reprisals after the 'bomb plot' badly affected the morale of his commanders in the West, and his policy of 'no withdrawal' nearly ensured a swift victory for the Allies. His forces were simply unable to defend all northern France against an enemy superior in numbers, in tanks and in the air. Early in August the Americans swung west, into Brittany, then turned east to head for the Rhine, while the British and other Allied forces advanced towards Belgium and the Netherlands as German armies collapsed under the pressure.

On 15 August American troops landed in the south of France in an invasion code-named 'Operation Anvil'. They advanced quickly, meeting little opposition; but it didn't really matter one way or the other: as in 1940 the battle for France would be won and lost in the north. Yet, according to the Americans and the British, it was going to be won without any part being played by the French. The Americans intended to impose a military government on France once the country had been liberated: they had already printed 'occupation francs' to pay their troops.

They reckoned without the French Resistance or the Free French and their leader, de Gaulle, who throughout the war had insisted on France being treated as an equal ally. On 16 August the Resistance in Paris organised an uprising against the Germans. De Gaulle urged the Allies to send relief to the city, and reluctantly Eisenhower agreed that a French armoured division should be diverted to the capital: on 26 August Charles de Gaulle walked in triumph down the Champs Elysées. The man who before the war had been a little-known colonel in the French army now proclaimed himself President of the Republic. France was once again an independent force in Europe.

In August the Allied armies liberated most of the rest of France and Belgium. By September there were over two million Allied troops in France, and there was a general feeling in the air that the war could be won easily. So, instead of pushing their advanced forces on through thin and disorganised defences and making straight for the Rhine, the Allies paused to 'refit, refuel and rest'; the Germans used the interval to reinforce their armies and their positions.

An attempt to outflank the strengthened German line at Arnhem on the River Rhine by the British commander, Montgomery, failed; and Eisenhower and Montgomery began to blame each other for not taking

The Second World War

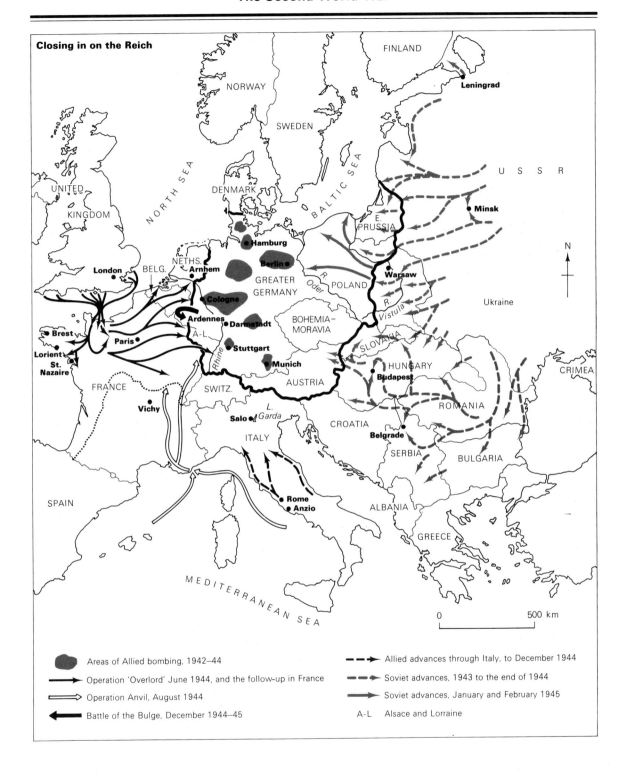

Closing in on the Reich

FINLAND

NORWAY

SWEDEN

Leningrad

NORTH SEA

BALTIC SEA

U S S R

DENMARK

Minsk

E. PRUSSIA

UNITED KINGDOM

Hamburg

Berlin

GREATER GERMANY

R. Oder

POLAND

Warsaw

London

NETHS.

BELG.

Arnhem

Cologne

Ardennes

Darmstadt

BOHEMIA-MORAVIA

R. Vistula

Ukraine

N

Brest

Paris

A-L

SLOVAKIA

Lorient

St. Nazaire

Stuttgart

Rhine

Munich

AUSTRIA

HUNGARY

Budapest

CRIMEA

FRANCE

SWITZ.

ROMANIA

Vichy

L. Garda

Salo

CROATIA

Belgrade

SERBIA

BULGARIA

ITALY

SPAIN

Rome

Anzio

ALBANIA

GREECE

MEDITERRANEAN SEA

0   500 km

- Areas of Allied bombing, 1942–44
- Operation 'Overlord' June 1944, and the follow-up in France
- Operation Anvil, August 1944
- Battle of the Bulge, December 1944–45
- Allied advances through Italy, to December 1944
- Soviet advances, 1943 to the end of 1944
- Soviet advances, January and February 1945
- A-L   Alsace and Lorraine

179

Bombed out. Refugees leave the ruined city of Aachen in western Germany in October 1944.

advantage of German weakness in September. The delay meant not only loss of life at the front but further civilian casualties in Britain. In September 1944, Hitler launched the first of his new faster-than-sound V2 terror weapons: long-range rockets, each carrying a tonne of high explosive. In the next seven months London would feel the impact of more than 500 rockets, and 2,754 people would be killed.

The delay in September was not the Allies' only mistake. Suddenly, on 16 December Hitler launched an offensive against the place where the defence of the Allies was weakest. As in 1940, the attack came in the Ardennes. The Battle of the Bulge got its name from the fearful swelling that erupted in the line of the German front and caused panic in Allied high places. But the Germans were short of men and fuel, and the Allies managed to flatten the bulge by the beginning of 1945.

In the East 1944 had seen some spectacular Russian successes. In January Leningrad was at last relieved from its ordeal by siege: nearly one million people had died in the city from starvation or from German bombing and artillery fire. As the Germans fell back they were able to shorten their lines of communication and supply in the north and hold up the Russian advance. But further south the Red Army rolled over the enemy's extended front. Early in January Russians crossed the pre-war Polish frontier; by April they had recovered the Ukraine; and in May they cleared the Germans out of the Crimea. Alarmed by this sudden threat to Central Europe and the Balkans, Hitler sent troops to occupy Hungary. And the Russians paused to refresh and re-fit their armies before committing them to the next wave of attacks.

In a new offensive which began on 23 June, seventeen days after the Americans and the British had at last opened their second front in France, the Red Army struck the centre of the enemy front and pushed the Germans back beyond Minsk. At the end of July Russian advanced forces reached the outskirts of Warsaw, where their arrival triggered off a rising by the Polish Home Army against the Nazi occupation forces. In the vicious local war that followed, the Russians gave no assistance to the Poles: they claimed that their forward troops were in no condition to mount another offensive, and they were probably telling the truth. Even so, they were later blamed for not trying to prevent what turned into the massacre of 300,000 Poles, most of them believers in an independent, non-Communist Poland.

As German resistance stiffened in the centre of the eastern front in August, Russian armies in the south began to advance again. Faced with the alternatives of joining the Allies or annihilation, the Romanians chose the wiser course and on 23 August announced that they were now at war with Germany. The victorious Red Army tanks now rolled into Bulgaria – which also hurried to declare war on Germany – and then began a colossal left wheel through South-Eastern and Central Europe. In October they advanced into eastern Hungary; liberated Belgrade, the capital of the old Yugoslavia, with the help of Tito and his partisans; and entered Slovakia. In November the Germans fled from Greece, and by the end of the month Russian troops were surging around the defences of Budapest. Mean-

while, in the north, the Finns had signed an armistice in September and Russian armies had swept through the Baltic states to place themselves on the border of East Prussia.

By the beginning of 1945 the German domination of Europe had been so thoroughly beaten back that the effective power of the Reich was limited to the land between two rivers: the Rhine in the west and the Vistula in the east. Behind the Rhine the Western Allies had been embarrassed, though not seriously wounded, by Hitler's Ardennes offensive. Behind the Vistula the Russians collected massive forces of armour and motorised infantry for an attack which by early February took them to within 65 kilometres of Berlin.

Germany herself was by now a virtually open target for American and British bombers. Air raids had crippled the German oil industry, and large numbers of the *Luftwaffe*'s new planes were grounded for lack of fuel. Allied control of the air and of the seas, together with Russia's conquest of the Reich's 'colonies' in Eastern Europe, were beginning to strangle the German war economy. Hitler's war had come back home with a vengeance. The Allies would accept nothing less than unconditional surrender, and the Führer would not give in. His defeat was certain, and he would drag Germany down to destruction with him.

32 People at War II

It was a war of blind brutality, of a filthiness that chokes the imagination.

For some people it was a good war: it gave them steady jobs in industry and actually raised their standards of living. For many others, including those sent away to fight in distant lands, it was an exciting time after the gloom of the Depression years. For the Jews the war brought an attempt to exterminate them with gas and fire; and Poland became a kind of slaughterhouse annexe to Hitler's Reich.

The war killed some of your grandparents, though most of them in Britain lived to tell their tales of blackouts and blitz, rationing and the Home Guard – recruited to resist an invasion that never came. In Poland and western Russia people of your grandparents' generation vanished by the trainload and by the trenchful.

The experience of war touched people in different ways at different times. At the end of 1940 it was much safer to live in Leningrad than in Liverpool: by the time twelve months had passed the German siege was turning the Russian city into an icy tomb. In the summer of 1942 the citizens of Japan were living safe and secure at the heart of a far-flung empire: three years later the Japanese cities of Hiroshima and Nagasaki would be suddenly transformed into the unhealthiest places on the face of the earth.

Among the few generalisations that we can confidently make about the war is the one that half the total casualties were civilians. All the combatant countries used bombing planes to terrorise cities and destroy industry and these targets were much easier to find than purely military ones. In general it was the people of towns and cities who were harder hit by bombing and enemy occupation. But there were grim exceptions. In western Russia thousands of square kilometres of countryside were laid waste as the armies moved to and fro carrying out 'scorched earth' policies to cheat the advancing enemy of food and shelter. In Yugoslavia, where there was an active resistance, both underground fighters and civilians suffered. Tens of thousands lost their lives, killed by occupying forces as resistance fighters, or by the resistance fighters as 'collaborators'.

People on the Move

It was a war in which more civilians moved across the map than soldiers. Some people moved of their own free will; for example, in the USA many workers and their families migrated from the south and the middle west to take part in the industrial boom which the war created in the factories of the north-east. In Europe most migrants were *forced* to move. Hundreds of thousands of foreign-born German-speaking people were pulled into Hitler's Reich; while Poles, Czechs, Slovenes and Frenchmen were expelled. And quite separate from those population 'exchanges' were people who were uprooted from their own lands and forced to work in Germany. By 1945 there were nearly five million of them, drawn from all the occupied countries but mostly Russians and Poles. They were put to work in the factories and mines of the Nazi Reich, in conditions which meant almost certain death for most of them.

In the USSR the government assumed that minority peoples in the west were disloyal to the Soviet Union. The Germans on the Volga and the Tartars in the Crimea were callously transplanted in Siberia; while Estonians, Lithuanians and Poles were dispersed throughout the vastness of the USSR. In addition, hundreds of thousands of workers were forced to move east when their factories were relocated in the Urals (see Chapter 31, page 169).

In 1944 and 1945 the westwards advance of the Red Army, and the collapse of the German empire in countries such as Czechoslovakia and Poland, brought about more migrations, and we shall see their effects in the next chapter.

Meanwhile, we must turn to look at a forced migration which took place between 1941 and 1945 and is unique in history. It involved the collection of a people scattered throughout the countries of Europe, priority use of railway networks for their transportation, the organisation of a system of camps for their reception, and the building of gas chambers for their murder and of ovens for their cremation. It was Hitler's "final solution" to the problem of the Jews: they were to be wiped out.

Of course, the Nazis were already well-qualified mass murderers by 1941. At home they had destroyed political opponents, such as communists and socialists;

Death in a Nazi camp, recorded by a camera team of the advancing Allied armies. Only when photographs like this were released to the general public did many people realise – after more than five years of war – the full horror of the Nazi Reich.

and they had learnt how to kill mentally defective children in hospitals and call it 'euthanasia' to promote the 'racial health' of the German population. Now, in war, they used their old techniques, and invented new ones, for the extermination of political foes and 'racial enemies' on a previously unimagined scale.

When 'Operation Barbarossa' was launched against the Soviet Union in the summer of 1941, the assault troops were followed into newly occupied territory by four *Einsatzgruppen* – 'Special Action Squads'. There were about 3,000 men in the *Einsatzgruppen*: their job was to hunt down and kill all Jews as well as any local Communist Party officials who had not retreated with the Soviet forces. At first they shot them; later they used specially built vans, in which the Jews were killed by exhaust gases from the engines. By the end of the year they had destroyed almost half a million Russian Jews.

Meanwhile, plans were going ahead for the killing of all European Jews. In late 1941 and early 1942 six concentration camps were turned into extermination camps (see map opposite) by the addition of gas chambers and either burning grounds or crematoria. In January 1942 Reinhard Heydrich (see Chapter 25, page 113) called political leaders and top civil servants to the Wannsee Conference, the first of a series of meetings to arrange the smooth functioning of the "final solution". Obviously the Nazis would need an efficient organisation to round up, transport and destroy millions of men, women and children. By the summer all six camps were in operation, and at Auschwitz the SS were using prussic acid gas, Zyklon B, instead of diesel fumes: it was an easier system to operate, it was quicker – and speed was essential when there were so many people to kill.

Between 1941 and 1945 more than five million human beings died in the extermination camps. Not all of them were Jews: the Nazis used the camps to destroy gypsies and other people they regarded as inferior beings, as well as their political enemies. But if we add the Jews of the six camps to those who were shot or gassed in the Soviet Union, and those who died by violence or starvation in the other concentration camps, we end with a total of almost six million dead Jews.

As you can see from the map, they travelled from all over Europe to their deaths – although the Jews of Poland didn't have to move far. It was a forced migration whose pace didn't slacken even when German armies were being pushed back towards the Reich. It was more important that skilled Jewish workers should burn in Auschwitz or Treblinka than that they should be spared to help the German war effort.

The "final solution" was an operation for which the Nazis needed the assistance of the governments and people of occupied, friendly and client states, in the round-up and deportation of their Jews. In some Central and Eastern European countries a long tradition of anti-Semitism (described in Chapter 14, page 60) made that kind of collaboration easy. In Western Europe there were startling differences in the ways people reacted to the Nazis' requests to take part in their atrocities. In crude terms, they either resisted the Nazis or they didn't kick up much of a fuss – which amounted to collaboration, for those Jews who were not protected from the SS died. And, again in crude terms, we can measure the degrees to which Jews were protected or abandoned by their fellow-citizens by counting, in each of the countries concerned, the proportion of the Jewish population destroyed in the "final solution".

Those figures – clearly marked on the map – suggest that the protection given to Dutch and Belgian Jews was not very effective. In the occupied zone of France police and civil servants helped the Nazis with their work; while the Vichy régime handed over to the Germans non-French Jews who had fled to France before 1940 seeking safety from persecution. In Belgium and the Netherlands members of the Nazi movements and collaborators helped in the naming and round-up of Jewish fellow-countrymen for the killing camps. In contrast, the people of occupied Denmark assisted their 8,000 Jews to flee the country. And although Italy fought on Germany's side in the war, and her Fascist government passed a number of harsh anti-Semitic laws, the Italian Jews were *not* handed over to the SS. Their migration to death in Poland only began when the Germans occupied Italy in 1943.

It is not the business of historians to pass glib moral judgements on whole peoples; and there were many examples of decent and brave behaviour towards the Jews in the Netherlands, in Belgium and in France, as well as in Italy and Denmark. Equally, it is not their business to ignore evidence that in some Western European countries there was complicity in the murder of Jews. No British Jews were sent to Poland – but then Britain was never occupied by the Nazis and put to the test.

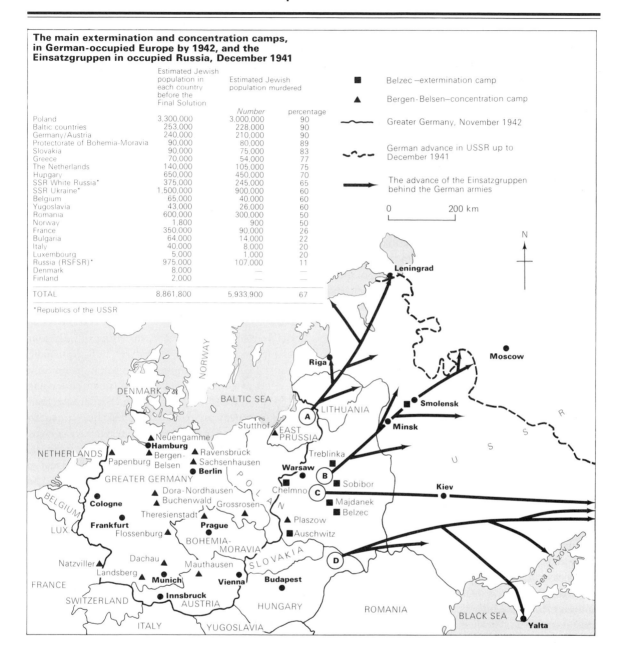

The main extermination and concentration camps, in German-occupied Europe by 1942, and the Einsatzgruppen in occupied Russia, December 1941

	Estimated Jewish population in each country before the Final Solution	Estimated Jewish population murdered	
		Number	percentage
Poland	3,300,000	3,000,000	90
Baltic countries	253,000	228,000	90
Germany/Austria	240,000	210,000	90
Protectorate of Bohemia-Moravia	90,000	80,000	89
Slovakia	90,000	75,000	83
Greece	70,000	54,000	77
The Netherlands	140,000	105,000	75
Hungary	650,000	450,000	70
SSR White Russia*	375,000	245,000	65
SSR Ukraine*	1,500,000	900,000	60
Belgium	65,000	40,000	60
Yugoslavia	43,000	26,000	60
Romania	600,000	300,000	50
Norway	1,800	900	50
France	350,000	90,000	26
Bulgaria	64,000	14,000	22
Italy	40,000	8,000	20
Luxembourg	5,000	1,000	20
Russia (RSFSR)*	975,000	107,000	11
Denmark	8,000	—	—
Finland	2,000	—	—
TOTAL	8,861,800	5,933,900	67

*Republics of the USSR

- ■ Belzec – extermination camp
- ▲ Bergen-Belsen – concentration camp
- Greater Germany, November 1942
- German advance in USSR up to December 1941
- The advance of the Einsatzgruppen behind the German armies

0   200 km

Britain played an honourable part in sheltering Jewish refugees who fled from Hitler's ever-growing Reich in the 1930s and 1940s, and after the war there was a widespread feeling of revulsion as the horrors of the death camps were revealed. Yet, the post-war record would show that her government was sadly quick to forget, even if no-one ever considered forgiving. The major Nazi leaders and most criminal generals were tried at Nuremberg for "crimes against peace" and "crimes against humanity"; and most of the accused were executed or sentenced to long prison terms. But historians have estimated that between 150,000 and 200,000 Nazis – soldiers, officials, industrialists – were responsible for the deaths of nearly six million Jews and six million others in the murder camps and slave barracks of the Reich. After 1945 only about 35,000 of them were tried and convicted. The British sent only three investigators to produce evidence for the trials of Nazis in their occupation zone, and in 1946 the investigations were dropped except in the case of war crimes directly against British citizens. The Americans had 320 investigators, but their work, too, was ended in 1948. One of the possible reasons for this may be found in what you will read in Chapter 35, pages 207–8.

When it was all over, when nearly six million Jews were dead, Rudolf Höss, the Commandant of Auschwitz, declared: "There was no escape for me. I had to carry on the process of extermination, of mass murder, to live with it, to be an unemotional spectator of something at which my whole soul revolts." That was the kind of plea for understanding made by other SS leaders when they were subsequently brought to trial. It made a kind of sense, in that Nazism was a political system which didn't allow disobedience – but neither does any government of a country at war. Nor was killing civilians as a matter of daily routine in any way connected with Germany's war-effort to defeat her enemies. So other questions must be asked. What was the connection between the horrors of the "final solution" and the long tradition of anti-Semitism in Germany and, for that matter, in most of Europe? Did all the jokes, the jealousy of successful Jews and the despising of their poor finally end up in a shrug of the shoulders as the cattle trucks passed by on their way to the killing camps? Knowing what we do now about these inhuman barbarities, we would be less than human not to need to seek answers to questions about their roots in the history of the people who committed them. The evil of the Nazis is not in dispute, but what was the responsibility of all those Germans who had voted for them in the early 1930s? They listened to the speeches and must have known something of the message of *Mein Kampf*, for it became a best-seller. Did they vote for Hitler because they were promised war against the sub-humans of the non-German people; or did they just not take that side of the Nazi movement seriously? If the latter, why give support to the Nazis? Had the huge votes of 1930 and 1932 more to do with the German tradition of unthinking acceptance of authority; did it begin with those people who wanted back the 'good old days' when the Kaiser and a handful of civil servants and generals had given the state 'strong leadership'? Perhaps this leads to a still broader question. Can the final responsibility for the "final solution" be traced back to those people who had misused their democratic rights as free citizens to

put in power those who had signalled that they had no respect for democracy, the rule of law, or the fundamental principle that all men should be free and equal?

Economies at War

The war which began with Britain and France defending themselves against the threat of German aggression turned, in 1941, into a much greater conflict in which a new alliance – Russia, the USA and Britain – aimed at nothing less than the unconditional surrender of the German armed forces and the destruction of Nazism, with the secondary target of breaking the military power of Japan. These new and far-reaching objectives meant that the war would be long as well as on a scale far greater than had appeared likely in 1939. The consequences for the economies of the countries concerned were also far-reaching.

Between 1939 and 1941 the German economy was not greatly affected by the war, for Hitler quickly won a European empire by *blitzkrieg* and diplomatic pressure. The need to mobilise the whole nation in a war effort arose only as late as 1942 when Hitler was forced to realise that 'Operation Barbarossa' had landed Germany in the kind of war he wanted to avoid – a long one. From then on Germany was geared up for war under the direction of Albert Speer, Minister of Armaments and Munitions, whose Central Planning Board was in complete control of the economy by 1943.

Despite intensified bombing of German cities, Speer was able to increase munitions production in 1943 and 1944; but even he was unable to overcome the crippling effects of Allied victories, particularly of those in Eastern Europe. For as the Russians advanced they broke into pieces the economic empire on which the German economy had lived, like a giant parasite, for four years. No longer was there a ready supply of raw materials for the Nazi war machine, nor an abundance of food for the German people. Nor, by the end of 1944, was Eastern Europe a German-dominated compound from which the Nazis could select the slave-labour they needed for their factories.

In the summer of 1944 Hitler appointed Joseph Goebbels Commissioner for Total Mobilisation of Resources for War. It was the beginning of the last spasm of the Reich. Goebbels could close restaurants and cinemas and order people to work longer hours: he could not conjure new workers out of thin air, especially while his Führer was drafting all available German males into a last-ditch defence force, the *Volkssturm*. Nazi Germany was at last living and fighting within her own means: given the opposition ranged against her, it meant that her defeat was certain.

Between 1941 and 1944 the fighting and occupation by the Germans made western Russia a ruin. When the Russians had time to pause and count the cost it amounted to the destruction or damage of over 1,700 towns, 70,000 villages, six million houses, nearly 32,000 industrial concerns, over 60,000 kilometres of railway track and close to 100,000 collective farms. In addition, the Germans took away seven million horses and seventeen million head of cattle.

Yet the Russians were able to fight back once they had relocated much of their heavy industry in the East (see page 169). Stalin's leadership in the Great Patriotic War against Hitlerite Germany was as ruthless and determined as you would expect from the man who carried through the economic revolution of the 1930s. Workers were forced to move to those areas of the Soviet Union in which they were most needed, hours of work were increased, and crash training programmes were developed to make up for the shortage of skilled labour. Standards of living went down, partly because of the havoc the Germans wreaked in the rich agricultural regions in the west but also because the output of munitions was made an absolute priority. The results, which you can see below, were extraordinary. As early as 1942 Russia was producing more military aircraft, more tanks and more artillery guns than Germany.

Russian war production, 1941–44

	1941	1942	1943	1944
Military aircraft	3,950	25,400	34,900	40,300
Tanks and machine-gun carriers	4,700	24,600	24,000	29,000
Artillery guns	–	29,600	130,000	122,000

German output in 1942 was: 15,400 aircraft, 9,300 tanks and 12,000 artillery guns.

Despite her cruel losses of people, territory, and supplies of food and raw materials, Russia was able to recover by drawing on a huge population to man her armies and factories and on her vast natural resources of minerals and energy to supply her war industries. In contrast, Britain was hardly in the same economic league. To pay for their defiance of the Reich in 1940,

for the shipment of food and other essentials across U-boat-infested seas, and for their campaigns in North Africa, the Mediterranean and the Far East, the British cashed their overseas investments, spent their gold and foreign currency reserves, and drew heavily on American Lend-Lease aid.

The strain of fighting in several theatres of a world war was too much for a nation with a small population and limited natural resources. The war solved Britain's long-standing unemployment problem, but then it could have solved it several times over. The new problem was a *shortage* of labour, and especially of the skilled labour which both the armed forces and industry needed. In 1942, British armaments factories turned out 8,600 tanks, but only 7,500 in 1943 and still fewer in 1944. As Britain approached the hour of victory in Europe, so she edged nearer to exhaustion and bankruptcy.

Across the Atlantic, the American economy thrived on a war the American people had wanted so desperately to avoid. The Depression vanished like a bad dream as industry tooled itself up and delivered the goods for making war in both the West and the East. By the autumn of 1943 America had achieved full employment of her labour force.

So great were American reserves of manpower, energy supplies and sources of raw materials that the war effort didn't eat into civilians' standards of living. And that war effort was truly prodigious. Between 1940 and 1945 American industries produced over 300,000 aircraft, 96,000 tanks, 61,000 artillery guns, seven million rifles and over two million lorries – not to mention the other paraphernalia of war they supplied to the twelve million men mobilised in the armed forces. To coordinate and control production on that scale Roosevelt created new government agencies, such as the Office of War Mobilisation and the Office of Economic Stabilisation, on the model of the 'New Deal' agencies of the 1930s (see Chapter 26, page 120). And to pay for it all the federal government had to spend much more than its income. It was a far cry from the days when American politicians and financial experts believed that massive budget deficits were a sure recipe for economic disaster.

The new surge of American power was evident abroad not only in the presence of millions of fighting men and the billions of dollars poured into Lend-Lease: it was also expressed in the tighter grip which Americans exerted on the economies of Latin American countries. In the Depression of the thirties, when the USA had little money available for foreign investment, that grip had been weakened. Now US money was pumped in to expand production of primary products. Where US business men helped this expansion they gained control of large parts of the industries, factories, oil wells and mines, which produced Venezuelan oil, Chilean copper, Peruvian lead, Cuban sugar and iron ore.

Roosevelt spoke of the need to "ensure economic prosperity in Central and South America" within a framework of "cooperation and economic interdependence", yet the new invasion of the dollar brought prosperity to only a small proportion of the people of the sub-continent, and roused nationalist resentment against the Yanqui 'big brother'.

In Argentina those grievances assisted the emergence of a fascist-style movement, led by Juan Perón. His support came from the urban workers in the meat-packing and other industries, and Perón played on their demands for social reform and their dislike for foreigners who made profits at the expense of Argentinians. He became President of Argentina in 1946. In the larger context of a war-torn world that was not, in itself, an event of great importance. But it was an indication that new political ideas were beginning to penetrate Latin America.

The Marvels of the Age

As governments mobilised the economies of their nations, so they employed the mass-production techniques of modern industry to create the weapons for the mass destruction of human beings that is the mark of modern war. You have already read of aircraft produced by the thousand, of 'flying bombs' and faster-than-sound rockets. For the war on the ground the factories turned out not only tanks and field-guns, but an array of portable weapons that made the infantryman a much more formidable figure than he had been in the Great War. Chief among them was the sub-machine gun, an automatic weapon light enough to be carried and used by one man. For reasons best known to its generals, the British army entered the war without such a weapon. But a new model was designed in early 1941, put into production in the summer – and by the end of the war over four million had been made. The gun was simple to construct; and it was so cheap –

about £2.75 – that even the hard-up British could afford to give it away in large quantities to their allies. It was called the Sten gun: soldiers referred to it as the 'Woolworth gun'.

The sub-machine gun had only one use – to kill people at short range. In contrast, other developments stimulated by wartime needs had obvious peacetime use. The large-scale industrial production of the new sulphonamide drugs and of penicillin (originally discovered in 1929) saved thousands of soldiers' lives, and would later save millions more; while the carnage of the battlefields encouraged research into the improvement of techniques for storing blood and plasma. Many victims of accidents in peacetime Britain owe the fact that they are not totally disfigured to the development of plastic surgery by surgeons working on badly injured or burnt soldiers and airmen. Radar had a vastly important future in air and sea navigation and traffic control; while synthetic fibres, such as nylon (used to make parachutes), would soon find their way into fishing nets, surgical thread, and dress and furnishing fabrics.

The German research for the V2 terror weapons led indirectly to the development of rockets for space exploration. The jet engine, developed independently in both Britain and Germany, would later revolutionise air travel – though curiously enough neither the British nor the German government was willing to invest enough resources in the production of jet-powered aircraft until it was too late for them to have much effect in the war.

The same could not be said of a research and development operation, code-named the Manhattan Project, which "is estimated to have cost as much as all the scientific research previously conducted by mankind from the beginnings of recorded time". Its purpose was to find a way of setting up a nuclear chain reaction in a lump of the metal uranium, so as to release vast amounts of energy in a single, colossal explosion. In short, the aim was to produce the world's first atomic weapon. The Manhattan Project was set up at Los Alamos in New Mexico in August 1942. Nearly three years and one billion dollars later, on 17 July 1945, one of three devices was successfully tested in the Alamogordo desert. Some scientists were delighted, others appalled at the enormity of the thing they had created. The world had entered into what some called the "atomic era", and others the "nuclear age". Whatever its name it was pregnant with threat:

in the mid-summer of 1945 the USA had two atomic bombs ready for use.

Who was going to Win?

That question looks so simple it hardly deserves an answer, for by early 1945 it was as certain as anything could be that the two remaining Axis powers would be defeated by the Allies. But there were other people involved as well; they included those political leaders who had gone into exile, mostly in London, when the Germans invaded their countries, as well as the members of resistance movements who had stayed on to wage their own underground local wars against the occupying forces.

For example, the King of Yugoslavia hoped to be returned to his throne, but the Yugoslav resistance fighters were mostly republicans. The leaders of the Polish and Czech governments in exile had to face the fact that other politicians from their countries were in exile in the USSR. These men all hoped to take power once the war was over, but the leaders of the partisan movements and home armies fighting the occupying Axis powers were not at all ready to see their countries return to a pre-war system of politics. Many of them were communists, and the German attack on the Soviet Union in 1941 had turned *all* communists, not just the Russians, into bitter enemies of the Reich. And in France, in Poland, in Czechoslovakia, in Italy, in Hungary, communists joined and stiffened the resistance to the Nazis; while in Yugoslavia Tito's communist partisans were the only effective opposition to the enemy. In Greece, by the end of 1944, the two main wings of the resistance, the Communists and Royalists, were fighting a bitter civil war to decide who would rule their liberated land.

The history of the communist parties suited them admirably for their new task of cooperating in or leading European resistance movements: they were well organised, tightly disciplined, and used to working undercover. Their deeds won them many admirers and new recruits; they became respected in their own lands; and they established claims to power based no longer on mere words but on the record of their part in the defeat of the enemy.

To reassure his allies that the Soviet Union was not interested in fomenting world, or even European, revolution, Stalin dissolved the Comintern in 1943. As you know from Chapter 14 (page 59), that body had long been a mere façade for Russian control of the European communist parties, so its disappearance in no way weakened Stalin's influence. Indeed, many leading communists spent most of the war in exile in Moscow – Walther Ulbricht from Germany, Klement Gottwald from Czechoslovakia, Georgi Dimitrov from Bulgaria, Boleslaw Bierut from Poland. And those star figures in the 'Who's Who' of European communism followed the Red Army as it liberated their countries.

As the Russians attacked Germany from the east, so the virtually bankrupt British and the immensely powerful Americans approached from the west. Between and behind them lay a devastated Europe. If anything was clear at the time it was that when the war against Germany came to an end another kind of brawling would begin. After all, what else held the Allies together but a determination to destroy Nazism? Only in their brief celebrations of victory over a monstrous evil would people imagine that universal peace and goodwill could be born out of a global war.

33 Conclusions in Europe

The Yalta Conference

From 4 to 11 February 1945 the Big Three met at Yalta in the Crimea. They came together to decide the consequences that would follow their certain victory over Nazi Germany. It was the last time all three of them would meet: the crippled Roosevelt, who had been elected President of the USA for the fourth time in the previous November, was by now gravely ill.

None of the three men came to Yalta with plans for a peace that would be generous to Germany or merciful to the Germans. In August 1944 Roosevelt had declared that "The German people as a whole must have it driven home to them that the whole nation has been engaged in a lawless conspiracy against the decencies of modern civilisation." And Henry Morgenthau Jr, the US Secretary of the Treasury, had even gone so far as to work out a scheme to strip the post-war Reich of all her industrial plant and turn her into a pastoral country.

That kind of talk appealed to Stalin, for the Soviet leader wanted compensation for the blood the Nazis had let flow and the ruin they had caused in Russia. He demanded payment of reparations which would amount to $20,000,000,000 – of which half would go to the USSR. He also reminded Churchill and Roosevelt of their agreement at Teheran (see Chapter 31, page 175) that the Russian frontier should be moved west at the expense of Poland; and he now suggested that Poland should be compensated by the grant of German territory up to the River Oder and the western River Neisse (see the map opposite).

The proposal that Poland should be lifted bodily so far to the west didn't please Churchill. He had no wish to give territory to a country whose government might well end up under permanent Soviet domination. On the other hand, Churchill was less concerned about the future of Poland than he was for countries of South-East Europe, such as Greece. They mattered to Britain's trading and strategic interests; Poland did not. There was, too, the question of what would happen to the millions of Germans living in the lands now claimed for Poland.

The question of an Oder–Neisse frontier for Poland was not settled at Yalta: the Allies agreed to leave that matter, and the fixing of a sum for reparations, until the peace conference. But they did decide that once Germany was defeated, she would be demilitarised and denazified; that the country would be divided into four zones for purposes of occupation – a zone for the French as well as one for each of the Big Three – and that the city of Berlin would be jointly occupied. And Stalin promised that the Russians would be ready to enter the war against Japan three months after the victory in Europe.

The Big Three also pushed ahead with their plans for a new organisation to replace the League of Nations. To begin with, only those countries that took part in the struggle against the Axis Powers would be allowed to join; and they would be invited to a meeting in San Francisco in April. That provoked something of an unseemly rush to declare war on Germany and Japan. Chile, Ecuador, Paraguay, Peru and Venezuela all entered the war in February, while Argentina followed in March.

The new body, to be called the United Nations Organisation (UNO), would inherit some of the work and even some of the agencies of the old League. It would have a General Assembly, in which all members would have equal voting rights; and a much smaller Security Council with the power to decide whether UNO should intervene in disputes which threatened international peace. The Council was to have five permanent members – the Soviet Union, the USA, Britain, France and China – each of whom would have a veto (the right to stop a decision being taken and acted upon). Thus, any one of five nations could paralyse UNO – which was realistic, for none of them would have accepted a world organisation which they would be bound to obey.

The post-war world would have not only UNO but three other international organisations to help recovery. At a conference at Bretton Woods in the USA in 1944, the Americans and the British had set up the International Monetary Fund and the World Bank. The Fund would lend money to countries whose economies were in poor shape and whose currencies might suddenly have to be devalued: its aim was to prevent repeats of those wild fluctuations in international exchange rates which had done so much damage to the world economy in the 1930s (see Chapter 22, pages 88–89). The Bank would lend money for re-building

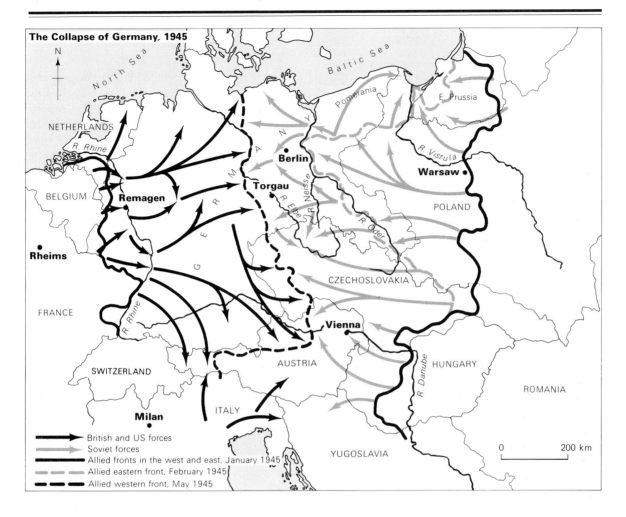

The Collapse of Germany, 1945

▬▬▶	British and US forces
▬▬▶	Soviet forces
▬▬▬	Allied fronts in the west and east, January 1945
▬ ▬ ▬	Allied eastern front, February 1945
▬ ▬ ▬	Allied western front, May 1945

war-torn Europe and for the economic development of the world's poorer nations. In addition, an International Trading Organisation was proposed for the task of persuading countries to get rid of their tariffs and quota systems which would otherwise hinder economic growth in the post-war world. The ITO never formally came into existence, but the job of freeing world trade from unnecessary obstacles was later taken over by GATT – the General Agreement on Tariffs and Trade.

So far, so good. At Yalta the Big Three appeared to be working together to assure the world of a sane and well-ordered future. The Russian newspaper *Izvestia* declared that "the conference would go down in history as a new example of how understanding had been reached on the most complex questions in the interests of peace, democracy and progress". Now it was a matter of bringing to an end the work that had

first brought them together as Allies – the war against Germany.

The Road to Berlin

It didn't take long. In January and February, as the Western Allies built up massive formations of troops, armour and aircraft for an assault towards the Rhine, Hitler diverted most of his forces to the east to hold the front against the Russians. In March the Allies launched attacks across the Rhine, and met little organised resistance from enemy soldiers who saw their defeat as inevitable. Away to the east, in his bunker in Berlin, the great destroyer turned on his own people and issued orders to turn Germany into a wasteland. "If the war is lost," declared Hitler, "the German nation will also perish. So there is no need to consider what the people require for continued

191

existence." But for the first time in over ten years the Führer's orders were disobeyed.

On 11 April the Western Allies reached the River Elbe, and there they halted. On the 16th the Russians, whose armies further south had been advancing through Hungary and into Austria, finally broke through in the north and advanced across country with great speed. On the 25th, Soviet and US troops met at Torgau on the Elbe. In Italy the British and Americans made swift progress against the demoralised occupying forces, and partisans took over the great industrial cities of the north. By the last week of April the bloody war against Nazi Germany was restricted to the streets of Hitler's ravaged capital, Berlin.

April 1945 was the last full month of German resistance to the Allies. It was also a month notable for the deaths of wartime leaders. On the 12th, Franklin D. Roosevelt died. He had led his country for twelve years, first through Depression and then through war; he had increased the powers of the Presidency and made the USA the strongest military power on earth. He was succeeded by Vice-President Harry S. Truman, a former senator who despite his vast inexperience of international affairs was determined to make full use of his presidential powers in war and peace.

On the 28th, Benito Mussolini was shot by partisans who had discovered him trying to leave Italy along with the retreating Germans. For good measure they shot his mistress too. The bodies of the *Duce* and Claretta Petacci were then taken to Milan and hanged upside down in a city square for public abuse.

On the 29th, Adolf Hitler prepared to leave the world by marrying his mistress. On the 30th, his bride, Eva Braun, took poison, and Hitler shot himself. Their bodies were taken upstairs, to the garden outside the bunker, doused with petrol and set alight. The Führer was followed in death by his most devoted admirer: Joseph Goebbels first murdered his wife and six children, then killed himself.

Hitler had appointed Admiral Doenitz as his successor. In his last testament he had declared, "Above all I charge the leaders of the nation and those under them to scrupulous observance of the laws of race and to merciless opposition to the universal poisoner of all peoples, international Jewry." But Doenitz had no power to oppose anything. In effect, he had become not the leader of the nation but the delivery boy, who would hand over the corpse of Nazi Germany, unconditionally, to the victorious Allies.

The Cost of the War

The surrender of Germany's forces came quickly. Indeed, the German generals in Italy had already signed a surrender document on 29 April: it came into effect on 2 May. On the 4th, German forces in the north surrendered to Montgomery at Lüneburg Heath; and a few days later the Russians took the surrender of German forces in the smouldering ruins of Berlin. General Jodl finally signed a document which covered the surrender of all Germany's armed forces at Rheims on 7 May 1945.

You may remember that after the Great War the numbers of the dead were not known for certain (see Chapter 8, page 37–8). Perhaps as many as twelve million lives were lost between 1914 and 1918. Estimates of deaths in the World War of 1939 to 1945 range between forty and fifty million. The conflict in the Far East accounted for roughly a quarter of that total figure, and for about half the American losses of 300,000 men. But the main killing ground was Europe, and in particular the eastern half of that continent.

Estimates of European war dead

USSR	20,000,000
Germany and Austria	6,500,000
Poland	6,000,000
Yugoslavia	1,600,000
France	600,000
Hungary	600,000
Romania	600,000
Italy	400,000
Britain	390,000
Czechoslovakia	270,000
Greece	200,000
The Netherlands	200,000
Belgium	30,000
Bulgaria	20,000
Norway	10,000
Denmark	3,000

In round, bald estimates – though not forgetting the wounded and the maimed, and the ruins of houses and of farms, of factories, cathedrals, roads, railways and harbour installations – that was the cost of the war to Europe by the early summer of 1945. And many more were yet to die. Suffering did not abruptly cease when General Jodl put his name to a piece of paper on 7 May.

War brutalises those who wage it; and the war in Eastern Europe had been a particularly filthy affair –

The eyeless city. The ruins of Berlin in May 1945.

a war of extermination as well as aggression. When the Red Army rolled west, through Hungary, Czechoslovakia and Poland, it advanced as an instrument of vengeance as well as a liberating force. German-speaking people who lived in those lands – many of whom had taken no part in the Nazi atrocities – were tortured or killed, or fled in terror. And now, as Poles and Czechs began to take over the responsibilities of running their own countries, so they straightaway began to persecute and expel the Germans from their midst.

In May and June Germans who had been expelled from the East entered the Reich in increasing numbers. It was not their homeland; it was an over-populated ruin. Children from Poland and from the Sudetenland ate garbage in the streets of German cities; and those who found no garbage died. It was not surprising that this was so; but it made a mockery of the notion that 'peace' had come in place of war.

The Potsdam Conference

On 17 July 1945 the three Allied leaders – Stalin, Truman and Churchill – met at Potsdam near Berlin. On that same day, in the Alamogordo desert, the Americans tested the world's first nuclear device (see Chapter 32, page 189). Stalin appeared to be less surprised by the news that the USA possessed a new, terrible weapon than by the result of the British general election which became known a little later. The Labour Party won by a landslide; Churchill was no longer Prime Minister; and Clement Attlee, the Labour leader, took his place at the Potsdam Conference table.

By this time it was clear that Stalin had no intention of letting the Americans or the British interfere in his plans for the future of those parts of Eastern Europe now occupied by Soviet troops. He had already paved the way for a Communist takeover in Poland by inviting non-Communist Polish leaders to Moscow, where they were arrested and imprisoned. Key posts in the Provisional Government of National Unity, set up in June, were in the hands of members of the Polish Communist Party. And now, at Potsdam, Stalin declared that he had "not been able to prevent the Poles from taking over the administration of the area up to the western Neisse".

The Western Allies had to accept that they were powerless to resist this move, short of going to war against the Russians. The expulsion of German-speaking people from Eastern Europe would now be on a greater scale than they had ever imagined. In Article XIII of the Potsdam Protocol [agreement] they tried to put a brave face on their predicament.

"The Three Governments having considered the question in all its aspects, recognise that the transfer to Germany of German populations, or elements thereof, remaining in Poland, Czechoslovakia and Hungary, will have to be undertaken. They agree that any transfers that take place should be effected in an orderly and humane manner."

As you can see from the map on page 195, Germany had been divided into the four zones of occupation proposed at Yalta; and Berlin, deep in the Soviet zone, was split into four sectors. Austria was separated from Germany and also held under joint occupation.

At Potsdam, the Allies agreed that Germany should be administered by a Control Council made up of the four military commanders of the occupied zones. Eventually elections would be held, to begin with at local government level. In the meantime Germany would be purged of her Nazi past: former SS men would be sought out and put on trial, while the wartime

Moving out with all that they could push or pull—three of the millions of Germans forced to migrate to the West.

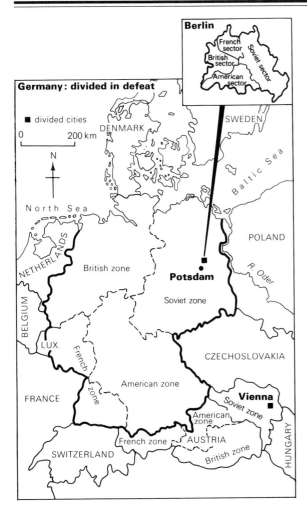

Berlin

French sector
British sector
Soviet sector
American sector

Germany: divided in defeat

■ divided cities
0   200 km

N

SWEDEN

DENMARK

North Sea

Baltic Sea

POLAND

NETHERLANDS

British zone

R. Oder

Potsdam

Soviet zone

BELGIUM

LUX.

French zone

CZECHOSLOVAKIA

American zone

FRANCE

Vienna

Soviet zone

American zone

SWITZERLAND

French zone AUSTRIA

British zone

HUNGARY

as the historian Richard Mayne has put it, "the crippling of France and the impoverishment of Great Britain ensured that the confrontation was essentially between America and the Soviet Union".

Towards Two Germanys

In November 1945 F. A. Voigt, a former Berlin correspondent of the *Manchester Guardian*, reported on the tidal wave of migrants from the East.

"Millions of Germans, Danzigers and Sudetenlanders are now on the move. Groups of 1,000 to 5,000 will take the road, trek hundreds of miles, and lose half their numbers by death through disease or exhaustion. The roadsides are dotted with graves. Children have arrived in Berlin looking like the emaciated creatures shown in pictures of Belsen [concentration camp].

One train, which arrived in Berlin on August 31st, started from Danzig on the 24th with 325 patients and orphans from the Marien Hospital and Orphanage in the Weidlergasse. They were packed into five cattle trucks, with nothing to cover the floors, not even straw. There were no doctors, nurses or medical supplies . . .

Between six and ten of the patients in each truck died during the journey. The bodies were simply thrown out of the train. When the train arrived in Berlin, sixty-five of the patients and orphans were removed to the Robert Koch Hospital, where nine of them died. We have no information as to what happened to the rest . . .

About the same time, a transport of Sudetenlanders – men, women and children – arrived from Troppau. They had been travelling in open cattle trucks for eighteen days. They numbered 2,400 when they set out and 1,350 when they arrived, so that 1,050 perished on the way."

In all, between 1945 and 1947 some sixteen million Germans were expelled from the countries of Central and Eastern Europe. At a rough estimate, one out of every eight died as a direct result of compulsory flight to the West. The war was supposed to be over, yet here were two million more corpses to add to the heaps of Europe's dead.

Those who survived settled down to the stark misery of existence in swollen Berlin or in the overcrowded American and British zones. And meanwhile the Allies, and especially the Russians, had begun to dismantle

leaders of the Nazi Party and the army would be brought before an Inter-Allied Special Tribunal to be set up at Nuremberg. As for reparations, each power would take what it wanted from its own zone, while Russia would also be allowed to remove a quarter of the industrial equipment in the British and American zones.

In fact, the Potsdam Conference decided very little. It was the last meeting of a disintegrating wartime alliance, not the first attempt at a partnership in peace. There would be no peace conference to settle the fate of Germany and Eastern Europe: that had really been settled by the positions the Allied soldiers had taken up before Potsdam. Complete victory had brought the Allies from the West face to face with their Ally from the East. Friendship had already given way to suspicion, and that would soon turn into open hostility. And,

and carry off German industrial plant. It was, to say the least, a short-sighted policy. Reparations were destroying Germany's capacity to earn her own living and feed herself.

The Americans and the British could not intend to make Germany into a vast camp of starving humanity, nor were they prepared to subsidise the Soviet Union by feeding Germany's people while the Russians stripped her industries bare. Their answer to the appalling problems of overcrowding, malnutrition and galloping inflation was to re-establish an economically viable Germany – which would also act as a buffer between the West and the Russian-dominated East. But the Russians had no intention of building up the strength of an independent or pro-Western Germany: twenty million Russian dead and the future security of the Soviet Union demanded that they kept control of at least their portion of the former Reich.

As the former Allies drifted apart so the partition of Germany began to look like a permanent feature of the map. The Russians ensured that the communist-controlled Socialist Unity Party was the dominant political force in their zone. In January 1947 the American and British zones were joined together. As the forms of the two Germanys began to harden, so the predicament of the citizens of Berlin looked less and less secure. To govern their city, in the heart of the Russian zone, they had elected an anti-communist mayor, Ernst Reuter. If the Russians and Americans came to a trial of strength in Europe, it was almost certain to begin here.

The "Iron Curtain"

In June 1945 Winston Churchill had told Harry Truman, "I view with profound misgivings ... the descent of an iron curtain between us and everything to the eastward." The phrase "iron curtain" explains itself, and you can see it marked as a thick black line on the map opposite. By March 1948 that "curtain", which was, in fact, a 2,000-kilometre stretch of barbed wire, sentry platforms and blocked roads, had become the dominant feature of the political geography of Europe. The curtain almost completely separated Eastern from Western Europe. It had been drawn at the furthest extent of Soviet military power.

In Eastern Europe after 1945 there had been Communist takeovers in a number of separate states, aided and abetted by the Soviet Union. Leading Com-

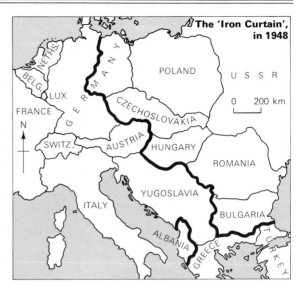

The 'Iron Curtain', in 1948

munists, having spent the war years in the Soviet Union, had returned to become members of coalition governments, generally in control of the police and radio services. To win complete power, they had first to drive their coalition partners, leaders of the Peasant and Socialist parties, out of government, despite the fact that they had the widest support from the people. In Bulgaria the apparently rigged elections of 1945 led to a Communist victory. In the following year the people voted in a referendum for the abolition of the monarchy, and Bulgaria became the first of the new "People's Republics". The wartime resistance hero, Marshal Tito, had already created a Communist republic in Yugoslavia. In 1947 Communists seized power in Hungary and Romania; and in the same year elections were held in Poland under the scrutiny of a Communist Minister of Public Security. In the next few years the only outspoken criticism of the new Communist government in Poland would come from the Catholic Church, led by Cardinal Wyszynski.

By the end of 1947 only three states east of the curtain were not ruled by Communists: Finland, Greece and Czechoslovakia. The Finns made their own arrangement with Russia – to remain independent but neutral. In Greece a civil war was being waged between Royalists and Communists, but Stalin did not intervene in an area which he had earlier agreed to leave to the British. Czechoslovakia appeared to stand a good chance of remaining independent. Beneš had returned as President, and Jan Masaryk, the son of the founder of the state, was Foreign Minister in a coalition government which included a number of Communists. Appearances were deceptive. In February 1948 Beneš was pressured into accepting a government dominated by Communists, though Masaryk stayed on. A few weeks later Masaryk fell out of an upstairs window to his death. The least credible report of the 'accident' suggested that the Foreign Minister lost his balance. He was either killed or possibly committed suicide to draw attention to his country's fate. What was certain was that Czechoslovakia had lost her independence.

Eastern Europe was transformed into a bloc of Soviet-dominated Communist republics whose leaders took their orders from Moscow and whose industries were 're-organised' so that the USSR could take the lion's share of goods she needed: Polish coal, Czech machine-tools and Romanian oil. Yugoslavia, by 1946, was well on the way to becoming a model communist state with public ownership of industry and collectivisation of agriculture. But Tito refused to accept Stalin's orders, or to allow Yugoslav industry to serve Russian needs. In 1948 Stalin tried to bring Tito to heel by ordering the Yugoslav Communist Party from the Cominform (a body of European communist organisations set up in 1947), believing that this would turn the rank and file members against their leader. He had calculated badly. Tito was a war hero, and had the loyalty of wartime partisans who now dominated the Yugoslav Communist Party. They backed him, and Yugoslavia became an independent communist state. Within a few years she was becoming the world's only partly liberal communist state, allowing some private ownership of land and workers' ownership of industry.

The Condition of the West

While the countries to the east of the "iron curtain" were being locked into a new political and economic system that was primarily for the benefit of the Soviet Union, the independent countries of the West appeared to be reverting to the classic European pattern of disunity. They seemed to be almost completely absorbed in their own problems. Italy needed to erase the nightmare memory of Fascism, to repair the

ravages of two years of war fought on her soil, and to halt runaway inflation. France had still to come to terms with the shock of her defeat in 1940 and the shame of Vichy; and she too had to repair the damage done by both occupiers and liberators. Belgium had to live with the fact that the extreme Flemish nationalists had collaborated with the Nazis. Britain was broke, her empire was beginning to break up and she no longer ruled the waves. Six years of war had left her a much poorer country but still a proud one: the leaders of both her major political parties could not bring themselves to believe that victory in a world war had brought about her decline as a world power.

Even so, there was one aspect of post-war Western European politics which gave general cause for concern. Except in Britain, which had not been occupied by the Nazis, the Communist parties had emerged stronger and more popular from their participation in the resistance movements. In both Italy and France the supposed threat of Communists coming to power led to the rise of large new Catholic parties pledged to social reform and the preservation of Western-style democracy – the Christian Democrats in Italy and the MRP (*Mouvement Républicain Populaire*) in France. There was, in the late 1940s, no guarantee that they would succeed.

The World War had dislodged Western Europe from its position at the centre of world politics. Its great powers no longer had any influence in the East of the continent; its overseas empires were beginning to crack up as nationalists in the colonies took advantage of their weakened masters. Some of its more far-sighted politicians believed that the best hope for the future lay in some form of economic and political union of the separate states. But by 1948 only Belgium, the Netherlands and Luxembourg were more closely integrated than they had been before the war: the Benelux agreement, signed in 1944, established a customs union between the three states. Until the separate nations of Western Europe could bring themselves to forget old antagonisms and plan together for the future, they would need aid from outside to strengthen their war-weakened economies. And that aid could come only from the one country strong enough to prop them up – the USA.

197

34 Conclusions in the Far East

The Defeat of Japan

When the Big Three met at Potsdam in July 1945 (see Chapter 33, page 193–5) after their victory in Europe, they still had half a war to settle. Ever since the Americans had entered the war, after the Japanese attack on Pearl Harbour in December 1941, the defeat of Nazi Germany had been given the first priority. Now it was possible for the USA to bring all her might to bear against the enemy in the East; and Soviet troops were being moved from European to Asiatic Russia to add their weight to the final assault on the Japanese Empire.

Japan was at the end of her tether. Since November 1944 the home islands had been attacked by America's new bombing planes – B29 Superfortresses – based in the Marianas. In March 1945 nearly 300 B29s devastated Tokyo in a fire-bomb raid which burnt out a quarter of the city and killed 80,000 people. By the time of Potsdam the bombing reached a terrifying crescendo which paralysed what was left of the Japanese economy and drove millions of city-dwellers to seek shelter of some kind in the countryside.

Most Japanese could see that their defeat was inevitable. In April, Admiral Suzuki took over as Prime Minister, and the government tried secretly to interest the Americans in a peace which would avoid the humiliation of 'unconditional surrender' and would preserve the position of the Japanese Emperor. Approaches were made to the still officially neutral Soviet Union to act as an intermediary to arrange a peace. Stalin did not pass on the Japanese proposals to the US government, but the Americans knew of them all the same: their Intelligence service had intercepted and deciphered the messages sent from Tokyo to Moscow.

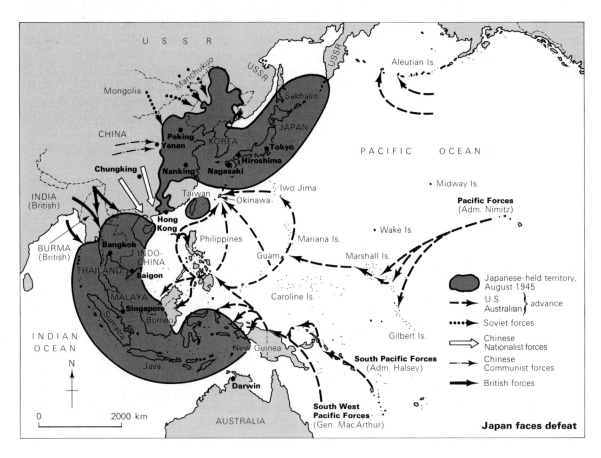

Japan faces defeat

A weapon of terrifying power: an atomic bomb explodes over Bikini atoll in the Pacific in a 1946 test explosion. It destroyed a fleet of obsolete warships moored there to test the bomb's power.

By the beginning of August 1945 the position in the Far East was as follows. Suzuki's 'peace party' wanted to end the fighting, but on terms that would not give fanatics in the Japanese army excuses to overthrow the government and lead the people in suicidal resistance to the Allied invasions that were bound to come. Stalin was poised to hurl his troops against Japanese positions in Manchuria, and was looking forward to a land-grab in China and a share in the occupation of Japan as the price of his participation. Both the USA and Britain were alarmed at the prospect of a Soviet penetration of Asia to match the takeover of Eastern Europe; and Truman's advisers estimated that the projected invasion of Japan would cost the lives of hundreds of thousands of American soldiers.

The invasion never came. At 2.45 a.m. on 6 August 1945 an American B29, piloted by Colonel Paul Tibbets, took off from the island of Tinian in the Marianas. The plane was called the *Enola Gay* after the pilot's mother. In its belly was "Little Boy" – an atomic bomb. At 8.15 a.m. the bomb was dropped over Hiroshima, an industrial city and the seventh largest in Japan. Forty-three seconds later, and still more than 500 metres above the city, the bomb went off. The following is part of an account by two historians of what it did:

"The initial flash spawned a succession of calamities. First came heat. It lasted only an instant but was so intense that it melted roof tiles, fused the quartz crystals in granite blocks, charred the exposed sides of telephone poles for almost two miles, and incinerated

nearby humans, so thoroughly that nothing remained
except their shadows, burned into asphalt pavements
or stone walls. Bare skin was burned up to two and a
half miles away.

After the heat came the blast, sweeping outward
from the fireball with the force of a five-hundred-mile-
an-hour wind. Only those objects that offered a minimum of surface resistance – handrails on bridges,
pipes, utility poles – remained standing. . . . Otherwise,
in a giant circle more than two miles across, everything
was reduced to rubble. . . ."

The bomb detonated with an explosive power equivalent to 20,000 tonnes of TNT. It killed in an instant
by fire and blast. It also killed slowly, by pollution: the
vast cloud of destruction that mushroomed over Hiroshima was radioactive. By one means or another, "Little
Boy" killed some 70,000 people and injured 80,000
more. On 9 August, a second bomb, "Fat Man", was
dropped on the port of Nagasaki, and another 40,000
Japanese died.

The Americans had run clean out of bombs: the
Manhattan Project (see Chapter 32, page 188) had produced only three nuclear devices. But the Japanese
were not to know that. The Emperor Hirohito proposed that they should surrender, provided they were
allowed to retain the imperial dynasty. On the 10th the
Allies replied that the "Emperor's authority would be
exercised under the supervision of the inter-allied C-
in-C"; and on the 14th the Japanese government
accepted the Allied terms.

One by one, in August and September, the Japanese
military leaders surrendered their armies; although a
few chose to avoid the humiliation by committing *hara-
kiri*, ritual suicide. On 2 September General Douglas
MacArthur accepted the formal surrender of all the
Japanese forces. The document was signed on board
the battleship *Missouri*, anchored in Tokyo Bay: a
short prayer for peace was then followed by a flight
of more than four hundred B29s over the Japanese
capital.

Like Germany, Japan was to be occupied by the
armies of her former enemies; but unlike Germany she
would not be divided into Allied zones. America had
won the war, and America would decide the peace. The
new power in Japan was Douglas MacArthur,
Supreme Commander for the Allied Powers (SCAP).
Under his military government, Japan was to be
demilitarised and democratised.

The East Indies

When MacArthur received the surrender of the
Japanese on board the *Missouri*, representatives of
Britain, France and the Netherlands were present to
watch the ceremony. You will remember from Chapter
31 (page 169–70) how the Japanese victories of late 1941
and early 1942 had swept white men out of Asia with
what looked like astonishing ease; how the legends
of European superiority and invincibility had died
a sudden death. Now, in September 1945, the Asian
imperialists had lost their war, and the European
imperialists had won theirs – mainly from the decks of
American warships. The white men had returned to
claim back what they believed to be rightfully theirs.
But it soon became clear that the colonial peoples had
no intention of shuffling back obediently under the rule
of their long-absent masters.

In the East Indies the Japanese forces surrendered
to the British, who held the islands in readiness for the
Dutch to re-assume control. By that time nationalists
had proclaimed an independent Republic of Indonesia,
with Sukarno (see Chapter 20, page 80) as President;
and had armed themselves with the weapons of the
former occupying forces. The scene was set for a
bloody struggle for power; and soon after the British
left the Dutch launched, in July 1947, what was known
as their "first police action". In straightforward language it was a full-scale attack against nationalist
forces, serious enough to cause the United Nations
Security Council to intervene. After a patched-up
truce between the two sides, a "second police action"
was mounted at the end of 1948, in which nationalist
leaders were captured and imprisoned.

The Dutch behaved as if the Indonesians had no
right to resist them. It was, perhaps, an odd opinion
to be held in a country where many people had become
national heroes for their resistance to an occupying
power. But the same men who called their resistance
leaders 'patriots' now dismissed Sukarno and his followers as 'rebels'. It was a conclusion which could not
stand up to the facts, not only because it was dishonest,
but because the Netherlands no longer had the economic and military power to back it. Nor were the
Dutch helped by the new power in the Far East, the
USA. The Americans, who had destroyed Japan's
Greater Asia Co-Prosperity Sphere, did not want the
reputation of being upholders of old-fashioned European colonialism.

Under pressure, especially from the USA, the Dutch gave up an old role they could no longer sustain. In December 1949, they recognised the independence of their former colonies as a federal country, the United States of Indonesia. But the nationalist leaders regarded the federal system as an attempt by the Dutch to leave behind a weak and divided Indonesia. So in the following year they re-organised their country into a centralised republic.

Indo-China

During the war the Japanese occupation forces in Indo-China had been harassed by a new movement, the Vietminh, which by the summer of 1945 was in control of Tonkin and most of Annam. A new government, led by the communist revolutionary Ho Chi Minh (see Chapter 20, page 80), was set up in Hanoi; and when the Japanese surrendered in September, the Vietminh took over more territory to the south and declared themselves rulers of the independent state of Vietnam.

When the French returned to Indo-China (some of them didn't have to travel far: they had been interned by the Japanese) they were able to re-establish control in the south but were confronted by a popular, well-entrenched nationalist régime in the north. The most they would offer the Vietminh was that North Vietnam should become a self-governing state within a French-controlled federation of Indo-China. It was not enough, and the hostility between the two sides erupted into violence: at the end of 1946 the French bombarded the port of Haiphong, and the Vietminh attacked Frenchmen still living in the north.

As the French could not bring the Vietminh to heel they now tried the old, familiar tactic of exercising power through a local ruler willing to cooperate with the Europeans. The front man in this case was to be Bao Dai, the former Emperor of Annam. In June 1949, a new state of Vietnam was set up, with Bao Dai as its head; and Laos and Cambodia were given a similar limited independence. The Vietminh prepared for war.

As an attempt to put the clock back to a pre-war style of imperialism, the French plan was almost bound to fail. The Vietminh were far stronger, better disciplined and armed than the nationalists of the late 1930s had been. As the historian D. K. Fieldhouse has stated, "the Japanese occupation finally destroyed the already weakened foundations of European power in South-

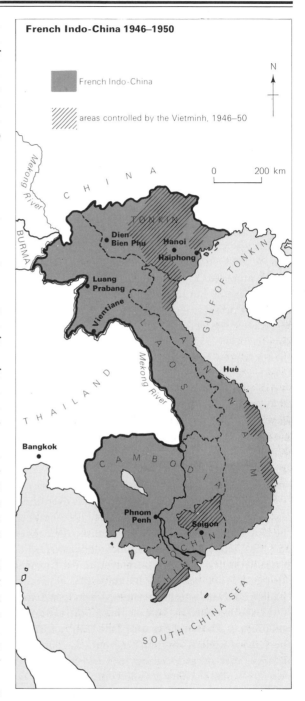

French Indo-China 1946–1950

East Asia". By 1950 the Dutch had been forced to recognise the new facts of life in the area: it would take four more years of mounting bitterness and violence to bring the French to the same conclusion – and we shall return to that story in Chapter 35.

India-"that most truly bright and precious jewel"

Britain was the only European power that had maintained a presence in Asia throughout the war. Malaya, Singapore and Burma had fallen to the Japanese, but the sub-continent of India had remained under British control, and the enemy had been swept out of Burma by May 1945. However, although British rule in India was not seriously threatened from outside, there were serious internal disorders as nationalists carried on their struggle for independence that had racked the country in the 1930s (see pages 71–2).

The Congress Party refused to cooperate in the British war effort and in 1942 turned down a new scheme for eventual self-government and Dominion status proposed by a mission led by Sir Stafford Cripps. Gandhi himself spoke contemptuously of the offer as "a post-dated cheque on a crashing bank", but his real fear was perhaps not that Britain was a ruined country but that she would break her promises once the war against Japan was over. After all, the offer had been made by a government headed by the arch-imperialist Winston Churchill, the man who had declared "I have not become His Majesty's first minister in order to preside over the dissolution of the British Empire". Under the new slogan "Quit India", Congress mounted a campaign of civil disobedience: British troops were called in to quell riots; and Gandhi, Nehru and other nationalist leaders were imprisoned.

But when the struggle against Japan was over, there was to be no tug-of-war in India like those between the Dutch and the Indonesian nationalists, the French and the Vietminh. The British people were tired of war, and the new Labour government, under Clement Attlee, did not see India in quite the light that Stanley Baldwin, a former Prime Minister, had seen it when he described the land as "that most truly bright and precious jewel in the crown of the King". Instead, the Labour leaders saw India not only as a political liability (after all, as socialists, they had not come to power to exploit the poor of India) but also as a possession that might prove too costly in money and lives to hold on to.

The British government hoped to grant independence to a united country, but the divisions between Hindus and Muslims and the rift between Congress and the League (see Chapter 17, pages 71–2) were by now far too deep to be papered over by fancy constitutional schemes which aimed to keep them together in one India. In August 1946 riots in Calcutta, Bihar, East Bengal and the United Provinces threatened to plunge the whole land into violence between the communities. When Attlee failed to persuade the party leaders to come to an agreement, he decided on shock treatment. Early in 1947 the government announced that they would hand over all power and responsibility for India not later than June 1948; and Lord Mountbatten was appointed Viceroy to prepare the transfer of authority.

It was a sobering prospect: the Indian political leaders now had to agree to a workable compromise or accept responsibility for the unthinkable – an India free at last but disintegrating into chaos and bloodshed. They chose the compromise. The land would be partitioned: India for the Hindus together with the Sikhs; Pakistan for the Muslims. Mohammed Ali Jinnah would get his "land of the pure". Gandhi was heart-broken at the decision, but he accepted it; the seventy-eight-year-old prepared himself for a last service to his land – to put his frail body between men intent on killing each other. Mountbatten, too, knew that every day's delay before independence would mean more violence in those districts where Hindus, Sikhs and Muslims lived as neighbours.

In June 1947 Mountbatten took the decision to bring forward independence – and with it partition – to 15 August, little more than two months away. In that time the parliament of each province of British India would have to decide whether to join India or Pakistan; so too would the 565 princes who, under agreements made between their ancestors and the British, ruled that many states, some of them larger than Wales but many not much bigger than a good-sized farm. At the same time British officials worked long days to draw boundary lines through the areas of mixed Hindu and Muslim populations in the Punjab and Bengal.

On 15 August 1947 the British relinquished their rule over nearly 400 million people: Nehru became Prime Minister of India, while Jinnah became Governor-General of Pakistan; and the people of the divided Punjab – Hindus, Sikhs and Muslims – let themselves go in a frenzy of slaughter.

Muslims killed Sikhs left in the new Pakistan, while on the other side of the frontier, Hindus and Sikhs massacred Muslims. Millions fled in terror, and the more ambitious of the murderers pursued the refugees

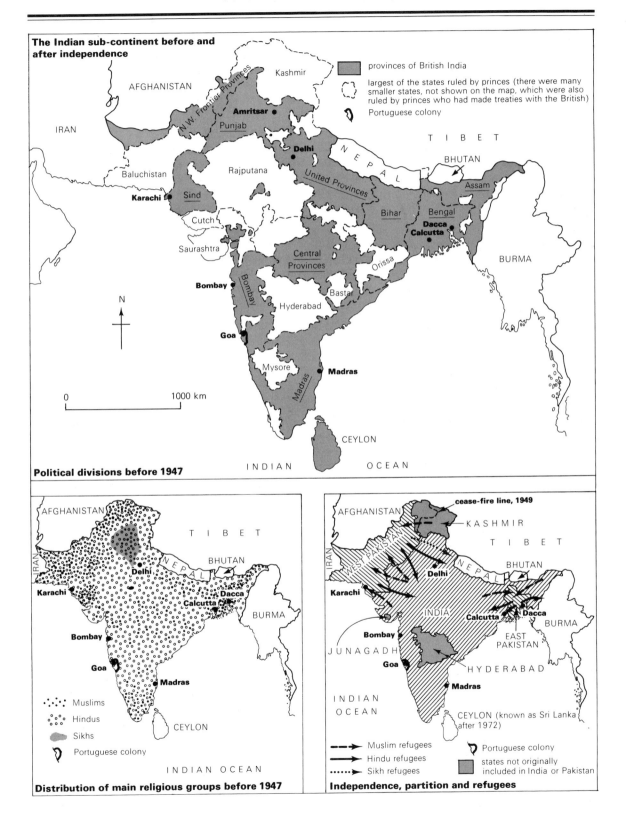

The Indian sub-continent before and after independence

provinces of British India

largest of the states ruled by princes (there were many smaller states, not shown on the map, which were also ruled by princes who had made treaties with the British)

Portuguese colony

AFGHANISTAN

Kashmir

IRAN

N.W. Frontier Provinces

Amritsar

Punjab

Delhi

T I B E T

N E P A L

BHUTAN

Baluchistan

Rajputana

United Provinces

Assam

Karachi

Sind

Bihar

Bengal

Cutch

Dacca
Calcutta

BURMA

Saurashtra

Central
Provinces

Orissa

N

Bombay

Bombay

Bastar

Hyderabad

Goa

Mysore

Madras

Madras

0   1000 km

CEYLON

INDIAN   O C E A N

Political divisions before 1947

AFGHANISTAN

T I B E T

N E P A L

BHUTAN

Delhi

Karachi

Dacca

Calcutta

BURMA

Bombay

Goa

Madras

CEYLON

·.·.·.·. Muslims

Hindus

Sikhs

Portuguese colony

INDIAN OCEAN

Distribution of main religious groups before 1947

cease-fire line, 1949

AFGHANISTAN

KASHMIR

IRAN

WEST PAKISTAN

T I B E T

N E P A L

BHUTAN

Delhi

Karachi

INDIA

Calcutta

Dacca

BURMA

Bombay

EAST
PAKISTAN

JUNAGADH

Goa

HYDERABAD

Madras

INDIAN
OCEAN

CEYLON (known as Sri Lanka
after 1972)

Muslim refugees

Hindu refugees

Sikh refugees

Portuguese colony

states not originally
included in India or Pakistan

Independence, partition and refugees

and killed them by the lorryful and the trainload. In all, about half a million people lost their lives. Of the panic-stricken migrants, about eleven million trekked across the frontier in the Punjab – roughly half each way; while over 400,000 Hindus moved out of Sind and a million more left East Pakistan for West Bengal. Many of the Hindu refugees found their way to Delhi where they threatened to annihilate the remaining Muslims; but Gandhi arrived in time to stop the bloodshed. He came straight from Calcutta where he had begun a fast which he had threatened to keep up until death, and had broken only when the Hindu and Muslim leaders called upon their people not to unleash violence in that overcrowded city.

And then, on 30 January 1948, came the news that shocked people out of their murderous hate. At 6 p.m. All India Radio made the following announcement: "Mahatma Gandhi was assassinated in New Delhi at twenty minutes past five this afternoon. His assassin was a Hindu." The newsreader might have added "Thank God he wasn't a Muslim". The little man had been gunned down by extremist Hindu nationalists – fanatics who couldn't stomach Gandhi's love for Muslims and Untouchables. On the following morning the *Hindustan Standard* made the moral clear to anyone who still hadn't seen it:

"Gandhiji has been killed by his own people for whose redemption he lived. This second crucifixion in the history of the world has been enacted on a Friday – the same day Jesus was done to death one thousand nine hundred and fifteen years ago. Father, forgive us."

You will see from the map on page 203 that in August 1947 three princely states had not declared themselves for inclusion in India or Pakistan. In 1948 Hyderabad and Junagadh were gathered, with a little compulsion, into the new India. But Kashmir was in a class of its own: it was a border state with a Hindu ruler and concentrations of both Hindu and Muslim peoples. In October 1947 the ruler appealed to India for help when Pathans from Pakistan invaded his land. In went the Indian troops, and there they stayed, not only to clear out the Pathans but to wage war against Pakistani forces sent in by Jinnah. In 1949 the United Nations managed to arrange a truce between them; and from then on the state of Kashmir was to remain divided along the frozen battle line, a land forcibly partitioned between two countries.

If the predicament of Kashmir showed the gulf that now lay between two peoples who had once lived together under alien rule, the geography of Pakistan was in itself the most extraordinary expression of the difficulties that had clouded the Indians' advance to independence. Look at the map. Even as the Pakistani crows flew, more than 2,000 kilometres of mainly Indian territory separated Karachi in the west from Dacca in the east; while East Pakistan was surrounded on three sides by India and her coastline was washed by an Indian sea.

As the British left India, and Pakistan, in 1947, so they left two more of their possessions, Ceylon and Burma, in 1948. In their withdrawal from most of their Asian empire the British had performed, overall, in a creditable manner. A measure of their performance was that few of their former subjects bore them much ill-will: of the four new independent states only Burma did not accept membership of the British Commonwealth.

China – One Man's Revolution

If the World War had hastened along the decline and fall of Western European imperialism in Asia, it had slowed down the struggle for power in China. In Chapter 18 (pages 73–4) we saw how a showdown between Chiang Kai-shek's Kuomintang and Mao Tse-tung's Communists was postponed in the late 1930s by the Japanese invasion. Since then the Communists had acquitted themselves better than their rivals.

By the summer of 1945 Mao's forces had liberated large areas of northern China from Japanese military control. Mao's million-strong army of guerrilla fighters was now backed up by a two-million-strong 'home guard' – a militia of peasants recruited to defend their villages against the Japanese. And in those areas under Mao's control peasants had been won over to the Communist cause by the seizure of land, especially from landlords branded as collaborators, and the sharing out of that land among poor villagers. By the end of the war the reputation of the Communists was strikingly different from that of the Kuomintang: while Mao's forces had harassed and stood up to the enemy, the so-called 'nationalists' had squandered their American aid and profited from black marketeering and corruption that was spectacular even by the standards of 'warlord' China.

Even so, when Japan was bombed into defeat in August, Chiang expected to benefit from a victory he had done nothing to bring about. He quickly signed a treaty with Stalin – which meant that Communist Russia accepted the Kuomintang as the legitimate authority in China – and insisted that only his armies should accept the surrender of enemy forces still in China. Mao ignored him and sent his men to accept the surrender of the Japanese in the east and in Manchuria.

Chiang turned again for aid from the ally he had tried to mislead throughout the war – the USA. Roosevelt was dead, but a powerful 'China lobby' in the States insisted on helping the Kuomintang to resist the further spread of communism. By courtesy of the US Air Force, half a million of Chiang's troops were ferried east and north to take over Japanese-occupied towns.

By 1946 the armies were in position, ready for their final contest. The American government attempted to stave off a civil war, and the alarming prospect that the Communists would win and control China, by sending General George Marshall to mediate between the two Chinese leaders. Chiang and Mao were persuaded to come together for talks, but too much history lay between them for any kind of coalition government to be possible. The future would belong to one or the other, but not to both.

The civil war erupted in 1947 as the Kuomintang mounted a three-pronged offensive against the Communists in the north. It failed. When Mao opened his counter-offensive in the following year, the enemy forces disintegrated. Chiang's armies had become weak legions of graft rather than formidable instruments of conquest. Soldiers deserted in their thousands; some Kuomintang cities surrendered without a fight. In April 1949, having secured the northern towns, Mao's armies advanced across the Yangtse River. What was left of the Kuomintang followed Chiang in a humiliating flight from the mainland to the island of Taiwan. On 1 October Mao announced the foundation of the People's Republic of China.

Mao's revolution had been a long and extraordinary affair. It had taken nearly twenty years and cost millions of lives. It had finally been won by an army that had matured as a fighting force in a nationalist war against an alien occupation. It broke all Marx's rules for when and where and how a communist revolution should take place. It had been based on the support of millions of peasants, not city workers. It had appealed to national feeling against the Japanese as much as to class feeling against men of property. It had been an open struggle, not a conspiracy. In comparison, the world's first communist revolution – that of Lenin in 1917 – looked like a terrorist takeover of a city.

While Kuomintang troops look on in the background, a Shanghai municipal policeman kills two political prisoners during street executions before the city fell to the Communists, 1949.

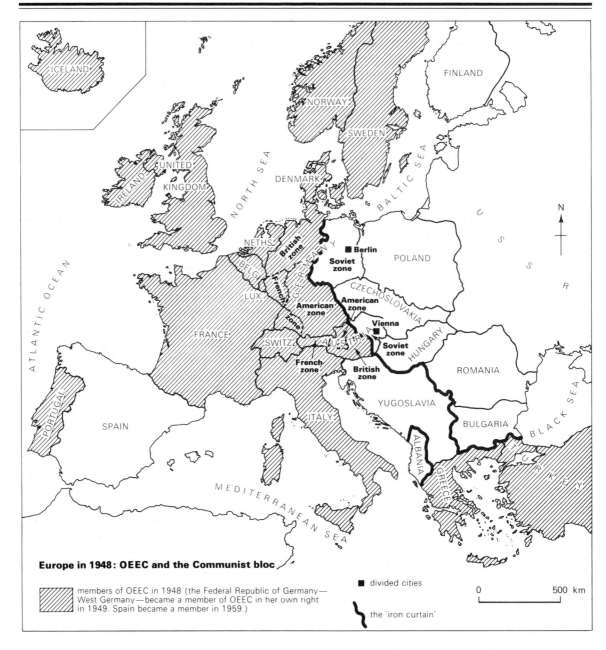

Europe in 1948: OEEC and the Communist bloc

| | members of OEEC in 1948 (the Federal Republic of Germany— West Germany—became a member of OEEC in her own right in 1949. Spain became a member in 1959.) |

■ divided cities

the 'iron curtain'

0   500 km

Americans and British were moving towards the creation of a separate Western Germany as part of the plan for the economic recovery of non-communist Western Europe. Even the façade of co-operation between the four occupying powers was falling apart. In March the Russians had walked out of a meeting of the Control Council, furious at the refusal of the three Western Allies to tell them their plans for the future of their zones. On 18 June 1948 a new currency – the

Deutschmark – was put into circulation in the Western zones to replace the old *Reichsmark*. The Russians responded by introducing a new currency in their zone – which included Berlin. On 23 June the West German *Deutschmark* was introduced into the Western sectors of Berlin. Russian retaliation this time came fast and hard: they declared that since the Americans, British and French were creating a new Germany in the West, they had no business interfering in the Germany of the

East. To make their position absolutely clear, on 24 June the Russians closed the roads, railroads and waterways that linked West Berlin to the Western zones.

The Western powers could have abandoned Berlin. That would have meant handing over two million West Berliners to Communist rule – and three years before, the Americans and the British had not been at all squeamish about the fate of German people, particularly those in the eastern lands. Although West Berlin was a useful 'listening post' behind the "iron curtain", was it really worth a confrontation with the Russians that might lead to a hot war?

The Americans declared, emphatically, that it was. The Commander of the American forces in Germany, General Lucius Clay, declared, "We have lost Czechoslovakia. Norway is threatened. We retreat from Berlin. When Berlin falls, Western Germany will be next." And then, presumably, the rest of Western Europe? Remember the dominoes? Harry Truman, the man whose Doctrine demanded that no ground should be given to the Communists, summed up the American position without wasting words: "We are going to stay, period."

Airlift to Berlin

At first, General Clay considered the possibility of breaking the blockade by armed force. It was not on: the Russians had far more ground troops in the area than the Americans. An answer was found instead in the form of an airlift of food, fuel, medicines and other necessities of life to the besieged citizens of West Berlin. The arguments behind the airlift, which began in the last week of June, were simple: the Americans and the British had enough large transport planes to make the operation feasible; and if the Russians were determined to stop the flights they would have to take the appalling risk of being the first to open fire. The shuttle of Allied planes over Germany was given a chilling back-up when two groups of American B29 bombers were sent to bases in England in mid-July. We still do not know whether those B29s were armed with atomic bombs. What everyone, including the Russians, had to believe was that those planes could carry nuclear weapons to Eastern European targets: they had, after all, carried them from Tinian to Hiroshima and Nagasaki.

The Berlin airlift went on into the autumn and winter of 1948. Truman's decision to see the operation

through, no matter how long it took, certainly didn't harm his political career. His closest political adviser, Clark Clifford, had told him over a year before that

"There is considerable political advantage to the Administration in its battle with the Kremlin.... The worse matters get, up to a fairly certain point – real danger of imminent war – the more there is a sense of crisis. In times of crisis the American citizen tends to back up his President."

In the Presidential election of November 1948, Truman polled twenty-four million votes to Republican Thomas E. Dewey's twenty-two million.

As the blockade continued into 1949, the governments of the USA and the Western European nations as well as Canada considered how they might cope best, together, with similar crises in the future. The outcome of their debate was the North Atlantic Treaty Organisation (NATO); the twelve founding members agreed on 4 April 1949 to defend each other from any kind of armed attack.

By the end of April it was clear to Stalin that the Berlin blockade would not succeed. The volume of supplies flown daily into the city was rising, not falling. On 12 May the Russians re-opened the land routes to the city.

For 318 days the Americans and the British had fed and fuelled West Berlin. The US Air Force and the RAF had flown in nearly 1½ million tonnes of supplies (roughly three-quarters of which were carried in American planes). Their phenomenal effort had maintained a Western presence in Eastern Germany, upheld the Truman Doctrine, and kept two million people free from communist rule.

New Fears and Alarms

On 23 July 1949, President Truman signed the NATO Treaty after Congress had discussed the pact and given its consent. On the same day Truman asked Congress for 1·5 billion dollars over the next year to help the nations of Western Europe strengthen their armed forces. But Congress was as reluctant to pay for military aid as it had been to pay for economic aid in 1947. Some Senators argued that they didn't see much point in spending vast sums of money on building up 'conventional' European forces. Since the USA had a

Steam rollers at Gatow Airfield, Berlin, making another unloading stage for aircraft during the Berlin airlift of 1948. In the background are American Skymaster aircraft which have brought supplies of coal into the besieged city.

monopoly of nuclear weapons, why not step up their production so that the USA could, by herself, defend the West with bombers based in the NATO countries? The answer to that question came on 22 September when Truman announced he had been informed that the Russians had successfully tested an atomic bomb. Almost overnight it seemed that the balance of military power had swung in Russia's favour. In Washington, as the historian Stephen Ambrose has recorded, "the urge to do something, anything, was irrepressible". Within the next week, Congress gave the President the money he needed for strengthening Western Europe's ground forces; and Truman ordered an acceleration of

the programme to develop even more devastating nuclear weapons.

As the winter of 1949–50 settled in, the temperature of the Cold War sank to new lows. As you already know from Chapter 34 (page 204–5) Mao's Communists set up their new régime in China in October. By December the new Chinese leader was in Moscow discussing with Stalin the terms of a treaty between their two countries. In the USA an anti-communist witch-hunt was under way. A young Republican from California, Richard Nixon, led a Congressional investigation into the allegedly traitorous activities of Alger Hiss, a former official of the State Department (the American

Foreign Office). After two widely publicised trials, Hiss was found guilty of perjury in January 1950; many American people were convinced that there were other 'reds' in the government; and Nixon had made for himself a national reputation. In February it became known that Klaus Fuchs, a British physicist, had betrayed secrets of the atomic research programme to the Russians. In the same month Senator Joseph McCarthy announced that the State Department was stuffed with communists.

McCarthy was a true creature of the Cold War – crude, irresponsible and vicious in the cause of one hundred per cent super-patriotism. According to him, China had fallen to the 'reds' because 'traitors' in the American government had worked to that end. America herself was in danger; the 'commies' must be rooted out of her government, out of the mass media and out of the education system. McCarthy operated on the simple, ugly principle that mud sticks. Those who dared criticise him were themselves branded as communists – so few people dared to risk the mud. In the state of Massachusetts an up-and-coming young politician, John F. Kennedy, took no risks at all. "McCarthy", he declared, "may have something."

With mounting hysteria at home about the 'red threat', Truman was determined to resist any hint of further Communist advances abroad. The USA flatly opposed the Russian proposal that Mao's government, not Chiang's exiled régime in Taiwan, should now represent China in the United Nations. In January 1950, after the proposal had been defeated, the Russian delegate walked out of the Security Council and announced his government's intentions to boycott further meetings of that body. In February the Russian and Chinese governments signed a treaty of friendship and "mutual assistance", though communist matiness did not go far beneath the surface. The Russians provided China with credit arrangements for the purchase of Soviet goods to the equivalent value of $300 million, spread over five years – chickenfeed compared with the Marshall Aid that America was pouring into Western Europe – and at the same time were reluctant to hand over control of Manchuria and Mongolia to the Chinese. In May President Truman announced that negotiations would soon begin on a Japanese peace treaty, in which the USA would claim the right to maintain military bases in Japan. In the same month there were reports of disturbances in Korea.

War in Korea, 1950–53

As you can see from the map on page 212, Korea was a divided land. Like the partition of Germany, the division of Korea was a war-wound: in 1945 the Japanese forces in the north of the peninsula had surrendered to Soviet armies, while those in the south had surrendered to the Americans. The two great powers had then set up two separate régimes – a Communist dictatorship under Kim II Sung in the north, and a form of democracy, corrupted and misgoverned by President Syngman Rhee, in the south. The USA and the USSR had then removed their own occupying forces, and left behind weapons and 'military advisers'.

In May 1950 there were small raids across the artificial border, in both directions. Early in June the Northern government proposed the reunification of the country after a general election and at the same time strengthened their army with more Russian-built tanks. Neither the USA nor the Soviet Union did anything to stifle the mounting risk of serious conflict in the peninsula. Whatever the final cause, the friction between the two Koreas erupted into war on 25 June when the Northern armies invaded across the 38th parallel.

If the South Koreans were surprised by the North's determined offensive, it was clear that the US government was fully prepared to act the moment it began. Within twenty-four hours President Truman re-affirmed that his Doctrine applied to Asia as well as to Europe; sent the US Seventh Fleet to patrol the sea between China and Taiwan; extended military aid to the French in their fight against the Vietminh in Indo-China; ordered General MacArthur in Japan to send supplies to South Korea; and put a resolution before the UN Security Council demanding that the North Korean aggressors should pack up and go back home. The resolution was passed unanimously: the Russian delegate was keeping up his boycott. Two days later, on 27 June, the Security Council passed another American resolution, by seven votes to one, recommending that members of the United Nations should help South Korea in restoring the peace: the odd man out was Yugoslavia, and she did not have the right of veto (see page 190). By that time the USA was already involved in the war: her bombers were being used in an attempt to slow down the North Korean advance.

On 30 June Truman ordered American troops stationed in Japan to move into South Korea. It was a unilateral action: the Americans did not consult their allies before the event. But one by one in the months that followed sixteen non-communist nations, including the UK, followed their leader and committed forces to the conflict. Their contributions made it look, provided you didn't get too close, as if South Korea was being rescued by a collective effort of the United Nations. In reality, it was a US – not a UN – operation. Douglas MacArthur had a new, additional rank as "Commander-in-Chief, United Nations Command": he would later admit that during the war he had "no direct connection with the United Nations whatsoever". Altogether, the USA provided half of the ground forces (South Koreans made up most of the rest), 86 per cent of the naval power, and 93 per cent of the air power.

As you can see from the map, the North Korean offensive was halted before it could sweep all the South's troops into the sea. As American forces poured into the bridgehead around Pusan, the US government considered not just pushing the invaders back to their border but advancing beyond it to 'liberate' the people of the North. The Cold War was about to enter a new, and risky, phase. The invasion of a Communist country in Asia might provoke Russian retaliation in Europe. On 12 September Dean Acheson, the new American Secretary of State, proposed strengthening NATO by sending more US troops to Europe – and by re-arming the West Germans! After their first astonishment at this proposal, the members of NATO agreed to eventual German participation; but meanwhile, in December 1950, an integrated European force was set up temporarily with General Dwight D. Eisenhower as Supreme Commander.

On 15 September 1950 MacArthur's troops outflanked the North Koreans by an amphibious assault at Inchon, far up the west coast of the peninsula. In a little more than a week they had taken the capital, Seoul, and trapped large forces of North Koreans in the south. On the 27th Truman instructed MacArthur to move through the North if there were no signs of Russian or Chinese resistance. On 7 October US troops crossed the 38th parallel, and on the same day the UN endorsed the American action. (Note that the UN "endorsed" the invasion: they did not authorise it.)

Three days after the invasion, on 10 October, the Chinese government stated that their armies would enter the conflict if the Americans continued to ad-

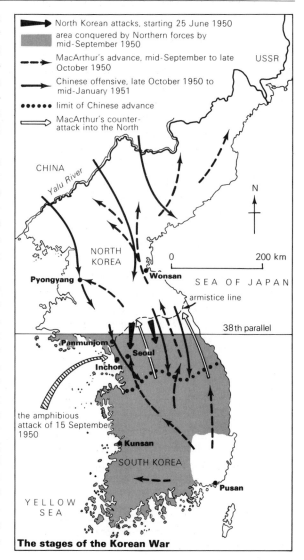

The stages of the Korean War

vance north. Later that month Truman met MacArthur at Wake Island in the Pacific, where the General assured the President that there was no danger of large-scale Chinese intervention. On 24 October MacArthur launched what he believed would be the last offensive of the war, towards the Yalu River.

The Chinese had already interpreted the movements of American ships and troops in June 1950 as acts of war against them. Had it not been for the US Seventh Fleet, Mao's forces would have crossed the Straits to Taiwan in an attempt to destroy Chiang Kai-shek's remaining base and "re-unite" the island with the rest of China. Now in October the US forces in Korea were driving towards the Yalu River, which was not only the border with China, but just a short march or bomber flight away from the only industrial region in Mao's republic. Chinese armies themselves crossed the Yalu on 26 October. Within a fortnight the Chinese had overrun US positions in much of North Korea; by mid-January 1951 the humiliated Americans had been thrown back well beyond the 38th parallel.

The US government was profoundly shocked. At the end of November Truman had lost enough of his cool to suggest that he might use nuclear weapons against the Chinese – a remark that brought the British Prime Minister, Clement Attlee, flying over to Washington. In the end the President didn't use the fearful weapons: he increased American spending on defence from $13·5 billion to $50 billion, vastly expanded the US air force, and raised the number of men in the army by fifty per cent to three and a half million!

At the beginning of 1951, in the second half of January and in February, MacArthur pulled together his forces and pushed the Chinese back to the 38th parallel. Truman prepared to negotiate a cease-fire, but MacArthur sabotaged that by crossing the border again and demanding that the enemy surrender. Truman, never a patient man, was livid. And then, in early April, the General called loud and clear for new initiatives in American policy. He wanted to reunify Korea, and help Chiang Kai-shek to mount an attack on mainland China. He declared:

"It seems strangely difficult for some to realise that here in Asia is where the Communist conspirators have elected to make their play for global conquest... that here we fight Europe's war with arms while the diplomats there still fight it with words; that if we lose the war to Communism in Asia the fall of Europe is inevitable.... There is no substitute for victory."

There was a substitute, and Truman, whose attempt to 'liberate' the North Koreans had come badly unstuck, was determined to have it. That substitute was the containment of communism within its then present boundaries – and one obstacle in the path of that policy was a loud-mouthed general who'd spent so long playing God in Tokyo that he believed he could ignore the orders of his Commander-in-Chief, the President of the United States of America. On 11 April 1951 Truman sacked MacArthur.

Many Americans felt somehow cheated of the prospect of "victory" that MacArthur had held out. He had proposed simple military answers to political problems that worried them, sometimes baffled them, and cost them money in the form of aid to unreliable allies. The General returned home to the greatest popular reception in American history. Joseph McCarthy, the red-baiting Senator from Wisconsin, enjoyed a new wave of popularity. Leading government officials, university lecturers and school teachers, journalists, film directors and actors – indeed, anyone whom McCarthy felt like accusing of "commie" leanings – were hauled before his investigating committee and faced with unsubstantiated charges of treason. Dealing in half-truths and smears, he and his accomplices ruined men and women's careers and broke up families. For President Truman they had only one recommendation: "the son of a bitch ought to be impeached".

Thanks to both McCarthy and MacArthur, Truman was out of favour with the American people. But his policy of containment, which MacArthur attacked as cowardice, was beginning to pay off in Asia.

To all intents and purposes the Korean War was over: the great ambitions of 1950 had been abandoned. It was now a tired, bitter struggle around the 38th parallel. The difficulty lay no longer in fighting it, but in getting out of it. Peace talks began in July, promptly broke down – and that pattern was repeated for the rest of the year. Early in 1952 the talks broke down again, this time over the repatriation of prisoners-of-war. The Chinese wanted all their men back: the USA would agree only to send back those who wanted to go. The fighting continued.

For the Presidential election of November 1952 the Republicans ran two men who together presented an unbeatable combination of a popular war-hero and an unscrupulous mud-slinger: Dwight Eisenhower for President and Richard Nixon for Vice-President. They won by a landslide. For his Secretary of State the new President chose John Foster Dulles, a man absolutely convinced that he was always right, that his country was morally superior to any other, and that all communists were utterly wicked.

Eisenhower had promised the electorate he would end the war. In early 1953 Dulles fulfilled that promise for him by making cold-blooded threats. Unless the Chinese agreed to a peace formula, he declared, the USA would use atomic weapons against them. The Chinese suddenly changed their attitude to the repatriation of prisoners. Only Syngman Rhee in South Korea objected to peace: as long as American troops were in Korea the safety of his régime was guaranteed against the Communists. In the end the Americans, the British and the French promised to support South Korea if the North attacked again, and a military armistice was finally signed on 27 July 1953. The war was over, although negotiations for a final peace were to drag on for many years at Panmunjom.

Containing Communism

By the time the conflict in Korea, the second great crisis of the Cold War, had come to an end in an uneasy truce, America had created most of a world-wide framework for the containment of communism. In the next two years she added a few more pieces to her complex structure of interlocking alliances and gave the world the political geography of 1955 shown in the diagram on page 215: the Communist states from the "iron curtain" to South-East Asia were hemmed in on all sides by client states of the USA.

Very early in the Cold War the USA had used her economic power in Latin America to persuade the separate countries of the sub-continent to join her in an agreement on collective security. In September 1947 a treaty was signed in Rio de Janeiro which declared that an attack on one American nation would be considered as an attack on them all. In the following March the Organisation of American States (OAS) was set up, and provision was made for the development of joint military strategy between its members. At the same time, wary of their big brother to the north, the Latin American governments insisted that the following article should be included in the Charter of the OAS: "No State may use or encourage the use of coercive measures of an economic or political character in order to force the sovereign will of another State and obtain from it advantages of any kind."

How little account would be taken of the Charter when the US government learnt of or suspected, any communist activity was seen in Guatemala in 1953. In that year, the Guatemalan leader, Jacobo Arbenz Guzmán, nationalised the property of the American-owned United Fruit Company, which dominated the economy of his poverty-stricken country. The fact that Arbenz was supported by local Communists was sufficient to goad the US government into helping a former Guatemalan officer, Carlos Castillo Armas, to

mount an armed invasion over the Honduras border in June 1954. Arbenz's government was ousted and a new conservative régime took over, supported by American aid.

For the confrontation with communism in Europe the OEEC and NATO were created – as you have already seen in this chapter. Neither the economic bloc nor the military alliance made much sense without the inclusion of a strong Western Germany; and the crisis over Berlin hurried along the creation of an independent state, by the amalgamation of the American, British and French zones. In September 1949 the new Federal Republic of West Germany was set up – a parliamentary democracy, with a Christian Democrat, Dr Konrad Adenauer, as Chancellor, and with the Social Democrats as the largest of the opposition parties. West Germany was allowed to rearm and became a member of NATO in 1955. By that time, Greece and Turkey had both joined NATO (in 1952), while in 1953 the Americans had persuaded Franco's government in Spain to lease them bases for the use of their air force.

Containment in South-East Asia

It was in Asia that American involvement took its most complex form. The war in Korea had raised American fears that another Asian peninsula, that of Indo-China, would fall victim to armed communism. As you saw on page 201, the French were at war with the guerrilla forces of the Vietminh, and between 1950 and 1954 the Americans gave them $1·2 billion worth of military aid. In the end, it made no difference. Worn down by the Vietminh's guerrilla tactics, the French decided to make a stand at the town of Dien Bien Phu and bring their enemy into open battle. They were outwitted and outfought and forced to surrender on 7 May. A new government in Paris, led by Pierre Mendès-France, decided that the time had come for a French withdrawal from Indo-China.

In July 1954 an agreement between the two sides was reached at Geneva. A truce was declared, and the French agreed to withdraw south of a partition line drawn at the 17th parallel. National elections were to be held within two years to unify Vietnam, while similar elections were also to be held in Laos and Cambodia. But to hold elections would be virtually to hand the whole of Vietnam on a plate to Ho Chi Minh; for the north contained a majority of the population, and

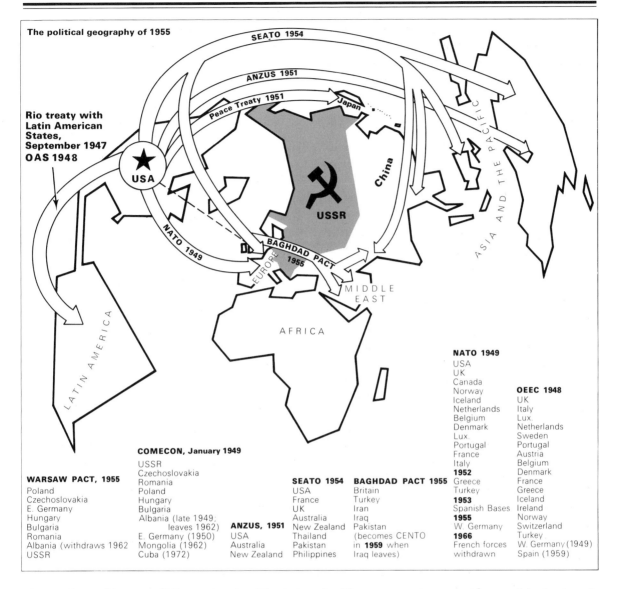

The political geography of 1955

Rio treaty with Latin American States, September 1947 OAS 1948

SEATO 1954
ANZUS 1951
Peace Treaty 1951
Japan
China
USSR
USA
NATO 1949
BAGHDAD PACT 1955
EUROPE
MIDDLE EAST
ASIA AND THE PACIFIC
LATIN AMERICA
AFRICA

WARSAW PACT, 1955
Poland
Czechoslovakia
E. Germany
Hungary
Bulgaria
Romania
Albania (withdraws 1962)
USSR

COMECON, January 1949
USSR
Czechoslovakia
Romania
Poland
Hungary
Bulgaria
Albania (late 1949;
  leaves 1962)
E. Germany (1950)
Mongolia (1962)
Cuba (1972)

ANZUS, 1951
USA
Australia
New Zealand

SEATO 1954
USA
France
UK
Australia
New Zealand
Thailand
Pakistan
Philippines

BAGHDAD PACT 1955
Britain
Turkey
Iran
Iraq
Pakistan
(becomes CENTO
in **1959** when
Iraq leaves)

NATO 1949
USA
UK
Canada
Norway
Iceland
Netherlands
Belgium
Denmark
Lux.
Portugal
France
Italy
1952
Greece
Turkey
1953
Spanish Bases
1955
W. Germany
1966
French forces
withdrawn

OEEC 1948
UK
Italy
Lux.
Netherlands
Sweden
Portugal
Austria
Belgium
Denmark
France
Greece
Iceland
Ireland
Norway
Switzerland
Turkey
W. Germany (1949)
Spain (1959)

the north would vote solidly communist. Elections would mean that the American investment in aid to the French would all have been for nothing, and a large hole would be punched in the policy of containment.

Dulles immediately set to work to create another anti-communist barrier – a kind of Asian NATO. In September the South-East Asia Treaty Organisation (SEATO) was formed by the USA, France, the UK, Australia, New Zealand, Thailand, Pakistan and the Philippines, in which they agreed to take joint action against aggression in a "designated area" – which included Vietnam, Laos and Cambodia. And to firm up

the Vietnamese resistance to communism the Americans transferred their aid programme from the French to the government of South Vietnam, under Prime Minister Ngo Dinh Diem.

In reality Dulles's barrier was less impressive than it seemed on the map. Britain was more concerned about Malaya than about Indo-China, Pakistan was chiefly interested in getting US support in her quarrels with India, while the French had not hopped out of the Indo-Chinese frying pan in order to jump into a fire stoked by Dulles and Diem. Nor were the two British Dominions, Australia and New Zealand, seriously committed to the containment of communism in South-

215

East Asia itself. Their membership of SEATO was an unavoidable consequence of the fact that they had become allies of the USA in 1951 when they had signed the ANZUS Pact by which the Americans agreed to guarantee their independence. It was an interesting example of a major shift in world power: two nations which had previously looked to London for protection now turned to the USA for their defence and, at least on paper, gave her their support in South-East Asia.

Even more dramatic was the changed relationship between the USA and Japan. By 1948, as vast amounts of American aid were being poured into Japan's war-shattered economy, it was becoming clear that the USA was developing a new role for her former enemy. Japan was not to be the peaceful pride of the Pacific: she was to be rebuilt as an ally against communism. (See Chapter 40, page 256.)

Containment in the Middle East

The USA's determination to contain communism meant that in Asia she took over much of the political, military and economic power once held by the Europeans in the area. A similar process took place in the Middle East, which before the Second World War had been dominated by British and French interests. In the immediate post-war years both Arabs and Jews rejected their alien rulers, and the area entered an explosive age of oil-fired nationalist conflicts. But what most concerned the USA in the Middle East during the years of containment policy was that the USSR might try to take advantage of the British and French withdrawal.

The first possible opportunity for a communist advance came in 1951 when nationalists gained control of Iran and the new Prime Minister, Dr Mohammed Mossadegh, undercut the power of the young Shah and nationalised the Anglo-Iranian Oil Company. That was a severe blow to the prestige of the British, who owned over half the shares in the company; but it also had a catastrophic effect on Iran's economy as her government found it next to impossible to find new markets in which to sell their oil. In 1953, as rumours spread of a Russian offer of aid to the hard-pressed Iranians, the American government provided the Shah

with sufficient military equipment to overthrow Mossadegh. By the summer of 1954 the Shah's government had signed a new agreement with an international consortium of oil companies, by which control of oil production was divided among the British (40 per cent), the Americans (40 per cent), the French and the Dutch (20 per cent). The Iranians were half pleased – in future they would receive half the profits from the exploitation of their own natural resource. The Americans were delighted: they had kept the Russians out, while their own oil companies had broken into what had once been a British monopoly.

The influence of the British in the Middle East was waning rapidly. Jewish nationalists had wrenched Palestine out of their control in 1948 and turned it into the state of Israel. In July 1954 the new revolutionary government of Egypt, under Prime Minister Gamal Abdel Nasser, negotiated an agreement by which all British troops would be withdrawn from the Suez Canal zone within two years, leaving behind only technicians to operate the partly British-owned waterway. In a further attempt to keep the Russians out of Middle Eastern politics, the American government supported the formation in 1955 of an alliance – the Baghdad Pact – between Britain, Turkey, Iran, Iraq and Pakistan. Dulles described the Pact as creating "a solid band of resistance against the Soviet Union".

In a sense it did more. The Baghdad Pact (which was transformed into CENTO – the Central Treaty Organisation – in 1959, after Iraq had left the Pact) completed the structure of American-dominated organisations and alliances: OAS, ANZUS, SEATO, NATO and the US treaty with Japan. 1955 was the high point of success for the policy of containment; the USSR and her allies might command colossal land armies, but they were enclosed by hostile states and their potential power was neutralised by the knowledge that, every minute of the day and night, American bombers were in the air with enough fuel to carry them far inside the Communist camp. And 1955 was significant in other ways: it was the year of the first post-war 'summit' meeting between the American and Russian leaders; and it was the year in which the Western world first became familiar with the name and the person of Nikita Sergeyevich Khrushchev.

36 Confrontation or Co-existence? East-West Relations, 1955–85

Joseph Stalin, the tyrant who had ruled the Soviet Union since 1928, died in March 1953. The new government, headed by Georgi Malenkov, was quick to bring an end to the worst excesses of Stalin's régime at home but no less eager to find new directions for Soviet foreign policy in a world which looked very different from Moscow than from Washington. The American government saw the USSR as a menacing power, dedicated to international revolution and ready to use any means to advance its frontiers: the Russian leaders looked out on a world in which they had scored no major successes since Czechoslovakia in 1948 – unless they counted China and North Vietnam, over which they had much less control than the Americans believed. Rather than being poised to seize world power, the Russians felt themselves threatened by the success of the Americans in building armed alliances. They also knew only too well how flimsy was the Soviet hold on the Eastern European satellites; only a few months after Stalin's death, tanks and armoured cars were needed to crush an anti-communist rising by the people of East Berlin.

What re-assessment of Soviet foreign policy went on in Moscow we can only guess at from hints in a few public speeches, but it's clear that the Russian leaders began with a consideration of the assets left by Stalin, the man who dragged the Soviet Union from the age of the wooden plough to that of the atomic stockpile. The USSR had exploded her first atomic bomb in 1949; and a much more powerful weapon, a hydrogen bomb, was tested in August 1953, less than a year after the Americans had set off their first thermo-nuclear device in November 1952. Still more important, enormous resources were already being spent on developing rocket missiles which might soon give the Russians a strategic advantage over the US air force. Secondly, by 1953 the Soviet Union's post-war economic recovery had put her in a position to enter into what Malenkov called "peaceful competition" with the USA in giving aid, with strings attached of course, to states around the globe. A third advantage to the new government was Stalin's corpse. Stalin had been feared and loathed in both the Western world and in the Communist satellite states; any Russian move to put relationships on a more open and equal basis would be immediately welcomed.

Georgi Malenkov did not stay in power long enough to carry out the new policies. In February 1955 he was overthrown and the new leading figure in the USSR was Nikita Khrushchev, the fifty-nine-year-old son of a peasant and now First Secretary of the Communist Party. He was clearly more powerful than the new Prime Minister, Nikolai Bulganin, who was, in any case, forced out of office in 1957. To all intents and purposes Soviet policies, at home and abroad, were made by Khrushchev between February 1955 and October 1964. They were to be turbulent years. It was not that the policies would have been much different if Malenkov had survived politically, but Khrushchev's blustering vigour, his love of travel and of argument and his willingness to take risks left their mark on these years.

Khrushchev and the Communist States of Eastern Europe

The death of Stalin was followed by a 'thaw' inside the USSR. Many political prisoners were released from labour camps and 'rehabilitated' – although often the investigating teams set up by the new government could rehabilitate only the memories of long-dead victims. Khrushchev hastened the emergence of the Russian people from the ice age of Stalinist terror. In a speech to a secret session of the Twentieth Congress of the Soviet Communist Party in February 1956 he roundly condemned the excesses and repression of Stalin's rule (except those in which Khrushchev had himself been involved) and promised a new era of Communist Party rule unsoiled by the Stalinist "cult of personality" which had presented a bloody tyrant as a benevolent superman. The speech did not remain secret for long: it was quickly spread throughout the Soviet Union and the communist states and was soon known in the outside world where it both confirmed what anti-communists had always said of Stalin's régime and shattered the self-confidence and unconditional loyalty to Moscow of other communist parties, especially those in Europe. The membership of the British Communist Party fell by about half in the following months.

De-Stalinisation was carried to Eastern Europe as Stalin's policies had once been put into effect – by order. Soviet leaders flew into the satellite capitals to insist that more liberal policies should be followed and to demand the sacking of the worst of Stalin's creatures. As a sign of the new relationship between the USSR and the Eastern European states the Warsaw Pact, a military alliance, was signed in 1955. Although the Pact was dominated by Russia, it recognised for the first time that the satellites had at least some control over their own armed forces. Even more dramatic was Khrushchev's visit in the same year to Yugoslavia, where he blamed the seven-year rift between the two countries on mistakes made by Stalin. The following year President Tito made a return trip to Moscow where a declaration was signed stating that it was possible for states to follow "different roads to socialism". It seemed that the Soviet Union was no longer the sole headquarters of the world communist movement.

There were, however, limits to the power Khrushchev was prepared to give up, and those limits were laid down in Poland and in Hungary in 1956. The first taste of de-Stalinisation produced demands for more in Poland, where strikes and demonstrations broke out in protest at the worst features of Soviet rule: industrial production designed chiefly to profit the USSR; agriculture ruined by over-hasty collectivisation; and the Catholic Church almost outlawed. To quell the riots the Polish Party appointed as First Secretary Wladislaw Gomulka, who had been imprisoned by Stalin. Khrushchev, probably under pressure from the Soviet army, threatened to move troops into Poland. Gomulka stood his ground, the Soviet leaders backed down, and Gomulka stayed in power for fourteen years – time enough to de-collectivise much of Polish agriculture, lift many restrictions on the Catholic Church and yet prove that his 'new course' did not include taking Poland out of the Communist bloc.

For Hungary, the way to freer communism was to be bloody and tragic. The Communist Party there refused at first to give in to demands for the sacking of the Party and government boss, the sadistic Matyas Rakosi. Revolt spread from the students to the trade unions and into the army. Government ministers and Party leaders fled from Budapest as the people's hatred spilled over into violence. It was a situation already beyond the control of the new Prime Minister, Imre Nagy*, who was, like Gomulka, a survivor from one of Stalin's prison camps. He was forced to meet the

* Pronounced 'Noj'.

Hungarians' most extreme anti-Soviet demands: to promise free elections, to set up a government which included non-Communists, and to order Soviet forces away.

On 28 October 1956 the Russians withdrew the tanks they had positioned near the Hungarian capital. The arguments in Moscow were intense: hard-liners argued that Nagy was no Gomulka, that he had lost control of the situation. The Chinese urged action to avoid the break-up of the Soviet bloc. And then Nagy announced that Hungary would withdraw from the Warsaw Pact. On 4 November Russian tanks entered the streets of Budapest. The fighting was fierce but quickly over: 30,000 Hungarians died and nearly 200,000 fled to the West. Shortly afterwards the Russians found their Hungarian Gomulka in Janos Kadar, who was to rule for more than twenty years and dismantle much of Rakosi's work, while remaining loyal to the Soviet bloc.

Khrushchev and the West

If you could forget Hungary, Khrushchev's policies were a kind of limited good news for Eastern Europe: for the rest of the world his first year in power brought a new excitement. Stalin had only once been outside the Soviet Union: here was a new leader bustling with eagerness to meet the world's leaders. In the summer of 1955 Khrushchev met the American President, Dwight Eisenhower, and the British Prime Minister, Harold Macmillan, at Geneva – in the first of what promised to be a series of summit meetings. The results were perhaps tiny, but they did include an agreement to end the joint occupation of Austria, Germany's enforced wartime ally, which now became an independent and neutral state.

In the next few months Khrushchev explored the possibilities of peaceful competition, or 'co-existence' as he preferred to call it. In September he broke across the Baghdad Pact by arranging an arms deal between Egypt and Czechoslovakia. Having bought one possible ally he went on to visit Afghanistan, India and Burma, making promises of Soviet aid and hoping to construct a line of Soviet client states to counter the influence of the USA.

The American response was swift, although clumsy. In December 1955, in an attempt to wean the Egyptian leader, Nasser, from undesirable friends the American government offered him the money to build a High

Dam at Aswan which would harness the Nile for irrigation and hydro-electric power. But that did not deter Egypt in April 1956 from forming a military alliance with other Arab countries obviously aimed at Israel, a client of the USA; and in May Nasser recognised Mao Tse-tung's Communists as the rightful rulers of China.

Dulles's reaction to Nasser's flirtation with the Communists was short-sighted: he cancelled the offer of money for the Aswan Dam. The long-term result would be to bring the Russians into Egypt to build the dam. The immediate effect was to trigger off a crisis which brought two of America's Western allies into conflict with Middle Eastern Arabs.

The Suez Crisis of 1956

Nasser had already angered the French by arming and encouraging the FLN in Algeria (see Chapter 44, page 283). In July 1956 he nationalised the Suez Canal Company, in which Britain owned over forty per cent of the shares, and seized control of the waterway through which vital oil supplies were shipped to industrialised Western Europe. Both the British and the French were enraged. Nasser had seized an operation from which he could expect to earn $25 million a year: worse, he now controlled an economic lifeline to the West. The two Western European powers tried, unsuccessfully, to negotiate him out of Suez; while the Americans, with their own oil interests to protect, stood aloof from the argument to avoid antagonising the Arabs. On 29 October the tension in the Middle East snapped into war as Israel's army invaded Egypt and smashed its way across the Sinai peninsula.

The Israelis were not acting alone. The whole operation had been planned at secret meetings in France with leading British and French politicians. On 30 October the British and French governments sent an ultimatum to the Egyptians, warning them to keep their forces away from the Suez Canal; they also sent an ultimatum to the Israelis, to make it look as if they were not taking sides. Nasser rejected the warning, and the air forces of the two European powers began bombing Egyptian military targets. On 5 November the paratroops went in and on the 6th more forces were landed from the sea.

The British-French adventure came to an abrupt end within a week, under pressure from the Americans who had been infuriated by the rash actions of their allies. The US government cut off the supplies of oil from Latin America the allies needed to replace the oil which could not now be shipped through the blocked canal; and the Europeans came meekly to heel and agreed to withdraw their forces.

All in all, the year 1956 had ended badly for the West. Hopes that the Hungarians would liberate themselves had been ground to a pulp by Soviet armour; the irresponsible and crude actions of the British and French had driven the Egyptians closer to the Russians; and the containment policy, so triumphant only a year before, had to be re-thought in terms of Khrushchev's 'peaceful co-existence' and the new confrontations it would produce in the next few years.

Peaceful Co-existence?

In the three years after Suez, the Americans and the Russians jockeyed for position in the Middle East. The Russians supported the claims of Nasser's Egypt to the leadership of the Arab states: the Americans were determined to protect their oil interests and shore up the anti-communist Baghdad Pact. In March 1957 the US government persuaded Congress to accept the Eisenhower Doctrine, giving the President the right to intervene in the Middle East, with troops if necessary, should a country in that area request help against "communist-instigated armed aggression". In April Eisenhower made quick use of his new powers by ordering the US Sixth Fleet to the estern Mediterranean and by sending $10 million to King Hussein of Jordan who had complained of subversion by pro-Nasser groups in his country. In July 1958, 14,000 American marines were sent to protect the 'friendly' government of the Lebanon against a similar threat.

But even that kind of fast-moving, heavyweight diplomacy could not compensate for the sudden sense of inferiority which afflicted the USA, nation-wide, on the morning of 4 August 1957. On that day the first man-made satellite was sent hurtling around the world at more than 25,000 km an hour. It was called 'Sputnik', and the men who made it were Russian. More to the point, a Russian rocket that could shove nearly 100 kilos of metal beyond the earth's atmosphere was also capable of carrying a nuclear warhead to the heart of North America. The 'space age' had arrived – in the middle of the Cold War, and on the back of a Russian ICBM (intercontinental ballistic missile).

From that time on, many Americans believed that the USA had lost the power to determine the destiny of the world. That their country never had such power was not quite the point: in the last two years of Eisenhower's second term as President critics pointed out American weaknesses which had been there all along but were now becoming starkly obvious. Khrushchev's use of his country's new-found power took the form of demanding new concessions from the Western powers while at the same time pressing his argument that the two super-powers could co-exist peacefully. In 1959 there was another summit, this time in the United States where Khrushchev met Eisenhower in September. This, we now know, enraged the Chinese who accused Khrushchev of selling out to the enemy, who were still pressing communism hard in Asia and still backing Chiang Kai-shek. As you will see in Chapter 39, page 250, that 'Sino-Soviet' split soon became an unbridgeable gulf between the two Communist powers.

At the end of 1959, partly in response to Chinese criticism that Soviet policy had gone soft, Khrushchev demanded the withdrawal of American, British and French troops from Berlin. That outpost of the 'free world' had become more than a political embarrassment to the Russians; since 1949 more than three million East Germans had escaped through Berlin to the West. However, despite Khrushchev's demand, arrangements were made for another summit to be held, this time in Paris in May 1960. It never took place. President Eisenhower's luck was right out: the Russians shot an American U2 reconnaissance plane out of the skies over their territory and Khrushchev refused to go ahead with the summit.

The USA and Central and Latin America

By that time the American President was faced with new worries nearer home. On New Year's Day, 1959, Fidel Castro overthrew the squalid dictatorship of Fulgencia Batista in Cuba after two earlier failures. Some of Castro's guerrilla fighters were Marxists: most were liberals eager to improve the lives of distressed peasants working in the cane fields and sugar mills of American-owned companies, and to put an end to the corruption and gangsterism in Cuban politics. By the end of the year Castro's revolution and his government had developed distinct left-wing, and anti-American,

attitudes. An extensive programme of land reform was begun; American companies were nationalised, without compensation for their former owners; and Communists were given positions in the government. In February 1960 Castro signed a trade agreement with the Soviet Union, whereby the Cubans exchanged sugar for Russian oil, machinery and technicians. In July the US government banned Cuban sugar from the American market, and shortly afterwards the President agreed to a CIA plan to train an army of anti-Castro exiles for an invasion of Cuba. It was one of Eisenhower's last major policy decisions. In the Presidential election of November 1960 the Democratic candidate, John F. Kennedy, won a narrow victory over his Republican opponent, Richard M. Nixon.

In January 1961 the new President, at forty-three the youngest in American history, made his inaugural address to the people. "Let every nation know," he declared, "whether it wishes us well or ill, that we shall pay any price, bear any burden, meet any hardship, support any friend, oppose any foe to assure the survival and success of liberty." It was the speech of an ambitious young man, determined to make up the ground he believed his country had lost in Eisenhower's later years. It was a speech which sounded brave and confident, but there were altogether too many "anys" in it.

The first price that Kennedy decided the USA should pay was a big increase in aid to Latin America. In March 1961 he announced the Alliance for Progress, a new relationship in which the USA agreed to pump $20 billion to the south over the next ten years, while the governments of Latin America agreed to invest four times that amount in their own economies and carry out various social and land reforms. The grand scheme was not as generous as it looked: the American loans had to be spent on American-made goods; and the Alliance did nothing to alter the fact that much of the profit from Latin American agriculture, mining and industry was sucked back into the bank accounts of North American investors.

Meanwhile, the first friends to whom Kennedy's government gave support were the Cuban exiles, trained by the CIA to launch an attack against Castro's régime. On 17 April 1,500 men, carried in US ships and promised cover from US aircraft, landed in the Bay of Pigs. They were utterly crushed by Castro's forces; and Kennedy, whose approval of the raid was an open secret, was made to look foolish.

The Berlin Wall

The next friends to whom the President made specific assurances were those veterans of the Cold War – the West Berliners. When Khrushchev met Kennedy in Vienna in early June 1961, the Russian leader again emphasised his determination to remove the Western powers from their outpost in East Germany and to stop the drain of manpower to the West. Kennedy was equally determined to stick fast, and to make his position clear he announced a considerable increase in American armed strength. On 13 August 1961 Khrushchev made his position so clear that no-one could possibly miss it: the Russians built a wall slap-bang across the middle of Berlin.

However ugly it looked, the Berlin Wall was to remain a feature of the political landscape of the Cold War. Kennedy was accused of being "soft on communism" because he didn't send troops to tear down the Wall; while some of the Russian leaders saw Khrushchev's bricklaying in Berlin as a weak and unsatisfactory alternative to the expulsion of the Americans and their allies from the city. Khrushchev responded to his critics by ordering a new series of nuclear tests; and in November 1961 the Russians announced the explosion of a hydrogen bomb whose destructive power was measured at 58 megatons – which meant, to anyone who could grasp such a gross obscenity, that it was 3,000 times more powerful than the Hiroshima bomb. In April 1962, Kennedy replied by ordering a new series of American tests.

So far, Kennedy had done little to distinguish his Presidency from Eisenhower's, except to step up the scale of America's armed forces, send more military aid to Vietnam, and – like Khrushchev – pollute the earth's atmosphere with the fall-out of nuclear devices.

But right in the middle of Kennedy's build-up of American troops in Vietnam came evidence of Soviet military traffic in a new, unexpected and alarming direction. In August 1962 an American U2 plane spotted a surface-to-air missile site on the island of Cuba. Early in October Russian planes, capable of carrying nuclear weapons, were observed on Cuban airfields. And then on 14 October, spy-planes took photographs of what appeared to be launch pads for long-range rockets which could destroy American cities. On the morning of 16 October American Intelligence experts informed Kennedy that the photographs showed, beyond any doubt, that Cuba was being made into a missile base. Suddenly, the young President had an unprecedented crisis on his hands.

Kennedy, Khrushchev and the Cuban Missile Crisis

On 16 October Kennedy set up a Committee of the National Security Council to consider America's response. They settled on three possible courses of action: a nuclear strike on the missile sites; or an air attack with conventional bombs, followed by an invasion of the island; or a naval blockade to prevent the Russians transporting more missiles to Cuba. The Committee, made up of government officials and defence chiefs, ruled out a nuclear strike, since the Russians would have probably struck back with similar weapons. For almost a week they debated which of the other two actions to recommend, and they made contingency plans for both. In the end, it seems that the President's younger brother, Robert, who was Attorney General in Kennedy's administration, persuaded the Committee to advise the President to decide on a naval blockade or 'quarantine'.

By Monday, 22 October, the decision was made, the plans were finalised, and America's allies were informed. At 7 o'clock that evening John Kennedy broadcast to the nation. The following extracts were among the most important parts of a speech that informed the American people, and many others throughout the world, that the USA and the USSR were now in desperate confrontation.

"Acting . . . in the defence of our own security and of the entire Western Hemisphere, and under the authority entrusted to me by the Constitution as endorsed by the resolution of the Congress, I have directed that the following *initial* steps be taken immediately:

First: To halt this offensive build-up, a strict quarantine on all offensive military equipment under shipment to Cuba is being initiated. All ships of any kind bound for Cuba from whatever nation or port will, if found to contain cargoes of offensive weapons, be turned back. This quarantine will be extended, if needed, to other types of cargo and carriers.

Second: I have directed the continued and increased close surveillance of Cuba and its military build-up . . . I have directed the Armed Forces to prepare for any eventualities . . .

Third: It shall be the policy of this nation to regard

221

MISSILE TRANSPORTERS

12 PROB GUIDELINE MISSILES

HEAVY EQUIPMENT

5 MISSILE DOLLIES

20 LONG CYLINDRICAL TANKS

MISSILE TRANSPORTER

OPEN STORAGE

A view from a U2 spy-plane. A high altitude photograph of a missile base on Cuba, labelled by US Intelligence experts.

any nuclear missile launched from Cuba against any nation in the Western Hemisphere as an attack by the Soviet Union on the United States, requiring a full retaliatory response upon the Soviet Union...

...*and finally*: I call upon Chairman Khrushchev to halt and eliminate this clandestine, reckless, and provocative threat to world peace..."

In a statement issued on the following day, 23 October, the Soviet government declared that they were taking "all necessary measures to prevent our

country from being caught unawares and to enable it to offer a fitting reply to the aggressor".

People now knew what was at stake. Somewhere in the Caribbean a naval incident could detonate a war of unimaginable horror. As Russian ships steamed towards the American blockade of Cuba, the Cold War seemed about to dissolve into a thermo-nuclear holocaust.

On Thursday, 25 October, the US navy intercepted the first of twenty-five Russian ships known to be sailing towards Cuba. But the oil tanker *Bucharest* was not

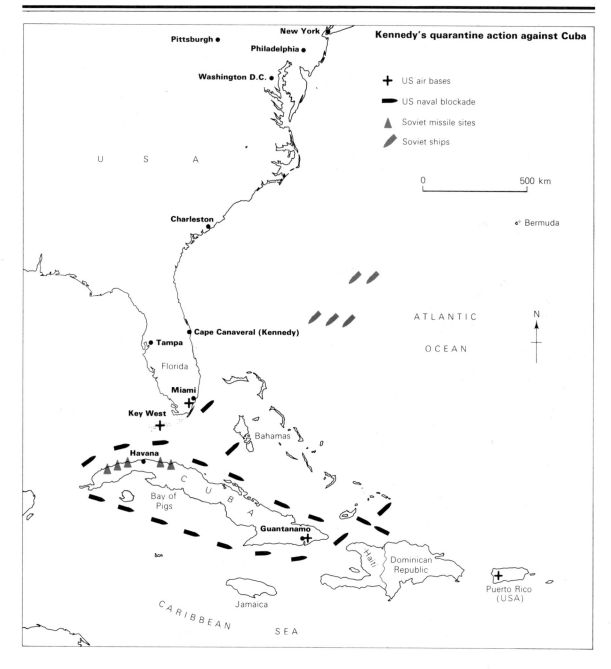

Kennedy's quarantine action against Cuba

+ US air bases

▬ US naval blockade

▲ Soviet missile sites

◢ Soviet ships

0 ————————— 500 km

boarded and she was allowed to go on her way: twelve other Russian vessels were reported to have turned round. But the tension did not slacken, primarily because American spy-planes over Cuba saw evidence of new construction work on the missile sites. And then, on the Friday evening, Kennedy received, over the wires from Moscow, a letter from Khrushchev. Its key passages were as follows:

"If assurances were given that the President of the United States would not participate in an attack on Cuba and the blockade [were] lifted, then the question of the removal or the destruction of the missile sites in Cuba would then be an entirely different question . . . we and you ought not to pull on the ends of the rope in which you have tied the knot of war, because the more the two of us pull, the tighter that knot will be tied . . .

Let us not only relax the forces pulling on the ends of the rope, let us take measures to untie that knot. We are ready for this."

Khrushchev appeared to be offering Kennedy a way out. But before the President and his advisers had time to draft a reply, a second letter from the Russian leader was delivered in Washington on the Saturday morning, 27 October – and this one had a catch in it.

"... Your rockets are situated in Britain, situated in Italy, and are aimed against us. Your rockets are situated in Turkey. You are worried by Cuba. You say that it worries you because it is a distance of ninety miles by sea from the coast of America, but Turkey is next to us ... I therefore make this proposal: we agree to remove from Cuba those means which you regard as offensive means; we agree to carry this out and make a pledge in the United Nations. Your representatives will make a declaration to the effect that the United States, on its part, considering the uneasiness and anxiety of the Soviet State, will remove its similar means from Turkey ..."

Kennedy refused to horse-trade missiles in Turkey for missiles in Cuba. To give in to Khrushchev would, he thought, do great damage to American prestige. Then the crisis suddenly deepened: on the Saturday afternoon came news that a U2 plane had been brought down in Cuba, presumably by a Russian SAM (surface-to-air missile.) Kennedy's Committee began to reconsider an airstrike against Cuba.

It was at that point that the President acted on an ingenious suggestion from Robert Kennedy – why not ignore Khrushchev's second letter, and instead reply to the first one? The President sent off his letter the same evening, promising to lift the blockade and not to invade Cuba, provided that the Russians agreed to remove their missiles from the island and not to install any more.

Khrushchev's reply came on the next day, 28 October:

"I have received your message of 27 October.... So as to eliminate as rapidly as possible the conflict which is endangering peace, ... the Soviet Government, in addition to the earlier instructions to cease further work on the weapon-construction sites, has given a new order to dismantle those arms which you have described as offensive, to crate them, and return them to the Soviet Union...."

The 'Cuban Missile Crisis' was over. The missiles were packed, loaded on to ships and despatched to the Soviet Union; and the sites were flattened and ploughed over. On 20 November Khrushchev agreed to remove the Russian bombers from Cuba within thirty days, and Kennedy lifted the American blockade of the island. There was a sense of relief all round, but still in the West a genuine puzzlement about why the crisis had developed in the first place. Why had Khrushchev decided to install nuclear bombers and missiles in Cuba, when their discovery was bound to provoke an angry, perhaps even a rash, response from the USA? Had the Russian leader gambled on getting the Cuban sites fully operational before the Americans found out about them – which would have presented the USA with a much stickier problem to solve?

Whatever its causes, Kennedy had come out of the crisis with a greatly improved reputation in his own country and throughout the West. He had acted quickly and firmly; he had controlled the hotheads in his own government and armed forces. He had stood up to the Russians, and he had won. Or had he? Before the crisis Castro had declared himself to be a Marxist, but Cuba was not a 'communist' state in the same way that, say, Bulgaria or Hungary was. After the crisis, Cuba was as dependent on Russian aid and protection as any of the Eastern European satellites.

The Cuban crisis was a sobering experience for both Kennedy and Khrushchev. At the brink of war they had no means of fast communication with each other. In June 1963 their two governments agreed to set up a 'hot-line', a direct and permanently open communications link, between the White House and the Kremlin which would give the two leaders instant access to each other in the event of another confrontation. The dangers of an uncontrolled arms race, now more obvious than ever, led to the signing of a partial test-ban treaty in August by the USA, the Soviet Union and the UK: the three powers agreed to ban all tests of nuclear devices, except those carried out underground. Even so, the American government remained determined to contain the spread of communism in areas where they believed they needed, and had a right, to act. One of those places was Indo-China.

Conflict in Indo-China

On page 214 in Chapter 35 you saw how Vietnam was divided by the Geneva agreement of 1954. The North was ruled by Ho Chi Minh, and the South soon fell into the hands of Ngo Dinh Diem, a Catholic politician governing a mainly Buddhist country. The opposition to Diem's corrupt régime was widespread. Sadly, he could ignore the Buddhist monks who protested by burning themselves to death in public; but he did have to reckon with better organised opposition – a political movement known as the National Liberation Front (NLF), and a guerrilla force called the Vietcong. Both received the encouragement of Ho's government in the North, which sheltered and supplied them.

The success of Vietcong operations forced the USA to give more and more aid to Diem, their embarrassing ally. The first massive rise came in 1962 when Kennedy increased the number of American troops, still called 'military advisers', in South Vietnam from 500 to 10,000. Diem's corruption, however, was a huge embarrassment and by the summer of 1963 there was a real prospect of civil war breaking out in a country which the USA was shoring up against communism. Early in November, with the approval of the American government, South Vietnamese army rebels overthrew Diem's régime and shot Diem himself.

US Intervention in Indo-China

Three weeks later, on 22 November, Kennedy himself was gunned down as he was being driven through the streets of Dallas, Texas. Lyndon Baines Johnson, the new President, had shared little in common with John Kennedy. He was from a southern state, Texas; he had not been born rich, and had little obvious charm. He was, however, a more experienced politician and was more successful in getting his own way. In Vietnam his policy was to follow Kennedy's, only on a much bigger scale.

Where Kennedy had sent thousands of troops, Johnson sent tens, and then hundreds, of thousands; where Kennedy had spent tens of millions, Johnson poured out billions of dollars; where Kennedy had threatened, Johnson bombed. Just as Eisenhower had inherited and followed Truman's strategy in Indo-China, and just as Kennedy had agreed with and developed Eisenhower's policy, so LBJ accepted and then escalated Kennedy's commitment of men, money and material to South Vietnam.

At the beginning of August 1964, North Vietnamese torpedo boats attacked an American destroyer in the Gulf of Tonkin. Johnson accused North Vietnam of unprovoked aggression on the high seas, and then asked Congress for authority to use "all necessary measures" to "repel any armed attack" against US forces. Congress obliged, and for good measure gave him the power "to prevent further aggression" and take "all necessary steps" to protect any nation covered by the South-East Asia Treaty (see page 215) which asked for help "in defence of its freedom". In effect, Congress gave Johnson virtually unlimited power to do as he wished in Indo-China.

Between 1965 and 1973 the conflict in Indo-China dominated American politics. In February 1965 the US air force began to bomb North Vietnam. The American government justified the action by declaring

"the war in Vietnam is *not* a spontaneous and local rebellion against the established government... In Vietnam a Communist government has set out deliberately to conquer a sovereign people in a neighbouring state... North Vietnam's commitment to seize control of the South is no less total than was the commitment of the régime in North Korea in 1950."

Americans refused to accept that the war had begun as a civil war and that what the Vietcong claimed to be a "war of liberation" was anything but part of a much bigger plan for the advance of communism. In a sense, the Americans helped to make their own fears come true. The more aid they gave to the South Vietnamese generals, the more support North Vietnam gave to the Vietcong; and North Vietnam's supplies of military equipment came from China and the USSR.

In June 1965 Johnson authorised American soldiers in Vietnam to drop the pretence of acting as 'advisers' and enter the combat on the ground. By the end of 1966 there were 390,000 US troops in Vietnam: by the beginning of 1968 there were 550,000. At the height of the conflict, one and a quarter million American and South Vietnamese troops, backed by the might of the US air force, were facing the guerrilla forces of the Vietcong and the North. Their aims were to destroy the enemy's capacity to wage war by bombing armaments and fuel dumps in the North and the supply routes to the South, and eventually to eliminate the guerrillas by both ground and air offensives. They failed, even though it was reckoned that by 1970 more bombs had been dropped on Vietnam than had previously been dropped, anywhere and everywhere, in the whole of the twentieth century.

And the war came home to America – every evening, on television screens. It came home to mothers and fathers who lost sons, to young men whose turn it would be next. It came home in inflation, as the government poured into the war effort sums of money not even the USA could afford – $2 billion a week by 1968. It came home in stories of drug-addiction on a massive scale among US troops, in sickening tales of boys fresh out of college massacring civilians. And Johnson became the culprit for a war which showed no sign of ending. Protesters attacked their President with the most terrible of slogans: "Hey, hey, LBJ!" they called, "How many kids did you kill today?" Johnson could give no honest answer. The President who had done more than any of his predecessors for America's poor, and for the civil rights of black citizens, was ruined by the war in Vietnam. Early in 1968 he announced that he would not stand for re-election. In November the Republican Richard Nixon, former Vice-President and dedicated anti-communist, narrowly defeated Hubert Humphrey in the contest for the Presidency.

The US Withdrawal from Indo-China

Nixon realised that the war could not be won by 'conventional' forces, and that the USA could not use nuclear weapons against a country supported by the Soviet Union. The problem was to get American forces out of Vietnam without sacrificing the South to Ho Chi Minh. Nixon's solution was the 'Vietnamisation' of the war, which meant building up South Vietnam's forces as American troops were steadily withdrawn. It was a vastly expensive solution, for the USA had to feed, clothe and arm a Vietnamese army which eventually included roughly half the able-bodied male population of the South.

The new President's way out of the war also, paradoxically, involved extending the conflict to other parts of Indo-China. In April 1970 American troops, supported by the US air force, invaded Cambodia. Nixon declared that the offensive was necessary to destroy North Vietnamese bases there: its only real effect was to help the propaganda of the local Cambodian Communists, the Khmer Rouge. In February 1971 the

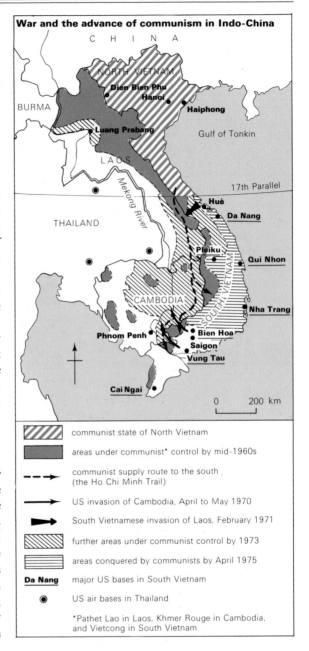

War and the advance of communism in Indo-China

- ▨ communist state of North Vietnam
- ▨ areas under communist* control by mid-1960s
- --→ communist supply route to the south (the Ho Chi Minh Trail)
- ⟶ US invasion of Cambodia, April to May 1970
- ▶ South Vietnamese invasion of Laos, February 1971
- ▨ further areas under communist control by 1973
- ▤ areas conquered by communists by April 1975
- **Da Nang** major US bases in South Vietnam
- ● US air bases in Thailand

*Pathet Lao in Laos, Khmer Rouge in Cambodia, and Vietcong in South Vietnam

South Vietnamese army, with American air cover, invaded Laos in an attempt to cut the North Vietnamese supply route to the South; but the Northern army won a decisive victory, much to the benefit of the Laotian Communists, the Pathet Lao. In the spring of 1972, after the North Vietnamese had launched a major offensive into the South, Nixon ordered the bombing of cities in the North and the mining of harbours.

However, despite the failures of aggression in Cambodia and Laos, Nixon's policy of 'Vietnamisation', accompanied by massive bomber attacks on the North, appeared to be working. Secret negotiations between the North Vietnamese government and Henry Kissinger, Nixon's chief adviser on foreign affairs, resulted in an agreement to end the war. A few days before the Presidential election of November 1972, Kissinger announced that "peace is at hand" in Vietnam. Nixon didn't just win the election: he buried the Democratic candidate, George McGovern, in an electoral landslide.

But the war was not over. The President of South Vietnam, Nguyen Van Thieu, refused to accept an agreement which would allow the North's troops to remain in the South. While Kissinger negotiated with Thieu, Nixon ordered the heaviest bombing attacks of the whole war on North Vietnam. Eventually, Thieu was won over by Nixon's secret assurance of "continued assistance in the post-settlement period", and the promise that "we will respond with full force should the agreement be violated by North Vietnam". In February 1973 representatives of the USA, the two Vietnams, and the Vietcong agreed to a cease-fire and to the creation of a Council of National Reconciliation in Vietnam to prepare for elections in that devastated land.

The war in Indo-China was an unqualified disaster for the USA. It was not just that the Americans had helped to kill nearly two million people in far-away Asia, nor that the expense of the war had led to the devaluation of the dollar, inflation at home, and the shortage of funds to pump into economic aid for poorer countries. It was a terrible lesson in the limitations of power. By 1973 the USA possessed enough weapons of mass destruction to kill every Russian citizen several times over, but still had to abandon her confrontation with a small, non-nuclear, Communist state.

Nor was the American government able to fulfil its promise of post-war aid to South Vietnam. The fighting between North and South continued, despite the 'cease-fire', until in 1975 Thieu's army disintegrated in the face of a Communist offensive. Congress refused a plea by the new President, Gerald Ford, for aid to South Vietnam, Laos and Cambodia. By the end of that year those three South-East Asian 'dominoes' had fallen into Communist hands.

'America's backyard': the USA and Central and Latin America since 1965

So far in this chapter we have looked at American-Soviet relations over a period of more than twenty years; and during that time there was only a single occasion when one of the two super-powers interfered openly in what we might call the other's 'backyard'. That was in 1962, when the Russians tried to turn the island of Cuba into a missile base. For the rest of the time, the Soviet leaders were content to leave Latin America and the Caribbean well alone, leaving the US free to deal as it liked with states in its 'backyard' that threatened its interests there.

In April 1965 civil war broke out in the Caribbean state of the Dominican Republic between on the one side the forces of the conservative government of Donald Reid Cabral, and on the other the liberal and radical supporters of Juan Bosch. The American President, Lyndon Johnson, chose to see Bosch as another Castro, his movement infested with communists; so he sent 23,000 American troops into the Republic to ensure that the rebels did not take over. In May Johnson declared his own uncompromising Doctrine for Latin America and the Caribbean: "American nations cannot, must not, and will not permit the establishment of another Communist government in the Western Hemisphere." In short, the USA would not tolerate another Cuba.

However, Johnson's successor, Richard Nixon, was faced with a new communist presence in Latin America when Salvador Allende, the Marxist leader of a coalition of left-wing parties, was elected President of Chile in 1970. Allende quickly nationalised a proportion of Chile's industry (much of it previously owned by American business men), signed a trade agreement with Russia, and established friendly relations with Castro's Cuba.

This time the US government did not use their own troops to destroy what they saw as a threat. Instead, they cut off economic aid to Chile; and Nixon ordered the CIA to encourage public demonstrations by Allende's political opponents. In September 1973 the Chilean government was overthrown by a military rebellion, in which the CIA played a murky part. Allende committed suicide, and Chile was taken over by a brutal right-wing régime led by General Augusto Pinochet.

In the late 1970s US fears of the spread of

communism in its 'backyard' focussed sharply on the states of Central America. In 1979 the anti-communist dictator of Nicaragua, General Somoza, was overthrown by the Sandinista Liberation Front, a left-wing movement backed by the Church and the trade unions. Fearing that the Sandinistas were receiving aid from Cuba and, indirectly, from the Soviet Union, President Ronald Reagan cut economic aid to Nicaragua in 1981. As relations between the two countries deteriorated, the CIA began to arm and train the 'contras' in Nicaragua, guerrilla fighters who opposed the Sandinista regime.

One of President Reagan's many complaints about the Sandinista government was that it was supplying arms to left-wing guerrillas in nearby El Salvador which had been racked by a brutal civil war since 1980. Reagan's response was to give US backing to an anti-communist Christian Democrat, José Napoleon Duarté. After four years of guerrilla fighting and grotesque political violence, with hundreds of political murders taking place every week, elections in 1984 put Duarté into power as President.

Reagan showed how determined the US government was to deal with the spread of communism in the Caribbean when, in October 1983, he authorised 'Operation Urgent Fury'. A joint force of US marines and paratroopers invaded the tiny island of Grenada after pro-Cuban members of the 'New Jewel' movement took power in a coup d'état and imposed military rule. The American forces quickly 'liberated' the island and installed a pro-US government. Reagan said shortly after the invasion that Grenada was "a Soviet-Cuban colony being readied for use as a major military bastion. ... We arrived just in time."

The Soviet Union and its Satellites since 1968

In 1956 the leaders of the Soviet Union had shown that they were prepared to slap down an Eastern European government that tried to take too independent a line (see page 218); and in 1968 they again used force to control one of the satellite states. In January of that year, Antonin Novotny, the cruel and repressive ruler of Czechoslovakia, was replaced as Secretary of the Czechoslovak Communist Party by Alexander Dubček. The new régime was much more liberal: censorship of the press was relaxed, some of the rigid state controls over industry were removed, and there was even talk of allowing other political parties to exist.

Dubček's brand of "socialism with a human face" proved to be attractive not only to the Czechs and Slovaks but also to the Romanians and their leader, Nicolae Ceausescu. There seemed to be a prospect of Czechoslovakia, Romania and Yugoslavia forming together an independent Eastern European bloc. That, in itself, was unacceptable to the Soviet leaders, for it would have greatly weakened their power in Eastern Europe. And the Czechoslovak Party's proposal to tolerate a degree of political freedom also alarmed the men in Moscow, for to them it looked like a question mark against their own right to rule. On 20 August the Soviet army moved in, accompanied by East German, Polish, Hungarian and Bulgarian troops. Dubček was eventually replaced by Gustav Husák, not exactly a Russian stooge, but a man who realised that in future Czechoslovakia would have to toe the Soviet line – if only because Soviet troops were stationed on her soil.

An entirely different kind of problem faced the Soviet Union on its southern borders. The 1970s saw a dramatic revival of the Islamic faith in Iran and Afghanistan as well as in the southern republics of the Soviet Union which shared borders with them. With the overthrow of the Shah's government in Iran (see page 294), extreme religious unrest spread throughout the region. In Afghanistan a Soviet-backed 'Armed Forces Revolutionary Council' failed to control the mounting religious excitement of the Muslim population which opposed its rule. With the threat of religious and political disturbance spreading north into the Soviet Union, the Russians decided on military intervention. In the last week of 1979 two airborne divisions of the Soviet army, 80,000 strong, began a full-scale invasion of Afghanistan. The invasion was condemned by most western countries and led, in 1980, to a boycott by the USA of the Olympic Games being held in Moscow.

In Afghanistan the Soviet Union met the same difficulties that had confronted the USA when she first became involved in Vietnam. Despite the use of tanks, helicopter gunships, napalm bombing and chemical warfare, the Soviet army was only able to gain control of the main towns and roads of the mountainous country; while the poorly-armed tribesmen who opposed them kept control of the rest.

While Russian troops were trying to make Afghanistan into a satellite of the Soviet Union, one of the existing satellites was threatening to break away again. Since the strikes and riots of 1956 (see page 218)

The inhuman face of Soviet Communism: a Czech girl runs for her life as Soviet tanks open fire in the streets of Prague on 21 August 1968.

Poland had suffered from recurring economic crises. Rising food prices had caused severe rioting in 1970 and 1976. Another series of strikes in 1980 led to the formation of an independent trade union movement, Solidarity, which demanded political as well as economic reforms. Continued unrest, food shortages, and the rapidly growing popularity of Solidarity and its leader, Lech Walesa, created fears that the Soviet Union would use military force to bring Poland into line. However, a new government led by General Jaruselski avoided this possibility by imposing martial law, breaking up Solidarity and imprisoning Walesa and other leaders.

From 'Sputnik' to 'Star Wars'

By the mid-1970s the USA and the Soviet Union had been contesting control of the globe for over thirty years. 'Cold War' was no longer an accurate description of their relationship, for their views of each other had matured, and to a certain degree warmed, after the confrontation over Cuba and the long bitterness of Vietnam. They continued to support their own clients, with arms and economic aid, but they were no longer willing to rush to the brink of nuclear war to hold on to, or to cancel out, a new advantage. It seemed that both the American and Russian leaders had learned something about great-power weakness and responsibility.

In 1957 the Russians had put 'Sputnik' into orbit and so took the lead in the first stage of the 'space race'. In 1962 Yuri Gagarin, a Russian, became the first man to be thrust into space. John Kennedy promptly promised that American technology would place a US citizen on the moon before 1970, and before any Russian Communist landed on it. In July 1969 Neil Armstrong, an American astronaut, walked on the lunar surface, returned safely to earth, and was greeted by President Nixon, who declared, "This is the greatest week in the history of the world since the Creation." Now you may remember that back in 1945 President Truman had said something similar about the atomic bomb—"This is the greatest thing in history"—and you can be reasonably sure that neither President was thinking in terms of the greater good of mankind at the time he spoke. Both men were speaking of new peaks in American power and prestige. The prestige came from being first: the power came from a technology which produced weapons of awesome destructive energy and faster delivery systems that were less vulnerable to the enemy's defences and means of detection. In short, the 'space race' was part of the arms race which by the mid-1970s had provided both super-powers with the means to annihilate each other – and the rest of mankind. And both powers had dispersed their nuclear armouries – underground in deep, secret silos; under the sea in nuclear-powered submarines; and in bombers permanently on alert or in the air – to ensure a 'second-strike capability' should the enemy attack without warning. Both had also invested heavily in early-warning radar systems, in anti-missile systems, and in MIRVs (multiple, independently targetable re-entry vehicles, which can be carried in clusters on land-based or submarine-launched rockets).

That capability to "overkill" each other resulted in the development of what the historian Peter Calvocoressi has called "a fearful intimacy" between the two powers. Both were concerned to reduce their armaments to levels consistent with self-defence, to avoid too much spending on ever more sophisticated weapons systems, and to prevent the manufacture of nuclear weapons by nations other than the five who already had them – the USA, the Soviet Union, China, the UK and France. In 1968 the two super-powers and the UK signed a Nuclear Non-Proliferation Treaty, which they invited other states to join. By 1975, ninety-three countries had accepted the invitation: but there were some notable exceptions, among them China, France, Egypt, Israel, Japan and South Africa.

In 1969 the governments of the two great powers agreed to discuss ways in which they might limit their own weapons systems. By 1972 their Strategic Arms Limitation Talks had produced a treaty, 'SALT 1', limiting the number of ICBMs (intercontinental ballistic missiles) that each country possessed. A second treaty in 1979, SALT 2, aimed to create a 'nuclear parity' between the two countries by limiting the number of missiles, short- and medium- as well as long-range, that they each possessed for launching nuclear weapons. By this time a new word had entered the vocabulary of super-power relations; the French word *détente*, meaning relaxation, was increasingly used to describe the improving relations between East and West. But following the Soviet invasion of Afghanistan in December 1979, President Carter asked the US Senate to delay giving its approval to the

SALT 2 treaty. At the same time, NATO took the decision to instal new kinds of nuclear weapons in Europe – Pershing II and Cruise missiles.

The 1980s therefore began with détente hardening into a new Cold War. Pershing and Cruise missiles, which could be moved around on mobile launchers, were for theatre warfare – to destroy everything in a region where enemy troops were concentrated. The USSR had its own version in the SS 20 missiles, which it planned to dot around western Russia and the satellite states. So the American negotiators came to the disarmament talks when they restarted in 1981 with a new and alarming view that theatre weapons made a limited nuclear war thinkable. If Cruise and Pershing missiles could be mobile in enough European states it might even be winnable.

The new round of talks proceeded hand in hand with the development of these and other new, ever more sophisticated weapons. While INF (Intermediate-range Nuclear Forces) talks and 'START' (Strategic Arms Reduction Talks) got under way in 1981–2, President Reagan ordered the production of neutron bombs – 'enhanced radiation' weapons which rely for their killing effect on massive amounts of radiation rather than explosive blast. And in 1983 he announced that the USA would try to develop a 'Strategic Defence Initiative' ('Star Wars', as the press immediately named it) involving the use of anti-satellite weapons to destroy incoming missiles as well as military satellites in space.

This revival of the Cold War led to protest movements in many western countries. Women established camps outside Cruise missile bases and membership of nuclear disarmament movements shot up. Then the relations between the super-powers began to improve again. Mikhail Gorbachev came to power determined to use diplomacy as well as arms to strengthen the USSR's security and standing in the world. Summit meetings with Ronald Reagan showed the two leaders committed to negotiations over nuclear armaments. The question of strategic arms limitation foundered over the issue of 'star wars' but both men knew they would strengthen their position in their own countries by agreement on Intermediate-range Nuclear Forces. In 1987 Gorbachev and Reagan signed an INF Treaty in Washington and in 1988 observers from the USSR watched Cruise missiles being dismantled while SS20s were inactivated under American inspection.

230

37 The USA since Roosevelt, 1945-85

President Franklin D. Roosevelt died on Friday 13 April, eleven weeks after starting his fourth term of office. No American before him had served four times as President and an amendment to the Constitution in 1951 made sure that no American will do so again. During his twelve years in the White House Roosevelt had made more impact on the American imagination than any President since Lincoln. He had taken office during the worst depression the country had ever known and, with his ambitious 'New Deal' measures, had kept it afloat without undermining the traditional liberties of the American people. He had taken the USA to war and, along with Stalin and Churchill, was a prime architect of the victory of 1945. He was by anybody's standards a supremely successful President – an almost impossible act to follow.

Harry S. Truman, 1945-53

Roosevelt's successor, 60-year-old Vice-President Harry Truman, said on 14 April to a news conference: "Boys, if you ever pray, pray for me now. I feel as if the sun, the stars and the moon have all fallen on top of me." Truman was rightly apprehensive. He had immediately to take over the conduct of the war in its final months, attend the Potsdam Conference and consider authorising the use of atomic bombs against Japan. His decisiveness in all three matters foreshadowed the impact he was to make on world affairs during the next seven years in office. With the 'Truman Doctrine' and with Marshall Aid in 1947, with American support for the Berlin airlift in 1948, with American membership of its first peacetime military alliance, NATO, in 1949, and with American intervention in Korea, 1950-53, Truman made sure that the USA would be recognised abroad as the first of the major powers during the coming decades.

Truman's handling of domestic affairs was much less remarkable, and he made no comparable impact. Even so, it is worth studying his domestic policies in some detail because they reveal a number of problems that have afflicted Presidents ever since.

Truman's primary domestic task in 1945 was to demobilise the armed forces – to 'bring the boys back home'. Within two years of the end of the war, the number of Americans in uniform fell from 12 million to 1·5 million. With the help of loans and retraining provided by the Servicemen's Readjustment Act – known to soldiers as the 'GI Bill of Rights' – over 10 million soldiers returned to civilian life. The American economy was able to adjust to this massive influx of labour without serious unemployment: wartime scarcity had made sure that there would be a post-war economic boom as workers who had accumulated savings during the war spent them on the consumer goods that industry could now start making again. The result was rapid industrial expansion. Between 1945 and 1948 the number of workers with jobs rose from 54 million to over 61 million.

But with jobs and wages came inflation. And as inflation eroded the value of workers' wages, industry was hit by a series of massive strikes in 1946. In response to strikes in the car, coal and steel industries, as well as on the railways, Republican Senators Taft and Hartley introduced an Act outlawing 'closed shop' trade unions, prohibiting the use of trade union funds for political purposes, and drastically reducing the protection acquired by trade unions in 1935 (see page 122).

Truman tried to use his Presidential power of veto to nullify the Taft-Hartley Act but there were enough Republicans in both the Senate and House of Representatives to over-ride his veto with a two-thirds majority. Truman found himself in a political stalemate that often occurs in US politics: that of a President belonging to one party finding it hard to introduce policies because the opposing party has a majority in Congress. It was for this reason that a '21 point programme' of social and economic reforms that Truman put forward in 1945 came to nothing. The programme aimed to continue a number of Roosevelt's 'New Deal' measures and so was rejected by the Republican majority in Congress.

Truman suffered just as badly from opposition within his own party. Some Democrats from the southern states, the 'Dixiecrats', disliked proposals that Truman made to improve civil rights for black people: Truman proposed a federal anti-lynching law and the abolition of the poll tax which denied the vote to black people who were too poor to pay it. The right-wing Dixiecrats threatened to break away from the Democratic Party at the same time as left-wingers in the Party organised themselves into a group of 'Progressives' who demanded more radical change. So when Presidential elections came around in 1948, Truman was opposed not only by a Republican majority in Congress but also by Dixiecrats and Progressives in his own party. Undaunted by the odds against him, Truman went on a 'whistle-stop tour' of the USA. Travelling 50,000 kilometres and making 356 speeches in the weeks before the election, Truman attacked the Republicans as a 'Do Nothing Party' and Congress as a 'Do Nothing Congress'. He promised a 'Fair Deal' for the American people if he was re-elected. Much to everybody's surprise Truman won the election by a comfortable margin. Even more surprising, the Democrats won a majority in both houses of Congress.

Despite these electoral victories, Truman had to struggle to introduce the 'Fair Deal' reforms he had promised. In 1948 he desegregated the armed forces. Rent controls were extended. Social Security was extended to an additional 10 million people, and a bill to assist public housing and slum clearance was passed by Congress. In every case, however, Truman had to struggle with Congress and, even then, not all his reforms became law. Part of the problem was that Truman, like Roosevelt before him, aroused fears of socialism in millions of Americans, both Republican and Democrat. They saw the invasion of the federal government into such areas as civil rights and welfare as a form of 'creeping socialism' that would strangle private enterprise and initiative.

Public fears of socialism were made the more real by the trial of Alger Hiss (see page 210) in 1950. It seemed to many that the government was at least partly in the hands of communists. Senator Joseph McCarthy traded on those fears when he announced on 9 February 1950:

"I have here in my hand a list of 205 names known to

Post-war prosperity in the USA: this 1951 photograph from Life *magazine claimed to show the yearly food consumption of an average American family, the Czekalinski family from Cleveland, Ohio.*

the Secretary of State as members of the Communist Party who nevertheless are still working and shaping policy."

In the wake of the Alger Hiss trial it was easy for McCarthy to discredit prominent Democrats and other public figures by falsely accusing them of belonging to communist organisations. 'McCarthyism' created a 'red scare' which in turn helped the Republicans win the 1952 Presidential election.

Truman later said of McCarthy:

"A man like that – it's like a sickness. It isn't going to disappear if you ignore it. And the people who know a man like that is up to no good but who encourage him . . . who'll do anything in the world to win an election, they're just as bad."

Truman, however, did not speak out in public against McCarthy, thinking it advisable during an election year to ignore the 'sickness'. At the same time, a scandal involving embezzlement in the Department of Inland Revenue suggested that there was a good deal of corruption in government departments. The Republicans found it easy to lambast Truman's record during the election campaign by using the slogan 'K1 C2' – by which they meant the Korean War, and corruption and communism in government circles. In the election, the Republican candidate, Dwight Eisenhower, gained the largest majority ever in American history.

Dwight D. Eisenhower, 1953–61

'Ike' Eisenhower was a household name long before he became President. He had served as Supreme Allied Commander for the invasion of Europe in 1944–45, as Chief of Staff in the post-war years, and as Supreme Commander of NATO forces from 1951 to 1952. For nearly ten years he had been America's most famous soldier.

Eisenhower was not, however, the hawkish militarist that many Democrats feared he would be. Tolerant, relaxed and easy-going, Eisenhower followed a policy of what he called 'modern Republicanism'. While trying to limit the interference of the federal government in the affairs of the 48 states (to become 50 in 1959 with the admission of Alaska and Hawaii to the Union), he made no attempt to turn back the clock by dismantling the New Deal – Fair Deal legislation of Roosevelt and Truman. In fact, Eisenhower's 'modern Republicanism' allowed a slight expansion of some federal programmes – in education, public housing, slum clearance and public health.

Nevertheless, Eisenhower was as committed to Republican principles as the Republicans of the 1920s had been (see page 85). His first cabinet was dominated by wealthy businessmen, eight of them millionaires. And although he began by introducing some decidedly *un*republican measures – such as establishing a federal Department of Health, Education and Welfare, raising minimum wages and refusing to cut taxes – he soon slipped into a more characteristic style of government. Like Calvin Coolidge in the 1920s he appeared to spend as little time as possible in the White House and as much as possible on the golf course. He delegated much of his domestic policy-making to his Chief of Staff, Sherman Adams, and left foreign affairs in the hands of John Foster Dulles.

Eisenhower, however, was ready to intervene personally in affairs when the occasion demanded it. Such an occasion came in May 1954. Senator Joseph McCarthy (see page 211) was by now Chairman of the Senate Committee on Government Operations. As he had already done while Truman was President, McCarthy took advantage of the fact that Senate committees have the power to interrogate public officials, including military officers, when they are investigating a government department. McCarthy now began to investigate what he called 'subversion' in the US army. For thirty-five days in May and June 1954 the Army–McCarthy hearings were given national television coverage. Most Americans were proud of the armed forces, units of which had recently returned from Korea, and were horrified when revered soldiers like General George Marshall were brought before the hearings for interrogation. But the very television coverage that gave McCarthy publicity also allowed the public to see for the first time what was really going on. As Daniel Snowman, a British historian explains:

"These were the early days of television and to those who had a set the new toy was often mesmeric. McCarthy knew that the eyes of the nation (more than 20 million pairs, to be precise) were upon him, and he revelled in his own importance. But if millions of people saw him bullying government officials and reprimanding army generals, they also saw him raising great numbers of ludicrously fastidious points of order and snarling cruelly at innocent victims. They saw him

233

scowling and fidgeting with obvious boredom whenever it was somebody else's turn to speak. They saw him turn on members of his own committee and accuse them of trying to hinder his efforts.''

While Truman in 1952 had not dared speak out against McCarthy, Eisenhower now made clear his distaste for the methods being used in the Army hearings. At the end of 1953 the Senate voted a resolution condemning McCarthy's activities and conduct. McCarthy reatreated into the political shadows as quickly as he had emerged from them three years earlier, and died in obscurity in 1956.

Eisenhower suffered a heart attack in September 1955 and was seriously ill in the following year – election year. Nevertheless, he stood again as Presidential candidate and won another landslide victory. But where his first term of office had been relatively uneventful, his second term soon became a time of acute social conflict.

We have seen (pages 81–82) that the Republican governments of the 1920s did next to nothing to tackle the problem of racialism, confining themselves to limiting the rate of immigration in three Immigration Acts. Some progress towards improving the civil rights of black Americans had been made during the Second World War when Roosevelt ordered an end to racial discrimination in factories producing war materials under government contract. In 1948 Truman had desegregated the armed forces and established a civil rights commission. But the outstanding development in civil rights for blacks came during Eisenhower's first term of office when the Supreme Court declared (in the Case of Brown v. the Board of Education of Topeka) that states must allow blacks to attend the same schools as whites so that they could have equal educational opportunities.

The Supreme Court ruling applied mainly to schools in the southern states where there was a long history of racial segregation. Although school authorities were instructed to desegregate schools 'with all deliberate speed', many of the southern states ignored the ruling. This led to a crisis in 1957 when Eisenhower ordered that the ruling must be obeyed throughout the USA. In Arkansas, Governor Faubus placed armed national guards around Little Rock High School to keep black students out. Eisenhower responded by putting the Arkansas National Guard under his own command and by sending 1,000 paratroopers to Little Rock where they enforced the black students' entry into the school.

Elsewhere in the USA the issue of civil rights dominated Eisenhower's Presidency. In December 1955, in Montgomery, Alabama, the black community organised a boycott of the city's segregated bus services. Led by a young Baptist clergyman, Martin Luther King, the boycott lasted a year until loss of fare-revenue forced the bus company to desegregate the city's public transport system.

Eisenhower introduced two civil rights Acts in 1957 and 1960, one designed to protect black people's voting rights, the other establishing a federal agency of six commissioners to investigate complaints that black citizens were being denied their legal rights. This agency pleased neither whites nor blacks, who felt that any progress it made was unnecessarily slow. Civil rights campaigners therefore resorted increasingly to direct action, mounting sit-ins in segregated public places such as cafés, lunch-counters, beaches, and even churches.

The ugly scenes of racial conflict in the southern states were not the only blows to Eisenhower's second term of office. In foreign affairs, Dulles was not able to prevent a series of blows to American self-confidence. As we saw (page 229), Russia's launching of Sputnik, the world's first man-made satellite, in 1957, made sure that Americans could no longer claim overwhelming superiority in all things, as many had grown used to doing in the twentieth century. The failure of Eisenhower's summit diplomacy and the shooting down of the U2 reconnaissance plane in 1960 (see page 220) were further blows to American prestige. In the Presidential election campaign the Democratic candidate, John Fitzgerald Kennedy, made much of America's loss of prestige in Eisenhower's later years, and was able to defeat the Republican candidate, Richard M. Nixon, by a small margin.

John F. Kennedy, 1961–63

Aged 43 when he came to office, Kennedy seemed to promise a more glorious future than had seemed possible under Eisenhower. When in his nomination speech to the Democratic Party he spoke of crossing a 'New Frontier' in the social and economic life of the country, he revived memories of Roosevelt's 'hundred days' and the excitement of the 'New Deal'. In his inaugural speech in 1961 he said that the USA would "pay any price . . . to assure the survival and success of liberty" around the world, recalling memories of the great days when Roosevelt had made America the 'arsenal of democracy'. Within two years, however, Kennedy was dead, assassinated on 22 November 1963 while driving in a motorcade into Dallas, Texas, allegedly by Lee Harvey Oswald for reasons that are still unclear.

By the time of his death, Kennedy had not managed to make much impression on the great social problems he had inherited. He had stimulated the economy by increasing federal government spending on the armed forces and on the space programme; and shortly before his death he had recommended big tax cuts to Congress. But Kennedy's own caution, and the opposition of many Senators and Congressmen to radical social and economic reform, meant that from 1960 to 1963 there was relatively little done for the human casualties of a white-dominated, aggressively capitalist America.

During that time the blacks' complaint against their treatment as second-class citizens developed into an impressive protest movement. Old organisations, such as the National Association for the Advancement of Coloured People (founded way back in 1909), were joined by new groups such as the SNCC (Student Non-violent Coordinating Committee) and CORE (Congress on Racial Equality) to press for the desegregation of education, public transport, cafés and restaurants in the southern states. In April 1963, Martin Luther King, whose deep Christian faith and passionate speeches were making him at once a national political figure and a target for the hatred of white racists, led a protest march through Birmingham, Alabama, where the police stopped the demonstrators with dogs, high-pressure water hoses, and electric cattle-prods. King was imprisoned, and the dignity of the man and his followers attracted even more support to the cause. Later in the year, after his release from prison, King led – and was able to control – a massive demonstration in Washington on 28 August. In his speech to a crowd of 200,000 protesters he said:

"I have a dream. I have a dream that one day this nation will rise up and live out the true meaning of its creed: 'We hold these truths to be self-evident, that all men are created equal. . . .'"

Belatedly, Kennedy asked Congress to pass a limited Civil Rights Bill; but before they could come to a decision, the President was dead.

In a very real sense Kennedy was more potent in death than in life. His murder in Dallas profoundly shocked the nation – and, indeed, the whole Western world – and the mystery which surrounded the killing still intrigues people today. His alleged assassin, Lee Harvey Oswald, was shot before he could be brought to trial: Jack Ruby, a nightclub owner, killed him in full view of television cameras. A Commission led by Chief Justice Warren was set up to investigate the President's death, and its members concluded that Oswald had acted as a lone, deranged murderer: there was, they said, no evidence of a conspiracy against the state or its leader. Later research discovered enough links between Oswald, the CIA and the Russian KGB, and between Ruby, American gangster bosses and anti-Castro Cuban extremists, to weave half a dozen theories of conspiracies to kill Kennedy. We do not yet know, for certain, who killed him or why: we are more or less sure that both the CIA and the FBI (Federal Bureau of Investigation), for their own undisclosed reasons, withheld evidence from, and lied to, the Warren Commission.

Lyndon B. Johnson, 1963–68

Whoever killed President Kennedy affected American history in ways that he, or they, could never have imagined. For the new President, Lyndon Johnson, took advantage of the nation's grief to push through laws that were associated with Kennedy's idealism – if not with his record in office. In 1964 Congress agreed to massive tax cuts, to the provision of money for a "war against poverty" programme, and to a new Civil Rights Act which banned discrimination against blacks in hotels and restaurants.

In the Presidential election of November 1964 Johnson romped home to victory over the Republican candidate, Barry Goldwater, defeating him by forty-three million to twenty-seven million votes. Ready and well prepared for four more years in office, Johnson unleashed on Congress a battery of proposals for reform, the like of which had not been seen since the early days of Roosevelt's "New Deal". The President declared that he aimed to create the "Great Society" which would improve every aspect of the nation's life; and to begin with, in 1965, Congress passed Acts which provided large amounts of federal aid to education, escalated the war against poverty, and set up the Office of Economic Opportunity (OEO) to administer the spending of billions of dollars on helping the needy and deprived. Congress also passed the Medicare Act, which provided subsidised medical facilities for some people over sixty-five; and a new Civil Rights Act, which outlawed the southern device of using literacy tests to prevent blacks from voting.

Instead of gratitude, Johnson's reward was mounting criticism – from Democrats as well as from Republicans, from blacks as well as from whites. The President had promised too much, and his reforms, however well-meaning, delivered too little. The OEO supervised an extraordinary variety of agencies to help the poor, but few of them offered more than advice, comfort and educational services. The unemployable poor – the sick, the old and the handicapped – still had to depend on inadequate welfare services; while the more militant blacks recognised that Civil Rights Acts had not brought an end to white racism, nor to discrimination in housing or education. The run-down centres of the northern cities had rapidly become black ghettos as the more prosperous white citizens had moved out to cleaner, 'white' suburbs. The facts of life in the USA meant that, with or without their full civil rights, blacks were poorer and more likely to be unemployed than whites, and their children got a raw deal in the schools.

One result of this new disenchantment was the rise of the Black Power movement, which aimed to end the reliance of blacks on whites for their jobs, their dignity and their culture. Some new organisations, like the Black Panthers, appeared to want an all-out war against whites. Established groups, like CORE, adopted harsh, unforgiving attitudes to whites. When Martin Luther King was awarded a Nobel Peace Prize in 1964 for his non-violent campaigns, a Black Power leader, Malcolm X, said:

"He got the peace prize, we got the problem. I don't want the white man giving me medals. If I'm following a general, and he's leading me into battle, and the enemy tends to give him rewards, or awards, I get suspicious of him. Especially if he gets a peace award before the war is over."

Among the more extreme Black Power groups were the Black Muslims, led by Elijah Muhammad, who combined faith in Islam with a fierce opposition to integration in a white-dominated society. Although the Muslims numbered perhaps no more than 20,000 in the mid-1960s, one of their converts became the most

famous black man of his time. Cassius Clay, the heavyweight boxing champion of the world, changed his name to Muhammad Ali, refused to be drafted into the US army, and had his title taken away.

The gathering racial tension broke into appalling outbreaks of violence in 1965. Riots in the Watts district of Los Angeles caused thirty-five deaths and damage to property estimated at more than $30 million. In 1967, twenty-six people died and more than a thousand others were injured in Newark; forty-three people were killed and two thousand injured in Detroit.

Those outbreaks of black anger took place in the years when Johnson was stepping up the war in Vietnam. That war cost the American people far greater sums of money than were spent on OEO, Medicare and all the welfare services combined. It brought into being its own protest movement, mainly among college students, who could see nothing "Great" in a society whose armed forces were making a wasteland of a small Asian country, and who feared that they would be drafted to fight for a cause they despised. American society had rarely been so angrily divided, or so tense. Appalled by the riots at home and the war overseas, Martin Luther King declared that the United States was "the greatest purveyor of violence in the world". In April 1968, King himself was shot dead in Memphis, Tennessee. Exactly two months later, in the run-up to the Presidential election, Robert Kennedy, brother of the assassinated President, was murdered in Los Angeles.

Richard M. Nixon, 1969–74 and Gerald R. Ford, 1974–76

In January 1969 Richard Nixon took over a badly shaken America from Lyndon Johnson. Surprisingly, black militancy appeared to subside – either because a number of its leaders were in jail or because the riots of the sixties had taken too heavy a toll of black lives and property. In the years that followed, they made some limited gains. The Supreme Court ruled in 1969 that the desegregation of schools should begin "at once", and soon many more black children were getting an education side by side with whites. However, a new problem quickly grew from this. Attempts to desegregate city schools were complicated by the fact that white people mainly lived in the suburbs while black people mainly lived in the centres of cities. City schools therefore tended to be either all-white or all-black, depending on whether they were in the suburbs or the centres. A common solution to this problem was to take pupils by bus from one area of a city to another, so creating a racial mixture in schools. This practice of 'bussing' became a major issue of the Nixon years. Many people were against it, including Nixon himself. The National Black Political Convention saw it as racist, saying that it was "a false notion that black children are unable to learn unless they are in the same setting as white children". White parents, for their part, claimed that the presence of black children in previously all-white schools caused a decline in academic standards. Nevertheless, bussing went ahead in many cities and the outcome was serious rioting, especially in Boston in 1974 and 1975.

Of all recent American Presidents, Nixon was perhaps the one least able to cope with criticism. He was secretive, suspicious and narrow-minded. He appointed to his Cabinet and to his White House staff men who were ambitious for power but who appeared to have no constructive ideas about what to do with it. As the anti-war protest movement grew in force, Nixon failed even to understand the passions roused by the offensive he ordered against Cambodia. His response to mounting criticism among students and in newspapers was to tap the telephones of government officials he suspected of 'leaking' information, and to try to set up a national security committee with powers to open students' mail and bug their rooms!

In 1971 and 1972 Nixon rescued his waning popularity with attempts to bring inflation under control by imposing limited controls on wages and prices and allowing the value of the dollar to fall – thus encouraging US exports and discouraging imports. Just as important, in February 1972 he became the first American President to visit China; and in May he travelled to Moscow for talks with Brezhnev. Suddenly he looked like a diplomatic giant, capable of talking in firm but friendly terms to the leaders of the world's most powerful communist states. In the Presidential election of November 1972 he beat George McGovern, the candidate of a disunited Democratic Party, by margin of forty-seven million to twenty-nine million votes.

You already know that in February 1973 Nixon and Kissinger finally managed to drag the USA out of the long agony of the Vietnam War. Later that same year the action taken by OAPEC on the outbreak of the Yom Kippur War (see Chapter 45, page 291) accelerated the pace of inflation throughout the world and dramatically

exposed the dependence of the USA on Middle Eastern oil. But even inflation and the urgent need to develop a long-term policy of energy conservation were overshadowed by a new crisis. In 1973 and 1974 the American people found that their own government was rotten to the core.

In October 1973 Vice-President Spiro Agnew was forced to resign when it was revealed that he had taken bribes and cheated on his tax returns. And by that time Nixon himself was under suspicion of having been involved in criminal activities, the most serious of which was burglary in 1972 of the Democratic Party's headquarters in the Watergate Building, Washington. Eventually, after a running battle with the courts, Nixon was compelled to hand over the tape-recordings of conversations he had held in the White House with his chief advisers during the 'Watergate' period. The tapes proved, to most people's satisfaction, that Nixon was guilty. To the embarrassment of many decent Americans, they also proved that their President was unscrupulous and foul-mouthed as well as a crook.

In August 1974 Nixon resigned – the first US President in history to do so – and was replaced by Gerald Ford, whom Nixon had appointed Vice-President after Agnew's disgrace. And Congress awoke to the realisation that for forty years it had surrendered power to a succession of ambitious Presidents. In the years of the "New Deal", the Second World War, and the Cold War, the men in the White House had all made special claims for new and ever-wider authority to deal with the nation's problems and security. Richard Nixon had misused and perverted that authority, and only the extraordinary fact that he had kept tape-recordings of incriminating conversations stopped him.

In November 1976 the American people went to the polls to elect a new President. Gerald Ford had provided the nation with a safe but unexciting interlude after Nixon, but most voters rejected him – perhaps because they wanted a complete break with the Vietnam and Watergate years – and chose instead Jimmy Carter, a former governor of the southern state of Georgia, who four years before had been a political unknown.

James E. Carter, 1977–81

Jimmy Carter later said of himself:

"I was not part of the Wall Street business Establishment, the Washington political Establishment or the Hollywood entertainment Establishment. I was not part of the Establishment in any way. I was a Southern peanut farmer, populist type."

At first, most people thought that being a Southerner, an outsider in Washington, was to Carter's advantage. Untainted by the 'Establishment' which had proved to be so rotten under Nixon, Carter would be in a position to sweep away all the evils of post-Watergate America and get the country back onto the path of greatness. In his inaugural speech in January 1977 Carter declared his intention to provide racial equality, full employment, a strengthening of the American family, and some measure of nuclear disarmament.

In fact, Carter's lack of experience in the ways of the 'Establishment' led him into difficulties from the start. His top priority in 1977 was to introduce a series of badly-needed energy conservation measures. He predicted a 'national catastrophe' if nothing was done to halt the country's dependence on imported oil (see page 291). In an Address to the Nation, he said:

"The energy crisis has not yet overwhelmed us, but it will do so if we do not act quickly .... Our decision about energy will test the character of the American people and the ability of the President and Congress to govern this nation. This difficult effort will be the 'moral equivalent of war', except that we will be united in our efforts to build and not to destroy."

As it turned out, fighting the 'moral equivalent of war' tested Carter's ability to govern much more than it tested that of Congress. When he put a series of proposals before Congress, he ran into major opposition from the Senate. The proposals seemed reasonable enough: he wanted to reduce oil consumption by raising taxes on petrol, by increasing domestic oil prices, by putting taxes on big 'gas-guzzling' cars, and by encouraging the use of alternative energy sources. But Carter had not appreciated the powerful influence that US oil companies have in the 'Washington Establishment'. Under pressure from the oil companies, Senate held up Carter's energy programme for the next eighteen months, amending it out of all recognition before allowing it to become law in 1978.

Carter had to deal with the thorny problem of energy conservation again in 1979, when a sharp rise in world oil prices led to a major petrol shortage in the USA. With massive queues outside filling stations becoming a daily news spectacle, Carter formed a new cabinet and announced an emergency programme of energy-saving measures. This time he aimed to increase domestic oil prices as a way of discouraging the use of oil, and to start a $88 billion programme to develop alternative and synthetic fuels. It was, he said to Congress, 'the greatest finance programme during peace-time in the history of the American people'. Although Congress eventually agreed to many of the new measures, they had not brought about any obvious benefits by the time of the 1980 Presidential election.

In the field of civil rights and race relations, Carter began by promising much. He pledged himself in his inaugural speech to make reforms, and he immediately brought a number of black people into his Administration, notably Andrew Young whom he made US Ambassador to the United Nations. No new initiatives followed this promising start, however. Race riots in Miami in 1980 showed how little things changed under Carter. The investigation that followed the rioting, in which twenty people died, revealed that 13 per cent of black people in Miami were unemployed while 40 per cent were living below the government's poverty line.

Unemployment and poverty were not confined to the black population. A serious economic recession in 1979–80 was accompanied by an inflation rate of 13.5 per cent and rapidly rising unemployment figures. Carter's response in 1980 was to make massive cuts in welfare payments and other government spending. While this eventually helped reduce the inflation rate it also led to further hardship among the poor and the unemployed.

Carter's lack of success in domestic policy was counter-balanced by a stunning diplomatic triumph in 1978. Talks about a Middle East peace settlement between the Israeli Prime Minister Menachim Begin and President Sadat of Egypt were held at Camp David, a Presidential holiday retreat in Maryland, under Carter's chairmanship, 5–17 September. As a result of the Camp David talks they signed an agreement on peace in the Middle East which later resulted in a peace treaty between Egypt and Israel (see page 292).

Carter also gained prestige from his handling of the second round of Strategic Arms Limitation Talks with Russia that had started in 1974. In June 1979 he signed an agreement, 'SALT 2' with the Russian leader, Leonid Brezhnev, to reduce the numbers and types of strategic missiles possessed by both countries. Senate, however, refused to ratify the treaty and so SALT 2, while demonstrating the desire for détente on both sides, did not achieve any reduction in nuclear arms.

In the end, foreign policy was Carter's undoing. On 4 November 1979, following the collapse of the Shah's government in Iran, Iranian students stormed the American embassy in Teheran, taking the American staff hostage. When peaceful negotiation failed to bring about their release, Carter authorised a daring rescue mission by helicopters in April 1980. When this failed, Carter's already fading popularity in the USA plummeted. His difficulties were made worse by a scandal in July when his brother Billy was found to have received $220,000 from the Libyan government in return for unspecified services given to Libya. When a Senate investigation revealed that the President had known for some time about his brother's Libyan contacts, talk of the 'Billygate' affair damaged Carter's reputation still further.

In the Presidential election campaign of 1980 Carter was opposed by another 'outsider' who could claim to be above the 'Establishment'–Ronald Reagan, Governor of California. Reagan had no difficulty in convincing the electorate that Carter was too liberal, too soft and, above all, incompetent. He won the election by a landslide.

Ronald Reagan, 1981–89

Aged 70, Ronald Reagan was the oldest American to take office as President for the first time. A former sports reporter and Hollywood film actor, he seemed an unlikely figure to restore the USA's flagging fortunes. As Governor of California from 1967–74, however, he had gained a reputation for tough talking and uncompromising policies, and his supporters now looked to him to bring these qualities to the White House.

Reagan began his term of office with an immense publicity coup. On the very day of his inauguration, 444 days after they had been taken prisoner, the American hostages in Teheran were released. When Reagan said in a speech that day "Let us begin an era of national renewal", it seemed that, at last, the USA was ready to emerge from the depths into which it had plunged since Watergate. Reagan's popularity was boosted still further when, ten weeks later, he was shot and wounded in an assassination attempt by John Warnock Hinckley. A remarkably rapid recovery turned the initial sympathy for Reagan into admiration for his obvious toughness.

Reagan had already made his toughness clear in launching a programme of economic measures several weeks earlier. Based on economic theories that the press called 'Reaganomics', the programme involved major reductions in tax and massive cuts in government spending. Taxes were to be cut by 25–30 per cent over the next three years, and government spending by 688,800 million dollars. The main savings were to come from Social Security which Reagan believed was being misused. Many Americans, he claimed, were living on Social Security payments rather than looking for work, and government money was therefore being wasted.

One area of government spending was not cut however. Spending on the US military forces rose to colossal heights as Reagan announced new plans for increasing the country country's armed strength. Plans were made for 100 'MX' missiles to be sited in hidden but movable launch-pads in Wyoming, for the building of 100 'B1' bomber aircraft, and for the building of a new Trident submarine each year. At the same time NASA, the National Aeronautics and Space Administration, was given extra finance for its 'Space Shuttle' programme: Reagan aimed to have a permanently manned American space station in orbit within the next decade. By 1985 defence spending accounted for more than one-third of all the federal government's spending.

One result of Reagan's economic programme was that the rich grew richer while the poor grew poorer. By 1984, households with incomes below the poverty line had gained an average of $20 a year from tax cuts but had lost an average of $410 a year in Social Security benefits. In contrast, households with high incomes–$80,000 or more per year–had gained an average of $8500 a year from tax cuts but had lost only $130 in benefits.

Despite the widening gap between rich and poor there was a mood of increased national confidence at the end of Reagan's first term of office. Inflation was dropping, industrial output was rising, unemployment was falling. The prospects of further improvement seemed good, and Reagan won the 1984 Presidential election with the largest popular vote in US electoral history.

38 Russia since the War, 1945–85

Post-War Reconstruction

The Great Fatherland War of 1941–45 devastated the Soviet Union. At the end of the war 20 million Soviet citizens were dead – a tenth of the pre-war population. The majority of the dead were young men of fighting age, so the survivors now included an unusually large proportion of women and children, of the old and the disabled. Seventy thousand villages and 98,000 collective farms had been wholly or partly destroyed. 4·7 million homes had been demolished. And the transport system had been shattered: 65,000 kilometres of railway track, 15,800 locomotives, 428,000 wagons, and half the railway bridges in lands occupied by the Germans had been destroyed.

Even before the end of the war it was clear that the survivors would be expected to make every possible sacrifice to help rebuild the country. In 1944,

"On the decision of the Leningrad city soviet . . . it was stated that the entire able-bodied population of Leningrad . . . was to work on reconstruction, with the following work periods: for workers and employees with an eight hour working day and those employed by military units: 30 hours a month; for workers and employees with a longer working day, and for students and schoolchildren: 10 hours a month; for citizens not working . . . 60 hours a month. Workers and employees are to work outside their normal working hours."

To direct the mammoth task of reconstruction Stalin announced a fourth Five-Year Plan in 1946. The Plan emphasised the rebuilding and development of heavy industry and rail transport: thus the building of factories came before houses; cement, tractors and pig-iron came before consumer goods. To help achieve the Plan, Manchuria and the areas of Eastern Europe occupied by the Red Army were stripped of machinery, railway equipment, raw materials and skilled workers. Money to finance the Plan also came from taxes on the collective farms. At the same time, peasants continued to receive low prices for their produce, so their incomes remained abysmally low. In 1948–50, according to the British economic historian Alec Nove,

". . . the average cash income from collective work was such that twenty-eight trudodni* (say twenty days' work) was needed to buy a bottle of vodka; a kilogram of butter equalled sixty trudodni; a poor quality suit required well over a year's average collective wage."

Nevertheless, by 1950 the planners were able to claim a real success. Many parts of the Soviet Union, even those most devastated by the war, were producing as much as in 1940. In many cases the Plan's industrial targets had been exceeded, as is shown in the following table.

Some industrial production figures for the fourth Five-Year Plan, 1946–50

	1945	1950 (Plan)	1950 (Actual)
Electricity (*milliard kilowatt hours*)	43·2	82	91·2
Coal (*million tonnes*)	149·3	250	261·1
Oil (*million tonnes*)	19·4	35·4	37·9
Pig-iron (*million tonnes*)	8·8	19·5	19·2
Steel (*million tonnes*)	12·3	25·4	27·3

Cultural Repression

To make sure that there was total and active commitment to the work of reconstruction, Andrei Zhdanov, the ruthless Party chief of Leningrad, was given the task of regimenting the country's artistic and intellectual life. In a campaign launched in August 1946, intellectuals and artists of all kinds were put under intense pressure to support the Party, the government and Marxist ideology. So anyone whose work was 'western' or 'bourgeois' in style was condemned as 'hostile to the people'. Instead, 'Socialist Realism' was encouraged; all artistic and cultural activity had to deal with the social and political lives of ordinary people, and to reflect the progress of Socialism. And in academic work and in scientific research, the Marxist theory of dialectical materialism – '*diamat*' – had to be followed to the letter.

The result was the suffocation of cultural life in the Soviet Union. Thousands of artists and intellectuals lost their jobs and thousands more disappeared into

* trudodni = work day units

labour camps. Those who remained free slavishly produced work of unmistakable socialist content. The composer Dmitri Shostakovich, for example, wrote *The Song of the Forests* in praise of a forestry plan announced by Stalin in 1948. The Institute for History at the Academy of Sciences hurriedly produced a Five-Year Plan of its intended future research and output. And the novelist Alexander Fadaev who won the Stalin Prize in 1946 for his novel *The Young Guard*, was forced to rewrite it in 1947 along stricter Party lines.

Along with all this went a campaign to glorify the Soviet Union and, especially, everything Russian. Most major discoveries and inventions of the past were said to be the work of Russians – the printing press, the steam engine and the radio, for example. Even the wheel was claimed to be the invention of prehistoric people living by the Moskva river! To prevent Russians from making unfavourable comparisons with the West, Stalin isolated the Soviet Union from the rest of the world. Russians were not allowed to marry foreigners or to travel abroad. Soldiers returning from occupation duty in Germany and Austria were forbidden to talk about their experiences. And Russian newspapers carried articles about conditions in the west that convinced Russian readers that conditions in the Soviet Union were overwhelmingly superior.

Stalin's last years

Public worship of Stalin had already reached incredible heights in the 1930s (see pages 135–6). The Soviet Union's victory in the Great Fatherland War raised his name to dizzying new heights. He was addressed variously as Father of the Peoples, The Greatest Genius in History, Shining Sun of Humanity, Life Giving Force of Socialism, and so forth. His name was given to countless cities, towns and villages, to public squares, streets and avenues, to schools and hospitals, to rivers, forests and mountain ranges. As *A Short Biography* written in 1949 by G. F. Alexandrov put it:

"J. V. Stalin is the genius, the leader and teacher of the Party, the great strategist of Socialist revolution, helmsman of the Soviet State and captain of armies. ... His work is extraordinary for its variety; his energy truly amazing. The range of questions which engage his attention is immense, embracing the most complex problems of Marxist-Leninist theory and school textbooks; problems of Soviet foreign policy and the municipal affairs of the proletarian capital; the development of the great Northern Sea Route and the reclamation of the Colchian marshes; the advancement of Soviet literature and art and the editing of the model rules for collective farms; and, lastly, the solution of the most intricate problems in the theory and practice of war."

Stalin himself vetted the manuscript of *A Short Biography*, and had only one thing to add:

"Stalin never allowed his work to be marred by the slightest hint of vanity, conceit or self-adulation."

Stalin increasingly ruled as a dictator in the years after the war. The Politburo and the Central Committee of the Communist Party never met as full bodies between 1947 and 1952. Instead, decisions were made and orders given verbally to whoever happened to be around at the time. Anyone who was rash enough to ignore an order or to misinterpret it risked being purged from the Party. When Zhdanov, the Leningrad Party chief, died in 1948, Stalin immediately purged the Leningrad Party: for some time it had been showing a tendency to ignore instructions from Moscow and to follow its own policies. In the 'Leningrad Affair' of 1948, over one thousand Party officials were arrested and executed.

From 1948 onwards Jews in the Soviet Union were particularly in danger of being 'purged'. The powerful traditions of anti-Semitism in Russia were now combined with Stalin's desire to prevent the creation of the state of Israel from whipping up nationalistic fervour among Russia's Jews. So, in 1948, many Jewish intellectuals were arrested. Jewish theatres, newspapers and journals were closed down. Mikhoels, a famous Jewish actor, was found dead in mysterious circumstances. In January 1953 it seemed as if a major new purge of Jews was about to begin. Nine Jewish doctors in the Kremlin medical centre were arrested and accused among other crimes of murdering Zhdanov five years earlier. In an anti-Semitic press campaign, *Pravda* claimed that the 'Nine Doctors' Plot' was part of a Jewish conspiracy to wipe out the Soviet leadership. But just as it seemed that new arrests were about to be made, the press campaign suddenly ended. The reason, which became public on 5 March 1953, was that Stalin had suffered a stroke and died.

The Succession to Stalin

Stalin's death was immediately followed by a struggle among the Party leadership to decide who should take his place. For a time it looked as if Lavrenti Beria, the loathsome head of the NKVD, would use secret police units to carry out a coup d'état in Moscow. But his colleagues in the Presidium, as the Politburo had been renamed in 1952, united to prevent this: Beria knew far too much about them and everyone else at the top. He was arrested and later executed as a traitor in December 1953.

The fall of Beria left power in the hands of two men: Georgei Malenkov as Prime Minister, and Nikita Khrushchev as General Secretary of the Party. Malenkov quickly took the lead in formulating policy. He announced in August 1953 that the production of consumer goods would be increased and the standard of living raised within three years. Money to finance this ambitious programme would come from major cuts in defence spending. This in turn would require more peaceful relations with the West. Khrushchev denounced this as 'Goulash Communism' and favoured the exact opposite: priority for heavy industry, an increase in defence spending and limited improvements in relations with the West.

Malenkov and Khrushchev also disagreed about agricultural policy. Production on farms was still low, and so too were peasants' earnings. There wasn't enough food. Malenkov's solution to the problem was to build up the country's engineering and chemical industries in order to provide farm machinery and fertilizers. Without these, he argued, there could be no real, lasting increase in output. Khrushchev, however, wanted much quicker results. His solution was to expand the area under cultivation – to create more farmland. After all, the Soviet Union is the largest country in the world and land is one thing that has never been in short supply. Khrushchev therefore put forward a plan to bring under cultivation at least 13 million hectares of virgin and fallow land in southern Siberia, northern Kazakhstan and south-east Russia.

Khrushchev's Virgin Lands Scheme was adopted as official policy by the Presidium in 1953. Tens of thousands of young people from Komsomol, the Communist Youth League, 'volunteered' to work on the Virgin Lands. Along with army conscripts, and helped by good weather, they brought in a good harvest at the end of the first year of cultivation. The success of the scheme led to the plan being doubled. 200,000 young people and conscripts worked on the Virgin Lands in 1956, increasing the cultivated area by 35·9 hectares – roughly the size of the British Isles. Another good harvest led to a record output in 1956, and this strengthened Khrushev's position considerably.

In February 1955 Khrushchev had enough supters in the Presidium to outvote Malenkov and force him to resign. In his place Nikolai Bulganin, a supporter of Khrushchev, was appointed as Prime Minister.

De-Stalinisation

The new, two-man leadership of Bulganin and Khrushchev – 'B and K' as they were known in the West – promptly adopted most of the defeated Malenkov's ideas: to increase the production of consumer goods, to raise living standards, to ease relations with the West. As these ideas were very different from those of Stalin, Khrushchev set about undermining Stalin's reputation in order to make his own policies seem more acceptable to the Party.

As we have seen (page 217), Khrushchev made a speech to the 20th Congress of the Soviet Communist Party in February 1956, condemning many features of Stalin's régime and promising a new kind of rule by the Communist Party. The 20th Congress was followed by a process of 'De-Stalinisation' in which life for many Russians became marginally more free as the shadow of the tyrant vanished.

De-Stalinisation began with the mortal remains of the man himself. On the third anniversary of Stalin's death, one month after Khrushchev's speech, only six bouquets of flowers were placed on his tomb; the year before it had not been possible to pile the mountains of flowers sent by mourners onto the tomb. Later, Stalin's body was removed from the tomb in Red Square and interred in the Kremlin wall.

Some of the seventeen members of the Presidium opposed the De-Stalinisation process. Malenkov and Molotov were alarmed by the unrest that Khrushchev's speech had stirred up in Poland and Hungary (see page 218) and they demanded his resignation. Khrushchev's supporters in the Central Committee of the Party managed narrowly to outvote this 'Anti-Party Group', and shortly afterwards they lost their seats in the Presidium. One sure sign that the Soviet Union was being 'De-Stalinised' was that the Anti-Party

Group lived to tell the tale: Molotov was despatched to Outer Mongolia as Soviet Ambassador, while Malenkov was sent to run a power station in Kazakhstan. Under Stalin, deposed rivals had invariably ended up dead. Later, in 1958, Bulganin was also forced out of his job by Khrushchev who then combined the post of Prime Minister with his own position as General Secretary, thus giving himself supreme power.

Perhaps the most reassuring feature of De-Stalinisation was a reduction in the power of the secret political police. Immediately after Stalin's death, the Ministry of Internal Affairs, the MVD, had been deprived of a number of its roles, especially the use of prison camp labour for public construction work. The MVD was forced to share its security and surveillance work with a new, party-run Committee for State Security, the KGB. Many of the forced labour camps were broken up. And in 1958 a new Criminal Code brought an end to the state's arbitrary use of arrest and imprisonment without trial.

Khrushchev's Russia

Khrushchev made energetic attempts to resolve two major problems of the Stalin years: the rigid over-centralisation of industrial planning, which had made for much inefficiency and waste; and the old, persistent difficulty of providing sufficient food for an increasingly urbanised society. In 1957 he set up 105 Regional Economic Councils throughout the country to take over from the Moscow planners much of the responsibility for directing industry and agriculture. In 1958 the sixth Five-Year Plan was abandoned and a new Seven-Year Plan was introduced with the aim of producing more consumer goods and raising the general standard of living.

Under Khrushchev living standards rose considerably. Wages increased and working hours were shortened. Maternity leave, old age pensions and disability payments were all increased, and taxes were cut. Improved medical and educational facilities and larger housing subsidies were also among the benefits of the Khrushchev régime.

Shortly after Stalin's death, in the summer of 1953, a rapid 'thaw' in the cultural life of the Soviet Union had begun. The loosening of controls on the theatre, films, broadcasting, music and literature produced a more liberal atmosphere in which criticism of Soviet government and society became possible once again.

However, Khrushchev's 1956 speech to the 20th Party Congress, in which he denounced Stalin's control of cultural life, was not followed by any further thaw. Although Khrushchev allowed the publication of novels criticising the Soviet industrial system (Vladimir Dudintsev's *Not by Bread Alone*) and the Stalinist prison camps (Alexander Solzhenitsyn's *One Day in the Life of Ivan Denisovitch*), he criticised the Nobel Prize-winning novelist Boris Pasternak, whose *Dr. Zhivago* was banned in the Soviet Union, for 'bourgeois individualism'. Strict controls on broadcasting and the press remained in force. Religious life came under even stricter control than before, with thousands of churches being closed down and their congregations even prevented from worshipping elsewhere.

Khrushchev announced in 1961, at the 22nd Congress of the Communist Party, that the Soviet government aimed to reach the goal of communism within the next twenty years. This would naturally require speeding up the development of both agriculture and industry. Accordingly, changes were made in the planning and administration of the economy. In 1963 the 105 Regional Economic Councils were reduced to 47. The Communist Party was split into agricultural and industrial sections. Many new planning councils and committees were created. And the early success of the Virgin Lands Scheme led Khrushchev to order another massive expansion of the cultivated area. The production of tractors was given a new, high priority. And orders went out to the collective farms to grow more maize to feed more cattle, and thus to increase the proportion of meat in the Soviet diet.

The result was chaos. Khrushchev had made haste too quickly; nobody knew exactly where they were or who was responsible for what. The Virgin Lands were unsuitable for wheat, no matter how much honest communist sweat was ploughed into them. In many areas maize yields were low: even the Communist Party could not command crops to grow in the wrong kind of soil. Tractors stood idle in the fields for lack of spare parts. And the enthusiasm of local party officials in the 47 Regional Economic Councils for new agricultural and industrial strategies was, in many cases, cancelled out by their inefficiency and ignorance.

By 1964 most of the other top Soviet Communists had had enough of Khrushchev's grand schemes, and equally grand failures. In October a majority on the Party's Central Committee voted to dismiss him from power.

Brezhnev and Kosygin, 1964–82

Khrushchev, who now went quietly into a tranquil retirement, had been a colourful figure, leading the Soviet Union through a period of rapid and important change. In comparison, his successors were dull and unadventurous. Leonid Brezhnev, the new General Secretary, and Alexei Kosygin, the new Prime Minister, promised an end to Khrushchev's 'hare-brained schemes' and introduced a stability and predictability into Soviet affairs that had been lacking since before the 1917 revolutions.

The new leaders moved quickly to undo some of Khrushchev's schemes. The Regional Economic Councils were scrapped in 1965, and planning was centralised in Moscow again. The Presidium was renamed the Politburo and the division of the Party into industrial and agricultural wings was abolished. However, within the general framework of the economy, factory managers and other industrial organisers were given more freedom to decide on production methods. Instead of factories delivering their products to the government they now sold them to State Purchase Agencies which had the right to refuse to buy poor quality goods. Factories could keep up to 40 per cent of their profits to invest in new machinery. The Kosygin Reforms, as these changes were known, were quietly abandoned in the early 1970s as a result of criticisms within the Party that they were a partial return to capitalism.

Brezhnev and Kosygin, like their predecessors, were unable to answer satisfactorily the old, recurring question of how the rural population could be made to feed the growing city population. Brezhnev made agriculture one of his chief priorities. In an attempt to increase incentives, crop prices as well as farmers' wages were increased. Restrictions on the farming of Russia's 50 million private plots were eased. Investment in machinery, fertilizers and irrigation was increased at a rate ahead of investment in industry. And the collective farms were amalgamated into much larger units: by 1980 there were 26,000 amalgamated collective farms, each with an average area of 6,500 hectares tilled by 550 households. State farms were also made larger by amalgamation. By 1980 there were 20,000 state farms, each of around 20,000 hectares tilled by 500 workers. However, agricultural output was disappointing throughout the 1970s and early 1980s, and poor harvests forced the government to import large quantities of wheat from the USA and from Canada in 1972, 1975 and 1979. And the private plots continued to divert a good deal of effort away from collective farming, accounting for one-third of all man-hours spent on agriculture although they covered only 3 per cent of the total cultivated area.

Just as Stalin and Khrushchev had achieved great power by eliminating their rivals in a collective leadership, so Brezhnev eclipsed Kosygin to make himself undisputed leader of the Soviet Union. By appointing his friends and supporters to key Party posts, and simply by outliving a number of rivals in the Politburo, Brezhnev built up enormous power inside the Party. In addition to his post of General Secretary, he also became President in 1977, making him Head of State as well as Head of the Party. However, under Brezhnev's leadership the Soviet régime became increasingly inefficient, slow and corrupt. Factory managers and Party leaders seemed unwilling as well as unable to solve the growing problems of drunkenness, absenteeism and indiscipline amongst the work force. The problem of corruption was highlighted in 1982 by the execution of a former fisheries minister, Vladimir Rytov, for 'economic crimes' involving the fraudulent export of caviar to Western countries. Another 'economic crime' in 1982 suggested that corruption had penetrated the highest levels of the Party: 'Boris the Gypsy', star singer of the Moscow State Circus, and close friend of Brezhnev's daughter Galina, was arrested by the KGB on charges of illicit dealings in diamonds.

Brezhnev died in November 1982 before these scandals had time to embarrass him politically. Brezhnev had intended that his successor should be a close colleague and friend, Constantin Chernenko, but the Politburo decided instead to try a new style of leadership by appointing Yuri Andropov as the next General Secretary.

Andropov and Chernenko, 1982–85

Yuri Andropov, 67 years old and suffering from a known heart complaint, had been head of the KGB from 1967 to 1982. In this capacity he had efficiently used police terror to crush dissidents (see page 245) and to deal with corruption in the Party. He brought the same toughness of approach to his position as General Secretary, launching a campaign against corrupt and inefficient managers in industry, punishing black marketeers, and tightening up factory discipline, particularly by punishing drunkenness on the shop floor. Andropov also attempted to breathe new life into industry by introducing what he called 'enterprise management'. Managers were given greater freedom of initiative as regards investment, pricing and wages within the framework of the Five-Year Plan.

Andropov's disciplinarian approach worried many Party workers who feared exposure and the loss of their positions. To overcome their opposition to his schemes Andropov began a campaign to replace 150 inefficient regional Party secretaries with new, lively, forward-looking secretaries. By 1983 it was clear that Andropov's reforms were starting to make an impact on the Soviet Union. Productivity in industry grew and the Soviet economy saw its best output figures for more than five years.

In August 1983 Andropov was taken ill, and he died in February 1984 after only fifteen months in office. He was replaced by Constantin Chernenko, Brezhnev's chosen successor who, at 73 years old, was of uncertain health and appeared to lack both ability and drive. He continued with Andropov's anti-corruption campaign, albeit without much enthusiasm, but he did not continue the shake-up of the regional Party secretaries. His administration soon proved to be little more than a stop-gap, for heart and lung disease forced him into prolonged absences from public life after July 1984. He died in February 1985.

The Soviet Union in the 1980s

Chernenko was succeeded by a much younger and more vigorous man. Aged 54, Mikhail Gorbachev came to power with possibly two decades of power ahead of him. Gorbachev had been groomed for top leadership by Yuri Andropov before the latter's death, and immediately took up Andropov's policies with gusto. In his first year of office he made it clear that economic reform would be his priority for the remainder of the 1980s. New technology in industry, a tightening of discipline amongst the work force, and a shake-up in the administration of industry were among his initial aims.

He began to speak of *perestroika* or 'reconstruction' of the Soviet economy and society along new lines of more efficient management. Along with this went the

principle of *glasnost* or 'openness' in discussion of political and social questions. *Glasnost* was seized on by the Soviet press which began to comment on political issues and made its first steps towards investigative journalism since the 1920s.

Glasnost revealed huge areas of dissatisfaction with the economy and a widespread desire to change the régime. Gorbachev skilfully used this public demand for change to strengthen his own position against the resistance of old guard Party leaders who saw their position under threat. In 1988, for example, he strengthened his position with the dismissal or forced retirement of many party officials of the Brezhnev era. A few were put on trial for corruption. Then, after meetings of the Party's ruling Central Committee and of the Supreme Soviet, he emerged as state President and head of a leadership openly committed to separating the work and the powers of the government and the Communist Party.

Many questions remained. There was a suggestion that voters might not be presented with only a single list of names in future elections; but how fundamentally would the USSR change the way it was governed? There was the problem which has affected many societies which set out to modernise their economy: would pockets of unemployment replace a situation where work is guaranteed but old-style methods mean that many do not have to work too hard?

Finally, there was the issue of how deeply individual freedom would go in a society which persecuted dissidents shamelessly. By the Helsinki Declaration of 1975 the USSR had immediately set up 'Helsinki groups' to monitor the Soviet government's observance of the Declaration, but the KGB vigorously suppressed them. Punishments ranged from internal exile in closed cities (those which foreigners were not allowed to visit), to imprisonment in labour camps and treatment in 'special psychiatric hospitals' where torture and drugs were used to alter the behaviour of victims. By 1988, in the new climate of glasnost, many of the dissidents were home, just as Jews were free, for the first time in decades, to emigrate from the USSR. But no-one knew where Gorbachev wished, or would be able, to draw the line between persecuting dissent and encouraging criticism.

39 China since Chiang Kai-shek, 1949–85

The "Mandate of Heaven"

The man who proclaimed the Chinese People's Republic on 1 October 1949 and became President of its Central Government Council ruling 540 million people was the son of a peasant from a village in the interior of China. To the Chinese that was not particularly surprising, nor did generals, civil servants, bankers and business men have many qualms about transferring their loyalty from Chiang Kai-shek to Mao Tse-tung. That had been the way of Chinese history for over two thousand years, ever since the First Emperor, the man who completed the Great Wall, became ruler of "all the land that lies under heaven ... " Since then China had known many dynasties, lines of emperors, which had lasted for years or centuries and in turn disintegrated, usually into the chaos of peasant unrest and rebellion. A new dynasty usually began when a rebel general with a chance of enforcing law and order over the whole land was accepted by the educated classes, who then quickly re-occupied the positions of civil servants, magistrates and local governors in the imperial service. It was clearly laid down by the ancient philosophers that the "mandate of heaven" – the right to rule – stayed with an emperor only as long as he could carry out the duties of government. China is the home of the Han people, and the 'sons of Han' (who still make up ninety-three per cent of the population) would know no peace unless the Great Wall and the passes of the north-west were fortified against barbarian invaders, and the neighbouring kingdoms in Korea, Mongolia, Tibet and Indo-China were compelled to recognise the emperor as overlord and send him tributes. Inside China, an emperor fit for the mandate of heaven kept the public grain-stores full of reserve foods against times of famine, suppressed the bandits who infested the mountain regions, and organised the upkeep of the dams and canals which prevented flooding and provided the irrigation waters essential to agriculture.

The work was done by ordinary village people who were allowed no part in decision-making and didn't seek one. Both rulers and ruled accepted the idea that there was a complete difference in the contributions that each made to society. This was expressed in many ways, but most Chinese would have been able to quote Confucius, a philosopher of the sixth century BC who had taught that "The people may be made to follow a path of action, but they may not be made to understand it". Was that the way it would be after 1949? It was clear that Chiang Kai-shek had lost fitness to govern: he had failed to defend China against barbarians, either the Japanese invaders or the Americans and Europeans who owned so much of China's industry and commerce, and the land was racked by famine and disorder. Now he ruled only Taiwan and a few 'off-shore' islands, which he grandly named the Republic of China. But were Mao Tse-tung and the 4,500,000 Communists simply a successful rebel force which would give the country strong government and a breathing space while the old privileges, of the educated over the illiterate and the city over the village, were re-established?

Democratic Centralism: the Government of Communist China

The Communist Party was small, but it was well disciplined along lines laid down by Mao in 1942:

"Some comrades do not understand the Party's system of democratic centralism, in which the minority is subordinate to the majority, the low level to the higher level, the part to the whole, and the entire membership to the Central Committee."

Democratic centralism is a Leninist idea; its short meaning is that the Communist Party on the point of seizing power gives total obedience to its leaders. The form of government devised for China in 1949 and 1950 had all the hallmarks of the ruthless central control which Lenin and Stalin had imposed on the Soviet Union. The eighteen provinces of the land were grouped into six regions, in each of which a bureau of the Communist Party was set up, headed by a leading Communist. Three of the bureaus were also responsible for controlling the army and Party teams which entered the non-Han regions of Sinkiang, Tibet and Inner Mongolia, and laid the foundations for the firmest control of these outlying areas for more than a century. Mao's Communist empire was as large as any in two thousand years of Chinese history.

Party members were placed at every level of power,

from county and market town upwards. Many, perhaps most, of them were People's Liberation Army fighters, and from the first the PLA provided the link which bound every district to the offices of the regional bureaus and to the Party's Central Committee in Peking. A new branch of government, the Supreme People's Court, was responsible for supervising the People's Trials in which henchmen of Chiang Kaishek, collaborators with the Japanese and rack-renting landlords were publicly accused. Some were unjustly punished; of the rest of the accused the majority were forced into the public humiliation of confessing to crimes and agreeing to serve the community in some lowly position; the most guilty were executed in numbers estimated from 150,000 to a million or more.

In mid-1950 the Agrarian Reform Law started another round of public investigation, this time of every villager's class position to decide whether he was landlord, rich peasant (one who hired labour), middle or poor peasant. Once the facts were established, land was re-distributed so that those who lived on the rents and labour of others almost disappeared as a class:

	Percentage of households	Percentage of crop area owned	
		Before reform	After reform
Landlords	2·6	28·7	2·1
Rich peasants	3·6	17·6	6·3
Middle peasants	35·8	30·2	44·8
Poor peasants and others	58·0	23·5	46·8

While the land went – temporarily – to the peasants, industry and business fell under state control. The Communists started from a strong position, taking over the major banks, the railways and about a third of heavy industry from Chiang's Nationalist government. The remaining private sector became the victim of a process of "ruthless high-pressure gradualisation". Firms were squeezed into bankruptcy by price controls, or their owners and managers found themselves forced to confess to crimes and anti-social activities in campaigns against the "three-antis" (corruption, waste and bureaucratisation) and the "five-antis" (bribery, taxdodging, fraud, theft and selling secrets to foreigners). By 1953, eighty-six per cent of Chinese industry and commerce was under at least partial government control, although some owners and shareholders continued to draw strictly limited profits.

The First Five-Year Plan

In 1953 the Chinese economy was organised very much like the Soviet Union's NEP (see Chapter 13, page 56) with the state controlling the major industries and peasants selling their surplus produce after tax to private traders. And it was to the Soviet Union that the Chinese turned for guidance and help with their first Five-Year Plan. Shortly after coming to power Mao had spent ten weeks in Moscow in hard negotiation. The actual aid he was given was tiny enough for him to describe it as like getting meat from the mouth of a tiger: the equivalent of a mere $300 million, mostly in the form of finance for joint undertakings from which the USSR would draw benefits. More useful were over ten thousand engineers and planning experts, plus another 1,500 from Eastern Europe. These advisers and the Chinese planners had a national economy to consider which was divided into three broad sectors: peasant agriculture, which occupied eighty-five per cent of the population, the light industry of the coastal towns and the heavy industrial region of Manchuria. Their decision was to give priority to heavy industry and especially to new production plants in central China. Light industry was starved of funds despite the fact that cotton manufacture and food processing had made up China's main exports. The Plan would be paid for by taxing the peasants.

By any standards the achievements after five years (1953–57) were remarkable: steel production was up by four times, the output of coal, cement, electricity and machine tools all more than doubled; China's first vehicles were coming off the assembly lines, and plant for aircraft manufacture had been laid down; small interior towns such as Sian and Wuhan were developing into vast industrial complexes. Yet, well before the completion of the Plan, Mao Tse-tung was occupied more with its flaws than with its successes.

The Plan was imposing frightful strains. The city working population rose by forty million and extra housing and food were needed for roughly the same number of people as there are in England. The planners and their Soviet advisers were unpopular; in 1956 Mao called for open public discussion in a movement to "Let a hundred flowers bloom and a thousand schools of thought contend". The result was an outburst of criticism from all sides, especially from writers and university teachers. Most of them paid for their outspokeness by losing their jobs and undergoing periods of re-education in labour camps, but the lesson was not lost on Mao.

Collectivisation of Farms

The most severe problems, however, were in the countryside; with a population increasing by fourteen million a year there was no way in which agriculture, with its manpower and mechanisation needs neglected, could continue to fuel the headlong industrial revolution with food, raw materials and taxes.

To this Stalin's answer had been collectivisation and so, in mid-1955, was Mao's. Up to then about half the peasant families farmed alone, the others worked in mutual-aid teams, a version of an age-old system whereby six or seven households would pool their labour and equipment at sowing and harvest times. The table shows how this pattern changed between 1955 and 1957.

Percentages of peasant families in:

	Mutual-aid teams	Lower-stage APCs (agricultural producers' cooperatives)	Higher-stage APCs (collectives)
1950	10·7	–	–
1951	19·2	–	–
1952	39·9	0·1	–
1953	39·3	0·2	–
1954	58·3	1·9	–
1955 (autumn)	50·7	14·2	0·03
1955 (year end)	32·7	63·3	4·00
1956 (January)	19·7	49·6	30·7
1965 (July)	7·6	29·0	63·4
1956 (end)	3·7	8·5	87·8
1957			93·5

Lower-stage APCs were created by pooling the labour of 30–50 households, usually the people of one small village. They kept ownership of their own land and the unit was far too small, and there were too many of them, for the over-stretched Communist Party to influence permanently. So in 1956 the higher-stage APC, or collective, was forged out of 200–300 households, grouping villages in clusters; small private plots were allowed, but the rest of the land was handed over to a managing committee. As in the USSR collectivisation was unpopular and Mao placed the blame on "a serious tendency towards capitalism

among the well-to-do peasants" and warned the Party not to relax its efforts. In the Soviet Union this had been the point at which Stalin turned collectivisation into a bloody business of killing and mass deportation. To travel this road was not possible for China where the number and proportion of peasants were both far greater than in the USSR in 1929, nor for Mao who pointed out that "In Russia the revolution developed from the cities to the countryside, while in our country it developed from the countryside to the cities."

The Great Leap Forward

In April 1956 Mao challenged the whole philosophy of the first Five-Year Plan in a speech on the "ten great relationships". He declared that in ten major areas the Party was over-emphasising the claims of one sector at the expense of another: the most important cases were industry over agriculture, the state over individual workers, Peking over the regions, and the Party over non-Party. The speech contained some sharp knocks at the Soviet Union and a call for a new approach: "Our theory is made up of the universal truth of Marxism-Leninism combined with the concrete reality of China. We must be able to think independently."

Independent thinking was evident in the Great Leap Forward which was launched in 1958 in place of a Soviet-style Plan. At the heart of the strategy of the Great Leap was the re-organisation of the countryside into 26,000 communes.

Most communes were set up within the boundaries of a rural local government district, a *hsiang*, and held on average about 25,000 people. Thus a commune was large enough to become an all-purpose unit for decentralised management of almost every activity in Chinese life. It was a local government area managing its own schools and medical services as well as a base for a small army unit which trained the commune's peasant militia. Cultivation was left to production brigades in the communes, based on the APCs set up in 1956, but the commune still could call on a lot of surplus manpower for other work, especially in the north where farming has to stop during the winter freeze; everywhere else too nurseries and public canteens could release women from their traditional tasks.

Thus the communes were to play a major part in the central idea of the Great Leap Forward, that China

Old and new China. A junk sails past the Hankow Bridge being built over the Yangtze River in 1957 with the aid of Soviet Engineers.

should practise "walking on two legs". One of those legs was industrial and scientific activity, advanced enough for China to explode her first nuclear device in 1964; the other was anything which could be done by the use of human muscles and ingenuity. The muscles were most evident in the massive irrigation works of the Great Leap; by September 1958 commune work forces dug the equivalent of three hundred Panama Canals. The ingenuity came with the nationwide rash of small commune factories making ball-bearings, cement, simple tools, and fertilisers, as well as 'backyard furnaces', each producing steel in small quantities. The extra town population built up during the Plan was sent back to the countryside to work in these commune schemes.

After only a year it was seen that heady enthusiasm and hard work were not solving all China's problems.

Many commune industries had sacrificed quality for quantity, and the political enthusiasm of some Communist officials had led to waste, for instance on building communal kitchens when people preferred their own. There was strong peasant opposition too, especially on communes which had forbidden private plots. In 1960 and 1961 severe droughts produced a grim food crisis, although famine was averted by rationing, the water storage schemes of the Great Leap and imported grain.

In December 1958, as it became clear that the Great Leap had produced as many problems as successes, Mao gave up the position of President of the Chinese government to Liu Shao-ch'i. This was probably no more than a tactful hand-over to a better administrator. Mao still kept the all-powerful post of Chairman of the Communist Party and Liu Shao-ch'i was probably not comfortable to hear that Mao was to spend his time considering the future development of Communism. Liu Shao-ch'i and others took the view that production would rise as a result of rewards, in the form of higher wages for the most skilled, higher education for the most promising young people and good prices for produce from peasants' private plots – which were brought back after the Great Leap. Mao became the figurehead for the ideas of the "mass line", that people would work best if fired with the desire to "serve the people" and if they were allowed a share in decision-making.

The Sino-Soviet Split

Less than a year after Liu Shao-ch'i had taken over the government, the Chinese and Russians broke apart. In effect the Chinese decision to go their own way was taken at a meeting of the Politbureau in August 1959 when P'eng Te-huai, the War Minister, who had consistently opposed communes and the Great Leap and favoured a return to Soviet-style methods, was dismissed and arrested.

Behind this decision lay several years of mounting disagreement with the USSR. The Chinese had keenly resented Stalin's failure to help them fight off the threat to their frontiers in the Korean War, his slowness in returning railways and industries in Manchuria seized by Soviet armies from the Japanese in the Second World War, and his obvious intention to treat them as just another satellite on the scale of Poland or Hungary. The death of Stalin and the coming of Khrushchev improved relations for only a brief while. As you have seen in Chapter 36 (pages 217–20), Khrushchev's foreign policy consisted of two main planks – trying to win allies among the world's poorer nations and, at the same time, reaching an agreement with the USA based on the fact that the world now contained only two fully armed super-powers. The first of these led straight away to conflict with China. Prime Minister Chou En-lai was pressing Chinese claims to leadership of the Asian nations and resented Khrushchev's tours of India and Burma in 1955 with promises of aid on a scale that China could not give. But it was Khrushchev's bid for 'peaceful co-existence' which touched the Chinese in their most sensitive area, their fear of the USA. When the Soviet Union launched 'Sputnik' in 1957, Mao had rejoiced and proclaimed that "the east wind is prevailing over the west wind"; with the Soviet Union leading the race for con-

trol of space the American atomic bomb was no more than a "paper tiger". Confident in the greater strength of the Communist "east wind", the Chinese launched an attack on tiny 'off-shore' islands held by Chiang Kai-shek between the mainland and Taiwan. But the USSR made no attempt to back the Chinese when the United States announced their firm support for Chiang Kai-shek; indeed Khrushchev set out to tame his restless ally by refusing to hand over promised samples of atomic weapons. In September 1959 Khrushchev flew to the USA to meet President Eisenhower. Days later he was in Peking for the celebrations of the tenth anniversary of People's China; behind the scenes of public rejoicing he was forced to listen to bitter complaints from the Chinese about Soviet foreign policy and about the scorn the Russians were pouring on the Great Leap Forward, which they had described as "a road of dangerous experiments, a road of disregard for economic laws and for the experience of other socialist states". Within a few months the USSR withdrew her specialist advisers and their blueprints from China and broke off economic aid.

The Cultural Revolution

In his many speeches after he had handed over his government post in 1958 Mao's most common concern was that Party officials had become more used to giving orders than encouraging persuasion and discussion. There were also, he thought, too many people occupying privileged city positions and failing to understand the aims of Chinese communism:

"We must drive actors, poets, dramatists and writers out of the cities and push them all off to the countryside. They should all periodically go down in batches in the villages and to the factories ... Whoever does not go down will get no dinner; only when they go down will they be fed."

"Going down" for periods of work in the countryside became one of Mao's favourite schemes for checking what he saw as the harmful results of Liu Shao-ch'i's policy of rapidly expanding the numbers of specialists with a lengthy period of training:

"From entering primary school to leaving college is altogether sixteen or seventeen years. I fear that for over twenty years people will not see rice, mustard, wheat or millet growing; nor will they see how workers work, nor how peasants till the field."

It was one thing to make these criticisms, it was another to be able to overthrow the Party officials, factory managers and other specialists from their positions of privilege. Strong support came from the new Minister of Defence, Lin Piao, a much-wounded hero of the PLA's struggle against the Japanese and Chiang Kai-shek, who, in 1965, began to apply Mao's ideas to the army. Ranks were abolished, as were special uniforms and badges. Every soldier was issued with a pocket-sized copy of the Little Red Book, containing snatches of quotations from Mao, especially those which emphasised serving the people and the benefits of self-discipline and self-criticism. Mao's other key supporter was his wife, Chiang Ch'ing, a one-time bit-part actress who claimed to be a specialist on cultural matters and led a campaign for abolishing the traditional theatre and ballet in favour of performances which served the people and glorified the communist "struggle".

Lin and Chiang Ch'ing could not on their own give mass support to Mao. For this Mao turned to the 'Red Guards', bands of schoolchildren and students whom he wanted to fire with the ideas of "going down" to the people. In the spring of 1966, students at Peking University began to criticise openly China's political leaders, notably the Mayor of Peking, a powerful leading figure in the Party. In June the Mayor was dismissed and, shortly afterwards, the Party agreed to Mao's proposal to set up a Cultural Revolutionary Committee and called on similar local committees throughout China to criticise the officials who ran the Communist Party, the factories and trade unions.

Why a cultural revolution? It could not be a class revolution in a country where the poor peasants and working classes were officially in power. The next stage in the development of Chinese communism was to be the victory of Mao Tse-tung's thought over 'revisionist' thought. 'Revisionism' was the "return to the capitalist road" which Mao saw in Khrushchev's policies for the Soviet Union which had strengthened the position of the Party as a privileged group ruling over the masses and also increasingly aimed at Western styles of life.

The Little Red Book was seen everywhere that summer in Peking, where a million young people, mostly between fifteen and nineteen, had been brought to camp with all arrangements carefully made by Lin Piao's PLA. Throughout China the schools and colleges were closed for six months while a new curriculum was worked out. In fact they remained shut for two years while the Cultural Revolution movement swept its uneven way through China, fired by Mao's declaration to the Peking Red Guards that, under certain circumstances, it was "right to rebel". The biggest targets for the mass parades of youngsters holding their Little Red Books and chanting slogans were powerful government leaders in Peking. Liu Shao-ch'i was branded as the "Chinese Khrushchev", placed under house arrest, and finally dismissed from the Party. Similar fates met other strong men, including the Party's secretary Teng Hsiao-p'ing.

These developments were copied in almost every city, and to a lesser extent in the countryside communes. Red Guard bands demanded the dismissal of "the handful of persons within the Party who are taking the capitalist road" and leaders in local government, factories and trade unions were replaced by revolutionary committees of citizens and workers. At times the Red Guard activities were vicious as they mauled and, in a few cases, killed alleged supporters of the "Chinese Khrushchev" and also foreigners – "imperialists and capitalists". They were often silly – at one time towns had all their street names changed to ones with revolutionary slogans. Everywhere, walls in factories and public places were festooned with huge "big character" posters screaming out some slogan. Inevitably the movement ran into anarchy; in some cities officials dealt with the Red Guards by forming their own Cultural Revolutionary bands and fighting broke out. The PLA was called on several times in 1967 to restore order. By the end of that year it had stabilised the country by setting up local "three-way alliances", made up of cultural revolutionaries, Party officials loyal to the new Maoist line and army representatives. Schools and colleges were re-opened in 1968, and in 1969 the Great Proletarian Cultural Revolution was officially declared over.

The Aftermath of the Cultural Revolution

The Cultural Revolution had begun as a power struggle between rival factions in the Communist Party but, by its end, the struggle had not been fully resolved. Lin Piao, who had so enthusiastically applied the Cutural Revolution to the PLA, was alarmed that the PLA-dominated revolutionary committees were becoming the weakest partners in the 'three way alliances'. He also disliked proposals made in a fourth Five-Year Plan for a massive mechanisation of agriculture which would be financed by a reduction in spending on the armed forces. Although Lin was named 'closest comrade in arms and successor to Mao Tse-tung' in 1969, the two men distrusted each other's intentions. Mao said that Lin was "one who while sitting at the table gave kicks and concealed his feet", while Lin wrote in a secret document circulated in 1971 that Mao was "a paranoid and a sadist . . . the greatest dictator and tyrant in China's history. Those who are his greatest friends today will be his prisoners tomorrow". On 12 September 1971 the charred body of Lin Piao was found in the wreck of an aircraft which had crashed 400 kilometres beyond the Chinese border in Mongolia. A government announcement later claimed that Lin had been trying to escape from China after a failed coup d'état in Peking.

After Lin Piao's death the PLA declined in importance and Communist Party officials began to emerge clearly as the strongest part of the 'three way alliances'. In many cases these were pre-Cultural Revolution officials who had been dismissed from office and who were now able to return to power. In the 'three way alliances' they had to face the radicals who had come to power during the Cultural Revolution. The friction that quickly grew between them was reflected in a split between moderates and radicals elected to the Politbureau in 1973.

The moderates were supported by the Party, the government administration and the armed forces. They were led by the Prime Minister, Chou En-Lai, who had quietly kept a grip on events during the Cultural Revolution, protecting valuable experts such as nuclear scientists from attack, and preventing the break-up of China into warring localities. Teng Hsiao-P'ing, who had been dismissed from high office in 1968, now returned as Chou's Deputy Prime Minister.

The radicals drew their support from the trade unions, the militia and the Communist Youth League. They also largely controlled the press and the radio. Chief among the radicals were Chiang Ch'ing, Mao's wife, and three Shanghai politicians. This 'Gang of Four', as the foreign press dubbed them, also had the advantage of access, through Chiang Ch'ing, to Chairman Mao, who was now in virtual retirement.

What divided the moderates and the radicals? The moderates wanted to achieve some kind of political stability in order to concentrate on economic growth and development. This, they believed, should take precedence over political arguments within the Party. As Teng Hsiao-P'ing put it, "What does it matter if the cat's black or white, so long as it catches mice?" For the radicals, however, class struggle was 'the key link'. Whilst they agreed with the moderates on the need for economic growth, they also thought that the 'elimination of bourgeois rights' must accompany it. This in turn would involve a revival of the Cultural Revolution.

The Rise and Fall of the Gang of Four

In January 1974 the start of a radical campaign seemed to herald exactly that. Known as 'Pi Lin, Pi Kung', the campaign attacked the thought of Confucius (see page 246) on the grounds that it had been the ideology of conservative and 'bourgeois' forces throughout China's history. Moderation in politics was equated with the Confucian 'doctrine of the mean'. Attacks were made on the Confucian style of learning by rote still being used in many schools. 200 million propaganda leaflets were distributed all over China. And all forms of western culture were denounced for their 'bourgeois and capitalist mentality'. However, no attempt was made to revive the Red Guard movement which had been dormant since 1965.

Chou En-lai, the leader of the moderates in the Politburo, died in April 1976. This turned out to be a growth point for the moderates, not a setback. When police removed wreaths placed in his memory in Tienanmen Square in Peking, 100,000 people rioted. The Tienanmen Square riots were a display of public support for Teng Hsiao-P'ing and other moderate leaders. The radicals, however, simply blamed the riots on Teng and had him stripped of all government and Party posts. A relative newcomer to political life was appointed in his place – the 55-year-old Minister of Public Security, Hua Kuo-feng.

With Chou and Teng out of the way, the radical Gang of Four seemed to be firmly in control of the political life of China. When, on 9 September 1976, Mao Tse-tung died, they intensified their propaganda campaign against the moderates and prepared to take power. On 7 October, however, the Politbureau elected the new Prime Minister, Hua Kuo-feng, to the post of Chairman of the Party. As Hua was already Prime Minister, and as the Party Chairman commands the armed forces, he thus acquired control of the Party, the government and the army, a concentration of powers that even Mao had never enjoyed. On the same day the Gang of Four was arrested and imprisoned.

The arrest of the Gang of Four was followed by a major propaganda campaign against them. In the press and on wall posters, their political attitudes as well as their personal behaviour were attacked. They were depicted as luxury-loving, callous, petty tyrants. Posters demanded such punishments for them as 'Deep-fry the Gang of Four in Oil!' And while they were being vilified in this way, Teng Hsiao-P'ing was restored to all the positions from which he had been expelled in April 1976.

At a Party Congress in 1977 Hua Kuo-feng brought a long and confused chapter in China's history to a close when he delivered this epitaph on the Gang of Four:

"The Gang of Four tried their hardest to cause damage and disruption. Now that the gang has been overthrown, we are able to achieve stability and unity and attain great order across the land, in compliance with Chairman Mao's instructions. Thus the smashing of the Gang of Four marks the triumphant conclusion of our first Great Proletarian Cultural Revolution which lasted eleven years."

The New Realism in China

Under the leadership of Chairman Hua, a steady return to moderate policies began. Although the Chinese leaders continued to pay lip-service to Mao Tse-tung and the Cultural Revolution, they quietly adopted policies which reversed some of the reforms of the Cutlural Revolution. At the end of 1977 competitive entrance examinations for university courses were held for the first time in over ten years. A more liberal approach to artistic and academic life became apparent as many Chinese as well as foreign books which had been banned during the Cultural Revolution were put back on the shelves of public libraries. Traditional Chinese plays, operas and films were revived. The ideas of Confucius were declared worthy of study again.

The return to moderation accelerated in 1978 and 1979. By this time Teng Hsiao P'ing, Vice-Chairman of the Party and Deputy Prime Minister, had emerged as the dominant figure in Chinese politics. A realist first and foremost, he said "One should not talk of class struggle every day. In real life, not everything is class struggle". Accordingly, a more tolerant attitude towards religion was adopted: churches, mosques and temples which had been shut in 1966 now reopened and religious services resumed. Many of the three-way alliances formed during the Cultural Revolution were abolished. Houses and bank accounts that had been confiscated from capitalists were returned to them. And, perhaps most significant of all, the cult of personality surrounding Mao Tse-tung was slowly dismantled. Less space was given to his 'Thoughts' in the press. Public pictures of him were gradually removed. Articles appeared criticising aspects of his 'Thoughts' and policies.

By 1981 the return to moderation had gone so far that even Chairman Hua was now seen as too radical for the Party. He was thanked for his 'useful work' in the struggle against the Gang of Four, and was replaced by 66-year-old Hu Yaobang. In the same year the Gang of Four was brought to trial. Unsurprisingly, all were found guilty of all the charges made against them. Chiang Ch'ing was sentenced to death (later commuted to life imprisonment) while the others received long prison sentences.

China's Economy since the Great Leap

As we have seen, there were different emphases among China's leaders at the start of the 1960s about how the Chinese economy should be made to work. The table showing production trends between 1952 and 1973 suggests that the emphasis stayed where Mao placed it with his call for balance in his speech in 1956 on the 'ten great relationships'. By 1973 China had an important heavy industry sector making her the world's fifth largest producer of steel and third largest of coal. But whereas steel output increased by more than four times after the end of the First Five-year Plan, chemical fertilizers were produced in quantities thirty-one times greater; and tractors, non-existent in 1957, were becoming a major industry in 1973. 'Walking on two legs' was still practised; about a third of China's coal was produced in quite small commune mines and much of the cement was made in the countryside. A good part of industrial employment was shared between town and country; many regions had

Production trends in China, 1952–1973

Product	Units	1952	1957	1959	1973
Crude steel	thousand tonnes	1,349	5,350	13,400	25,500
Crude oil	thousand tonnes	436	1,458	3,700	54,500
Coal	thousand tonnes	66,490	130,732	300,000	377,000
Cement	thousand tonnes	2,861	6,680	12,300	29,900
Chemical fertiliser	thousand tonnes	194	803	1,880	24,760
Electric power	million kilowatt-hours	7,261	19,340	42,000	124,800
Machine tools	units	13,734	28,297	35,000	80,000
Tractors	units	–	–	9,400	133,263
Motor vehicles	units	–	7,500	19,400	100,000
Bicycles	thousand units	80	806	1,479	4,859
Cotton cloth	million linear metres	3,829	5,050	6,100	8,660
Grain	thousand tonnes	166,000	185,000	165,000	250,000

plants where city-manufactured truck, tractor or electric-pump components were assembled. By such means China kept her town population down to the figure of 110 million which had been established after forty million were sent back to the countryside in the Great Leap Forward. Even when a new modern industrial activity was introduced, the exphasis lay on keeping a balance between town and country. Throughout the sixties and seventies the Chinese were encouraged to "learn from Taching", the new oil field in the north-east where wheat fields ran right up to the drills.

Taching became one of the main sources of China's spanking new export trade, selling oil to her industrialised neighbour Japan. This was an example of the re-direction of China's trade since the 1950s when about three-quarters was with the Soviet Union and her satellites. By 1974 nearly eighty per cent was with the non-Communist world, with Japan as the leading partner. The trade was directed at making the best possible use of exports to pay for import needs, rather than to boost a claim to great power status through giving aid to poorer nations.

Yet although China did not follow the two superpowers into the large-scale aid business, she claimed that her economic development was a model for other mainly agricultural countries struggling to draw nearer the so-called 'advanced' nations. The key place which she gave to combining agricultural and industrial activities showed how countries in many parts of Asia, Africa and Latin America could use their own great reserves of manpower.

From 1978 onwards new priorities for the development of the economy began to replace those originally laid down by Mao. In that year, Chairman Hua announced details of a Ten-Year Plan (1976–85), already under way, which put less stress on heavy industry than any previous Plan. The emphasis was now on creating a more modest economic structure – one appropriate to the semi-developed country that China actually was. The most noticeable change was a new emphasis on the payment of workers for work actually done. Before, piece-rates and bonuses had been condemned as 'material incentives' appropriate in a capitalist economy. Now they were paid to workers for high productivity and high standards of work. In place of the old Marxist motto 'To each according to his needs', the new motto was 'To each according to his work'.

By the mid-1980s the greatest unsolved economic problem facing the government was that of excessive population growth. With a population in 1982 of 1·008 thousand million, growing by 14 million each year, even the most optimistic forecasts suggested that there would be more people in China than could be fed by the end of the twentieth century. The government therefore adopted a campaign to persuade married couples to limit their families to one child only. Parents with one child only were to receive generous family allowances and privileges, while those having second children faced cuts in pay and loss of privileges. Many foreign observers of the Chinese scene condemned this attack on the most basic of human freedoms; others admitted that the populations of most agricultural countries were limited in far harsher ways – by flood, drought, disease and famine. And whatever else they said, the critics agreed that China under Communist rule had found answers to these.

40 Japan since the War, 1945-85

The Shock of Defeat

Japan took the aggressive way out of her problems at the start of the 1930s (see pages 103–4). Until June 1942 the policy of aggression was most successful. Japanese armed forces, without ever losing a major battle, conquered a colossal area of the Far East and the Pacific, creating a 'New Order' there, and prosperity at home. The defeats of 1942–45 therefore came as a profound shock to a nation accustomed to victory.

The physical destruction of Japan in 1945 was appalling. Some two million Japanese were dead. Around 40 per cent of all urban areas had been flattened by American bombers. Some 13 million workers were unemployed and a large part of the country's industry was at a standstill. There was no oil. Raw materials were in desperately short supply and food was so short that mass starvation threatened.

The American Occupation

The Americans had played the major role in Japan's defeat, and insisted in 1945 on a virtually free hand in dealing with her after the surrender (see page 200). General Douglas MacArthur, the Supreme Commander for the Allied Powers (SCAP – a term used also to describe the occupation authorities in general), largely ignored an Allied Council and a Far Eastern Commission which were intended to provide for allied cooperation in Japan's future development. Instead he ruled the country as an 'American Shogun', remote and mysterious, autocratic, hard-working, and highly effective. Typical of MacArthur's approach was his attempt to avoid the mass starvation that threatened to engulf Japan in 1945. Fearing that starvation might lead to social breakdown, MacArthur used the US Army to set up soup kitchens all over Japan. When criticised for this apparently generous treatment of a recent enemy, he said, "Starvation creates unrest and violence. Give me bread or give me bullets."

MacArthur's first task as SCAP was to disarm and disband Japan's armed forces. The demobilisation of the army was achieved peacefully, with Japanese commanders carrying out the orders themselves. Subsequently arms factories, arsenals and military bases were taken apart and scrapped. Organisations devoted to militarism were suppressed, including the state-supported Shinto religion. Over a thousand war criminals were rounded up: a trial of the major suspects resulted in the execution of seven of them, including former Prime Ministers Tojo and Hirota. A purge of militarists led to 200,000 people being expelled from government jobs. The police force, feared during the war as much as the Gestapo had been feared in Germany, was reorganised and its top officers dismissed.

The disarmament of Japan was quickly followed by measures to liberalise the country's political life. Press censorship was abolished. Political prisoners were released. Elections were held for a new Diet, or parliament. And the Emperor Hirohito, in a radio broadcast on 1 January 1946, renounced the claim of the Japanese emperors that they ruled with divine authority, and that the fate of the Japanese people was to rule the world. Hirohito became a figure-head emperor with no real power, but this did not mean that his importance was diminished. The American occupiers were well aware of the profound loyalty that the Emperor commanded. Hirohito could make or break American policy with the lead he gave his people. With his support a peaceful transition to democracy would be possible. Without Hirohito – if, for example, he was tried and executed as a war criminal – there would be the prospect of violent resistance and social chaos. A new constitution, the Showa Constitution, introduced in May 1947, therefore recognised the Emperor as 'the symbol of the State and of the unity of the people'. It vested power in an elected Diet from which a Prime Minister and a cabinet were to be chosen, and it also defined the civil rights of citizens and renounced war as a means of settling disputes.

The Showa Constitution added to the power of Yoshida Shigeru, Japan's most senior politician who had become Prime Minister early in 1946. Yoshida had already gained the approval of the Americans for demanding an early peace in 1945, while the Japanese respected him for standing up to SCAP and insisting that MacArthur watered down some of the more extreme ideas for 'Americanisation'. Now that he was Prime Minister of a democratic country, his reputation among both the Japanese and Americans increased. With a brief interlude in opposition, he remained as Prime Minister until his resignation in 1954.

The Americans poured relief aid into Japan at a rate

which reached $400 million a year by 1947. It was clear that thorough economic reform was needed if Japan were to support herself without American help. An important step towards economic recovery was a Farm Land Reform Act passed in 1946. Before this act, almost half Japan's farmland was cultivated by landless share-croppers who had to give 50 per cent of the harvest to their landlords. Over the next three years, landlords now had to sell over 2 million hectares of farmland to the government which then sold it to the share-croppers at low prices. As a result more than two million landless farmers became property-owners, farming the land more efficiently than before and with a vested interest in supporting the government that had allowed them to do so.

In industry MacArthur attempted to break up the giant cartels known as *zaibatsu* which dominated the Japanese economy. These family-owned financial, commercial and industrial combines controlled 80 per cent of Japan's business activity. Some had clearly defined areas of activity – for example Kawasaki in shipbuilding and steel – while the largest, such as Mitsubishi, were vast banking, trade and industrial empires working through hundreds of smaller firms and employing hundreds of thousands of workers. A series of laws in 1945 broke up the *zaibatsu* and sold off their assets. At the same time, laws were passed to protect workers and to encourage trade union membership which grew rapidly as a result.

Socially, Japan experienced some important changes under American occupation. A number of laws passed by the Diet improved the status and rights of women and gave them the vote, while a Eugenics Law of 1948 made abortion legal and easy to obtain. The educational system was thoroughly reformed, with the curriculum, teaching methods and textbooks being subjected to American-style changes. A purge of the teaching force removed supporters of the war-time militarist régime. Compulsory school attendance was increased from six to nine years, and many new schools and colleges were built.

In 1948 the aims of the American occupiers underwent an important change. Up until then the Americans had intended to sign a peace treaty with Japan and then evacuate her, leaving her disarmed and demilitarised. But the alarming development of a Cold War between the Capitalist West and the Communist East (see page 210) embroiled Japan in the American policy of containing Communism. The Communist seizure of

power in China in 1949 and the Communist invasion of South Korea in 1950 persuaded the Americans that Japan must become the key link in a chain of defences against Communism in the Far East. To strengthen Japan's economy, the American government therefore provided huge new quantities of aid. American-financed food imports doubled. The *zaibatsu* were allowed to re-establish themselves. The right to strike was denied to government employees, while Communists were purged from trade unions. Although the Constitution had renounced war and the creation of armed forces, a National Police Reserve was created in 1950, consisting of 70,000 well-equipped men who looked remarkably like infantry soldiers armed with mortars, machine-guns, tanks and aircraft.

The Korean War of 1950–53 brought Japan ever closer into America's schemes for containing Communism. It also brought great benefits to the Japanese economy. The islands of Japan provided an excellent base for thousands of affluent US troops on their way to or from Korea. Japanese industries quickly geared themselves up to provide for the needs of the Americans and their allies. And in 1951 the victors of the Second World War, with the exception of China and the USSR, signed the peace treaty of San Francisco with Japan. Japan was to become a fully independent nation in April 1952. She would not pay reparations for her actions in the Second World War. And while the Americans occupied the Ryukyu Islands, including Okinawa, and were granted long leases on military bases in Japan, the country remained intact and did not suffer division of the sort inflicted on Germany in 1945.

Japan's economic miracle

By the time the Americans left in 1952, the Japanese economy had largely recovered from the war. The economy then entered a twenty-year period of growth which averaged 9·7 per cent each year. This was nearly twice the rate of growth of any other major industrial nation in the post-war period. Shipbuilding, textiles, electronics and car-manufacturing were the industries that grew most quickly. By 1968 Japan's Gross National Product was the third highest in the world. By 1978 she had a steel industry as big as America's and nearly as big as that of the EEC. By the mid-1980s Japan had overtaken them in many areas of new technology – computers, telecommunications, nuclear power, electronics, robotics – and had become in some respects the world's leading industrial power.

There were many reasons for Japan's remarkable economic growth. The American occupation and the stimulus of the Korean War allowed Japan to recover quickly from the Second World War. Her friendship with the USA meant that Japan could rely on American military protection and thus spend relatively little on armaments. A low level of government spending on social services and a lack of overseas commitments meant that there was plenty of capital to invest in new plant. The labour force proved to be exceptionally hard-working, and its willingness to accept wage-restraint helped to keep production costs down. A high rate of personal saving meant that banks had vast amounts of capital to lend to industry. A series of stable governments, mostly of the conservative Liberal-Democratic Party, ensured that government economic policy was consistent throughout the 1950s and 1960s.

Economic growth, however, brought with it some unwelcome social developments. Although the growth of the population was levelling out by the mid-1960s, a steady movement of the rural population into the cities meant that by 1970 a quarter of all Japanese people lived in the Tokyo-Nagoya-Osaka urban belt. Overcrowding was accompanied by the pollution of rivers, the sea and the atmosphere, by poor sanitation in cramped housing complexes, by traffic congestion and road accidents, by the disruption of village communities and family ties, and by growing industrial ugliness in a land renowned for its beauty.

Awareness of these issues led to a national debate in the early 1970s about whether to continue with all-out economic growth, or to aim instead at an improved quality of life. Public opinion increasingly demanded a slower rate of growth and greater emphasis on welfare provision and environmental control. At the same time, the oil-price rise of 1973 resulted in high inflation and a renewed awareness that Japan is dangerously dependent on the rest of the world for raw materials and for energy. Since the oil 'shokku' of 1973 Japan has therefore experienced the same difficulties as many other oil-hungry industrial nations: increasing unemployment, a decline of her traditional industries, currency inflation and a reduction of trade.

Japan and the World

At the time of the 'sneak' attack on Pearl Harbour in 1941, no one could have foreseen that ten years later America and Japan would be allies in the defence of the 'free world'. Yet this is exactly how the relationship between them appeared in 1951. Within hours of signing the Treaty of San Francisco in that year, the Japanese government also signed a Security Pact with the USA, agreeing to supply military bases for American forces and allowing some of the occupying forces to remain on Japanese soil.

There was no shortage of critics of this intimate relationship. Japanese socialists led protests against the American presence. When the 1951 Security Pact was renewed as the Mutual Security Pact in 1960, violent left-wing demonstrations caused the Prime Minister to resign. American occupation of the Rykuku and Bonin Islands, and the maintenance of nuclear weapons on Okinawa, led to further violent protests in 1968 and 1969, as did the renewal of the Mutual Security Pact in 1970. (However, Okinawa was returned to Japan in 1972.) Although American-Japanese relations cooled in 1971 when the US government imposed a 10 per cent surcharge on Japanese imports, Japan has remained firmly under the strategic umbrella of the US armed forces, and their dependence on the USA is regarded by most Japanese as one of the facts of life.

Japan's relationship with America led to difficult relations with her Communist neighbours, Russia and China, neither of whom signed the Treaty of San Francisco. Although Russia had not gone to war with Japan until August 1945, diplomatic relations between the two were not restored until 1956, and today there is still no official peace treaty between them. In the economic sphere, however, there has been some co-operation. The Russians have welcomed Japanese investment and technology in opening up oil, gas and mineral deposits in Siberia, and this has provided the Japanese in return with a new source of energy and raw materials.

As an ally of both America and Taiwan, Japan followed a policy of non-recognition towards the People's Republic of China during the 1950s and 1960s. But following President Nixon's visit to China in 1971, Japan established diplomatic links with the People's Republic and trade between them increased rapidly. In 1972 Japan made an official apology for war-crimes committed during their occupation of China, and China gave up all claims to reparations in return. The signing in 1978 of a Treaty of Peace and Friendship normalized relations between the two countries.

41 Western Europe since the War, 1945–85

At the start of this century Western Europe was the very centre of the world. Although the USA had already outstripped the leading European countries in the league tables of industrial output, she had hardly begun to compete with the collective influence of the old nations of Western Europe in terms of commercial and financial weight, of military and naval power, of control over the lives of other people in other lands.

One of the major themes of this book has been the decay and the destruction of much of that influence. In 1945, at the end of the second great war of this century, Western Europe lay in the tatters of its former glory – virtually bankrupt, facing the grim prospect of a long struggle to reach pre-war levels of production and standards of living, and apparently dependent for its very survival on the goodwill of the USA. Half of Germany was now controlled by Communist Russia, along with the eastern half of Europe where the Western nations had once enjoyed great political and economic influence. The United Kingdom, once the world's supreme trading power and the great lender of money to other lands, was now a debtor nation. The war had overtaxed her resources: in victory she lifted up a begging bowl.

There were further shocks in store. By the middle of the 1960s the great colonial empires had disintegrated (see Chapters 34, 43, and 44). There were no longer such places as British India, French Equatorial Africa, the Dutch East Indies, and the Belgian Congo. After so many years of worldwide, lordly authority, the nations of Western Europe suddenly possessed little more than themselves. The subject of this chapter is the story, so far as we can tell it, of how those nations have learned to live with the fact that, separately and together, they have come down in the world.

Political Reconstruction

The war in Europe had been fought against anti-democratic régimes of the extreme right – the German Nazis and the Italian Fascists; and now, after 1945, the Cold War was to be waged against a totalitarian régime of the extreme left – the Soviet Communists. It was hardly surprising, therefore, that the nations of Western Europe returned to parliamentary democracy as their form of government; although some picked up their old patterns of politics faster than others.

In Britain Churchill's coalition government, which had taken emergency powers to wage war against the Axis Powers, soon came to an end. In the general election of July 1945 (held even before the defeat of Japan) the Labour Party, led by Clement Attlee, won by a landslide. For the first time Labour came to power with an absolute majority of seats in the House of Commons. With the election had come the ending of the emergency powers of the coalition and it was now back to business as usual with two major parties (Labour and the Conservatives) forming, respectively, the Government and the Opposition in a democratically elected Parliament.

The French took longer to get back to normal. Their old constitution, that of the Third Republic, had been discredited by the rapid collapse of the army in 1940 and by the ways in which the Vichy régime had collaborated with Hitler's Reich. In October 1945, elections were held for a Constituent Assembly to write the country a new constitution. The parties which gained most votes were a new conservative Catholic party, the *Mouvement Républicain Populaire* (MRP), the Communists, and the Radicals. As the Constituent Assembly settled down to its work, a Provisional Government, headed by Charles de Gaulle, set about the business of restoring a disturbed society to normal.

The "guilty men" of Vichy were quickly dealt with: Laval was executed and Pétain imprisoned for life. Writing a new constitution was a much more difficult matter to find agreement on. Some politicians wanted all power given to the Assembly, while others proposed a clean break with the old constitution. De Gaulle wanted to make the future Presidents of France more powerful and free of the need to seek support for their policies from political parties which were often divided along regional and religious, as well as class, lines.

Two attempts to form a new constitution resulted in a compromise by which the National Assembly was given the power to approve or reject a government and its policies. The trouble was that France had many political parties, none of which won enough seats in an election to be able to form a majority government. Any government, therefore, was bound to be a coalition dependent on its loosely organised supporters in the Assembly. A disagreement between them could mean the end of the government. To de Gaulle's disgust the Fourth Republic was not very different from the

Third. The General took himself off to Colombey-les-deux-Églises, a village in eastern France, far away from the political squabbles in Paris, to await the time when France might need him again.

After the new elections to the National Assembly of 1947 the three main political parties to hold the stage were the MRP, the Communists and the Socialists, with a fourth party started by de Gaulle's supporters – the *Rassemblement du Peuple Français* (RPF) – on the sidelines. In 1947 the Socialists, Radicals and the MRP joined together to exclude the Communists from a share in power after they had supported anti-government strikes. This new alliance, called the Third Force, had an overall majority in the Assembly and politicians from within it were to form the governments of France until 1958. The very different interests of the three member parties led to much instability. De Gaulle's fears were borne out: between January 1947 and June 1954 alone, France had fifteen governments.

Of the two defeated Western European powers, Italy and Germany, the former returned to parliamentary democracy the more quickly. By early 1948 the Italian Parliament was working again for the first time since Mussolini had suspended the constitution and put in its place an authoritarian, Fascist régime. Only the king was missing: after all the dubious antics of Victor Emmanuel III, the Italians had decided that an elected President was a safer bet as head of state.

The constitution of the new West German state set up in 1949 (see Chapter 35, page 214) was in many respects similar to that of the Weimar Republic of the 1920s. Every adult citizen had the right to vote in the elections to the *Bundestag* (the German equivalent of the House of Commons). In addition the constitution gave considerable power to the Republic's eleven *länder* (states): each had its own elected government and also sent representatives to the upper house of the Federal Parliament, the *Bundesrat*. There were, however, some new rules. The President was to be merely a ceremonial head of state, elected by both houses of parliament, and the Chancellor (prime minister) could be dismissed only by "a constructive vote of no confidence" – that is, after the parliament had already chosen a candidate to succeed him. The new Republic came into being in September 1949, with Bonn as the new capital, since Berlin was now well to the east of the "iron curtain".

The conservative Christian Democratic Union (CDU), led by Dr Konrad Adenauer, had won a majority in the elections of August 1949, forming a strong coalition with the smaller Free Democratic Party (FDP), and leaving the Social Democrats (SPD) under Dr Kurt Schumacher as the official opposition.

Economic and Social Reconstruction

In each of those four major Western European countries – Britain, France, West Germany and Italy – there was an urgent need to reconstruct war-damaged economies, and evidence of a desire to create better, fairer societies; and the patterns of both reconstruction and reform would be decided by central governments. Before and during the war some governments had taken control of basic industries, of communications systems, of central banks. Now, in peacetime, some of the new governments decided to extend such controls by 'nationalising' – that is, bringing into state or public ownership – certain other vital industries and services.

In Britain the new Labour government nationalised not only the coal industry, the railway network, the Bank of England, the generation and distribution of electricity and gas, and more of the civil aviation industry (the British Overseas Airways Corporation had already been set up in the 1930s), but also the iron and steel industry and road transport. The newly nationalised industries were to be run as public corporations, with their day-to-day management in the hands of boards, whose members were appointed by the government. Although a Conservative government later returned both iron and steel and road transport to private ownership, it was significant that they did not attempt a grand sweep of de-nationalisation. For Britain, as for France and Italy, a mixed economy – part capitalist and part state-owned – was here to stay.

Labour also went ahead with a programme for social reform that had been outlined in a wartime report prepared in 1942 by a committee under Sir William Beveridge, a former senior civil servant. The report proposed a comprehensive scheme of insurance to meet the costs of sickness and unemployment benefits, and old-age pensions. Beveridge further argued that the state had a responsibility to provide a minimum income and basic standards of medical care, housing and education for its citizens. Put simply, his aim was to do battle with the "five giants" of want, idleness, disease, squalor and ignorance.

The struggle against one "giant" – ignorance – had begun before the war against Nazi Germany was over.

In 1944 R. A. Butler's Education Act was passed, which laid down that there should be free secondary education for all, and suggested that local authorities should set up three types of school – grammar, modern and technical. Children were to be allocated places in those schools according to their age, ability and aptitude: but in practice that meant selection at eleven-plus by examinations which attempted to test intelligence.

In their 1945 election manifesto, Labour promised to carry out the rest of Beveridge's proposals. The Family Allowances Act (1945), giving a money allowance for every child after the first, had been passed before the election: the rest followed in the legislation of the Attlee government. The Industrial Injuries Act (1946) and the National Insurance Act (1946) provided for insurance against industrial injury, unemployment and sickness. Provision was also made for maternity and funeral grants and an improved scheme of old-age pensions. All those welfare benefits were to be paid for by contributions from workers, employers and the government. The National Health Act (1946) set up the National Health Service, which from July 1948 provided free medical treatment in hospitals as well as by general practitioners, dentists and opticians.

The National Assistance Act (1948) transferred responsibility for the relief of poverty from local bodies to a new National Assistance Board. People whose incomes from welfare benefits were below what was judged to be subsistence level could now apply for supplementary benefits, to be paid out of the government's tax revenue, not out of rates. That financial assistance was still subject to a personal 'means test', but the Act firmly put an end to the pre-war system of cutting the 'dole' if there was an earning lodger, or even furniture which might be sold, in the house. While Beveridge's "five giants" had by no means been defeated, Attlee's Labour government had created what was, for its time, a humane and comprehensive system of welfare for British citizens.

No other Western European government was able to put new policies and reforms into effect as quickly as Labour did in Britain. In France, Italy and Germany the first priority in the immediate post-war years had to be given to creating workable political systems. But soon the governments of those countries began to improve their welfare schemes and to re-organise aspects of their economies. As you would expect, they made progress in their own ways, in their own time.

The French were already used to some degree of public ownership of industry: before the war the French state had controlled most of the railway network and had owned, wholly or partly, about eighty industrial enterprises. In 1946 the Provisional Government set up a Commission (the *Commissariat du Plan*) to devise a programme for the country's long-term economic development and to see that the programme was carried out. The *Commissariat*, headed by Jean Monnet, was virtually an independent organisation within the state: while governments came and went, its planners carried on, more or less undisturbed, with their work of modernising French agriculture and directing investment to where it was most needed – at first into heavy industry and the supply of energy. An extension of public ownership played an important part in this re-shaping of the French economy. The whole of the rail network was nationalised; so were the electricity and gas industries, the biggest companies in the air-craft-construction and petroleum industries, and the major banks and saving institutions. The state also took over a number of enterprises whose previous owners had disgraced themselves by collaborating with the Nazi occupiers during the war. Of those, the Renault car company was the largest and most important.

As in France, so in Italy the public ownership of large industrial concerns had begun before the war. In the early 1930s the state-controlled IRI (*Istituto per la Riconstruzione Industriale*) had taken over a large number of manufacturing and commercial firms. In the twenty years after 1945, IRI grew in a very big way as its subsidiary companies penetrated all the key sectors of the Italian economy. One company, *Finsider*, came to own most of the steel industry; another, *Finmare*, controlled the major shipping companies; while *Fincanteli* dominated shipbuilding, and *Finmeccanica* took over many engineering firms, including Alfa Romeo. IRI also took over the state airline, *Alitalia*, radio and television, a number of large banks and the developing network of toll-paying motorways. Outside the control of IRI were two other big nationalised concerns: ENI (*Ente Nazionale Idrocarburi*) ran the Italian petroleum industry after 1953; while from 1962 ENEL (*Ente delle Imprese Ellettriche*) was in charge of the generation and distribution of electricity.

When the new state of West Germany was created after the war, its Federal government inherited control of the railways and of a few industrial concerns, the largest of which were the Volkswagen car firm and

VEBA (*Vereinigte Elektrizitäts- und Bergwerke*), a company with interests in the electrical, mining, chemical and metallurgical industries. However, the attitude of the new German government to public ownership was the opposite of that taken by the British, the French and the Italians. Instead of nationalising more industries, the Germans *de*-nationalised those already under state control. By the mid-1960s both Volkswagen and VEBA were back in private ownership: the only large industrial concern left in the hands of the state was the railway system.

As you have just seen, there was considerable disagreement in Western Europe about the desirability of extending state control over industry. In contrast, all governments were generally in favour of improving the scale and quality of their countries' welfare schemes. As in Britain, the pre-war levels of social services in France, Italy, Germany and other countries were raised; and new standards were set in education, medical care and housing. Again, different governments moved at different paces; and their spending on welfare was decided by how great a proportion of national income they believed could be diverted to improve social services. By the late 1950s, Germany would be ahead of all the others in terms of the cost of the services and the scale of the benefits provided for her citizens.

The Revival of Europe

However they began to re-organise their economies, the Western European governments were unable, by themselves, to resolve their countries' post-war economic problems. But, as we have already seen (in Chapter 35, page 207), early in the Cold War the USA decided to prop up the states of Western Europe with 'Marshall Aid'. The bulk of that aid was made available between 1948 and 1952, amounted to about $13·5 billion, and was distributed by the OEEC. Britain received the largest share, over $3 billion; France took $2·7 billion, Italy $1·5 billion and West Germany $1·4 billion. And at the same time as they were receiving those injections of American aid, the countries of Western Europe were also benefiting from the effects of an economic boom in the USA. The rising demand for manufactured goods led to increased European exports to the States, while more American money was invested in European industry. By the early 1950s Western Europe was enjoying a remarkable success: industrial output was already way ahead of pre-war

levels; the grim post-war years of austerity and rationing were fading into memories; and people's living standards had begun to rise.

Only a few countries in the OEEC did not share fully in the general prosperity of the booming fifties – countries such as Portugal, Norway, Iceland and Turkey – and two of those could hardly be described as Western European. The customs union between the Benelux countries (see Chapter 33, page 197) stimulated both production and trade, while both West Germany and Italy enjoyed such rapid increases in manufacturing output and trade that their performances were referred to by some as "economic miracles". And along with the new prosperity – with the new cars and new clothes, with television sets and washing machines on the never-never – came political conservatism, a general desire to limit radical changes for the time being and to enjoy a better life.

In West Germany, Konrad Adenauer's Christian Democratic Union established itself as the governing party. In Italy the Christian Democrats held on to power, though in coalitions with smaller parties, while in France the more conservative parties all made gains in elections to the National Assembly. In Britain, Winston Churchill led the Conservative Party to only a narrow electoral victory in 1951; but thirteen more years would pass, and three more Tory prime ministers – Anthony Eden, Harold Macmillan and Alec Douglas-Home – before the Labour Party came to power again.

By and large the new conservative mood in Western Europe was not an expression of a wish to turn the clock back, to abolish welfare reforms, or to undo nationalisation where it had been carried out. Two political slogans illustrate the mood of the times. In the West German elections of 1957 the main CDU slogan was "No Experiments – Konrad Adenauer". In the British general election of 1959 the governing party declared "Life's better with the Conservatives – don't let Labour ruin it." But the general quality of life for many people in Britain was by now underpinned by a social security system and a Health Service that had been introduced by the Labour Party more than ten years before. And we can note at this point that the attractions of the European Communist parties declined after November 1956 when the general quality of life in Budapest (see Chapter 36, page 218) was seen to be decided not by the Hungarian government, but by Soviet tanks.

Building a New Europe on Coal and Steel

Western Europe was still a collection of separate sovereign states finding their own ways to economic salvation, although they worked together in the OEEC to administer the Marshall Plan, and by 1955 all of them were members of the same defensive military alliance – NATO. Now we must look at the ways and means by which some of them came into a closer relationship in the ten years after the war.

That war had been, in part, the result of the crude, aggressive nationalism which had been rampant in the Europe of the 1930s. One lesson of Hitler's war was, therefore, that nationalism had somehow to be tamed. A second lesson was that the Führer's attempt to impose a "new order" had resulted in the vilest oppression. Yet where he had pulled most of Europe together by force, surely the free countries in the Western half could now form a new community in peace?

Besides drawing the fangs of nationalism, such a community could have other advantages: it could present a united front against the advance of European communism; provide a huge, tariff-free market for the industries and agriculture of its member countries; and preserve a true European identity which tasted neither Soviet nor American.

In August 1949 a new organisation was created, the Council of Europe, whose aim was "to achieve a greater unity between its Members for the purpose of safeguarding and realising the ideals and principles which are their common heritage". Its members were Belgium, Denmark, Ireland, France, Italy, Luxembourg, the Netherlands, Norway, Sweden and the UK. Other countries joined later – Greece, Iceland, Turkey, West Germany, Austria, Cyprus, Switzerland and Malta. The Council was a further step in European co-operation, but it was not a move towards integration. It had no authority over its member states, and its most important work was to be its recommendations on the protection of human rights rather than in bringing about any closer political or economic relationships.

But in May 1950 Robert Schuman, the French Foreign Minister, proposed a plan for setting up a new, though limited, community of nations in Western Europe – a plan which would, at the same time, provide a solution for a difficult economic problem. The boom

in the West had created a sudden increase in demand for steel; yet the only quick way to expand steel production was to bring back into operation German industrial plant which had been kept standing more or less idle since the war for fear that it might be used for rearmament. The 'Schuman Plan', which was really the brainchild of Jean Monnet, proposed a new organisation to manage all steel and coal production in Germany and France; while certain other countries would be invited to take part in the scheme. It was a bold and imaginative idea: it would bring two old enemies together in a common concern; it would stimulate two heavy industries, which would themselves encourage further economic expansion; and it would set up a new 'supranational' authority to create a kind of tariff-free 'common market' in which there would be no customs barriers to restrict trade in coal and steel across Western Europe.

The French asked the six governments of Belgium, Britain, West Germany, Italy, Luxembourg and the Netherlands to discuss the plan with them. Five accepted and they, with France, signed the Treaty of Paris in April 1951 that set up the European Coal and Steel Community (ECSC), which would begin operations from the end of July 1952. Britain was the odd man out.

British attitudes to Europe were complex. There were the coarse British, who believed that all foreigners were suspect, whether they came from Calais, Cologne or the Congo – and it was best not to get too closely involved with them. In contrast, there were those who pointed out that the two world wars had drawn Britain into very close involvement with Europe and that after both wars her troops had acted as armies of occupation on the continent. They argued that a closer British association with Europe might help to prevent future wars. Others again, including many influential people in government and in the two major political parties, agreed with Winston Churchill's old definition of Britain's relationship with the continent: "We are with Europe but not of it."

They considered that to enter a European community, to become part of the continent, would place intolerable limits on Britain's role in the wider world. For at the beginning of the 1950s Britain still had a large overseas empire and a growing Commonwealth; and her leaders believed that she had a 'special relationship' with the United States, based on language and something of a common culture, which had been strengthened by the close cooperation of the two countries during the war.

So Britain did not join the ECSC and did not, therefore, take part in the first experiment in a limited form of European integration. The day-to-day running of the Community's business was in the hands of the High Authority, located in Luxembourg. To pay for its own upkeep the Authority had the right to levy taxes on coal and steel production – a right which national governments had previously reserved for themselves. A Special Council of Ministers – one from each of the six member countries – helped to coordinate the work of the Authority with the policies of their governments; while a Court of Justice was set up to decide arguments which arose between the Authority, coal and steel companies and the six governments. And lastly there was a Common Assembly, made up of seventy-eight people nominated from the six national parliaments. That Assembly could not make laws; but it provided a link between the non-elected Authority and the democratically elected parliaments. All in all, the ECSC officials learnt a great deal about organising a relationship between the heavy industries of different countries, but the Community was very limited in scope and a long way from the kind of full integration of the European economy towards which people like Monnet wanted to move.

Towards a European Community

Almost before the ink on the Treaty of Paris was dry, the six countries that were to form the ECSC had begun to consider setting up a European Defence Community (EDC). The outbreak of the Korean War in June 1950 (page 211) had raised alarms that the Soviet Union might take action against Western Europe. The EDC, suggested by the French Prime Minister, René Pleven, in October 1950, was to be a six-nation answer to that possibility: it would establish a combined European army, into which West German forces could be integrated. It would, at one and the same time, strengthen the West's defences and also bring France and Germany into an even closer partnership. A draft treaty setting up the EDC was signed in Paris in May 1952; but that did not satisfy Europeans like Monnet. A combined European army had to mean an agreed European foreign policy – otherwise the new Europe would have no body to decide on the use of its armed force. Thus, an EDC must lead to an

EPC (European Political Community) – so why not immediately set up a single EC (European Community) which would integrate industry and trade as well as defence and foreign policy!

It was too much to ask too soon. By the time the French parliament debated the question of France's membership of the EDC, in August 1954, the Korean War was over and Stalin was dead. There was no longer the same urgent need to rearm the recent enemy, Germany, especially since Britain was clearly unwilling to commit herself to keeping an army permanently in Europe. The French parliament rejected the EDC, and in doing so it killed off the EPC too. Instead the six countries formed together with Britain the much looser Western European Union. But since NATO had already been set up, with American backing, as the main military alliance in Western Europe, the WEU was doomed from the beginning to be of secondary importance.

Even so, the governments of the six countries decided to take West European integration a stage further than the ECSC. In May and June 1955 the foreign ministers of the six countries met at Messina, in Sicily, and drew up proposals for sharing information and work on the uses of atomic energy and for setting up a full customs union, or common market. Early in 1956 those proposals were approved by the Common Assembly of the ECSC; and one year later, in March 1957, two treaties were signed in Rome by representatives of the six nations. One treaty established the European Atomic Energy Community (Euratom); while the other – usually referred to as *the* Treaty of Rome – set up the European Economic Community (EEC). By the end of the year the parliaments of all six countries had approved the treaties, and the two new communities officially came into existence on 1 January 1958.

The task of the EEC (which most people called the Common Market) was to pull its member countries into a much closer relationship than they had ever before experienced. For example, the Treaty of Rome clearly set out the aim of abolishing all "obstacles to freedom of movement for persons, services and capital" between the six member states. Each country entered the new Community expecting benefits for its own economy from a customs-free market which would be protected against goods from outside 'the Six' by a common external tariff. Tariffs within the Community were to be phased out in six stages over twelve years to ensure that none of the manufacturers and farmers of 'the Six' would be damaged by sudden exposure to trading competition on equal terms.

The administration of the EEC was based on that of the ECSC. The day-to-day business of the Community was to be decided by a Commission of nine members – two each from West Germany, France and Italy; and one each from the three Benelux countries. The major decisions of policy, based on recommendations from the Commission, were to be taken by a Council of Ministers from the member governments. The Parliamentary Assembly of the EEC was similar to the Common Assembly of the ECSC; while a Court of Justice was set up to give judgement in cases of disputes between members.

Seven into Six Won't Go

Attitudes to the new EEC varied. Within the Community itself there were people who thought that the integration of six European states had gone far enough; that to aim at more than a 'common market' would threaten national parliaments and governments with a loss of power they could not and would not accept. Others, who now saw themselves as Europeans first, and as Frenchmen or Italians or Belgians second, insisted that integration had a momentum of its own and that the EEC was merely a stage in the development of the 'United States of Europe'.

The Western European countries outside the EEC viewed it with mixed feelings. Some of them refused to consider applying for membership because they could not accept any loss of their own sovereignty – control of their own affairs. Others believed their economies would have been too weak to stand up to equal competition in the Common Market, and now feared that their highly priced products would be excluded from it by the EEC's external tariff. The British government regarded the Community with irritation and resentment. They refused to become involved in a set-up which they were sure would limit Britain's world role, downgrade the powers of her parliament and government, and weaken her trading links with the Commonwealth. At the time three-quarters of Britain's trade was with countries outside Europe: her government believed that Western Europe needed Britain more than she needed the EEC. Yet there was an uneasy feeling that the EEC would grow into a community of great economic, commercial and political power over which Britain would have no control.

In 1958 Britain tried to persuade the members of the newly created EEC to join in a much looser and wider association of countries, which together would work towards customs-free trade in industrial goods. 'The Six' turned down the proposal, but Britain continued her negotiations with six other members of the OEEC – Austria, Denmark, Norway, Portugal, Sweden and Switzerland. In January 1960 representatives of those six countries and the British signed the Stockholm Convention, which established the European Free Trade Association (EFTA), within which all tariffs on industrial goods were to be abolished by 1970. Western Europe now had an Outer Seven as well as an Inner Six.

The OEEC, which had been set up to aid post-war European recovery, had outlived its purpose. In 1961 it was replaced by a new body with a much greater geographical scope, the Organisation for Economic Co-operation and Development (OECD), to which would eventually belong all the industrialised countries of the 'free world', including the USA, Canada, Australia and Japan.

Making Six into Nine

In 1961 Harold Macmillan's government applied for British membership of the EEC, and the governments of Denmark, Ireland and Norway followed suit. Conservative leaders knew the Community was on the way to economic success and that 'the Six' were already discussing closer forms of integration, and they wanted to exert British influence over its future shape and policies.

The Labour Party opposed this new 'European' policy, chiefly on the grounds that it would damage trade with the Commonwealth and limit the sovereignty of the Westminster Parliament to decide British affairs. They needn't have worried. In January 1963 President de Gaulle announced that he didn't want Britain in the Community – and that, despite the anger his statement aroused in the other five EEC countries, was that. De Gaulle declared that if Britain were allowed in, and insisted on retaining her close relationship with the USA, then "in the end there would appear a colossal Atlantic Community under American dependence and leadership which would soon swallow up the European Community".

Four years later, in 1967, Harold Wilson's Labour government made a second attempt to get Britain into the EEC. Britain's worsening economic performance during the sixties, compared with the steady progress of those inside the Community, had wrought a marvellous change in the attitudes of Labour Party leaders to Europe. Yet before the year was out Charles de Gaulle had done it again – a loud French "Non" to the British application.

In 1969 de Gaulle retired, to the relief of the British leaders, and by the end of that year 'the Six' had agreed that British membership of the Community was desirable. De Gaulle died in 1970, and in May 1971 the new British Conservative Prime Minister, Edward Heath, received a firm assurance from the new French President, Georges Pompidou, that this time France would not stand in Britain's way. The negotiations on the terms of Britain's entry – how she would adapt to Community ways and how much she would contribute to the Community budget – were quickly completed. Similar negotiations were held between 'the Six' and three other countries – Denmark, Ireland and Norway. In January 1972 Britain and the other three newcomers signed treaties by which they would enter the Community as full members on the first day of 1973. Before that day came, referenda* were held in Denmark, Ireland and Norway, to give the final decision on entry to the people. The Danes and the Irish voted for membership of the Community: only the Norwegians voted against. A referendum had never been held in Britain and Heath's Conservative government saw no good reason to break with tradition; so Britain's entry into Europe was simply approved by Parliament. On 1 January 1973 'the Six' became 'the Nine'.

Britain's long, roundabout journey to the Market was not quite over. Harold Wilson, the Labour leader, insisted that the terms of entry secured by the Conservative government were not good enough. They could be, and would be, renegotiated by the next Labour government, which would then hold a referendum on the new terms. Accordingly, in 1974, the new Labour government began its discussions with the Community, mainly in an attempt to cut the amount that the Conservatives had agreed that Britain should pay into the central budget. James Callaghan, the Foreign Secretary, persuaded the Community to make concessions; the British government approved the new

* A referendum is a vote by all electors on a single question.

terms; and in June 1975 the British people voted, in the first referendum in their history, by two to one to accept the terms and stay in. Britain had finally become part of Western Europe exactly twenty-five years after Schuman announced his Plan. Back in 1950 the British could have had membership of a European community on virtually any terms they chose to make.

The New Community

In 1967, before 'the Six' became Nine, the independent organisations of the ECSC, Euratom and the EEC were merged into a single European Community, with its Commission in Brussels, its Parliament in Strasbourg, and its Court of Justice in Luxembourg.

By July 1968, eighteen months ahead of schedule, tariffs on trade within the Community had been abolished. In the late sixties and early seventies discussions began on ways of moving towards political and monetary union, but they decided very little. Although the Community was a supranational organisation, with the task of integrating the economies of its member countries, the power to take major economic decisions still remained in the grip of national governments.

In the early 1970s, when 'the Six' became Nine, two significant changes occurred. In 1973 the Community's Regional Development Fund was set up to help the poorer parts of the EEC by providing money for investment in industry and in essential services such as better roads, railways and electricity supplies. It was surprising that it had taken so long to develop a policy aimed at narrowing the gap in standards of living between the Community's richest and poorest regions; yet even by 1978 the money available for investment by the Fund was small compared with the sums allotted to other purposes.

The second change was in the Community's relationships with the developing countries. Until Britain became a member in 1973, the EEC had been accused of being a "rich man's club", not overmuch concerned about poorer, non-European states. But now it was decided that the aid and trade agreements which Britain had previously extended to developing Commonwealth countries should form part of a new Community policy towards those and other former colonial territories. The result was the Lomé Convention of 1975, agreed with forty-six African, Caribbean and small Pacific (ACP) states, which declared that the EEC would impose no import duties on the industrial

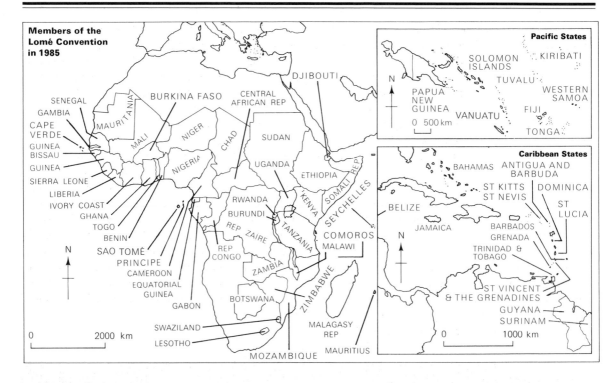

Members of the Lomé Convention in 1985

Pacific States

SOLOMON ISLANDS · KIRIBATI
PAPUA NEW GUINEA · TUVALU
WESTERN SAMOA
VANUATU · FIJI
0 500 km
TONGA

Caribbean States

BAHAMAS · ANTIGUA AND BARBUDA
ST KITTS ST NEVIS · DOMINICA
BELIZE · ST LUCIA
JAMAICA · BARBADOS · GRENADA
TRINIDAD & TOBAGO
ST VINCENT & THE GRENADINES
GUYANA
SURINAM
0 1000 km

SENEGAL
GAMBIA
CAPE VERDE
GUINEA BISSAU
GUINEA
SIERRA LEONE
LIBERIA
IVORY COAST
GHANA
TOGO
BENIN
SAO TOMÉ PRINCIPE
CAMEROON
EQUATORIAL GUINEA
GABON
SWAZILAND
LESOTHO
MOZAMBIQUE

MAURITANIA
MALI
NIGER
CHAD
NIGERIA
REP CONGO
REP ZAIRE
ZAMBIA
BOTSWANA

BURKINA FASO
CENTRAL AFRICAN REP
SUDAN
UGANDA
RWANDA
BURUNDI
TANZANIA
KENYA
SOMALI REP
ETHIOPIA
SEYCHELLES
COMOROS
MALAWI
ZIMBABWE
MALAGASY REP
MAURITIUS
DJIBOUTI

N

0   2000 km

products of those states, nor on most of their agricultural products. The Lomé Convention also created an export stabilisation scheme, 'Stabex', guaranteeing the ACP states a certain level of income on exports of their primary products. At the same time the Community's aid programme to the ACP states was substantially increased. The Lomé Convention was renewed in 1981 and again in 1985: Lomé II and Lomé III aimed to continue, strengthen and make more effective the provisions of the 1975 Convention. Lomé III also attempted to define the human rights of citizens of the member states, and to provide better development policies aimed at increasing the self-reliance of the ACP states.

That new sense of responsibility towards the poorer countries outside industrialised Western Europe was a welcome development, which most people could understand. But another aspect of the Community's work provoked puzzlement, a good deal of anger and some incredulity; this was its Common Agricultural Policy (CAP). The Treaty of Rome had laid down that the Community should aim to provide stable and regular supplies of food for all and at the same time ensure a guaranteed livelihood for the farmers. The trouble was that in most of the six original member countries agriculture was small-scale, over-manned, inefficient,

over-protected and over-subsidised. The French, in particular, did not intend suddenly to strip their farmers bare of protection and leave them naked to face the competition of the more efficient Dutch and of large-scale farmers outside the Community. The French demanded that the family structure of small-scale farming should be preserved as far as possible; and once that was agreed, it followed that Community food prices would be high.

Eventually the Six agreed on a policy that would decide agricultural prices centrally in an annual review, use tariffs to exclude cheap imports into the Community, and provide for the purchase of surplus foods – which would be stored and disposed of later, either within the Community or on world markets. That CAP, which came into operation in the late 1960s, generally set high prices to protect the smaller farmers. Its effect was to encourage farmers to produce more, which should have led to lower prices – except that the Community was committed to a policy of buying surpluses to keep prices artificially high. The result was that in the late sixties and early seventies the EEC paid out vast sums of money to amass in its central stores what outraged critics of the CAP called "mountains" of butter, beef, wheat, sugar and milk powder, and the occasional "lake" of wine. And it was difficult to get rid of mountains and lakes, except by selling them at knock-down prices on world markets or by making them into animal feed.

Such spectacular and expensive scandals gave the CAP a bad name and affected the way the man-in-the-street in Milan or Munich or Manchester looked at the European Community. In 1981 an opinion poll conducted in all member countries by the Community newspaper *Eurobarometer* showed that fewer than half of those polled thought the Community was 'a good thing'.

Despite the arguments caused by the CAP, the Community in the late 1970s appeared to be moving towards closer political and economic integration. In March 1979 a new European Monetary System came into being. Following a proposal by Helmut Schmidt, the German Chancellor, the currencies of member states were linked by a European Currency Unit (ECU). The value of the separate currencies could only go up and down against each other by small amounts. A support fund of $50,000 million to spend on keeping currencies in line was created by pooling the gold and foreign currency holdings of the members of the European Monetary System. Although three countries, Britain, Ireland and Denmark, decided not to join the European Monetary System for the time being, the Finance Ministers of those that did join were able to declare only a year later that they were happy with the working of the new system.

This important move towards the economic integration of Western Europe was accompanied by a significant political advance. 1979 was the first year in which direct elections for the European Parliament in Strasbourg were held. Although the turn-out of electors was disappointingly low in most countries, the very fact that the election could be held showed that Western European democracy was capable of transcending national boundaries to become a supra-national political community.

An EEC 'mountain' of barley in a Lincolnshire warehouse, 1980.

The Community in the 1980s

The achievements of the 1970s were over-shadowed in the early 1980s by increasingly bitter arguments between the governments of member states. In particular, the election of Margaret Thatcher's Conservative government in Britain in 1979 signalled the start of a long drawn-out debate on how much Britain should contribute to the Community's annual budget. Mrs Thatcher's argument, which other European heads of government only grudgingly accepted as fair, was that Britain was paying far too much. Britain was scheduled to contribute £1,180 million in 1980, making her by far the biggest net contributor to Community funds, ahead even of West Germany, the richest member of the Community, while Britain was the third poorest of the Nine. Mrs Thatcher's demands for a refund of £1,000 million caused heated and angry discussions between the heads of government. Although Britain was eventually promised a substantial refund of £1,577 million over the next two years, the bitterness of the arguments showed that national interests, however reasonable they might be, could seriously undermine relationships within the Community.

Arguments about the Community's finances dominated its affairs in the mid-1980s. The problem was that the CAP continued to set high prices to protect small farmers. By 1983 its runaway spending on farm subsidies seemed certain to bankrupt the Community. Although it was clear that a major reform of the Community's finances was urgently needed, no progress towards reform was made. The Thatcher government was still not satisfied with the long-term arrangements for a reduction in Britain's contribution to the Community budget, and so refused to agree to any increase in Community spending. At the same time the European Parliament in Strasbourg increasingly exercised its one effective power – the power to veto the Community's annual budget. Angered by the failure of the Council of Ministers to reform the CAP, it first vetoed the budget in 1980. Caught between the Parliament's demands for thorough reform and the conflicting demands of national governments – particularly those of Britain – the Community had failed by 1985 to produce any agreement about any of its financial problems.

None of this, however, prevented the Community from expanding in the 1980s. Greece joined as the tenth member in 1981. Spain and Portugal joined in 1986 despite fears that their small-scale agricultural systems would add to the already grievous problems of the CAP.

Forty Years On: the Main Features of Post-War Western Europe

The most striking feature of Western European history in the forty years after the Second World War was the creation and enlargement of the European Economic Community. For a continent whose previous history had been scarred by vicious rivalries between nations, that Community was a new and hopeful departure. It brought not only cooperation in place of hostility, but it offered to nations whose empires were disintegrating the compensation of influencing the future direction and policy of an integrated continental bloc. Its vital statistics were impressive. It brought together over 270 million people in an area of over 1,700,000 square kilometres. It had a bigger population and produced more wealth than either the Soviet Union or the United States of America. Yet, as we have seen, by the mid-1980s it was nowhere near to being a true federation of states under a central authority. Those 270 million people thought of themselves as nationals first, and as Europeans second – if they thought of Europe at all. Nationalism had not been smothered in Western Europe: it was still alive and kicking, both inside and outside the Community.

In contrast to the years before the war, parliamentary democracy seemed generally healthy. Generally, it survived throughout the greater part of the Western half of the continent. In only one country, Greece, which was politically associated with the West rather than geographically part of it, did an extremist group take power. In 1967 a handful of fanatical, anti-communist army officers overthrew a reasonably democratic government which they believed was veering too much to the left. In its place "the colonels" put themselves, to rule in a simple-minded fashion by censorship, brutality and not a little torture. Eventually, in 1974, when the bungling colonels proved they couldn't even organise the Greek army in a confrontation with the Turks over the island of Cyprus, their régime collapsed; and Greece returned to free democratic ways under the leadership of Constantine Karamanlis, who served as Prime Minister until 1980 and was then elected President of the Greek Republic.

Even in South-Western Europe there were moves towards more democratic forms of government. The dictatorship in Portugal was first to fall when in 1974 a group of army officers, critical of the government's policy of hanging on to the country's African colonies at any cost, seized power. A tussle for control followed between left- and right-wing groups in the army and a number of new political parties, and Portugal was threatened with civil war. Eventually a minority Socialist government, supported by senior army officers, was installed after free elections had failed to give any party majority support. Although the Socialist government lasted only fourteen months, and was followed by a further five minority governments in two and a half years, Portugal survived the 1970s without suffering civil war. Elections in 1980 brought to power a centre party coalition government which soon provided the country with greater stability than it had known since the revolution of 1974.

In Spain General Franco died in November 1975 and was succeeded as the Spanish head of state by the young king, Juan Carlos. A wave of fresh air swept through Spain, which had long resembled a locked and barred political museum. Censorship was relaxed, political parties that opposed the government were permitted to exist openly, and free elections in 1977 – the first in forty years – brought the Democratic Centre Party under Adolfo Suarez to power. A new constitution in 1978 made Juan Carlos a constitutional monarch, and this encouraged the steady development of a democratic climate. Despite an attempt by army officers to stage a coup d'état in 1981, Spanish democracy continued to flourish and, in 1982, elections produced the first Socialist government in Spain since the Civil War.

With the exception of de Gaulle's rise to power and the foundation of the Fifth Republic in France, there were no other substantial changes in the forms of government of post-war Western European countries. Their internal politics were mostly struggles for power within the constitutional frameworks that had been established either before or immediately after the war.

Political parties adapted to the new times, to new voters, and to some extent changed their characters. In both Britain and West Germany the conservative mood of the 1950s not only ensured long periods in power for conservative political parties (the Tories in Britain and the CDU in Germany), but also changed the thinking and electoral tactics of the non-revolutionary parties of the left. Both the British Labour Party and the German Social Democrats (SPD) com-

peted with their opponents for the support of voters who were neither staunch socialists nor solidly conservative. And the tactics appeared to pay off, at least in the short term. Britain had a Labour government between 1964 and 1970, and again in 1974; while the SPD dominated West German governments after 1969 under Chancellors Willy Brandt and Helmut Schmidt.

In France and Italy the presence of large Communist Parties made for different political patterns. In both countries conservative parties held on to power in the sixties and seventies – the Gaullists and their allies in France, and the Christian Democrats in Italy – but during that time the Communists shifted their ground. By the end of the 1960s it was clear that hard-line Communists, obedient to Moscow as the centre of a world revolutionary movement, were out of date. The Sino-Soviet split, and the independent stances of the Yugoslavs and Albanians in Eastern Europe, made nonsense of any suggestion that there was, or should be, a monolithic unity in the communist world. It was also clear that the old brand of European communism, which opposed any kind of parliamentary democracy, was on a hiding to nothing in the West. And out of those realisations came something called "Eurocommunism", which was to say that the Western European parties declared their independence of the Soviet Party and stated they were prepared to work, like other parties, within the framework of democratic constitutions. Thus, after the elections of 1976, in which the Christian Democrats failed to secure a parliamentary majority, the Italian Communist Party was prepared to support a minority government (though not in a coalition) in power while it attempted to deal with the country's economic problems. In France the Communists formed a temporary alliance with the Socialists against the parties of the right in the elections of 1978. Their alliance was decisive in the 1981 Presidential elections when François Mitterand became the first Socialist President for twenty-three years.

Of all the states of Western Europe, West Germany made the most notable progress in the post-war years. In 1945 she was physically separated from her eastern half and former capital city; her former leaders had been universally condemned for their "crimes against humanity"; and many of her towns lay in ruins. Thirty years on, she was among the most powerful industrial nations in the world; and, in terms of economic strength, the dominant partner in the European Community. Yet Germany remained split in two; and many people preferred to see the division continue rather than raise the question of how the people of the largest European nation outside the USSR could live in permanent peace with their neighbours. The West Germans could hardly be expected to see it that way. In the 1950s and for most of the 1960s the West German government refused to accept the new facts of Central European life – that the "iron curtain", Poland's Oder–Neisse frontier, and the state of East Germany were all there to stay for a very long time. It was not until the Social Democrat, Willy Brandt, became Chancellor in 1969 that West German foreign policy took a different line. Brandt's *Ostpolitik* (eastern policy) was, in brief, to accept the new facts of life while not ruling out the possible and desirable re-unification of the two Germanys at some later date. Between 1970 and 1973 his government signed agreements with the USSR and other Eastern European states, including East Germany, by which the post-war frontiers in Central and Eastern Europe were recognised.

In August 1975 the representatives of the USA, the Soviet Union, France, the UK and thirty-one other nations signed a Declaration at the end of a conference in Helsinki in which they tried to come to terms with a Europe that was split, geographically and politically, right down the middle. They all agreed to accept the existing frontiers in Europe as fixed, to respect human rights, and to make possible the freer movement of people across national frontiers. But the most important conclusion of Helsinki was that Europe and the two Germanys and the city of Berlin should remain as the war had left them – divided.

42   A United Kingdom? Britain since the War, 1945–85

In the forty years after the Second World War the British lost their empire and entered a Community among whom were peoples they had previously regarded as, at worst, enemies, and at best, competitors. Their leaders found it difficult to fashion a new role for Britian in a changed world which swept much of her global influence into history.

Problems of the British Economy

For the British economy the post-war years were a period of growth – but the rate of growth stubbornly refused to rise to the levels enjoyed by other Western European nations. For example, between 1948 and 1962, the rate of growth of output per head of population in the UK was 2·4 per cent a year: in France it was 3·4 per cent; in Italy 5·6 per cent; and in West Germany 6·8 per cent. Many reasons, and some excuses, were put forward for that relatively poor performance. Some people accused the trade unions of using their power to protect inefficient workers and to undermine management's attempts to promote greater productivity per man-hour. Others pointed the finger at inadequately trained managers and at lethargic salesmen who let Britain's overseas markets fall into the clutches of the more energetic Germans, Frenchmen and Japanese. Yet others claimed, particularly from the 1960s onwards, that Britain's ills could be cured by the *planned* use of her resources and man-power and by the direction of investment, either by government or by a central planning agency, to those sectors of industry which needed it most. Politicians of both major parties generally blamed each other for their inability to get Britain moving at a respectable rate of progress.

All those claims and accusations could be justified in particular instances, but they left largely untouched and unresolved the basic problem of the post-war British economy, which was how to keep the country's balance of payments in credit. Britain's balance of trade (the difference between what the country spent on imports and what it earned from exports) had been in deficit for many years before the war, but that deficit had been made good by earnings from investments overseas and from services such as shipping, insurance and banking. The balance of trade had been in the red;

but the balance of payments had been kept in the black. However, the war had destroyed that comfortable way of staying in credit. Overseas investments had been sold, and Britain's ability to provide profitable commercial and financial services to other parts of the world had been much reduced. More than ever before the country depended on the export of goods to stay solvent. The balance of payments became the iron master of the economy: if it went into deficit – that is, if the country earned less than it spent – measures had to be taken to drive it back into credit; and those measures affected every man, woman and child in the land.

Basically there were two ways of pushing the balance of payments back into the black – devaluation of the pound, and deflation of demand at home – and both had unpleasant side-effects. Devaluation meant cutting the value of the pound in relation to other currencies, in order to make British goods cheaper and more attractive to foreigners. In 1949 the pound was devalued by thirty per cent against the dollar; in 1967 it was devalued by a further fourteen per cent; and in 1972 it was allowed to 'float', that is, it was allowed to find its own level against other major currencies such as the dollar, the mark and the yen. Of course, devaluation of the pound also made imports dearer, which encouraged inflation and raised the cost of living. You might like to think of the effect this way: cheaper British cars in world markets could mean dearer Japanese TV sets in British shops.

Successive governments used a number of methods to deflate, or reduce, demand at home. Hire-purchase restrictions, such as increasing the required deposits on goods, meant that fewer people could afford to buy expensive consumer durables. Higher interest rates discouraged people from taking out loans, while higher indirect taxes on goods raised prices in the shops. Higher direct taxes, such as income tax, simply took more money out of workers' pay packets; while cuts in government spending could reduce demand for anything from new houses to guided missiles. In theory, deflation of demand should have led to increased exports as manufacturers diverted their goods from a slack home market to overseas buyers. In practice, higher interest rates could put a business man off borrowing money to invest in new machinery; and higher income tax was hardly an incentive for anyone to work harder.

The use of deflationary measures to meet a balance of payment crisis, and the lifting of curbs on home demand once each crisis was past, became a feature of the economic policies of the Conservative governments of 1951–64. 'Stop-go', as it was called, provided no solution to the basic problem of how to keep the balance of payments in credit. But neither could later governments, Conservative or Labour, find an answer. In the mid-1960s, and again in the mid-1970s, governments borrowed vast sums from the International Monetary Fund to tide Britain over particularly bad patches – and on both occasions the IMF insisted on deflationary measures, including cuts in public spending, as conditions of the loans. Only in the later 1970s, when oil companies began to tap the wells in the North Sea, did there appear to be a real prospect of the British economy moving out of the shadow of recurrent payments deficits. The oil, it was said, would cut Britain's import bills, earn foreign currency, and provide enough money for a lavish re-equipment of industry.

Britain became self-sufficient in oil in 1980, but this was too late to prevent the economy from floundering in the later 1970s. At the start of 1975 Britain's worst-ever balance of payments deficit was recorded – £534 million. At the same time the inflation of the pound went from bad to worse: with an inflation rate of 20 per cent in early 1975, employees in every sector of the economy were demanding wage increases of up to 30 per cent. The Labour government under James Callaghan (1974–79) gradually reduced the rate of inflation with a policy of voluntary wage restraint agreed with the Trades Union Congress, but this did not survive a 'winter of discontent' in 1979 when widespread strikes during an exceptionally cold winter ruined Callaghan's plans to limit wage rises to 5 per cent.

A Conservative government which took office in 1979 under Margaret Thatcher attempted to apply a new set of remedies to the ills of the British economy. Leaving behind the 'Stop-go' approach of the fifties and sixties and the incomes policies of the seventies, the Thatcher government adopted a 'monetarist' economic policy. This meant cutting public spending, reducing the amount of money borrowed by the government or the public sector industries, and restricting the growth of the supply of money. But before 'monetarism' had time to show whether or not it would succeed, the British economy was hit in 1980 by the deepest recession in over fifty years. Output fell sharply, factory closures and redundancies soared, and a 64 per cent increase in the number of people out of work was the largest rise in a single year since 1930. As a result of this recession the most visible single result of the government's new economic policy was widespread, long-term unemployment. By 1985 an economic recovery was under way, with inflation remaining low and investment increasing rapidly. However, the increased efficiency it brought was applied to a smaller area of industry than had been at work in the 1970s. Overall, Britain was not quite producing what she had done in 1979; and there were still more than three million people without jobs. Those with the least chance of finding work in the foreseeable future were mostly concentrated in the north of England, in Scotland and in Northern Ireland, suggesting that, in economic terms, the United Kingdom was actually two nations: a depressed and deprived North, and a relatively prosperous South.

For many people, then, the forty years after 1945 were a period of missed opportunities, incompetent leadership, and always promises of jam tomorrow. In fact, it was a time in which Britain was cut down to size – a small part of the Earth off the western coast of Europe – and to the resources of her own natural wealth and labour force. And that sudden reduction to actual size, no longer seen through the magnifying glass of a vast empire, opened up questions which before had been present but generally ignored. The most important of those questions concerned the relationships between the various nationalities who together made up that United Kingdom whose shorthand name is 'Britain'. They boiled down to a straightforward proposition: should the kingdom be taken apart?

Problems of Nationalism

It seemed that the proposition was first raised in Northern Ireland. In Chapter 20 (page 78) we saw how in 1920 the British Parliament passed the Government of Ireland Act, which gave a regional parliament to Northern Ireland – the six counties within the province of Ulster, where Protestants outnumbered Catholics by two to one. Since that time political power in Northern Ireland had remained in the hands of one party, the Protestant 'Unionist' Party, not only in the parliament at Stormont, but also at local level where some people were denied the right to vote by a property qualification and yet business men were allowed multiple votes. One result of that long history of one-party rule – and the Unionists were not above rigging constituency boundaries to retain their control over local government – was discrimination against the Catholic minority of the population, in particular in the crucial matters of the allocation of council houses and appointments to jobs. In 1968–69 the unemployment rate among Catholic workers was three times as high as the rate among Protestants.

In 1967 the Northern Ireland Civil Rights Association was founded, a non-sectarian organisation which campaigned for the same rights as those enjoyed by citizens elsewhere in the United Kingdom. In August 1968 they held their first peaceful demonstration in Dungannon; to be followed in October by a march in Londonderry,* a town where a high rate of unemployment and inadequate housing had led to much criticism of the Stormont government by both Catholics and Protestants. The march was broken up by the police, with considerable brutality.

In January 1969 a march by civil rights supporters from Belfast to Londonderry was ambushed by Unionist supporters at Burntollet, and there followed a frightening attack by the police on the Catholic area of Bogside in Londonderry. In August the police again attacked the Bogside; while in Belfast a battle between the police and Catholics in the Falls Road area of the city resulted in seven people dead, four hundred wounded, and many houses burnt down.

Disorders between rival religious groups and nationalist factions had been a common feature of life in Northern Ireland before and after partition. In August 1969, after the particularly violent riots in Londonderry and Belfast, the British government felt that they could no longer trust the local police to deal fairly with serious disorder, and they sent in troops. The Catholic population welcomed the British soldiers as protectors against the savagery of the forces of 'law and order' in their own country.

Under pressure from Westminster, the Stormont government now hurried through the reform of the voting system and abolished the 'B Specials', the wholly Protestant auxiliary police force that had come to be hated and feared by the Catholics. But it was too

* Called 'Derry' by Irish nationalists on both sides of the border.

late. As riots continued in early 1970, Stormont's ability to control events was rapidly being undermined by the activities of extreme nationalist groups.

In June and July the Irish Republican Army (IRA) defended Catholic areas in Belfast for the first time. Until then they had played no open part in the civil rights campaign, and had been more concerned by the split in their own movement between the 'Official' wing, who aimed to work peacefully for a united, socialist Ireland, and the 'Provisional' wing, whose policy was to unite the country by turfing the British out of it. Both the IRA (especially the 'Provisionals') and militant Unionist organisations, such as the Ulster Volunteer Force (set up in 1969), were now aiming for nothing less than the overthrow of Stormont. The UVF and their like intended to establish an undiluted Protestant supremacy: the IRA's objective was to sever all Northern Ireland's links with Britain. The issue was no longer civil rights: the extremists had taken the initiative out of the hands of parliamentary politicians and people whose protests were made with nothing more lethal than posters and banners.

At the beginning of 1971 both wings of the IRA began to attack British troops: at the same time they fought each other in a struggle for control over the Catholic areas of Belfast. In August Stormont tried to break the growing influence of the IRA by ordering the arrest and internment without trial of people suspected of terrorism. The army arrested only Catholic suspects – 342 of them – and in doing so appeared to reinforce the Provisionals' claim that British soldiers had been sent to Northern Ireland to uphold the Protestant cause.

The IRA responded by making vicious attacks on civilian targets; and then, on 'Bloody Sunday', 30 January 1972, British soldiers opened fire on a demonstration in Londonderry and killed thirteen people. As the threat of civil war and massive loss of life loomed nearer, the British government finally assumed direct rule over the province. The Stormont parliament was dead; and Protestant extremists celebrated its end by opening up a campaign of sectarian murders.

The British government did not relish their new role – which they had not sought and for which they received few thanks from anyone. They searched for a way of handing power back to the elected representatives of the people of Northern Ireland, recognising that Stormont could not be resurrected. Instead, elections were held in January 1973 for a new Assembly, which was to have an executive in which the moderate Unionists would share power with the leaders of the Catholic minority. But the new power-sharing executive – the first real attempt to include Catholics in the government of the province – was condemned by the militant Unionists; and in May 1974 a general strike called by the Ulster Workers Council ensured its downfall. The British government had no option but to re-assume direct control of Northern Ireland.

Subsequent attempts to find a political solution to the province's problems failed. The British, caught between fanatical Irish nationalists and equally unscrupulous Ulster 'loyalists', remained in Northern Ireland on the grounds that to pull out the army would lead to a bloodbath into which the extremists who posed as the people's champions would drag the two still unreconciled nationalist-religious communities of the province. However, the price of failure to find a solution was high. Following the reintroduction of direct rule in 1974, the IRA began to bomb civilian

targets in mainland Britain, bringing the 'troubles' to the very doorstep of the British government. By 1976 the killings in Northern Ireland as well as on the mainland had reached such a level – over 1,000 dead since the start of the 'troubles' in 1969 – that widespread public support grew for a Peace Movement founded by two Belfast women, Betty Williams and Mairead Corrigan, who subsequently received the Nobel Peace Prize for their efforts. Although the number of killings steadily diminished thereafter the British government never seriously contemplated withdrawing the army from Northern Ireland. The passions involved in the question of the future of the province were amply demonstrated in 1981 when ten IRA prisoners in the Maze prison near Belfast starved themselves to death in a series of hunger strikes.

Nevertheless, by the 1980s, the British government was willing to recognise that the question of Northern Ireland did not affect the UK alone. The Republic of Ireland had a legitimate concern for the lives and well-

Death in Belfast, August 1984: 22-year-old Sean Downes is killed by a plastic bullet fired from close range during a Republican demonstration, the 2394th victim of the 'troubles' in Northern Ireland.

being of people in the province. Its political leaders also had a genuine interest in not letting the IRA's secret terrorist army affect stability and democracy in their state as well as in the north. In 1981 Mrs Thatcher began a series of talks with the Prime Minister of the Republic, Dr Garrett Fitzgerald. In 1986 the two governments signed the Hillsborough agreement to cooperate over Northern Ireland on issues such as terrorism and economic development. The agreement alarmed unionist leaders who feared that the British government was taking the first steps towards handing the province over to a united Ireland.

The people who died by the gun and by the bomb in Northern Ireland were the victims of fanatics who inherited the mutual centuries-old hatreds. They were also the victims of British imperialism in the strict historical sense that British–Irish antagonisms, with their religious echoes, began with the English takeover of Ireland centuries before. But the Welsh and the Scots had also been subjected to the rule of the English. And when the British Empire was lost, it was not surprising that they should ask themselves what continuing benefit there was for them in association with the small rump of that empire, England.

In the 1970s, therefore, British politics gained a new nationalist dimension. In the general election of October 1974 nationalists won 24 seats (10 Ulster Unionists, 11 Scottish Nationalists and 3 Plaid Cymru), compared with the single Scottish Nationalist elected to parliament in 1970. The two major parties, Labour and the Conservatives, were forced to enter a debate for which British imperial history had not prepared them. It was a debate about domestic relationships, about the future arrangement of the homeland, about the devolution of government in a kingdom which had become part of a new community of European nations. The debate, which was conducted with growing intensity throughout the 1970s, came to a sudden end in 1979. In response to the demands of the Scottish Nationalist Party for a devolution of power, the government held a referendum in Scotland to find out what support there was for a proposed Scottish Assembly. Fewer than 33 per cent of the electorate voted in favour of the Assembly; and as Parliament had agreed that the Assembly proposal must have at least 40 per cent of the vote in order to succeed, the attempt at devolution had failed – apparently because large numbers of the Scottish people themselves did not want it.

Multi-cultural Britain

British imperial history was over. In the next chapter you will see how not only Britain but also the other colonial powers of Western Europe retreated from their overseas possessions. Here we must look at how people from the old British Empire, now the New Commonwealth, made their own impression on post-war Britain.

The Commonwealth Citizenship Act of 1947 allowed any citizen of an independent Commonwealth country the right to enter and settle in the UK. And at a time of shortage of both skilled and unskilled labour in the fifties and early sixties, the British government encouraged considerable numbers of Asians and West Indians to claim their right of entry and settlement. That 'right' was then severely restricted by the Immigration Act of 1962 and by further legislation in 1968 and 1971. As a result of those Acts the numbers fell dramatically and the pattern of immigration changed. Instead of the young, and mostly male, workers of the fifties and early sixties, the immigrants of the 1970s were almost entirely the young children of adults already settled in Britain, and some grandparents, husbands, wives and fiancées.

Recent estimates of the numbers of 'New Commonwealth and Pakistani' immigrants and their descendants – children born in the UK – involve some guesswork, for British population statistics are not collected on the basis of colour, race or ethnic origin. However, the following are the official estimates for mid-1984:

Place of origin or parents' origin	Total numbers living in the UK
Africa	109,000
Sri Lanka, Hong Kong, Malaysia, Singapore, and small Commonwealth territories in Asia and the Pacific	118,000
Mediterranean Commonwealth countries – Cyprus, Gibraltar, Malta and Gozo	112,000
Pakistan	371,000
Bangladesh	93,000
India	807,000
West Indies and Guyana	529,000
Total	2,139,000

Let's express those statistics in another way: in 1984 around three out of every hundred citizens of the UK were immigrants, or the descendants of immigrants, from countries of the New Commonwealth and Pakistan. By itself, that ratio was no kind of recipe for strife, particularly since about forty per cent of the total 'immigrant' population had been born in Britain; but problems did arise in those places where there was a higher than average concentration of immigrant families.

Most immigrants came to the industrial areas of England, where there was a shortage of workers in factories and in public services. Like all movements of population, the arrival of these migrants caused difficulties, both for people living in the 'inner cities' who had to learn how to get along with new neighbours with different customs and sometimes speaking different languages, and for the newcomers, who found themselves in areas where welfare services, schools and housing accommodation were already among the poorest in Britain.

The poverty of Britain's decaying 'inner-city' areas was sharply highlighted in 1981 when riots broke out in St Paul's (Bristol) and Brixton (London). In these riots police came under fierce attack and a great deal of property was wrecked by fire and looting. Although both young and old and black and white took part in the looting, the attacks on police were mainly by young black people. An enquiry led by Lord Scarman tried to explain why this was so:

"Unemployment and poor housing bear on them very heavily; and the educational system has not adjusted itself satisfactorily to their needs. Their difficulties are intensified by the sense they have of a concealed discrimination against them, particularly in relation to job opportunities and housing. ... Their sense of rejection is not eased by the low level of black representation in our elective political institutions. ... The recipe for a clash with the police is therefore ready-mixed, and it takes little, or nothing, to persuade them that the police, representing an establishment which they see as insensitive to their plight, are their enemies."

In the five years following the Scarman Report (1981) police forces made attempts to overcome the racial prejudice which had disfigured their relations with black people. Many local authorities attempted to follow 'Equal Opportunities' policies, particularly in the appointment of local government employees. Government funds were used to improve inner city services and to provide some jobs. But by 1986 none of these measures appeared to have made any real impact on the problems described by Lord Scarman. Further serious rioting in Handsworth (Birmingham) and Tottenham (London) in 1985, and again in St Paul's in 1986, indicated that a more fundamental approach to the problem was needed.

43 Towards a Third World: the Twilight of the Empires

One of the most far-reaching changes in world politics after 1945 was the break-up of the old colonial empires. Just as the 'New World' of North and Latin America had broken free from old Europe in the late eighteenth and nineteenth centuries, and as the subject nationalities of Eastern Europe had won their independence in the early twentieth century, so the peoples of the 'Third World' rejected colonialism after 1945.

Their struggle for independence from alien rule was often violent, and by the late 1970s, it was still incomplete. But the colonial empires of Britain, France, the Netherlands, Belgium, Spain and Portugal, which still dominated the maps of Asia, Africa and the Caribbean in 1945, had largely disintegrated by 1975. In their places they left, for the most part, a mass of new, and mostly poor, states that belonged neither to the 'First World' of industrial, capitalist nations, nor to the 'Second World' of the Soviet Union and her satellites, but to the non-industrial, non-aligned 'Third World'.

The First Phase of Decolonisation

We saw in Chapter 34 (pages 200–1) how the Second World War dealt the first blows to the colonial empires. Apart from Portugal, all the major colonial powers were involved in the war against Germany and Japan. The Japanese overran huge areas of the Far Eastern empires, and the Germans invaded North Africa, breaking the links between many colonies and the 'mother countries'.

After the war, Britain, France and the Netherlands were in no condition to re-impose their rule everywhere by force. Moreover, the post-war world was dominated by the USA and the USSR, both of whom were hostile to old-style colonialism. And for Western European countries, the attitude of the Americans was crucial, since they depended on the USA not only for economic aid to finance reconstruction and to pay off war debts, but also for military support to contain the threat of a Russian advance from the east. The Americans harked back to their own fight for independence from the British, and saw their own great influence and power in the post-war world as something quite different from the imperialism of old Europe. Much as the British and the French resented American criticism

of their empires, they were in no position to take an independent line.

The first phase of decolonisation, which you can see on the map, took place in the twelve years after the defeat of Japan, 1945–57. In Asia, India and Pakistan became independent in 1947; Ceylon (Sri Lanka) and Burma in 1948; Indonesia in 1949; and Malaya in 1957, after the British had defeated a local communist guerrilla movement. In 1949 the French granted Vietnam, Laos and Cambodia a form of independence which did not satisfy Indo-Chinese nationalists, especially those in the north of Vietnam. For the story of subsequent developments in Indo-China you should look at pages 214–6, and pages 225–7.

In the Middle East and North Africa, Jordan and Syria were granted independence in 1946; Palestine (which the leaders of the Jewish population proclaimed the state of Israel once British troops had left) in 1948; Libya in 1951; and Morocco, Tunisia and the Sudan in 1956. In 1954 the British agreed to pull their troops out of the Suez Canal Zone by June 1956, and thus brought to an end over seventy years of military interference in Egyptian affairs.

The Uncertain Future of the European Empires

For various reasons, these first grants of independence did not, at the time, appear to signify the beginning of the end of the empires. Most of the peoples who gained their freedom by 1957 appeared quite capable of governing themselves. Their leaders were experienced politicians; and some of the new states had already enjoyed a considerable degree of self-government within the old empires. Before the end of the Second World War, the British had started to transform their colonial Empire into a Commonwealth of self-governing countries. India, Pakistan, Ceylon and Malaya all became members; and the British hoped that through such an association of former colonies they might continue to reap many of the benefits of empire. The French aimed to develop a similar framework, within which colonies could achieve internal self-government without breaking their economic and political ties with the 'mother country'. That was the purpose of the French Union, set up in 1946, and of

Towards a Third World: the Twilight of the Empires

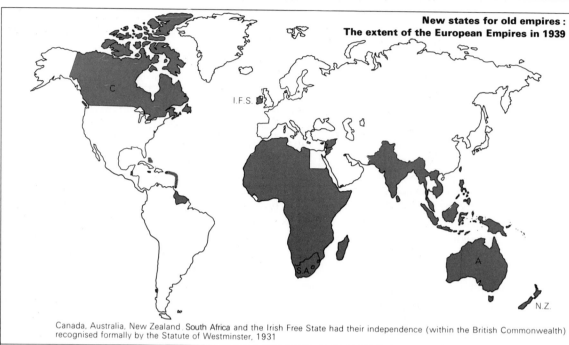

**New states for old empires:
The extent of the European Empires in 1939**

Canada, Australia, New Zealand, South Africa and the Irish Free State had their independence (within the British Commonwealth) recognised formally by the Statute of Westminster, 1931

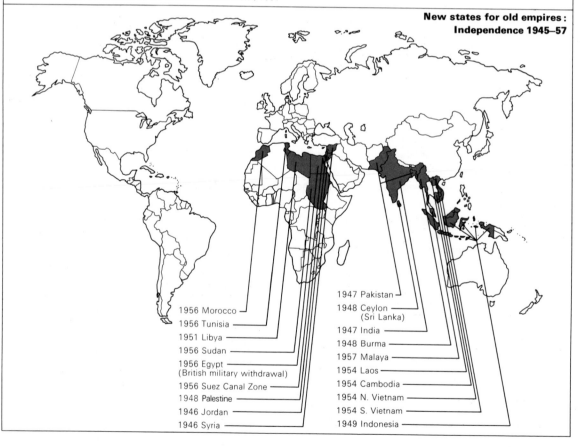

**New states for old empires:
Independence 1945–57**

1956 Morocco
1956 Tunisia
1951 Libya
1956 Sudan
1956 Egypt
(British military withdrawal)
1956 Suez Canal Zone
1948 Palestine
1946 Jordan
1946 Syria

1947 Pakistan
1948 Ceylon
(Sri Lanka)
1947 India
1948 Burma
1957 Malaya
1954 Laos
1954 Cambodia
1954 N. Vietnam
1954 S. Vietnam
1949 Indonesia

Towards a Third World: the Twilight of the Empires

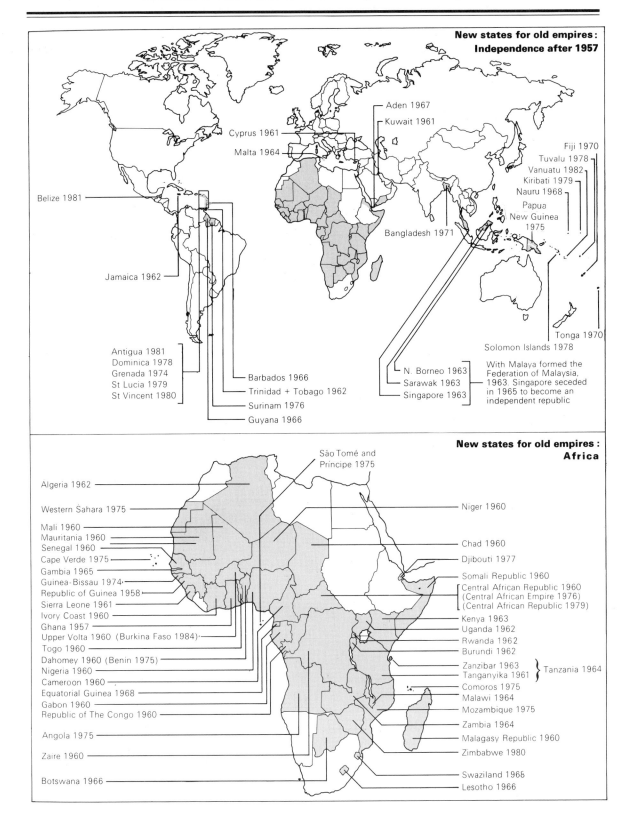

New states for old empires:
Independence after 1957

Aden 1967
Kuwait 1961
Cyprus 1961
Malta 1964

Fiji 1970
Tuvalu 1978
Vanuatu 1982
Kiribati 1979
Nauru 1968
Papua New Guinea 1975

Belize 1981

Bangladesh 1971

Jamaica 1962

Tonga 1970
Solomon Islands 1978

Antigua 1981
Dominica 1978
Grenada 1974
St Lucia 1979
St Vincent 1980

Barbados 1966
Trinidad + Tobago 1962
Surinam 1976
Guyana 1966

N. Borneo 1963
Sarawak 1963
Singapore 1963

With Malaya formed the Federation of Malaysia, 1963. Singapore seceded in 1965 to become an independent republic

New states for old empires:
Africa

São Tomé and Príncipe 1975

Algeria 1962

Niger 1960

Western Sahara 1975

Mali 1960
Mauritania 1960
Senegal 1960
Cape Verde 1975
Gambia 1965
Guinea-Bissau 1974
Republic of Guinea 1958
Sierra Leone 1961
Ivory Coast 1960
Ghana 1957
Upper Volta 1960 (Burkina Faso 1984)
Togo 1960
Dahomey 1960 (Benin 1975)
Nigeria 1960
Cameroon 1960
Equatorial Guinea 1968
Gabon 1960
Republic of The Congo 1960
Angola 1975
Zaire 1960
Botswana 1966

Chad 1960
Djibouti 1977
Somali Republic 1960
Central African Republic 1960
(Central African Empire 1976)
(Central African Republic 1979)
Kenya 1963
Uganda 1962
Rwanda 1962
Burundi 1962
Zanzibar 1963
Tanganyika 1961
} Tanzania 1964
Comoros 1975
Malawi 1964
Mozambique 1975
Zambia 1964
Malagasy Republic 1960
Zimbabwe 1980
Swaziland 1968
Lesotho 1966

279

the French Community, which replaced it in 1958.

Thus, the newly independent states were regarded as special cases, fit to be let off the imperial leash. On the other hand, the British, French, Belgians and Portuguese still retained many colonies which, in Western eyes, seemed ill-suited for immediate self-government. Most of them were tropical countries in Africa and the Caribbean, with weak economies, low levels of education, and often little sense of national unity. Their economic development, such as it was, had been based on the exploitation of mineral resources and cash crops (such as cocoa, coffee, groundnuts and rubber) for export by European companies: very little had been done to improve the production of food crops for home consumption, or to develop better balanced economies. Educational progress was equally unimpressive. In the Gold Coast, West Africa's most educationally advanced colony, only forty-four per cent of children were enrolled in primary schools in 1947; in Nigeria the proportion was twenty-one per cent; in Dahomey, ten per cent. Moreover, tropical African colonies were made up of peoples, who were different in language and culture, and often had long-standing hostilities towards each other. This made it difficult to see how they could create workable political systems of their own, if and when they gained their independence. The colonial powers had done little to encourage local politicians. Men like Kwame Nkrumah in the Gold Coast, Jomo Kenyatta in Kenya and Hastings Banda in Nyasaland were imprisoned for their activities in post-war years; and in some colonies the right to form political parties was denied.

The prospect of native rule seemed particularly alarming in colonies where large white settler populations would face a very uncertain, and perhaps a dangerous, future if independence were granted. In the British colony of Kenya a liberation movement called Mau Mau waged a campaign of terrorist violence against British settlers between 1952 and 1959, and bloodily illustrated the plight of white farmers in a hostile countryside. In Algeria the war between the French *colons* and the nationalist FLN (*Front de la Libération Nationale*) lasted from 1954 to 1962 (see page 281), and caused massive loss of life.

Finally, and particularly for the British, there were overseas possessions that were vitally important as bases from which British forces could protect trade routes and maintain a military presence outside Europe: for example, Malta, Aden, Cyprus and Singapore. Before the 1950s, to grant independence for colonies such as these would have been unthinkable.

Yet, in the years after 1956, the most unlikely candidates for independence in European eyes were granted their freedom. The chapters that follow show the extraordinary impact that this made on Africa, the Middle East and the Indian sub-continent.

44 Africa Since 1945

The first of the African colonies to be freed was the Gold Coast (re-named Ghana). This territory looked as if it would make a stable new state because of the wealth it could create from gold mines and vast cocoa plantations, and also because of the growing reputation of its British-educated black Prime Minister, Kwame Nkrumah, who impressed Westerners as an articulate leader of men. Ghana became independent in 1957. In 1958 the people of French Guinea opted out of the new Community set up to replace the French Union. Two years later the colonial empires began to collapse.

The Collapse of the French Empire

Algerian nationalists had for a long time wanted their independence from the French Empire, like the Vietminh in Indo-China before them. The trouble was that in Algeria there were very large numbers of white settlers – *colons* – who had no intention of letting Muslim nationalists take over a land which was, constitutionally, part of France. As the struggle between *colons* and nationalists became violent, the French sent in more troops to restore order.

The French army, still smarting from the disaster of Dien Bien Phu (see Chapter 35, page 214), waged a brutal war against the nationalists, became deeply involved in Algerian politics, and decided to resist the possibility of France giving Algeria independence. In Paris the weakness of the Fourth Republic became clear as successive short-lived coalition governments proved incapable of finding a solution to the problem.

And then, in May 1958, the *colons* took over control of the government in Algiers and, backed by senior army generals, threatened to seize power in France itself, where many army officers were prepared to help them. In desperation politicians turned to the one man who could save the situation because he stood above party politics and was acceptable to the army. On 1 June 1958 Charles de Gaulle emerged from his retreat in the village of Colombey-les-deux-Églises to become Prime Minister of France, with power to rule as he saw fit for six months. By September a new constitution for a Fifth Republic was worked out, which gave more power to the President and to the government, at the expense of the National Assembly. And once de Gaulle was duly elected President, he set out to use his power to settle the Algerian problem.

The army generals who supported the rebels soon found out they had been wrong about de Gaulle. He was not a man of the extreme right who secretly yearned for a military government: he was a realist, and in the end he was prepared to let Algeria go. As the policies of the new President became clearer, and as more Frenchmen were seen to want an end to the dirty war across the Mediterranean, so the *colons* and extremist army officers attempted two more revolts against the government, in January 1960 and April 1961. Both failed, and de Gaulle's negotiations with the nationalists eventually led to Algerian independence in July 1962.

In 1960 President de Gaulle began to liquidate the rest of France's African empire. Countries whose peoples had grown restless and dissatisfied with the limited degree of self-government they were allowed in the French Community were now granted full independence. French West Africa and French Equatorial Africa fragmented into eleven separate sovereign states, while the island of Madagascar became the Malagasy Republic. The two trust territories of Togo and Cameroon also became independent.

The Wind of Change in the British Empire

In the same year, 1960, the Belgians were forced out of the Congo, which became an independent state (it was re-named Zaïre in 1971): they had made no plans to leave the colony, but were too weak to resist a sudden and violent upsurge of nationalist feeling. In contrast, the British tried to bring their colonial rule in Africa and the Caribbean to a more orderly end, leaving the new states with democratic constitutions and locally born, trained élites. The British Prime Minister, Harold Macmillan, showed that he was aware of the new strength of African nationalism when in a speech delivered in South Africa in February 1960 he declared that "The wind of change is blowing through this continent, and, whether we like it or not, this growth of national consciousness is a political fact". As you can see from the maps on pages 278–9, the wind was blowing too hard to allow the British to delay their departure too long. You can also see that in the 1960s similar winds drove the British from colonies in the Mediterranean, the Middle East and the Far East.

The British tried to safeguard the interests of white minorities in Kenya and Southern Rhodesia. They planned to group colonies together in federations – Kenya, Tanganyika and Uganda in one, and Southern and Northern Rhodesia and Nyasaland in another – hoping that the more prosperous whites would be able to dominate their poorer black neighbours, and, indeed, rigging the constitutions so that the whites would be given more powers than their numbers warranted. But when those plans collapsed, British settlers, like the *colons* in Algeria, found themselves abandoned.

After the Federation of Rhodesia and Nyasaland (sometimes called the Central African Federation) broke up in 1963, only two of its member colonies were granted independence – Northern Rhodesia (Zambia) and Nyasaland (Malawi). Britain denied independence to white-controlled Southern Rhodesia, which refused to meet African demands for black majority rule. In 1965, the Rhodesian whites, led by the Prime Minister, Ian Smith, took matters into their own hands and made a unilateral declaration of independence (UDI). Although the British government refused to intervene by force, as the leaders of Black Africa demanded, they asked the United Nations to support worldwide economic sanctions against Smith's illegal régime, and froze Rhodesian assets in Britain. Faced with a choice between white and black rule in Africa, the British government did not hesitate by 1965 to side with the latter.

The End of the Portuguese Empire

There remained the oldest of all the European empires in Africa – that of the Portuguese. Although Portugal was, by Western European standards, a poor country with a small population, peculiar circumstances made it possible for her to cling on to her colonies longer than any other country. First, Portugal had not taken part in the Second World War and her rule in Africa had not been interrupted. Second, the US government was more tolerant of Portuguese colonialism than of British or French – mainly because the Americans did not want to offend a country whose naval bases were vital to NATO's strategy for the defence of the West. And third, Portugal's brutal, authoritarian government (controlled by Dr. Antonio

Salazar until 1968, and then by Professor Marcello Caetano) was able to order the ruthless repression of black nationalist movements in Mozambique, Angola and Guinea (Bissau) without fear of public criticism at home. Although the colonies became increasingly costly to defend – in the 1960s more than forty per cent of Portugal's national budget was spent on the armed forces – they were valuable as food producers and as markets for the mother country's exports. Even after most of the African continent had fallen to the black nationalists, the Portuguese government continued to encourage large-scale emigration to Angola and Mozambique to bolster white colonial rule.

Finally, in 1974 and 1975 the Portuguese Empire fell apart, under pressure from two directions. In Africa, Portuguese rule was under direct attack from armed black nationalist organisations, such as the Mozambique Liberation Front (FRELIMO), the Popular Movement for the Liberation of Angola (MPLA), the National Union for Complete Independence (UNITA) in Angola, and the African Independence Party of Guinea and Cape Verde (PAIGC). Back home, the economy was hit by international inflation and also by the entry of Portugal's main European trading partner, Britain, into the EEC. In April 1974 the army overthrew the Caetano régime, and the new government wanted a quick end to the colonial wars in Africa. Guinea (Bissau) became independent in 1974, and Mozambique and Angola in 1975. Something like 800,000 white Portuguese settlers fled in panic.

African Nationalism

Why was the disintegration of colonial rule so sudden? As we have seen, some European governments were under pressure, from the Americans and from public opinion inside their own countries, to withdraw from empire; and they were, in any case, not rich enough to pay the price of repressing liberation movements without sacrifices which their own people were not prepared to make. But the force which in the end took even the Portuguese by storm was the rise of nationalism among colonial peoples whom Europeans had previously thought too primitive to assert themselves.

Many factors contributed to the rise of black nationalism. The bigger concentrations of blacks in African towns and cities – both workers for big firms and surplus people from the countryside in search of jobs – offered new audiences for politicians and were easily mobilised in support of radical change. The growth of African élites, composed of independent professional men, civil servants, army officers and clergymen, provided nationalist movements with leaders. The more that educated Africans were exposed to Western political influences, the more clearly they saw the contradictions between the ideals of parliamentary democracy and the reality of colonial rule. For many of those men, Western socialist ideas appealed because of their emphasis on social justice and modernisation.

Finally, decolonisation was a cumulative process: from the point of view of the imperial Powers, one concession paved the way for another. If Algeria could not be held, what was the point in hanging on to other, less valuable, colonies in tropical Africa? And, with each nationalist gain, the colonies that remained became harder to hold down. Ghana inspired liberation movements throughout Black Africa; President Nasser of Egypt armed and encouraged the Algerian FLN in their struggle against the French; the anti-Portuguese nationalist movements operated from bases in the black states of Zaïre, Zambia and Tanzania.

The Problem of South Africa

Although black nationalism triumphed over the European empires throughout Africa, it met with one major defeat: South Africa. In the richest and most fertile state of the continent – which produced three-quarters of the world's gold, as well as other valuable minerals (diamonds, uranium and copper) – a white minority held on to exclusive power over the other eighty per cent of the population.

For Black Africa, white rule in South Africa represented a last stronghold of colonialism: yet South Africa was not a colony. The Boers, or Afrikaners, who formed a majority of the white population, had broken their links with the Netherlands, their country of origin, way back in the early nineteenth century. From 1910 the country was a self-governing Dominion within the British Commonwealth (see Chapter 2, page 10); and in 1961 that last connection with imperial Europe was broken when South Africa left the Commonwealth. The white South Africans were left with sovereign control over their own defence and the policies of their state, but with no possibility of retreat – unlike the French, Portuguese or British settlers – to a European homeland, before the rising tide of black nationalism. Moreover, they had an aggressively nationalist and racist philosophy of their own, claiming that the land belonged to them rather than to the black African people whom they had defeated and subdued in the colonial period. As the Prime Minister, Mr Vorster, put it in 1970: "South African nationhood is for the Whites only."

Throughout most of the world, the old doctrine that Europeans were a 'master-race', destined to govern non-European peoples, lost ground in the second half of the twentieth century. In South Africa, however, it flourished, gaining new support after the Second World War when the Afrikaners became the dominant group in politics, displacing the richer minority of English-speaking whites. Like the 'poor whites' of the American South, the Afrikaners stood for the principle of white supremacy in its crudest and most brutal form, and they were untouched by European liberal influences. The Afrikaner version of Christianity, taught by the Dutch Reformed Church, declared that God had made white men superior to blacks, and had ordained the white élite to rule and the blacks to be their servants. In the 1948 elections, the Afrikaner National Party, led by Dr D. F. Malan, came to power, pledged to the cause of white rule, and the separate development or 'apartheid' of different races. The Party held on to power for the next thirty years, wearing down the resistance of English-speaking liberals in the 1950s and early 1960s until it emerged as the only effective governing party in South Africa. Malan's successors as Prime Minister of South Africa – all of them hard-line Afrikaner nationalists – were J. G. Strijdom from 1952, H. F. Verwoerd from 1958 and B. J. Vorster from 1966. In 1979 Paul Botha was the first to use the overwhelmingly strong position of the Nationalist Party to carry out tiny relaxations of apartheid.

The System of Apartheid

The Afrikaner nationalist movement was, in fact, part of the nationalist surge which swept through the Third World after the Second World War. Yet for the non-white population of South Africa, it resulted in a more complete racial oppression than even they had ever known before (see Chapter 16, page 70). Apartheid deprived them of all civil liberties and all hope of progress, and kept them desperately poor in one of the world's richest countries. An Act of 1953 banned strikes by African workers (they had already lost the right to form trade unions in 1937) and by 1959 all non-whites had had their right to vote taken away. Rigid segregation was enforced in every aspect of life: to marry someone of a different race became a crime, and so did any mixing of the races in sport. Public transport, cinemas, post offices, restaurants, and churches were all segregated by law. After the Bantu Education Act of 1953 schools were segregated and the government gradually took over African schools from Church missions and enforced limitations on the syllabuses, so that most black children were trained only for manual work. From 1959, Africans were not allowed to attend white universities.

Perhaps the most far-reaching aspect of apartheid was the territorial segregation of the races. A series of Acts, starting with the Group Areas Act of 1950, limited the freedom of non-whites to live, own land and establish businesses in areas designated as reserved for whites – and those 'white' areas amounted to eighty-seven per cent of the country's land. The Bantu Self-Government Act of 1959 lumped the remaining 'African' land into eight reserves, or Bantustans, each supposed to act as a 'homeland' for one of South Africa's black tribes. Within the Bantustans Africans were given the right to elect their own governments – but the white government in Pretoria kept control of the police and a veto over legislation, and attempted to ensure that conservative tribal chiefs controlled Bantustan affairs. Blacks lost all right to live outside those reserves, and in the 'white' mining and urban areas where they provided cheap labour they became no more than migrant workers, without the right to bring their wives and children to live with them. After 1963 blacks could be – and were – moved by force to a Bantustan from any 'white' area, no matter how long they had lived there. The white government promised the Bantustans independence in due course, yet the reserves were so poor and overcrowded that they could not hope to break away from their dependence on the South African economy. Without South African aid, and jobs for migrant workers, their people would have starved.

The system of apartheid was enforced by pass laws, requiring all non-whites to carry identity cards with them at all times, and by a brutal police force with very wide powers – including, since the early 1960s, the right to keep suspects in prison indefinitely. Moreover,

the 1950 Suppression of Communism Act gave the Minister of Justice wide powers in suppressing radical opposition to the Nationalist régime. Not only did he ban the tiny South African Communist Party, but he also branded as Communists all who stepped outside the law in speaking out against apartheid, and introduced harsh measures against them.

The imposition of apartheid in the 1950s provoked opposition from the non-white population, which led to riots and civil disobedience campaigns. On the whole, the protest was non-violent, influenced by leaders like Chief Albert Luthuli of the African National Congress (see Chapter 16, page 70), who hoped for white liberal and Christian support. Even the Pan-African Congress, a more radical breakaway organisation formed in 1958, at first proposed peaceful methods of opposition to apartheid. But even peaceful protest was met by violent repression.

In 1960 it seemed that the police had gone too far. They opened fire, without authorisation, on a crowd demonstrating against the pass laws at Sharpeville, in Transvaal. That massacre, in which 67 blacks were killed and 186 injured, had a profound effect on South African politics, and for a few months the future of apartheid seemed uncertain. It led to widespread demonstrations by the blacks; and new leaders of the ANC and PAC broke with non-violence and started campaigns of arson and bombing. Alarmed by such developments, foreign investors withdrew funds from the country, and some white families emigrated. However, the South African government stood firm. The spectacle of near-anarchy and civil war in Zaïre, which had just become independent under black rule, reinforced its determination to resist attacks on white rule. It banned the ANC and PAC and either imprisoned their leaders or forced them into exile. After 1963 no radical opponents of the régime remained free for long inside South Africa: the police state had established control.

South Africa's Foreign Relations

The confidence of foreign investors was restored quickly, too, once the threat of revolution had faded. In the 1960s South Africa achieved a faster rate of economic growth than ever before in her history – and a faster rate than any other country in the world, except Japan. Her rich natural resources and cheap labour costs attracted massive investment from overseas and a new wave of white immigrants from Europe. The governments of Verwoerd and Vorster set out to make South Africa more self-sufficient, by developing her manufacturing industry and by finding new trading partners, so as to make her less dependent on Britain and the USA.

Western Europe responded enthusiastically: the West Germans provided larger amounts of investment and high-technology imports (such as computers and military communications systems), while the French supplied the South African government with arms after 1964, when the British Labour government cut off supplies. However, British and American investment also increased after 1963, and even the

Black and white in South Africa. Black children begging on a street in Cape Town in the 1960s.

assassination of Verwoerd in 1966 failed to shake confidence in the South African economy. That was hardly surprising, for investment in South Africa offered a rate of return of 15 to 20 per cent, far above the profits which could be made anywhere else. In 1967 the price of gold in world markets also began to rise, reaching a peak in 1974, partly as a result of the weakness of the dollar in the later stages of the Vietnam War, and partly because the South Africans deliberately mined less. Between 1967 and 1974, the value of their gold output rose threefold.

In 1970 South Africa's position seemed all but unassailable. In that year, white South Africans overtook the inhabitants of California as the richest people in the whole world. Their income per head was about fourteen times higher than that of the country's blacks, most of whom lived in dire poverty. All that had been achieved in the way of world protest was an ineffective UN embargo on arms sales to South Africa in 1963; and in 1966 an equally ineffective decision to bring to an end South Africa's authority in the black territory of South West Africa, or Namibia, a colony over which she had been given a mandate by the League of Nations after the Great War of 1914–18. In 1971 the new British Conservative government resumed arms sales to South Africa.

There was one area, however, where Mr Vorster's régime remained vulnerable. That was in its relations with the new Black African states. South Africa needed to sell exports to those states in order to pay for high-technology imports from the West. She also needed to avoid getting involved in expensive wars. Although in the 1960s her northern frontiers were made safe by the friendly white governments of Angola, Mozambique and Rhodesia, as you can see from the map on page 279, it seemed prudent to seek good relations with Black African states too. The South Africans did establish open trading relations and friendship with Malawi, and rather more surreptitious relations with Zambia, and with some of the former French colonies, led by the Ivory Coast. But those black nationalist régimes could not afford to be branded as clients of white colonialism. South Africa's trade with the rest of the continent did not grow very much in the sixties. To make matters worse, in courting Black African friendship Vorster's government upset the extremists in their own country. A hard-line or *verkrampte* wing of the National Party broke away, in opposition to the *verligte* or 'enlightened' policies of the government.

After 1970 developments outside and inside Africa brought South Africa's golden years to an end, and sharpened the dilemma of the white supremacists – how to survive in a black continent without compromising their own ideals. South Africa was hit first by Britain's entry into the EEC in 1973, which meant that her exports now became dearer in the British market because of the higher EEC customs duties. Second, the oil crisis which began in 1973 greatly increased her import bill; and her support for Israel in the 1973 war (see page 291) angered the Arab nations and brought the threat of a loss of oil supplies, which she avoided only by a deal with the conservative government of the Shah of Iran. Third, there was a temporary halt to the gold boom, which had helped to cushion South Africa against the rise in oil prices in 1973–74, when the IMF, with American backing, took steps in 1975 to make the world's monetary system less dependent on gold, and the price of the metal fell for a while. Fourth, and worst of all, the Portuguese colonies on South Africa's northern frontier fell to black nationalists.

South Africa tried hard to establish friendly relations with the FRELIMO régime in Mozambique; but she allowed her troops to become involved in Angola in a fight against the communist-backed MPLA, hoping that a more friendly African government might be established there in place of the Portuguese. The MPLA, helped by troops from Cuba, defeated all opposition, and South Africa's intervention only hardened Black African hostility towards her. The governments of Mozambique, Malawi and Zambia took steps to stop South Africa recruiting migrant workers in their lands, and all hopes of *détente* with Black Africa seemed at an end.

Pressures on Apartheid

This external crisis left South Africa vulnerable for the first time to guerrilla raids from border states, and it happened just as a major internal crisis was developing. In 1975 economic growth ceased, the currency was devalued twice, and both inflation and unemployment mounted. The recession put new stresses on the African population, who had already begun again in the early 1970s to assert their grievances – through strikes in factories and mines, and through the new, student-based Black Consciousness movement. On the other hand, Vorster had, under pressure, made concessions to the *verkrampte* Nationalists. In particular, he had taken into his government one of the *verkrampte* leaders, Dr Andries Treurnicht, as Deputy Minister of Bantu Education. Treurnicht insisted on enforcing the rule that in African schools, fifty per cent of the instruction should be in Afrikaans – a language which many black teachers did not speak fluently, and which they and their pupils hated as the language of their oppressors. In June 1976 schoolchildren in the township of Soweto, which housed about 1·5 million of Johannesburg's black workers, held a demonstration against the fifty per cent rule: police fired on them, and at least 25 were killed and 200 injured. Riots, strikes and demonstrations spread throughout South Africa in the following months, and by the end of the year over five hundred blacks had been killed by the police. Foreign investors once again took fright at this new evidence of South Africa's instability, and capital flowed out of the country, deepening the recession.

In the course of this crisis of 1975–76 new pressures were brought to bear on South Africa to relax her white-supremacist policies. Within the country, businessmen pressed for modifications in apartheid which might reduce world criticism of the régime and help to restore confidence in the economy; and the government agreed to relax segregation in sport and in public amenities, and to abolish the fifty per cent rule in black schools. From outside came pressure from the USA to stop South Africa propping up Ian Smith's government in Rhodesia, where a tiny majority of whites imposed their rule on the black majority. This pressure led South Africa to prod Ian Smith in 1976 to make progress to black majority rule, which followed in 1980 when Robert Mugabe became Prime Minister of independent Zimbabwe, as Rhodesia was now re-named.

Shortly before, in 1978, the white Nationalist Party was discredited in a political scandal and the President, Johannes Forster, was forced to resign. As a result of this 'Muldergate Scandal', in which the Minister of Information, Dr Connie Mulder, misused secret government funds, a new Prime Minister, Paul Botha,

came to power. Botha quickly adopted a more liberal policy in an attempt to make apartheid more acceptable to its critics, both at home and abroad. Over the next five years some of the restrictions on segregated sport were removed. The Mixed Marriages Act and Section 16 of the Immorality Act, which banned sexual relations outside marriage between whites and non-whites, were both abolished. In some areas the segregation of public amentities, such as trains, buses, cinemas, hotels, restaurants and beaches, was relaxed. Blacks gained the right to join trade unions.

In most respects, however, the system of apartheid remained intact. Compulsory race classification of all citizens, the pass laws and the sytem of land ownership all remained untouched by Botha's reforms. Blacks were as disadvantaged as ever by a high rate of unemployment, unequal education, poor housing, low wages, and inadequate medical and welfare facilities. In the mid-1980s the government therefore found itself under increasing attack from black political organisations dedicated to the destruction of apartheid. In the ghetto townships that fringed the cities of 'white' South Africa, increasingly violent protests were organised by the African National Congress – whose leader, Nelson Mandela, remained in prison – by the Inkatha Organisation of the Zulu tribe, by the Azanian People's Organisation and by the United Democratic Front. In 1985 more than 800 people were killed in riots and battles with the police. As rioting, murder and arson, as well as police violence, became an almost daily spectacle on television screens around the world, the government banned foreign pressmen from filming scenes of 'unrest'. Nevertheless, unseen by the rest of the world, the violence continued after the ban. Added to pressure from Black organisations was the threat that foreign investors would close their businesses. In 1988 the government faced pressure to release Nelson Mandela, now seventy years old and sick but still unprepared to renounce violence unless the state abandoned the use of force to keep apartheid in being.

45　The Middle East Conflicts since 1947

The Palestine War of 1948–9

Before the Second World War hundreds of thousands of Jews, many of whom had fled from persecution in Europe, settled down in the British mandate of Palestine (see Chapter 15, page 67). The post-war future of that land was quickly and violently decided in 1948, when the British left.

Neither the British government nor the United Nations could persuade the Arabs to agree to the partition of the land between Arabs and Jews. When the Jewish leaders proclaimed the state of Israel in May 1948, the Egyptians, Jordanians, Syrians and Iraqis invaded, to support the resistance of the Palestinian Arabs and to wipe the new Jewish state off the map. But the Israelis, armed with Czech weapons and with the desperate knowledge that their very survival was at stake, defeated the Arab armies and gained more territory – including the western part of the Negev Desert, which had not been assigned to the Jews in the partition plan drawn up by the UN in 1947.

The very creation of Israel gave rise to a refugee problem that brought real difficulties for those states – chiefly Egypt, Jordan, the Lebanon and Syria – to which the Palestinian Arabs fled. According to UN estimates, there were nearly a million Palestinian refugees by 1958, well over half of them in Jordan. Both Israel and the Arab states refused to attempt any permanent solution to the problem on the grounds that a general settlement of the whole Palestinian question and the future of Israel must come first.

Meanwhile, the refugees lived in camps, in acute poverty; and some of them set out to fight their own battles, by terrorist action against Israel. The Israelis decided at an early stage that their only protection against Palestinian guerrilla warfare was to hit back with massive reprisals against the states which protected the refugees. So the Palestinians became a threat to the security of Israel's neighbouring Arab states, as well as an economic burden and a moral reproach.

Israel won the Palestine War, which ended in January 1949, but her enemies remained in strong positions to harass the new state. First, the port of Eilat, Israel's only outlet into the Red Sea, was blockaded by the Egyptians, who controlled Sinai and the Straits of Tiran; and since Egypt also refused to allow Israel's ships through the Suez Canal, her trade with the East was effectively stopped. Second, the Arab League – an organisation that had been set up* in 1945 – imposed economic sanctions against Israel. Its member governments banned direct trade with Israel, and boycotted ships and planes that called at Israeli ports and airports. Third, Israel was subjected to armed raids by Palestinian refugees from neighbouring states – and, particularly in the 1950s, by the *fedayeen*† from the Gaza Strip and Sinai.

The Suez War of 1956

In July 1952, the royal government of Egypt, Israel's most hostile neighbour, was overthrown by a revolt of army officers, led by General Mohammed Neguib and Colonel Gamal Abdel Nasser. The new régime was intensely nationalist; and Nasser, who replaced Neguib as Prime Minister in April 1954, aimed not only at the eviction of all remaining British troops from his land, but also at Egyptian leadership of the whole Arab world.

The new ruler of Egypt soon began to cut a formidable figure in Middle Eastern politics. In July 1954 the British government agreed to remove their troops from the Suez Canal Zone within two years. Late in 1955 an arms deal was announced, by which Egypt received from Czechoslovakia substantial numbers of modern fighter planes, bombers and heavy tanks. Viewed from the Israeli side of the Egyptian frontier, Nasser had become by early 1956 alarmingly well equipped to lead a new Arab attack on the Jewish state. The Israelis looked for ways of strengthening their own armed forces, and in April 1956 the French government, angered by Nasser's support of nationalist rebels in Algeria, supplied Israel with their most up-to-date jet fighters.

The way in which Israel and Egypt came to fight a second full-scale war, the Suez War of late October and early November 1956, has already been told in Chapter 36 (page 219). This time it was the Israelis, backed by the British and the French, who struck first.

---

* The member states of the Arab League were Egypt, Iraq, Syria, the Lebanon, Jordan, Saudi Arabia and Yemen.
† *Fedayeen:* armed fighters, or guerrillas.

And whereas the short war ended in political disaster for the Europeans, it was a major victory for the Israelis. They had aimed to clear out the *fedayeen* bases and to free the port of Eilat from blockade: and not only did they capture Sinai and the Gaza Strip, but their spectacular defeat of the much bigger Egyptian army severely battered the prestige of Nasser, who had become President of Egypt in June.

In March 1957 Israeli troops marched out of Sinai and a United Nations Emergency Force took up its positions in the area. The UN had guaranteed to prevent further raids into Israel from the Gaza Strip and to stop Egyptian threats to Israeli shipping in the Straits of Tiran. UNEF units were therefore stationed both in the Gaza Strip and at Sharm-el-Sheikh.

The port of Eilat grew and flourished in the years after 1956; and so did the Israeli economy, despite the continuing Arab boycott. But a new organisation of Palestinian nationalists, *El Fatah*,* now emerged, which trained guerrillas and mounted attacks on Israeli villages from its bases in Syria, Jordan and the Lebanon. It was simple for Israel to make reprisal raids against Jordan and the Lebanon, even though their governments did not support the guerrillas. However, the Palestinians found their chief support in Syria, which was dominated after 1963 by the radical pan-Arab Baath Party – and the Syrians controlled the Golan Heights, from where they mounted artillery bombardments on Israeli settlements. The Syrian government's attitude to Israel was made absolutely clear in radio broadcasts directed at the enemy to the south: "We have decided to drench this land with our blood, to oust you, aggressors, and throw you into the sea for good."

The Six Day War of 1967

Early in 1967, war fever began to mount again. Israel's raids into Jordan and the Lebanon were violently condemned; and Nasser, in a new bid for the leadership of the Arabs, mobilised his troops on the Sinai border, ordered out the UN forces that had patrolled the frontier since 1957, closed the Straits of Tiran to Israeli shipping, and called for a new holy war to eliminate Israel. Syria, Iraq, and even Jordan, rallied

* 'Fatah' means 'conquest', and was formed by the initial letters, in reverse order, of 'Harakat al Tharir al Falastin', which meant Palestine Liberation Movement.

to Nasser's call, and a full-scale Arab invasion of Israel looked inevitable.

Instead, the Israelis attacked first, after the 'hawks' in the Israeli government, led by General Moshe Dayan, had persuaded their colleagues that attack was the best form of defence. In the Six Day War of 1967, which was all over between 5–10 June, Israel's victory was swift and complete. Her planes destroyed the Egyptian air force on the ground, while her army took the whole of Sinai, the Old City of Jerusalem and the West Bank of the Jordan, and then captured the Golan Heights.

From that war the Israelis gained stronger frontiers, and new confidence in their fight for survival. But, like the Suez War, this third conflict solved no basic problems. The Palestinian nationalists were as determined as ever to fight for their cause, and although Syria and Iraq gave them full backing, the main effect of the war was to strip the refugee organisations of any illusions that the Arab states could win them what they wanted – resettlement in Palestine.

The Palestinian Liberation Organisation

In the twenty years after their unwilling departure from their own land, the Palestinians had become a powerful force in the internal politics of other Arab states. King Hussein of Jordan eventually had to establish control over the Palestinians in his country by war in 1970–71; and in the Lebanon the Palestinians played a key role in the bloody civil war of 1975–77 between Christian right-wing and Muslim left-wing forces. Yassir Arafat, the *El Fatah* chief, was treated more and more as an independent nationalist leader; and the new broadly based Palestine Liberation Organisation (PLO), formed in 1964, was quickly taken over by *El Fatah* leaders. Breakaway terrorist organisations, like the Popular Front for the Liberation of Palestine, led by George Habash, began to mount independent commando raids and hijacking operations, often against targets outside Israel, in attempts to keep up the pressure on world opinion to back the Palestinian cause.

More serious from Israel's point of view were the problems created by her new conquests. In the Old City of Jerusalem and on the West Bank of the Jordan she had gained lands that were inhabited by hostile Arabs, and which the Israeli government planned to

The Middle East Conflicts since 1947

The Middle East in 1985

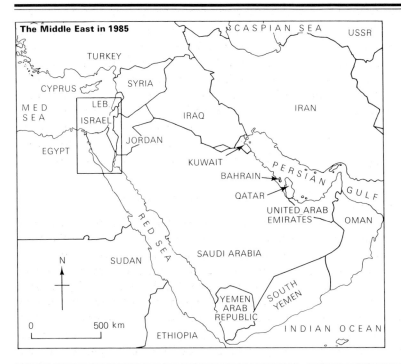

TURKEY

CASPIAN SEA

USSR

CYPRUS

SYRIA

LEB.

ISRAEL

MED SEA

IRAQ

IRAN

EGYPT

JORDAN

KUWAIT

PERSIAN GULF

BAHRAIN

QATAR

UNITED ARAB EMIRATES

OMAN

RED SEA

SAUDI ARABIA

SUDAN

YEMEN ARAB REPUBLIC

SOUTH YEMEN

INDIAN OCEAN

ETHIOPIA

N

0   500 km

Israel in Palestine, 1948 to 1967

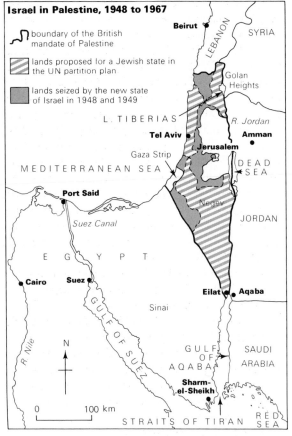

boundary of the British mandate of Palestine

lands proposed for a Jewish state in the UN partition plan

lands seized by the new state of Israel in 1948 and 1949

Beirut

LEBANON

SYRIA

Golan Heights

L. TIBERIAS

R. Jordan

Tel Aviv

Amman

Jerusalem

Gaza Strip

DEAD SEA

MEDITERRANEAN SEA

Negev

JORDAN

Port Said

Suez Canal

E G Y P T

Cairo

Suez

Eilat

Aqaba

Sinai

GULF OF SUEZ

GULF OF AQABA

SAUDI ARABIA

N

0   100 km

Sharm-el-Sheikh

R. Nile

STRAITS OF TIRAN

RED SEA

Israel at war, 1967 to 1985

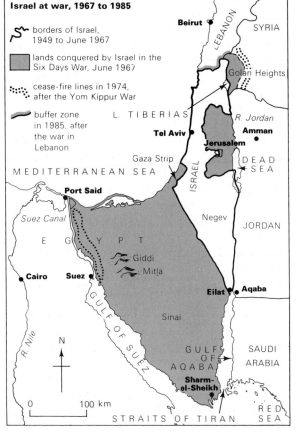

borders of Israel, 1949 to June 1967

lands conquered by Israel in the Six Days War, June 1967

cease-fire lines in 1974, after the Yom Kippur War

buffer zone in 1985, after the war in Lebanon

Beirut

LEBANON

SYRIA

Golan Heights

L. TIBERIAS

R. Jordan

Tel Aviv

Amman

ISRAEL

Jerusalem

DEAD SEA

Gaza Strip

MEDITERRANEAN SEA

Negev

JORDAN

Port Said

Suez Canal

E G Y P T

Giddi

Mitla

Cairo

Suez

Eilat

Aqaba

Sinai

GULF OF SUEZ

GULF OF AQABA

SAUDI ARABIA

N

0   100 km

Sharm-el-Sheikh

R. Nile

STRAITS OF TIRAN

RED SEA

treat as bargaining counters in exchange for an agreement with the Arab states which would guarantee Israel's future in the Middle East. Yet to the Jews those lands were precious for religious and historic reasons: they would not readily give back the Old City and the Wailing Wall; and they were eager to establish Jewish communities on the West Bank.

The Yom Kippur War of 1973

Nasser died in 1970 and was succeeded by Anwar Sadat. The new Egyptian President appeared to be a subtler statesman than the old revolutionary leader. He inherited a country in which the twin pressures of expensive war and a rapidly increasing population had permitted only a marginal improvement in the general standard of living. Clearly, the Egyptian government could not afford to go on indefinitely spending vast sums of money on their armed forces, for such a policy would not only drag Egypt further into debt and make her even more dependent on the Soviet Union – her chief armaments supplier – but it would make her already severe economic problems even worse. Yet at the same time Sadat could not shrug off the fact that the Israelis were occupying huge areas of Egyptian and Jordanian territory and establishing settlements there. On the one hand, he had to look and be aggressive: on the other, it was essential to search for some arrangement with Israel that would make it possible to halt the ruinous expenditure on armaments.

The first two years of Sadat's régime were remarkable for a new flexibility in Egyptian policy. He tried, and failed, to persuade the Israelis to withdraw, at least partially, from the occupied lands: the Israeli government were not interested in handing anything back without first getting Arab recognition of Israel's right to exist. In 1972, dissatisfied with the reduced flow of arms and aid from the USSR, Sadat expelled all Soviet specialists and 'advisers' from his land. Then, in the autumn of 1973, to everyone's surprise, he launched an all-out attack on Israel.

On 6 October, just before the Jewish festival of Yom Kippur, the Egyptian army advanced across the Suez Canal and broke through the Israelis' forward positions. Shortly afterwards, the Israelis were faced by a two-front war as the Syrians, helped by other Arab states, made a grab for the Golan Heights. The Soviet Union supplied Egypt, Syria and Iraq with arms; but massive American military aid, together with the

greater efficiency of the Israeli armed forces, enabled Israel to beat back her enemies within a fortnight.

The Yom Kippur War left Israel's frontiers more or less unchanged, but it did have very important political consequences. It made the Western powers, as well as the Egyptians, much more anxious to bring about a settlement in the Middle East. And behind the new urgency to calm down this explosive part of the world was an acute concern about oil supplies.

The Arab 'Oil Weapon'

In 1970, about sixty per cent of the world's known crude oil reserves were located in the Muslim states of the Middle East and North Africa. The enormous increase in consumption of crude oil by the developed countries of Europe, North America and Japan after 1945 had brought great wealth to the major oil-producing states, such as Saudi Arabia, Kuwait and Libya. They had greatly improved the terms under which foreign companies extracted and exported their oil. They had become independent of foreign aid: indeed, they had become rich enough to give their own aid to the poorer Arab countries, such as Egypt.

In 1961 the Organisation of Petroleum Exporting Countries (OPEC) was set up to coordinate and strengthen the policies of the oil producers, and in 1968 the Organisation of Arab Petroleum Exporting Countries (OAPEC) was formed, to promote greater solidarity in the Middle East. By the early 1970s OAPEC was using its power not only to jack up the price of oil, but also as a political weapon to influence the attitudes of Western governments towards Israel. When the Yom Kippur War broke out in 1973, the Middle East oil producers raised their prices by no less than seventy per cent, and made threats – some of which were carried out – that they would restrict sales to countries which backed Israel against the Arabs.

So, turmoil in the Middle East could now threaten the very livelihoods of industrialised countries round the world – from Britain (then without North Sea oil on tap) and France, to the USA and Japan. Not only that, but the Yom Kippur War had brought from the USSR the alarming proposal that Soviet and American troops should be sent to the area. The sooner a settlement was reached, the better – especially for the Americans, whose ever-increasing consumption of energy had made their economy dangerously dependent on foreign supplies of oil.

291

From the end of 1973, the American Secretary of State, Henry Kissinger, worked strenuously to bring peace to the Middle East; and he eventually succeeded in bringing about the disengagement of Egyptian and Israeli forces in January 1974. In 1975 they reached a further agreement by which Israel withdrew her troops from the Mitla and Giddi passes and part of Sinai, and in turn received increased American aid and Egypt's agreement to allow Israeli cargoes through the Suez Canal. In 1977 President Sadat took the bold step of going to Israel and stating Egypt's terms for a permanent settlement directly to the Israeli parliament.

Sadat's peace initiative led to talks in 1978 with the Israeli Prime Minister, Menachim Begin, at Camp David in Maryland, USA, under the chairmanship of President Carter, and a peace treaty was finally signed between Israel and Egypt in Washington in 1979. The Washington Treaty provided for Israel to evacuate all the land taken from Egypt, except for the Gaza Strip, and to end Israeli settlement in those lands. The treaty also envisaged Israel's eventual withdrawal from the West Bank. Although Israel finally left Sinai in 1982, there was no indication that Israeli settlers would withdraw from the West Bank. Indeed, new Israeli settlements continued to spring up there during the mid-1980s, infuriating the Palestinians still further.

Sadat's peace initiative aroused the hostility of most of the other Arab nations. Hatred for him in the Arab world increased when he offered refuge to the deposed Shah of Iran (see page 294) in 1980. He was assassinated in 1981 by Egyptian soldiers no longer prepared to tolerate his moderation.

War in Lebanon, 1975–85

Despite the new Egyptian attitude, the Israelis and the Palestinian Arabs were further away than ever from a negotiated peace after the Yom Kippur War.

By 1974 the PLO had been recognised by the Arab states, including Jordan, as the official representative of Arab Palestine; and Yassir Arafat persuaded the UN General Assembly to support the rights of the Palestinians to sovereignty inside Palestine and to independent representation at a peace conference. The PLO had thus gained new prestige and confidence, and some of its leaders were ambitious enough in 1975–77 to back the Muslim left-wing forces in the Lebanese civil war – hoping they could help to overthrow the predominantly Christian government and turn Lebanon into a pro-Palestinian stronghold. But the Syrians intervened in the Lebanon in 1976 and, jointly with the PLO, made war on the Christian Phalangists.

Israel was naturally alarmed by the growing instability of her northern neighbour, particularly as the PLO used southern Lebanon as a base from which to make attacks on Israel. In March 1978, 26,000 Israeli troops invaded Lebanon after Israeli civilians had been killed in a bus hijack by the PLO. Their aim was to protect the villages of southern Lebanon from infiltration by PLO guerillas. In an attempt to restore peace, the United Nations Security Council sent a peace-keeping force to the area. But Unifil (the United Nations Interim Force in Lebanon) was unable to create a neutral buffer zone between Israel and Lebanon. For the next three years Israeli aircraft continued to make bombing raids on Lebanese territory.

In 1981 the UN successfully negotiated a cease-fire. Four nine months there was relative calm on the Israeli-Lebanese border. But by now Lebanon had become a tangled collection of enclaves controlled by many rival political and religious groups. Beirut, the capital, was divided by conflicts between Muslims and Christians, between Shia Muslims and Sunni Muslims backed by the PLO, between Christians and Druze. Each sect had its own private army. And the PLO, based in the Palestinian refugee camps of west Beirut, were heavily armed with anti-aircraft guns and tanks.

In June 1982 Israel began a full-scale military invasion of Lebanon. The aim was to destroy the PLO, to re-establish Christian rule throughout Lebanon, and thus gain a more friendly northern neighbour. By the time the Israeli army reached Beirut in September, 17,000 Lebanese were dead. But once the Israelis had encircled Beirut they found it was almost impossible to dislodge the PLO whose guerillas now occupied civilian areas and fired their anti-aircraft guns from within them. During the siege of Beirut the Israeli air force demolished whole apartment blocks in bombing raids, killing countless civilians. The Israeli army allowed, if not actively encouraged, Christian Phalangists to murder hundreds of civilians in the Palestinian refugee camps. Such tactics enabled the Israelis to drive out the PLO, who left Beirut under American supervision in August 1982 for dispersal to Tunisia, Syria, Jordan and other Arab states. They also provoked an unprecedented degree of hatred of the Israelis among the Muslims of southern Lebanon.

Israel began a slow withdrawal of her forces in 1983. In the areas vacated by the Israelis, Syrian forces arrived to occupy the country along with the Muslim and Druze forces which they backed. The Christian forces which Israel had hoped to strengthen dwindled and retreated to the areas north of Beirut. And as the Israelis retreated south they found themselves increasingly under attack from fanatical Shia Muslims who inflicted spectacular defeats on them with suicide bombing missions. In Israel itself, anti-war protesters organised the biggest demonstrations in the history of the country and Menachim Begin resigned as Prime Minister. In April 1985 the Israelis withdrew their last forces behind a heavily fortified buffer zone along Lebanon's southern border, suffering their first defeat.

Israel after the Lebanon War

Defeat in Lebanon was not the only problem facing the Israeli government in the mid-1980s. After a stalemate in elections in 1984, Israel's main political parties had to share power in a 'government of national unity'; Shimon Peres, the left-wing Labour leader, taking a turn as Prime Minister before handing over to the right-wing Yitzhak Shamir in 1986. Shamir was under pressure from his supporters not to negotiate with the Arabs over the future of the West Bank. Jewish settlers continued to build new villages there, contrary to the Camp David agreement, warning they would oppose any attempt to remove them.

Faced with such attitudes, the government found it impossible to satisfy the demands of both Israeli settlers and Palestinian Arabs, and tension rose in the West Bank and Gaza during 1987. Demonstrations and protests by Arabs became everyday events. In December the demonstrations turned into a full-scale *intifada*, the Arabic word for uprising. The *intifada* spread rapidly. In Gaza, young Palestinians set up barricades and ran the streets behind them as 'no-go areas' closed to the Army. As the uprising spread to the West Bank, Palestinians also mounted a campaign of strikes and economic boycotts.

The Israeli government responded to the *intifada* with what Shamir called an 'iron fist' policy. The Army used live ammunition as well as riot-control equipment to put down demonstrations. Thousands of young Palestinians were arrested and detained and many severely beaten. By mid-1988, 220 Palestinians had been killed and 5,000 detained. With many stories of Israeli brutality appearing in the foreign press,

Israel was condemned by the UN Security Council for violating human rights, while the Arab League resolved to give all possible support to the uprising.

The conflict reached a critical point in 1988. The PLO, having re-established itself as a political and military force after leaving Beirut, gained widespread international support when its leader, Yassir Arafat, condemned terrorism and recognised Israel's right to exist, thus removing a long-standing barrier to peace negotiations. However, close results in the 1988 Israeli general election gave the balance of power to ultra-orthodox, right-wing religious parties. Led by Shamir, this coalition viewed the PLO's peace initiative with deep suspicion. As the 1980s drew to a close, the problem of Palestine seemed as far from a just and lasting settlement as ever.

Problems of the Arab World

Looking back over more than forty years of Middle Eastern conflict, it seems puzzling that the Arabs achieved so little in their struggle against Israel. Clearly, the Israelis depended heavily for their very survival, on Western aid: yet the Arab states were armed with modern weapons, provided not only by the Soviet Union and other Communist countries, but also (and particularly since the mid-1960s) by France and Britain. In manpower, artillery and combat aircraft, the Arab states always had an enormous advantage over the tiny state of Israel. Yet the Arab League had real political weaknesses. Faced by an enemy with an iron will to survive, the Arabs were divided among themselves and distracted by internal problems of their own. They experienced the struggles between ruling and subject nationalities and religious groups, between modernisers and conservatives, and between rich and poor, that affected the rest of the post-colonial Third World.

One dominant theme in Arab politics was the conflict between monarchists and republicans. Hereditary rulers held on to power not only in those countries which remained outside the British and French Empires – Iran and Saudi Arabia – but also in Egypt, Iraq, Jordan, Yemen, Kuwait, and the North African states of Libya and Morocco. After the Second World War, those monarchies came under attack from nationalist, republican movements, for whom kings were symbols of the colonial past and obstacles to modernisation and progress. The King of Egypt was overthrown in 1952, the King of Iraq in 1958; in 1967 republicans in the Yemen deposed the hereditary

Imam; two years later the King of Libya was ousted.

The division between monarchist and republican regimes hindered Arab unity from the early 1950s. President Nasser of Egypt was treated with suspicion by the rulers of Jordan, Saudi Arabia and the smaller Arbian states because he stood for republicanism and all the elements of 'Arab socialism' which they deeply disliked—modernisation, land reform, and soaking the rich by progressive taxation. Between 1962 and 1967 Egyptian troops were involved in fighting in the Yemeni civil war against troops sent by Saudi Arabia and Jordan to support the royalist side. Between 1970 and 1971, when Hussein of Jordan attempted to establish control over the Palestinian refugees in his country and reach a settlement with Israel, the Syrian government sent troops to support the Palestinians.

Another source of division in the Arab world was conflict between rival republican nationalist movements. In the 1950s and 1960s the chief rivalry was between the supporters of Nasser on the one hand, and the Syrian Baath (or 'national regeneration') movement on the other. Both agreed on the same objectives – Arab unity, modernisation, and opposition to Western influence – and both aimed at the leadership of the Arab nationalist cause. In 1958 the Egyptians and Syrians took a step towards Arab union by merging their two countries in a new United Arab Republic. But in 1961 Syria withdrew from the union, in protest against Nasser's policy of centralising government under Egyptian control. Proposals for union between Egypt and Iraq also came to nothing, mainly on account of opposition from the Iraqi Baathist and Communist Parties. In the later 1960s and 1970s the growth of Marxist influence in some republican nationalist movements produced yet more friction in Arab politics. Devout Muslims, whether royalists or republican Baathists, opposed Marxism as a godless, un-Arab creed: one reason why the Syrians refused to support left-wing forces in the Lebanese civil war.

The Arab states were further hampered in their struggle against Israel by internal problems and the instability of their governments. The Western model of parliamentary democracy proved a complete failure in the Arab world; and armies overthrew governments in many Middle Eastern states – in Egypt, Syria, Iraq, Libya, Sudan and the Yemen. Most states ended up with unstable coalitions between military groups and civilian parties. In some countries dissatisfied national or religious minorities caused trouble, or even chaos. The Iraqi government and army were at war with the

Kurds in the northern provinces of their country between 1958 and 1970. Above all, in Lebanon it proved impossible for the wealthier and Westernised Christian population to live in peace with the Muslims.

By the mid-1980s a new and very potent factor in Arab affairs had emerged: a major resurgence of the Islamic faith. Following a revolution in 1979, the Shah of Iran was toppled from his 'Peacock Throne' and replaced by an 'Islamic Republic' headed by the Ayatollah Khomeini. Under his guidance, a Revolutionary Council composed of Mullahs, or priests, took control of Iran and set about creating a fully Islamic society freed from western influences. This involved imposing Islamic law upon the country, including the banning of alcohol, the compulsory veiling of women and their exclusion from public employment, and the use of the strict penal code of Islam. The result was a reign of terror carried out against the 'enemies of Allah'. Thousands of political opponents of the Ayatollah, racial minority groups such as the Kurds, Sunni Muslims, and supporters of the Shah, were executed. Countless others were imprisoned and tortured.

Although the Iranian revolution inspired Shia Muslims throughout the Arab world, particularly in southern Lebanon in their war against Israel, the resurgence of Islam did not prove to be a unifying force. In September 1980 Iraq declared war on Iran, hoping to gain control of the oil-rich Iranian province of Khuzestan. The Iraqis won some early victories but after an Iranian counter-attack in 1982 a stalemate settled in. By 1985 this 'Gulf War' between Iraq and Iran had killed over one million people on both sides. Iraq took to attacking oil tankers in the Persian Gulf, hoping to ruin Iran's oil export trade, while Iran attacked Saudi Arabian and Kuwaiti oil tankers in order to deter them from giving aid to Iraq. Many ships of other nations were sunk. In 1988 a fierce Iraqi offensive led Iran to agree to a ceasefire and negotiations for peace under UN chairmanship.

It was not, therefore, only because of Israel that Arab unity remained a dream. Although the Arab peoples were drawn together by a common language and a common religion – bonds which were missing in Black Africa and the Indian sub-continent – they could not act together for long because of political differences and the conflicts aroused by non-Muslim minorities in their midst. And Arabs who could unite in denouncing Israel were themselves divided over solutions to the Palestinian question.

46 India, Pakistan and Bangladesh

Nowhere else in the world did people have greater hopes of independence, and of the benefits it might bring, than in the Indian sub-continent. As Jawaharlal Nehru, the first Prime Minister of the new state of India, declared just before midnight on 14 August 1947,

"At the stroke of the midnight hour, when the world sleeps, India will awake to life and freedom … It is fitting that at this solemn moment we take the pledge of dedication to the service of India and her people and to the still larger cause of humanity."

The Social and Economic Development of India

Although the joy of independence was overshadowed by partition and by hideous violence, Nehru remained true to his ideals as a socialist. He hoped to modernise the country, to raise the living standards of the people and to do away with inequality in Indian society. He attacked the privileges of the princes, the wealth of great landowners, and the caste system. His government gave full civil rights to women and to the Untouchables.

India achieved a great deal after 1947. Almost alone among the Third World countries that gained independence in the post-war period, India remained a parliamentary democracy; and her constitution was suspended only once, during Mrs Gandhi's 'state of emergency' between 1975 and 1977. There was impressive progress in the 1950s in modernising agriculture and in industrial development; and as a result of Nehru's five-year plans India's national income rose by forty-two per cent between 1951 and 1961. However, over the whole post-war period India's successes fell far short of the original hopes; and in the sixties and seventies the country's problems attracted more attention than its achievements.

By far the greatest problem was the growth of population – from 360 million in 1951 to 439 million in 1961, 515 million in 1968, and over 590 million in 1975. Economic growth could not keep pace, and in the 1960s *per capita* income stopped rising. India could not produce enough food for her own people; costly imports of food put pressure on the country's balance of payments, and made it difficult to pay for imports of machinery and to maintain levels of investment in industry and in the mechanisation of agriculture. In the late 1960s, the government gave priority to increasing food production by developing new strains of corn and rice, which yielded heavier crops, and by using more fertilisers and pesticides. But even the dramatic results of that 'green revolution' (food production rose from 74 million tonnes in 1966–67 to 100 million tonnes in 1968–69) could not solve India's problems. Her people remained among the poorest in the Third World, and in years of harvest failure Indians starved to death in their thousands in the more backward provinces of the country.

The people resisted government attempts to persuade them to have fewer children. For centuries it had been true that an Indian peasant family benefited from its children – the more hands to work the family's land, and to support the mother and father in old age, the less likely the parents were to starve. As many babies and young children died, there wasn't much incentive for parents to calculate how many children they actually wanted. So the new programmes of education in birth control, backed by free provision of contraceptives and with rewards, like transistor radios, for men who agreed to be sterilised, clashed with the requirements of an agricultural society, often provoking angry resistance.

In other ways, too, Indian society resisted modernisation. Millions of peasant farmers clung to their traditional ways of life and it was difficult to get them to take part in programmes for the improvement of agriculture. Bigger farms, that would produce efficiently for the market, were needed to boost food output: but for the peasants that meant the loss of their land and independence.

Political Problems of India

The obstacles to the successful working of parliamentary democracy were also very great. India had been more thoroughly penetrated by Western liberal influences than most colonies, since British rule there had lasted so long (nearly two centuries in Bengal and Bihar, and in parts of the south and west). Unlike most Third World countries, India also had a relatively

295

large, educated middle class of professional and business people. However, even by the mid-1960s over four-fifths of her people were illiterate. Her vast population was, moreover, made up of many different ethnic and religious groups, speaking more than sixty different languages. Many years passed after independence before Hindi, the country's most widely spoken tongue, was established as the official language. Nehru, whose native tongue was not Hindi but Urdu, tried unsuccessfully to keep English as an official language alongside Hindi, hoping in that way to ensure that at least the educated Indians would have a common means of communication. When his successor, Lal Bahadur Shastri, proclaimed Hindi as the official language in 1965, riots broke out in Madras and in other areas where it was not the language of the people. There were other difficulties – not least of which was the continuing hostility between Hindus and the Muslim minority who had stayed in India at partition; and some political parties which gained most of their support within particular regions of that vast land had little national appeal.

However, it did seem for a long time that the enormous problem of uniting the people of India under democratic rule had been overcome by the Congress Party, which had led the struggle for independence and had supporters in every region of the country. In Nehru's time, Congress won large majorities in elections to the national parliament (*Lok Sabha*); but even before his death in 1964, conservative opponents of modernisation and socialism had gained ground within the Party. The leader of those conservatives, Morarji Desai, made an unsuccessful bid to succeed Nehru, and then opposed the choice of Nehru's daughter, Indira Gandhi, as Prime Minister when Shastri died in 1966. Soon afterwards, in 1969, the Congress Party split; but in the elections of 1971 Mrs Gandhi's Ruling Congress Party won an absolute majority of seats in parliament and nearly obliterated Desai's Opposition Congress Party.

Even so, criticism of Mrs Gandhi's government mounted in the early 1970s; and in 1975 a High Court Judge ruled that the Prime Minister had offended against the Corrupt Practices Act in the 1971 elections and that she should be disqualified from political activities for five years. Mrs Gandhi responded by declaring a "state of emergency" and imprisoning most of her leading critics, including Jaya Prakash Narayan who had been working to unite all non-communist opposition parties into a Janata (People's) Front against her.

This unusual period in the history of independent India saw not only the use of state power to silence opposition, but also attempts to deal with some of the country's most pressing problems. In 1975 Mrs Gandhi announced a twenty-point programme, which included the planning of new power stations and vast new irrigation schemes, the distribution of more land to landless peasants, and promises of severe action against food-hoarders in times of shortages. In the same year she promoted a scheme to establish regional banks to provide credit for small farmers.

However, Mrs Gandhi's suspension of democracy united opponents from many different Indian communities and regions. In March 1977, she miscalculated her personal popularity and held elections that led to a landslide victory for the opposition groups, including the conservatives of the old Congress Party, who combined to form a new, national, Janata Party. The state of emergency was immediately ended by the new government when Morarji Desai became Prime Minister. However, Janata government was brief and, after elections in 1980, Mrs Gandhi and her Congress Party once again took office.

Problems of Race and Religion

The India that Mrs Gandhi led into the 1980s was cruelly divided by racial and religious hatreds. In 1983 hundreds were killed in Hindu-Muslim riots in Bombay, while more than 3,000 people died in racial violence in the north-eastern state of Assam. But the most serious threat to the unity of India came from the Punjab, in the north-west of the country, where 20 million Sikhs were coming increasingly into conflict with the Hindu population. In 1983 the Sikh political party, the Akali Dal, made demands for religious and political autonomy. Extremist Sikhs went further, demanding that the Punjab be made a separate Sikh state, to be called Khalistan. The extremists used their headquarters in the Golden Temple in Amritsar as a base for terrorist attacks on the Hindus of the Punjab.

In June 1984, when the Akali Dal announced that it would cut off supplies of wheat grown in the Punjab to the rest of India, Mrs Gandhi ordered the army to clear the Sikh extremists out of the 30-hectare site of the Golden Temple. During four days of fighting that followed, more than 300 Sikhs were killed and the Golden Temple itself was desecrated. Sikhs all over the world, moderate as well as extreme, united in condemnation of Mrs Gandhi; and in October 1984 two Sikhs in her bodyguard assassinated her.

Mrs Gandhi was succeeded as Prime Minister by her son Rajiv, who quickly demonstrated considerable political skill in calming the widespread violence that followed his mother's death. By the end of 1985, however, his skill had not managed to find any kind of solution to the problem of the Punjab, where Sikh terrorism continued to claim hundreds of lives.

India's Foreign Affairs

Back in 1947 Nehru had a vision of India, the newest and largest democracy in the world, as a nation that would align itself with neither of the two great power blocs but would, instead, take an unselfish lead in a movement for world peace. However, such a fine ideal proved impossible to maintain in the face of the harsh realities of government. India's leaders felt bound, like any other government, to defend their country's frontiers. Nehru himself was prepared to use force to back Indian rule: against the Nagas in the north-east, who wanted to break away from India; against the Portuguese, whom he expelled from their colony of Goa in 1961; and, more seriously, against Pakistan, who disputed India's claim to rule the predominantly Muslim border state of Kashmir. In 1965, shortly after Nehru died, Pakistan invaded Kashmir to fight what turned out to be a second unsuccessful war against the Indian army.

Thus Nehru's neutralist policies were undermined by his own nationalist concerns. That was particularly evident when rivalry flared up between India and her great Asian neighbour, China. Both states had taken a leading part in the Bandung Conference of 1955 (see page 301), but shortly afterwards they quarrelled over Tibet, which the Chinese had conquered in 1950. In 1959 the Tibetans mounted an unsuccessful revolt against their new rulers, and the Chinese resented the fact that Nehru allowed the Tibetan leader, the Dalai Lama, to take refuge in India. For its part, the Indian government was alarmed by the Chinese building a road from Tibet to Sinkiang, which ran through land claimed by India. An increasingly sour relationship resulted in a border war in 1962 – a war in which India failed to drive the Chinese from the disputed territory.

By the time Nehru died, his foreign policy was in ruins.

Mrs Gandhi continued her father's neutralist policies, successfully avoiding entanglement with the super-powers while at the same time taking aid from the Soviet Union. By the time of her death she had gained a considerable international reputation through her chairmanship of the Non-aligned Movement. She had already won the respect of Indians by giving India its first military victory in war when she went to war with Pakistan in 1971 (see below).

Pakistan and Bangladesh

We have seen that India faced great economic and political problems after independence. Pakistan faced even greater difficulties. Above all, that new state was made up of two territories, geographically separate, and united only by the Muslim faith of the majority of the people. Mohammed Ali Jinnah, the founder of Pakistan, died in 1948, soon after independence, and there was no-one left to whom the two halves of the state could look with the same admiration and respect.

By 1954 the people of the poorer but more heavily populated Bengali territory of East Pakistan had rejected domination by the Punjabi Muslim League, and they were brought to heel only by military rule. In 1958 the army took control in West Pakistan too, abolished direct elections to parliament, and set up a presidential government under General Ayub Khan. But the failure of the invasion of Kashmir in 1965, and Ayub Khan's inability to bring about economic progress, led the army to persuade him to resign in 1969. General Yahya Khan, his successor, restored parliamentary democracy, but in doing so he merely illustrated how destructive democracy could be in a deeply divided country. In the 1970 elections, Sheikh Mujibur Rahman's Awami League, which supported Bengali separatism, won a massive victory in the East, while Zulfiqar Ali Bhutto's People's Party won a majority in the West. A working relationship between them was not possible: Bhutto wanted to maintain a united Pakistan, while the Awami League wanted independence for the East. Early in 1971 Sheikh Mujibur was arrested and civil war broke out.

The Indian government could hardly stand aside from the conflict, especially since a flood of refugees crossed the border from East Pakistan. They numbered not far short of ten million in all, and many of them were Hindus, fleeing from reprisals for their opposition to rule by the Muslims of West Pakistan! Faced with the impossible task of absorbing that many extra people, and not sorry to settle some old scores with Pakistan, Mrs Gandhi's government ordered the Indian army into East Pakistan on 4 December 1971. By 16 December it was all over in the East. The Pakistani army surrendered, and the independent state of Bangladesh was established.

The war with Pakistan was immensely popular with the Hindu majority in India: it also meant a decisive break with the Indian policy of non-alignment. The American government, which supported Pakistan, denounced India's intervention and cut off aid to her. Mrs Gandhi retaliated by making a treaty of friendship with the Soviet Union in return for arms and aid. Meanwhile, Pakistan and Bangladesh went their separate ways. When, early in 1972, Bangladesh applied for and was granted membership of the British Commonwealth, Pakistan withdrew.

The wars between India and Pakistan illustrated two of the tendencies at work throughout the Third World: the conflict of rival ethnic or religious groups; and the exploitation of such conflicts by the great powers. And the Indian sub-continent itself revealed some of the extreme contrasts that emerged in the Third World in the post-war period. Independence brought anarchy and economic chaos to Bangladesh, a desperately poor and over-populated country. Sheikh Mujibur proved unable to control other forces in the state, and he was murdered in 1975 in the course of a military revolt. The leader of the rebels, Brigadier Khaled Mosharraf, was himself assassinated in further violence in 1975. So too was his successor, Major-General Zia Rahman, in 1981. West Pakistan was ruled for a time by a civilian government, headed by Mr Bhutto. But in 1977 he was overthrown by the army and replaced by General Mohammed Zia ul-Haq.

At the same time as giving assurances that he would hold free elections for a new civilian government within three months, General Zia placed Pakistan under martial law. Political and trade union activities were banned. The press were censored. And traditional Islamic punishments such as whipping and the amputation of the left hand were imposed for some offences.

General Zia kept Pakistan under martial law for the next ten years, governing the country as a virtual dictator, and assuming the Presidency in addition to his offices as Army Chief of Staff and Chief Martial Law Administrator in 1978. In 1979 the deposed Prime Minister, Zulfiqar Ali Bhutto, was hanged.

In the summer of 1988, shortly after announcing that free elections would be held later that year, Zia was assassinated in an aircraft explosion that also killed many top army generals. In the power vacuum created by their deaths it was unclear whether the armed forces would try to re-establish military rule. The army, however, did not stop the promised elections from taking place. As a result, civilian government was restored when the Pakistan People's Party won the election in November 1988, and its leader Benazir Bhutto, daughter of the deposed Zulfiqar Ali Bhutto, became Prime Minister.

47 Problems of Independence and Non-alignment in the Third World

It proved far easier for Third World nationalists to throw off colonial rule than to build a secure future for themselves and to satisfy the hopes that people had invested in independence – hopes of prosperity and freedom. Most of the newly independent countries included peoples of different nationalities, tribes or religions, speaking different languages, and often bitterly hostile to each other. The struggles for liberation had tended to unite non-European peoples against white rulers; but independence brought conflict, and, in some instances, separatist movements dragged the new states into civil war.

Separatist Movements

In Africa the causes of conflict were mainly tribal disputes. Zaïre, for example, included 150 major tribes speaking 38 different languages; and Nigeria's numerous small tribes were dominated by three major ones – the Yoruba, the Hausa and the Ibo – each at odds with the others. Both countries experienced bloody civil wars. Between 1960 and 1963 the prosperous province of Katanga, led by Moïse Tshombe and supported by Belgian mining interests, attempted to break away from Zaïre, which was then known as the Congo. In Nigeria between 1967 and 1970 the Ibo leader, Colonel Ojukwu, led his people's struggle to make the Eastern Region of the country (Biafra) independent of the Hausa-dominated federal state.

Zaïre and Nigeria survived those attempts to break away; but tribal conflicts continued to dominate their internal politics, as they did in most Black African states. The hostility between rival tribes was one major reason why parliamentary democracy seemed almost unworkable in Africa; and the single-party régimes and military dictatorships which took over almost all the new states in the continent shortly after independence generally meant arbitrary rule by one tribe over all the others.

Africa also saw conflicts, on national and religious lines, of a kind which were more typical of Asia and the Middle East. In the Sudan there was conflict between the Arab Muslim peoples of the north and the black Africans of the southern province, who resisted northern rule by guerrilla warfare in the early 1960s and by full-scale civil war between 1963 and 1972. For the Muslims of north east Kenya, and of the Ogaden and Eritrea in Ethiopia, independence simply didn't come. The Somalis of the Ogaden and of Kenya continued their struggle to join the independent state of Somalia, which supported their cause; while Arab states backed the Eritreans in their struggle for independence. In the late 1970s these nationalist struggles in the Horn of Africa were poisoned by great power politics when the Soviet Union first supported the Somalis and then provided the Ethiopians with massive military aid.

The rise of militant nationalism stretched to breaking point the age-old tensions between Hindus and Muslims in the Indian sub-continent (as you saw in Chapter 34, pages 202–4), and between Muslims and non-Muslim peoples in the Eastern Mediterranean – chiefly the Jews in Palestine, and the Christians in the Lebanon. Cyprus too had no hope of a peaceful independent existence after the British left in 1960. Conflict between the Christian Greek majority and the Muslim Turkish minority over the island's future led to civil war in 1963 and to an invasion by Turkey in 1974 when the Greek colonels and Cypriot army officers tried to unite the island with Greece.

In Asia and the Middle East a number of countries faced attempts by aggrieved minority peoples to break away, and had to fight to preserve the unity of their states. The Kurds of northern Iraq fought for independence from 1961 to 1970; and the Naga tribes of northeast India rebelled against Indian rule between 1956 and 1969. They both failed, but the Bengalis of East Pakistan successfully broke away from a state dominated by the more prosperous Punjabis of West Pakistan. East Pakistan became, with Indian help, the independent state of Bangladesh in 1971.

The belief in the right of national self-determination, which had inspired anti-colonial liberation movements, proved impossible to apply in countries of mixed nationality as well as posing other problems. For the people who had supported nationalist movements had expected independence to bring in its train a new prosperity and national regeneration. As Kwame Nkrumah told his followers, "Seek ye first the political kingdom and everything else shall be added unto you." But independence did not change the facts of life.

Economic difficulties

Most of the new states were extremely poor countries, with little manufacturing industry and backward agriculture and they faced a difficult future in a world still dominated by the technology and capital of the developed states. It was an unfortunate paradox that Western medicine added to their problems by reducing mortality rates and causing massive population growth throughout the Third World (see also Chapter 48, page 303). The prices paid to primary producers for their mineral exports and cash crops were fixed in world markets – and prices often fluctuated wildly from year to year, giving rise to uncertainty and frequently to real hardship. The only way in which the new states could hope to escape from poverty and from dependence on the powerful foreigners who bought their primary products was by industrialising and modernising. Yet many of them were desperately short of both capital and technical and business know-how. Population growth drained their resources and made it all the harder to accumulate capital without help from foreign investors and governments. The foreigners who had exploited their resources in the past stood for colonialism, and the nationalists wanted to be rid of them; and rid not only of the white oil-men and mining bosses and plantation owners, but also of the wealthy non-Europeans, such as the Asians who dominated the trade of Kenya and Uganda, and the Chinese who controlled business in Malaya.

Sometimes the new governments took over foreign capital by nationalisation. The government of Zaïre, for example, nationalised foreign businesses in the late 1960s, including the Union Minière which controlled Katanga's copper resources. In other cases foreign business men were expelled – most notoriously by President Amin of Uganda, who in 1972 threw out all Asians who had not given up British citizenship. But such nationalist policies set back economic growth, and most Third World governments eventually accepted that they could not develop their economies without foreign capital and expertise.

Political difficulties

Most of the former British and French colonies began their independent lives with parliamentary forms of government. Looking back, it is clear that such régimes stood little chance of success in deeply divided countries with low literacy rates and grave economic problems. Very few survived as genuine democracies, and most were either quickly changed into single-party régimes, which retained a democratic front but banned all organised opposition (for example, Nkrumah's Ghana, and Nyerere's Tanzania), or they were taken over by their armies. Between 1958 and 1969, twenty-two out of the thirty-eight African states, and fourteen of the twenty-six Asian states, were taken over by military régimes. Clearly, the new professional armies of the Third World had an advantage over civilian politicians in imposing their wills on divided peoples; and, on the whole, they worked for modernisation and economic progress. But some were more brutal than even the worst of the old colonial régimes.

Marxism was also influential in Third World politics. In a few special cases, nationalist movements were taken over by Marxist leaders. Castro's régime in Cuba turned to the Soviet Union for support against American subversion. North Vietnam and Cambodia were near enough to Mao's China to draw inspiration from her example, and suffered terribly in war against the USA. In Africa in the 1970s there emerged a number of régimes controlled by hard-line Marxists and supported by Soviet and Cuban aid – in Angola, Mozambique, Somalia and Mengistu's Ethiopia – but it remained unclear whether Soviet-style communism would last in those countries. In a Black Africa dominated by tribal rather than by class divisions, and in the Middle East and Asia, where religion continued to have great social and political importance, Marxism did not easily take root.

Many Third World régimes were attracted instead by socialism, which justified government intervention in the workings of a country's economy. Leaders like Nyerere and Nasser made it clear that they were not adopting the alien ideas of Marxism, but rather developing new forms of 'African socialism' and 'Arab socialism' to suit the needs of their peoples. Régimes such as those in Tanzania and Egypt did not ban all private enterprise, but nationalised some large industries, introduced measures of land and tax reform and tried to plan economic development.

Whether or not such policies worked depended in part on the efficiency and honesty of the people who put them into practice. Kwame Nkrumah proved less competent as a pioneer of African socialism than as a leader of the struggle against colonialism. In Ghana, between 1961 and 1966, his government came near to bankrupting one of Black Africa's most prosperous countries. Massive corruption, mismanagement of nationalised industries, and the waste of funds on prestige projects stopped Ghana's economic growth and burdened the country with huge overseas debts. On the other hand, socialist planning was successful in Nehru's India; and in the poor country of Tanzania, Nyerere established a genuinely fair society.

The Non-aligned Movement

In international relations, the countries of the Third World tried to find ways of asserting their independence of the Western and Eastern power blocs. Regional organisations were formed in the Middle East and Africa to promote solidarity between the nationalist régimes. The Arab League was set up in 1945, and the Organisation of African Unity was created in 1963. Both organisations set out to coordinate policies on specially important regional problems – the Arab struggle against Israel, and Black African opposition to South Africa.

In 1955 a more ambitious attempt was made to combine the newly independent countries of Africa and Asia in a third, non-aligned, bloc. Alarmed by the growth of American influence in Asia and the Middle East, Sukarno and Nehru called the representatives of twenty-nine countries to a conference at Bandung in Indonesia. But although the participants could agree on their opposition to colonialism, they were unable to reach agreement on what 'non-alignment' as such meant in practice.

Chou En-lai, the Chinese Prime Minister, visited Bandung and tried to persuade the anti-colonial powers to follow the lead of China – a poor Asian country which had thrown out the imperialists but had no plans, so he said, to use communism as a means to world-wide domination. He influenced some of those present, and although others remained hostile to any brand of communism, Nehru's hope that the Third World would remain neutral between East and West was slowly eroded as communist influence increased in the next few years. At the second conference of 'non-aligned' countries, held in Belgrade in 1961, the mood of those present was markedly anti-Western.

Behind such divisions among the new states of the Third World lay not only political differences, but also bread-and-butter issues which prevented some of them from acting independently of the Eastern and Western blocs. Poor countries needed economic and technical aid; countries at war with their neighbours needed arms. East and West competed to provide both in strategically important areas. The new states needed trading partners too, as markets for their exports. Most of the former British colonies remained within the Commonwealth after gaining their independence, chiefly for the economic advantages it offered. They were also able to exert some influence on Commonwealth policies: in 1961, for example, they forced South Africa to leave by their concerted attack on the evil of apartheid. And as you saw in Chapter 41 (page 266), no fewer than forty-six African, Caribbean and small Pacific states signed the Lomé Convention of 1975 which gave them a valuable trading connection with the European Community.

The hope that the Third World might form a third power bloc, or even maintain united and effective regional leagues, was doomed to fail. The new states achieved their greatest international impact at the UN where, by the late 1960s, they had a large majority in the General Assembly. Yet little was achieved by UN resolutions against colonialism, even though they were passed by massive votes, combining Afro-Asian support with that of the Communist countries. The UN could only denounce: it could not use force against states intent on maintaining alien rule. The military role of the UN in Third World conflicts was therefore confined to supplying peace-keeping forces to hold rival armies apart in trouble-spots like Zaïre, Cyprus and the Middle East.

In the 1980s many observers of the international scene drew a distinction between the 'Third World' of developing countries, many of which were relatively prosperous, and a 'Fourth World' of desperately poor and declining nations. The least fortunate of these were the Sahelian states, the nine countries south of the Saharan and Egyptian deserts which constituted a 'famine-belt' stretching across the whole of Africa. In these countries a combination of factors – drought, the encroachment of the desert, civil wars, poor government – combined to produce a state of continuous famine. In Ethiopia and Sudan, the worst affected of the Sahelian states, more than three million people starved to death in 1984–85.

Other observers of the international scene have criticised the notion of First, Second, Third and Fourth Worlds as dangerously misleading, pointing to the interdependence of all parts of the global

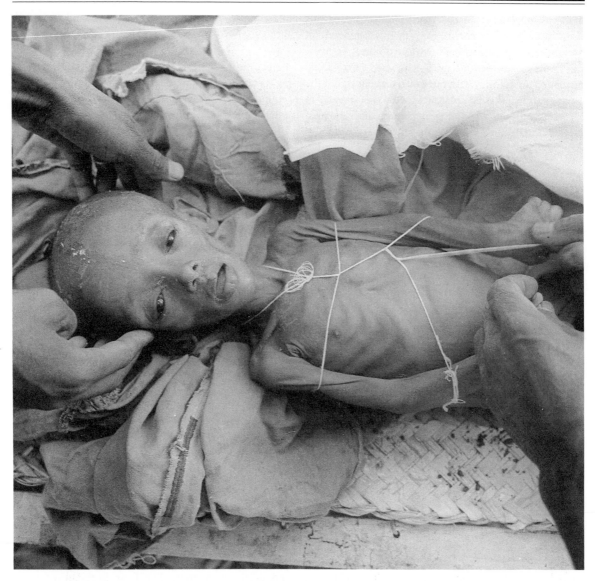

The 'Fourth World'. El Fau refugee camp in Tigray province, Ethiopia, February, 1985. The little boy, who had lost the ability to eat through starvation, died in front of the camera as a doctor tried to attach a nasal drip. His body was bound, according to local custom, before being put in a shroud for burial.

community. The 'North-South Report' produced by the Brandt Commission in 1980, for example, drew attention to the interdependence of the relatively prosperous northern hemisphere and the much poorer southern hemisphere. For each to survive inevitable economic disaster in the future, the 'North-South Report' argued for a massive transfer of financial resources from the northern to the developing countries, for a world food programme, for a global energy strategy, and for a reformed international economic system. But by the mid-1980s it seemed that no progress had been made towards achieving any of these objectives. And there was a bitter irony in the fact that European governments in the EEC spent more in 1985 (£265 million) on destroying surplus food as part of the Common Agricultural Policy (see page 266) than on providing emergency aid to the Sahelian states.

48 People and Societies III

In Chapter 1 we discovered the world as it was when your great-grandparents came into it; and in Chapter 28 we looked at the changed world into which they brought their children. In this final chapter we shall look at the world which greeted their children's children—you.

The People

We noted in Chapter 28 that before 1940 the number of people in the world was increasing rapidly. Between the Second World War and the mid-1980s numbers grew so fast that people talked of a 'population explosion'. In 1950, the total world population was 2,501 million: within ten years 485 million people were added to that figure; while the next ten years saw the addition of no fewer than 624 million. In just five years after 1970 a further 357 million brought the total to 3,967 million; and at some historic, unrecorded moment in 1976 the world's four-thousand-millionth citizen was born. In that same year for every one person alive in 1930, there were now two. By 1981, the world population was distributed as you can see opposite. If you compare these figures with those on page 139, you will see that population had grown faster in the developing areas—in Africa, Latin America and Asia—than in the mainly industrialised regions of North America and Europe.

Between 1985 and 2000 the world's population is expected to grow by nearly 2 thousand million, reaching 6 thousand million by the year 2000. This means that more people will be born in those fifteen years than were born in the twelve thousand years of human civilisation up to 1920.

In Chapter 28 you saw how two population trends appeared in the twentieth century: a general decrease in the numbers of children dying at birth or before the age of one; and a general increase in life expectancy. Both those trends were exaggerated after the Second

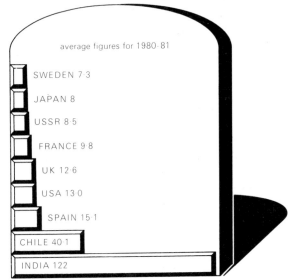

Where the 4,684 million people lived in the world in 1983

increase between 1900 and 1930

increase between 1930 and 1975

ASIA 2731 millions

EUROPE and the USSR 761 millions

AFRICA 521 millions

LATIN AMERICA 388 millions

NORTH AMERICA 259 millions

OCEANIA, AUSTRALIA and NEW ZEALAND 24 millions

Death in infancy: the number of children who died before the age of one (out of every 1,000 born alive)

average figures for 1980-81

SWEDEN 7·3
JAPAN 8
USSR 8·5
FRANCE 9·8
UK 12·6
USA 13·0
SPAIN 15·1
CHILE 40·1
INDIA 122

Life expectancy at birth in selected countries in the early 1980s

Country	Males	Females
India	46	45
Chile	60	66
Poland	67	75
Australia	68	74
USA	69	76
West Germany	69	76
England and Wales	69	76
France	70	78

World War – far fewer babies died and more people lived longer – as standards of medical care improved and as scientists found means of controlling mass-killers such as malaria and smallpox. If you compare the information at the bottom of page 303 and above with that on page 140, you will see for yourself the progress that was made in such a relatively short period of time.

These national averages conceal the existence of grim pockets of human misery where infant mortality rates were much higher and expectations of life were very short. Even so, the figures tell us that by the early 1980s men had achieved an impressive degree of 'death control' which appeared to benefit people all over the world. But unfortunately death control outstripped birth control with the consequence that developing countries in particular saw a sudden surge of population which used up resources that might otherwise have been used to raise levels of investment in agriculture and industry and to improve standards of living, as you will have seen in the case of India, in Chapter 46 (page 295).

Town and Country

In the countries that had long been industrialised the numbers left to work the land were, by the 1980s, very small. In France fewer than 9 out of every 100 workers were employed in agriculture; in the USA the proportion was down to 4 out of every 100; and in England and Wales 3 out of every 100. The other workers in those countries were employed in manufacturing industry and, in ever greater numbers, in 'service' jobs – for example, in shops, schools and hospitals, and in the offices of companies and of local and central governments.

The post-war years saw a similar movement away from the land in the rapidly industrialising Communist states. By the 1970s the USSR had fewer workers on the land than in manufacturing and service industries; and other Eastern European countries closely followed the Soviet example. By 1980 only thirty per cent of Poland's working population, and thirty-one per cent of Romania's, were employed in agriculture. Elsewhere in the world the movement of labour into industry generally proceeded more slowly than the rise in population so that the proportions of people who earned their living from agriculture remained very much the same as in the 1930s.

In the forty years after the Second World War the industrialised Western societies became still more urbanised, especially as factories using electric power were sited on the outskirts of cities or filled the spaces between already large towns. Often these merged into each other, helped by motorways and express roads, and the new conurbations or urban sprawls were re-named and given new systems of local government to cope with the problems of providing services for much larger populations. This happened in the UK in 1974 when the six largest urban regions each became a metropolitan county.

Multi-million cities appeared in the developing countries too, often providing no more than a shack or a pavement home for people driven from the land by over-population. In Latin America, North Africa, India, the Philippines and Indonesia giant cities grew by the addition of people to whom they could offer little support in the way of jobs and few, if any, of the basic amenities of city life. On a world scale, urbanisation was now as much a consequence of over-population as of industrialisation.

On page 141 we looked at the contrasts between the world's rich and the world's poor towards the end of the 1930s, measured in terms of *per capita* income. Now let's look at some examples of *per capita* income in 1980 to see just how wide the 'wealth gap' grew.

Per capita incomes 1980

Kuwait	$11,300	Spain	$2,663
Sweden	$8,043	Brazil	$1,100
Canada	$7,341	Peru	$700
USA	$6,996	Paraguay	$574
West Germany	$6,451	Nigeria	$350
Australia	$6,288	India	$132
France	$5,859	Zaïre	$124
Japan	$4,465	Mali	$90
UK	$3,550	Bangladesh	$85

Just as in the 1930s, these figures conceal the wide

The six industrial heavyweights, 1980

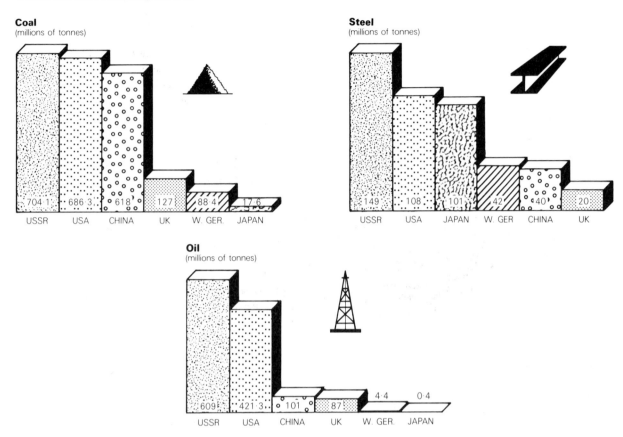

Coal
(millions of tonnes)

USSR 704·1 | USA 686·3 | CHINA 618 | UK 127 | W. GER. 88·4 | JAPAN 17·6

Steel
(millions of tonnes)

USSR 149 | USA 108 | JAPAN 101 | W. GER. 42 | CHINA 40 | UK 20

Oil
(millions of tonnes)

USSR 609 | USA 421·3 | CHINA 101 | UK 87 | W. GER. 4·4 | JAPAN 0·4

gaps in wealth within each of the countries shown. For an example of a state with one extremely rich and one very poor community see the section on South Africa in Chapter 44.

Among the world's industrial powers the USA still held pride of place. In Chapter 1 (page 3) we compared some of her industrial outputs at the beginning of the century with those of the UK and Germany, her two chief competitors. In Chapter 28 (page 142) we repeated that exercise for the years 1936–38, and included figures for a new industrial giant, the Soviet Union. And to our list of great industrial powers in the 1970s we must now add Japan and China. In the forty years after the Second World War, the Japanese enjoyed an almost continuous 'boom', based on the export of cheap, high-quality products of large-scale, efficient manufacturing industries. Among those products, as you may well know, were motor-cars, motor-cycles, television sets, cameras and hi-fi equipment.

China had begun an industrial and agricultural revolution as recently as 1952. In the chart above the industries compared are the same as those in Chapter 28.

New Faces, New Places

The post-war world saw migrations on a huge scale, some for short distances and some taking people half-way round the world. Among the new movements were fearful migrations, as when Hindus, Sikhs and Muslims fled for their lives into new India or new Pakistan; and forced displacements, as when minorities in Eastern Europe were herded west in the wake of the Nazi defeat, and the government of Uganda expelled Asians from its land. There were also, of course, refugees from the Second World War, and from later conflicts in the Middle East, in Southern Africa, in Korea, and South-East Asia. And there were those who fled from revolutions – in Eastern Europe, Asia and the Caribbean.

Emigrants from selected European countries, 1951–60

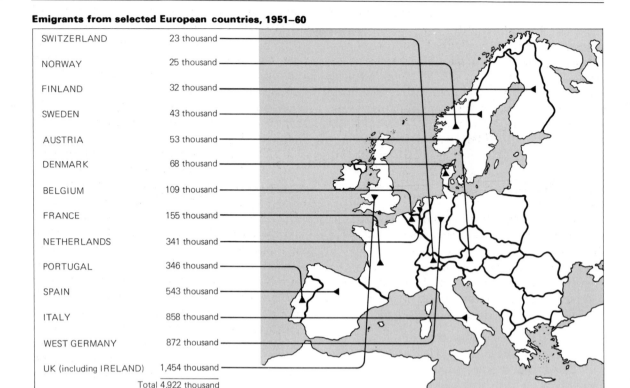

SWITZERLAND	23 thousand
NORWAY	25 thousand
FINLAND	32 thousand
SWEDEN	43 thousand
AUSTRIA	53 thousand
DENMARK	68 thousand
BELGIUM	109 thousand
FRANCE	155 thousand
NETHERLANDS	341 thousand
PORTUGAL	346 thousand
SPAIN	543 thousand
ITALY	858 thousand
WEST GERMANY	872 thousand
UK (including IRELAND)	1,454 thousand
Total	4,922 thousand

Old patterns of migration continued, or were re-established after the Second World War. People in the USSR continued to move to the eastern regions of the country; and in the USA other millions found their way west, and especially to California, while black people from the southern states moved into the great industrial cities of the north-east. Jews from all parts of the world took themselves to Israel.

You can see from the map that Western Europe continued to pump out people. The numbers of emigrants did not match the extraordinary level reached in the first ten years of the century (page 4), but they were far higher than in the years immediately before the Second World War. Many of the migrants went to countries which not only had long-established traditions of European settlement but now more than ever welcomed new citizens, especially young, skilled workers. Among those countries, which included Canada, Argentina and New Zealand, Australia stood out as the land which received most immigrants in proportion to population. In the most intensive period of immigration, the ten years after 1945, no fewer than one million 'foreigners' arrived to graft themselves on to an existing population of only seven and a half million. Not all stayed to become good Australians, but the majority did, and more than half of them were non-British. That, in itself, was a real break with pre-war tradition – the acceptance of large numbers of Italian, Dutch, German, Polish and Greek Australians – but 'White Australia' then did not admit Asians and blacks.

Canada, too, experienced an immigration boom, taking in no fewer than 1·2 million people, mostly from Europe, between 1946 and 1955, and substantial numbers after that. The USA relaxed the severe restrictions that had been imposed in the 1920s. An Act of 1965 limited the number of immigrants from any one country to no more than 20,000 a year, but no longer discriminated against people from Southern Europe and Asia. Yet of the more than seven million newcomers who entered the USA in the forty years after the Second World War nearly half were from Canada and Mexico, while about 650,000 were refugees from Castro's Cuba. In the face of rising levels of immigration from the United States' neighbours, and some from Asia, Europe no longer provided a majority of new American citizens.

In the same forty years the industrialised countries of Western Europe were also on the receiving end of large-scale immigration. Many of the new migrants were simply following the trails blazed earlier in the century as they moved in search of work from the poorer lands of the Mediterranean, such as Italy, Spain and Greece, to countries which, especially in the fifties and sixties, were short of labour. By 1970 those migrant workers, many of whom did not intend to settle permanently, accounted for more than half the nine million or so newcomers living in France, West Germany, the UK, Austria, Belgium, Switzerland, Sweden and the Netherlands.

The rest of Western Europe's immigrants came from outside the continent. Many were of European origin; for example, the French *colons* from Algeria and the former settlers of Portugal's African territories. The others were non-European people born in lands which had made up the Empires of the French and the British (see also Chapter 42, page 275).

The Other Half

In earlier chapters of this book we looked for means of measuring how women were making progress towards the goal of being treated equally with men. We suggested that such progress might be measured in terms of the right to vote, opportunities for employment outside the home, the availability of artificial means of contraception to enable them to limit the size of their families, and the mass-production of appliances which could free them from the drudgery of housework. Clearly, those indications of progress were most firmly established in the Western societies. Some, but not all, were adopted as goals generally throughout the Third World.

By the mid-1980s the right to vote was commonplace, in developing countries as well as in the industrialised nations. But that did not, in itself, give women the power to change fundamentally the societies in which they lived. Even in the advanced countries politics remained a man's game, in which women played only a limited part. Few women were elected to parliaments, and even fewer became members of governments in either the Western or the Communist world. Between 1945 and 1985 only four women gained supreme political power in their own lands – Mrs Indira Gandhi in India, Mrs

Bandaranaike in Sri Lanka, Mrs Golda Meir in Israel and Mrs Margaret Thatcher in Great Britain.

In the industrialised countries women's employment was boosted by the growth in the numbers of 'service' jobs. Many more were taken into clerical work, the distributive trades, nursing and teaching. In China, the Soviet Union and other Communist countries women were also recruited for work of all kinds, including heavy manual tasks. By 1974 roughly sixty million Soviet women had jobs outside their homes – nearly eighty-five per cent of all women of working age, in comparison with about fifty per cent in America.

In Communist countries equal pay for equal work was firmly established as a principle, although whether women had equal opportunities to obtain equal work was another matter. In the West, the increasing dependence of industrial economies on the employment of large numbers of women was making it more difficult for employers to justify the profitable nonsense of paying them at lower rates than men for equal work. In the mid-1970s female workers in Britain were helped by new laws which established the principle of equal pay and made it illegal to discriminate against women in appointments to jobs.

Women's right to decide for themselves the number of children they would bear was, at last, generally recognised in the West, though the teaching of the Roman Catholic Church, as expressed in the encyclical *Humanae Vitae* of 1968, remained firmly opposed to all artificial means of contraception. Condoms, diaphragms, coils and, above all, contraceptive pills provided Western women with a battery of highly reliable techniques to avoid unwanted pregnancies, although they were not openly available in predominantly Catholic countries, such as France, until the late 1960s at the earliest. The right to have an abortion – the destruction of an unborn foetus – on demand was nowhere near so widely accepted.

In the Soviet Union and Eastern Europe the availability of contraceptives and the ease or difficulty of obtaining an abortion depended, as did most things, on the current policies of governments. When they felt a need to restrict population growth, as they did in the late fifties and early sixties, abortions and contraceptives were easy to come by. In the late sixties, when governments began to get worried about the effects of low birth-rates on future supplies of labour in the People's Republics, policies were changed and abortion,

tion, in particular, was discouraged, although whether government action was effective was another matter. The decline in the British birth-rate in the later 1970s was, so far as we can judge, the consequence of individual decisions taken by women – and their husbands.

Most developing countries began to organise public campaigns for birth control as their population increases were seen to outstrip food supplies and the development of public services. Often, however, there was a lot of resistance, especially in lands where infant mortality rates were still high or where there was no real prospect that one fewer child to feed or educate would make any real difference to the rest of the family. Family planning was still most successful in societies where people could see that a smaller family would mean real gains in their standards and styles of living and where women had a real chance of a second occupation in addition to motherhood.

Modern Times

When we last looked at the general impact of this inventive century of ours upon very different societies in Chapter 28 (page 145), we noted that after forty years it had not made much of an impression on the ways in which very large numbers of people lived. More than forty years later there was plenty of evidence that the styles and paces of many people's lives were still based more on the customs and observances of a remote past than on the fleeting fashions of recent times.

Americans and Canadians, Western Europeans and Japanese, and, to a lesser extent, Russians and Eastern Europeans had all exported to other lands the products of their high-technology industries – motor-cars and tractors, radios and television sets, telephones and pocket calculators. But the take-up of those products by the vast and increasing populations of the developing world was nowhere near large enough to alter significantly the day-to-day lives of most of their people. In 1980, there were more than 125 million motor-cars in the USA – roughly one car to every two people: in Peru there were fewer than 20 cars to every 1,000 people; in India fewer than 2. In America there were 77 telephones to every 100 people: in Britain there were 41; in Yugoslavia 7; in Paraguay 1·7. In America there was one television set to every 2 people: in Britain there was one to every 3; in Ghana one to every 200, and in Mozambique one to every 1,000. More important, while the farmers of North America used nearly thirty per cent of the world's tractors, the farmers of Asia used only seven per cent, and those in Africa had just two per cent to share between them. In the industrialised nations applied science and advanced technology pervaded everyday life – in the machines of factory and office, in the kitchen and the sitting room at home, in transport, in entertainment, in computerised bank accounts and bills.

When you compare this short survey of the very recent world with those of Chapters 1 and 28, there are some hard questions to answer. Who has, after all, gained from the twentieth century's technical progress? Did the poorer majority of the world's people benefit from the development of a world economy in which primary producers and manufacturers were tied together by trade? Did the great revolutions and independence movements make any human beings any happier? Not all the answers need be negative; the twentieth century can too easily overwhelm us with the scale of its violence, the mechanisation of slaughter, the very number of its people. This book has tried to contain those excesses in a wider perspective of history. Your task is to see your times and society, and yourselves, in that perspective.

Glossary

This glossary defines or explains many of the historical terms and phrases used in the text. An arrow before a word (→) shows that there is a separate explanation of it in the glossary. 'cf' after a word means 'compare with' another word in the glossary.

Allies In general, the partners in a pact or alliance. The term is most often used for the countries which fought the → Central Powers in World War 1 and the → Axis powers in World War 2.

Alphabetical agencies Government-financed bodies created as part of the → New Deal in the USA between 1933–36. So called because people generally referred to them by the first letters of their titles, e.g., 'The Three Cs' for the Civilian Conservation Corps.

ANC (African National Congress) Oldest and largest black political organisation in South Africa. Banned in 1960 after the → Sharpeville Massacre, and its leaders (notably Nelson Mandela) imprisoned or exiled, it aimed to overthrow white rule in South Africa and to destroy → apartheid.

Annexation The act by which a country adds to its own territory by taking land from another country, usually by force or coercion – e.g. Germany annexed Czechoslavakia's Sudetenland in 1938.

Anschluss (German) The union in 1938 of the two German-speaking nations, Austria and Germany, despite this being forbidden by the Paris Peace Settlement of 1919.

Anti-Comintern Pact Treaty between Germany and Japan, signed in 1936, to block the spread of Soviet communism by the → Comintern. In a secret clause they also agreed they would stay neutral if either went to war with the USSR. Italy joined the Pact in 1937.

Anti-Semitism Hostility towards, hatred of, or discrimination against Jews. Anti-Semitism was a central feature of the → Nazi régime in Germany, leading eventually to the killing of six million Jews in the → Holocaust.

ANZAC Australian and New Zealand Army Corps in World War I.

ANZUS Pact Treaty between Australia, New Zealand and the United States, signed in 1951, providing for their mutual defence against armed attack in the Pacific region.

Apartheid (Afrikaans) The policy of the white South African government, developed and refined since 1948, of dividing South Africans into racial groups according to their skin colour, and of segregating them by racial groups in work, housing, civil and legal rights, transport, recreation, etc.

Apparatchik (Russian) Employee of the Sovist Union's state apparatus' – that is, the institutions which administer the USSR. Apparatchiks are always members of the Communist Party, thus allowing the Party to control the state.

Appeasement Foreign policy followed by the British Government, and later by the French, in their dealings with the → Axis powers from 1937–39. It was designed to avoid war by giving way to some of their demands and by conceding territory to them, notably the Sudetenland area of Czechoslovakia by the → Munich Agreement in 1938.

April Theses Outline of → Bolshevik policies delivered by Lenin in a speech following his return to Russia in April 1917.

Armistice Agreement by countries at war to stop fighting while a permanent peace settlement is arranged.

Arms race Competition between states or → blocs to build up their weapon stocks. Examples in the twentieth century have been the → Naval Race between Britain and Germany before World War 1 and the race between → NATO and the → Warsaw Pact to build more powerful nuclear weapons from the 1950s onwards.

Autarky The policy of making a country self-sufficient in agriculture and industry so that it need not depend on foreign supplies. A key economic policy in both → Fascist Italy and → Nazi Germany.

Authoritarian An authoritarian government keeps strict and forceful control of the population, with little regard for the rights and freedoms of individuals. Its authority is chiefly maintained by a strong police organisation and/or armed force which enforces obedience to the state.

Autocracy A system in which one person, or a group with a single strong leader, has political power without legal constraints, and is not answerable to electors or any other group. Usually used with reference to leaders of the earlier part of the twentieth century, e.g., Nicholas II of Russia and → Kaiser Wilhelm of Germany.

Axis Term coined by Mussolini in 1936 to describe the close relationship between Rome and Berlin, capitals of → Fascist Italy and → Nazi Germany. The Rome-Berlin Axis became a three-way, or → Tripartite Axis Pact, when Japan joined it in 1940.

Baath Party (Arabic) Literally 'The Party of Arab Renaissance'. Based in Syria, and with associated Baath parties in countries such as Iraq, this Arab political movement is not confined to any one Arab state. Its aims are to unite all Arabs in one nation, to free the Arab world from outside interference, and to create a socialist system in the Arab world.

Balfour Declaration Announcement made in 1917 by the British Foreign Secretary, Arthur Balfour, that the British Government had agreed to support → Zionist demands for a Jewish homeland in → Palestine.

Balkans Region of Europe south of the Danube and Sava Rivers, comprising present-day Albania, Bulgaria, Greece, Romania, Turkey-in-Europe and Yugoslavia. Renowned for political and territorial instability, especially in the early years of the twentieth century, when these states were competing with each other for existence.

Baltic states Collective name for Estonia, Latvia and Lithuania on the east coast of the Baltic Sea. Part of Russia until 1918, they were independent nations from 1918 until 1940, when they were annexed by the USSR.

Bandung Conference Conference of 29 African and Asian states in Bandung, Indonesia, in 1955, at which the → developing nations began to develop a common approach to foreign relations, → colonialism and → non-alignment.

Benelux Short for Belgium, the Netherlands and Luxemburg, and for the economic union of these countries started by the Benelux Agreement of 1944.

Berlin blockade A blockade, or siege, of West Berlin by the Soviet Union from March 1948 to June 1949 by cutting road, rail and canal links between West Germany and West Berlin, deep inside Soviet-run East Germany. The blockade was defeated by supplying West Berlin by air (the Berlin Airlift).

Berlin Wall heavily fortified, guarded barrier dividing East Berlin (capital of the German Democratic Republic) and West Berlin (belonging to the Federal German Republic). Built in 1961 by the GDR to prevent its citizens leaving to live in the west, it has been a potent symbol of the → Cold War ever since.

Beveridge Report A proposal drawn up in 1942 by Sir William Beveridge as to how the British government could provide social security and social insurance for all.

Big Three The dominant political figures in the peace negotiations of the two World Wars: Wilson (USA), Clemenceau (France) and Lloyd George (Britain) at the Paris Peace Conference of 1919; and Roosevelt (USA), Stalin (USSR) and Churchill (Britain) at the Teheran (1943) and Yalta (1945) Conferences.

Black Tuesday 29 October 1929, the day when share values on the New York stock market in → Wall Street crashed to an all-time low.

Black Power movement Militant black American → civil rights movement of the later 1960s and the 1970s, comprising the Black Panther Party, the SNCC (Student Non-violent Co-ordinating Committee) and others. It aimed to achieve greater power for American blacks using direct action methods, including violence where thought necessary.

Blackshirts Uniformed para-military members of the Italian → Fascist Party under Benito Mussolini, renowned for their violence and brutality towards opponents.

Blitz (German) The bombing of British cities, especially London, by German aircraft from September 1940 to May 1941.

Blitzkrieg Literally, 'lightning war' – the swift, mobile, mechanised style of warfare used by the German armed forces in their conquest of Europe, 1939–41

Bloc (French) Alliance or grouping in politics, especially international politics – e.g. the 'Communist bloc' of Eastern European states and the USSR, or the → developing nations bloc of → Third World countries in the UN.

Bolshevik The section of the Russian Social Democratic Party led by Lenin after the party split in 1903. Literally means 'majority'. After gaining power in 1917 the Bolsheviks renamed themselves the All-Russian Communist Party, becoming the Communist Party of the Soviet Union in 1952.

Brownshirts See SA (Sturmabteilung).

Capitalism Economic system based on (1) the private ownership of property, business and industry, (2) the employment of workers by private employers producing goods to sell for profit, (3) a free, competitive market.

Central Powers The countries fighting the → Allies in World War I – Germany, Austria-Hungary, Bulgaria and the Turkish Empire.

Cheka (Russian) Abbreviation for Extraordinary Commission for Combatting Counter-Revolution and Espionage. It was the state security police force set up by the → Bolsheviks in 1917 to deal with their political opponents. It was renamed → OGPU in 1923 and → NKVD in 1934, eventually becoming the present-day KGB in the 1950s.

Civil rights Freedoms and privileges of citizens within a society, for example the right to vote, the rights of free speech and free association, freedom of religious belief, and the right to be free from discrimination in social life and opportunities of work. Denial of such rights led to the growth of civil rights movements in many countries in the twentieth century, notably the USA in the 1950s and 1960s.

Cold War State of extreme hostility between the USA and its allies on one hand, and the USSR and its allies on the other, involving an → arms race, diplomatic conflicts, spying, → propaganda and hostile actions of every kind short of actual war.

Collectivisation Process by which farm land in → communist countries is transferred from individual ownership to common ownership in collective farms. Collectivisation was carried out on a massive scale in the USSR in the 1930s and the People's Republic of China in the 1950s.

Colony Territory beyond the frontiers of a country that is occupied and ruled by the people of that country for their own advantage – e.g. to gain access to food and raw materials, to provide markets for exports, gain room for their people to settle and live, or to possess military and naval bases.

Colonialism The methods and policies by which a country gains → colonies and maintains or extends its control over them. The term implies that colonies have no real political independence and little control over their economies; it has therefore become a derogatory term in the twentieth century.

Colons (French) White setters or colonists in Algeria when it was a French colony from the mid-nineteenth century until 1962.

COMECON Short for Council for Mutual Economic Assistance, an economic organisation established by the USSR in 1949 to co-ordinate the economies of the eastern European states with the economy of the USSR.

Comintern Short for Communist International, also called the Third International. Founded by Lenin in 1919 to help communist parties in every country to organise → revolutions. Abolished 1943.

Common Market An economic union of nations in which trade is stimulated by the removal of tariffs and other trade barriers. The European Economic Community, often called 'The Common Market', is one of the most successful of such unions.

Commonwealth An association of independent nations, → dominions and dependent territories which once belonged to the British Empire and which now accept the British monarch as a symbol of the association between them

Commune In China, a commune is a group of → collective farms as well as being a unit of local government, of Communist Party organisation, and of education and welfare provision. In 1980 there were some 50,000 people's communes in rural China, with an average of 16,000 people per commune. In some western European countries, e.g. France, a commune is the most basic unit of local government, equivalent to a British parish or local district council.

Communism Has many meanings; chiefly (1) the concept of a classless society based on the common ownership of property, business and industry, and (2) the method of government used in countries governed by communist parties, e.g. the USSR, People's Republic of China, North Korea, Cuba, etc.

Concentration camps High security prison camps in which large numbers of inmates are concentrated. Introduced by the British during the Boer War, they are most usually associated with → Nazi Germany, where some 2,000 KZ (Konzentrationlager)

camps were used to imprison and kill political opponents of the Nazis as well as racial, social, religious and sexual 'undesirables'.

Congress In general, a meeting or assembly of representatives for debate or discussion. Specifically, the term is used for (1) the parliament of the USA, consisting of a Senate and House of Representatives (2) the Congress Party, the main political party in the Indian struggle for independence and the dominant party in India since independence in 1947, and (3) the Congress of the Communist Party of the Soviet Union – the occasional meetings of delegates from all parts of the state.

Containment United States policy used from 1947 to contain the spread of communism from the → Communist bloc to other regions of the world.

Coup d'état (French) Literally, 'seizure of state' – the sudden and violent overthrow of a government, usually by the country's own armed forces, and its replacement by a new ruling group. A coup is different from a → revolution, in which the social and political order is changed, whereas a coup results only in a change of leadership. cf → putsch.

Cultural Revolution Political, social and cultural upheaval in China, 1966–68, caused by Mao Tse-tung's attempt to stimulate revolutionary enthusiasm among young people as part of a power struggle between Maoists and their more moderate opponents.

Decolonisation Process by which the peoples of European → empires gained the power of self-government and independence after 1949.

Deflation Economic measures taken by a government to reduce the prices of goods and services. Usually involves cuts in government spending, reduced industrial activity and decreased demand for goods.

Demilitarised zone Area in which no troops, weapons or fortifications are allowed. The most notable example of a 'dmz' was the German Rhineland (all German land on the west bank of the River Rhine, and on the east bank to a line drawn 50 km east of the Rhine) from 1919–36.

Democratic centralism Doctrine by which the Soviet, Chinese and most other communist parties are run. By this doctrine, (1) all party officials must be elected by members, (2) there must be full, free and open discussion of policies by members before a decision is made, and (3) once a decision has been made it must be unquestioningly accepted and carried out by all party members.

De-Stalinisation Process in the USSR after 1956 by which Stalin's reputation was discredited and some Stalinist policies reversed, resulting in greater individual freedom and a 'thaw' in cultural life.

Détente (French) The easing of tension between states. Especially used for changes in the relationship between the USA and USSR in the → Cold War, especially in the 1970s as a result of arms reductions talks.

Developing nations Term used by the United Nations to classify countries in which large parts of the economy are under-developed, the majority of the population are very poor, and public services such as medical care, education, welfare and transport are inadequate. cf → Third World.

Dictatorship Form of government in which one person has sole and complete political power. Notable twentieth century examples are Hitler, Mussolini, Stalin, Franco and Chiang Kai-shek.

Dominions Self-governing territories of the British Commonwealth. The term was used most commonly before 1947 to distinguish dominions from colonies and then applied to Canada, Australia, New Zealand and South Africa.

Domino theory The idea that if one country becomes communist, other countries in the same region would automatically follow suit, 'falling' to communism like a row of dominoes knocking each other down in turn. The term was first used by US President Eisenhower in 1954, and was used to justify US intervention in South-East Asia, especially Vietnam.

Duce (Italian) Leader. The title adopted by Benito Mussolini as Head of Government, Prime Minister and leader of the → Fascist Party in Italy. Pronounced 'doochay'.

Duma (Russian) Parliament established in Russia after the Revolution of 1905, surviving until 1917.

Dyarchy System of government with two levels of power, one Indian, one British, introduced into India by the Montague-Chelmsford Reforms of 1919.

Empire Colleciton of territories ruled by one authority (headed by an emperor or empress) and consisting of an imperial state and independencies such as → colonies, → dominions and provinces.

European Community Group of three economic organisations linking twelve European countries; the European Coal and Steel Community, the European Economic Community (also known as the → Common Market) and the European Atomic Energy Community.

Falange Spanish → fascist party founded in 1933, emphasising national tradition, loyalty to the nation and obedience to the leader.

Fascism Either the political movement which Mussolini led to power in Italy in 1922, or the doctrine which inspired it and similar movements abroad, e.g. the → Falange and → Nazi parties. Characteristics of fascism include: violent dislike of → communism; belief in → authoritarian government; leadership by a single, powerful figure; nationalism; existence of only one party.

Final Solution Nazi German plan drawn up in 1942 to exterminate all Jews in Europe, leading to the final and worst stage of the → Holocaust.

Five-year plan Method of economic planning used in communist countries to increase industrial and agricultural output. Targets to be achieved by each sector of the economy are set for five year periods. Five-year plans were used most notably in the USSR in the 1930s and in China in the 1950s.

Fourteen Points US President Woodrow Wilson's 14-point plan (January 1918) setting out principles for a more peaceful world after World War 1.

Freikorps (German) Literally means 'free corps" – unofficial, volunteer fighting units made up of demobilised German soldiers after World War 1. They were ruthless, often violent nationalists, supporting various right-wing parties in an effort to destroy → communism in Germany.

Front Either the line along which fighting takes place in a war – e.g. the Western Front in Belgium and France, 1914-18, or a coalition of political parties or groups – e.g. the → Popular Front, National Front, or Popular Front for the Liberation of Palestine. Other usage; the → Home Front, → second front.

Fuhrer (German) Leader and guide – the title adopted by Hilter in 1934 when he become President of Germany as well as its Chancellor. cf → Duce and → Generalissimo.

Gang of Four Chinese propaganda label for the leaders of a radical group who become prominent in China during the → Cultural Revolution, who attempted to take power after the death of Mao Tse-tung, but were arrested and imprisoned in 1976.

Generalissimo Literally 'greatest general' – a title adopted by various twentieth century → dictators, notably Franco of Spain and Chiang Kai-shek of China.

Gestapo (German) Short for Geheime Staatspolizei, the secret political police in → Nazi Germany. It had unlimited power to deal with political opponents, becoming the most feared and hated branch of the Nazi police as a result of using that power to arrest people without warrant, to imprison people without trial, to torture and to kill.

Glasnost (Russian) Literally 'openness' – a trend towards greater freedom of information and discussion in the USSR, begun in 1985 by the new Soviet leader M. Gorbachev. It involved the reappearance of investigative journalism in the media, the ending of censorship of many publications and films, and greater frankness about previously unmentionable subjects such as disasters, social problems and historical controversies.

Gold Standard System by which currencies of different countries were each exchangeable for a fixed amount of gold. The system was general in the world's trade dominated by Europe and the USA until 1914, but inflation during World War 1 virtually destroyed it. It was revived during the 1920s but collapsed again during the → Great Depression.

Gosplan (Russian) Centralised economic planning agency established in the USSR in 1921. Short for State Planning Commission.

Great Depression World-wide economic slump, lasting from 1929 to 1934, and marked by a big decline in trade between nations, the collapse of banks and other financial institutions, high levels of unemployment, and generally reduced prosperity.

Great Leap Forward Chinese → propaganda slogan describing the ambitious economic policies adopted by the Chinese government in 1959, chiefly a massive increase in agricultural and industrial output, associated with the creation of → communes.

Great Society Slogan coined by US President Johnson in 1965 to describe the general aims of his domestic policy, notably an attack on poverty, improved → civil rights, urban renewal, educational reforms, and environmental improvement.

Great Terror A campaign of repression, organised by the → NKVD, by which Stalin got rid of all leading political opponents in the USSR, 1934–39. Involved the use of indiscriminate arrests, extraction of confessions by torture or brainwashing, show trials, imprisonment in labour camps, and execution with and without trial. Also known as the Great → Purge.

Greater East Asia Co-Prosperity Sphere Japanese → propaganda title for the Asian territories it acquired by conquest between 1937–42 – Eastern China, French Indo-China, Malaya, Indonesia, the Philippines, and the islands of the western Pacific. cf → New Order in East Asia.

GULag (Russian) Acronym for Main Administration for Camps. The term is most often used to describe the whole Soviet detention system of forced labour camps, prisons, psychiatric

hospitals, and internal exile, especially during the Stalinist → purges of the 1930s–50s.

Hoare-Laval Plan Secret British-French plan to solve the Abyssinian crisis of 1935–6 by giving part of Abyssinia to Italy. Publication of the plan in the press led to the resignation of both Hoare and Laval as foreign ministers of Britain and France.

Holocaust Death and destruction on a massive scale. In 20th century history, the term is used to describe the persecution, deportation and extermination of some 6 million Jews in Nazi-occupied Europe from 1938–45.

Home Front The activities and experiences of civilians in their own countries while their armed forces are engaged on the military → front.

Hoovervilles Shanty-towns established by destitute Americans in or on the edges of cities during the → Great Depression. The term was a critical reflection on the leadership of President Herbert Hoover.

Hot line Direct telecommunications link between the White House in Washington and the Kremlin in Moscow. It was set up in 1963 after the Cuban Missiles crisis of 1962 to allow the US and Soviet leaderships to communicate more easily in any future international crisis.

Hundred Days The first three months of F.D. Roosevelt's presidency in 1933, during which he initiated a large number of programmes designed to relieve the worst aspects of the → Great Depression.

Hundred Flowers campaign Campaign in China in 1956 to encourage free public debate about the political, economic and social development of the country. The campaign was abandoned when debate developed into widespread criticism of Mao Tse-tung's leadership.

Imperialism The extension of a country's territorial and/or political and/or economic control over other countries. (cf → colonialism.) The term refers especially to the creation in the 19th century of colonial empires by European countries, and to the rivalry between those empires.

Imperial Preference See → Ottawa Agreements.

Inflation Rise in prices and fall in the purchasing power of money. Very rapid inflation, as in Germany in 1923, is known as hyperinflation.

International Monetary Fund Specialised agency of the United Nations set up in 1945 to help world trade by lending money to countries suffering from balance of payments problems.

Iron Curtain Frontier dividing communist eastern Europe from western Europe. The term, first used by Nazi propaganda minister Goebbels, was popularised in 1946 by Winston Churchill in various speeches.

Isolationism US foreign policy, particularly strong between the two World Wars, of keeping out of foreign conflicts and of avoiding involvement in the affairs of other countries.

Kaiser (German) Emperor of Germany during the period 1871–1917. Derived from Caesar (Latin) and similar to Czar, or Tsar (Russian).

Keynesianism The economic theories and governement economic policies associated with British economist J.M. Keynes (1883–1946) from the 1920s onwards. The term implies especially the idea that governments could counter the effects of an economic depression by spending money to create jobs, thus increasing public purchasing power and raising demand for industrial and agricultural products.

Kolkhoz (Russian) Collective farm in the USSR, as established by Stalin during the process of → collectivisation.

Kristallnacht (German) Literally, 'night of glass' – the night of 7 November 1938 when Jewish shops, homes and synagogues throughout Germany were attacked and destroyed by → Nazis. The term is a reference to the broken glass which resulted from these attacks.

Ku Klux Klan Racist organisation in the USA, founded in the 1860s and reaching its largest membership in the 1920s. Dedicated to the preservation of white, Protestant supremacy in the USA, it violently opposed blacks, Catholics, Jews and any other group it considered 'alien'.

Kulak (Russian) Class of peasant farmers who became more prosperous than average peasants in Russia before World War 1 and then gained most through the private enterprise encouraged by → NEP. The Kulaks did not support → collectivisation and were destroyed by Stalin.

Kuomintang The 'National People's Party' – a Chinese political party organised by Sun Yat-sen which helped overthrow the Manchu dynasty in 1911. The KMT (as Kuomintang is abbreviated) was the governing party of China under Chiang Kai-shek from 1928 until its overthrow by communists in 1949.

Lebensraum (German) Literally, 'living space'. The word was used as a slogan in → Nazi Germany to describe the territory in eastern Europe which Germany allegedly needed to house and feed its growing population.

Lend-lease Term derived from the Lend-Lease Act passed by the US Congress in 1941, making it possible to lend military equipment to Great Britain and her allies. Ownership of the equipment remained American, and payment was either deferred until after the war, or was cancelled in return for the lease of military bases to the USA.

Little Entente Czechoslovakia, Romania and Czechoslovakia formed this alliance in 1922 to discourage Hungary from trying to recover lands which it lost at the end of World War 1.

Locarno Treaties Five treaties, drawn up at Locarno, Switzerland, in 1925 and signed by Germany, Belgium, France, Britain, Italy, Poland and Czechoslovakia. The most important of these treaties, the 'Rhineland Pact', guaranteed the inviolability of the frontiers between France, Belgium and Germany, and confirmed the → demilitarised status of the German Rhineland.

Lomé Convention Agreement signed in Lomé, capital of Togoland, in 1975 between the European Community and the ACP (African, Caribbean and Pacific) states. The Convention allowed ACP exports to enter the European Community free of import duties or quotas, and made arrangements to stabilise ACP export prices. It was renewed in 1980, 1985 and 1990.

Long March A retreat by the communist forces of Mao Tse-tung from Kiangsi in Southern China to Shensi in Northern China, in order to escape extermination by the → Kuomintang.

Maginot Line A line of massive fortifications and defences along the border between France and Germany, built by the French between 1927 and 1936 to defend France from invasion.

Mandates Territories taken from the defeated German and Turkish empires after World War 1 and placed under the temporary administration of the victorious powers because they were not considered able to govern themselves.

Manhattan Project Code name for the secret US project for research into and development of atomic weapons during World War 2.

March on Rome The Fascist seizure of power in Italy in 1922, achieved by threatening to depose the government in Rome by armed force.

Margin, on the American phrase referring to the purchase of company shares on the stock exchange using borrowed money – a common practice in the USA before 1929.

Marshall Plan American programme of financial aid devised by US Secretary of State George Marshall to help the economic recovery of Europe after 1947.

Mau Mau Secret society of the Kikuyu people of Kenya which aimed to drive white settlers out of Kenya in the 1950s by the use of → terrorism.

McCarthyism Anti-communist attitudes and practices associated with US Senator Joseph McCarthy in his attempts to uncover communist 'subversion' in the USA in the early 1950s. McCarthy's practices included Congressional investigations into people's political backgrounds, often ruining their careers, the black-listing of suspected communists, and the administration of 'loyalty oaths'.

Mein Kampf (German) Literally, 'My Struggle' – a book written by Adolf Hitler in 1924 outlining the story of his life and his political ideas.

Mensheviks (Russian) Moderate Russian socialists opposed to the Bolsheviks after the split of the Social Democratic Party into Bolsheviks and Mensheviks in 1903.

Munich Agreement Agreement in 1938 between Chamberlain (Britain), Daladier (France), Hitler (Germany) and Mussolini (Italy), compelling Czechoslovakia to give up its Sudetenland area to Germany and to give land to neighbouring Hungary and Poland. It was the high point of the policy of → appeasement.

Nationalism Movements to strengthen the common bonds of language, religion, history among people especially in states where these are not recognised. In such cases nationalists attempt to gain the right of → national self-determination or become states in their own right (e.g. Poland for Polish-born, Polish-speaking people) or to press for greater recognition of national culture (e.g. the assertion of French language and culture in Quebec).

National self-determination The right of a nationality to exist, independent from foreign interference, in its own nation state, and to govern its own affairs.

NATO North Atlantic Treaty Organisation. Established in 1949 in response to → Cold War developments such as the Berlin Blockade. Founder members were Belgium, Canada, Denmark, France, Iceland, Italy, Luxemburg, Netherlands, Norway, Portugal, UK and USA. Greece and West Germany joined later, while France withdrew.

Naval race The first international → arms race of the twentieth century, a competition between Britain and Germany to build larger and more powerful battleships in the years before World War 1.

Nazism Short for National Socialism – the ideology of the National Socialist German Workers' Party (Nazi Party), becoming the ideology of the entire German state under the → dictatorship of Hitler, 1933–45.

Nazi–Soviet Pact Agreement between Nazi Germany and the Soviet Union in 1938 not to fight each other in the event of a European war. In a secret addition to the Pact, they also agreed to divide Poland between them. Also known as the Ribbentrop–Molotov Pact after the German and Soviet foreign ministers who negotiated it.

New Deal Election slogan coined in 1932 by Franklin D.Roosevelt to describe his plans for overcoming the → Great Depression if elected President of the USA. The term is also used to describe the economic and social policies which he put into practice between 1933–37 during his first and second terms as President.

New Economic Policy (NEP) Lenin's policies, adopted in 1921, for restoring the Soviet Union to economic stability after its economic collapse during the Civil War.

New Frontier Election slogan coined by John F.Kennedy in 1960 to describe the ambitious social and economic policies which he intended to pursue if elected President of the USA. cf → New Deal.

New Order in East Asia Japanese programme announced in 1938 for a political, economic and cultural union of Japan, Manchukuo and China. It was extended in 1940 to include south-east Asia, becoming the → Greater East Asia Co-Prosperity Sphere.

Night of the Long Knives Hitler's elimination of Ernst Röhm, leader of the SA, along with other SA members and political figures opposed to his → régime on 30 June 1934.

NKVD The People's Commissariat of Internal Affairs – the state security police in the USSR from 1934–43, chiefly reponsible for the → Great Terror of 1934–39.

Non-aligned movement International grouping of countries, mostly in Africa, Asia and Latin America, which avoid commitment to any of the military → blocs. It was initiated at the → Bandung Conference in 1955 and formally established by the Belgrade Declaration of 1961.

North-South International term, used especially by the United Nations, to describe the economic division of the world into a developed northern region and a mostly under-developed southern region.

OAS The Organisation of American States, an international orgaisation of 32 states in North, Central and South America and the Caribbean. Established in 1948 to provide for the peaceful development of disputes, the strengthening of security and the promotion of economic development throughout the region.

OAU The Organisation of African Unity, an international organisation consisting of all African states except the Republic of South Africa. Created in 1963 to promote unity and development in Africa to eradicate → colonialism, and to co-ordinate the economic, social, defence and foreign policies of the African states.

Oder-Neisse line Demarcation line in central Europe along the rivers Oder and Neisse which became Poland's new frontier with Germany after World War 2.

OEEC The Organisation for European Economic Co-operation, an international organisation created in 1948 to co-ordinate the use of → Marshall Aid in Europe. Replaced in 1960 by the OECD (Organisation for Economic Co-operation and Development.)

OGPU The United State Political Administration – the state security police force in the USSR from 1923–34.

Order No 1 Order issued by the Petrograd → Soviet in March 1971 requiring soldiers to take their orders from elected, regimental committees.

Ostpolitik (German) The 'East Policy' adopted by Willy Brandt, West German Chancellor, in 1969 in an effort to normalise diplomatic relations with East Germany.

Ottawa Agreements Customs arrangements agreed by the Imperial Economic Conference in Ottawa, Canada, in 1932, by which goods from the Empire entering Britain were exempt from customs duties while duties were imposed on all other foreign goods entering Britain. These arrangemants were known as → Imperial Preference.

Palestine Part of a provicne of the Turkish Empire until 1920, then a British → mandate until 1948 when the United Nations partitioned it between its Arab and Jewish populations. In wars in 1948–49 and 1967 the Jewish state, Israel, → annexed the Arab state, making the Palestinian Arabs a stateless nationality.

Peaceful co-existence Soviet Russian slogan coined by Khrushchev in 1956, referring to the possibility that the capitalist and communist → blocs could co-exist without war between them. This helped to relax some → Cold War tensions between East and West, but it helped cause the → Sino-Soviet split.

Perestroika (Russian) Literally means 'restructruing'. It is the policy introduced by M. Gorbachev in the USSR in 1985 for a major reorganisation of the Soviet economy, political structure and society.

Phoney war The period of World War 2 from Germany's defeat of Poland in September 1939 up to April 1940 when no fighting took place between Germany and the western European states which had promised to defend Poland.

PLO The Palestine Liberation Organisation: largest and most influential of the Arab political movements which aim to re-establish Arab control of → Palestine, using diplomatic pressure, propaganda and (until renouncing its use in 1988) → terrorism.

Politburo The Political Bureau of the Central Committee of the Communist Party of the Soviet Union. It is the most important policy-making body in the USSR.

Popular Front Popular Fronts were alliances of left-wing parties in the 1930s, formed to combat the advance of → fascism and → Nazism. The most famous Popular Front was that established in France and which formed a government led by Leon Blum in 1936–7 and 1938.

Prohibition A nation-wide ban on the manufacture, sale and transportation of alcoholic drinks in the USA from 1920 to 1933.

Proletariat The industrial working class as described by Karl Marx and Friedrich Engels in *The Communist Manifesto* in 1848, and by many left-wing writers thereafter.

Propaganda Persuasive, usually emotive form of providing information, using any or all of the mass media, to change or reinforce people's political views and behaviour.

Purges The expulsion from the Communist Party of the Soviet Union of corrupt or politically unreliable members. Under Stalin, purges led not only to explusion from the party but often also to the imprisonment and execution of many party and armed forces leaders, particularly during the → Great Terror.

Putsch (German) The sudden and violent overthrow of a government by armed opponents, and its replacement by a new, non-elected ruling group. cf → coup d'etat.

Quisling Term used to describe a person who co-operates with an enemy occupying his or her country. Derived from Vidkun Quisling of Norway who collaborated with German forces occupying his country during World War 2.

Reds Slang term for → communists. Derived from the colour of the flag of international communism.

Red Army Bolshevik military force, commanded by Trotsky, created in January 1918 to defend the Bolshevik government in the Russian Civil War. Commonly used for the armies of the Soviet Union.

Red Guards (1) Armed groups of Russian workers, mostly in Petrograd, formed after March 1917 to oppose counter-revolutionaries and to defend the gains made by workers in the March Revolution. They played a key part in bringing the Bolsheviks to power in November 1917. In 1918 they were absorbed into the → Red Army. (2) The name was also used in China from 1966 to about 1976 for the millions of uniformed young piople who supported Mao Tse-tung during the → Cultural Revolution and who carried it out on his behalf.

Red Terror Policy adopted by → Sovnarkom during the Russian Civil War to suppress counter-revolution and to eliminate political opposition. Carried out by the → Cheka, it involved the use of mass as well as individual executions without trial, imprisonment in → concentration and labour camps, torture, hostage-taking, etc.

Régime (French) Term describing the form of government in a stat – e.g. a 'military régime' is government by the armed forces; a 'Marxist régime' is goverment by communists; etc.

Reichstag (German) The German parliament from 1871 to 1918 and from 1919 to 1945.

Reparations Money and goods paid by a defeated nation to victorious nations for the repair of war damage.

Republic Form of government in which the head of state is not selected by heredity but is elected by the country's voters. The word is sometimes also used as a synonym for the country which has this form of government – e.g. Germany from 1919 to 1933 is referred to as the Weimar Republic.

Revolution In the political sense, a revolution is a sudden, often violent, change in a country's → regime, accompanied by major changes to the political and social order, and involving large numbers of people as direct participants.

SA [Sturmabteilung] (German) Literally, 'Storm Troopers'. The SA was the paramilitary wing of the German Nazi Party, founded in 1921 to protect party meetings and rallies, and to fight political rivals. Also known from the colour of their uniform as → Brownshirts.

Salt March A march to the Indian Ocean to collect free salt, led by Gandhi in violation of British law regarding the manufacture and sale of salt (1930).

Sanctions Measures taken by the League of Nations or by the United Nations against a country that has broken international law. Economic sanctions involve a ban on trade with the offending country. Military sanctions, never so far used, would involve collective military action by the United Nations against the offending country.

Second front The idea, favoured by Stalin, that the USA and Britain should invade western Europe in 1942 to take the pressure off the Russian front, where German forces were close to defeating the Soviet Union. This 'second front', however, was not opened until the D-Day Landings in France in 1944.

Self-determination See → national self-determination.

Sharpeville Massacre Killing by South African police of 67 black Africans demonstrating against → apartheid in the township of Sharpeville, near Johannesburg, on 21 March 1960.

Sino-Soviet split Ideological dispute between Communist China and the USSR, originating in 1956 when Khrushchev announced a policy of → peaceful co-existence with the West, and began a process of → de-Stalinisation. The Chinese resented this attempt to re-interpret communism without consulting them. The split deepened in 1958 with disagreements between the two over Chinese foreign policy and the → Great Leap Forward. Sino-Soviet relations remained bad until an easing of tension in the later 1980s.

Socialism Belief that the community should own and control the means of production (e.g. factories and farms) in order to satisfy the needs of the community rather than just individual needs.

Soviet (Russian) A council of workers' deputies. Soviets were first formed during the 1905 Russian Revolution to represent the workers in each locality.

Sovnarkom (Russian) Short for Council of People's Commissars – the government created by the → Bolsheviks in Russia in November 1917, with Lenin as its chairman.

SS [Schutzstaffel] (German) Black-uniformed military wing of the → Nazi Party, founded as a bodyguard for the Nazi leaders in 1925, and becoming a vast police and security organisation in the 1930s after suppressing the rival → SA in the → Night of the Long Knives.

Stresa Front Agreement by France, Britain and Italy in 1935 to uphold Austrian independence in the face of Nazi German aggression and to condemn Hitler's announcement of German rearmament.

Successor states Nine states in central and eastern Europe created from territouy belonging to the former empires of Russia, Austria-Hungary and Germany at the end of World War 1. They were Finland, Estonia, Latvia, Lithuania, Poland, Czechoslovakia, Austria, Hungary, and Yugoslavia.

Sykes-Picot Agreement British and French agreement in 1916 to divide the Arab territories of the Turkish Empire between them at the conclusion of World War 1.

Terrorism The use by minority groups of, e.g., random bombing, hijacking, hostage-taking, assassination and extortion to create a situation in which their political opponents or the state authorities are under strong pressure to agree to their demands. The term is a pejorative one; 'terrorists' generally describe themselves differently, e.g. as 'freedom fighters'.

Third Reich Term used by the → Nazis to describe their → régime in Germany from January 1933 to May 1945. It implied continuity with the first Reich (Empire) of the middle ages and with the 'Second Reich' of 1871–1918.

Third World Collective term for countries belonging neither to the developed capitalist world (the First World) nor to the developed Communist World (the Second World). They are mostly → developing nations in Latin America, the Caribbean,

Africa and Asia, sharing a → colonial past. Some (recognised as a separate Fourth World) are desperately poor. In foreign affairs, many Third World countries follow the policy of → non-alignment.

'Torch' Code-name for the joint British-American invasion of North Africa in November 1942.

Tripartite Axis Pact Alliance between Germany, Italy and Japan, signed in 1940, promising to help each other should they find themselves at war with another major power.

Truman Doctrine An announcement by US President Truman in 1947 that the USA would give military and economic aid to European nations to help them resist the spread of communism. This marked the start of the US policy of → containment.

Vichy France The cintral and southern portion of France not occupied by Germany after the fall of France in 1940, and governed from the town of Vichy by French collaborating with the Germans.

Vietcong Communist, South Vietnamese guerilla force that operated against the South Vietnamese government and American forces during the Vietnam War.

Vietminh North Vietnamese communist organisation founded by Ho Chi Minh to drive the French out of Indo-China after 1945.

Vietnamisation US policy developed during the Presidency of R. Nixon to have the South Vietnamese government take over the conduct of the war against North Vietnam from the US armed forces.

Volk (German) A term used by Nazis to describe the racially pure German people (volk) who would be loyal to their leader, Hitler.

Wall Street Crash Sudden, massive fall in the prices of shares on the New York stock exchange in Wall Street, Manhattan, from 24–29 October 1929. The Crash led to the failure of many banks and companies, and hastened the onset of the → Great Depression.

War communism Strict economic system with state control of industry and forced collection of foods, established by the Bolshevik government during the Russian Civil War (1918–21).

Warsaw Pact A treaty (the 'Eastern European Mutual Assistance Treaty') signed in Warsaw, Poland, in 1955 by Albania, Bulgaria, Czechoslovakia, the German Democratic Republic, Hungary, Poland, Romania and the USSR, creating a unified military command for these countries and agreeing to respond to an attack on any one of them as an attack on all.

Whites Forces opposed to the → Bolsheviks during the Russian Civil War (1918–21).

Yom Kippur War The war between Israel and neighbouring Arab countries which began with surprise Arab attacks on Israeli forces on the Jewish festival of Yom Kippur (Day of Atonement) on 6 October 1973.

Zionism Jewish → nationalist movement founded in 1897 for the recreation of a Jewish nation in → Palestine.

Index